Becoming Van Morrison: It's Too Late To Stop Now, 1973-1974

BECOMING VAN MORRISON:
IT'S TOO LATE TO STOP NOW, 1973-1974

by HOWARD A. DEWITT

With the editorial and layout assistance of
Scott Amonson

HORIZON BOOKS
2023

Book design and layout by
Scott Amonson.

ISBN: 978-0-938840-14-5 (Paperback)
Library of Congress Control Number: 2023918200

Printed by Kindle Direct Publishing in the USA.

Published by

Horizon Books
P. O. Box 4342
Scottsdale, AZ 85261
www.howardadewitt.com

10 9 8 7 6 5 4 3 2 1
(First Edition Printed 2023)

Printed in the United States of America

✧ Book Titles By Howard A. Dewitt ✧

ROCK N ROLL

1 **ELVIS *the* SUN YEARS**
The Story of Elvis Presley in the Fifties *Revised Ed.* (2023)

2 **FATS DOMINO**
Blueberry Hill To Millions (2021) *KINDLE ONLY*

3 **VAN MORRISON**
Astral Weeks To Stardom, 1968-1972 (2020)

4 **SEARCHING FOR SUGAR MAN II**
Rodriguez, Coming From Reality, Heroes & Villains (2017)

5 **SEARCHING FOR SUGAR MAN**
Sixto Rodriguez' Mythical Climb To Rock N Roll Fame and Fortune (2015)

6 **VAN MORRISON**
Them and the Bang Era, 1945-1968 (2005)

7 **STRANGER IN TOWN**
The Musical Life of Del Shannon (2001)

8 **ELVIS: THE SUN YEARS**
The Story of Elvis Presley in the Fifties, *1st Edition* (1993)

9 **PAUL MCCARTNEY**
From Liverpool To Let It Be (1992)

10 **BEATLE POEMS (1987)**

11 **THE BEATLES**
Untold Tales (1985, 2nd edition 2001)

12 **CHUCK BERRY-ROCK 'N' ROLL MUSIC**
(1981, 2nd Edition Revised 1985)

13 **VAN MORRISON**
The Mystic's Music (1983)

14 **JAILHOUSE ROCK**
The Bootleg Records of Elvis Presley (with Lee Cotton) (1983)

Available through Amazon Books and other online book retailers
or contact: Horizon Books P. O. Box 4342 Scottsdale, AZ 85261

✧ **Book Titles By Howard A. Dewitt** ✧

HISTORY AND POLITICS

1 **TRUMP'S PLOT TO DESTROY DEMOCRACY (2021)**

2 **TRUMP**
Destroying America (2020)

3 **TRUMP AGAINST THE WORLD**
Foreign Policy Bully, Russian Collusion (2018)

4 **SICILY'S SECRETS**
The Mafia, Pizza & Hating Rome (2017)

5 **MEETING HITLER**
A Tragicomedy (2016)

6 **OBAMA'S DETRACTORS**
In The Right-Wing Nut House (2012)

7 **THE ROAD TO BAGHDAD (2003)**

8 **A BLOW TO AMERICA'S HEART**
September 11, 2001, The View From England (2002)

9 **JOSE RIZAL**
Philippine Nationalist As Political Scientist (1997)

10 **THE FRAGMENTED DREAM**
Multicultural California (1996)

11 **THE CALIFORNIA DREAM (1996)**

12 **READINGS IN CALIFORNIA CIVILIZATION**
(1981, 4th Edition Revised 2004)

13 **VIOLENCE IN THE FIELDS**
California Filipino Farm Labor Unionization (1980)

15 **CALIFORNIA CIVILIZATION**
An Interpretation (1979)

16 **ANTI-FILIPINO MOVEMENTS IN CALIFORNIA**
A History, Bibliography and Study Guide (1976)

✧ Book Titles By Howard A. Dewitt ✧

17 IMAGES OF ETHNIC AND RADICAL VIOLENCE IN CALIFORNIA POLITICS, 1917-1930
A survey (1975)

SPORTS, NOVELS AND MEMOIRS

1 SALVADOR DALI MURDER (2014)

2 THE PHOENIX SUNS
The View From Section 101 (2013)

3 STONE MURDER
A Rock 'N' Roll Mystery (2012)

4 COFFEE & HEMINGWAY MADE ME A WRITER
A Travel Memoir (2023)

5 MY BIRTHDAY WITH VAN MORRISON IN SPAIN
A Memoir (2023)

Available through Amazon Books and other online book retailers or contact: Horizon Books P. O. Box 4342 Scottsdale, AZ 85261

Table of Contents

INTRODUCTION

"In order to win you must be prepared to leave one or two cards showing."

VAN MORRISON

"There's always got to be a struggle. What else is there? That's what life is made of. I don't know anything else. If there is, tell me about it."

VAN MORRISON

"I never felt like I was born with a silver spoon…I felt like howling at the moon a lot of times."

VAN MORRISON

"I saw the danger, yet I walked along the enchanted way."

VAN MORRISON

Van Morrison's artistic soul is the subject of this book. He has searched for ways to express meaning since **Astral Weeks**. What is Van's creative soul? It is how he expresses himself. That is in his songwriting. He has another level to this talent. That is in the concert arena. When performing his songs, he will vary the words and the music in length and interpretation. Why? It is in his psyche to perform the songs as he views them. The same song can be interpreted many times. He makes it a new song. That is his creative soul.

The use of words is a Morrison trait. The beauty of "Warm Love" contrasted with "Why Must I Always Explain?" is an example of another Morrison direction. He can write a romantic song and a short time later pen a biting criticism.

When he settled in the rustic village of Fairfax in the early 1970s, he began an evolution filling out his time in Marin County where he was "Becoming Van Morrison." Bucolic leafy images of Marin County showed up in songs composed alongside a rant, a complaint or settling a score. Van's inner creativity runs a broad spectrum. One that is never definable.

That is a special love song can be written in beautiful lyrics. The next song can be about getting even or being angry about being disrespected. A good example is "Whatever Happened to P. J. Proby." The artistic soul realizes the finished product must have a life of its own. Van has said many times his songs are timeless. A life in song is a manifestation of his deep soul and inner talent.

Van's creative soul is not easily defined. He writes without concern for approval or disapproval. He stays true to his heart. His inner feelings radiate. Van will write in unknown areas as his literary output demonstrates. He accomplished the definition of his inner soul from 1973 into the summer of 1974. By that point he perfected his artistic vision. From 1973 into 1980 Marin County was the laboratory for his creation. The two volumes from 1973 through 1979 may seem like too much material. It isn't! It is necessary to define how "Becoming Van Morrison" took place.

While Irish themes increasingly dominated, the definition of this creation in 1973-1974 was formed on a hill at his Fairfax home and then in the San Geronimo Valley, where he fled with Carol Guida, to escape a divorce, a curious press and a record label he detested. The result? "Becoming Van Morrison" with the It's Too Late To Stop Now tour and album with the Caledonia Soul Orchestra inaugurating the legend.

As a writer Morrison's journey from school boy prose to legendary intellectual visions was a curious one. He expanded intellectually while watching others in his field becoming the flavor of the month.

SOME WRITERS EXPAND OTHERS BECOME INTELLECTUALLY DEEPER: WHICH ONE IS VAN MORRISON?

How could a young Belfast kid who dropped out of school at fourteen become an acclaimed singer-songwriter? The operative wisdom is he couldn't. But he did. Today in his finely tailored suits, replete with the blues fedora, Van strolls on stage for ninety minutes of pure r & b-soul with references to his Irish heritage. Van Morrison cuts a titillating public figure with his rants about those who would prevent him from performing due to Covid. Are you listening Robin Swann?

It is Morrison's flair for over the top behavior that attracts the press. Along the way they miss the essence of the man. He is a brilliant songwriter, performer and businessman.

He has flaws. To ignore his at times out of step behavior is to write from the hagiographer's viewpoint. Are you listening Ritchie Yorke? Or to write from the standpoint of the critic who does little than complain about his behavior. Are you listening Clinton Heylin? The biographer who trudges on with the useless facts, the inane material and the over the top analysis is a concern. This type of biographer goes down too many rabbit holes. Are you listening Johnny Rogan?

Today Van lives in Belfast years after a shocking, contentious divorce from a former Miss Ireland Michelle Rocca. Her job was marrying rich men. Van didn't see it coming. Now after two kids with her Van is paying through the nose. Now damn you die hard Van Morrison fans, I don't want to hear any complaints that Rocca is a gold digger. She isn't a gold digger! She used a pile driver to extract gold from his soul. She needs money for two au pairs, for two personal assistants, for two cleaning nannies, for two dog walkers, for two driveway sweepers, for two chimney cleaners and for two lawyers to extract more money when needed. She is not evil. Nasty? Not my concern. Just ask her next door neighbor.

How nasty is Rocca? She sued a neighbor alleging the couple next door didn't respect Van's privacy. In an Irish court she sobbed and wailed about people intruding on their private life. In that Dublin courtroom she came almost to tears suggesting how Van's privacy was violated. Rocca even acted out a scenario where Van was getting a drink of water as the neighbor waved to him. Rocca allegedly told a Belfast reporter Van sued. She made her husband look like an angry, bilious, spoiled rock star. Van lived in Belfast. None of this took place while he was enjoying his marriage to Rocca. She sued after he left the family abode. While Morrison can be a pain in the ass with his detractors, he has never had a nasty word to say about Michelle Rocca or any of the women in his life. He is private. Stay away from his personal life. Does Rocca deserve some nasty words? I asked the fifteen people I interviewed from Belfast. They answered: " Love can blind you. Van was blinded. He is now paying the piper."

WHY ARE YOU OBSESSED WITH VAN MORRISON? I AM NOT, I AM A PROFESSOR WITH SERIOUS ACADEMIC INTERESTS

"Why are you obsessed with Van Morrison?" Ray Ruff asked. I looked at him. It was 1976. I was working on my first book on the Belfast Cowboy. He asked me this question during our third interview. I responded: "I admire him for his willingness to attack the record labels, and to never backdown in an industry that eats its young." Ruff, who booked Them into the Whiskey A-Go-Go in 1966, was unruffled. "I helped Van in his early career. Now he won't say hello to me," Ruff continued. "How do I explain that?" I was uncomfortable. I said: "It is simply Van." I didn't know what else to say. My book **Van Morrison: The Mystic's Music** arrived in 1983. I continued to attend Van's concerts. I collected bootlegs, vinyl albums and memorabilia. Over the years I talked to Ruff for other projects. His words resonated with me. How could I explain Van? I decided to look at his early years.

Who was Ray Ruff? He was a friend to Buddy Holly. Ruff's dalliance with rockabilly as a performer ended. He was a recording artist. He was never a star. Ruff left Texas to settle in Los Angeles. He became an industry insider. His relationship with Van began when he booked Them into the Whiskey-A-Go-Go. My relationship with Ruff began when I wrote for **Blue Suede News**. Ruff was a fountain of information for my rockabilly articles. His relationship with Warner Bros. was an ongoing one. He introduced me to a number of key recording executives.

He worked at ABC-Paramount producing Brian Hyland. When I wrote a book on Del Shannon, Ruff was an indispensable source. He enjoyed my early book on Van Morrison. He encouraged me to write a multi-volume biography. The three books I outlined with Ruff evolved into the present six volume work. Like me, Ruff was a Van fan.

The fan part is what the biographer must ignore. To present a fully developed picture of Morrison as a unique writer, charismatic performer, and brilliant observer, it is necessary to delve deeply into his life. Why can he take a mundane, short term, out of character event and make it into a hit song? How can he audition fifty musicians and make eleven of them the Caledonia Soul Orchestra? How can he take analog tapes and edit them into what is arguably among the best live rock music albums? How can he beat the record labels at their own game? Keep reading these questions will be answered.

When Ruff died in 2005 my first Van Morrison multi-volume book was just published. He loved reading the manuscript. There was one thing Ruff did for me that was indispensable. He told me to concentrate on the facts. Ruff warned Morrison would attempt to

control the narrative. "If you bend to Van's demands, you will be no more than a factotum," Ruff continued. "If you stay away from his behavior, you will get closer to the truth. I am not sure there is a truth with Van."

I didn't ignore Ruff's advice. I came to realize if you spend enough time with a subject, you understand that person. Ruff was correct in describing Van as a creative, but complex, individual with a mercurial personality. I took that advice. I tried to explain why and how he reacted during his career.

In the first volume **Van Morrison: Them And The Bang Era, 1945-1968**, I found the period from his birth until **Astral Weeks** was a means of understanding his early creativity. The second book, **Van Morrison: Astral Weeks To Stardom, 1968-1972** took the story to the precipice of reorganizing his career.

This is the third book in the six volume multi-Morrison biography. **Becoming Van Morrison: It's Too Late to Stop Now, 1973-1974** is the first step in defining his early career. It is an examination of a year and a half in Morrison's life. I told Ruff what I intended to do. He laughed loudly. "You will never be able to do this the right way," Ruff continued. "Morrison is a fierce competitor; a private guy and he will eat you alive." I pointed out to Ruff this was a literary biography. I said it wasn't "a hit job." He chuckled. Ruff was in ill health the last time I talked to him in 2004. He passed the next year.

Before he left us to go see John Lennon, Ruff listened to my plans for the multi-volume biography. I told him I was going to be the rock 'n' roll Robert Caro. "Never heard of him," Ruff said of Caro.

VAN AND MICHELLE ROCCA

My conversations with Ruff defined these early books. When I told him the theme of two lengthy volumes on the 1970s was "Becoming Van Morrison," he screamed: "What the hell do you mean?" I explained the Van Morrison of the early 1970s was an artist training for long term stardom. I pointed out how much work Van put into his songwriting, with increasingly sophisticated themes, and a professional business structure. Ruff screamed: "Who cares!" I responded: "You don't understand Ray," I continued. "Van wore egg stained shirts, when he left a San Francisco Boarding House show in the early 1970s because he thought the audience wasn't paying attention. He ended his appearances at the Great American Music Hall because a guy who stood in line drinking all day got in and proceeded to be too loud. I told Ruff the quirks in Morrison's performing, the glitches in his writing, and the erratic behavior were demons the Belfast Cowboy conquered by 1980. When I informed him the sequel to this volume, covering 1974-1979, had the theme of

"Becoming Van Morrison's" trademark, he looked at me like I had lost my mind. Then just before he passed, he read volume one, **Van Morrison: Them And The Bang Era, 1945-1968**. Ruff responded: "Damn, Howard you are not the dumb shit I thought, nice work." Michael Hayward, reviewing the book wrote: "It will be an important addition to the library of any serious Van Morrison fan." My three volume biography grew to six thanks to Ruff.

What, then, is the role of the biographer? To peer into Van's soul one should examine the careers of other artists, notably D. H. Lawrence and William Faulkner, to understand his creative character. Like the famous authors, he is the ultimate contrarian. His ex-wife described him as a "creative genius." When Janet Morrison Minto was asked about Van personally, she told the **Los Angeles Times**: "The man was like a prickly pear." Then I came into the picture. It was time to write a six volume biography of the prickly pear.

I decided to write a short warm up book on Van's early years. It was not a part of the six volume multi-biography. I could test the waters for the longer project. I had hundreds of great sources. There were two hundred plus interviews with varying memories, experiences and thoughts on Van the Man. After collecting the material, I had conceived the two volumes stretching from 1973 to 1980. Was this too much material? No! The more than fourteen hundred pages on seven years of Morrison's life was necessary to examine and analyze his emergence as a fifty year plus music star and rock and roll legend.

I was asked: Why so much material? Why the 1970s? Why the notion of "Becoming Van Morrison?" This book and its sequel answers those questions.

In 2020, **Van Morrison: From Astral Weeks To Stardom, 1968 To 1972** was published setting the tone for the following two volumes on the 1970s. This was the second volume in my multi-biographical work. As the first book **Van Morrison: Them And The Bang Era, 1945-1968** came my marriage and grown children allowed me more time to research and write. I began to understand Van's travails and personal concerns. After Dan Hicks took me through the Fairfax home, while Van was on tour, and Carol Guida hadn't entered the picture, I thought of abandoning the project. I was a fan. I wasn't interested in discussing Van's deep dark secrets. I didn't even care about them. Just before Dan Hicks, passed from a lifetime of boogie woogie, he suggested I finish the project. I went through my three file cabinets. I had spent my life collection the material. Then a young kid came into my life. I became friends with Pat Thomas. I told Dan Hicks no more Van Morrison. The joy, the excitement, the knowledge that Thomas possessed concerning Morrison made me get back into the project. I decided to write a full length six volume biography, up from the three I planned in the 1980s.

The collection of materials, the interviews and the writing continued with a more sporadic concert schedule. Now I have finished four of my projected six volume Morrison biography. How can I defend four thousand pages on a rock 'n' roll singer who daily screams he is not an artist in that genre? I can defend the six volumes as necessary to understanding Van Morrison's life, career and musical genius. These books are also a window into the often murky, insidious record business. Myth and reality is difficult to define within the record business. My books define myth and reality.

Van's friends and musical cohorts provided valuable insights. One person, in particular, was locked into Morrison's life. He was an extraordinary guitarist. His name was Chris Michie. He lived and breathed the Marin County music scene. For much of the 1980s, he was Van's lead guitarist. He was not only an observer of Morrison's growth as an artist, he was an active participant.

He was praiseworthy of Van and his accomplishments since **Astral Weeks**. I asked Michie: "How can you explain the contradictions in Van's life?" He did in detail. That material is in the next three books.

What is it about Van Morrison? He is mercurial. He is alternately helpful, hateful, contradictory, but he is loyal to long-time friends. Explaining his fragmented personality is impossible.

The way to understand Van Morrison is through a maximalist biography. There is no event too small, or seemingly insignificant, that didn't influence Morrison. The expansive power of Van's mind deserves more than simple observations. Readers like the brain fried critics screaming Van is a difficult asshole need to step back and look in detail and depth at his work. His personality? That is a different story.

Does Van expect too much from his listeners? He does! That needs to be addressed. This thick volume covers less than two years of Van's life. To understand him it is necessary to peer inside his mind. How does the biographer do this? Read every spoken and print interview. In his songwriting, he drifts nostalgically back into the 1970s. When I tell you what Van thinks these conclusions emanate from copious interviews. Van goes down rabbit holes. Hs does discuss his life. It is during print interviews. YouTube has a plethora of Van interviews opening his mind to the biographer. His comments open previously closed windows into a complex soul.

Finally, to understand Van, the biographer must look at the critics, and the previous books with a jaundiced eye. Why? Morrison's complex nature befuddled them. The war between the Belfast Cowboy and reviewers, biographers and journalistic interpreters has mellowed. It is still present. That is why the story remains interesting, relevant and mysterious. To understand Van is not easy. The following pages will walk you through the joys, the contradictions and the mysteries of his complex life. In the process, you will appreciate Morrison's oeuvre. The biographical details of the Belfast Cowboy's life are not in dispute. What is not known is how, at least for this volume, Marin County influenced him. My conclusion is it was the seminal influence on his art. The memoirs of musicians are sketchy, often unreliable, and sometimes taken from articles in **Rolling Stone**. There are two Van Morrison's. One is the private writer. The other is the public performer. This book blends these two disparate themes into a volume of a year and a half suggesting why and how he evolved as an artist.

There is a wall Van has erected around his life. His continual threat is don't discuss my private life or all hell will break loose. I am not interested in analyzing his love life, his personal finances, his letters to friends or his peccadillos, whatever they may be, that is unless it is understand his oeuvre. To analyze the man, his music, his writing, his battles with the music industry, his dust ups with promoters, concert staffs and the press, it is necessary to examine his at times self- imposed exile.

In a sense this book is living history. I was following Van Morrison from one show to the next. I realized he was a unique talent. He was waging a war on the music business for his artistic freedom. He was "Becoming Van Morrison." I spoke in depth with many of the people who were there in 1973-1974, while interviewing, in the last four decades, many who remain in the Belfast Cowboy's orbit. The focus is on Marin County. This small settlement shaped him. It runs deeply throughout this book. Without the bucolic beauty of his Fairfax home and the appearance of the beautiful, understated Carol Guida, Van would not have achieved the enormous successes of this brief period in his life. Enjoy the ride. I did!

Remember this book tells you how Van Morrison adjusted to the rigors of the rock 'n' roll life, while maintaining his privacy, sanity and innate creativity. The rock 'n' roll life is not an easy one to describe, analyze and follow, but here is an attempt to view a brilliant artist who survived and defined his life in the murderous trenches of rock and roll.

PREFACE

"I believe that an artist does not belong to the public but to himself. I don't want anyone to know anything about my personal life because it is my personal life to do with what I wish, like anyone else."

Van Morrison to Ritchie Yorke

"The only thing that stands up is whether you've got it or not. The only thing that counts is if you're still around. And I'm still around."

Van Morrison to Ritchie Yorke, the 1970s

"A man's life of any worth is a continual allegory."

John Keats

"Biographers are burglars, robbing the lives of their subjects."

Janet Malcolm

Its Too Late To Stop Now

Hard Nose the Highway

T B Sheets

Warner Brothers

St Dominics Preview

Bang Records

Veedon Fleece

This is my third release in a six volume Van Morrison biography. It covers the period from 1973 into mid-1974. A companion book will take the story through 1979. Why two volumes on this brief period? After completing the rough draft, I believed a new Van Morrison emerged in this seven-year period. Hence, the title "Becoming Van Morrison." Initially, this seemed preposterous. Then I realized what other biographers (myself included) missed. Marin County's influence was missing. This book takes an in-depth look at the people the places and the events that shaped Van in Marin County.

A new muse emerged. She was an elusive figure. Carol Guida was a normal, well educated, bright, thoughtful twenty-year-old when she came into Van's life. From 1973 until early 1977, when she left, her spiritual, intellectual and personal guidance influenced the person and artist. He became, by 1980, an internationally acclaimed star. As she sat down with me for more than a dozen interviews, Guida talked of Van's sophistication as a singer-songwriter. "We read and talked about all the books he used to increase his prolific songwriting," Guida recalled. She gave Van all the credit. Her insights. Her thoughts on things of a spiritual nature were important contributions. Her Zen qualities. Her yoga. Her Buddhist chanting. Her knowledge of philosophy, religion and history intrigued Morrison. Guida wasn't a hippie muse. She was an equal intellectual partner. Van blossomed.

When **Common One** arrived the indication to the fans (me included), it was a new Van Morrison. That artist was formed from 1973 through 1979 with the influence of Marin County musicians, San Francisco Bay Area clubs, local business professionals, a ukulele playing Sausalito attorney, a cast of ne'er do well dope smoking intellectuals and an adoring fan base.

For nineteen months Van molded the earliest part of his legendary career. Throughout the 1970s he beat the industry at its own game. That is he figured out how to protect his intellectual property, collect royalties and publicize his musical output while developing a legendary in concert persona.

By 1980, at the ripe old age of thirty five, he was an increasingly mature songwriter. He was also a feisty little devil countering the industry bullies. Van had more fun, more freedom, more creativity, and more personal growth than at any time in his career. It wasn't until he moved from Woodstock to Fairfax that the bucolic California countryside finalized his professional growth. Although only in his mid-twenties, when he arrived in the Golden State, he had been a touring musician for a decade.

Since 1960, at the tender age of fifteen, he was a professional musician. He spent a few years touring with Irish show bands. Then, he emerged as he lead singer of Them. They were advertised as a British Invasion group. They weren't. They were a rhythm and blues or quasi blues band from Belfast. After going solo with Bert Berns and Bang Records, Van signed a lucrative major label deal with Warner Bros. Ray Ruff, who booked Them in California, remarked: "Van was cast into the cauldron of the devil. He survived." Ruff meant that Morrison learned the ins and outs of the record business early in his career.

After a landmark album that initially didn't sell well, **Astral Weeks**, Van turned out a series of hit albums and chart singles for Warner Bros. Despite these successes he was unhappy.

There were five influences bringing changes to Van's career. These forces created his legend by his mid-thirties. First, he finalized a business structure necessary to protect his intellectual property. Second, he experienced musical and personal changes in Marin County impacting his songwriting and performing. Third, the It's Too Late To Stop Now tour and the double album carved out a legendary in concert niche for the Belfast Cowboy. Fourth, Van has always written from life experiences and geographical locations. These are his major sources of inspiration. Fifth, his albums from **Hard Nose The Highway** through **Into The Music** were personal, less pop and more analytical. They hinted at future literary references. The albums were more sophisticated and less predictable.

Van Morrison grew musically in this brief period. He redefined his sound and stage persona. Until 1973, he was a hit and miss performer. He was a brilliant songwriter. As his guitarist, Chris Michie, suggested a decade later, he became Van Morrison.

That is when he evolved into the performer he is today. The musicians making the new Van accelerate his career included Mark Isham, Jack Schroer, Tony Dey, David Hayes, John Allair, Jef Labes, Mark Naftalin, Jon Gershen, John Platania and dozens of other Marin County performers. Van's friends, select industry insiders, and his fiancée, Carol Guida, were instrumental in his transition to a legendary career. The influence of Marin County was the catalyst to his songwriting and performing genius. This small, rural county across the Golden Gate bridge to Sausalito and beyond became Van's training ground. He finalized and finessed his career into stardom.

When Van moved from Woodstock to the small, bucolic California town, Fairfax, his wife, Janet, mentioned his stage fright. This move didn't end his performing reluctance. "He was terrified to go on stage," Janet remarked. She talked with him at length to help him overcome performance anxiety.

Janet Morrison Minto was the catalyst to relocating to Marin County. Her mother was there taking care of her son, Peter, from a previous relationship. She believed Marin County was much like Belfast geographically. She reasoned this might help Van overcome performing anxiety and accentuate his writing.

Van conquered his stage fright in the small clubs in and around San Francisco. Early on, he turned his back to the audience. He was known to leave the stage in a huff if the audience wasn't paying attention. If it was too noisy, he was irascible. He fought stage fright. He conquered his demons.

By November and December 1979, Van's personal journey took a road toward a new commercial future. He rehearsed "Summertime In England" and "Haunts of Ancient Peace." These tunes formed the core of Van's increasingly sophisticated jazz sound with mature lyrics. "Becoming Van Morrison" led to **Common One**.

By 1980, when **Common One** appeared, Van was a twenty plus year veteran of the music business. He was an established star. He could do what he pleased musically. He had a professional business organization. He performed with a wide variety of musicians. This was possible because of the watershed years 1973 through 1979. The blue print for the next forty plus years emerged.

Becoming Van Morrison: It's Too Late To Stop Now, 1973-1974 and **Van Morrison: The Marin County Subculture Transformation Period, 1974-1979** argue the drive, hard work, vision, sacrifice and persistence of the Belfast Cowboy which laid the ground work for decades of stardom. It was in the San Francisco Bay Area, not London, New York, Boston or Woodstock, that Van found and perfected his musical niche.

The San Francisco Bay Area clubs weren't without their problems. One Marin County club sold pizza. Once in the middle of a plaintive Morrison solo, the microphone from the kitchen announced: "Pizza number nine is ready." In the blue collar town of Hayward, California, south of Oakland, Van played Frenchy's. The club manager interrupted Van's show to request that the Hell's Angeles move their motorcycles from the front entrance. When Van played a bowling alley south of Stanford University the cocktail lounge show, with leopard skin wall ornaments, was interrupted when the public address system boomed: "Will the Hewlett Packard Bowling team report to lane 7." Van loved these small clubs. It was there he perfected his live shows.

In the 1970s, Morrison's business affairs grew into major corporations. Suddenly excellent management, a stable of top flight lawyers, a defined corporate structure, and a litigation minded Van held the reigns of Caledonia Productions. Van said: "The producer made all the money." Van became the producer. The rise of the legend ensued. He intensified that path. It eventually led to Cleveland's Rock 'N' Roll Hall of Fame.

By 1973, he was taking stock of his commercial direction. He worried he would become the "flavor of the month" if the hits continued. Warner Bros. disagreed. Van vowed to write albums giving him complete control. He eschewed the hits.

Hard Nose The Highway was the initial album where he achieved total mastery of his craft. Van produced it his way. The critics were flummoxed. The fans were mystified. It was the first step in the independent, non-predictable Van Morrison.

He never chased trends. There was no dance Van. There was no disco Morrison. There weren't duets with Lulu, Petula Clark or Cilla Black. There were constant signs of musical innovation. His personal growth accelerated. He developed a dedicated fan base. His fans respected his privacy. That trend persists. Except, of course, with the press who ran hot and cold on his music, his songwriting, his performing and his personality.

Van Morrison's fans have an eerie, almost mystical, attachment to the Belfast Cowboy. One fan, Pat Corley, wrote a book **Vanatic** chronicling his passion for Morrison's music. He subtitled the book "The Story of a Van Morrison fan." When he was twenty-eight, in 1973, Pat discovered Van's music. Like many of the fans, Corley personally connected to Van's albums. The fans remain constant.

Why is fandom important? The fans see Van as a blue collar, hard-working musician who has paid his dues. They love his blues-soul-rhythm mélange. From 1973 through 1979, the birth of a legendary career originated. He had been around musically for half a decade when at eighteen he wrote "Gloria." The road to Becoming Van Morrison accelerated.

The Vanatics exhibit a concert loyalty combined with a record purchasing love for his music. Pat Corley's **Vanatic: The Story Of A Van Morrison Fan**, published in 2016, begins: "To me it is only the music that matters." This is the mantra of the Morrison fan. They love the music. The man? Some are faithful followers of his life. Others do little more than imbibe the music. After 2000, there was a noticeable younger tinge to those watching Morrison perform. There are numerous Van fan sites. Pat Thomas has my favorite fan site. He is a music insider and a scholar of African American and counterculture politics. He is presently working on a book on Morrison's songs. Not his life. Just his albums, singles and other aspects of his recording career.

Pat Thomas' Facebook page, **Listen To The Lion: Musings on Van, His Band And Street Choir** is insightful. Thomas is a professional musician. He is a seasoned producer. He is a seasoned drummer. He has a free form jazz aggregation, Mushroom, where he experiments in clubs, concert venues and in the studio. He is an acclaimed record producer, as well. He provided unique Van insights. Thomas posts album thoughts, random points of interest, and anything that fascinates him. He is typical of Van fans. They provide a wealth of knowledge outside the usual cornucopia of musical wisdom. Where else can you hear Glen Hansard performing "Astral Weeks" from Austin, Texas? Van will discuss his music during interviews. He is adamant about his private life. Respect it! Don't invade it! Don't cross the line! The fans don't! The writers do! Clinton Heylin's biography is the best and Johnny Rogan's two book have special insights into the Morrison phenomenon. For specialty volumes, Eric Hage and Peter Mills provide academic brilliance and thoughtful interpretations. Their scholarly contributions to the Van Morrison story clarifies the man. Heylin and Rogan are first rate researchers, brilliant writers and knowledgeable historians with a literary flair.

There is a joy to listening to, writing about, and placing Van Morrison in the context of popular culture. He hates to be identified as a rock musician. He is! Or is he? He will do what he can to protect his intellectual property, his privacy and his view of his life. Ask Clinton Heylin!

The biographer finds Van tells a story in each song. It is usually about his daily thoughts. Often it details his interaction with others. Sometimes it is just a song. As Van said it doesn't always have a deeper meaning. Van tells you to interpret it for yourself. The songs are unique. They are produced from fragments in and around his daily experiences. There is usually a complaint, maybe a bit of praise, or an axe to grind. It is observational. It is esoteric. It is invariably personal. It is, at times, the product of his reading. It is impossible to write about Morrison without following the small paths, the secret alleyways and the public musical-business successes, and failures he experienced. In Morrison's life and music there are conflicts, successes and a few dry periods. They all yield biographical gold.

When Clinton Heylin's **Can You Feel The Silence: Van Morrison, A New Biography** was in its planning stage, he sent out his researchers on a mission. They were tasked with finding intimate details of the Belfast Cowboy's life. Then, as the book was in its embryo construction stage, Clinton wrote: "The aura of intimidation Morrison has built around his life, the question of whether his wishes should be respected remains." This comment suggested a pissing matching between Morrison and Heylin. When Heylin's book appeared the first sentence read: "It's not like I wasn't warned. To steer clear or to stir it up, that is always the biographer's conundrum." Van's lawyers threated Heylin during the research period. The war between Heylin and Morrison was colossal. The result was the best biography of Morrison. It was not without warts.

Heylin took on Morrison with the venom of a poisonous snake on steroids. He is an established writer with ten plus books on Bob Dylan. He has literary style. He is an even better researcher. He hired researchers who combed the vineyards of the music business. They come up with new material. Heylin's interviews and archival research at Warner Bros. was a plus. He had a complete discography, thanks to Warner's cooperation. The result was enough material to fill a phalanx of biographies. Heylin claimed it was hard to find anyone who had a good word to say about Van. That may tell one more about Heylin than Morrison. Threats of lawsuits, some court room bantering, and bad blood on all sides, made Heylin's biography a runaway best seller. Everyone made money. That is except Van Morrison.

His elegant prose exposed deep, dastardly dark secrets in Morrison's life. Heylin hurt his book with his barrage of charges, real and imagined, against the Belfast Cowboy. Heylin writes: "I hope that this volume does not come across as the petulant repast of a spurned writer." It does! That comment diminished his brilliant book. What is it Heylin cannot accept? Van is shy! He is private! He is critical of music journalists. His life evolved 24/7 around his music. His career and his constant need for critical acclaim makes for a unique personality. Heylin cannot accept the veil of secrecy.

What are Heylin's faults? He failed to analyze in-depth Van's reading and writing, as well as his pursuit of religion and literary influences beyond his rock 'n' roll life. In the 1970s, as Van ramped up his personal education, he took a slow drift toward subjects that had more in common with T. S. Eliot than Chubby Checker. Heylin doesn't believe it is important. This is unfortunate. The swirling intellect that is Van Morrison defines his life, his writing, his music and his persona. Unlike, Johnny Rogan, Heylin doesn't give enough credit to Van's peripatetic wanderings. How Van's journeys shaped his music is the story of his life. But, make no mistake, Heylin's book is brilliant.

The emphasis on Van's drinking is an unfortunate aside. It borders on the obsessive. Heylin has twenty four pages of drinking stories. Are they important to the story? Some are! Some aren't! Morrison's drinking tales leads into a derogatory direction. What do these stories tell us about his music? Nothing! What do they tell us about his creative process? Even less! Did Heylin make up these stories? No! They are accurate. The simple truth is Van was terrified walking out on stage. That is when a bit of drinking took place. Did it impact his long term career? No! Did it provide Heylin with fodder? Yes! Was it consequential? No! End of drinking stories. They took place. Who cares! If the drinking didn't impact his career what is the point? Heylin concentrated on these tales without a conclusion. Venom is not easily disguised.

Heylin describes Van as a "self-confessed curmudgeon and part time misanthrope." He is right. There is no question there is a cranky Van. There is no question there is, at times, a cooperative Van. Does this have anything to do with his career? Not really! Well maybe for a few pissed off journalists, music executives, airline employees, rental car people and waitresses who have told tales of his volcanic eruptions. Is any of this important to biography? Probably not! Then again, maybe!

What is the purpose of the biographer? The biographer's task is to blend Van's traits, career, music and writing into a coherent narrative. The biographer presents an examination into the soul of the artist. That soul is influenced by his environment, his family, his personal life, and it examines influences in and beyond the music world. Van's complexity is revealed in a portrait of a complex individual with stories and a creative energy.

Van's literary craftsmanship. His perception of life. His sense of his art. These forces suggest why he has written and performed at such a high level for almost seven decades. What has occurred in and around Van's life influenced his musical themes. His biographers, those who host websites, some who write intelligent blogs, and some who turn out lengthy articles, often bend to Morrison's wishes for total privacy. This bastardizes the biographical process. They don't report the forces, the facts, or the idiosyncratic circumstances surrounding his life as it influenced his songwriting. These authors act as proselytizers. The result is hagiography not biography.

The Belfast Cowboy is dead set against anyone using his name for profit. This has led to some unfortunate misunderstandings. Why am I introducing volume three of my six volume biography with this story? It is not to suggest Van is difficult. He can be. He can also be friendly. He attacks through his barristers. He attacks only those he believes have violated his personal space. Using his intellectual property, without licensing it, or stealing a portion of his musical copyright sends his lawyers scurrying to halt publication. He believes biographers steal his intellectual property. Van is insistent on collecting royalties. He can't conceive the biographer is not the enemy. He imagines Clinton Heylin has a Florida winter home from the royalties writing about Van. It is from writing about Bob Dylan. Sorry Van!

Why did Morrison sue Heylin? Van's lawyers spent two years litigating in Britain over copyright infringement. In England it is easier to stop the publication of a book due to libel laws. The British laws on damaging stories, quoting from song lyrics and the written word, as well as unflattering statements that are potentially libelous, makes it easier to halt publication.

Van's lawyers alleged "outrageous false accusations, malice and reckless disregard for the truth and employing quotations from disgruntled lovers, friends and music industry insiders." The real issue was Van wanted to control the narrative. His story, he says, can only be told by him. "Morrison isn't interested in winning the case," Clinton Heylin continued. "There is no way he would ever get on the stand and address any of the issues in the book. He's got too much to lose. It's about stalling the publisher and trying to suppress the book." Heylin is right. In matters of intellectual property, Van does not bend. Is a biography intellectual property? No! Is a biography dangerous to a performer's reputation? Maybe! Maybe not!

After Van sued Heylin's London publisher his barristers descended upon the Chicago Review Press. Fortunately, the Chicago lawyers let Van know there was a First Amendment. Van's lawyers responded with a charge of copyright infringement for quoting a few lyrics. The fair use guidelines prevailed. Van lost. The operative wisdom was rock and roll publishers didn't have the money to fight in court. Before the book was published, Morrison complained Heylin spent too much time on the women, the boozing, and the record deals, as well as attacking his personal life. There wasn't a great deal about the music. Van's lawyers argued no one read the book. This turned out to be a surreptitious argument. It was a runaway best seller. Heylin provided the most complete and in-depth analysis and critique of Morrison's life and career. His book was brilliant on the music side. It contained the most in-depth analysis of his records. Heylin was unusually laudatory about everything Van recorded. Heylin's discography was so complete Warner used it for a variety of legal challenges. Rumor has it even Van consulted it. Heylin seemed to know more about Morrison's music than the brain trust at Warner Bros.

Heylin allegedly was granted access to internal Warner documents. This explains the lack of criticism toward the label. Why? When he was allowed to examine song sheets from the Warner Bros. archives to compile a discography, he did so with a frenetic zeal. One company employee told me Heylin provided a more complete discography with un-released and alternate recorded material. Warner has never said whether or not he updated the Warner discography. Stan Cornyn said at times Warner ignored some of Van's best material. No one at Warner confirmed that. When the case hit the courts there was no luck for Morrison's attorneys. They lost every round.

Warner did not allow Heylin into the archives with tapes, unreleased material and a bevy of released and unreleased recordings as well as demos. Selected company records allegedly were provided to Heylin. The reason Van was so upset with the Heylin book is he allegedly believed there were people inside Warner Bros. out to get him. That explains Van's fury with the Heylin book.

As Van's lawyers screamed of "false allegations," or "malice prose" the judges yawned. Did Van hope for a book that was flattering, not serious and praiseworthy? He did! What he got from Heylin was a brilliant interpretation. It was, in places, belligerently hostile. What Heylin got was continual harassment. He vowed never to write again on the Belfast Cowboy. He has kept that vow.

A good example of Van's control of his music occurred when a vocal track he cut with Frank Zappa, "Dead Girls of London," was prepared for release. Zappa found out how carefully Van controlled his intellectual property. His lawyers and Warner Brothers would not give Zappa permission to release it. When Zappa asked Van about it, the Belfast Cowboy told Frank to talk to Warner Bros. The news reports Van prevented the release of the song may not be accurate. But they could be accurate. Van may have blamed Warner Bros. to maintain his friendship with Zappa. This doesn't sound like Van's typical behavior.

When he met Zappa, sometime later, Van said it was a management decision driven by his lawyers. Ray Ruff told me Warner Bros. did not want Van's music associated with Zappa. The real story? Who knows!

Van's vocal was replaced by Zappa in the final production. The song came out on L. Shankar's 1979 album **Touch Me There** without Van's vocal. L. Shankar, was the arranger and orchestrated the album. Why didn't Van's vocal appear? Zappa was in litigation against Warner Bros. at the time. Ray Ruff said this was the reason for axing Van's vocal. What we know is Stucky Holmes sang the lead vocal. Who was Holmes? Frank Zappa! Van probably felt like he needed a bath after dealing with Zappa. So did everyone else.

The actions of Van's attorneys cowered and intimidated writers for decades. The courts have ruled the public life of a celebrity is fair game for the biographer. Personal issues influenced his songwriting, his performing and his nascent career abounded.

At times Heylin treated Van fairly. He didn't mention Linda Gail Lewis's in-depth law suit. There was no mention of Gigi Lee. He knew about her. He considered it an intrusion upon Van's privacy to discuss her role in his various businesses. Heylin was not a Fleet Street purveyor of indiscriminate facts. He was, and has always been, an outstanding reputable writer. I have great respect for his Morrison book.

The gossip and innuendo it created for Van in the London tabloids over the Linda Gail Lewis incident was a constant source of irritation. It led to a settlement. The non-disclosure agreement excluded the media from the facts privy to the case. But the NDA applied only to the U. K. Linda Gail was allowed to tell her story in America. She had already done that in the U. K. In a 2001 issue of the **London Daily Mirror**, Linda Gail detailed her affair with Van. She charged sexual discrimination. She claimed wrongful termination of concert revenue. I have avoided these issues. They are not germane to Van's career. She settled her law suit. Linda Gail accepted a settlement of $22,500 with a confidentiality agreement. Heylin never discussed the details.

At other times, Heylin was a nasty critic. He was getting even with Morrison for attempting to prevent publication of his book. Heylin's conclusions are intriguing. Here are my favorites. He accuses Van of striving to become a "pop singer." My thoughts are Van would opt to become an ax murderer before a pop singer. Van did everything he could to avoid pop records. When he had a pop hit, he bitched. He told reporters he didn't like the song. Heylin's descriptions of Van in concert leads me to believe the biographer avoided his concerts. There is little understanding of Morrison's life-long spiritual quest. Heylin didn't read in-depth on the litany of Van's religious ideas, philosophy books or quirky history tomes influencing him. Morrison's extensive reading shaped his songwriting. Heylin fails to address this in an in-depth manner. He labels Van's "spiritual quest," as one fraught with "a personal settler of accounts, repaying those who had crossed him before the more mundane matter of saving humanity got in the way." (p. 473) This is excellent writing. It is also accurate. Van went so far recently to license all of his albums to Spotify except for the one his former wife, Janet Morrison Minto, graced the cover on. Van never forgets. Petty? Yes! Being Van? Yes!

Van has good reason to be angry with the Heylin book. This is due to the faulty tale the Belfast Cowboy lacked social skills. He doesn't. He does at times lack tact. He does at times explode over business. He is a contrarian. Van is an individualist. He is a survivor in an industry that eats its young. The faulty logic in Heylin's description concerning Van's personality influenced other writers. Van is not a Saint. Neither is he an unrequited Sinner. The truth lies somewhere in the middle.

Heylin fails to recount the best Van stories. Those that are humorous. Those that show Morrison's humanity. Those that demonstrate his playful quirky nature. Those where he is mistaken for a common person not a celebrity. When Morrison showed up at a London press party, he was dressed in an old tweed jacket, his shirt had an egg stain on it, his hat was worn and dirty. A London journalist hollered: "Did anyone order a mini-cab?" When a reporter asked Van who he was, Van responded: "Bozo the fucking clown." Van was largely anonymous at times in London. He loved it.

There are hundreds of stories where Van is agreeable. He can act as a cultured gentleman. He has had fun. Bob Neuwirth told me Van was "an unrequited Leprechaun." Those tales didn't make Heylin's book. When Van played the Ottawa, Canada Bluesfest in 2015 the staff heard he liked hot apple pie. They found a local bakery. They heated a piece. Van ate it. He had a second piece. He came out of his dressing room to talk to the person who brought in the apple pie. He congratulated the baker. He talked to her for over half an hour after she delivered the pie. That is Van on a good day. The person who delivered the pie, Sandra Mansour, laughed. She looked at Van and said: "You know I was expecting you to be real nasty but this has been a pleasant surprise. You're kind of cool." Van erupted in laughter. He commented: "Ignore the press."

The problem with writing about Van Morrison was shown when Greil Marcus, in his introduction to **When The Rough Gods Go Riding: Listening To Van Morrison**, in 2010, observed: "Consumed by the resentment over the swindle of stardom, fame, records, money, debt, and oblivion, caught in the trap of performing and publishing contracts after Bern's death at the end of 1966, Morrison found himself in Boston." (p. 6) Marcus is brilliant. That statement summed up Van. In my previous book, **Van Morrison: From Astral Weeks To Stardom, 1968 To 1972**, I found in that five year period Van beat Bert Berns and Bang Records at the game of not paying the artist. He secured his intellectual property. He sent the production team of Schwaid-Merenstein packing. He convinced Warner Bros. to grant his commercial freedom. By 1973 a new Van Morrison emerged. Then Janet Planet left and Carol Guida arrived. Women intensified his writing.

While things were better at Warner Brothers, the war with the industry never ended. During the early Warner years, Van produced a bevy of 1970s hits. This established his commercial appeal. Van was conflicted over hit records. He didn't like the Warner Bros. pop sound. The singer-songwriter label frustrated him.

He said repeatedly, he didn't want to be "the flavor of the month." When Greil Marcus concluded Van released an "endless stream of dull and tired albums through the 1980s and 1990s" (p. 9), he missed the point. Those albums reflected Van's creative drift. He moved into writing from a stream of consciousness position. Why? Van said it enhanced his intellectual integrity. Those albums were the product of living in Marin County in the 1970s. The pastoral countryside. The isolated house on a hill. The whirlpool in the yard. These were symbols of a new life. It was a long way from Hyndford Street. At least this is how Van's friends joked when they visited. Chris Michie was observant. He told me possessions weren't important to Van. A good environment was a constant force driving his writing. Van worked to maintain a lifestyle he only dreamed about a few years earlier. By 1973, he saw the gold ring of fiscal rewards in the rock 'n' roll world. He worked hard to succeed.

His home was high on a hill in a remote section of Fairfax with a large gate hiding him from a prying public. Then his wife, Janet left. A few months later a new lady came into his life. She wasn't interested in fame. She care very little about money. She was a student of religious philosophical themes. She was perfect for Van. Her name was Carol Guida.

It was at the Fairfax home, where Guida placed rubber ducks in the whirlpool for his daughter, Shana, to play with, as she settled in for almost three and a half years of a life with the Belfast Cowboy. Van's beautiful new muse accentuated his creativity. She was also her own person. He had never met such an independent woman. She was not only a muse. Guida was an observer of Van's writing habits and thinking.

Van writes for the moment. What he feels is what he writes. "I remember standing in line with Van in a bank. He looked at his surroundings. He grabbed a bank deposit slip. He furtively wrote lyrical fragments," Carol Guida remarked. She was amazed at the media rumors Van was semi-retired. "He read, wrote and continued his creative journey with me," Guida concluded.

What goes on around him is combined with a photographic memory of visual images. This created the constant production machine highlighting Morrison's record releases. He detests biography. An academic, Michael Fishman, published a short lived newsletter he handed out at concerts. This indicated the level of attraction Van's music had for concert goers.

Greil Marcus got it right. Who else got it right? Simon Gee's fanzine got it right. **Wavelength** was a fair minded critic, as Van's career flourished. Art Siegel and Pat Corley were brilliant analysts who wrote about Van and contributed to the various fanzines. Michael Seltzer was a super fan as was Roma Downey, Jeanette Heinen and Bernard McGuinn. Corley's posts and his book had more to say than the biographers. Why this outpouring of words? People want to know what makes Morrison's creativity so vast? There is no answer.

Simon Gee's brilliant magazine, **Wavelength**, was more than a fanzine. It was laced with professional writing. The superb layout and design spared no cost. The in-depth stories analyzed Van's songwriting, his performing and his life. This coverage was friendly to Van without being hagiography. Van persisted. He believed Gee was making a fortune from writing about him. End of the magazine. Van's lawyers eviscerated it.

"Van was on a mission to make sure no one took advantage of him. He didn't see that Gee's magazine was in fact a benefit to his career," Chris Michie continued. "As a person and performer, Van came alive with a level of analysis befitting his lyrical depth. He made sure that direction was never compromised. Van had tunnel vision."

The fanzines often were more accurate. They represented a more sophisticated analysis. The mainstream media emphasized strive and conflict. When Van was angry, concerning press coverage, he had a valid point. There were two sides to the press war that began when Van told a **New Musical Express** writer to fuck off in 1964. Van's media complaints continue to occupy the press. Over the last two decades, there has been a kinder, gentler Van.

There was one fan who stood out as a supporter trumpeting Van Morrison's nascent genius. He was an Englishman. His name was Simon Gee. A tall, quiet, self-deprecating person, he was on a mission to trumpet the musical genus of the Belfast Cowboy. That mission was one he took seriously. He established the most comprehensive, fair minded, intelligent and analytical magazine in rock 'n' roll history.

Simon Gee's fanzine, **Wavelength**, was a source of musical, never private, information on the Belfast Cowboy. Van shut it down claiming Gee was making a fortune. He said his privacy was compromised. The truth is Gee was lucky to break even. This wonderfully analytical and intelligent magazine was filled with the one thing Van Morrison abhorred. The unvarnished truth. It was fair and impartial. It was the work of a super fan. With a literary flair, and a dedication to quality, Simon Gee was taken to court for what was his commitment to interpretive excellence. **Wavelength**, which began in 1994, was published three times a year. Every concert, recording date, record release and personal appearance was analyzed creating an accurate picture of the Belfast Cowboy's genius. In 2008, after legal difficulties with Morrison's barristers, Gee shut down his magazine. His magazine remains the best Morrison tome. But it wasn't the first one.

Another Van fanzine, Stephen McGinn's the **Van Morrison Newsletter**, was produced at a Western Canada University, where McGinn was a professor. The McGinn newsletter began in the late 1980s with the notion of sharing tapes and gossip. After placing an ad in **Q** magazine, McGinn received almost fifty replies. That was enough to put out his mimeographed newsletter. This turned into ten interesting and highly readable issues. Simon Gee was one of his co-conspirators. They formed a bond and a friendship. In 1994, Simon Gee took over the publication renaming it **Wavelength**. It went on to become the premier Morrison magazine.

Stephen McGinn was a fan. He had no intention of making money. My understanding is he lost a great deal of money. When Van's lawyers went to the professor's administration, at the University of British Columbia, they threatened the institution with an intellectual property theft lawsuit. The university folded. The professor was on the verge of losing his job. The newsletter ceased publication. What is the point? Van may have had no idea his lawyers went as far as they did. I have had numerous Morrison band mates, two road managers, people inside the Bill Graham Organization, and others, telling me of Van lamenting some of these moves. To a person, they said if he believed others were profiting from his talent, he sued. One source chuckled and said: "He would sue his mother." One Belfast insider claimed that Van considered suing his mother, Violet, for performing his songs. I bought this ne'er do well half a dozen pints of Guinness. I realized he was shining he me on. Mervyn Solomon arrived to rescue me from Eric Wrixon. The point is Van was correct. There are those who continued to make excuses for themselves by going after Morrison. As a founding member of Thin Lizzy, Wrixon said he had a rock and roll pedigree. The British press loved these interviews. The truth was Wrixon spent very little time with Van. They lost touch over the years. It didn't matter. The press reported his comments verbatim. What the press didn't report is Wrixon left Them and Thin Lizzy before they achieved commercial success. As Van said the memory and recollection of some sources are suspect. I asked Mervyn Solomon: "Were Van and Wrixon friends?" He looked at me for a moment. Mervyn smiled: "How could they be. Eric left to live in Italy and Germany. He left every group before it achieved success. He told the press tall tales. He didn't work hard like Van. Wrixon was a gossip and lay about." That answered my question. At Wrixon's 2015 funeral there was no word from the Belfast Cowboy.

It was only fitting the first fanzine reporting on Morrison originated from Ireland. When **Into The Music** came out in Dublin it had the requisite Irish flavor. The first issue was in April 1990. I had never heard of Donal Caine and I never could find him. After ten publications it folded. Caine was an elusive figure. He vanished into the rock and roll foothills. Another fanzine, **No Guru**

Newsletter, was an American effort with attention to Van's mysticism. What is the point to these fanzines? They provided some of the best material for fans. In 1983, when my book, **Van Morrison: The Mystic's Music**, came out sales increased yearly due to these publications. Morrison's fans knew his music with a complete command of it. His life and his intellectual pursuits were better known by the fans than some biographers.

The **No Method Newsletter** was an Arlington, Virginia effort by a group known as the Van Morrison Appreciation Society. Michael Fishman and Jack Turner were the brains behind this project. It had a literary bent, a superb level of analysis and brilliant writing. Fishman, a dedicated academic, set a high standard. This short lived newsletter was an indication of the depth, intellectual prowess and continual growth of Van's literary skills.

The story behind the Michael Fishman newsletter is a fascinating one. The idea for this newsletter began after Fishman left a Morrison concert thinking someone should organize a publication to examine the "music and philosophy of Van Morrison." Fishman wrote to Caledonia Productions on December 4, 1988 describing the purpose of the newsletter. His letter described the notion of examining "Morrison's music…as well as poetry, philosophy and Zen Buddhism." Caledonia Productions answered with a polite response. They would be in touch. Fishman began the mimeographed newsletter. Biographers found gold in their pages. A donation of five dollars was requested to become a member of the Van Morrison Appreciation Society.

The **No Method Newsletter** came out in the summer of 1991. The mention of Morrison books, the insightful letters from fans, and the collaborations that Van had with Tom Jones and Bob Dylan graced this issue. The Turner-Fishman newsletter demonstrated the loyal fan base and the increasingly intellectual maturity in Morrison's writing.

Peter Viney's blog contained some wonderfully personal reviews. He also included visuals of ticket stubs, photos and concert shows. Viney's blog from 1998 through 2019 provided a wealth of information on Van's concerts. Much of this material was in Simon Gee's **Wavelength**. Viney lived in Poole in the U. K. He has been a full time writer since 1980 with a list of publications making me look like a dilettante. Viney, with an advanced degree in American Studies and English, reviewed Morrison's shows with the skilled eye of a serious professional.

For the terminally factually induced fan concerned with statistics, the Vanomatic.de site is a must. In Germany this site has a complete discography, official statistics, a list of key career facts, in-depth descriptions of live shows, and a lengthy glossary. This description doesn't do credit to Gunter Becker's website. His section entitled, "Info," lists useful links which includes Visions of Pat, which is Pat Corley's take on Van and other artists. Pat entitles his blog: "Just A Hobby On The Internet." But, in reality, it is a prized musical site including much more than Van's music.

Pat Thomas, an industry insider and a talented writer-musician, has many analytical blog postings on Van Morrison. He continues to work on his inclusive book on Van's songwriting with brilliant postings on **Astral Weeks**, **Moondance** and a host of other Morrison albums. As a professional writer, Thomas is able to dissect what Van's words mean and why they are important.

For the 1970s there are many great reviews. There were two that helped me to formulate some of my arguments. See Pat Thomas' 2015 reviews "Van Morrison's Moondance: A Perfect Album" and "Come On People, It's Van Morrison's Astral Weeks" for examples of incisive analysis at East Portland blog. While not a fanzine, Thomas's writing is an important source.

Simon Gee's thirty issues, his organizing of the fans, a bed he gave me for a few nights when I was in a town near London doing research, and his enthusiasm inspired my six volume biography. As I completed this third volume, I am indebted to Art Siegel, Bart Hendriks and Michael Seltzer's wisdom, Russ Dugoni's encyclopedic musical mind, Bernard McGuinn's affable countenance, Hamlet de Los Santos's Spanish tales, Ron Sexton's Southern charm, Chris Brandsetter's photos, Jeanette Heinen's observations and a host of other Van fans many of whom wish to remain anonymous helped go formulate this volume. They all made this volume possible. I respect that they, as I do, honor Van's privacy. If the story of the music is to be told accurately without interference from Van there can be no threats to those analyzing his career. Those threats produce hagiography. Otherwise, how it does his amazing talent shine? Enjoy this book! I love rabbit holes, side bars and small bits of seemingly minor points in the Belfast Cowboy's life. Hopefully, the result is an understanding of his songwriting and performing.

Why is this period significant? There are ten reasons that helps one understand Van Morrison's evolution as a singer-songwriter, businessman and as a person. After you read these ten points it is apparent why two books were needed to cover this period.

First: He gained complete control over his production beginning with **Hard Nose The Highway**. It gave Van a sense of his future musical direction. He looked back. This means he mined his personal experiences in lyrical form. He translated those observations into song. There is no need to interview the Belfast Cowboy. He laid out his life in a collection of print interviews. Then along came the Internet. The myriad interviews on YouTube suggest how Van thinks. How he writes is important. Van is described in his own words. Why does he detest biography? He answers during interviews. If only Clinton Heylin and Johnny Rogan had the last two decades of interviews. They would have appreciated Van's life and career in more detail.

Second, The Caledonia Soul Orchestra and the Caledonia Soul Express answered the question regarding his experiences formatting a band. He formed, molded, instructed and brought together two of the tightest musical aggregations of the 1970s. Van never stopped re-inventing his stage persona. He evolved into a well-oiled performer (no pun intended) who continues to delight his audiences. The ninety minutes of Van Morrison in concert, with little interruption from the promoter, the fans, the record labels and the fledgling rock and roll press, established his brand.

Third: He archived everything he wrote, collected and produced. When **The Philosopher's Stone** was released, the word was out. The Morrison archives were a treasure trove. The cache of unreleased material remains virtually untouched. The storage sheds, Van rented in Marin County, were recipients of his un-released treasures. Much of this material allegedly has been moved. There are people, rumor has it, working on box sets. What is archived? To the present day it remains an unsolved mystery. Van's cache of unreleased songs is a commercial blockbuster.

Fourth: He interviewed and hired new managers at will. Was this capricious? Maybe yes! Maybe no! It is a character trait. One musician claimed, it was Van's way of taking his music into new directions. He needed a manager who understood his mercurial musical changes. His whims persisted. He remains demanding. He makes the decisions. The result is an unbreakable will to protect his intellectual property. Others claim he is laid back and friendly in the studio. Mark Isham said it best: "When Van is happy with your playing there is no problem." That is, as Isham suggested, true as long as you are talented and on his wavelength. Matt Holland, Jay Berliner, Ronnie Montrose, John Allair, David Hayes, Teena Lyle, Chris Michie and John Platania among others found Van an eager collaborator. Those who have worked with Van in the studio seldom complain.

I interviewed over two hundred people in preparation for my six volume biography. I found no consensus. Some people love him. Some people are uneasy with him. There is agreement only on his musical genius. Why? Van's life is first and foremost about his career. It is always about the music. When he recorded and toured with Linda Gail Lewis, Van asked her to take piano lessons. He told Linda Gail she played too much like her brother, Jerry Lee Lewis. He told her she had to expand her repertoire. Van told her she had to learn to play in a broader direction. She was not happy with these suggestions.

Fifth: He made sure his intellectual property was protected. He did this through a phalanx of lawyers, accountants and business managers. He is a major corporation. In matters of business, Van demonstrated an expertise belying his youth. Caledonia Productions was the prototype for other rock artists to combat the industry.

Sixth: Van hired various public relations specialists to re-do his media image. They arranged requests for interviews. That is if the interviewer discussed his new release. These interviews often turned into reflections of his moods and concerns. Some media questions set him off. Reporters often vilify Van. A case in point was the Laura Barton interview in the **London Independent**. Barton couldn't wait to talk to Van. She said it was a life-long dream. It turned into a petulant nightmare. Barton was there to discuss Van's new album **Three Chords And The Truth**. It was October 2019. Van was tired of these interviews. "I have the feeling that Morrison is curling up into a ball before me and closing his eyes so that I might not see him," Barton wrote. Van reacted negatively to some of her questions. She knows how to follow up. A case in point was when Barton asked him about new jazz musicians. Van made it clear. He didn't listen to new artists. She asked him if he has heard of Moses Boyd? Van answered: "No." It was all downhill after that.

She infuriated Morrison by suggesting he was obliged to answer her questions. He sat stunned. What the hell is going on? Van took the offensive. "Well, what are ya? Are you a journalist, what are ya?" There was a stunned silence. Barton observed: "He looks at me with a kind of disdain. I dutifully reel off the various components of my career," Barton wrote. She was angry and defensive. "Ok, well, I do music," Morrison responded. Barton thinks of telling him to grow up. She doesn't. She writes it. What is the point of this exchange? The sixteen minutes and twenty eight seconds Barton spent with Van suggests his complicated nature, the pressures of the music business, and the perils of sitting with Van in a media interview. Should he be excused for his behavior? No! Should it be considered? Yes! It gives us the picture of the complete man. There are other interviews where he is a prince. To understand him, however, it is necessary to examine his puerile thoughts. The Barton saga reveals an at times on going war with the press.

Why was Van difficult? On August 31, 2021, on her Twitter account, Barton wrote wishing Van a belated Happy Birthday: "Let's all listen to this and remember how goddamn sublime the man can be when he's not being a curmudgeon or a covid-denier or spoiling for a fight." Whether or not Van knew of that tweet in unknown. What is known is she posted a video of "Linden Arden Stole The Highlights," after she made this comment. Barton declared war on Morrison. He responded. The Barton-Morrison exchanges tells the biographer all one needs to know about Van and the press.

The **London Times** weighed in on Van. In an interview with Bill Hodgkinson, Van complained he found himself without support for his anti-covid comments. He viewed himself as a "lockdown refusenik." It bothered him to be heavily criticized. He doesn't take criticism well. Despite the press, Van defended his right of free speech. "Freedom of speech used to be OK-what's happened?" Van commented. No one reminded Van it was a double edged sword.

Seventh: After the divorce from Janet, he doubled down on his private life. He made sure the press realized what he did apart from the music was no one's business. That course is consistent to the present day. His time with Carol Guida, 1973-1977, was without a media presence. That was the way Van liked it. The result is Guida remained a mysterious figure in Van's life. The truth was less complicated. Carol is a typical California vixen. She is beautiful. She is smart. She is talented. She is spiritual. She was never a druggie. She was supremely intellectual. Nothing has changed as these traits still define Carol Guida.

Eighth: Van realized he needed to balance his professional successes with a private life. He has done that in spades. He developed a persona that kept the media and fans away. He is aloof. He maintains a select coterie of insiders. They provide a well-adjusted, if somewhat boring, life. This is the way he likes it. Van remans a shy loner with good friends.

Ninth: Despite his fame and fortune, Van leads a relatively normal life. He remains centered with an often combative personality. There are no minders or bodyguards. There is no entourage. I heard from several band members Van might have had writer's block in the 1970s. This wasn't true. He was stoic and quietly productive. He rearranged his career for the long haul. He was relaxing. Enjoying his life. He was determined not to be a rock and roll casualty. Writer's block was a myth. Who perpetuated it? Van Morrison! He did so to isolate himself from the press.

Tenth: He lives the creative life. He worries about his intellectual development. He doesn't need advisers to tell him what to do. He dropped out of school at fourteen. His songwriting became a college English 101 course. It is a part of his life to the present day. Read! Read! Read! That was Van's mantra. It still is. The songs roll of his pen due to his voracious reading. His blue collar work ethic makes him productive 24/7.

Van Morrison is a rock and roll survivor. In 1978, Van told Davitt Sigerson: "I've been around for quite a while." From his showband days, to Them, to an early solo career, to the legendary wisdom of **Astral Weeks**, and finally, superstardom. For Van it was a dream come true. He worked hard to get there.

As Van said: "Fame is not good for creativity." When Anthony Mason on CBS Sunday Morning on March 3, 2009 asked Van: "Are you uncomfortable with fame." Morrison responded: "Fame is a complete negative for me." Then Van suggested he accepted it. He said he needed people to buy his records so he could continue to do the work. One of the nuggets from this brief conversation was his appreciation for Charles Mingus. No one has explored Mingus' influence.

How, then, has he balanced fame with the desire for a normal life? It has not been an easy process. He has been cranky at times. Intimidating on other occasions. He makes it clear; it was his way or the highway. Over time, with age and experience, he mellowed. He prospered. He modified his act. His life resembles perfection. The press is still after him. Real or imagined? You will have to ask Van.

Van told Mason the music lived. It had a life. That was the way Van wanted it. In the 1980s Van confessed stage fright came and went. "I stopped doing it for a while," Van said of the mid-1970s. He intimated the performance with The Band, at the Last Waltz, began his road back to performing. As he looked back in 2009 with Mason it was obvious the mid-1970s was a watershed in his performing life.

What does this volume do? For my third installment from 1973 through a portion of 1974 Van cemented his songwriting legend. He fine-tuned his in concert persona. His business successes were woven into this narrative. As he said concerning his acclaimed 1973 tour and 1974 album, **It's Too Late To Stop Now**, he set the template for a double live album for a legendary tour. The next volume completes the 1974 through 1979 story. The result? Becoming Van Morrison.

Carol Guida was a fountain of information on the Marin County chapters. She refused to talk about her private, personal relationship with Morrison. She respects his privacy. She had no ill will toward him. When one of my interviewees told me she was stalking him. I laughed! Guida has a full and rich life. She is bright. She is successful.

She has moved on. Her book will tell her full story with Van. She has other highlights of her life. She combined them with her time with Morrison into an intriguing and interesting manuscript. She corrected only the misconceptions about her role in Van's life vis-à-vis the music, her role as a muse and her intellectual partnership with the Belfast Cowboy, which lasted until early 1977, when she left him.

Van Morrison from 1973 to 1974 was a product of Marin County. The California sub-culture, which he detested, shaped his rock 'n' roll persona. The wealth of new material on Van in Marin County, a lengthy compare and contrast series of chapters on the It's Too Late To Stop Now tour, and the subsequent double live album provide the gist for his emergence as a major creative force. That led to a chapter on Van's writing. Not just songwriting but his evolution as a prose stylist. When I broke the book into two parts Carol Guida's introduction to the story was a necessity. She was there until early 1977. For that period Van was obsessed with forming a business structure to protect his intellectual property. He did! He triumphed! Guida was with him every step of the way. She was his muse. She tells her story.

Why break the period into two books? This book analyzes and explains how Van took his career, business and music wise, into a permanent zone of success. It was about "Becoming Van Morrison." The next step 1974 through 1979 was making the Van Morrison trademark permanent.

I have tried to construct, with copious detail, the forces, pressures and cultural influences shaping Van's songwriting. I did this while contrasting his lyrical brilliance with an in-progress concert genius. Van was like Shakespeare. The playwright left a huge, distinguished body of work. We know very little about the man. Van fits into the same mold.

Biography is not Van Morrison's favorite topic. He hates it. Why? He claims no one gets it right. His outrageous behavior, tantrums, boorish remarks and pissing matches with journalists have never ended. This is a good thing. It gives the biographer insights. He has a psyche strewn with musical innovations, petty hatreds and brilliant ideas.

Van presents a tough exterior when it comes to his intellectual property. His ability to get paid is his foremost goal. That is what this book is about. To get to that story Van's specious work ethic, and his intellectual evolution tells the story.

There is a rich, rewarding context to Van's life biographers often miss. His graciousness with his band. His high wage to those supporting him in concert. His treatment of those who open for him is spectacular. Sam Butera told me he didn't know a thing about Van when he appeared with him in San Francisco. "Van Morrison was a class act. He treated me and my Las Vegas band with dignity and world class accommodations. He paid us handsomely. Van said there was a car waiting 24/7 to take me around San Francisco. I ate at two Italian restaurants. I couldn't believe his humility," Butera concluded. He shook his head. He smiled as he left Bimbo's.

When Butera appeared with Van at Bimbo's, he was amazed at the fan base. "I couldn't believe it," Butera continued. "We were playing on this small little side stage and Van comes out to join us for a song. I thought Frank Sinatra entered the stage, what a great act, he covered Louis Prima better than anyone. Crazy!" The biographer can carp and complain about Van. Those who play with him see another side to his personality. He is not always a rascal. When he is on stage there is a window into his creative soul. When he is off stage, as he demonstrated in the Leo Green interviews, he can provide a personal look inside his musical genius. It is not easy being Van Morrison.

Van's enigmatic lyrics define his haunting prose and brilliant musical style. His scintillating word magic is a constant insight into his psyche. His frustration with the music business is an integral part of his personality. Following Van's life is a wonderfully disorienting experience. It is much like a roller coaster ride. The ups and downs are thrilling. The end of the ride dispels a legendary talent if a bit piqued by life.

The spectral aspect of Irish, English and American images run through Van's enormous catalogue. He is a new kind of rock writer. He is a musician with a flair for the past, think Bobby "Blue" Bland, Irish music, the Chieftains and John Lee Hooker.

To quote from his lyrics is to court a law suit. His personal life is sketchy. He is not above leading the biographer or fans astray. Only when he is outed by the press, unfairly maligned, overly criticized, or when he goes off on reporters does this become important.

The purpose of this book is to demonstrate how the forces in his life influenced his songwriting. A good example was in "Fair Play," when he used the name "Geronimo." Those who interpret his work said it as a reference to the Native American warrior. It wasn't. Van's use of Geronimo was in reference to a home he lived in with Carol Guida in the valley area of Marin known as San Geronimo. This is why Van does not want his songs interpreted. Only he knows the meaning. This book interprets his songs. I am sure I don't always get it right. I tried. Research for a rock and roll book is nothing like my doctoral dissertation research and the other books I have written. Why? There are no Van Morrison archives. The major obstacle to rock 'n' roll biography is the lack of collected materials. Interviews are important. The printed word is more precise and helpful. Combine them! Viola! An interpretive book.

To overcome a lack of archive material is not a problem After in-depth research and using hundreds of sources, I flushed out a talented, but enormously complex, singer-songwriter. The raw data is there for a book. This method was necessary to describing the inner Van. His voluminous writing is a treasure trove of personal information flushing out Van's thought processes. His mind is an astonishing one. He combines carping criticism with a poetic beauty. If Vladimir Nabokov had been a rock 'n' roll singer, he would have been the first Van Morrison. There is a defined mystery to Van's life. That makes his personal and musical journey intriguing. It also makes it difficult to interpret. That is why this book analyzes the germination of the Caledonia Soul Orchestra in the last few months of 1972. Van sat on the top of his hillside Fairfax home looking out at the valley fuming about what Warner Bros. hadn't done to promote his records. He told close friends he would form a band to make his tours world class. He started the process. Jack Schroer, Van's horn man, talked about the Caledonia Soul Orchestra long before Van organized the band. "I knew it was special," Schroer continued. "I did not realize what Van was doing. He was a genius."

It was in this time frame, early 1973, Van began the process of reinventing himself. He thought for years about how the old blues guys reinterpreted themselves on stage. John Lee Hooker, a close friend, became the model for this transition. Van followed John Lee's formula. This created, by 1980, the Van Morrison who is still performing with a gusto in his late-seventies. The Shakespeare of Telegraph Avenue, Greil Marcus, said it best when he wrote of the Belfast Cowboy: "Van Morrison was as intense and imaginative a performer as any to have emerged in the wake of the Beatles....What he lacked in glamour he made up in strangeness...."

Greil Marcus' brilliant prose, carved in stone, ignored a part of the real Van Morrison. Sitting in his lofty hillside Berkeley home, Marcus cast aside Van's blue collar, hard-working, dedication to his craft. It is a complicated story. "Strangeness" is a part of the story. But only a small part. Intelligent prose makes Greil Marcus's book on listening to Van Morrison a must for the fans. For the biographer it is a brilliant tool. It reminds us of how much more there was to Van's life.

The period from 1973 into the summer of 1974 established Morrison's career. "Becoming Van Morrison" was the result in the midst of releasing a double vinyl masterpiece. Van created the business model, the songwriting and the performing brilliance continuing to the present day. He had no idea the plan would work. The future Sir Van Morrison was in the dim recesses of history. The honorary doctorate, the Grammy and Songwriter awards, a star on the Hollywood Walk of Fame, a place on Presidents George W. Bush, Bill Clinton and Barack Obama's playlists and Van's induction into the Rock 'n' Roll Hall of Fame were in his future. That path began with the release of **It's Too Late To Stop Now**. He had other albums and hit records prior to this live masterpiece. It was when he began his 1973 tour to support the album there was a new Van Morrison. The title of this book **Becoming Van Morrison: It's Too Late To Stop Now, 1973-1974** pays tribute to his business-creative-performing genius.

Why does Van Morrison matter? He is one of the few singer-songwriters to beat the record business. The major labels were ruthless ignoring royalties, selecting who would and who would not be a star, while bankrolling and paying only those who were fiscally responsible for millions of dollars in corporate profits. Morrison turned the tables.

"The producer made all the money. I became a producer," Van told Leo Green. After dropping out of school at fourteen, Van's attention in the 1970s to detail, his voracious reading habits, his blue collar work ethic and a 24/7 commitment to his career produced a legendary Hall of Fame path.

Van Morrison is elusive. "Silence, exile, cunning-and so on," Stephen Dedalus wrote. Who was Stephen Dedalus? He was James Joyce's alter ego in **The Portrait Of The Artist As A Young Man**. Why the alter ego? To escape detection in a world of celebrity and material goods. The alter ego allows one to be left alone. Van Morrison never invented an alter ego. This book tells you why he should have developed one.

Van worried about the power of the media. He fought it for decades. In the last twenty years, he has, at times, embraced the media. He tells his story to most journalists. He rants and raves to a few. As a performing and songwriting legend, he has that platform. His attempts to distance himself from the media spotlight have failed over the years. Since 2000 he has attempted a modicum of cooperation. When he has a new album, he gives interviews. Otherwise, he demands a private life.

In the late 1960s, he lived amongst average folks in New York, Boston and Woodstock. Van appeared lost in America. Then Janet Planet wanted to move to Marin County. Van purchased a house in Fairfax. The early 1970s Warner Bros. albums sold massively. Then, as the money rolled in like a veritable hurricane, Van had the means to reinvent his life. By 2016 he was transformed into Sir Van Morrison. Suddenly he lived amongst bankers, businessmen, lawyers, editors, doctors and retired millionaires. Not surprisingly, he remained the same person who resided in a dingy New York hotel in 1967. That is the beauty of Van Morrison. He is the same person who went to bed in second hand sheets as the Van Morrison who wakes up in silk sheets. As this story encapsules two volumes in seven years of his life from 1973 through 1979, it highlights his dramatic evolution as a person and artist. His Irish character, combined with Marin County influences, a new muse Carol Guida, and a continued obsession with American music finalizing his songwriting and performing genius.

There is an emotional side to Van's life. If you understand that his story makes sense. He is a brilliant songwriter. He is a performing genius. That comes with warts. To understand Van the man the warts must be considered.

The purpose of this book is to convince the reader of three things. First, the Caledonia Soul Orchestra was the first step in Van Morrison's fifty plus year journey to rock 'n' roll performing immortality. Second, Marin County formed his art and its influences continued his development into a Rock 'n' Roll Hall of Fame writer-performer. Third, Van won the battle against the record labels, the media critics, the fluctuating fans, the critical musicians, and, along the way, he became one of the most authentic voices in the history of rock 'n' roll.

The role of San Francisco remains an integral part of the Van Morrison story. Most biographies pay lip service to the California Dream. That is a mistake. Van wrote from his physical surroundings. He imbibed the local culture. He reflected the changing landscape.

Van's persona is central to the story. He was never predictable. He was often difficult to work with and understand. This was a plus in refining his natural talent. Van's unyielding view of his art. The need to hide his personal life. The constant pressure to prevent any interpretation of who he was and why he was a creative genius is his unique story.

Morrison challenged the rock 'n' roll world from the first day he stepped on stage with the Monarchs. By the time this book ends in mid-1974, he established his songwriting genius. His age? He was twenty nine in 1974. He was ready to make the rock and roll world look like fools. Mission accomplished!

Van With Daughter Shana Receiving His Knighthood

PROLOGUE

"Freedom is not a fruit of every climate, and it is not therefore in the capacity of every people," The Social Contract.

JEAN JACQUES ROUSSEAU

"He doesn't like a lot of people around him. Really he is a recluse. He is quiet. We never go anywhere."

JANET MORRISON MINTO

"Where is the Life we have lost in living?
Where is the wisdom we have lost in knowledge?
Where is the knowledge we have lost in information?"

T. S. ELIOT

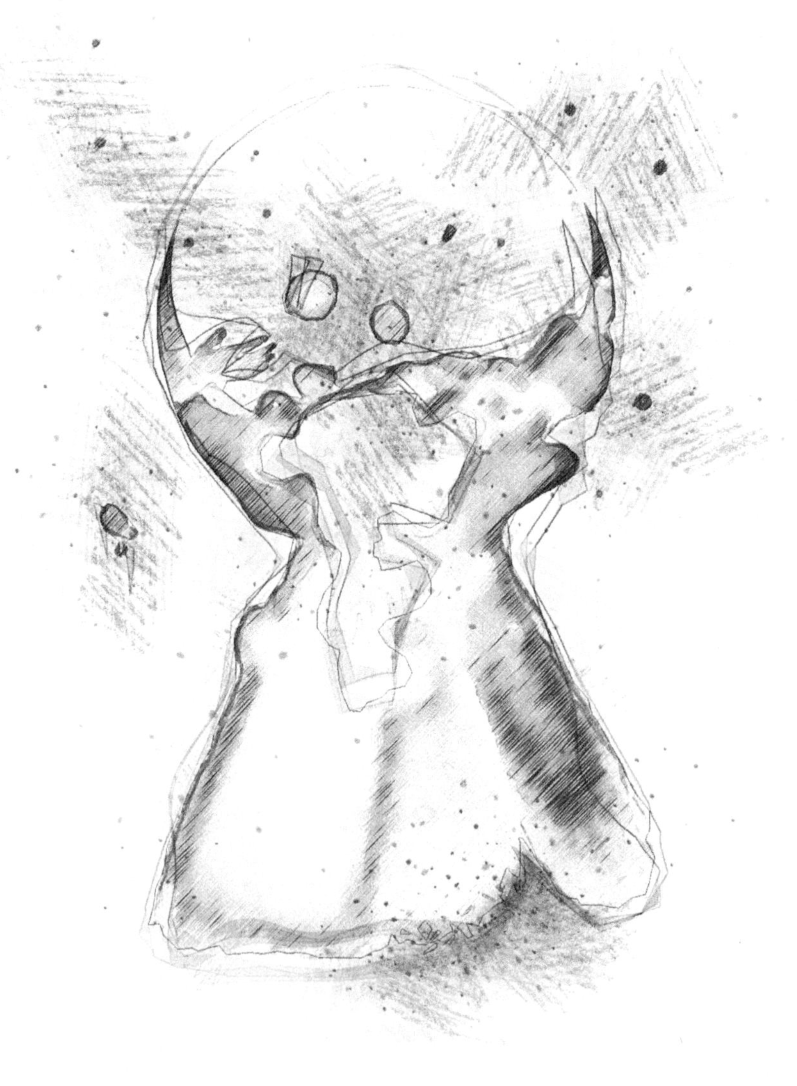

The changes in Van Morrison's music in 1973 resulted from a visit to Ireland. The Emerald Island was his muse. Belfast was forever his home. The Troubles kept him living elsewhere. Van was apolitical. He remained private. He was perpetually creative. He was concerned about Northern Ireland. He wasn't interested in droning on about political problems. His heart remained in Belfast. Van never felt he belonged in America. Marin County nursed his creativity. The lack of comfort, due to financial difficulties, in New York, Boston and Woodstock ended with a move to the bucolic, country oriented lifestyle north of San Francisco. By the early 1970s fame, fortune and a calm life came with stardom. As Van found out fame and fortune was a mixed blessing.

As Van stood in the window of his Fairfax home the shining, gibbous moon inspired him. At the top of the hill, where his house was located, he had privacy, a leafy atmosphere, weather much like Belfast and a garage converted into a recording studio. Isolation! Harmony! Solitude! These were the forces creating a hard working songwriter destined for lyrical greatness. Carol Guida arrived in the Fall of 1973 providing him with an intellectual partner.

Fairfax's inspiration led, a decade later, to a creative binge into the 1980s giving birth to the modern day Van Morrison. As a blustery wind blew in from the Pacific Ocean daily, Van had fleeting memories of Belfast.

Marin County was the first place in the U. S. Van felt comfortable. He didn't have fond memories of living in a small hotel in New York. He cringed at the thought of a student flophouse apartment in Boston. His dingy rental home in Woodstock accelerated his creativity while depressing him.

When he lived in these disparate locations, his creative juices were energized by the American landscape. Songwriting was his greatest joy. Performing? He was ill at ease with it. Was Van inordinately shy? Yes! What solved this problem? He came to terms with his stage appearances in the late 1970s. By the 1980s, he was a seasoned, already legendary, performer. He was refining his place in the business and performing side of the music industry. He told people it wasn't easy. Being a professional musician mattered. He pursued it diligently.

In the 1970s, Van was in an American exile. It was to perfect his craft. He watched performers and bands with enormous talent wither and die in Belfast. He left Ireland. He had bigger dreams. He planned his career. He worked hard on his craft. He made sure his songwriting and performing matured. He said what he does is not easy. The amount of work going into his show business persona wore Van out. He was inordinately cranky.

Over time he grew more personable. He was increasingly at ease on stage. He allowed his accompanying musicians greater freedom. He was settled. He was happy. These musical changes from 1973 into mid-1974 had an enormous impact upon his songwriting. He strayed from hit songs to personal visions. Did his voracious habit of listening to music change? No! If anything, it intensified. The music he listened to in the 1970s was no different than in the past. It was the same mélange of blues, rhythm and blues, traditional Irish music, a bit of country, roots rock and an eclectic mix of obscure, often arcane, singers-songwriters. These influences fed his lyrical brilliance. He never succumbed to musical fads. He remained true to his artistic vision. That vision was personal. A hint of the new Van came in a December, 1970 interview with **Sounds**. He talked of a live album. The planning for **It's Too Late To Stop Now** was a few years in the works. That was only one part of his creative genius. He discussed his desire to work with the Modern Jazz Quartet. He hoped to produce an album by an unknown singer Lorraine Ellison.

The brilliance in Van's appreciation for new music was shown when he became friendly with Elvis Costello. A Marin County band, Clover, backed Costello on his first album. Van took note of the bespeckled Costello, who looked like a latter day Buddy Holly, but sounded like a unique performer with a cache of brilliant songs. John McFee, a member of Clover, was the conduit for Morrison's introduction to Costello's New Wave sound.

The 1970s was a watershed in his career. The 1973-1974 touring established his concert brilliance. After a decade of performances with show bands and Them, Van perfected his solo act. He found working with the right musicians, molding them, creating a solid stage show and performing ninety to one hundred and twenty minute shows guaranteed a lengthy career. This philosophy drew in Van's fans. The release of the double album in 1974, **It's Too Late To Stop Now**, cemented the bond behind Morrison, his fans, the critics and the increasingly sophisticated music press. Success brought new pressures. The continual loss of privacy, and a demanding media, created Van's inner turmoil.

The music press said he was a legend. He said he was too young to be a legend. It bothered him. He met the challenge by withdrawing from the business for two and a half years. In isolation, with Carol Guida by his side, he worked diligently on new songs.

WHY THE 1970s WAS A WATERSHED

The 1970s was a watershed. It was because of changes in the music industry. This was a time Van's artistic maturity blossomed. Independence was the key to Morrison's persona. He didn't think or act like other rock artists.

Van never allowed the music business to define his direction. He remained true to his unique musical vision. That spelled horror for his managers. After Woodstock's Mary Martin rescued Van's career from the street gangsters, Bert Berns' slavery contract, Warner's unique bookkeeping and the mysterious names on Van's copyrights, she continued the fight to maintain his intellectual property. Then he took matters in his own hands. Van fired Martin. He became his own manager. He believed this was the road to controlling, protecting and expanding his career.

Van observed: "I feel I'm not the type of artist who can have a manager. That puts the music business through quite a few changes. It means they have to deal with somebody who's not a puppet, who doesn't function like a clockwork robot." That explanation frightened Mary Martin. Every executive at Warner Bros. recognized

Morrison's intellect. Warner executives complained too many of his songs were non-commercial.

By 1979, he was a creative force emerging as a wunderkind from the 1960s into an accelerated career. By 1973, Van was a respected producer. At least as far as his musicians were concerned. Stan Cornyn was a strong supporter of allowing Morrison into the recording studio anytime of the day or night. He urged Warner to grant him funds to record at home, in Sausalito or in the numerous San Francisco studios. Cornyn told me the corporate brains, under Mo Ostin and Joe Smith, didn't get it. They thought Van needed studio supervision. When Cornyn asked: "Why?" There was no answer.

Warner Bros. assigned a house producer, Ted Templeman, to work with him. Morrison did the bulk of the production. Templeman gave advice. He drove Van to and from the studio. Working with Van remained a nightmare for many in the industry. Templeman included. He vowed never to work with him again. He would in hindsight, in his autobiography, talk about how much he learned from Morrison. By the late 1970s, the Belfast Cowboy was an established artist and regarded as a continual fountain of creativity. Van said it best when he described what he hoped to do musically: "I was trying to show the dynamics of the music. ...Rock and roll is a mind trip now. It's not music anymore...I definitely think we need some new music."

The 1970s were a strange time. Not just for Van Morrison but for many of the old rockers. When the Rolling Stones went on tour, there were so many musicians on stage, it was hard to tell if the Stones were playing their instruments. Morrison continued to perform with small, musically tight groups. He was seldom booked in larger venues. That changed over time due to the financial demands of touring.

The music business is vicious and unfriendly. It wore Van out by the mid-1970s. He took time off to concentrate upon writing. Then twenty years later, he sat down in a reflective, 1995 Dublin interview with Michelle Rocca. Van said he never wanted to be a rock star. "I work for a living. When I started," Van continued. "I just wanted to play blues." This video segued to Van performing a cover of Sonny Boy Williamson's "Help Me." He observed he started out as a blues singer with a Bobby Blue Bland soul emphasis.

Van complained rock music was too broad. "Anything can sell, it has always been that way, it is just more so today," Morrison continued. "Rock and roll is still active it is just pushed underground." A clip of Jimmy Witherspoon came on during the interview. It made the point the old blues singers were Van's dominant influence.

WHAT DID SITTING DOWN WITH MICHELLE ROCCA TELL US?

In this series of interviews in 1995, with Michelle Rocca, Van sat down resplendent in a white hat, a stylish ascot and an Armani suit, looking like a country gentleman. Van spoke freely, honestly, and with a relaxed countenance to his wife. The result was four YouTube interviews explaining his career. These interviews reflected on Marin County, without mention of it. The 1970s were highlighted. This 1995 interview resulted in a picture of Van's evolution from Marin County songwriter-performer to his Dublin country home life with the glamorous Rocca. As he looked back fondly, without trepidation, he realized Marin County was the watershed in his evolution as a singer-songwriter. Rocca was too busy looking at herself in the mirror to realize her husband's confessional state of mind. She had a glass of champagne on her mind. By 1995 Van clearly was living a lifestyle making him uncomfortable. Chris Michie said: "Van's nostalgia for the 1970s continued to occupy our conversations." When Michie made these comments to me in the 1980s, he believed Van found himself in a "milieu of strange Marin County influences."

As he looked back on the 1970s, Van "pondered" his songs. He observed he dried up in the mid-1970s. Why? Too much thinking! Too much writing! Too little self-control! Too much Carol Guida! That was a good thing! She centered him!

He told Rocca he needed a period of exile. He took that exile from 1974 into early 1977 with Carol Guida at his side. He kept writing during his time off. He was escaping the industry. This was to answer some San Francisco Bay Area critics who claimed he had writer's block. Van said if he didn't write consistently, he would get writer's block. "I had a period where I thought I had dried up. I lost interest during that period." That was in the mid-1970s in Marin County. Looking back on these years he remarked: "If I write anything, I keep writing." He said he was determined to finish anything he started.

As he ruminated about his life, Van rephrased old complaints. He supplied new information. Of the music business, his attitude has never varied. "I have always gone out of my way not to be a rock star. I work for a living." This explains why he goes off during interviews.

Van's independence, as well as his wandering soul, made it difficult for him to tolerate the rock 'n' roll subculture. He worked in a medium he detested. Van commented to Rocca he entered the music business to perform what he liked, when he liked, and how he liked. The sense of independence he exhibited was evident from day one in his lengthy career.

He believed many new fans had little interest in his early career. He was wrong. He realized it. In time, Van closed most shows with "Gloria." The crowd was up dancing. Van performs a few minutes of it. He exits the stage. By the time the band ends their extended musical jam on "Gloria," Chris Michie said: "Van has met his ninety minutes on stage."

Van reflected he was never a poet. "I describe myself as a singer and songwriter." He doesn't like being labeled a poet. He doesn't consider Bob Dylan a poet. "Words are words with or without music. There is no benefit for me to say I am a poet," Van concluded. That conclusion would change over time.

Rocca asked Van: "Who were the first singers your father had you listen to?" He said: "Bing Crosby, Mahalia Jackson, as well as a batch of gospel and blues records. I was singing when I was three. It was a natural thing for me to do." He recalled no one believed he was going to be a professional musician. Van envisioned this career goal early.

Van lamented the changes in Belfast. "The Belfast I knew was a completely different place." His fame robbed him of a portion of his creative essence. "The whole creative process is about moving into new directions," Van said.

"You can't go back, you grow and you change," Van remarked to Rocca. When she asked him if he would like to return to the good old days, he took umbrage with the question. A clip of "Crazy Love" suggested he reinterpreted the romantic side of his music.

On performing! He said it was natural. "The energy starts with the band," Van continued. He thought for a moment. "I like the interaction between the musicians and the singers."

Van was asked why he performed? He said he was compelled to do it. "Singing is this form of communication...." He continued: "Rock music is not growing. You have to go way back to get that." The masters, as Van defined them, provided a road map for his approach to writing, recording and performing.

He remarked Ray Charles, John Lee Hooker and Lightnin' Hopkins remained his favorite artists. A clip of "One Irish Rover," with Bob Dylan, followed as a program interlude.

During the fourth part of the interview with Michelle Rocca, Van discussed fame's burden. That question led him into his early business failures. He said he had terrible business advice when he started out. "I don't like touring," Van said. Then twenty five years later he said he loved playing while bemoaning tours. That has changed as a private plane often takes him to gigs. His musicians know his songs inside out. Touring in the seventies was not a pleasure. It was essential to perfecting his craft.

VAN AND BUSINESS: HE IS A GENIUS AT IT

Although Van owns the copyright on his life, to borrow a phrase from Clinton Heylin, he had as much trouble as anyone surviving the 1970s. He wrote the music. He copyrighted his material. He protected his intellectual property. He took care in the recording studio to turn out a commercial product. He worked closely with Warner Brothers while touring. Carol Guida observed Van did not have big money when she was with him from 1973 into 1977. She observed, he was reorganizing his fiscal affairs.

His business structure became more complex. It was difficult for him to interpret the early Warner Bros. royalty statements. Hidden costs were a factor. Warner Brothers, like most major labels, had hidden expenses. In Van's case storing his outtakes and songs not included on albums became a major expense. Van joked the charges for storing often came close to a record royalty.

By 1973, he had enough clout to contest past royalties. He sued the Bert Berns estate for past royalties. The sum was substantial. The idea was to go after the Bert Berns estate and the Web IV management-production contract. In the process Van's lawyers dragged Warner Brothers into this business mess. Warner was forced to pay Web IV Music and the Berns estate past due royalties for material included on **Astral Weeks**. Warner Bros. was not happy.

His 1973 touring schedule guaranteed increased record sales. The flow of money was important to his lifestyle, his creativity, and his ability to forge ahead as an independent artist. The money machine was being designed for future payoffs.

THE CRITICS NOTICING THE COMMON THEMES

Some of Van's biographers do him a disservice. They come up with careful definitions of his work when complex analysis is required. They ignore the esoteric songs. They deride his common themes. The primary theme? Fame was a bitch. Another constant was Van's question: "Why am I always being disrespected?" That drove him. No one understands me! That was another thought dominating his thinking for decades. What I do is tough! That drove his blue work ethic. These themes echo throughout his 1970s career explaining a great deal about character. They continue to the present day. They prioritize his songwriting. Clinton Heylin does an excellent job explaining that when pressured Van retreated, hunkered down or he went silent. He didn't always answer his critics. Or surreptitiously, he would do so a decade later in a song.

As Clinton Heylin analyzed Van, in the early 1980s, he entitled a chapter "Down By Avalon." He suggested Van retreated emotionally to Ireland. The operative wisdom is he had never left Belfast emotionally or psychologically.

In Marin County he experienced new influences taking his songwriting away from his Belfast roots. If Morrison did retreat to Ireland, it was in the private recesses of his mind. Heylin missed the

California influences. Marin County and Carol Guida were the mantra to his new creativity. His meteoric popularity. His careful planning from 1973 into mid-1974 made Van an industry icon. His genius in concert emerged. His successes bore all the earmarks of California's influence. Van slowly lost his thick, impenetrable Belfast accent. Or perhaps he modified it.

The search for respect was a continual theme. When he was inducted into the Songwriters Hall of Fame, in 2003, that feeling ebbed. He believed songs, like "Bulbs," were overlooked. The years of honors reside in the mind of an ever expanding writer. He was continually searching for new lyrical adventures.

THE ART OF THE OLD BIOGRAPHY

While research and writing this multi-volume Van Morrison biography, the joy was listening to his music. I used no research assistants. I hired no lawyers. I avoided using song lyrics. The approach was one designed to explain Van's life from the creativity of his albums, the images from his everyday life, and his reaction to his surroundings. I integrated his life into the broader fabric of the music industry. I began hanging out on the periphery of the Morrison soundstage. I enjoyed the process. In my view his personal interaction with his environment was necessary to understanding him. To define the mystery of his creative genius is to go down small, minor rabbit holes in his life.

The media hounded Van at every turn. Part of it was his fault. He was often unforgiving in interviews. He had little time for ill-informed media hacks. He was petulant. He was at times nasty. He was uncooperative. In the right setting, he was an easy interview. That was his charm. His behavior was one of his many contradictions. He was alternately cooperative, kind and loyal to family and friends. He needed diverse people. They fueled his attitudes. The rock 'n' roll world is one of entitlement. That explains more about Van than anything else.

THE CHARACTER AND THE CONTRADICTIONS

In Van Morrison's case it was his single-minded devotion to his craft that defined his character. The press often described Van as a taciturn character. That is accurate. Morrison likes to hide behind his lyrics while remaining anonymous personally. John L. Wasserman told me at times Van acted like a spoiled child.

Van's complex character makes it difficult to analyze his life. The contradictions in his public statements go a long way toward creating biographical confusion. He claims he channels songs. He states he writes songs that have little to do with his life. This is of course utter nonsense. Songs like "Don't Go To Nightclubs Anymore," "Whatever Happened to P. J. Proby" and "Why Must I Always Explain?" provide a platform for personal messages or grievances.

He blanches at the notion "Brown Eyed Girl," with its more than eight million radio airplays, is a song defining him. He said the song was the beginning not the definitional end. He preaches it is impossible to categorize his music. This volume is an attempt to do just that for nineteen months in the 1970s. His character and contradictions define that period. His artistic growth and evolving intellectual maturity was evident in the 1970s. He had money. He had a home studio. He could write what he wanted, and how he wanted it to play out. He could perform when and where he desired. Was he happy? Who knows! In some interviews, he was witty and engaging. In others, he couldn't wait to finish. He became alternately cooperative during interviews and, at times, sullen. It was simply Van being Van.

SHOULD VAN HAVE THE LAST WORD?

It is appropriate for Van to have the last word. In "New Biography," he sets out his objections to those writing about him. "How come they've got such good memories?" Van remarked. He said he can't remember last week. That observation suggests why he needs a new biography.

Van complained, to Carol Guida, other close friends and even strangers about biographers. He said most people are not on his wavelength. This was one of his persistent themes. He accused the biographer of reinventing many of his friends' stories. The facts. They are always in dispute when Van answers questions on his career.

He said repeatedly he had to have the last word. In his lyrics is where Van sees truth. Nowhere else.

An ironic observation is Van doesn't like stories "so far away, way back when." He obviously doesn't want to be reminded of Bert Berns or Phil Solomon. That is except when he bitches about them.

From time to time Van goes off the rails with anti-commercial records. This is a part of his charm. Then, decades later, these albums achieve gold status. The critics fall all over themselves praising the product. That is after it achieves gold. Before that the barbs, the insidious remarks, and the barbaric prose often degrade the project. Van follows the reviews. He will articulate his opinions on critics in his songs. Invariably, he is decried as a sore loser. Van believed the only way to answer the critics is in lyrical form. When Van writes: "Why Must I Always Explain?," he has a point. Maybe he is correct. He concluded playing the name game "is a crying shame." But he continues to do it. That is his writing mantra.

Morrison combined kindness with grudges, cruelty, long simmering feuds, as well as love and support for friends. Is this a contradiction? No! It is Van being Van. Cranky! Introspective! Shy! Brilliant! These are some of the Belfast Cowboy's traits. These observations are spot on. They are not easy to analyze.

Astral Weeks was a breakthrough. It was also a millstone for his future success. Van has always met a challenge with a hard working answer. He vowed to make better music than **Astral Weeks**. Instead of being a burden, **Astral Weeks** spurred Van into new creative directions with hit oriented pop songs like "Moondance." It was as if Van was saying it's a marvelous night to keep my hit making career in high gear.

His appeal in concert reached an increasingly varied and larger audience. When he took the concert stage in the San Francisco Bay Area at twenty-six, he was an uncaged Lion with a shy demeanor. By the early twentieth-first century, he no longer smoked, drank and partied into the early morning. He was now a controlled Lion. He has two glasses of water on stage. One is hot. The other is cold. This is a lesson from his voice doctor. What does this tell us about Van? He is the ultimate professional. Whether in concert, in the studio, or directing his career, Morrison as a writer-performer lyrically provided a window into his creative process. He did so with a mixture of Irish and Marin County influences. The San Francisco Bay Area was like a literary professor. American images, blended with Irish influences, creating one of the most unique performers in rock music.

In 2007, Van sat down for a twenty-seven minute interview where he looked back on his formative years. He talked at length about his early influences, Ray Charles, Bobby Blue Bland, Louis Jordan and Sam Cooke. He waxed nostalgically about buying 45s at Solly Lipsitz's Atlantic Records. When Lipsitz passed in 2013, Van was there to pay respect to and mourn his friend. He told reporters Solly was there for him in the early days.

As Van recalled his early environment, he pointed out Hyndford Street was alive with music. In 1960, while playing with the Monarchs, he discovered Bobby Blue Bland in Germany. He heard African American soldiers playing his records and singing like him. This was a revelation. He was fifteen years old and began his search for the blues sounds defining his life.

When asked about Elvis Presley, Van responded: "He didn't have any impact." He continued pointing to Ray Charles' influence. He said: "When I heard rock 'n' roll it was Gene Vincent and Carl Perkins."

Van said much of what he did musically was bohemian. It was against pop music. He mentioned Jack Kerouac and Jean Paul Sartre as early literary influences. Did he listen to pop hits? "I was absolutely opposed to pop music. I grew up in this family where my father had this record collection...pop music to me was just that....The real thing was Muddy Waters and Leadbelly...."

"Rock 'n' roll is really boogie woogie in disguise," Van continued. "Rock 'n' roll was image...that wasn't my...thing." As Morrison discussed his early interest in American music, he connected with it.

By 1972-1973 the American influences coalesced in Marin County. This small enclave, a few miles north of San Francisco, influenced Morrison's future. Van's biographers pay passing interest to Marin County's tree lined suburb with a foliage much like Belfast and a bursting rock 'n' roll subculture.

When Van arrived in Marin County the rock 'n' roll population was huge and growing daily. Rockers, blues singers, Bob Dylan wannabes, country rockers, pop maestros and an amalgam of musicians who dipped into numerous genres lived in rustic homes and in neighborhoods with a wild life or in suburbs with young children.

Van learned of the blues before the British blues revival. Belfast was not a blues town. When he played the blues for local friends, they asked him: "Is this Chinese music?" Van said. His friends didn't understand the blues.

In March, 2007, Van sat down with a trumpet player cum journalist, Leo Green, to look back on his career. The result was twenty-seven minutes of thoughtful, incisive comments on his career and unwittingly his life. In part one of this multi-interview with Green, posted on Van's website, he explained a great deal about his career. While he continually shouts his private life is off limits, this interview saw Van postulate on and explain key moments in his personal life. Sitting comfortably in a chair wearing sun glasses, a cap and a blue, wrinkled work shirt, Van looked more like a casual blue collar worker than a famous songwriter.

Green has played in Van's band. They have been friends for decades. Morrison was relaxed. At sixty-two he had accomplished everything he set out to do. Yet, he was still working 24/7 on writing and performing. He was reflective as his old friend asked him questions that would cause Van to explode if an unknown writer posed them. He answered quickly. There was a clarity in Morrison's voice. He loved looking back. Nostalgia has never interested him. But Van talks about it. It is one of his many contradictions. He considers truth more important. The Green interview was about truth. At least truth as Van perceived it.

Van explained the heart break of trying to make a living with the group Them. He reminisced about their manager without naming him. It was Phil Solomon. I sat in Phil Solomon's Penthouse in Bournemouth thanks to his brother, Mervyn, who demanded Phil grant me an interview. Solomon did more than that. He directed me to take the train from London to Bournemouth and to stand outside the train station. He picked me up in his Jaguar. I spent the afternoon talking with Phil and Dorothy Solomon. It was decades after he managed Them. Phil had a warm spot in his heart for Van. He had little to say that was negative. He recognized Van's enormous talent. The remaining members of Them were dismissed.

I sat at a beautiful table being served fresh salmon, root vegetables and at the end a souffle cooked by the Filipino maid. Then we drank brandy, coffee and tea. We talked about the music business. The Solomon's described the acts losing them money. The singers who had little talent, like Twinkle, who Phil spent huge sums of money to guarantee hits. "I never had to spend much on Them, you looked at them. You heard them, they were special." He admitted this irritated Van. He talked about Van's reputation for being difficult. Like Van, Phil was Irish. He grew up in Belfast the son of a Jewish father who housed World War II Jewish European refugees.

Phil Solomon: "Van was difficult. He was not impossible. I understood him. He was too much trouble." As Phil and Dorothy reminisced about the musical mélange that was the British Invasion, they suggested there was so much talent they didn't need Van Morrison. That takes us back to the 27 minute interview with Leo Green. Unwittingly, Van responded to a number of things Phil and Dorothy told me in this 2002 Bournemouth interview.

Van remarked he left Them to get paid. That is he approached Solomon about the lack of money. The Belfast Cowboy told Green they were paid enough to keep up the rent. Some months even that didn't happen. The only way for Van to move forward, he claimed, was to become a solo artist. Van said Solomon told him: "I have you as a lead singer. That is all I need." At that point, Van decided to go solo.

I asked Solomon: "Why was Van Morrison so successful?" He answered cryptically: "Talent, perseverance, business sense." Solomon didn't look happy. I asked him: "Why the sour look?" He thought for a long time. He said Van had to figure out how to be himself. I wasn't sure what he meant. I asked: "What do you mean, Mr. Solomon?" He took some time answering. Finally, he said: "I have wondered why Van wasn't a bit more civilized at times." That comment continued in interviews with others close to Morrison. Joe Smith remarked he never understood the mercurial temperament that blossomed within the Belfast Cowboy.

Green asked Van about his soul voice. Van couldn't define it. "It's not just the voice. It's the energy. I actually prefer James Brown, the slow stuff....Solomon Burke...it isn't just the voice it is the whole thing." Van said the question had no answer. "Bobby Bland was very influential....there were other people too."

Van remarked to Green he loved the music of Solomon Burke, Joe Tex and Wilson Pickett. Initially, he claimed they were not direct influences. He loved listening to these artists. Sam Cooke was described as a key influence. That seemed odd as Cooke was a pop, crossover artist with soul. That is also the route Morrison took in the early 1970s.

Politics is not a Morrison interest. He didn't return to Northern Ireland until the Troubles were settled. He had nothing to do with anti-war politics while living in Marin County. He was asked about politics. The question bored him. He always gave the same answer. Move on! Don't ask me! Finally, he gave Leo Green a definitive answer on the political question. Van said the American civil rights movement didn't influence him. He was not into the hippie political nonsense. He was a professional musician. He was concerned about his career. His music wasn't political. End of discussion!

The umbrage he displayed over political questions was obvious. To the Belfast Cowboy it was about his music. His sensitive point was could a white man sing the blues? Green knew better than to ask that question. Van told Green John Lee Hooker said: "Your skin color didn't matter. It was about the truth." Business was more important than any topic during the Green interview.

Van talked of getting ripped off. When he arrived in America it was basic survival. "It was like starting again....I didn't have time to think about a bigger picture," Van recalled.

Jazz came up. Van said the jazz sound always was important. Louis Armstrong was an early influence. "There was a guy called Slim Gaillard who I got to know later in life. He lived in London," Van said. Where did Morrison discover Slim Gaillard? It was in Jack Kerouac's **On The Road**. As a friend of Kerouac's, Gailliard had a connection to the 1950s hip subculture. Ironically, Morrison and Gaillard performed an excerpt from **On The Road** in a rare 1989 BBC Arena film "How High The Moon."

Gaillard, who died in 1991 while living in London, in the last decade of his life, became Van's friend. Morrison's quest for the hip, jazz, poetry of the 1950s was spurred by his appearance with Gaillard. As Van recited a brief section from Kerouac's book, Gaillard played the bongos chanting. The BBC film was a remarkable insight into Morrison's consistently evolving intellectual persona.

In remarks to the **Herald Scotland**, Van said the beat experience and memories of Gaillard inspired him to write "In Tiburon." Van said the second verse was about the beats. "I met people involved in this scene like Vince Guaraldi, who I did some gigs with, he was a great jazz player. I also met guys like Allen Ginsberg and Lawrence Ferlinghetti a few times." The Green interview opened windows into Van's psyche previously closed to the biographer. Van hung out with, thanks to Carol Guida and Alan Watts and Ali Akbar Khan.

Green asked Van how he took black music into the mainstream? "I felt the white working class situation was like the black experience," Van concluded. He finished the interview lamenting about "the pop world." "We all got caught up in the pop world," Van said. He pointed out one had to remain disciplined and stay away from the pop sound. "People were constantly hammering away at you to get you to do what they wanted you to do." Van told Green. Van paused for a moment. He intimated it was the record labels that controlled everything. That demon remains in his psyche.

On April 20, 1988, Van participated in a panel with Derek Bell of the Chieftains, Martin Lynch, Clive Culbertson and Professor Bob Welch. He sang and discussed his music. He talked openly, and, at length, about his career. In this discussion his private life seeped into the conversation. The Riverside Theater in Coleraine was the site of this event. The audience was students. No one was disappointed. Van sat playing a harmonica and singing the blues to a rapt and attentive audience. It was almost an hour of a revealing look into the private Van Morrison.

A relaxed Morrison displayed an intellect searching for truth while his musical numbers drew raves. The lack of pretense, an intense humility, and an honest reflection suggested his personal growth. This was a decade after exiting Marin County. As Van looked back on the 1970s, and forward to the future, his complexity intensified.

At this discussion, Van performed "A Sense of Wonder" to the hushed and appreciative audience. The other songs "Celtic Ray," "In The Garden" and "Raglan Road" were augmented by Derek Bell who Van had known since the early Belfast days. Bell was a member of the Chieftains. His connection to Van was a lengthy one.

Bell grew up in Belfast. He was a musical child prodigy giving his first concert at twelve. He was manager of the Belfast Symphony Orchestra. When he appeared with Van, he accompanied him on "Raglan Road." Van spent hours talking with Bell about musical instruments, traditional Irish music and the hammered dulcimer, which was introduced into Irish music in the 18th century. Bell was a devotee of eastern religions. His first album **Mystic Harp** was right out of Morrison's handbook. As a practicing Buddhist, Bell was a friend and influence upon the Belfast Cowboy.

One of Van's more interesting tales is when he talked of giving a sound man a book he was reading by Alice Bailey. This was in the early 1980s. This book told the story of why and how he wrote some songs. He needed another song for an album. He didn't have one. He gave the sound man a short bit of writing or a statement "Dweller On The Threshold." They talked. The sound man took Bailey's book home. The next day he and Van discussed the book. Then Morrison took the phrase and words of encouragement from the sound man and wrote "Dweller On The Threshold" for the **Beautiful Vision** album. This story was apocryphal. Recalling it, years later, Van provided a window into his creative process. There are many incidents in his life where interaction with others led to a song.

Van talked of the "dark side" of one's mind and how to confront it. This discussion had Van analyze Carl Jung on how to confront creativity. They talked about the threshold of intellectual growth. The idea of the borderlands of creativity was discussed by Professor Bob Welch. He turned to Van asking him about creativity. "I relate it to a death experience," Van continued. "I died several times." The audience laughed. Van's humor told a serious tale. He worried about failure. It drove him mercilessly. There was never time off. That personality trait continues to drive him.

The spirituality of Ireland came in 1982 with **Beautiful Vision**. The panel asked him about the decade of living in California and how it influenced his Celtic images. These images became pronounced in the 1980s. Ironically, Van never answered the question of Marin County influences. His Irish images were redefined in a California setting. This was geographically similar to Belfast but culturally different.

The University of Ulster discussion with Derek Bell, on piano, was one where Van was asked about his poetic lyrics. He talked of reading a book on meditation and explained why he wrote "No Guru, No Method, No Teacher." Van said he was exploring his spiritual roots. Van said the 1970s was a time without spiritual roots. He talked of Wordsworth and Blake's influences. When asked who was the singularly most important poetry influence, Van said: "I'd say Blake…his sort of song poems I connect with the most."

Derek Bell provided a window into Van's enormously complicated personality. They had common Belfast roots. They had a singularly love for Irish influences. They hung out. The pair went on ice cream binges. Back in the drinking days? No one knows! "In the days when I first met him," Bell remarked of Morrison. "He was really looking for some sort of a spiritual answer to things." Bell said he made a record with material from a British mystic, Cyril Scott. "Van had read the information on the back of the sleeve and he made contact with me—this was before we ever teamed up musically." They met and discussed mysticism. Van asked if there was anything he should be studying. "He had read something like 3000 books on mysticism, during a period of personal crisis," Bell continued. "Anything I mentioned was covered somewhere in those 3000 books," Bell concluded. Bell said Van was so well read, so versed in religion, philosophy and mysticism it demonstrated bis drive to educational perfection. That is a theme of this book.

Another important aspect of this book is Van's business brilliance. His commitment to protecting his intellectual property runs through the 1973-1974 time frame of this book. It continues to the present day.

Bell recalled a business dust up that Van had with another Chieftain, Paddy Moloney, and how it illustrated Morrison's commitment to firm business practices. The Chieftains and Van were publicizing the **Irish Heartbeat** album and Moloney was slow to sign a contract. Van came after him with a furry of insults demanding the contract be executed. This European tour to publicize the album became a rough one when they didn't talk. Then one night in Scandinavia a crisis ensued. "They each poured a bottle of wine over each other's head," Bell remembered. The crisis abated. The tour continued.

As Bell looked back on his relationship with Van, he talked about how the Belfast Cowboy delved into a topic. Learned everything he could about the subject. Then he moved on. "I share his interest in mysticism," Bell recalled. "However, after we teamed up with Cliff Richard, he went back to Hallelujah Christianity again and that doesn't hold much appeal for me. He always says to me: 'Ah, I have to go in a new direction.' We no longer share an interest on that level but we still get on real well as people." Bell's comments are illuminating. Van is bright, complicated and uncompromising.

In January, 1995, when Bell made these comments, he concluded: "I think he has loosened up a lot in recent years. He's gotten back into society a lot more." That was Bell's way to proclaiming middle aged adjustment was on Morrison's horizon. Bell recalled that Van looked back to the 1970s when figuring his life out. He said Van still mattered after almost half a century in the forefront of the record business.

The elusive mysterious nature that is Van Morrison continued. "Anytime he's in town, he comes up to us and we take him out for coffee and buns or ice cream. I live very close to where he's supposed to live but, of course, he never tells you. I live in Bangor. He is, supposedly, very close to that, maybe four miles away or something. He never tells when he's coming. He just rings up on the portable telephone and says: 'Coming for a scoop? I'm here.'" Bell, like many others, was baffled by Van's behavior.

To examine Van's personality is to dissect his music. One goes with the other. He is a brilliant, complicated writer with a unique vocal gift. His mind erupts daily in volcanic creativity. That story continues with a look at why Van matters.

Van Morrison and Janet Planet

ONE

Why Van Morrison Matters

"Blues isn't to do with black or white; blues is about the truth, and blues is the truth."

Van Morrison In Conversation With Mike Figgis

"I stopped being an artist in the 1970s."

Van Morrison, In Conversation, March, 2007

"Knowledge came to me through pleasure."

Oscar Wilde

"Van believed in the separation of art and personality."

Mervyn Solomon In Conversation With The Author

Joseph Campbell, the mythologist, coined the phrase "follow your bliss." What did he mean? He suggested each person had to find meaning in life. That explains Van Morrison. At thirteen, he formed his first band. At fifteen he was on the road with a show band, the Monarchs. He toured Germany. He found the blues when he heard African American G. I.'s sing soul music. His journey began to perfecting a soul-blues sound. Then years later, Van celebrated his seventieth birthday performing on Hyndford Street. He was now Sir Van Morrison. He had grown up. He followed his bliss.

Why does Van Morrison matter? He is a blue collar, hard-working songwriter who just happens to be one of the world's premier blues performers. Aren't blues artists supposed to be African American from Clarksdale? They are! Van is the exception. From the moment he crawled out of the cradle his desire to sing the blues dominated his life. This music is the essence of his life. Everything else takes a back seat.

To understand Van Morrison is not an easy task. He is mercurial. He is prone to mood swings. He is a defined personality. He can alternately charm and disarm a critic, a friend, an acquaintance, a member of the music industry, a promoter or a fan. Some who write about him never utter a critical word. They are little more than hagiographers. Think Ritchie Yorke. Others emphasize only the critical word. Think Clinton Heylin or Johnny Rogan. Both are excellent biographers. They told the truth as they saw it. How does one understand the Belfast Cowboy? If Van Morrison is to be understood, there is one element deserving constant analysis. That is his mercurial world view. As he sees the universe, it explodes in song form. His complexity must be addressed. Since the 1980s, a new and more understanding Van has emerged. He took on an air of sophistication from Marin County. His cranky nature abated slightly. It resurfaced with a vengeance during the world wide coronavirus pandemic.

The biographer views his snits as a window into his soul. Janet Morrison Minto commented: "The man is a prickly pear." She is right. Or is she? Are there reasons for the prickly pear? There are! Should the biographer ignore his behavior? No! Why! Because of his personality, he percolates with wisdom then denigrates it with venom. Accept that and you understand the man. His writing genius is another matter. The writing took some time to evolve and mature.

In 1973, Van took firm control of his career. The early road was a rocky one. **Hard Nose The Highway** was the first album where he had complete control. The reviewers were neutral, if a bit confused. There were some positive comments. **Rolling Stone** called the album: "psychologically complex, somewhat uneven musically." As Van said: "His listeners would have to catch up with him."

Van's control was firm. He didn't have a muse. His wife Janet was emotionally absent. Soon she was physically absent. He hadn't met his new muse, Carol Guida, but he was continually refining his songwriting genius. When Guida arrived she provided a personality finishing school for Van. He was never in better hands.

Ideas were percolating in Van's psyche. At times, they boiled over into a creative rage. His albums came complete with new themes. Spiritualism, the blues, Irish influences and obscure themes based on his life, dominated his music. The new songs were not always commercial ones. It was critical acceptance, not commercial success, Van sought. If there is a persistent theme to Van's life, it is leave me alone. Listen to my music. That's it. Van loves live gigs. He can take his songwriting into a public forum. He enjoys being on stage. It shows!

Why does Van Morrison matter? He connects personally with his dedicated followers. Think Michael Seltzer, Art Siegel, Pat Thomas, Bernard McGuinn, Michael Fishman, Simon Gee, Jeanette Heinen, Pat Corley, Russ Dugoni and Ron "The Dude" Sexton, as well as hundreds of others. Who are these people? They have nothing in common. That is until you start talking Van Morrison. Then they share a common bond. That is they are Vanatics. This is why Van matters. He connects with a wide variety of people. That passion is in his music not his personal life.

IDEAS MATTER IN ROCK 'N' ROLL: CALEDONIA EMERGES

Ideas matter. In the rock 'n' roll world ideas often give way to commercial success. Bob Dylan employs his talent to play with words. Bruce Springsteen has the same freedom. Where does Van Morrison fit into the creative mélange? The ideas and personality that make up the Morrison psyche stands out in a cascade of contrarian ideas. His critics interpret the lyrics, which at times irritates Morrison.

Religion and spiritualism are themes to understanding the Belfast Cowboy. His personal growth accelerated in October, 1973, when in the company of Carol Guida, he travelled for a three week Irish vacation. The trip to Ireland provided material for **Veedon**

Van Morrison: Veedom Fleece Album Cover (Photo Taken by Tom Collins)

Fleece. The past was like a horse collar strangling his creativity. Mervyn Solomon told me **Astral Weeks** was a burden. It was in Marin County in 1973 he came to realize it was an early, but defining, moment in his creative life. He confessed to Chris Michie he built on **Astral Weeks** after his divorce.

Poetry, literature and pop culture found their way into Morrison's notebooks. There was a conscious effort to concentrate upon songwriting. He intensified his plan to master the producer's role.

THE POET IN EXILE

In Marin County Van became a poet in exile. By 1973, with thoughts of leaving the music industry, he entered a period of semi-retirement. He reoriented his life into a more normal pace, he quietly intensified his career direction. There was, initially, a creative wilderness. Janet Morrison Minto, in a **Los Angeles Times** interview, observed Van had a difficult time securing representation. Other factors were in the mix. He was in charge. No more bad contracts. No more interference in his music. No more slick industry insiders. Van was in charge in the 1970s in Marin County.

Janet Planet's interview wasn't mean spirited. But, when she gave it in 1998, she was still conflicted over her relationship with Morrison. The **Los Angeles Times** reporter, Louis Sahagun, entitled the article "The Clouds Have Lifted." Her comments were heartfelt. "I would have done anything for the man who wrote those songs, who whispered in the night that they were true," Planet remarked decades later. That reference was to songs Van wrote for her. They included "Ballerina," "Beside You," "Crazy Love," "You're My Woman" and "The Way Young Lovers Do." Here is where Van has an argument. He repeatedly told close friends, who remarked to me, that he wrote songs without reference to Janet. Many of those close to him in Marin County remarked Van had "a romantic soul." The "prickly pear" she described to friends had little room for compromise. Van denied writing songs for her. Janet allegedly if the songs were written for her that was fine. If not, she said, that would also be fine. She had fond memories of his creativity. Van told Chris Michie he wrote songs daily to make a living. His ex-wife, and the press, came in for Van's criticism.

From 1973 into mid-1974 he dramatically retooled his life, and his career. Van feared, close friends told me, the stagnation of his life due to the pressures of writing, recording and touring. He was adamant, the music business would not control his life. He envisioned his personal life intertwined with the pressures of making a living was the loss of his soul.

Van's personality is open to interpretation. He is not as dogmatic as Johnny Rogan suggested. He is not as malevolent as Clinton Heylin concluded. The Belfast Cowboy is an open book. His themes. His intellectual direction. His bands. His moods. They all remain an integral part of his lyrics. There is a consistency to his life. It is in musical themes. They harken to his childhood. The early Belfast years defined him. "Van was like an encyclopedia soaking up local lore here in Belfast," Mervyn Solomon observed. Whereas Johnny Rogan sees "dogmatic stubbornness," and a "Belfast long lost in time," others see a local poetic-literary brilliance. In Belfast the wonderous wooden crates filled with records no one heard of were sitting on the floor of Atlantic Records. Van would search for hours into these musical treasures. This inspired him This record store, owned by Solly Lipsitz, became Van's second home. Lipsitz recalled how Van talked about his reading habits while sifting through boxes filled with obscure records from America. "Van was reading quietly at an early age," Lipsitz continued. "Maybe he was sixteen, I am not sure." The path to spiritual enlightenment began long before Marin County. It was in this bucolic, leafy, tree lined playground he finalized his writing. "Becoming Van Morrison" was the mantra.

The notion Van, as Rogan claims, has "a lack of grace" is a misnomer. He is not an easy person to understand. The Irish literary, musical, historical and mythological traditions run through Morrison's music, lifestyle, personality and approach to daily life. He is a hard ass curmudgeon who is unpredictable.

Who named Van Morrison: The Poet? It was Jonathan Cott in **Rolling Stone**. His November 30, 1978 article had a sub-headline: "The Scholar, Dancer And One Of The Few Originals In Rock Parses Out His Lyrics Blues." That said it all. At thirty three years of age,

Van arrived as an acclaimed musical poet. He cringed. Fame was intruding. He clung to his Belfast past while refining his musical make over.

BELFAST IS THE INSPIRATION: THEN MARIN COUNTY FINISHES THE ARTISTIC MAKE OVER

Images of East Belfast abound in his lyrics. The lack of opportunity to pursue a mainstream music career in Ireland drove the Belfast Cowboy to New York. Then it was off to the first many musical exiles in Boston. This was followed by inexpensive living in Woodstock, and finally he and Janet settled in Marin County. Here he found a semi-permanent home in Fairfax at 89 Spring Lane. He later purchased a home in Mill Valley. The single family Fairfax home, built in 1927, was 3038 square feet with six bedrooms.

Those forays completed his American musical journey. Belfast influences dominated. The confluence of Marin County completed the artistic makeover creating a fifty year career after the apprenticeship with Them and Bert Berns at Bang Records.

The California interlude tells one why Van matters. What were the myriad influences forming Morrison's creative genius? These influences coalesced in Marin County to create his legend. Van discovered hundreds of ready for prime time songwriters, musicians and performers. The good news was semi-famous acts like Ramblin' Jack Elliott and talented, but unknown, musicians, like Estrella Berosini, bonded with the Belfast Cowboy. They brought him a creative serenity.

CAROL GUIDA'S CREATIVE ROLE

Carol Guida's seminal role as Van's fiancée, after Janet left, is an untold story. This book tells the beginning of that story. It is an important one. She was a companion. More significantly, she was Van's first literary partner. She possessed a developed intellect inspiring him. She calmed Van as his life cascaded into an intense devotion to his career. Her influence on the music from late 1973 into the first few months of 1977 saw the Belfast Cowboy evolving into a creative nirvana. She made the period that she was in his life from August, 1973 until early 1977, one where Van defined the next fifty years of his career.

What did she provide? Guida was a strong, independent and intellectually curious person. She was a reader. She was a thinker. She was philosophical. She practiced Zen Buddhism. Van had never met a woman like this. She also had no interest in money.

This beautiful vixen with rock 'n' roll roots, and a bubbly personality, created one of the calmest, most creative chapters in his life. She was the influence in Marin County putting the finishing touches on "Becoming Van Morrison." She understood the depths of his moods and nourished his talent.

Guida was only twenty years old when she moved in with Morrison. She had an intellectual maturity beyond her years. It didn't hurt that she was drop dead gorgeous. She was low key, calm, and the antithesis of Van. Her study of Indian music, her selective reading habits, her interest in discussing literature, and her lack of star struck acceptance of the rock 'n' roll lifestyle sealed Van's relationship with her. He admired her intellect as much as her beauty.

Make no mistake Guida's influence was as much on Van's mind as his youthful libido. When **Veedon Fleece** arrived there was an accelerated maturity to Morrison's prose. That resulted from his October 1973 trip to Dublin's Sutton Place and then the trip around the Irish countryside. It was a therapeutic journey to extended creativity. She freed Van of the guilt of his divorce while accentuating his writing.

The songs in **Veedon Fleece** pay tribute to Guida's influence. It appeared Van had every intention of marriage. "Fair Play" suggested he and his partner (Carol Guida) were debating whether to live in California's San Geronimo Valley or relocate to Belfast. While visiting Arklow, Van and Carol marveled at the local architecture. There are hints of petty disagreements in the album, but Van was clearly infatuated with Guida's statuesque beauty. It came with a clam demeanor and a razor sharp mind. The playful and friendly repartee with Guida freed Morrison's intellect.

At the time of the Irish visit, Van read and digested Gestalt theory. Barry Stevens' writing resonated due to Guida's continual spiritual quest. When Guida helped Van interpret the complex language in the poetry of William Blake, that accentuated a new songwriting direction.

A good example of Van's resurgent creativity was the "Streets of Arklow," which unlocked the wandering soul in his songwriting. The Belfast years resonated with Van as he recalled the leafy beauty, not of Marin County, but of the Northern Irish countryside.

The trip brought visions of Edgar Allan Poe, Oscar Wilde and Henry David Thoreau into Morrison's writing. The beauty, history and Irish inspiration led to furtive writing spurts. A new artistic vision of Ireland emerged with flashbacks to a simpler time. Visions of a mythical Ireland danced in Van's head. The tranquility of the Irish trip set the tone for the next eighteen months of "Becoming Van Morrison."

AFTER WRITING THREE BOOKS: HERE IS THE KEY TO VAN

After writing three books about Van Morrison in the last forty years, I arrived at the conclusion 1973 through 1979 was the pivotal phase in establishing his long term career. It was the 1973-1974 era that was most important in creating the structure for and forming of Van's long term success. The period from his divorce through the It's Too Late To Stop Now tour and album brought a commercial renaissance. Then his business acumen blended with his songwriting, performing and intellectual interests began his professional structure. This freed Van from the shackles of the record industry. The intense devotion to his career in 1973-1974 was the first step in creating his permanent place in the rock 'n' roll marketplace.

The It's Too Late To Stop Now tour and album brought a commercial renaissance. It came with hard work. Van realized his place in the industry. His undying thirst for new musical directions accelerated. To continue working he had to please his audiences. He did that in spades.

Why does Van Morrison matter? For multiple reasons. He is not as acclaimed as Bob Dylan. Yet, he occupies a Dylanesque niche. He was not as brilliant in concert as Bruce Springsteen. Then things changed. He polished his concert repertoire from 1973 through

1974. This brought sell out shows and ecstatic reviews. From the It's Too Late To Stop Now tour, his professionalism evolved into brilliants ninety minute shows. Like any performer, there were great songs, average tunes and a few bottom-of-the-barrel songwriting disasters. Overall, over the years, Van has been brilliant in concert.

To understand Van, it is necessary to examine, in critical depth, the cities where he has lived. He mines local history. His eye toward religious-spiritual themes, quirky incidents, strange restaurants, different night clubs, non-typical churches and weird off the wall local sights defines his emotional and literary creativity. These forces directed his writing.

It is this cornucopia of images that seep into his songwriting. There is a hidden Morrison. It surfaced in **The Philosopher's Stone**, a 1998 compilation of previously unreleased outtakes from 1969 to 1998. This musical treasure was another window in Morrison's creativity.

One of the curious sidebars to **The Philosopher's Stone** was Van's most perceptive biographer got into a pissing match with him over when, and where and with whom, many of the 1970s tracks were recorded. At the time it seemed childish. In retrospect, it tells us a great deal about Van and his biographer Clinton Heylin. They are both difficult.

Heylin was given access to the recording logs at Warner Brothers. He used them to find every major, minor or personal discrepancy in the Van Morrison story. Why does this matter? Heylin was setting the record straight. It mattered to Van. He said Heylin obfuscated the record. Not true! He corrected it.

IN THE VAN MORRISON FOG

Re-creating Van Morrison's life is like writing in the fog. Like Bob Dylan, Van is a trickster. He continually reinvents himself. His mercurial intellect knows no bounds. His songs are the raw material of his surroundings, and those he interacts with in daily life. "Van was in a productive, creative fog in the mid-1970s," Chris Michie said.

When did the Van Morrison fog lift? It was in the 1974 **Veedon Fleece** album. He was working his way out of the **Astral Weeks** acclaim. He headed into another songwriting phase. The fog was lifting. Then, after a brief period of retirement, the fog continued to lift with the aptly titled **A Period Of Transition** album. By 1979 **Into The Music** erased the past sending Morrison's music into new thematic directions. Like writer's block, there was no creative fog. That was an invention of the press.

Paul Vincent, a San Francisco disc jockey, explained the conversation that made it difficult to describe Morrison. "I felt like I was in the Van fog," Vincent remarked to me. What did he mean? "When I interviewed Van at the K-Mel FM studio, we sat alone in an empty studio. He was relaxed. He mentioned the "fog in his life," I didn't pursue it. He would look out our window at Alcatraz or the edge of Sausalito. The conversation was relaxed. He opened up in a great interview." The fog Van spoke of was in the 1970s. This November 1981 interview on a blustery, cold San Francisco day was replete with insights about Marin County's influence. There were also comments suggesting what Van believed he had to do to survive in the music business.

VAN'S BAT SHIT CRAZY BEHAVIOR: IT IS BAD NEWS: IT IS ALSO GOOD NEWS

The Van Morrison story is often a horror show. Journalists who meet Van can have issues with him. He is prickly, imperious and full of himself. He can also be calm, reserved and cooperative. You never know which Van will be present at an interview. He can be insulting. He can be cooperative. He can be rude. Why is this important? The good news is we find out the real Van Morrison might be like us. A guy who gets pissed but who has happy moments.

When an Irish journalist, Liam Mackey, interviewed Van, the Belfast Cowboy said: "Is it okay if I go to sleep?" The poor guy was flummoxed. If he knows a journalist, like Donal Corvin, butter melts in Van's mouth. If not, watch out!

When I interviewed Johnny Rogan, he told me he had stories for legal reasons he couldn't report. But, unlike Clinton Heylin, Rogan had sympathetic windows into Van's private life. "Van was not as nervous about my book," Rogan continued. "I think Clinton Heylin paved the way for the end of the lawsuits."

Rogan followed Van around like A. J. Weberman dogged Bob Dylan. When Rogan took notes from Van's friends, they spoke of his total commitment to the music. He also told me Van had unyielding ambition. His unbreakable work ethic and attention to detail intrigued Rogan. A sense no one understood him drove Morrison's, at times, vindictive prose. These were factors influencing Rogan's mellifluous prose. There was a self-righteous attitude, Rogan said, to Van's persona. Rogan believed Van had a difficult time making the transition from a blue collar, shotgun house to Dublin high society with Michelle Rocca. She was a former Miss Ireland. She had never worked a day in her life. Her job was marrying rich men. Van found out that when the bills for the divorce arrived. She had a retinue of personal assistants, an entitled existence and a need for money to maintain her multi-million dollar lifestyle. Champagne and the good life was not Van's thing. He paid the bills. No wonder he was difficult during covid. He was still paying for an egregious mistake. Rocca had little interest in his music career. It was all about the money. After two husbands, the richest soccer player in Ireland and the scion of the Ryan Air family, Van was the third millionaire in the mix. No one said Rocca was stupid. Conniving? In love? You decide!

Van was a long way from East Belfast. He yearned to return. Rogan concluded Van was an entitled loner. That was an oversimplification. He is private. He has a wide circle of friends. He is a multimillionaire. This is not the life of an entitled loner.

How does one explain the mercurial Morrison? It is simple. He grew up Protestant in a Catholic dominated city. Everyone I interviewed said he was temperamental long before fame and fortune. East Belfast was a Protestant oasis. His view of the world originated there. Van's interest in local geography inundated his songwriting. Rogan said Van was "chained to Belfast." Not true! If anything, the Belfast influences were molded by Marin County experiences. His marriage to Janet Planet ignited his initial creativity. The relationship with Carol Guida extended his writing. His old friends from Woodstock, John Platania and Jon Gershen, were important in developing his musical chops. A host of poets, authors and itinerant intellectuals swirling around Marin County brought him a literary touch. These were the factors molding the Belfast Cowboy. There were two Van Morrison's evolving in Marin County. One was a singer-songwriter. The other had the persona of a public intellectual without a platform.

THE GOOD VAN, AND THE ERRATIC VAN

Van was staunchly loyal to friends and employees. He kept Stephen Pillster on as an employee a decade after his usefulness expired. He ignored Pillster's management charges, which half a dozen of Van's musicians told me, were outrageous. The other side was Van's blind loyalty to employees, when a tongue lashing or firing was more appropriate. "You never know what you are going to get personal with Van," Chris Michie observed.

His pen had a different influence. There was a romantic side to his writing. The joy of listening to beautiful songs like "Crazy Love," "Sweet Thing" and "Warm Love" suggested the sensitivity in a soul that at times appeared dour. The contrast between his personal behavior and the love rolling off his prose described his multi-faceted personality.

On **Hard Nose The Highway**, "Warm Love" suggested Van had no idea divorce was imminent. He and Janet, per revelations in the divorce agreement, had been going to couples therapy for some time, and Chris Michie and others told me "Warm Love" was Van's way of saying let's keep the marriage together. The song, at least a dozen people close to Van told him, was a "love letter to his wife." Images of "you're dressed up in lace" seem to support the positive nature of the marriage on the cusp of divorce. As Van describes "the ivy on the old clinging wall" there is a sense of nostalgia for the hilltop Fairfax home. Years earlier, in 1970 on the **Moondance** album "Crazy Love" evoked how Janet mended his heart. He writes of needing her in the daytime as well as at night. This type of romantic song began with "Sweet Thing" on **Astral Weeks**. The words caught Greil Marcus's attention. Marcus made Morrison's music a staple of his writing in **Creem** and **Rolling Stone**.

Once he became a legend the critics were in for a rough ride. That is except for Greil Marcus. He knew Van personally. He understood him better than any critics. He was an honest reviewer with depth of knowledge and the pen of a literary giant. Not only was Marcus the most important rock critic, he was the best. A giant of an analytic reviewer of rock 'n' roll music.

Greil Marcus: "Van Morrison is heir to a tradition of mysteries, and he knows it. He is a Celt, and at least a spiritual descendant of the Irish prelate St. Brennan, who set out from Ireland 1500 years ago…reached America itself….So there may be a sense in which Morrison can understand that he was always an American…." Marcus makes the point "in the history of rock and roll, a singer who cannot be pinned down, dismissed, nor fitted into anyone's expectations" is a rarity.

One of Van's writing traits is to look back upon his life. He did that for his ninth studio album in 1977 **A Period Of Transition**. He looked back to the hard work in 1973-1974 in this album. In one song, "You Gotta Make It Through The World," he sang of his "survival" and the need to find a "real spiritual song." He was angry that a host of young artists, Bruce Springsteen, John Cougar Mellencamp and Bob Seger were influenced by Van, but they failed to acknowledge him. He viewed it as ultimate disrespect.

Van began a new career path with **A Period of Transition**. This album began a creative direction challenging the critics, complaining about those he influenced and railing on about his life. Many critics dismissed the album. Why? One London reviewer said it sounded like someone singing in a local pub. It was pub rock. Van did not invent pub rock. Dave Edmunds and Nick Lowe might disagree. Graham Parker also owed a debt to Van as did Bruce Springsteen, Bob Seger, Elvis Costello, John Cougar Mellencamp and Tom Petty. Van is pissed about it. He wants his share of the royalties. He doesn't understand the similarities in genres or styles. You can't copyright style. Van would disagree.

To this day he rants and raves "copycats ripped off my soul." His anger at those he influenced was controlled but persistent.

WHAT DOES VAN'S PERSONALITY DO FOR HIM IN THE MUSIC BUSINESS?

Van should be thankful he is a crabby little bugger. He gets a pass for his over the top behavior. He can insult. He can berate. After all he is Van Morrison. The good news is since turning sixty he has been overly cooperative with the press. Well except for the journalists who pose inane questions. The press can receive his vitriolic criticism. A case in point was Ryan H. Walsh's article: "What Happened To Van Morrison: The Fall From Eccentric Genius to Conspiracy Theorist?" This journalist posits the question: "Outside of the circles of his most dedicated fans, has the arrival of a Van Morrison album in the twenty-first century been a news event?" The Belfast Cowboy didn't react. Van acted in a surreptitious manner to avoid controversy. The mercurial Morrison has mellowed with age. There are exceptions. The Belfast Cowboy's creative juices still flow from a personality dealing withs six decades of show business. Van often looks back to look forward.

CLINTON HEYLIN'S DISDAIN AND JOHHNY ROGAN'S RANTS: GOOD BOOKS WITH AN ATTITUDE

In writing a multi-volume Van Morrison biography wading through Clinton Heylin's disdain and Johnny Rogan's rants is a joy. The two biographers are the best in the rock music industry. They give out a message important to this multi-volume biographer. That message is it is difficult to understand the impenetrable Morrison. Or is it? He can be understood as an enormously talented, blue collar, hardworking and continually creative product of 124 Hyndford Street, Belfast. But don't ask his biographers to write it simply. This results in disdain and rants from Van. He claims biography is a distortion of his life and career.

To close friends, Van is boringly normal. His band, will at times, hide out in a local bar without him while on tour. They need a rest from the ranting and raving. His outcries concerning the music business are ignored in private moments. His legendary accomplishments are seldom discussed. He is a mystical stylist. Over the years the evolution of theme, content, direction and perception took him into new creative modes. There is no easy way to explain Morrison. His artistry is the key to understanding him.

He views the local landscape. He encapsules it in his lyrical beauty. Clinton Heylin sees another side to Morrison. Kevin Mitchell reviewing Heylin's book wondered if Van's thrown wine glasses, the indiscriminate firing of managers, musicians, girlfriends, wives and musicians indicated a problem? Of Heylin's biography, he wrote: "It is not a biography; it is a quibble, a long-far too long-and humorless snarl of a book, detailing Morrison's crimes and misdemeanors, his foibles and flaws." After finishing Clinton's book, Mitchell concluded: "I felt slightly dirty when I put it down, as if I'd been part of an assassination plot." I think it is safe to conclude Mitchell was outraged by Clinton's prose. Why is this important? Right or wrong the Mitchell review illustrates the passion of those who write about the Belfast Cowboy.

To understand Morrison, one must examine his inspirational landscape. Van frequently looked back on his career. He dismantled those he disliked. He praised those whom he needs. He is open one minute with journalists and at odds with them at other times. Van is a brilliant contrarian. That alone is not a reason to write about him. Then why are two books on seven years of Morrison's life necessary? The reasons are many and varied. Van waged a one man war against the music business. Did he win? Probably! Did it make him happy? Probably not! Did Van protect his intellectual property? He did! Was he happy about it? No! He continues to grieve over lost royalties. A few years ago his ex-wife, Janet Morrison Minto, wrote a lengthy e-mail asking him to get over his complaints. What was Janet talking about? She said he owned ninety-nine percent of his musical catalogue. She pondered why was he still complaining? Even Janet Morrison Minto didn't realize it was Van being Van. He continues to complain while suing those who deign to disagree.

What are Van's positive points? He writes like a poet while bringing back long lost artists in concert like Charlie Gracie, Jimmy Witherspoon, Sam Butera, Taj Mahal, Bobby Blue Bland, George Benson and developing artists like Brian Kennedy and James Hunter. They open for him. Few performers can match Van on stage. Van's genius is to take the mundane and make it beautiful. His relevant and personally intoxicating words are the work of a wunderkind.

What about Johnny Rogan? David Sinclair, in the **London Guardian**, labelled Rogan's 2005 biography "almost comically unflattering." What did he mean? Sinclair claimed Rogan had "an almost neurotic attention to detail." That is how one understands Morrison. The Belfast Cowboy is characteristically petty and vindictive while maintaining a righteous attitude. "Whatever Happened To P. J. Proby" was not a hit. It was a window into Morrison's psyche. He wondered if P. J. Proby faded into obscurity because he was a teen idol?

What did Johnny Rogan accomplish in two brilliant biographies? No one got inside Van's head better than Rogan. In two scintillating, breakthrough biographies, he provided brilliant prose, in-depth research, and his consummate analysis never ended. There are rare bits of information, trivia and obscure occurrences other books ignore. As a master researcher, Rogan is brilliant. For that he took Van's anger and ire to his grave. Rest in peace Johnny Rogan. You paved the way for future biographers.

THE VOICE, THE VOICE, THE VOICE

This book demonstrates Van Morrison is complicated. There are peaks and valleys in his career. There are points of contradiction. He is a rascal. He is also kind, considerate and loyal to friends. There is one constant. "The voice, the voice, the voice," Delbert McClinton told me when I interviewed him. What is a singer of McClinton's vocal prowess doing bringing up Van Morrison? He, like other artists, paid tribute to the amazing singing voice that defines Morrison.

Today Van sounds much like he did when he belted out "Here Comes The Night" with Them. Some say he sounds better. Morrison's voice is an extraordinary one. It gets better with age. Why? He works on it. A glass of cold water on stage with a glass of hot water. He has a vocal coach. He takes care of his voice. While in his late-seventies in 2023, his weight loss indicated his commitment to good health and to his career longevity.

For decades Van has said what he does is not easy. He is right. He continues to work 24/7 on his career. This book is about nineteen months of his life in 1973-1974. He had the goal to stabilize and finalize his songwriting and performing. He did it. His themes have never varied.

When Van's forty-second studio album **Latest Record Project: Volume 1** arrived with twenty-eight tracks in 2021, he said: "I'm getting away from the perceived same songs, same albums all the time." The irony is he made similar comments in 1973-1974. There is a continuity to Van critics miss. It is more than his voice. It is the absolute unyielding commitment to his career.

There is one absolute in Van's life. That is accept his opinions. He goes off the rails if he sees or imagines censorship or disrespect. Once during a 2014 GQ awards ceremony, Van looked over to see a TV personality, Piers Morgan, staring at him. Van looked away. A few days later Morgan wrote Van was glaring at him. The point of the story, Van told punk poet cum musician John Cooper Clarke, Morgan complained Van did not tolerate other people and their opinions. In a private moment, Morgan allegedly called Morrison "a world class asshole" in a production meeting. Van was calm. He said of Piers Morgan: "He's an advocate for free speech, but he's obviously not very accepting of mine. I've always done my own thing," Van continued. "I've been independent of the music business since the late 1970s, so I fund everything. I am not funded by any record company. Nobody is my boss. I'm self-employed."

From 1973 through 1979 Van established this brand in Marin County. What was Morrison doing? He was perfecting a vocal style for the ages. "The voice, the voice, the voice," Delbert McClinton said. "You never forget it." That is true. What is also true is Van has taken extraordinary care of his vocal instrument.

VAN HAS THE LAST WORD: SORT OF!

Van never acknowledged the debt he owed Marin County. This fervent musical cauldron, in a small county north of San Francisco, defined Van's early songwriting. For one **Los Angeles Times** reporter, Van morphed into a conspiracy theorist during the coronavirus pandemic. This criticism was a bit over the top. It illustrated the continual war between Van and the press.

The press war continues to the present day. Van has the last word every day of his life. That is a good thing for the biographer. Why? The story never ends. Van's life is like visiting a museum where his artistic achievements provide new daily insights. Van's life creates a level of attention exhausting the critics and enabling his fans.

When Van sat down with a fellow musician-cum journalist, Leo Green, to discuss songwriting, it was revealing. It was a fourteen minute look into his writing process. The interview began with Van discussing the movies. "People don't want to record new songs," Van continued on the movies. "I've got...like a dozen songs that keep getting recycled...." He observed: "They always put the same songs in the movies." Van commented he has written over four hundred other songs. No one in the industry is interested. "It's always about the past," Van concluded.

Before he arrived in Marin County, he had had only written a few dozen songs. Van observed everyone was writing their own songs. The record company wanted the publishing. "I never lost the thing I was a singer; I am doing my own songs. I was a singer first." He believed the 1960s changed everything in the industry. It was necessary to learn the business side of the industry to survive.

Bibliographical Sources

For a recent examination of Morrison's up and down spiritual life, see, Erik Hage, **The Words And Music Of Van Morrison** (New York, 2009). Hage, an assistant professor of Journalism, Mass Media and Cultural Criticism at SUNY, Cobleskill, is a perceptive critic. His literary prose provides cogent analysis. Hage is an academic writing brilliantly for a popular audience. His strength is illustrating how Van's dark songwriting moments were buttressed with, at times, uplifting and celebratory lyrics. This is a complicated explanation of an enormously talented artist. Hage writes: "If you're looking for me to sum up or define the work of Van Morrison....I simply can't do it....Van Morrison seems to constitute an entire universe unto himself." That is a problem for the biographer, as Hage states, there are "too many identities." That is also window into Van's complicated life. He won't talk about his personal life. He does so in lyrics. Hage reflected on how the artist who wrote such poignant love songs like "Have I Told You Lately That I Love You?" could also have written and growled out "Listen To The Lion."

Where Hage gets it right is when he analyzes Van's relationship with his audience. The majority of his fans had never heard of Bobby Blue Bland. After a few Morrison concerts they bought his old blues records. It is Van's musical world that his fans enter. They never leave his lyrical world. Michael Seltzer, a young Detroit kid on the way to a storied career as a Notary and local politician, attended his first Morrison concert in the late 1970s. Today he continues to see virtually every Van show. Being a retired Notary must pay well. The Irish actress Roma Downey is another Van fan. She tells people she is the number one Morrison fan in the world. Rumor has it Seltzer is considering legal action.

As a cultural critic, Hage, using a sense of minutiae, detailed Morrison's lyrical diversity. He concluded it was is the product of a wide variety of American musical styles. Hage sees Van mining his early life for themes. He places these images in detail in his lyrics. Hage impressively described Morrison's apolitical nature. He discussed Morrison's spiritual quest in copious detail. He suggested it was the force shaping his talent. By analyzing Hage's views of Morrison it is possible to see how significant the 1970s were to forming and launching "Becoming Van Morrison."

Hage writes of Van: "He is one of the most idiosyncratic songwriters in the history of popular music." The professor concluded his songbook is "an expansive and diverse canon." Hage believes the Belfast Cowboy "doesn't have too much of an existence outside of music." That is a popular view. It is also not correct. Van has always lived a rich private life with two wives, half a dozen serious girlfriends and a group of friends, many dating from more than a half a century. Van popularizes the fiction music is his entire life. It isn't. He is as normal as anyone else. Some remark he is boring. While Professor Hage says he works in a musical world that is his own, he doesn't recognize Van's personal life is a mirror image. There is "no "feral existence" as Hage suggests. The professor recognizes Van's intellect: "He is extremely intellectually curious." He fails to analyze why the Morrison phenomenon has lasted for more than sixty years. Perhaps there is no answer. One answer is the influences in Marin County from 1973 through 1979. "I also tried to get past the myth of Morrison by really trying to get at what makes him tick as a songwriter." Hage got this right as he demonstrated how Van's environment completed the lyrics making his songs special.

See Stephen Holden, "Hard Nose The Highway Music Review," **Rolling Stone**, September 27, 1973 for a critique of the first album Van said he produced completely on his own. Also, see, Howard A. DeWitt, **Van Morrison: The Mystic's Music** (Fremont, 1983), passim.

For comments on Van's dogmatic nature and love affair with the past see, Johnny Rogan, **Van Morrison: No Surrender** (London, 2005) pp. 1-4. Rogan's book has a detailed description of the Caledonia influences, the Troubles and how these forces impacted Morrison spiritually, intellectually and creatively. For a general history of California, see, Howard A. DeWitt, **California Civilization** (Dubuque, 1979, revised edition, 1981). Also, see, Howard A. DeWitt, **The Fragmented Dream: Multicultural California** (Dubuque, 1996) for the Irish influences in the Golden State.

See Peter Mills, **Hymns To The Silence: Inside The Words And Music Of Van Morrison** (New York, 2010), Chapter 1. The first chapter, "Imagining America: Jazz, Blues, Country And The Mythology Of The West" is a brilliant account of how American music infatuated, shaped and blended Morrison's music with his Irish roots. By including Jack Kerouac's influence there is a sense of how Beat literature produced the Belfast Cowboy's unique music. As Mills writes: "Van Morrison was well placed next to Belfast's thriving port to catch the new music." (p. 2) He continues linking the blues, with an illustration of how Huddie Ledbetter's music contributed to Van's artistic development. Mills analyzes how Robert Johnson and English folk-rock icon Lonnie Donegan added another ingredient into Morrison's musical stew.

For Van reflecting on his career as he entered looked back in 1990, see, David Wild, "Conversation With Van Morrison," **Rolling Stone**, August 9, 1990. https://www.rollingstone.com/music/music-features/a-conversation-with-van-morrison-232640/ Van's comments on MTV set the tone for the precipitous growth of how he viewed the new music.

The reviews are at times excessively picky, often unfair and overly critical of Clinton Heylin's 2002 biography. This highlights the divide among Van Morrison biographers and the critics.

For a brilliant, incisive, and analytical review of Heylin's tome, see, for example, Kevin Mitchell, "How To Make Van Ordinaire," **The London Guardian**, December 2, 2002. https://www.theguardian.com/books/2002/dec/08/biography.vanmorrison.

The brilliance of Mitchell's argument is he charged Heylin with ignoring Van's strengths. There is a beauty to his songwriting. As a wordsmith the Belfast Cowboy has the facile pen of a nineteenth century poet. Mitchell's review acknowledged Van's at times inexcusable behavior. Mitchell argued there was a stark need for a book understanding Van. Lastly, Mitchell rightly points to Van's ability to employ his environment to frame his art.

See Greg Haymes, "Erik Hage Peels Away The Myth From Van Morrison's Music," **Nippertown**, August 31, 2009. This is a revealing interview with Hage by a local outlet where he shares his views on his book and Morrison.

Johnny Rogan was rock 'n' roll's most obsessive biographer. For criticism and faint praise for Rogan's Van Morrison biography, as well as some valid criticism for Rogan's idiosyncratic reporting in an in-depth and fair minded article, see, David Sinclair, "Angry Man In The Van," **The London Guardian**, May 27, 2005. https://www.theguardian.com/books/2005/may/28/highereducation.biography

For the Van Morrison-Slim Gaillard segment where Van reads from Jack Kerouac's **On The Road**, while Gaillard plays the bongos, while singing and ripping off his shirt, see, "Van Morrison Reads From On The Road," **BBC.co., UK**, posted August 10, 2011. https://www.bbc.co.uk/programmes/p00jqk8s This is a four minute segment from the BBC Arena film "How High The Moon." Recalling the 1989 film Morrison reflected: "I got to know him quite well-he's the singer who is referenced in Kerouac's **On The Road**. For more on Van and his remembrance of beat influences, see, "Van Remembers The Beat Poets," **FYI Music News**, December 6, 2016. https://www.fyimusicnews.ca/articles/2016/12/06/van-morrison-remembers-beat-poets

There are a number of YouTube videos highlighting the Gaillard-Morrison friendship. As Van reads from Jack Kerouac's novel Gillard is sitting next to him with a smile. He is having fun. Van stops in deference to Gaillard. It is a wonderful moment. Then Van comes back in with his reading of **On The Road**. There is a spiritual sense to the reading. See the YouTube video "Van Morrison And Slim Gaillard Read Jack Kerouac's On the Road." At the interview's conclusion, Gaillard provides some insights into his long term friendship with Kerouac. On October 21, 2014, Van's official website released a three minute and forty seven second video "It Has Been 45 Years Since Today Since...." This celebrates the Slim Gaillard reading on YouTube in another format. Van is obviously pleased with his time with Gaillard. Van Morrison's Twitter account also contained a post. Also, see, "Jazz Spotlight: Morrison Takes Familiar Path, But It's Not Jazz," **Los Angeles Times**, January 7, 1996 for another Gaillard-Morrison reference.

For the Piers Morgan story that Van was a nasty bloke and for the conversation with John Cooper Clarke, see, Dylan Jones, "Van Morrison And John Cooper Clarke On Life And (anti) Lockdown," **GQ**, May 11, 2021. https://www.gq-magazine.co.uk/culture/article/van-morrison-john-cooper-clarke\ This is a revealing Morrison interview. He explained his opposition to the covid-19 lockdown. He believed it was a government conspiracy. Van was clear it was an abuse of government authority. This comment drew a great deal of criticism. One journalist suggested Van was overly conspiracy minded. That is a life-long trait. Van also explained how this CD **Latest Record Project, Volume 1** explained his point of view. During this interview, Van briefly mentioned Joel Selvin's book on Bert Berns. Van said when he got to the part about his relationship with Berns, he closed the book and threw it away. He saw Selvin's descriptions of him as pure fiction. Selvin's deeply researched and brilliantly written book told the story of Berns and Bang Records accurately, in-depth and it was fair to both sides. For some reason, Van will not answer, correct or address inconsistencies as he sees them in people who write about him.

In writing this chapter conversations with Paul Vincent, Mervyn Solomon, Delbert McClinton, Carol Guida, John Goddard, Mark Naftalin, Tony Dey, Chris Michie, the Barsotti brothers, Larry Catlin,

Paul Vincent and Nick Clainos helped to flush out this material. A special thank you to Marie Bainer for local music history.

There is very little serious scholarship on rock 'n' roll lyrics and poetry. For some examples of how to view this subject see, for example, P. Astor, "The Poetry of Rock: Song Lyrics Are Not Poems But the Words Still Matter, Another Look At Richard Goldstein's Collection of Rock Lyrics," **Popular Music**, volume 29, Issue 1, 2010, pp. 143-148. Goldstein's book is the best example of why rock 'n' roll lyrics are poetic.

There are a number of music or rock 'n' roll insiders who have espoused Van Morrison's talent and why it matters in the larger scope of rock 'n' roll history. There are so many examples of why Van catches the eye of those in the industry it would take a book to catalogue them. In 1980 a documentary on Martin Scorsese's career, "Movies Are My Life: A Profile on Martin Scorsese," where he talks with The Band's Robbie Robertson as he was editing the documentary for "The Last Waltz," a clip appears with a drunken, virtually incoherent Robertson telling Scorsese to wanted to play the director a song. Scorsese didn't look interested. Robertson persisted. "I wanna play you a song before we knock off here. This song…has got nothing to do with anything, but you'll know exactly what we mean, this is by Van the Man," Robertson blurted out in a drunken stupor. As Scorsese listened to Morrison, he tilted his head back, he smiled and he enjoyed the lilting vocal refrain. The video, on YouTube, is a clip of Morrison performing "Tupelo Honey." See "Robbie Robertson & Martin Scorsese Vibing To Van The Man."

https://www.youtube.com/watch?v=1tJqk4XWJRE&t=176s

For Van's creativity those close to him, notably Derek Bell, Solly Lipsitz and Mervyn Solomon, provided information on how Belfast influenced his psyche and by extension his creative process. Irish influences on Van's songwriting coalesced with the Marin County influences in the 1970s to dominate his art. For an examination of how the Chieftains and individual members of The band helped Van fulfill his songwriting goals, see, for example, John Glatt, **The Chieftains: The Authorized Biography** (New York, 1997, 2000, revised edition).

Paul Vincent offered copious insights into how easy it was to deal with Van in a room with no other people while they were on San Francisco premier FM radio station for an interview later transcribed in **Bam**. A brief conversation with Solly Lipsitz added to this chapter. Blues singer Delbert McClinton spoke briefly and glowingly of Van's talents in two interviews I did for magazine articles on him in **Blue Suede News** and **Rock 'N' Blues News**.

TWO

Looking Back To Look Forward: 27 Minutes Of Van Redux And Reconsidered

"We seek the absolute dream. We are forced back continually to an acquiescence in all that is hallucinatory and wasteful to a rejection of all norms and gods...."

Joyce Carol Oates

"Do not judge it. Do not try to understand it. Do not censor it."

Philip Roth, *Operation Shylock*

"Van Morrison the person is not for public consumption."

Van Morrison in a 1985 interview with Al Jones

What is meant my looking back to look forward? The answer is a simple one. When cornered by a journalist Van says: "I don't talk about my private life." Or perhaps he will remark: "I don't discuss my music." Is this Van being difficult? Of course! So how does one examine the elusive Belfast Cowboy? The answer is in multiple subjects. All of which I will discuss in this chapter.

When Van reached the middle of 1974, his career had taken more twists and turns than most fifty year show business veterans. Clinton Heylin labelled this period "Naked To The World." Not necessarily wrong! More complicated than that. What Heylin meant remains a mystery. The prevalent wisdom is Van reinvented himself. He was escaping the hit records. One of the strangest conflicts is when he informed the press he was through with pop hits only to confront Mo Ostin at his home demanding that Warner Bros. guarantee "Bulbs" would hit the Billboard Hot 100.

Joe Smith was behind the drive to promote "Bulbs" as a pop hit. He arranged for jazz musicians to re-record it in New York. Van had rewritten the song. When Warner Bros. released "Bulbs" as a single in eleven countries it failed to chart. Van looked back on his early 1970s hits with a nostalgic feel "Bulbs" would reignite his hit records. It didn't. In a twenty-seven-minute interview posted on his website; Van was adamant about the 1970s. He intimated this period of his life made him what he was when this 2007 interview surfaced.

Van's belief was he had to look back to look forward. That explains the rhythm and blues, blues and oldies rock hits in concert. Wilbert Harrison's "Kansas City" and Chris Kenner's "I Like It Like That" were by artists Van's knowledge of and interest in was deep. Not only because of their music, but it was due to the way the industry treated them. Van protested the treatment of the African American pioneers. He was making a statement. American music was increasingly the foundation of his 1970s metamorphosis into a superstar.

VAN'S CAREER DOMINTES: PERSONAL RELATIONS SUFFER

For support Van will call upon a friend. As Janet Planet was preparing to end their marriage, he flew Jon Gershen from Woodstock to San Francisco. He picked him up at the airport. Why? Van needed a sympathetic ear. A listener to the trauma of his marital nightmare. Gershen became that sympathetic listener. Van claimed to be surprised by the divorce.

He was! Why? Van focused so much attention on his career he forgot personal relationships. His marriage ended. His professional career exploded into a hurricane of creativity.

As Van revised his music career to escape the traumatic change in his life, the muse with no money, Janet Planet, was gone. The euphoria of moving to California was lost in the tendentious marital atmosphere. That down time in his life accentuated a 24/7 creativity. Then decades later, in a twenty-seven-minute interview, Van recalled that time. He intimated he had to look back in his life to look forward. He confided to friends in the 1970s his career goals. He never discussed his personal life. Had he considered his personal life his path to fame and fortune would have slowed. That was not an option. The window into Van's 1970s soul came when he sat down for interviews with Canadian journalist Ritchie Yorke. Facts and truth emerged.

VAN'S EARLY CONFIDANTS: WHAT THEY MEAN FOR THE BIOGRAPHER

A Canadian journalist, Ritchie Yorke, was another confident. Van talked to him numerous times. A book resulted. It was hagiography. Yorke's book ranks as the worst Van Morrison biography. Ironically, it tells future biographers a great deal. How? It repeats Van's interviews verbatim. The conversations with Yorke led to Van's renewed Irish influences. Belfast was back in his psyche. Pronounced Irish influences were lost in the hippie subculture in and around Marin County. Soon Van emitted what he labelled "a brighter side of Irish culture."

The professor's showed up in Van's life. Gerald Dawe, a Belfast lad who went on to become an acclaimed poet and a University Professor, watched Van's every move. Decades later he would write about it. Other writers were influenced by the 1970s Van Morrison.

One of the unpopular subjects biographers, pundits, journalists and even the Shakespeare of Telegraph Avenue ponder is the loquacious question of can white boys sing the blues? It is a harmless, needless and mind-numbing argument. The **New York Times** jazz critic, Stanley Crouch, wrote of African American cultural authenticity. Guess what? He didn't think white men could sing the blues. One wonders if he had heard of Joe Cocker.

When Crouch died, he was in the process of redefining black music. When he passed in 2020, he had never analyzed Van Morrison's music. He had heard Van on the 1997 B. B. King record **Deuces Wild** in which Van covered "If You Love Me" along with King. We have no idea what Crouch thought of Van. He probably didn't follow Van's career. What is the point? The idea of a white man not being able to sing the blues is an argument in ignorance, anarchy and cultural deprivation. When Crouch passed away in 2020, at the age of seventy-four, he was the doyen of conservative jazz critics. His writing on white people singing the blues popularized the term cultural miscegenation. That is unfortunate. Music is music. Like Van, Crouch was an intellectual contrarian. He was continually asking why he had to explain?

The last part of this chapter brings Mick Cox into the mix. He helps Van evolve as a musician and songwriter, as does his constant companion Carol Guida. Then Van picks up a book by Elizabeth Clare Prophet and viola the transition to the spiritual subjects he increasingly favors.

HOW DOES ONE UNDERSTAND VAN?

To understand the Belfast Cowboy all of the above subjects, influences, attitudes and local markers must come together. I have established a Top Ten List of Van Morrison traits. The reason? To understand the man, one must consider his geographical influences, those around him, and the stimuli driving his career. Public relations is not a Morrison forte. Some of the most obvious insights come from the revolving door of public relations experts who fled Van in ultimate terror.

Keith Altham, an early public relations specialist, defined Van: "The man is an arse," Altham wrote. Then he fired himself. A Van Morrison fan who helped Janet Morrison Minto fight a legal action where Van wanted to stop her from selling her home-made jewelry, told me from his sumptuous Virginia home with pictures of Van adorning the game room: "Van is a world class asshole." Harsh? Yes! Warranted? No! Explaining Morrison's, at times, boorish behavior is the best way to understand him. To ignore it. To praise his every uttering is not the way to analyze his musical genius. One of the best sources for Van being Van is a Cameron Crowe interview for **Creem** in which he discusses the 1970s.

To musical cohorts like David Hayes, John Platania, John Allair and dozens of others there is a commonality to Van's behavior. They say if you leave him alone, he is a prince. If not, watch out. Van has never compromised his privacy. He has since 1985 in dozens of interviews provided his thoughts for understanding him as a writer and musician. This book, and the next three to follow, will use that material to show that one can understand the Belfast Cowboy. He is not unexplainable. It just appears that way.

There is more to Van than the March 2007 twenty-seven-minute interview from Van's website. This interview shows Van in a plaid shirt wearing a brown hat with sunglasses, relaxed and talking easily about his career. What that interview did was to validate everything in this chapter. He answered the question: "Why Van Morrison matters."

VAN LOOKS BACK ON HIS CAREER IN A 27 MINUTE INTERVIEW: A NEW PERSONA

In March 2007, Van Morrison looked back on his career with satisfaction in a twenty-seven-minute interview. The YouTube heading for this extraordinary piece of film, was "What's The Question? Part I." As Van talked about his early career, he had fond memories of Marin County and the San Francisco Bay Area. He was mildly complimentary concerning the role Warner Bros. played in his career. Whoever is in charge at Woolhall released this video to suggest how and why Van may not need a biographer. He can tell his own story. What did this tape suggest? Plenty!

After signing with Warner Brothers, Van produced a series of commercial and critically acclaimed albums. He remarked he did this to guarantee his commercial future. In the mid-1970s, he took two and a half years off to recharge his personal and writing life. He had time to think. He wrote furtively. It brought one major change. The intellectual side to Van created a new persona. That is, he developed an even more intense interest in mysticism and spiritual matters. He eschewed the trendy Maharshi's the Beatles and Beach Boys favored. Van was, and has always been, a private person. No one talked of his intellectual side. Rock 'n' roll was not a career for aspiring brain surgeons.

The Belfast Van knew was a simple place. That changed as he fled to America to find a career and escape the Troubles. Belfast from 1973 into mid-1974 was a city of religious divisions, security checks, shootings and restricted areas due to the Troubles. The juxtaposition of violence and justice made it unsafe. Van fled the confusion. He lived in an American exile. When violence with the Troubles declined, the Belfast Cowboy sporadically visited Belfast. He settled in London, as well as in Bath, and in North East Somerset. In time, he returned semi-permanently to Ireland.

His mercurial ways succumbed to age. His passion for privacy intensified. His personal muse was driven with a Belfast countenance. Van never articulated why he fled Ireland. Was it the Troubles? Was it his wandering creative muses? Was it his penchant for finding songwriting inspiration in varied geographical settings? Was it a 24/7 drive for success? What was he searching for and why? He has never said. We will never know. But, as he sat down with Michelle Rocca, in 1995, for lengthy discussions, he answered why Belfast remained his primary creative muse.

Looking back on the 1970s, Van reflected to Rocca: "You start writing songs...and you get these reviews and these people are saying 'well that means this is about that,'" Van sighed. He couldn't understand the critics. He believed his writing was private. Don't analyze it. It may mean nothing. It may mean something. "You get to the point where you are out of it," Van concluded. There was a dogmatic frustration. He said he was "unanalytical." He was tired of the reviews. The questions were insipid. The fledgling rock journalists knew very little about his music. "The whole show business trip," Van complained to Rocca, "was a disaster."

When Van was asked about the truth. He looked dumbfounded. It was about family. It was about observing the erratic 1970s. It was about his business interests. Van's observations indicated his songwriting stew was complicated. His level of talent, seldom seen at such a young age, matured. He wanted the critics to leave him alone. He claimed to channel his songs. He was a consummate, consistent blue-collar writer. A workaholic in rock music was not the norm.

JON GERSHEN HELPS VAN WITH FAME'S BURDEN

Fame took its toll in the early 1970s. Van needed someone to talk with about his career. When he flew in his old band mate, Jon Gershen, from Woodstock, it was an attempt to rethink his career. He was fretting over his personal life. His future? He was equally concerned. When Gershen arrived, Clinton Heylin claimed, it was in the midst of the Morrison's marital difficulties. Others in Woodstock and Marin County disagreed. The differences between Van and Janet were private. No one knew! No one cared! Everyone was surprised by the divorce. Van confided to Gershen he was surprised by Janet's abrupt departure. Her words hurt. One musician said Van was lost "in a fog of doubt." Hence, the untrue writer's block rumors surfaced.

Gershen was typical of Van's friends. He was a musician. In the 1969-1970 period, while in Woodstock, Van played with members of Gershen's group, the Colwell-Winfield Blues Band. When he relocated to Marin County, Van took their horn players Jack Schroer and Colin Tilton with him to California. Tilton's flute on "Moondance" received critical acclaim, as did Schroer's saxophone.

For Van, Gershen was a shoulder to cry on while he reinvented his music. "He had an incredible mistrust of the business," Gershen continued. "Before we moved to California, we took him into the city

(New York) to talk to our lawyer." This was when Van found out how much money he was owed. Then he moved to Fairfax. Then the divorce. Van's contract with Schwaid-Merenstein was close to penury. Van's new manager, Mary Martin, broke it. In this atmosphere Gershen was close to Morrison providing a needed friend in time of despair.

Jon Gershen: "When he moved there (Fairfax) he used to call me-in the middle of the night-and say, 'What's happening? What's going on in Woodstock?" He missed the whole scene." Gershen made it clear. Janet wanted to relocate to Marin County.

The uncertainty of relocating to Marin County clouded Van's marriage. His creativity was inspired by the hundreds of musicians making a living in California while living in a country setting north of San Francisco.

Jon Gershen: "He invited me out to stay for a week. It was right after **St. Dominic's Preview**...." After they had dinner, high on the hill in his Fairfax home, Van drove Gershen to a local hotel. He told his friend a divorce was imminent. "I listened to her side of it, and it was just clear that things had reached an end," Gershen concluded. During interviews with Clinton Heylin, Gershen blamed the divorce on Van's career. There was a steady income. "Van didn't have the money he later acquired," Carol Guida continued. "I didn't care! We had our books. We talked about literature. We lived fine." Van wasn't a spender. He was frugal. As the muse with no money, Janet rebelled. She left.

Gershen told Heylin: "He invites me out there in the middle of this thing that's going on between them-oblivious to the fact that this is not a good time to hang out." These observations were made before Janet moved out on November 17, 1972. When Janet filed for divorce on January 26, 1973, Gershen's friendship with Van was important. Clinton Heylin said Van wrote "songs of bitterness and need, but precious few lyrics displaying regret or remorse." "I Paid The Price" showed a sense of regret and remorse. Local Fairfax residents weren't interested in the divorce. Van had his privacy.

VAN'S DIVORCE SURPRISE

Many Woodstock observers were surprised when Van and Janet

Caledonia Productions
presents
VAN MORRISON 1957
and
RUBBER DUCK
in concert

at Bermuda Palms
737 Francisco Blvd.
San Rafael, Calif.

$3.00
8:00 P.M.
Fri., November 17, 1972

THE DIVORCE CONCERT

divorced. They concluded fame and fortune led to the split. They grew apart artistically. They retained strong family values. The ensuing publicity drove Van crazy. He craved privacy. That was impossible. It was not the contentious divorce Heylin described. California's no fault divorce law divided up the assets with negotiations between the parties. Van and Janet had few disagreements over money. Then why is the divorce important? It goes to Morrison's creativity. The divorce inspired new songs, new themes and a renewed sense of his songwriting craft.

When Janet moved out on November 17, 1972, Van was playing in San Rafael at the Bermuda Palms. Those around him said he was flummoxed. He had no idea a divorce was imminent. Clinton Heylin over dramatized the situation. "Janet finally moved out on her increasingly difficult husband." Van was moody, Janet allegedly remarked. He went into rages about the music business. He still does that. She was tired being a muse without money. When Shana was born Van was a devoted father. He remained a hands-on parent. To this day Van is a private and model father. This is the reason no one could figure out why the marriage ended. As Van said many times it was no one's business.

There were enormous pressures on Van. Warner Brothers demanded hit records. His Woodstock manager, Mary Martin, was controlling and personally erratic. Martin was in the mode of her mentor Albert Grossman. She was an even bigger asshole. She had a one-way mode. My way or the highway. Van fired her. Then he hired a new manager, Stephen Pillster. He knew the San Francisco Bay Area music scene. He was lazy, ill prepared and entitled. He allegedly had one goal. It was to get rid of Carol Guida. Van kept them both around. Pillster was not what you are looking for in a manager. The October 20, 1973, **Billboard** announced Pillster as Morrison's newly appointed general manager.

Pillster was tough minded. He was paid handsomely. One musician told me when Pillster left Morrison's fold he had made more money than anyone except Van. But, for a time, Pillster was adequate at his job.

The divorce was barely mentioned in the San Francisco media. John L. Wasserman and Phil Elwood told me it had no place in their columns. This is why Van appreciated Marin County. He had his privacy. He had extensive airplay on FM radio. Morrison was one of the initial major stars of the FM radio boom. "We loved Van at K-Mel and he in turn was a prince to us when we met him," Paul Vincent said.

HOW VAN ESCHEWED ROCK 'N' ROLL AND MUTED THE GUITAR: MARIN COUNTY WAS THE MONSTER INFLUENFCE

While still in Woodstock, Morrison eschewed rock 'n' roll. "I personally don't have anything to do with rock, in any shape or form," Van said. It was when he moved to Fairfax that Van was able to intensify this comment. Marin County was rock 'n' roll central. Exceptional guitar riffs with country and rock influences dominated Marin's musical groups with Commander Cody and the Lost Planet Airmen, Clover, the Quicksilver Messenger Service, Michael Bloomfield, the Sons of Champlin, the Rowen brothers and a host of others, dominating local clubs. They flooded the recording studios, toured and provided an identification for Marin County bands.

The Grateful Dead and Jefferson Airplane received inordinate publicity for their music. When Carlos Santana and Bill Graham moved there the music was defined with over-the-top production. Van liked the groups, the musicians and many of the sounds. But Van, being Van, he had his own musical direction. He was always the contrarian. He loved the creative atmosphere. He eschewed the hippie life style. He ignored the politics.

Van purposely brought in the soft mellow guitar picking of John Platania from Woodstock. Later, Chris Michie would be the master of the subtle guitar. Van's saxophone was another primary instrument. The Fairfax home recording studio was an element in the road to "Becoming Van Morrison."

Before he moved to Fairfax, Van enjoyed Woodstock. Those who hung around him in Woodstock, and who came to his home, described him as unusually mellow. Why? Bob Neuwirth believed he was happy with his creative life. His family life? Neuwirth had no idea that tension was in the air.

Everyone remembered Van concentrated 24/7 on his career. To do this, musicians arrived and departed with a ferocious regularity. San Francisco and Marin County studios combined to provide a working atmosphere. These influences led to a commercially productive period in his career from **Moondance** through **St. Dominic's Preview**.

Van was paying attention to new sounds. He listened to the Rolling Stones' **Exile On Main Street** and the Who's hard driving **Who's Next**. What did Van learn? Plenty! From the Stones he discovered they recorded a portion of the album in a studio in Southern France. He eventually did that. From the Who he discovered the Moog synthesizer, which allowed him to duplicate a moog like interlude on "Almost Independence Day."

Chris Michie claimed Van was a student of the hit charts in the early 1970s. Then he rebelled against pop hits for **Veedon Fleece**. "Van didn't want a 45 release on that album," Michie recalled. Joe Smith convinced him to go to New York to recut "Bulbs," which Warner would make a hit. When it didn't happen, Van was vindicated. "He told Smith he wasn't a rock 'n' roll artist," Michie concluded.

The early 1970s created the angry, disillusioned and cantankerous Morrison. Why? As his fame increased, the money flowed in, and the acclaim accelerated, he was frustrated by the re-release of the Them material.

TEMPORARY HAPPINESS IN MOVING TO CALIFORNIA: THEN DISASTER

Things appeared idyllic for Van. He had money. He had a new life. Until Janet moved out, he was happy. No one was more surprised by the divorce than Van. He never complained. He hunkered down working feverishly until the mid-1970s. Then he took almost three years off to retool his career and enjoy life with Carol Guida.

Clinton Heylin's take on the divorce suggested Van's recently built home recording studio was somehow responsible for the divorce. It wasn't! Heylin wrote the home studio "was completed just in time for Morrison to record a number of new songs—songs of bitterness and need, but precious few lyrics displaying regrets or remorse." Van wrote songs with those lyrics before the divorce. When he went into the studio, he didn't reflect on the divorce. It was about the music.

Heylin's notion Van lacked "regrets or remorse" is literary license. In his November 1972 recordings, Van had songs that made no mention of marital difficulties. Janet moving out was the furthest thing on his mind.

The musicians, who recorded with Van in late 1972, were as shocked. As Chris Michie told me: "Van was remorseful." How and why I asked? Michie said: "I have no idea. He is private. He never said." That explained Van Morrison. Divorce is traumatic. Heylin failed to capture that obvious fact.

Johnny Rogan's **Van Morrison: No Surrender** had the best version of Van and Janet's divorce. He didn't interview Janet. Rogan's source was Janet's artist bio for a record she released in 1998. Rogan believed it provided an insight into the marriage. It didn't. "I was a sweet tempered innocent," Janet explained in her 1998 bio release. She recorded an album with Lauren Wakefield for the group Fake Id. Janet commented: "I know to a certain extent my physical appearance played a part." She was right. Warner Bros. used her visual image, her pictures and her sense of style, when appropriate, to promote her husband's records. She believed her image perfectly described how the label envisioned her as Van's love child. She was described as a muse. "Everybody knew I played some part in what was going on creatively," Janet continued. "Van wasn't talking, and he couldn't be pushed for details." Her comments suggest how little she understood about her husband's complex personality.

Van needed to talk to someone. He hoped to find a knowledgeable and responsible journalist. He found that journalist in a Canadian rock and roll writer Ritchie Yorke. He was a blonde haired hipster with an almost hero worship of Van's music. He became Van's first biographer after meeting and interviewing him in Vancouver, British Columbia. For a brief time Yorke worked as Van's publicist.

RITCHIE YORKE AND VAN MORRISON (courtesy Ritchie Yorke)

TALKING TO RITCHIE YORKE AND A VACATION IN IRELAND

By looking back, Van told Ritchie Yorke, he would move forward. He meant his mistakes in the early Warner Brothers years told him where his music and business interests were headed to fulfill his vision. When the long haired, blonde hippie writer from Canada sat down with Van, to talk about 1973, there was a revelation. Van said his new album, **Hard Nose The Highway**, was his first independent production. He did it alone. Talking to Ritchie Yorke, Van speculated on his career. "I was just trying to establish how hard it was to do just what I do," Van remarked. This theme runs through Morrison's career. His blue collar work ethic persisted.

The discussions with Yorke were revealing. Van told him one side of his recent album had a hard edge. The other side had lighter touches. Van glowed with creativity. He hoped to release a double album. Warner Brothers nixed the idea. They were concerned the Belfast Cowboy wrote too much about Ireland. He certainly talked too much about Belfast. This began Morrison's furtive cataloguing of materials with Irish themes. **The Philosopher's Stone** was born. This cataloguing of material, whether unreleased demos, alternate cuts, recording fragments, or concert cuts began in earnest. To this day no one knows what the Morrison vault contains. The operative wisdom is it is a cache of gems. "Van Morrison's music has always had a timeless quality...we discover one reason why....Van is a man who will serve no song before its time," David Wild in **Rolling Stone**.

Steve Turner recalled Van talked of reconnecting with his Irish influences. Long before he discussed this with Turner, Van told California friends he needed to return to Ireland. The pronounced Irish influences surfaced dramatically in October 1973 after a brief trip to Dublin and the nearby countryside.

When he arrived at Sutton Place with his fiancée, Carol Guida, it was a relaxing time. Van hung out with Belfast journalist Donal Corvin. They stayed at Sutton House; a stylish, romantic hotel dominated by Irish influences. It was during what Van labeled a vacation that the Irish countryside beckoned in Dublin. Carol Guida and the Irish countryside inflamed his writing passion. This led to **Veedon Fleece**.

When he talked with Ritchie Yorke, it was extensive, honest, forthcoming, and there was a heartfelt description of his life. Yorke's 1975 book **Van Morrison: Into The Music** was the first Morrison biography. After he read it, Van hoped it was the last biography. He complained Yorke didn't get anything right. That trend persists. The time talking with Yorke was a revelation for Van's biographers. The images of Ireland's political problems drove him to California. The seeds of intensified Irish songwriting influences were planted At Sutton Place. **Veedon Fleece** germinated. With friends Van would never answer or even discuss a permanent return home.

RITCHIE YORKE AND VAN MORRISON
(photo courtesy Ritchie Yorke)

Once Van's parents arrived in Fairfax they talked constantly to their son about the dangers of sectarian violence in and around Belfast. This didn't lessen Van's Irish influences. They dominated his music, his life and his outlook. In numerous interviews, Van observed the leafy atmosphere in and around Fairfax reminded him of Northern Ireland.

PRONOUNCED IRISH INFLUENCES

In 1973-1974 images of Celtic history swirled in his head. He was no longer concerned about hits. He wanted to do it his way. He loved Marin County. It was a refuge. He missed Belfast. Carol Guida remembered the small scraps of paper on which he wrote lyrics. These almost illegible scripts were often romantic, always poignant and overwhelmingly heart felt.

Mervyn Solomon: "When I talked with Van, he had a nostalgia for Belfast. He talked lovingly of Solly Lipsitz's Atlantic Record's on Belfast's Main Street." Mervyn went on explaining Van spent hundreds of hours searching the crates, the stacks and the shelves holding the vinyl masterpieces from America. "The sailors who came into Belfast from New York brought cheap records to sell. These were the blues rejects ignored in the U. S.," Solomon continued. "These records were Van's education. He also bought traditional Irish music."

Van is Irish through and through. He always recognized Northern Ireland as his intellectual core. His creative juices flowed from the Emerald Island. It was during the 1973 trip to Sutton Place that he embraced his heritage. The result was a profound set of songs making up **Veedon Fleece**. The songs were largely set in and celebrated Ireland. A decade later, Roddy Doyle's novel turned movie, The Commitments, was close to the Van Morrison story.

When the film was in its planning stage Van auditioned for the role of Joey "The Lips" Fagan. This character was a trumpet-playing aging lothario. The **London Times** reported during the audition "things did not go smoothly." Van complained about the script. The director, Alan Parker, took exception to the criticism. Van didn't get the role. Those around Van disputed the **Times** story suggesting Parker and Van got on well. There was no comment from the Belfast Cowboy. The operative wisdom from those close to Van was he didn't want the role.

VAN ON THE BRIGHTER SIDE OF IRISH CULTURE

Van looked at the brighter cultural side of Northern Ireland. Its economic growth, technological abundance and Irish themes crept into his musical landscape. His lyrical sophistication grew. He increasingly weaved literary illusions into his musical tales.

Although he was living peripatetically in California, in London, in the English countryside and in Bath, he had an Irish epiphany. Van saw the new Ireland emerging. The increased wealth! The demographic changes! The modernization of industry! The mechanization of the ports! The technological advances! These characteristics led to the rise of a sophisticated business structure. The positive movement in government altered the political landscape. These factors made Belfast virtually unrecognizable from his youth. It piqued Van's interest. He continued employing Belfast landmarks in his writing.

HOW VAN INFLUENCED IRISH POET GERALD DAWE

At Orangefield School, while living in East Belfast, another artistic young man came of age. His name was Gerald Dawe. Like Van, he had writing and singing aspirations. A slight, bespeckled young man with a gift for poetic lyrics, he grew up to become an internationally recognized poet. He was a college professor ending his career at Dublin's Trinity College, where he retired as Professor Emeritus.

Dawe was another example of the fertile Protestant, intellectual tillage in East Belfast. Like Van, he was a blue collar, hard-working literary professor whose 2014 collection of poems, **Mickey Finn's Air** were so extraordinary that Richard Ford described these poems as "a finely made book." It is in Dawe's writing, observations and mammoth list of publications one can see his debt to Van Morrison.

Gerald Dawe wrote while he was in Belfast, as he said, he "spent time listening to Morrison's music." What did that do for Dawe? It convinced him to become a writer not a musician. As Dawe recalled he "spent time listening to jazz, folk and rhythm and blues." Like a lot of kids, he envisioned a musical career. He realized he wasn't a musician. He was born only seven years after Van in 1952. When Dawe became one of Ireland's most acclaimed writers, he credited Morrison's music. His collection of poetry in 1978, **Sheltering Places**, began a storied writing career leading to **Another World: Van Morrison And Belfast** in 2017.

The Dawe book was a strange hybrid. It was also a brilliant piece of interpretation. It was advertised as part memoir and part history. It turned into more history than memoir. When Dawe attended Orangefield School, he learned in the same classrooms as Van. As Dawe wrote the book, it was more about himself than Morrison. He observed he took the same poetic path as Van. Dawe was also in a band, the Trolls, and it became apparent he wasn't the next Belfast Cowboy. He gave up rock 'n' roll for poetry and literature. **Astral Weeks** was another influence on Dawe. "You can be a Belfast guy and still be lyrical," Dawe wrote. Poetry of the working class became Dawe's avocation. Poets are not well paid. Dawe became a legendary professor and a prolific writer. He was a sought after speaker. He thanked Van Morrison. He recalled the night he heard Van perform a cover of Bob Dylan's "Like A Rolling Stone," in Sammy Houston's Belfast jazz club. "You could…bypass the sectarian bile" Dawe wrote of the freedom of listening to Van with The Troubles cascading around him. When Dawe watched young Van perform, he said he was "defined by work." He was destined for stardom.

Over the years, as their friendship deepened, Van decided to cooperate with Dawe on an autobiography. Why not a biography? Van said: "No." He wanted to control the narrative.

In 1985 Random House announced a 288 page Morrison autobiography, **The Burning Ground** with Gerald Dawe as co-author. The manuscript has never been explained. The ISBN was registered with the Library of Congress. The author was listed as Gerald Dawe.

Random House stated the book was "written with the cooperation of Van Morrison." A check of the International Standard Book Number (ISBN) indicated it was properly registered. There has been no further revelations. This book was announced for a German book festival. That never materialized. One suspects that Dawe's 2017 book on Van and Belfast was the progenitor for this elusive volume. But who knows? There is no more information.

Dawe believed Van also influenced other local Belfast writers. Stewart Parker in his book, **Dramatis Personae & Other Writings**, compared his interest in music and writing to Van Morrison's infatuation with the blues. Parker concentrated on his writing after performing at a teen age dance hall gig. He realized he was not the next Van Morrison. When Parker's first television script "Catchpenny Twist" premiered he was called the "Van Morrison of Irish Theatre." On Van's seventy-fifth birthday, Dawe connected Morrison's writings to not just Parker, but also to Lynne Parker, Lucy Caldwell, Wendy Erskine, Leontia Flynn and David Ireland.

Parker, who passed in 1988, is the penultimate example of Morrison's influence. He began writing the "High Pop" column for the **Irish Times** often paying tribute to Van. He was the first Irish pop critic with a literary flair. His view of rock music was much like Van's. This was thanks to Morrison's songwriting.

STANLEY CROUCH AND MORRISON'S CULUTRAL MISCEGENATION

Morrison is the product of what Stanley Crouch labels "cultural miscegenation." What is "cultural miscegenation?" It is a mix of influence, Crouch wrote, without specifically mentioning the Belfast Cowboy while questioning race in the performance of blues songs. He posited the question: "Was it authentic for white boys to sing the blues?" Then Crouch, ever the intellectual contrarian, asked: "What is the blues? How does one sing the blues?" Crouch's book **The Artificial White Man: Essays On Authenticity**, published in 2004, was a collection of essays examining the question of race writing. Crouch, a noted contrarian, argued it was the message, the product, not race, that created ethnic authenticity. Morrison had it. He was categorically an original blues shouter. Crouch appreciated Morrison. We know that from a cover of a B. B. King song he recorded for a tribute album. He never wrote about him. But Crouch, in his writing, described Morrison's extraordinary vocal gifts.

While not writing specifically about Van Morrison, Crouch makes a point. Was it possible for a working class kid from Belfast, with a minimal formal education, to write and sing about the blues? It was! If it was about jazz, Crouch wrote, it was o. k. Who was Crouch? He was the most noted **New York Times** jazz critic. He examined cultural miscegenation by reading Philip Roth, Ernest Hemingway, Saul Bellow and listening to Duke Ellington. What a minute! Duke Ellington? Yes! Crouch says if you simplify by race. If you remain in your own cultural orbit. If you simplify music to black and white. If you simplify culture, you overlook authentic artists. Crouch suggested "cultural miscegenation" created Van Morrison. How? Where? What was the artistic mix?

In Van's case, it was the Marin County influence. It melded with a mix of Celtic soul, as well as the luminous image of East Belfast. That provided the grist for his writing mill. It is in his intellectual makeup that Van provided the road for the 1973-1974 era of self-improvement. There was one firm influence. That was Van Morrison was completely culturally Irish. A bit of the English and a tad bit of America crept into his soul. There was a melting pot in his lyrics. That was the cultural miscegenation Crouch defined. Like Stanley Crouch, Morrison does not suffer fools easily. Like Crouch, Van sees in literary influences the road to his writing and performing. Words matter!

As an intellectual contrarian, Van's superior intellect created trouble. He brooks disagreement if he sees anything potentially obstructing his intellectual journey. Van stood apart from America's racially neurotic society. He was an observer. This is why Van Morrison matters? He tells us things about America that are new musically and culturally. As Stanley Crouch said: "There are many ways to interpret our culture." Van provided a new means for understanding the blues and the soul influences creating an inner vision of the world.

VAN AND THE COMPLEXITY OF IRISH HISTORY

The complexity of Irish history runs through Morrison's oeuvre. As Van wrote of the leafy streets of Cyprus Avenue, there was a simplistic message. "If you want to know about Belfast listen to my music. Interpret my lyrics and you will understand my life."

For the Northern Irish it is a liberating message. For those of us in the colonies we are still trying to understand. Van as he celebrates his Irishness. He does this to protest the stereotypes, the Troubles and the feeling Belfast and Northern Ireland remains a second class enclave. Irish roots, Van said, defines the history of the Emerald Island.

What does Van mean by Irish roots? In the early 1980s, Phil Coulter answered this question. Coulter said Van began frequenting a San Francisco pub owned by an itinerant Irishman. He said Van began visiting his Irish friend sometime in the 1970s, he wasn't sure when. It was in these drinking establishments Irish influences became more predominant. Van was secretive. Everyone who hung around him in Marin County had a different story. These differences swirled around the intensity of his Irishness. In his music and writing most observers believed Irishness drove him creatively They all agreed he could veer off in many writing directions. Coulter intimated the early 1980s brought Van's Irish nature to the forefront of his music. Van has never addressed the idea. We can only speculate.

Phil Coulter credited Van's interest in a Northern Irish poet, James Simmons, as one of the jumping off points for his writing on Irish themes. Van said it best: "There's just a big part of me that's just strictly involved with the island of Ireland." It was 1982 that Van's friends, associates, critics, hangers on and more than forty musicians believed began his intense Irish period.

HOW BEAUTIFUL VISION VALIDATED MARIN AND PREDICTED THE SOUNDTRACK TO BELFAST

By 1982 the **Beautiful Vision** album was the first in a long line dominated by Irish influences. The combination of Celtic themes and jazz ideas melded into a brilliant thirteenth studio album featuring songs recorded at Sausalito's Record Plant. It indicated Marin County influences were present but waning. In many respects **Beautiful Vision** validated the calm nature of Van's 1970s life. Steve Turner captured this notion suggesting that Van had "captured the balance between his contentment of work and his aspirations to learn more about music." That summed it up perfectly. The use of uillean pipes, the national bagpipe of Ireland, brought Morrison back to traditional Irish folk music. As Van imbibed Irish history, musical folklore and traditions enhancing local culture, he became interested in movie soundtracks. He built his credentials in the movie business placing his songs on a number of important movies. From 1983 to 2006 the number of songs Van licensed to the movies led to a 2007 album **Van Morrison At The Movies-Soundtrack Hits**.

The benchmark for Van's licensing his songs for soundtracks came when the Academy Award winning movie "Belfast" heralded his reputation in the industry. Van provided the soundtrack for "Belfast." Winner of the Best Original Screenplay Oscar, the 1969 setting and what the Troubles did to the locals suggests why Van migrated to America.

"Down To Joy" bears a resemblance to a 1970 song "Coming Down to Joy" and that has set off a debate over whether Van recycled an old melody and fiddled with the lyrics. It didn't matter the "Belfast" movie soundtrack version fit the time and the place. The bootleggers loved "Down To Joy" and released an eight song album with forty minutes of some released and some unreleased Van material. The "Coming Down To Joy" cut, according to Zaire, was found in a dumpster. This is probably an urban legend. What is known is that Zaire was selling a three CD bootleg with the ubiquitous title **Van Morrison Gets His Chance To Wail**. Van turned a three song demo into Warner Bros. sometime in the early 1970s which included a demo of "Coming Down To Joy."

He didn't return to Northern Ireland until the political differences subsided. Throughout the movie Van's subtle saxophone and gravely-voiced lyrics explain the pain and trauma of the Troubles. When Kenneth Branagh talked with Van, he remarked he was impressed with Morrison's desire to "honor" Belfast. Branagh was stunned by Van's original opening song "Down To Joy." He remarked that this was why the film received an Oscar nomination for the "Best Musical Score." The film didn't win. It didn't matter. After more than sixty years in the music business, the film industry finally recognized Morrison.

Van was tired of the perception Belfast was guns, bombs, suffering and the Troubles. His music celebrated Belfast. Morrison complained songs about Belfast are written by people who don't come from there or had never lived in the city.

A DUBLIN 1973 TRIP: FINNEGAN'S WAKE, WORDSWORTH, YEATS, ELIOT AND COMMERCIAL SONGS WITH CAROL GUIDA

Van planned a three week trip to Ireland in October 1973. It was a catalyst to reconnecting with his Irish roots. He had never departed from them. The influences upon his songwriting, his intellectual pursuits, and his quest for personal understanding was an inspiration. It was time for songwriting inspiration. Traveling with his new girlfriend, Carol Guida, he was comfortable. They checked into hotels as Mr. and Mrs. Guida. No one recognized him. He was ecstatic.

He looked back on his Irish life. He did this to maximize his songwriting. He hated pop music. He despised hits. He worked on a diverse musical direction to avoid continuing in that direction.

The October, 1973, trip to Sutton Place was the first step in "Becoming Van Morrison." What was missing in Van's life? It was the spark to create. He needed inspiration. He searched for a muse. He found both in Carol Guida and a trip to Ireland.

Van has never discussed Irish stereotypes. He seldom explained his view of Irish history and literature. That is until he reached his sixties. Then there were glimpses of his private Ireland. He displayed a personal privacy for things Irish. Personal privacy guided his life. Like James Joyce, Morrison often goes on too long for those who do not understand his Irish condition. He has gone out of his way to condemn those who do not appreciate Ireland. His songwriting! His music! His personality! The Belfast Cowboy remarked these factors

A BOOTLEG ALBUM COVER

created his place in the music world. Van is a defender of his tough road to success.

Carol Guida: "Sutton Place was magnificent. The fire place was massive. The beds were so tall you had to climb up from a stool onto the bed, it was an estate property." While at Sutton Place Donal Corvin, a Belfast friend and journalist, and Sam Smyth, another journalist of note and a close friend, from the old Belfast days arrived to celebrate Van's return.

Sam Smyth negotiated Van's first appearance with Them in Belfast. He was a lifelong friend. As a journalist he wrote about Van while becoming Ireland's top investigative reporter on business malfeasance. One can only imagine their conversations concerning Van's business dealings with record labels.

His songs had an Irish bent since his early solo years. He has done this through educating himself on literature, history, folk lore and with a keen sense of his observations, he believes he elicits new views of Northern Ireland.

The attempts to establish a political Van Morrison failed. Johnny Rogan tried that approach with dire straits. Van wasn't shaped by Irish politics. He was aware of the Troubles. Van was more complicated. He's an Evangelical Protestant. What does that mean? He is a professor lecturing to the flock. That is the opinion of Belfast poet Tom Paulin. "He's testifying," Paulin said of Van's music.

Van samples renowned Irish literature. Then he will reshape these fragments into a heartfelt song. Rumor has it Van allegedly only read a few pages of James Joyce's Finnegan's Wake. He retreated into a long songwriting session. The influences from Finnegan's Wake weren't obvious until 1980 when "Summertime in England" was released. Some say he worked on the song for ten years. Others told me he wrote it in ten minutes. Only Van knows! He hasn't shared how long it took to compose "Summertime In England." The operative wisdom is a decade.

REHEARSING 'SUMMERTIME IN ENGLAND': THE NEW VAN 1979

By 1979, when Van began rehearsing "Summertime In England," there was a pronounced influence from his reading, thinking and from discussions with the now departed Carol Guida. She was gone by early 1977. Guida talked daily with Van about their reading. The philosophy that emerged in his 1980s songs was rooted in this time frame.

From 1973 into mid-1974 the maturation of his thinking crept into his writing. Van was conflicted. He pursued commercial success. He realized he needed it to maintain his lifestyle. He didn't want pop hits to compromise his intellect. This set the stage for the departure in 1980 with the Common One album. That departure, in his twelfth studio album, was a major career turning point. The album, recorded in the south of France, near Nice, took its title from a line in

"Summertime In England." The album's jazz overtones came from a newly found creative feeling due to Marin County. Chris Michie intimated Common One declared his freedom from California influences. The Van Morrison trademark was underway. The inclusion of lyrics by William Wordsworth and Samuel Taylor Coleridge was a paean to his recently discovered literary influences. This album contained the phrase: "Can you feel the silence?" Clinton Heylin loved it.

For the **Common One** album, when he formulated "Summertime In England," performing it with "Haunts of Ancient Peace," his music evolved into a new direction. He told Chris Michie and others he found a new sense of freedom. This was the earliest sign of leaving the Marin County inspiration. Yet, he was there on and off through 1988 visiting his daughter in Mill Valley, while performing where and when he desired. His hidden home, in a small valley north of Fairfax, provided the isolation he needed to create.

He finalized an Anglo-Irish intellectual direction. For some unexplainable reason he needed the leafy local Marin County countryside to finish his creations. Writing was easy in this bucolic setting. Van didn't leave Marin County creatively. He returned in concert to experience the rustic California setting inspiring his arrival as a songwriter. He has performed, visited, wrote and sat the same type of coffee shops every year since fleeing Marin County. This leafy, enclave was no different for Van than the English countryside or Belfast. A sense of defined territory drives Van's creativity.

He lived for more than a decade in the area. "The ambiance moved him into a new and carefully defined musical direction," Chris Michie told me of the 1980s. "When he was in Marin County it was not like he ever left," Michie concluded. Van had a connection with the locals. After he purchased a house in Mill Valley in the 1980s, Shana came of age. It was her place. She still lives there.

The old days of "Domino," "Moondance" and "Wild Children" created, what his long-time friend Mick Cox called, "the new Van Morrison." Then the Van Morrison trademark triumphed by 1980. The journey through the trenches and joys of Marin County was the difference maker in maturing his talent.

The transition from 1979 into 1980 was a dramatic one. It was not just Van's songwriting that made the transition. It was his artistic maturity thundering into the commercial marketplace. His stage presence was that of a caged lion. The lion was trained at the Inn of the Beginning and the Lion's Share. The pursuit of his craft and his personal freedom triumphed. He was a new person; one who was perpetually creative. His visions of the U. K. and Northern Ireland freed him from the mundane and the trite. That gave him a permanent creative freedom he intended in writing and performing in 1973-1974.

The striking, raven haired vixen by his side, Carol Guida, provided the emotional stability lacking in the early years of his marriage. Creativity exploded! Free at last. He went into a frenetic writing mode that continues to characterize him.

Van's writing goes well back into the 1960s. He presages his future writing in letters. There were six letters Van sent to Mick Cox from New York's Marlton Hotel at 58th St, and in these letters, he states "Bert Berns & Bang was a F***** up bad scene." He also talks at the length about attempting to find his niche in the music business. These letters were sold at auction and suggest they were written before Janet Planet showed up. The Christmas card Van signed included the name "BRENDA." These letters are important in illustrating the unending drive Van had in his search for a musical career. How many times has he said? "What I do is not easy." Hundreds! He does have a point. When Cox passed in 2008 his heirs, or someone close to him, auctioned off this material. It is a treasure trove.

MICK COX SEES SAUSALITO PUT THE FINISHES TOUCHES ON THE NEW VAN MORRISON: COMMON ONE EMERGES

Mick Cox: "In 1979 I went to the States…I rang Van, who was in Sausalito…he invited me to his place. I stayed a couple of weeks and we mucked about playing bits and pieces, and working on the early stages of **Common One**." That was the beginning of the new Van as Cox observed a creative zeal buttressed by Van's blue collar work ethic created a whirlwind of brilliant music. As Cox looked back

King Edward Hotel
120 West 44th St
New York

Dear Mick,

This may come late
or right the cat and the mouse
mistakes to take uncover and
cover. The trails that lead
to one the space between
the crowds of thoughts that
don't see trouble come the
freedom songs they sing but
when can I come into those
dimly lit afternoons alone
avenues to encounter new
dreams once more I answer to
myself the selfish self but
with cause I've seen me be
minipulated and holed and
paralysed right in my own
mind I do want to know

Come through for you and I
My heart waits.

Van.

One of six letters Van sent to Mick Cox from New York's Marlton Hotel at 58th St.
(circa 1960s)

upon 1979, he told Simon Gee the lengthy rehearsals, and careful attention to the music, while working with fellow musicians, at his home in Fairfax, was a training ground for future in concert brilliance. Cox believed these jams or rehearsals were better than the shows at the Inn of The Beginning and the Great American Music Hall. Either way, Cox observed, Van worked day and night on his music.

By 1979, as Van prepared new music, he wrote "Summertime In England." He was reading William Wordsworth and Samuel Taylor Coleridge. He displayed the ferocity of a converted scholar. He took a trip to England's Lake District to personally experience where Wordsworth and Coleridge wrote. He was inspired. Van Morrison: "Summertime In England' was actually part of a poem I was writing, and the poem and the song sorta merged...." That was it. Marin County was now in the creative rear view mirror.

In and around Marin County he was a familiar sight in coffee shops. The locals left him alone. They also marveled at his constant reading, writing and thoughts on spiritualism and philosophy. "Van wrote all the time when he was with me," Carol Guida said. He could write a song in a few minutes. He took years with other tunes. They all emanated from a prodigious reading habit. It was formed in California and spurred on by Marin County's bucolic calm. The intellectually stimulating atmosphere created "Becoming Van Morrison."

THE ELIZABETH CLARE PROPHET INTERLUDE

Van read voraciously. From 1973 through 1974, he increased his knowledge of spiritual subjects. He pursued explanations of channeling songs. He developed mind altering prose. He mastered mysticism. He had an up and down relationship to studying religion. He believed in unexplainable occurrences. These facets of his life surfaced in his writing. Van grew into a quasi-intellectual with a skepticism for the material world. Money wasn't a concern. Ironically, he paid close attention to the money, when it involved his intellectual property. Creative thoughts were his mantra. That led him down some strange rabbit holes. None stranger than his infatuation with Elizabeth Clare Prophet.

Nothing was more interesting to Van than mystical or enlightened thought. No book was more important than Elizabeth Clare

Prophet's **The Science Of Rhythm For The Master Of The Sacred Energies Of Life**. None of Van' s friends had ever heard of Prophet. They asked who she was and how he acquired her books?

Prophet, the leader of an embryo religious movement her husband founded, was a cult figure. She died in 2009. She founded the Summit Lighthouse and the Church Universal And Triumphant in Southern California. She was a local cult leader perfectly situated to take advantage of the counterculture revolution. Her time as a religious leader blended with Van's search for spiritual truth.

Why was Van attracted to her spiritual views? The answer was a simple one. She taught enlightened spiritualism. She was an early New Age guru with a message promising self-enlightenment. After Janet Planet left him, he found her message a balm for his lost soul. Her message was attuned to Morrison's future intellectual direction.

Prophet took over the religion after her husband died on February 26, 1973. Prophet was known as "Guru Ma Mother of the Flame." She was an extreme religious fanatic. She eventually settled in the Montana wilderness. She lectured to her disciples nuclear war was inevitable. She predicted the end of the world by 2000. She began these sermons in 1975.

Although she was a religious nut case, Prophet came from an entitled, wealthy background. After earning a B. A. in political science from Boston University in 1961, she had ambitions to write. Her prodigious writing was of dubious quality. Her content bordered on the ridiculous. Prophet described herself as philosophical, holistic and as a person with a "deep message." She claimed to have visions. She taught a doctrine the soul had a one on one relationship with God through Christ. After her husband's death, she continued her career directing the Church Universal and Triumphant.

Where and how Van found her writing is not known. The Prophets published more than seventy books on what they called the "Teachings of the Ascended Masters." Wisdom! Spiritualism! Mysticism! These forces shaped Morrison's intellectual direction. Her writing was an offshoot of theosophy. Van adopted the tenets of theosophy. But not her writings. Why? He believed there was a deeper spirituality and a direct connection with God. The use of intuition and meditation led to revelation. That is how Van viewed his intellectual direction.

Those who followed this movement argued enlightened people were ordinary ones. Why? They had undergone a process of spiritual transformation without a formal church, a teacher or a set of guiding lights. In other words no guru, no method, no teacher. They were blue collar philosophers. Van told David Tame, the author of **The Secret Power Of Music: The Transformation Of Self And Society Through Musical Energy,** he believed 95% of Prophet's arguments were solid. Van showed the influence of her books by arguing there was a healing power to music. In the 1980s, this theme emerged in **Common One**. He would reflect these New Age influences with more intensity in the 1980s and 1990s. Again without Marin County's influence this would have been impossible.

Van's religious beliefs delved into literature and philosophy. That Van is spiritual is established to the present day. That he has studied a wide range of religions is well known. The mystical writings of Alice Bailey was one of many influences. There were a number of other roads to spiritualism. Van read and assimilated Alice Bailey to understand spiritualism. Bailey's **Glamour a World Problem** influenced him. In this book she described "oppressive humanity" then goes to lecture about "deflecting the light of truth." Whatever she meant was lost on many of her followers. Van picked up a message from her. She highlighted his search for a spiritual path. That path intensified in the mid-1970s. Fewer concerts! Isolation! Personal time! That was the new Van.

THE TRANSITION IN THE MID-1970s

In the mid-1970s, Van slowed down. Clinton Heylin misrepresents Morrison's decision to some take time off. Heylin writes: "The fall out, personally, for this troubled man continued to be an almost total absence of normality in his life." He wasn't a troubled man. As his long time road manager, Ed Fletcher, commented: "Van didn't like the set of clothes he was granted at birth." But, like Fletcher said, the man was creative. Close friends told me he was calm, relaxed and productive. He was intensely private. Some said Van was "boringly normal." Others described him as "brash and insolent." Everyone agreed he was moody.

"If only Van would stop dining at the International House of Pancakes," Chris Michie observed with a sly smile. "He would have been the perfect reclusive intellectual." Michie suggested post-divorce Van was grounded with his usual blue collar work ethic. "I think Carol Guida enhanced his writing," Michie continued. "When Van looked back on the **It's Too Late To Stop Now** album, he told me Carol sat next to him and listened to every edit or cut." Michie jokingly said: "Maybe she should be listed as a co-producer."

He continued to make music, if more privately. Heylin concluded: "Morrison's sense of isolation was now exacerbated by a rapid curtailment of musical activities." Van rented a storage space in Sausalito. He stored a wealth of unreleased material there. He had to rent two spaces. He was more prolific than ever. Mark Naftalin told me the storage in Sausalito was a treasure chest of unreleased material.

During 1976, Van played eight shows with two at San Francisco's Winterland. The rest of his appearances were in London with sporadic recording at the Los Angeles Shangri La Studio. In 1977 he wasn't interested in performing. There were seven appearances and five of these were television appearances. There were two shows at Maunkberry's, a trendy London club. That was it. Van had a life. He lived it to the fullest. Privacy! Creativity! Personal time! These traits defined Van in the mid-1970s.

Once again Van took stock of his monetary needs. While his contract with Warner Brother didn't end until 1985, there were constant strains on the relationship. He would not accept their demands for pop ditties. He continued to work in a solitary manner. Van told Warner he would work at his own pace.

In the early 1980s, Warner Brothers experienced financial difficulties. When they signed Prince that helped alleviate their fiscal problems. Lenny Waronker believed when Van's contract came up for renewal, they couldn't meet his financial demands. That statement may be an excuse for making one of the most disastrous financial decisions in Warner's storied history. Waronker defended his decision. Van made a separate distribution deal with another label. He was alternately uncooperative and then butter would melt in his mouth when dealing with Warner. Waronker, those close to him suggested, was tired of the Van Morrison soap opera. This became more obvious as Morrison searched for other opportunities.

In a move other record companies had made, Warner pared back its artist roster. The label dropped more than 30 performers. "We realized we were just too big and had to make some hard decisions," Waronker said. The hardest of those decisions, he said, was opting not to renegotiate with singer Van Morrison, who subsequently signed a new contract with Polygram Records. "Van Morrison wasn't dropped," Waronker said. "We were in a position to renew our contract with Van, but we knew he'd been offered a deal by another company that we couldn't afford to match."

To understand the next volume, it is necessary to examine the 1979 watershed year. It was at this point Van's career thrived as he returned to the U. K. and Ireland in theme and content. When you arrive at 1979 there is a new an unrecognizable Van Morrison. The years in Marin County created his transformation from a performer into a recognizable star. In this metamorphosis from performer to perfectionist, he was aided by some unwitting allies. Dan Penn and John Rockwell were two music insiders producing what Peter Mills labelled Van's road to "Imagining America." When Van released the **Wavelength** album, Mills concluded it was "a kind of love letter to, and from, America." It was also a departure from Morrison's American influences.

WAS 1979 A WATERSHED? DAN PENN AND JOHN ROCKWELL: VAN IS BACK

In 1979, Van's career spiraled into a number of new directions. When **Into The Music** was released in 1979, one critic called it "an erotic/religious cycle of songs...." Van was back, if temporarily, with a batch of potential hits. He was ready in 1980 to head into jazz religious-philosophical directions. Van demonstrated he could still turn out pop hits.

The song portending change from **Into The Music** was "Bright Side of the Road." It prompted Van to recall his early songwriting influences. He revisited his previous hits. One American songwriter Van loved, Dan Penn, also wrote in isolation in Muscle Shoals, Alabama. He had this in common with Van who began writing in isolation in Belfast. Penn wrote of cultural change and good times with common folks. He recalled his brilliant Southern influences. Penn was a hidden role model who Van adopted in his quest for inspiration.

After Van listened to a number of Dan Penn songs, he focused on "The Dark End of The Street." He wrote an answer to it. He had also apparently read Jack Higgins' 1967 novel **Dark Side of The Street**. From these influences Van furtively composed "Bright Side of the Road." It was an apocryphal tune suggesting his uncharted musical and personal journey.

When the **Vanthology: A Tribute to Van Morrison** album came out in 2003, Penn covered Morrison's "Bright Side Of The Road." This album showcased his appreciation for the Belfast Cowboy's songwriting wizardry.

When **Into The Music** was released, some critics compared it to Dylan's **Slow Train Coming**. John Rockwell, in the September 2, 1979 **New York Times**, praised the two veteran rockers for serious themes. Rockwell wrote: "Morrison never really approached Mr. Dylan's status as voice of a generation. But he has a passionate, if smaller cult, one that this writer has never been a part of." Later, Rockwell complained Morrison was cool to him. I wonder why!

LOOKING TO THE U. K. AND IRELAND IN 1979: CONFUSION AND MISUNDERSTANDING, BELFAST I AM COMING

Was 1979 the last year of Morrison's confusing management? Was 1979 the last year Van had to deal with rank amateurs? Was 1979 the last year Van prevented outsiders from interfering with his albums? Was 1979 the last year of inadequate concert management? Was 1979 the last year of putting up with wanker journalists asking questions to produce drivel? Was 1979 the last year of business problems? The answer? An unequivocal; "Yes."

What changed in 1979? Plenty! The business model was operational. Van's marriage, girlfriends, business problems, label-production disagreements and difficulties with backing and touring musicians were behind him. As he prepared to turn thirty-five in 1980, he had honed his career path with precision. He had done this without sacrificing the independence of his music. Why is this important? He was free to concentrate upon songwriting. The result was **Into The Music**. In the next volume the period from mid-1974 through 1979 will reflect on how the brief nineteenth month 1973-1974 interlude established the perimeters and freed Van's mind, body and soul for the next half century of brilliant production.

The result? The confessional Van Morrison emerged. In "You Know What They're Writing About," he discussed love. A song title that didn't seem to celebrate love did just that. He writes about the joy of love, as he had or would soon find a new muse in Ulla Munch. That was still some time up the road.

Sporadically from 1980 to 1983 Van loved in and around Copenhagen. Van immortalized the forty steps down to the catch the S-train at the Vanlose Station. The quaint imagery of "Vanlose Stairway" found Van placing his Copenhagen metro station in his lyrics. What does Van's third muse, Ulla Munch, tell us? That he needed female companionship to write love songs.

VAN AND LOVE SONGS: NEW THEMES

What was the mantra for Van writing love songs? The love songs drew in every lady in his life. In recent years Kim Cottrell attests to the lifelong attraction of his love oriented lyrics. There are dozens of others, beginning with Brenda in New York, but the emphasis is on how these love lyrics prove a window into Van's soul.

The love lyrics tell one all they need to know about how Belfast images populate his songs. When he writes of "downy by the pylons" it is a stark reminder of Northern Ireland. As he was freeing himself from Marin County images, wanderlust brought Van back to touring the U. K. He looked to Northern Ireland to end his California exile. A portent of changing themes, a new environment, and a glimpse of his future arrived in **Common One**. But it was still 1979. What happened? Van was headed increasingly into love songs, when he wasn't writing in a spiritual philosophical vein.

The roots of "Someone Like You," which wouldn't appear until 1987 on **Poetic Champions Compose**, took place. Was Ulla Munch, Van's girlfriend in Copenhagen, the muse for this song? No one knows. What we do know is that after Janet Planet and Carol Guida, Munch was the third and last muse in Van's early writing. The new Van Morrison emerged in the late 1970s, and into the 1980s, with increasingly sophisticated literary themes crafted into his lyrics. He still had to tour.

By 1979 a reinvigorated Van Morrison prepared for a twenty one-date U. K. tour. He spent an inordinate amount of time planning the return to the U. K. and Belfast. The Belfast shows were scheduled for two nights on February 20 and 21, 1979, at the Whitla Hall. It had been twelve years since the Belfast Cowboy appeared in his hometown. He was apprehensive but excited. He was ready.

Van's welcome to Belfast was that of returning royalty. "I went down to see Van," Mervyn Solomon continued. "He was happy to be back home. The press followed him everywhere. He was surprisingly good humored."

In his preparation for the return to Belfast, Van left no stone unturned. He wasn't yet the Irish Rover, but he was on his way.

Mervyn Solomon told me Van was tired of Warner Brothers. The American lifestyle no longer excited him. He had learned all he could in the San Francisco Bay Area. By hanging out with beat poets, fine-tuned authors, experimental musicians and a bevy of counterculture intellectuals, Van's literary persona evolved.

His increasingly sophisticated songwriting themes helped him mature intellectually. As Solomon talked with Van, he realized Morrison was homesick. But not for Ireland. He wanted to return to London. Why not Ireland? The Troubles remained on his mind.

The Northern Ireland political situation, the barbed criticism, the garrulous comments and the general ineptness of the music press accelerated his disinterest in returning to Northern Ireland. The sectarian violence, in and around Belfast, privately impacted Morrison. "Van was a solitary person," Mervyn Solomon continued. "The police presence frustrated him. He longed for the old Belfast." Nostalgia is a defined Morrison trait.

Asgard Events Promotion
Van Morrison Concerts

THE PRESS: ENTER KEITH ALTHAM

The press bothered him. He felt in control and he used a number of high end publicity firms to smooth over his image. Some firms worked. Others didn't. There was a soap opera to Van and public relations. He vowed to conquer the media beast. He looked for an experienced writer to take over his public relations. He found a former music journalist, turned public relations guru, with a brilliant reputation for providing his clients excellent press. His name was Keith Altham. He hired him to enhance his public image. That did not go well.

Van remembered in 1966, when the **New Musical Express** sent over Keith Altham for an interview. He liked him. He discovered Altham opened a public relations firm. Why not hire him? Van did! Impulsively!

When Morrison hired Keith Altham, to direct his public relations, he was looking to reconnect with the U. K. market. Altham, a legendary public relations figure, made his reputation as a no nonsense writer with the London based **New Musical Express**. He branched out as a public relations specialist with such high profile clients as Sting, the Rolling Stones, the Troggs, Rod Stewart, Phil Collins and the Who.

Morrison coveted Altham's media contacts. For a time Altham's radio show on BBC 2 "Scene and Heard," in the late 1960s and early 1970s, made the career of numerous rock stars. He was innovative. He had a degree of honesty rare in the music business. His book, **The PR Strikes Back**, included honest appraisals of his clients. Altham told the world fame had done little, if anything, to change the behavior of or alter the perceptions of the Belfast Cowboy. Altham was honest to a fault. He commented: "What a talent. What a singer. What a pain in the arse."

Altham's firm, K. A. Publicity, was well thought of in the U. K. It was considered one of the best London offices for positive publicity. Altham had no idea how difficult it would be to work with Morrison. He tried. He failed.

Altham attempted to clean up Van's image. To that end he booked a photo session. Altham hired photographer Brian Aris to shoot some publicity shots. Van didn't see why it was necessary to have publicity photos. He said it was a waste of money. Altham was strong minded. He told Van he should hire a parrot not a publicist. Van held steadfast. No interviews. No interruptions. No pictures. Didn't his music do the talking? Altham left the fold. Van said he had a better way to create public relations.

Keith Altham should have the last word. "I think he's been fairly consistently difficult. The most disturbing thing about Van is that he's disturbed, and it's unsettling to deal with someone like that," Altham continued. "I think he's a man who's gonna be searching all his life for something that he'll never find...."

Van would eventually find a media expert who could bamboozle the press. That didn't happen immediately due to Morrison's predilection to fear press conspiracies. Reclusive by nature, Van didn't understand public relations. In later years, Van hired a Los Angeles public relations specialist Phil Lovel. This high level professional solved his problems with the media. In San Francisco he didn't need a publicist. The local press and radio stations were his public relations.

VAN SOLVES THE PUBLIC RELATIONS GAME WITH LOBELINE

By the 1990s, Van solved his American public relations concern by working with a West Hollywood company, Lobeline Communications. This office dealt with press requests for interviews. They created a positive press image. "Van has never done interviews about his personal life," a PR spokesperson remarked. Lobeline, a major public relations firm, represented Brad Pitt, Sasha Cohen, George Michael and the Trans-Siberian Orchestra among others. Frank Keel, a London based publicist, said it best: "The pettiest musical genius of his time." There is no sugarcoating it. Morrison does not handle the media well. But eventually things did improve public relations wise for the Belfast Cowboy. Lobeline is still his U. S. PR firm. They have been impressive.

The Lobeline professionals contracted for a CBS Sunday Morning Special with Anthony Mason, which aired on March 8, 2009, and thirteen years later, it was re-broadcast to a broader audience. This interview and profile of Van suggested his legendary growth within the music business. Lobeline crafted a new Van Morrison. He remains a work in progress. But if you provide first rate journalists, with intelligent questions, he was an easy interview.

"He has suffered the weight of a press that has, perhaps out of spite over his insistence on privacy, chosen to stress the idiosyncratic nature of his past performances and depict him as an on-again, off-again rock 'n' roll performer," Cameron Crowe wrote in the rock magazine **Creem**.

THE TOP TEN LIST OF VAN MORRISON TRAITS

In Van Morrison's life there were few absolutes. Like most people, he has a set of personality traits dominating his life. Some biographers ignore these peculiar traits. Others expand upon them.

FIRST: Van hasn't the ability to handle any form of criticism. He rails against it.

SECOND: He is a brilliant artist who changes his music direction to avoid stagnation.

THIRD: He is adamant about his personal life. It is private. Don't invade it! The barrister will call. The Web Sheriff will terrorize you. Just ask Janet Morrison Minto. Van had the Web Sheriff threaten her with legal action if she continued to sell her jewelry on the Internet. He said she was exploiting his name. Van's bullying caught the eye of a super Morrison fan who Van had thrown out of a Utrecht concert for drunken behavior. The fan wasn't a drunk. He was a multi-millionaire software pioneer who had his lawyers talk to Van's legal team about the First Amendment. "Van is a bully," the Dude continued. "Stand up to him and he goes away."

FOURTH: He continually criticizes the music industry for its lack of creativity, refusing to pay a fair royalty and beating a musical style to death to accommodate the times. It was not just Warner Bros. who experienced his personal quirks. The jazz label, Blue Note, years later, worked well with Morrison. Then he had lockdown arguments with a Blue Note executive, not Don Was, and there was a contentious atmosphere over promotion. There were a few tiffs over lack of sales. A Blue Note executive told me Van didn't back down. Blue Note listened to him and worked their media magic on two critically acclaimed albums.

Blue Note went out of its way to promote Morrison. Even though he was, at times, unhappy, Don Was, the label chief, understood the lengthy jazz history in Morrison's career. The result was sophisticated promotion and a deep understanding of Van's talent. Over time, Morrison attitude softened toward Blue Note.

Blue Note understood Van's evolution from the 1970s into the 1980s. In copious publicity releases they highlighted his growth. In 2003 when Blue Note released **What's Wrong With This Picture**, Van told the press he was happy to be at Blue Note. Don Was was all over the press, and the Internet praising Morrison for his jazz roots. Was brought Van back for **Born To Sing: No Plan B**.

Was called **Born To Sing: No Plan B** amongst Van's finest songwriting. In a YouTube conversation, Was and Morrison discussed how Morrison created his songs. Was talked, a year earlier, with Van about making an album of jazz standards. They decided on an album of new songs. "Whenever you are famous you automatically become a mark," Van continued. "You become a target for grifters. Pop and rock magazines never address this stuff." Van said. Was and Van got on fine. **Born To Sing: No Plan B** did well. But Van remained Van. There was no discernible pattern. His personality differs from day to day. At least for the public Van. The private Van! I have no idea. Van Morrison did have thoughts and praise for Don Was. "I am happy to be working with Don Was and the team at Blue Note," Van continued. "To have such a creative music person as the head of my record label assures me that all the effort taken to write and record this new album will be rewarded with a music based focus and marketing approach."

FIFTH: Van remains mercurial. He is never predictable. To friends, he is a life time supporter who you can call on in time of need.

SIXTH: He is an inveterate collector. His studio tapes, his records, his books and his ideas form a solid intellectual core. Collecting and preserving is important to Morrison. His legacy is always on his mind. He preserves it.

SEVENTH: He has wanderlust. He can't sit still. He finds it difficult to live in the same place. He constantly needs new musical collaborators. Those factors enhance his creativity.

Eighth: He established strong, lasting and healthy relationships with women. With two marriages and a number of long-term girlfriends he solidified his personality with ladies who are long term muses. He has been a good father to his three children.

NINTH: He loves the arcane. His interest in various wide ranging religions, his quirky reading habits, and his general intellectual makeup suggests the obscure is the norm.

TENTH: He defines reality in his own terms. That is not open to negotiation. These traits are common in biographical subjects. With Van, however, they define his life.

SITTING DOWN WITH CAMERON CROWE AND CREEM: VAN GOES IN DEPTH ON HIS PERFORMING

In October, 1973, Van sat down with Cameron Crowe for a **Creem** interview. He was looking ahead. Crowe remarked Van no longer had a cult audience. He was now a mainstream commercial entity. This interview took place before a show at the Santa Monica Civic Auditorium. The reason for the interview? Van's new album **Hard Nose The Highway** was about to be released. Crowe was impressed. Van opened up on a number of topics. Surprisingly, he was critical of Bill Graham Presents. Most artists hoped to work with BGP. Van described Graham's self-interest as a detriment to his career. He smoldered at Graham's controlling nature. He had doubts about BGP's level of professionalism. Those close to Van told me he had a concern about the empresario usurping royalties. Ironically, it was Graham's erratic personality and his penchant for stretching the truth that was the last straw for the Belfast Cowboy. Van fired Graham on stage during a performance. When Graham has been interviewed over the years about his relationship with Van. What he has said it closer to fiction than truth. It emboldened the ego driven machine that BGP manufactured for his legacy. Graham never understood Van. It was all about Bill Graham Productions.

Why did Bill Graham come in for Van's criticism? "Bill Graham is your friend. But if things aren't going groovy man, he's just not around. You don't see him," Morrison told Crowe. The relationship between Graham and Morrison was rocky. Nick Clainos described it as "two control freaks trying to solve a problem." Morrison repeatedly told friends he was rethinking his role with Bill Graham. He left. To this day the real story is unknown.

Van complained about the economics of the rock music industry. "I prefer to play small clubs…you don't make any money playing small halls. You barely make any money playing big halls." Van listed a litany of people he supported. He talked about not wanting to be predictable. "You're supposed to be this stereotype," Van continued. "I don't fit the mold. I think the truest part of what I do is making records."

The rock and roll tag attached to Van sends him into a snit. "I don't know why they keep writing me up as a rock 'n' roller. I was never in rock 'n' roll. I'm a singer. And I'm a musician," Van bellowed.

Crowe commented: "Van talks back." This is one of the earliest interviews where the Belfast Cowboy vents about the music business, performing and his life style. It suggests why he took a few years off.

What does one take away from this free flowing Morrison interview? When asked about his performing, Van replied: "The stage show has always been and will always be good when the music's together. Right now, the music is together and the live shows have been going great." Van talked of what he termed his problems on stage. "That whole thing about my inconsistency on stage, what happened was that I did a couple of shows last year that just got blown out of proportion," Van continued. "You see the press picks up and publicizes all the negative things....You can't be on every night. But I honestly say that with this group of people, it's mostly on."

In looking at his career in 1973, Van was forthcoming about what to expect when he was on stage. "What I am trying to say is that it's not a rock 'n' roll show," he told Crowe. "I just think that what people expect is not what they should expect from what I do." Van was emphatic. He would not bend to playing the flavor of the month hits. "I prefer, like I have always said, to play smaller halls," Van said. He did that. The press, except for John Wasserman, didn't cover his small gigs at the Inn of The Beginning or the Lion's Share. Van had a beef with the press. He intimated they missed his best shows.

"What does a person's personal life have to do with music?" Van asked Crowe. In a tirade, Van blamed the labels and the press for the constant invasion of privacy, and the loss of innocence. Crowe was mute. In an abrupt shift, which remains a typical Van trait, he praised the press. "There have been a few good articles written about me. Maybe a dozen that I've read that were talking what we were saying." This tells you Van read the embryo rock 'n' roll press. Greil Marcus, John Wasserman and the pipe smoking guru of jazz, Ralph Gleason, were critics Morrison praised. Van didn't care for the music industry. The critics who extolled its virtues weren't praised. "I'd prefer to remain anonymous but that's not the way it is. You're a vehicle for music to come through," Van continued. "I'm a musician and leave it at that."

MORRISON TALKS OF THE PHONY RETIREMENT THING

Every biography of Van, including mine, discusses the "retirement thing." It was in 1973, and the Belfast Cowboy hadn't slowed down. He wasn't considering retirement. Here is the weird part. The retirement rumor came from comments Van made repeatedly to the press during his greatest period of productivity from 1970 through 1972. Why is this significant? Van wanted to control the narrative. While he comments there are excellent articles about him, he never identifies the writers. He played with the press.

"That retirement thing was the phoniest thing that ever happened. I never retired. I was still working. I was working in clubs. A certain writer thought up this thing about my retirement. I haven't taken a holiday in a long time. I don't go very long before I'm playing....These journalists are writing about their game." Van took a breath. He continued. "And it doesn't have anything to do with the cat that's living the life." That cat was Van Morrison. After thinking about it he embraced the so-called "retirement myth" while working 24/7 on his career. That was Van being Van.

The odious retirement myth is repeated in every Morrison biography. In 2016 Kim Carr, writing in the **London Mirror**, repeated this myth. It was too good a story to vanish into the journalistic wilderness. The **Mirror** headlined Carr's story: "Van Morrison Says He Returned To Music After Quitting For Two Years Because He Ran Out Of Money." The truth was Morrison took time off because Warner Bros. royalties provided a living. Van complained about the retirement myth while benefitting from it.

VAN LOOKS BACK ON YOUTUBE: INVITING THE BIOGRAPHER INTO HIS LIFE

Morrison reminisced on his career in a number of YouTube interviews. These discussions explain his biographical journey. Since 1995, when he talked at length, with then wife Michelle Rocca, Van has opened up about his life. His thoughts! His fears! His successes! His failures! These are elicited with great candor and personal insight. Van has sat for many interviews during the last thirty years. He is in some interviews an open book. The contradiction is he continually screams "stay out of my private life. My personal affairs are none of your business," he told Crowe. Then he explains in depth the aspects of his life creating his genius. It is as if Van is inviting the biographer into his life. That is with the exception of Clinton Heylin. Or perhaps Johnny Rogan. Or perhaps Steve Turner. Or perhaps Erik Hage. My sources told me he loved Peter Mills book. Van has never commented positively on any book. That is with the exception of the two brilliant books of lyrics from his pen with introductions by literary luminaries. If you look hard there were hundreds of nuggets from Morrison interviews.

One of Van's more interesting comments was delivered at the 41st Montreux Jazz Festival on July 18, 2007, when he observed if **Astral Weeks** had been a breakout million selling album: "I would have quit the business had that happened," Van continued. "I just wanted to be a songwriter and a singer. I did not bargain for all the rest of it." This interview was illuminating. Why? Van said each song was "a fictional story." He intimated, to Crowe, he made stories to obscure his craft as a songwriter. The rest of the stories people say about my music is fiction as well. Not really, Van. When you reference "Geronimo" it is not about the Native American warrior. It is an oblique nod to living in the San Geronimo Valley, near a former Paul Butterfield musician turned solo artist, Elvin Bishop, with super Van fan, Ron Sexton, living nearby, while he was haunting the local bars. Van brings the biographer into his life. Since 1988, in-depth, lengthy and revealing interviews illuminated his life. Van presented revealing insights into his writing themes. He had a tranquil life thanks to Carol Guida and the San Geronimo Valley.

Carol Guida: "After I moved in with Van, he bought Janet a home in nearby Terra Linda. He looked around and found this beautiful home with acreage at an estate sale. We moved in. It was lovely. Van had isolation. He went to work like a blue-collar lumberjack ready to cut down a forest."

BIBLIOGRAPHICAL SOURCES

For the Elizabeth Clare Prophet influence, see, for example, her book, **How To Work With Angels** (Gardiner, 1998). She taught her disciples from this book. Many of whom, like Van, found her ideas in the midst of his quest for a profound spiritual life. Prophet's ideas were nurtured by Van. They slipped into his life and writings. When Van told the author David Tame he believed 95% of Prophet's ideas, it suggested he had read her abundant literature or heard her speak in the 1970s when she appeared on Larry King Live or on Nightline. Prophet was an esoteric astrologer and healer. She was a disciple of Alife Bailey who Van also studied. Prophet didn't die until 2009. She was all over television. His album, **The Prophet Speaks**, which was released in 2018, may be an example of her continued influence. Morrison stated in a number of interviews he was completely familiar was probably through his writing. When he writes he looks back on literary influences. She was only six years older than Van and her career was cultish. Van does not have anything to do with cults. He was influenced by her ideas. See, Elizabeth Clare Prophet's **The Science Of Rhythm For The Mastery Of The Sacred Energies Of Life** (Gardiner, 1978) for a book that Van told interviewers he read and appreciated.

David Tame, **The Secret Power of Music: The Transformation Of Self And Society Through Musical Energy** (Rochester, 1984) is important to understanding Van's infatuation with things philosophical, religious and spiritual in the 1970s. That infatuation intensified his spiritual and mystical writing quest.

See, Clinton Heylin, **Can You Feel The Silence?: Van Morrison, A New Biography** (New York, 2002), p. 260 for Heylin's comments regarding Janet Planet leaving Morrison and newly recorded songs of bitterness Van composed afterward. See p. 304-305 for Heylin's comments on what effect this had Morrison's musical activities. See p. 355 for information on Prophet and Tame and how Van believed it impacted his life. Heylin had excellent insights into the subject of spiritualism on Morrison's life and career. These insights suggest mysticism became a lifelong quest.

The analysis of the "erotic/religious cycle of songs" is taken from a review of the **Into The Music** LP by Dave Marsh in the **Rolling Stone Album Guide** (New York, 4th edition, 2004). Also, see, the bootleg CD of Van on October 6, 1979, at the Capitol Theater in Passaic, New Jersey for the boundless energy he continued to display in concert with a clear path to future mystical writing, recording and performing.

See the **New York Times**, September 2, 1979, "Arts and Leisure Section," page D-20 for the review comparing Dylan and Morrison. Also, see, Bill Holland, "The Musical Sparks of Van Morrison," September 5, 1979, **Washington Post**, p. C6. Holland comes closest of any American critic to understanding the Marin County Van Morrison and the influences of this bucolic countryside oasis north of San Francisco on his emerging musical genius. He writes: "A lugubrious, uncompromising man at times, Morrison is steadfast in his refusal to become a rock entertainer. At the core of his songs there is a determination to make spark, to celebrate the pulse and breath of living, to grab at the gristle of real life." Holland perfectly described the Belfast Cowboy, and his transition into an independent artist who refused to compromise.

See Johnny Rogan, **No Surrender: Van Morrison** (London, 2005), chapter 18 for the return to Belfast and for the divorce. Rogan alludes to it in pp. 275-285. Also, see, **Melody Maker**, November 18, 1978. Rogan's book benefits from deep research with close Belfast friends. One of Rogan's coups was to interview as many of Van's school mates as possible. Since Van left school at fourteen it was unbelievable when Johnny Rogan sat down with almost a hundred of Van's classmates or their families to discuss his life. How much new, useful information did he gleam? Rogan's answer was: "I never thought about that."

For Janet Morrison Minto's comments on her life, after the divorce, she was thoughtful, non-judgmental and kind in her memories of life with Van. For her comments, see "Fake ID Press Release," reprinted in **Wavelength**, Issue 18. She was thoughtful and fair in a discussion with a Los Angeles reporter. This interview in the **Los Angeles Times**, with Louis Shaguan, is one in which she talks at length about regrets, happiness and the difficulty of her journey with Van and her thirty-year career as a songwriter. She did this interview, as she was preparing for the release of her own record with a musical partner. See Louis Shaguan, "The Clouds Have Lifted," **Los Angeles Times**, November 7, 1998. This is an interesting article where Janet looks back on her life with Van. She analyzed the years since the divorce. She is neither accusatory nor praiseworthy. A wonderful look into her life, from a talented person, who found her way after the divorce. The lack of rancor and bitterness makes this a worthwhile look back at the Morrison's life. This was a rare interview, as Janet seldom discussed her marriage. She is a wonderful person. Janet has no rancor toward Morrison. What she fears, according to close friends, is Van's wrath talking to the press. She has never talked to me. She is also blithely intelligent with a long-term marriage to a sound engineer and a calm, relaxed life in Orange County. To this day Janet is lively, creative and well adjusted. She is a sweet person who has found her own way in life.

For a view of Janet Planet, from London, almost three decades after the divorce, see, for example, Barry Egan, "Love Lost In The Myths Of Time," **London Independent**, January 30, 2000. https://www.independent.ie/woman/celeb-news/love-lost-in-the-myths-of-time-26253156.html The Egan article is an interesting one. It details the trip from Fairfax to Albuquerque, New Mexico when a fortune teller told Janet California was about to be swallowed up by an earthquake. This article lifted material from the **Los Angeles Times** article a few years earlier. Egan talks about a conversation he had with Van about UFOs. After researching and writing on Van for fifty years I have never heard him or anyone close to him discussing UFOs. Egan describes Janet Planet's "drug addled recollections." This was a fabrication. Egan went on to write glowing pieces on Van. To Morrison's credit he ignored this wanna-be factotum.

See Howard A. DeWitt, **Van Morrison: The Mystic's Music** (Fremont, 1983) for a brief glimpse at Morrison in the late 1970s.

See Keith Altham, **No More Mr. Nice Guy** (New York, 2000) for an appraisal of the difficulty of working in public relations with Morrison. This is a brief, but heartfelt, explanation of why Altham had difficulty working with the Belfast Cowboy. Altham's chapter praises Van's talent while recounting the difficulty of working with him.

For Van's early creativity, see, Howard A. DeWitt, **Van Morrison: From Them To The Bang Era, 1945-1968** (Fremont, 2005), passim and Howard A. DeWitt, **Van Morrison: From Astral Weeks To Stardom, 1968-1972** (Scottsdale, 2020). The more than 1200 pages in these two books suggest the high level of Morrison's intellectual growth.

For cultural miscegenation see, for example, Howard A. DeWitt, **The Fragmented Dream: Multicultural California** (Dubuque, 1997), passim, and, for a brilliant critic analyzing how and why performers are difficult, see, for example, Stanley Crouch, **Always In Pursuit: Fresh American Perspectives** (New York, 1999) and **Considering Genius: Writings On Jazz** (New York, 1997). Also, see, Crouch's, **The Artificial White Man: Essays On Authenticity** (New York, 2004) for the cultural miscegenation theory.

The late 1960s was a time when Van filled his notebooks with scribbles that turned into gold. These fragments continued into the 1970s when Van became obsessed with the writing life. When he hung out one day with the actor, Sterling Hayden, they discussed and analyzed the writing life. Hayden told Van when he began his memoir, **The Wanderer**, he needed help developing his writing style. Hayden said he brough in a mentor or a coach. Hayden's memoir, and late in life writing, was lauded by critics. His memoir has never gone out of print. The conversations with Hayden impressed upon Van the power, the timeliness and the permanence of the printed word. Hayden became an unwitting mentor to the Belfast Cowboy. For Warner and Van parting ways see, Lenny Waronker's comment in the **Los Angeles Times** by William K. Knoedelseder, Jr., "Turnaround After 2 Years of Setbacks: Warner Bros. Records Plays A Happier Tune," **Los Angeles Times**, February 14, 1985. https://www.latimes.com/archives/la-xpm-1985-02-14-fi-2620story.html

See David Burke, **A Sense of Wonder: Van Morrison's Ireland** (London, 2013) chapters 6-7 for Ireland's influence. The Irish influence was the centerpiece driving Van's creative impulses.

For the McPeake Family, Belfast local culture, and other influences on Morrison, see, the in-depth interview by, Robin Denselow, "Van Morrison: People Who Say Others Are Difficult Are Usually Difficult Themselves," **London Guardian**, June 4, 2015. https://www.theguardian.com/music/2015/jun/04/van-morrison-people-who-say-others-difficult-are-difficult-themselves-lead-belly-lonnie-donegan

The review comparing Bob Dylan's **Slow Train Coming** to **Van's Into The Music** is John Rockwell's, "Dylan And Morrison In A Religious Vein," **The New York Times**, September 16, 1979, p. D-20.

For Cameron Crowe's comment on Van and the media, see, **Creem**, October, 1973. This is an interview Van granted prior to a Los Angeles show with the Caledonia Soul Orchestra. The questions were excellent. Van was a cooperative open book.

For the Morrison quote on "Summertime In England," see Clinton Heylin, **Can You Feel The Silence?: Van Morrison, A New Biography** (Chicago, 2002), p. 359 and for Heylin's take on "Cul de Sac," as well the material before and after his songs which helped to perfect it, see, chapters 17-19. The genesis of the 1980 Van Morrison began in the later part of 1979, when he appeared at the Rancho Nicasio, the Inn of the Beginning and the Berkeley Community Theater as his long-term fans noticed a shift into a pronounced literary style. Van's reading and his approach to writing "Summertime In England" was in the earliest stages. Mick Cox told Clinton Heylin Van performed the song in local San Francisco Bay Area clubs. He didn't. He was still writing it.

For "Cul de Sac," see, John Collis, **Inarticulate Speech Of The Heart** (New York, 1997), p. 140. Dan Penn's songwriting and vocal expertise may well have been a more pronounced influence than Collis and others imagined. Another aspect of "Cul de Sac" is Morrison appears to be growing tired of the rock and roll lifestyle. For a defense of Belfast's distinct nature, see, Matthew O'Toole, "Northern Irishness Must Be Celebrated As Distinct Identity," **The Irish Times**, November 5, 2018. The O'Toole article is illuminating concerning how Morrison's lyrics reflect not just his Protestant point of view on Northern Ireland but how people fail to understand the Emerald Island. O'Toole argues Van is a fountain of wisdom reflecting and interpreting local history. See the 1981 video "Van Morrison In Ireland" for a concert recorded in 1979. It was directed by Michael Radford who went on to mainstream movie success. By using images of Belfast, Van's band, some live performances and shots of Hyndford Street and Cyprus Avenue the atmosphere so important to Van's lyrics and music is highlighted. Tony Stewart, writing in the **New Musical Express**, compared the video to shows Van did with the Caledonia Soul Orchestra. Bobby Tench's guitar brought the critics out with praise, as did Tony Marcus' exquisite violin. The band was the one on **Wavelength** and when Van opened with "Moondance," he had the audience with him. Katie Kissoon's backup vocals on "Crazy Love" and John Altham's sax on "Checkin' It Out" was a critic's favorite. A ten minute "Caravan" was another highlight. Also, see, Brian Hinton, **Celtic Crossroads: The Art of Van Morrison** (London,1997), pp. 215-216.

The anger that grew and erupted in the early 1970s from Van was apparent to a large number of local Marin County musicians and those close to the music scene who commented to me they couldn't understand Morrison's frame of mind. These musicians included Charlie Musselwhite, Mark Naftalin, Chris Michie, George Frayne, John Goddard, Nick Clainos and Terry Dolan among others.

For Lobeline Communications, its founder, the company history and their work with Van Morrison, see, for example. **Lobeline Communications.**
https://z-p3-upload.facebook.com/LobelineCommunications/posts/5203506726407745 Lobeline is a top-of-the-line PR firm. They have treated Van well for almost thirty years. Phil Lobeline, who founded the company, was a college concert promoter at the University of Colorado presenting shows from the Rolling Stones to the 1983 legendary U2 concert video shot at the Red Rocks Amphitheater. Morrison has never remarked about Lobeline but they remain an essential part of his modern public relations arsenal.

For a revealing interview-story on how Van views his career, songwriting, **Astral Weeks** and his life, as well as a defined view of his songwriting, see, Dean Goodman, "Van Morrison's Career Almost Over Before It Began," **Reuters**, June 10, 2009.
https://www.reuters.com/article/us-morrison-idUSTRE5596XB20090610

The difficulty analyzing and reporting on Van's songwriting is a topic journalists shy away from for obvious reasons. For a brilliant article suggesting how difficult it has been over the years to write brilliant songs about Belfast and Northern Ireland, and those who have and haven't done so, see, the incisive reporting with a touch of literary panache by Matthew Collin, "Belfast: The War against Cliché," **The London Guardian,** January 24, 2003.
https://www.theguardian.com/culture/2003/jan/24/artsfeatures.vanmorrison

For material on Woodstock, before he moved to Fairfax, interviews with Artie Traum and Tom Pacheco were important. The leafy atmosphere in and around Fairfax was a massive influence upon the Belfast Cowboy. For a critique of pastoral influences upon Van, see, for example, G. Smyth, "Gardens All Wet With Rain: Pastoralism In The Music Of Van Morrison, **Irish University Review**, Volume 49, Issue 1.

On the film "The Commitments," **The London Times** reported that Van auditioned for the role of Joey "The Lips" Fagan and things did not go well between Morrison and the director. See, "Van Morrison Was Up For Commitments Role," **The London Times**, April 17, 2005.

https://www.thetimes.co.uk/article/van-morrison-was-up-for-commitments-role-7jlv0gdfgbs

The notion Gerald Dawe is a protégé of or was influenced by Van Morrison is suggested in Fintan O'Toole's review of Dawe's **In Another World: Van Morrison & Belfast** (Irish Academic Press, 2020). The O'Toole review suggests how and why Belfast symbolism blew like a furtive wind through Morrison's writing. Dawe is seldom mentioned in Morrison biographies. This is unfortunate. He is the Michael Seltzer of Ireland. That is, he considers himself Van's biggest professor fan. I am sure Peter Childs would disagree. Like Van, the bespeckled Dawe grew up in East Belfast. When Dawe returned to Belfast in 1972 his future writing on Morrison reached a literary fever pitch. Upon walking into the Orangefield Boy's School, Dawe saw images of Van not of himself. The poet's prerogative. Even stranger, Dawe equated Morrison's breakout song "Gloria" with what the poet termed "my street, my house, my door, my room." The point? It suggests Van's influence on those pursuing the intellectual life. There is a brilliance to Dawe's writing. He suggests what many writers miss. They fail to understand East Belfast. The result is they misinterpret Morrison. Dawe hints, but does not write, that too much attention is placed on his personality. Dawe acknowledges the unexplainable outbursts; the guttural blow ups and he posits there is not enough analysis available on the lasting East Belfast influences. The professor-poet protests too much attention is placed on Van Morrison hanging out at Atlantic Records. There is not enough analysis of the physical beauty in and around Belfast. Again, a fair point. As Fintan O'Toole's review of the Dawe book suggested there is a need to look closely at "local color or social realism." The religious culture emanating from East Belfast needs more emphasis. Or does it? O'Toole writes Van emphasized "the language of being healed" as he speculates there is almost too much in the spiritual realm in Van's writing. The reviewer, Fintan O'Toole and the author, Gerald Dawe, seemingly engage in a dance of interpreting those influences creating Van Morrison. In their own way they employ my "Becoming Van Morrison" thesis in a symbiotic dance in allegorical prose.

The religious culture in and around Belfast is a determining influence upon Morrison. O'Toole's review understands this better than Dawe explains in his book, **In Another World: Van Morrison & Belfast**. This is the nature of those writing about Morrison. They view the spiritual realm differently. Dawe interprets Morrison's religious zeal as the search for a simple life. Calm! Detached! Stoic! Dawe believes these are the traits Morrison emanates from his religious views. It is about Van, not spirituality, Dawe alleges. This is a poignant insight. "His songs are about rapture, not radicalism," Dawe writes. Professor Dawe demonstrates his scholarly direction writing that in the small Belfast night clubs like Sammy Houston's Jazz Club you could "bypass the sectarian bile" and simply enjoy the music. However, one interprets Van Morrison is not as important as his influence upon those who write about him. That is his genius. Van takes the biographer, the journalist, the critic and the analysts into his world influencing them. That is not an easy task. Van does it with elan. The authorized biography that Dawe envisioned writing with Van never materialized. Why? Only the Belfast Cowboy can clear up that story.

See, Fintan O'Toole, "Bittersweet Insights Into Van Morrison's Belfast: In Another World Is A Lively Exploration Of Morrison's Music And Its Impact On The Poet Gerald Dawe, **The Irish Times**, December 16, 2017.
https://www.irishtimes.com/culture/books/bittersweet-insights-into-van-morrison-s-belfast-1.3322104

For Van's road manager, Ed Fletcher, who had not only insights into Morrison but to the industry in general, see, Richard Ames, **Live Music Production: Interviews With UK Pioneers** (London, 2019). This book describes Ed Fletcher with Van in the U.K. and retells the story of his jumping into an unruly audience to protect Morrison. The book also makes a case for the hidden role of the tour or road manager. In Van's case his road manager, Ed Fletcher, was among the best in the business. Fletcher, who has retired to a farm north of Marin County, is one of the most important observers in Morrison's 1970s resurgence does not do interviews. Fortunately, his friends do.

For validation Marin County and Van's Fairfax home provided inspiration for his enormous growth as a writer in the 1970s, see, Steve Turner, **Van Morrison: Too Late To Stop Now** (London, 1993), p. 31. Turner was adamant about the skill Van possessed in mining his life in song form. That brought an angry letter from Van stating the book contained "lies, gross exaggerations and innuendo." Turner responded: "You may not think you are difficult...but other people do and have the right to express their opinions." That brief exchange is one where Van has never varied his attitude toward or inability to accept the biographical process. For reporting of this exchange between Morrison and Turner, see, for example, "Diary-Books," **London Sunday Times**, July 10, 1994, pp 7-8, Martin Wroe, "Rock Star Tries To Bring His Unofficial Biographer To Book," **The London Independent**, September 25, 1993.

Nick Clainos offered a great deal of information on the Bill Graham Organization before Van was officially with BTP and he helped me to understand their stormy relationship.

Mervyn Solomon provided in depth anecdotes and real-life observations on Morrison. In five lengthy interviews with Mr. Solomon, he went into great detail about Van's talent, his personality and his drive to success.

For David Wild's comment on **The Philosopher's Stone**, see, **Rolling Stone**, May 1, 1998 for an incisive review.

Most of what has been written on Bill Graham and Van Morrison's relationship reeks of hagiography. Graham was a narcissist with a personality that was driven to egregious self-promotion. He had little regard for the truth when it came to Van Morrison. As a result, his pronouncements on Van bear little resemblance to reality. He has had the benefit of first-rate writers, who deal in fact not fiction, and the result is Graham looks better historical than his career deserves. For Bill Graham, see, for example, Bill graham, **Bill Graham Presents: My Life Inside And Out** (New York, 2004) for an interesting and well documented autobiography. He pays short shirt to his brief time managing Morrison. Also, see, Rita Gentry, Stefan Gosiewski, et. al., **Before I Forget: Moments And Experiences With Bill Graham** (Santa Rosa, 2022) for a delightful compilation of people and experiences in and around Graham. Rita Gale Gentry lived in Fremont, California, where I taught at Ohlone College, and her compilation of materials on Graham is an outstanding piece of work. She escaped Fremont to live in San Francisco and she eventually became a booking agent for the Grateful Dead. She lived for a time in Marin County. Her book is a dictionary of primarily people in and around BGP and, as a result, it contains raw material for this book. Her insights are amazing. She catalogs Graham's eccentric nature, his over-the-top personality and his dictatorial methods. She also shows how professional, brilliant and attuned to the rock audiences Graham was as a promoter. As he human being, she is kind. It was his way or the highway. The people who worked for Graham highlight this book with love and hate.

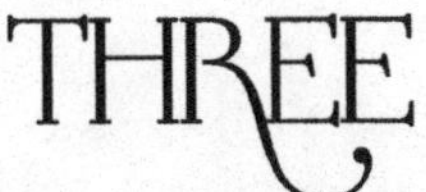

Biography Three: From Mainstream Stardom To Sanity

"I come from a working class background…If you're like me, there's nothing to battle against….Just be yourself."

Van Morrison, 1993

"Some of my works are just straight poetry."

Van Morrison commenting to Martin Chilton March 30, 2020, London Independent

"Literature is the salvation of the condemned."

John Cheever

"Biography gives a new dimension to terror to dying."
Oscar Wilde

VAN MORRISON
VAN MORRISON
Them and the Bang Era
Becoming
VAN MORRISON

There have been a number of full scale Van Morrison biographies. Why another one? He is a fascinating contrarian with a creative genius. That doesn't answer the question. Van has said he will write his autobiography. Don't hold your breath. His quest for privacy and working in isolation is an indication he will not complete his story.

Like many writers, Van created a semblance of his life in his lyrics. If you combine his words with interviews from close friends, musical associates, concert promoters and record label insiders you have a road map for a biography. Then along came the Internet, major newspaper and magazine interviews, and YouTube confessions. There is enough material to fill six biographical volumes.

Van has never sugarcoated his life. He tells it like he sees it. He is a hard-nosed survivor of the music business. In nineteen months from January 1973 through July 1974, Van established his brand. Even with a self-imposed period of retirement, 1974-1977, Van had unparalleled success. His prolific output accelerated throughout his career.

The enthusiastic and loyal audience following Van from **Astral Weeks** on has grown. He has never forgotten the need to tell a story. It can be about warm love, the autumn leaves or any number of romantic themes. He can also be a tough critic screaming "why must I always explain?" What does this do for the biographer? It provides a biographical journey.

WHAT IS THE VAN MORRISON STORY?

The Van Morrison story is not a simple one. The past is necessary to understanding the person. Marcel Proust said it best when he observed: "We are not provided with wisdom. We must discover it for ourselves...after a journey through the wilderness which no one else can take for us." That comment defined the Belfast Cowboy's progression from mainstream stardom to legendary performances.

Van's journey through the wilderness of life has not been a smooth one. He is often viewed as an arrogant contrarian. That is not necessarily incorrect. The number of times he is friendly, cooperative and at ease is seldom mentioned in biography. When there is too much information Van explodes. The press loves it. After all complaints, rants and controversy sell more than the relaxed good times in Morrison's life.

Clinton Heylin and Johnny Rogan made their writing bones describing Morrison's volatile behavior. This is why writing about him is fascinating. When you are hanging out with Martin Scorsese at his birthday party, while talking with Robert DeNiro, you can be a happy guy. Van achieved that in 2023. "The hardships and low points in the road," Mervyn Solomon told me, "are not important to the story. What is important is Van's music. Never lost sight of that."

The hardships were conquered in Van's survival in the rock 'n' roll business jungle. He was fashioned into a brilliant storyteller by his environment. The unfortunate aspects of Van's life made him the legend he is today. His lyrical brilliance came out of conflict not consensus.

Biographers have come to grips with the volatile Van. They have paid less attention to the romantic Morrison. Why? "Warm Love" is not as interesting a song to write about as songs settling a score. There is a duality in Van's writing that makes him two people. The is a conundrum the biographer faces.

For all of Van's interest to biographer's no one concluded when and where he found his métier. Some say the **Astral Weeks** album, some say **Common One**, some say he always had his métier. The truth is he discovered his writing rhythm and perfected it in Marin County from 1973 through mid-1974.

In the early 1970s his writing exploded with a sophisticated content and a poetic direction. He chased success. The result surprised him. He became a celebrity. The term legendary emerged. Fame was not good for his career. He complained about it before he was thirty. His biography is that of a life of flashes of brilliance, combined with some droll writing, and sporadic complaints of personal grudges. Put all that aside and concentrate upon his brilliance. But never forget the quirks. Over the years the last half of Van's life is more relaxed. He no longer has to explain. He is more content. He has nothing to prove. But unremittingly, he continues to work, into his late seventies, like a blue collar truck driver in the music business. The sheer volume of his work in his seventies belies the notion he is content in middle age. By 2023, a half a century later, Van continued to work like he was a young man beginning his career in the music business. He didn't go on tour with his greatest hits in 2023. He believed his greatest hits were in the future. He remained, as he was about to celebrate his seventy eighth birthday, the same hard working musician he was at twenty-seven in Marin County.

THE PARAMETERS IN WRITING ABOUT VAN MORRISON

When writing about Van Morrison the first rule is to remember he has micro-managed his songwriting, his performing, his business, his personal life and his intellectual development. Don't tread on those areas. He will send in an army of lawyers. That said, since he turned sixty in 2005, he has mellowed. During interviews, at times, he makes an effort to work with the press. Van remains cantankerous. This is essential to his creativity. To understand who Van Morrison is and what he is about, his lyrics tell the story. He is a dissident. He is a superb songwriter. That dissidence is personal. He has nothing to do with politics. He remains unconcerned about musical trends. His dissidence is directed at his writing and performing life. As a songwriter, his pen is that of a novelist. He is a determined writer. His creativity is endless. That is the story this book concentrates on from 1973 into 1974. Becoming Van Morrison was the end result.

Never forget Van's mantra in this brief period 1973-1974. That mantra was a frenetic zeal to control his musical output, refine his in concert persona, and to isolate from the press, while establishing a rich, private life. It bears witness to his indefatigable sense of micromanaging his career. To many outsiders it looked like a fool's journey. How could a kid in his late twenties beat the music business at its own game? He did while crafting a concert genius. Impossible! Improbable! But it happened! He is now on a fifty plus year run after propelling his career from the bucolic Marin County countryside into become Sir Van Morrison.

Let's examine the biographer's pitfalls. In this third of my six books, in this multi-volume biography, I discovered the road Van took and the plans he put into his music for a half-century career. Why so many books? Why so many words? For a biography to be successful, the writer must get inside Morrison's psyche. How does one do this without an interview? You interview the people around him. You read every word written about him. You watch his YouTube videos since 1985. They tell you more about the man, in his own words, than the articles and books. You go to as many concerts as possible. You listen when he mentions a writer, an event or a curious incident in his life. You read what he reads. You take these sources, combine them with his Internet confessions, and you have multiple sources for an in-depth biography. Warts and all! Why warts? Van Morrison is a complicated contrarian. He is a genius in songwriting and performing. If you asked him to go to Safeway to buy a quart of milk, he would have no idea how to do it.

As the sorcerer of syntax, Van's talent for storytelling is one few rock 'n' roll performers possess. His writing, while elusive and opaque, has a beautiful cadence with romantic twists. In love songs like "Warm Love" there is a brooding sensitivity with a blue collar view of the world. His sensitivity, combined with the trained eye of a historian, makes Van a superlative writer. He is an intriguing observer with unique insights.

As he settled in Marin County, he was inspired. Marin was like Belfast geographical. He was caught between two different cultural communities. They provided the same inspiration.

Van surveyed his career. There were too many cooks in the business stew. There were too many loose ends stifling his creativity. He streamlined his business organization. He refined his shows. He took the distractions from his life. He was "Becoming Van Morrison." Writing, writing, writing. That was Morrison.

By 1973, Van made a decision. He would control his music through a sophisticated business structure. He would control his touring. A first rate management team with multiple companies to protect copyrights, secure bookings, conduct public relations, analyze legal issues and to manage his archives emerged. As Van set up a flowing professional support team, he learned to fund his recordings, lease the masters and control the product. That story in the 1970s remains largely untold.

The in concert sound was one Van worked on 24/7. As he told Cameron Crowe, in a 1973 **Creem** interview, he was in the process of putting together a band that would back him flawlessly. That band, the Caledonia Soul Orchestra, remains a legendary group. Even on an off-night, Van speculated, this collection of musicians would carry him through tough times.

He continued to play small clubs. The Inn of The Beginning and the Lion's Share where his training ground. In San Francisco the art deco Great American Music Hall was another venue accentuating his drive to literary perfection. To bring an eleven piece group like the CSO into a club setting with two hundred people didn't make for financial success. It made for creative perfection.

While living in Marin County, Van avoided music industry insiders. There was another side to the Belfast Cowboy. It was his personal life. From September 1973 into the first few months of 1977 Carol Guida shared this life. She was an attentive listener. She was an articulate, intellectual equal. This was a first for Van. Guida was a thoughtful, well educated person with a spiritual countenance. She was also one of the most beautiful women in Marin County. She knew everyone. Van evolved personally.

When Van arrived with Guida at a party it took some pressure off of him. He loved Carol for her ability to light up a room. She put everyone at ease with her sultry good looks, engaging personality and quick wit. In the tree lined, blue-sky, casual suburban atmosphere of Marin County, Van came of age spiritually, mentally and emotionally. A spiritual seeker of truth is how Chris Michie described Carol Guida.

The questions surrounding religion and spiritual matters were of concern to Morrison. He discovered serious literature. The changing 1970s California social culture prompted him to reorder his life. The period from 1973 through mid-1974 was a protest against mainstream stardom. It was a journey into sanity. Van was determined to live his life his way.

He was saved from the excesses, musically and sartorially, by his inner psyche. Van was never a tortured artist. He grew up in a normal Belfast family. His dad was an avid music aficionado. His mother was a brilliant singer. He was raised in a happy, well-adjusted household. Molly Fee, Van's neighbor, told me he loved to lay on his back playing the saxophone late into the night. Fee said: "He was quiet." Molly Fee commented: "Shyness was his personality."

He was inordinately shy. Janet Minto Morrison, his ex-wife, talked at length about the terror he felt before concerts. She asked the fans to understand. There were no scars from his childhood. Belfast was the creative fountain providing eternal inspiration. California was the final ingredient creating the artist known as Van Morrison.

The anger and outrage that was early Van Morrison was partially controlled by the 1980s. "Fuck off " was no longer the phrase of choice when the media approached him without an invitation. The seminal influences of the 1970s were personal maturity, songwriting depth, business acumen and a carefully designed performing genius. The package that was the Belfast Cowboy was formed and finalized in the midst of his first decade at Warner Bros. In Marin County from 1973 into mid-1974 the final polish to his career was carefully applied. Then from late 1974 through 1979 the rough edges in Morrison's career were polished to perfection. Van Morrison's trademark emerged.

As Van matured, his songwriting reflected the influences around him. He was never political. Yet, he couldn't escape the Troubles in Northern Ireland. He wasn't a minority. He came to feel like one in Marin County. He read California history. The Irish were a much discriminated San Francisco minority in the nineteenth century. Then they established a prominent position in California's economic and political growth. As he visited San Francisco's Irish restaurants and pubs, they provided another lesson in how persistence created economic success. Whenever Van imbibed the Golden State's culture and local history, it guided his songwriting. California was a classroom for Van's developing intellect.

Van's divorce, in the early 1970s, didn't change him. He was angry before the divorce. He was angry after the divorce. His anger was directed at the obsequious music industry. As the 1970s formalized the man, he emerged as a singularly powerful and independent artist.

What have biographers spent too much time discussing? Drinking! That part of Van's life was no better nor no worse than the average rock musician transitioning from his twenties into his thirties. One of Van's closest friends told me the 1970s was a time when Van became "boring," then "uplifting," then "difficult" and finally a "formed personality." A contradiction! Not really! It was just Van Morrison. Clinton Heylin spent too much time on drinking. His book contains thirty seven pages of references to his drinking. None are tied to his career successes or failures. None are tied to others around him, None are tied to the pressures surrounding his life. None are tied to his relationship with record labels. Why, then, so many stories. Heylin was pissed. It was about the legal threat he endured from Van. He got even. The press took note. The English tabloids were their usual quarrelsome selves. Van said he was into truth and ultimately facts. That truth about what was left behind in the 1970s surfaced in **The Philosopher's Stone**. The songs in that 1998 album of unreleased material was autobiographical. Most, but not all, songs had a Marin County connection with a name checking of his life.

VAN ON FACTS, TRUTH AND THE PHILOSOPHER'S STONE

The 1970s brought significant changes. Van was not just about things spiritually. He was not just about discovering a performing genius thanks to the It's Too Late To Stop Now tour. What Van was about, according to Carol Guida, was centering his life. That centering created an intellectual persona brought recognition for his writing. He was suddenly more than the music.

His songs were increasingly interpreted and praised for their poetic direction. He was not just about channeling his music. Van increasingly complained about twisted facts and lost truths. He believed he had to set the facts straight to amplify the truth. He did so in song. The 1970s produced a singer-songwriter with an intellectual aura unique in rock music. The first album he had total control over was **Hard Nose The Highway**. It was a misunderstood masterpiece. Why? As Peter Childs wrote: "One of the problems with the reputation of **Hard Nose The Highway** is simply a lot of great material remained in the vaults."

He told close friends he was learning the production process. That was obvious when the album was released. It was a learning process. That album celebrated his continued emotional maturity, his production path, and his oblique dealings with Warner Bros. These forces inspired Van to complete a double album. Warner wouldn't release **Hard Nose The Highway** as a double album. The songs were archived and turned up in 1998 in **The Philosopher's Stone**. The tiff over a double vinyl masterpiece led to one. The impetus for the **It's Too Late To Stop Now** double album was born. As Van told Chris Michie: "I won, Warner lost." No one disagreed.

What was in **The Philosopher's Stone**? A portion of it was leftover songs from 1973-1974. Many of these tunes were destined for **Hard Nose The Highway**. They provided insight into the Belfast Cowboy. There were eight songs on the album that revealed what the 1973-1974 period meant to Morrison's writing, career direction and his growth as a featured entertainer. There were so many gems from the 1973-1974 period in **The Philosopher's Stone** that it is important to examine, analyze and suggest what these songs meant for Morrison.

"Wonderful Remark" was recorded in Marin County in 1973 with local musicians. When it appeared on the soundtrack album for the 1983 movie "The King of Comedy," those close to Van wondered why it was not released on **Hard Nose The Highway**. The tune was originally recorded during the **Moondance** sessions in August 1969 and then Van recut it at the Church in San Anselmo in 1973. The original release was less than four minutes and **The Philosopher's Stone** version was eight minutes. There were reportedly at least five versions of this song Van recorded. The importance was in the lyrics. The song also featured Ronnie Montrose's guitar. Van said it was about a difficult time in New York. He was lamenting Bert Berns and the lack of funds to live. "It was about people who were supposed to be helping you," Van remarked. The themes in the songs recorded for but left off **Hard Nose The Highway** were lost love, nostalgia and hard **Times**. Some of those themes influenced the direction of Morrison's future releases.

LOST LOVE, NOSTALGIA AND VAN'S ALBUMS

On **Hard Nose The Highway**, Van lamented lost love. He reached into his nostalgia bag to comment on Frank Sinatra and Nelson Riddle. He talked of lost youth in "Wild Children." He made fun of the hippies in "The Great Deception." This paean to the Haight-Ashbury mentality illustrated Van's creative observations. He did so at a time the counterculture celebrated itself.

By 1974 there was a new truth. One emerging from Ireland. His trip to Ireland in October 1973, with Carol Guida, accentuated his songwriting. This led to the Irish themes in **Veedon Fleece**. Van's favorite song from the album, "Bulbs," seemed innocuous. It wasn't. "Bulbs" was the 45 released from **Veedon Fleece**. The original track was cut for the **Hard Nose The Highway** album. Then it was re-written and re-recorded. Jef Labes commented Van didn't like the direction of the initial "Bulbs." When he re-recorded it, the result was a distinct rock and roll direction. Van was once again searching for **Billboard** hits. "Bulbs" was released eleven times, as a 45, in the world market. It failed to chart. The song showed a duality in Morrison's songwriting. He mixed America and Irish themes. That wasn't surprising as American song images emerged from 1966 at the Whiskey A Go Go. Van was on stage with the self-described American Shaman, Jim Morrison. That night Van and the members of Them realized they had something special. Van also came to the conclusion he didn't need Them. "When I managed and traveled with Van and Them," Phil Solomon told me, I said to Van: "I have got you, I don't need the rest of the group." Solomon told me he believed his comment spurred Van to a solo career. His brother, Mervyn, disagreed. "Van was going solo from the day he began his music career. He just had to wait for the right moment."

When Them left Los Angeles they drove to a small club, that had once been a roller rink, in San Leandro, California. It was here Van met Janet Planet. What is overlooked is the club owner told Van he needed to pursue a solo career.

THE SO-CALLED TWO AND A HALF YEARS OF RETIREMENT: HOW DOES IT FIT INTO THE BIOGRAPHICAL BANE?

In the process of writing this book, and the previous volumes on Van Morrison, I talked with almost a hundred people about the period of Van's so-called retirement in the mid-1970s. In an interview with the **London Mirror's** Kim Carr, Van said he quit the music industry in the 1970s but he returned to performing to pay the bills. Carr reported Van was shocked Warner's royalties were not enough to sustain his Marin County lifestyle. "I had to come back because my accountant called me up and said: 'You don't have any more (money) left. You're going to have to do it all again." Van went on remarking he had "people to support...." He continued, explaining to Carr, he would never be able to retire. "I'm trapped. I've got so much product that even if I stopped public appearances, I'd still have to manage my catalogue, so I'd still be working." How does one interpret Van's statement?

For starters this is typical Van. He loves to work. The recent outpouring of albums suggested his blue collar work ethic is on overtime. He bounded into his late seventies with the energy of an artist beginning his career. These comments took place as Van released his thirty-sixth album **Keep Me Singing**.

What is the real story? Those who worked with Van in the mid-1970s have a different view of the so-called period of retirement. Tony Dey, who lived in Sacramento, was Van's drummer in 1975 in the midst of the retirement. He recalled the two in the morning phone calls requesting that he come into the studio by five or six in the morning to begin recording. It was no problem. Dey loaded up a coffee cup, stopped in Fairfield for a second cup and met Van in the Fairfax studio. Many people close to Van didn't realize his frenetic work habits continued.

The operative wisdom, according to Chris Michie, was the "retirement myth" was a convenient way to get the media off his creative path. In the two and a half years he lessened his concert appearances, he worked on his career and enjoyed his new life with Carol Guida.

Van planned his future in the music business with the precision of a kamikaze fighter pilot. That is he didn't leave a stone unturned in planning his future. He envisioned his future with original tunes supported by covers of blues, rhythm and blues tunes and an odd assortment of personal favorites. While original compositions highlighted his albums the cover songs in concert brought in a new and varied audience.

As he planned his future in the mid-1970s he showed Warner Bros. they would not dictate, direct or influence his albums. He was death on any sort of meddling in his career. The proof of that? The **Hard Nose The Highway** album left his best songs unreleased. To this day no one knows why. Neither Van nor Warner Bros. has commented. The operative wisdom, according to those close to Van, was the album was his creation for better or for worse. Future albums suffered.

When **Rolling Stone** labelled **A Period Of Transition**: "Sluggish," it was a criticism emanating from **Hard Nose The Highway**. Why did **Rolling Stone** make this comment? Ironically, it was due to the horns. The new Van Morrison, as the premier rock magazine concluded, should not be concerned with horns. That was for the Muscle Shoals folks. That was fine with Van. He had continually new directions. That was his future mantra.

The Shakespeare of Telegraph Avenue, Greil Marcus, weighed in with a pronouncement from the God of rock 'n' roll critics. From high on a hill in Berkeley, California, Marcus appeared like a God on High declaring: "Flamingos Fly" "was the only tune to which the horns added anything..." Even faint praise from Marcus brought raucous applause. From his multi-million dollar home in a leafy, bucolic Berkeley suburb, Marcus saved the day for Van. At least one of the interpretive giants was with Van if only on one song.

VAN LOOKING BACK TO LOOKING FOREWARD IN MARIN COUNTY

By 1977, the fashion police hadn't arrived. Van was pictured on **A Period Of Transition** in a blue leisure suit. He still performed wearing shirts with egg stains or coffee splotches. The Van in a suit, top hat, shined shoes and looking like a blues man was in the future.

His ninth Warner Brothers studio album, **A Period Of Transition**, was a lackluster seven song attempt to get back into the musical mainstream. Carol Guida had left. That may have been the problem. The reviewers had trouble finding a song that stood out.

There was an exemplary tune. "You Gotta Make It Through the World." It was a marvelous tune. No one knew what to do with it. Van reflected on this song. He said it was: "a survival song." As I interviewed musicians in and around Marin County, for my 1983 book **Van Morrison: The Mystic's Music**, there were comments about Van having writer's block. Chris Michie laughed. "Van worked quietly, solitarily, there was no writer's block. It was rumor not fact." Van loved the writer's black humor. It took the heat off him. He was quietly productive with a fierce competitive zeal.

Fact not fiction became Van's mantra. He believed facts had to be set straight in song form. The Belfast Cowboy controlled the narrative. The triumph and despair Van lived with for his entire career drives him. In my last book, **Van Morrison: Astral Weeks To Stardom, 1968-1972**, in chapter two, "From Cult To Mainstream Stardom," I asked the question why **Astral Weeks** was not a best-selling album? Then why the sudden splurge of hit Warner releases from 1970 through 1972? The answer was money. Van needed to continue his commercial successes to support his lifestyle. He realized record sales guaranteed his fiscally secure personal and professional life.

He demanded privacy! He demanded to be paid fairly. There is no need to recount the lawsuits, the over the top behavior and the difficulty Morrison brought to record labels.

Van will sue for invasion of his intellectual property. What is important is Van was suing those he deemed were profiting from writing about him. Clinton Heylin comes to mind. Simon Gee is another. Gee lost money on his fanzine. Van sued his ex-wife over a website selling jewelry believing she profited from his name. Those, like Johnny Rogan, Steve Turner, John Collis, Brian Hinton, Peter Mills, Clinton Heylin and Eric Hage, who admired his work, were rewarded by fans and critics with thanks for their thoughtful insights. Van never threatened to sue any of them. Or did he? Who knows!

Van's close friends describe him as "loyal, supportive, low key and private." There is no question they are right. To write a full biography, that captures the person, it is necessary to include some of the ribald episodes.

If Van Morrison has a fault, it is pointing his finger at his critics and those who disparage him. He does it regularly. He remarks, with arduous venom, he has reasons. The inane questions! The snarky observations! Interpretive malfeasance! These factors infuriated him. If he has a point, he will write about it. Van's songwriting is disguised autobiography. Some critics postulate it may simply be observations. Nothing more! Nothing less! Who knows! Only Van can tell us.

VAN'S CRAFT IS CENTRAL TO HIS BIOGRAPHY

Van's craft as a songwriter and performer is central to his biography. There are often boring aspects to the Belfast Cowboy. He withdraws. He is shy. He is reclusive. He is into himself. Phil Solomon told me he rode with Van in his car to a show an hour outside of London. Van looked out the window. He didn't say a word during the entire trip. When Solomon attempted a friendly chat, Van turned the radio up. He looked, with boredom, outside the car window.

It is in the songwriting and performing that he emerges. Otherwise, he remains a quiet, unassuming Irishman. The inner life of Van Morrison is the story. Perhaps only he can tell it. Then again, his songs contain lyrical fragments of the happiness and grief reflecting on his inner soul. By charting Van's emotional and spiritual life, one can see his musical direction.

To understand Van Morrison is not an easy task. I have been writing about him since the 1970s. My first book **Van Morrison: The Mystic's Music**, in 1983, was when I conceived this six volume biography. In 2005 the first volume covered the years 1945 into 1968. In 2020, the second tome covered the period from 1968 through 1972. This volume analyzes the 1973 into mid-1974. Why three volumes and roughly almost two thousand pages on Van' life in the 1970s until he reached the ripe old age of twenty-nine? Those years defined his art, his writing, his business ventures, and his place in the music business. His organizational zeal to protect his intellectual property reached epidemic proportions. To Van's chagrin, by the late 1970s, Warner Bros. advertised him as "a legend in concert." He considered himself first and foremost a songwriter. Since 1980, he has built upon his reputation. He enhanced his career while remaining the loveable curmudgeon. He is an entitled contrarian in a business where one or two hits is the norm. Van eschewed the hits. He marched to the beat of his own drummer.

Who are the writers who have analyzed Van's soul? There are many. These writers searched out his foibles, praised his eccentricities and in the process defined him? My choices are Erik Hage, Johnny Rogan, Clinton Heylin, Pat Thomas, Peter Mills, Simon Gee, Steve Turner, Pat Corley, Brian Hinton, John Collis, Peter Childs and last, but not least, the Shakespeare of Telegraph Avenue, Greil Marcus. They have analyzed Van's extraordinary impact upon our culture. Van is more than rock 'n' roll. He claims he is not a rock music artist. He is right. He is more than a rock and roller. That is the conundrum the biographer faces.

HOW DOES ONE WRITE ABOUT VAN?

How does one write about Morrison? To concentrate on what interests him is to understand the man. He is a multi-layered personality. His peccadillos, contradictions, intellectual depth, a shy arrogance, and a need to be left alone makes the biographer's task an onerous one. The beauty, tragedy, ornery behavior, law suits, whiney complaints, happiness, fulfillment and grievances over sleights, real and imagined, in Morrison's life, are the biographer's bane. This biography examines his youthful drive to stardom, and how he won the battle to control his intellectual property, his career and his life. In the 1970s, Morrison set up a musical empire lasting to the present. As his songwriting and performing talents matured so did his themes.

Because of his distaste for biography and biographers, Van published a short version of his life, **Reliable Sources**, a seventy-two page booklet, in the 1970s. It was dreadful. Stephen Pillster sugar coated Van's life. The editor, Cynthia Copple, did a marvelous job on production. She cleaned up the writing. If not for Copple, it would have been a failure. Copple is a New Age guru. She is the type of woman contrary to Morrison's lifestyle. One assumed Stephen Pillster's hand was in this mix. But Copple was talented. She single handedly turned **Reliable Sources** into an interesting read. Despite his disdain for biographers, this brief memoir had value. It demonstrated how Van visualized himself. Or more precisely what he didn't want to share with reviewers and biographers. It taught us that he will never appoint an authorized biographer.

A biography is often a travesty. Why? Misinterpretation! Misrepresentation! Missing material! Malpractice in writing! There are dozens of subjects in the great manhole of biography. Getting people right is the task. To get Van Morrison right from 1973 into mid- 1974 made it necessary to scurry down rabbit holes. That is to investigate the mundane, which is often a determining factor in Van's creative gestation.

What was the biggest influence ? Was it Marin County or Carol Guida? It was neither. It was spiritualism. Van's intellectual development was followed by self-awareness and the cultivation of his art and his intellect. Along the way he figured out the meaning of life. In the mid-1970s he asked to be left alone.

The second task was to analyze Van's work habits. Why all the time in the recording studio? The answer is experimentation. A number of musicians mentioned when they arrived to record with Van the Oakland Children's Youth Chorus, drummer Tony Dey, a string quartet or a newly auditioning guitarist, like Chris Michie, was in the studio and the result was the person arriving to talk with Van was alternately confuse and impressed.

When Van talked with Guida, as well as close friends, and those who had a literary lineage like Alan Watts, he discussed how to use language. This leads into looking at his lyrics. They surround his life. It is an examination of his creative psychosis. The third task was to allow Van's personality, perhaps sometimes the lack of it, to intrude upon this manuscript when and where it influenced his musical, intellectual and creative direction. Those who write about Van have a myriad number of ways of interpreting him. He has frightened biographers to leave out large segments of his life. He wants to control the biographer. Steve Turner's coffee table biography, which was a major re-interpretation, was helped by meetings with Van. At the time they talked Morrison and Turner were discussing a book on Christian writers. When Turner came out with the Van coffee table book, he was unhappy. He would not have agreed to talk with Turner if he knew his biography was in the works. When Turner's tome was released, it was disparaged by the Belfast Cowboy. When he read the final product, Van felt betrayed. He accused Turner of misdemeanors and high literary crimes. Turner laughed. Van argued Turner took undue liberties with their discussions, which he deemed "partially private."

WHAT DOES BIOGRAPHY THREE REVEAL?

Explaining Van Morrison's fame is a difficult task. When the fame game burst upon Morrison in the 1970s, his concert advertisements stated: "The legendary Van Morrison." He hated the term. This made the 1970s alternately a period of commercial explosion and a gut wrenching time of re-evaluation. This was the reason for the so-called period of retirement. The burden placed on Van from fame and fortune strangled his creativity for brief periods. This is why he took time off, while remaining out of the limelight. Van said many times there was no period of retirement. The retirement myth defined the mid-1970s. It was too good a story to ignore. An excellent example of interpreting Van, when there was no need for interpretation, centered around his mid-1970s album, **Veedon Fleece**. In an attempt to link this vinyl masterpiece to the past critics looked to **Astral Weeks**.

Veedon Fleece, Van's eighth studio album, released on October 5, 1974, was hailed as the second coming of **Astral Weeks**. Van was mystified. This comparison startled him. He was determined to write independently. He prided himself in not recreating his music. For that reason he didn't include a hit, pop single. Joe Smith remedied that problem. He came to Van with a suggestion to re-record "Bulbs" in New York with two jazz musicians.

Smith told Van; "Bulbs" was the hit he needed to sell **Veedon Fleece**. Van reluctantly agreed. After "Bulbs," was re-recorded and Warner Bros. issued eleven worldwide 45s. "Bulbs" did not chart. Van was vindicated. He didn't need a hit to sell an album. Van was running his career not his label. The tensions were enormous over "Bulbs." This portended future problems.

Van's songs are a collection of stories reflecting his public and personal concerns. The malicious, often gratuitous, press attacks were ongoing. Van's combative personality accelerated differences with Warner Bros. and the press. He viewed the media as a constant source of irritation. He blanched at the media's unfair criticism. He said conclusions about him and his music bore no relationship to reality. That said, when a knowledgeable, non-confrontational journalist showed up, Van was a calm, cooperative interview. There were only a few of such interviews from 1973 into 1974. Controversy with the media continued.

Contempt and cruelty are traits often associated with Morrison. He has contempt for egregious stupidity. He eschews egocentric behavior. His cruelty is an unfair charge. His personality is associated with perfection. When I interviewed musicians who recorded and performed with him, they said cruelty was a word Van didn't understand. It was about making the music perfect. It was about the right type of stage presence, the clarity of the performances and understanding how to present his music in concert.

"He has never treated anyone with cruelty," Chris Michie continued. "When Van wanted to change musicians, it was due to his desire for a new sound. It was nothing personal. It was about the music. It wasn't about the musician."

There is a self-righteous moralizing to Morrison. This leaves the door open for critics to question his actions. They don't realize he is not an open book. He runs a tight ship. He has a perfectionist gene. The proof. His business corporations run through nineteen LLCs. The structure of his corporate entities ran with the precision of a well-oiled machine.

STEVE TURNER AND VAN MORRISON: THE CHRISTIAN WRITER AND CONTROLLING THE BIOGRAPHER

In an attempt to control his biography, Van decided to work with a Christian writer, cum excellent rock biographer, Steve Turner. He would eventually write a Van Morrison coffee table tome filled with pictures. Turner met Van in 1985. He interviewed forty plus people associated with the Belfast Cowboy and Penguin Books made it appear like Van cooperated with Turner when the coffee table tome arrived. Van sent a letter to Turner stating those he interviewed were not friends. He made his unhappiness with the book known.

When Turner met Van in 1985, they got along quite well. Steve is tall, calm, soft spoken, religious and he emanates integrity. He is a brilliant writer. He is also a detached English intellectual with a penchant for careful analysis. His writing never overstates. He appeared to be the perfect Morrison biographer. He was also a stone cold fan. Some years later, he secured a contract with the U. S. Penguin group and the English Bloomsbury publisher for a coffee table book.

The term "coffee table book" was an insult to Turner's research, writing and careful attention to detail. The press, a large portion of the fans, and the general public, ignored or dismissed Turner's biography. That was unfortunate. Turner's assessment of Van's mother, Violet, and her spiritual journey, was brilliant. Turner's book was a Christian critique. He wrote similar books on Eric Clapton and Cliff Richard. As Turner pointed out, Van name checked T. S. Eliot and John Donne alongside Otis Redding and Wilson Pickett. Van was more than a pop-rock-blues musician. There was something else going on. Turner identified it. It was originality. Van blended soul, jazz, pop, blues, and rhythm and blues sounds in his unique musical direction. Turner described and analyzed Van's intellect with precision.

The critics were hard on Turner. Half the book concentrated on Them. There are only eighty pages on Van's solo career. When Turner labelled **Veedon Fleece** "a plodding, meddlesome affair," the critics ranted and raved. This was unfortunate. Someone liked the book. The 25,000 print run sold out in few months. Morrison was infuriated with the book. He hated it. Turner's reaction was frustration and bewilderment.

When Turner's **Too Late To Stop Now** appeared in 1993, Van tried to purchase the entire print of 25,000. Why? He said Turner got it wrong. What did Morrison object to in the Turner book? He was unhappy with flautist John Payne discussing **Astral Weeks**. Van sent Turner thirty-six examples of what he termed "lies, gross exaggerations and innuendo." Turner replied: "You may not think you are difficult or an introvert and other people do and have the right to express their opinions." Chris O'Donnell, Van's manager, weighed in commenting: "He is not happy about books period. He is an artist and stands up for himself—he doesn't want his private life raked over." Turner didn't invade Van's privacy. To Van writing is an invasion of his privacy. Any writing is unacceptable.

In a 1990 podcast David Wild detailed his hilarious and at times frustrating attempt to complete a **Rolling Stone** piece on Van. Caledonia Productions called **Rolling Stone** and told founder Jann Wenner Van was ready to do an interview for the release of **Hymns To The Silence**. When Wild showed up in New York to interview Van, the **Rolling Stone** writer said the Belfast Cowboy ran away from him. A Warner executive standing nearby looked flabbergasted during his attempt to introduce them. It caused bewilderment. Wild was only twenty-seven. Then Van's management told Wild to come to Boston where he was performing. He would do the interview. Wild met him. Van fled again. "I was chasing Van around Cambridge. Finally, we did the interview." Then Van called him and asked: "Are we ok?" Wild said: "Yes." A few days later Van's management called and asked Wild if he would like to write the liner notes for **Hymns To The Silence**. To this day, now sixty years old, Wild considers this his strangest journalistic assignment. It is a tale suggesting the biographer's woes in writing about Van. The irony is those woes define his brilliance. What does this have to do for a book on Van in 1973-1974? Plenty! In **Hymns To The Silence** he continues to beat to death the themes of the 1970s. That is the nostalgia of the leafy places he has lived. He also complains in "Professional Jealousy" about those who don't understand him. The point is a simple one. In 1990 in **Hymns To The Silence**, Van reflected on the lessons he learned in Marin County. His attraction to Steve Turner, his books and his writing was the product the street corner Marin County gurus, the itinerant, but functioning, Marin County intellectuals and a bevy of religious-philosophical thinkers. Van's furtive reading continued. Spiritualism and religion were engrained in his psyche.

It was the influence of spiritual forces and religious motivation that highlighted Turner's approach. Van believed this violated his privacy. Religion and spirituality abounded in Turner's elegant prose. Van believed this was his private domain. That led Morrison to question Turner's objectivity. It appeared he was upset with references to the Jehovah's Witnesses, and how they influenced his mother. Why? His mother had a brief flirtation with the sect. She quickly returned to traditional Protestantism.

Turner's biographical strengths makes his book brilliant. He analyzed how and why Van fit in with Bob Dylan, Neil Young and members of The Band. Turner described Van's antipathy to organizations, rules, structure, and any form of corporate restraint as restraining. This prompted Van to complain about the book. When Turner employed Van's quotes: "I hate organizations" or "I'm just groping in the dark," Morrison allegedly told a friend these comments had no relationship to his music. These quotes, Van said, were to sell books. He went to a party in San Francisco where Turner's book was on a coffee table. Van picked it up, grabbed a pen, and he began writing "untrue" throughout the book. He was angry.

The photos, the illustrations and the coffee table look took away from a solid biography. Turner asked questions others didn't. On matters of Van's reluctance to be interviewed and his difficult nature, Turner didn't mince words. That didn't sit well with critics or fans. That is unfortunate. Turner's insights into Van the person eclipsed those of Brian Hinton, Johnny Rogan and Clinton Heylin. The only reviewer to get it right was David Lister in **The London Independent**. He concluded Van was a "reclusive singer-songwriter whose non-stop touring is a spiritual quest."

HOW DOES VAN SEE PEOPLE, HIS ART AND THE BIOGRAPHER?

Van's everyday life is like no other. His mind works constantly. His thoughts evolve from reading, reflecting, taking in historical sites, analyzing the local landscape, and with in-depth discussions with friends. Then he writes about these encounters. Like many creative individuals, he doesn't see people clearly. He views them on his own terms.

Then he enters the public arena with a product. Acceptance or rejection! That is on his mind. Then Morrison reacts. The critics often find him prickly, contentious, sullen, petty and abrasive. He has survived. Why? He refuses to compromise his art. That is he takes exception to many interviews while freely talking to select journalists. Is this a contradiction? No! It is Van being Van.

In "Why Must I Always Explain?," a song from his 1991 album **Hymns To The Silence**, he complained about the press. In a 2019 interview, Van said: "I don't need to explain what I do or how I do it, I don't need to. It's OK if it's a mystery."

Van intimates he channels songs? He claims he can't understand how his creative muse works. Van misses one key element. His lyrics are grounded in his life. This is the window to interpret his work. "There's not a lot of intellectual pondering about what I'm doing…. It's…kind of instinctive," Van commented to **The London Guardian**. He remains his own biographer. That will never change.

Van's imaginative genius speak to us. To understand Van, one must turn to the less familiar songs, the overlooked concerts, and the people his biographers ignore in his evolution to forming his persona.

THE COMPLICATED VAN MORRISON: ULLA MUNCH AND VAN IN COPENHAGEN

When analyzing Van Morrison, it is necessary to remember his one dimensional drive. He makes decisions, at times, without considering the needs of others. The best example was replacing drummer Peter Van Hooke. Why replace Van Hooke? Because Van wanted a new sound. Van Hooke was distraught. Morrison couldn't understand why. The Belfast Cowboy valued Van Hooke as a friend. When it came to his music, Van followed his muse. Early on it was Janet Planet, then Carol Guida, Ulla Munch and finally Michelle Rocca. After that Van had enough confidence to be his own muse. Munch was gone, as Clinton Heylin said, by Van's "choice of beverage." Clinton's less than sly remark concerning drinking was a low blow. It was also untrue. They mutually agreed to part ways.

As Munch climbed up and down the Vanlose Station every morning and evening it inspired Morrison. Munch was Van's girlfriend and for a period of three years. He lived in or around the Vanlose Station. Munch was a concert promoter for the Arne Worsøe company, ICO Concerts. Van met her because of ICO.

Munch, a raven haired beauty, with curly hair, was much like Van's previous muses. She was thin, beautiful, highly intelligent, quiet and intellectually inclined. Allen Ginsberg took a picture of her and Van suggesting their compatibility. When Ginsberg snapped the photo on April 27, 1985 Munch was introduced as a photographer. That was typical Van. Blur the story. Can the biographer find the truth? Probably not!

Ulla Munch provided another window into Morrison. She lived in Copenhagen. Most people remember her from Van's song "Vanlose Stairway." There is more to the story. It is complicated. The London press followed Van around and concluded he lived for a time in Copenhagen. The press looked for his apartment in Vanlose. He remained elusive and private. The black, wide brimmed hat Van wore, when in downtown Copenhagen, guaranteed his anonymity.

Van Morrison, Michelle Rocca, Hillary And Bill Clinton

The press discovered Van collected records. He shopped at Superlove purchasing special order records as well as **Rolling Stone**, **Melody Maker** and the **New Musical Express**. Van wrote furtively while in Copenhagen. In 1982 "Vanlose Stairway" appeared on **Beautiful Vision**. The Denmark Radio Big Band provided a musical outlet. By 1983 Van was gone from Denmark. There were only a few Ulla Munch sightings. By 1989 she was out of the picture.

But Van did write "Scandinavia" and "Beautiful Vision" while with Munch. The muses continued to define him. The muse, without a day job, who married rich guys, Michelle Rocca, was on the horizon. Van should have seen it coming. He didn't. Ouch!

CREATIVITY AND VAN

The press spends less time on Van's creative process and more time on what they think is important in his private life. When he is asked about subjects, he deems private there is an eruption.

The justification for Van's occasional erratic behavior was his art. Here is how Van explained it to one of his band mates. If those who buy his records, those who review his material, those in the record business who don't understand him don't get what he is doing they don't deserve respect. Van doesn't see his erratic behavior. All he envisions is his music and where it is going commercially. At least that is the perception until you look deeper into his soul.

When you look deeply into Van's creative process there are no easy answers. There are lots of questions.

Creativity is his driving force. Like Bob Dylan, Van will say of a particular song it is nothing special. It is just a song. In 2021, after a monster year, plus a lockdown due to the coronavirus pandemic, Van released a new double album, **Latest Record Project: Volume 1**. The single "No More Lockdown" prompted a London newspaper to headline that he went from a genius to a conspiracy minded person for ignoring coronavirus dangers. The old days of berating the press once again erupted.

In 2021, the Woolhall people placed a twenty-seven minute interview on the Internet. Van looked back on his life reflecting on what influenced him. He clarified how he arrived as an artist. He recalled he didn't initially listen to or understand black music. He said that changed in 1960 in Germany. When the show band, the Monarchs, travelled to Germany, he heard a wide variety of soul artists. He talked to black soldiers. It was there, Van said, he discovered Bobby Blue Bland. The black soldiers, whether playing records or singing, influenced young Morrison.

He commented Eric Burdon and the Animals and the Rolling Stones opened commercial doors for him. Van could play in small clubs with show bands. He did this in 1961 prior to joining Them. The influence of Ray Charles, James Brown, Sam Cooke, Bobby Blue Bland, Sonny Terry and Brownie McGhee and Leadbelly made Van a performer with a blues edge.

WHAT DOES VAN MORRISON EXPECT FROM HIS BIOGRAPHERS?

Ted Hughes, the poet married to Sylvia Plath, remarked: "I hope each one of us owns the facts of his or her own life." Hughes made this comment to **The London Independent**, as a series of authors eviscerated his life. The freedom a biographer takes with a person's life is a concern. No one worries about this more than Van Morrison.

There is a constant fight over facts. That is the crux of Morrison's complaints. To portray the subject in the act of living is difficult. In Van's case, he won't allow it. Getting a feel for the real Van is a problem. His mercurial personality. His diffident attitudes. His cranky nature. His last minute business decisions. His inability to analyze other viewpoints presents problems. These are contradicted by Van's at times warm personality. With friends he is calm and relaxed. He is a contrarian with personal contradictions. He is also a good person. He is neither greedy nor cruel. He has a delicate personality prone to sensitive feelings. The contradictions in Van's life make for an interesting biography.

What does Van Morrison expect from his biographers? Strict adherence to the facts. A sense of understanding. That understanding, Van argues, does not emerge from close friends and associates over more than half a century. Van is adamant personal interviews flaw the biographical narrative. He has addressed this in "New Biography." He does not believe biography elicits truth. He views biography as the best way to muddle, confuse and misinterpret the subject.

What does Van expect from his biographer? There are cautionary signs of what he would like. He hopes for someone to explain his intellectual direction. Greil Marcus did in commenting on some of his songs. Steve Turner explained Van's religious direction. Stuart Bailie concentrated on seventy-five songs highlighting a wordsmith with Shakespeare like overtones. Clinton Heylin argued there was a brilliant, if flawed, Van. Johnny Rogan views him in the light of myriad influences. The art of Van's music is Brian Hinton's view from a literary perspective. Ditto for Erik Hage. Peter Mills is the analyst placing Morrison's music in a brilliant academic context with a literary flair.

Morrison's life never evolved in a straight line. For years a wanderlust guided his creativity. He flipped-flopped on religion. He studied philosophy. He lived out personal stories. He wrote about those adventures. He made references to dance halls, churches, blue collar restaurants, his friends, his foes, his beloved Belfast and his Irish heritage. His writer's life emerged.

Van's songwriting subjects are in front of him. Whether it is record company executives, think Bert Berns, obscure rock stars, think P. J. Proby, his ex-wives, think Janet Planet and Michelle Rocca, his intellectual muses, think Carol Guida and Ulla Munch, or other subjects, think disapproval, a search for respect and isolation is foremost in his psyche.

He has avoided, being as he said: "The flavor of the month." The complexity of survival in the rock and roll business jungle has made him a recluse with an antenna looking for signs of those attempting to destroy his career. His relationship with record labels have been laboriously contentious. He is demanding. Just ask the Blue Note executives. "We loved working with Van," a Blue Note company employee told me on the condition of anonymity, "In the end we vowed never to work with him again. Don Was overruled our brain trust." Viola! A commonly heard tale.

The growth of the poet is a common theme in Morrison's life. His words ring true. Van is now in his mid-seventies. His songwriting themes remain personal. As Oscar Wilde said: "Biography is the mesh through which our real life escapes."

Van Morrison has the last word. What is it? It would be in song. It would be in an observation. It would be in analysis. He is a master of language. He has the vision of Chekov. He has the storytelling skill of Shakespeare. Telling stories is Van's mantra. Interpreting them is the biographer's role. That is the biographer's forte. Complexity is a roadblock. Interpreting it is a joy.

His observations on Belfast recall a simpler time. He presents descriptions of those who have made the Irish literary tradition a worldwide phenomenon. While living in New York, and later in Boston, Van imbibed folk influences. Then he blended these with rhythm and blues, traditional blues and a mélange of soul sounds to create his music.

VAN LECTURES HIS BIOGRAPHERS: BEWARE OF INTERPRETING WHEN THERE IS NO INTERPRETATION, THE FACTS ARE BULLSHIT!

In a 2015 interview, with Gavin Martin, at London's Portobello Hotel, Van discussed the myths, the misinterpretations and the bull-shit peddled by journalists, professors, biographers and a host of literary giants. He didn't believe any of them got it right. They never would. They didn't understand.

When Gavin Martin asked Van if there were myths about him and his music, he wanted to say: "Do we have a week?" He didn't. He dispelled many myths. The idyllic childhood on Hyndford Street was close to the truth. It was a blue-collar working class upbringing. Van said it was no different than any other kid growing up in Belfast after World War II. Hyndford Street wasn't special. The fans and writers made this an idyllic place. He said it wasn't. It was typical. A hard working, hard scrabble family adjusting to post World War II Northern Ireland was his story. Van downplayed the Troubles. He said they didn't impact him.

On his Belfast youth, Van observed: "Was it idyllic? I don't know I'd have to ask some of the people I knew as a kid who are still around if they thought it was idyllic. I don't think it was idyllic...."

On references to Belfast songs, he is adamant he used poetic license. "Do you actually think I am writing about Cyprus Avenue?" Van continued on his Belfast life. "It was pretty hard at that time," he remarked to Martin.

Van sat looking out the Portobello Hotel lost in his past. "They used to call it poetic license—what happened to that? It's not the real place and no song is...maybe the stuff I was writing later on idealized the situation."

When he reflected on school, Van was specific: "I was learning more on my own, reading outside of school. I don't think they knew what they were doing...."

THE BIOGRAPHER IN THE TRENCHES: DEFINING CREATIVITY

I have been asked why I was so intrigued with Van Morrison's music. I was a fan in the trenches when Van moved to Marin County. I spent a great deal of time at John Goddard's Village Music, as a vinyl record collector. I had just finished a PhD in history. I was busy writing academic books. By 1975 I had turned out the first five of my thirty-five books. As a record collector, I began acquiring bootlegs, articles, handouts from Warner Bros. and anything else on Van.

As I observed Van, I realized the tale of a man from Belfast beating a major label at its own game was a once in a lifetime story. That journey needed to be told from 1973 through 1979. I am telling it in two volumes with almost four hundred thousand words. Too much? No! Not enough! The complicated artist, known as Van Morrison, was going through a careful, almost surgical, defining of his songwriting and performing.

In **A Period Of Transition** one song, "You Gotta Make It Through The World If You Can," explained his 1970s mindset. He was coming off a divorce from Janet Planet and a relationship with Carol Guida. It was his ninth studio album. The songs were a reflection of who he was and how he had gotten to this place in his life. Some say working with Dr. John on this album had more to do with his diminished confidence than his search for a fresh sound. The point was Van needed collaborators to finish his tasks. Van defined his creativity through others as he needed affirmation. When he edited the tapes for the **It's Too Late To Stop Now** album, Carol Guida was by his side. For **A Period Of Transition**, he had Dr. John.

The album wasn't praised. As he worked with Dr. John, AKA Mac Rebennack, there was a renewed vigor in his writing. It seeped over into his production. Van has always been and will always be inspired by unexplainable incidents. Guida leaving him was not a divorce. Her abrupt departure to live for a time in his Fairfax home set his songwriting into a renewed direction.

For the next three years Van went into a hot writing mode with a brief return to the writing magic of the early 1970s.

I went to over one hundred 1970s shows and watched early on as he delivered average, a few bad, and many excellent shows. From 1973 through 1979 I realized he was crafting his stage shows with more precision. In concert, at small clubs, he lost his shy nature, as his inhibitions declined. He became polished on stage while seldom acknowledging the audience. His years of working audiences morphed into a concert brilliance.

He was expanding his writing. That is he examined topics, influences and forces previously alien to his skilled pen. By 1979 **Into The Music** provided insight into what he had learned or how he had developed his craft. One song "You Know What They Are Writing About," explains his craft and reaction to print criticism. The lyrical repetition that is Van Morrison made this a simple song. He wrote songs the critics, the biographers and the fanzines loved. When he answered those who invaded his private life, he did so in song.

This is what he accomplished in Marin County. Carol Guida's influence helped him open up and mature. She listened to him. She gave her opinions. She became his new muse. His life in Fairfax and the San Geronimo Valley, as the divorced progressed, was a positive, therapeutic one. The intellectual influence of Carol Guida, the freedom from business constraints, and his increased intellectual drive made Van a new person.

THE SOPHISTICATED BUSINESS STRUCTURE

He set up a sophisticated business structure. Since 1971, when Caledonia Productions Inc. was founded and based in Sausalito California, it became Morrison's corporate arm. There were more companies to follow. This one was where he dipped his feet into the business quagmire. Leslie I. Weiner was the only employee of Caledonia Productions in 1971. He was acting as his own management. The other employee was George Ivan Morrison. California tax records indicated a taxable return of $140,000 the first year in business. Today the Sausalito based Caledonia Productions is listed by the State of California as "inactive." Van set up an even more sophisticated business structure in the U. K. and Ireland.

Chris Michie: "I admired Van's blue collar work ethic, his organizational planning and his attention to detail. He was only twenty-eight when he established his business base. He was experimenting and refining his brand. This was apparent in shows paying very little. They taught him about the intricate nature of the concert business. When he arrived to play a small club, it was not about the money. It was about perfecting his stage show. At times there wasn't enough money to cover expenses. He ponied up to pay The band. He paid them well. He was learning to control the music business."

The complexity in Morrison's life intrigued me. I got to know Paul Vincent, at KMEL-FM, a popular disc jockey, who shared his thoughts on Morrison's life. That led me in 1983 to publish **Van Morrison: The Mystic's Music**. This was the second biography on Morrison. Ritchie Yorke's was the first. Johnny Rogan's two excellent books, deeply researched and brilliantly written, became the answer to Clinton Heylin's work. Peter Mills covered the songwriting. Eric Hage provided the view of a professor looking into Van's cultural life. Brian Hinton went in-depth in the heart of the art of Van's music. The doyen of Van's biographies remains Clinton Heylin. He put out a marvelous book. It is beautifully written. It is meticulously researched. It has all the knowledge fans needed. What did it lack? The only thing missing was the real Belfast Cowboy. After reading the Clinton Heylin book three times, I realized his vendetta against Morrison was unacceptable. It was a vendetta perpetrated on both sides. I have remained away from the Van Morrison wars. I do talk to the super fans who know more than most biographers. Originally, a three volume biography was in the works. I wrote it. The rough draft was just over a million words. That was acceptable. I had to divide it into a more equitable package. This decision I am blaming on an industry insider, a working musician, a brilliant writer and a staunch critic. His name is Pat Thomas. He is the catalyst to the now six volume biography. If it grows beyond that blame Pat, not me, and if it does it will be a joy to research and write.

When I decided to write a six volume biography it was after the first two volumes were published. This is when Pat Thomas entered my life and, unbeknownst to him, he inspired me to go down rabbit holes and throw in the kitchen sink. Pat's comment was "do not go down rabbit holes, do not throw in the kitchen sink." What role, then, did Thomas play? He was an honest, kick ass critic who never bullshitted me. I can't say that of all my critics.

When I met Pat Thomas, he was a working musician fronting Mushroom, a record producer, a reissue guru, and he is a well-educated writer with an MFA. As a writer he has a vast body of published work in history, ethnic studies and of course music with praiseworthy reviews. Pat's compilation genius, his extraordinary encouragement, his shared writing skills and his knowledge of the record business became a catalyst to four of my Van Morrison volumes. He is aware of everything about Van Morrison. It was his none rock 'n' roll books that initially intrigued me. Thomas' books include, **Listen Whitey: The Sounds of Black Power, 1965 to 1975** and **Did It! From Yippie To Yuppie: An American Revolutionary.** They rekindled by interest in finishing the multi-volume Morrison biography. Then as we talked over the years, he completed books on Ernie Kovacs with the ubiquitous title **Ernie In Kovacsland: Writing, Drawings And Photographs** and Allen Ginsberg, **Material Wealth: Mining The Personal Archive Of Allen Ginsberg**. He also was one of the editors on **Invitation To Openness: The Jazz Photograph Of Les McCann, 1960-1980**.

WHEN MY SECOND VOLUME ON VAN ARRIVED IN 2020, I REALIZED WHAT I HAD MISSED: MARIN COUNTY

In 2020 **Van Morrison: From Astral Weeks To Stardom, 1968-1972** arrived. I decided that was it. I had written three books on Van. It was time to enjoy my retirement. Then I came into contact with Van's fans including Art Siegel, Michael Seltzer, Pat Corley, Bernard McGuinn, Russ Dugoni, Chris Bradford, Simon Gee, Paul Vincent, Ron Sexton, Boom Baker, Jeanette Heinen and dozens of others. I received bootleg CDs. I was sent obscure clippings. I had a manuscript I had written from 2006 to 2011. The length was overwhelming with just over one million words. It covered Van career to 2020, Then I took the remainder of the 1970s and turned the manuscript into two volumes. The third volume **Becoming Van Morrison: It's Too**

Late To Stop Now, 1973-1974 gestated in its final form, after swirling in my head since the 1980s. The companion volume out next year covers the period 1974 through 1979. Why so many words? It was necessary as Marin County created Van's lengthy career. When I broke the last seven years of the 1970s into two volumes there was a quantifiable list of sources, influences, materials, environmental and personal factors influencing the Belfast Cowboy. He rages on about leaving his private life alone and then he covers it during intimate interviews with Leo Green, his ex-wife Michelle Rocca and his conversations on YouTube and social media. The irony is Van grants interviews to the world as he says don't invade my private life. A contradiction? No! It is Van being Van.

This book, which is volume 3, covers 1973-1974, and it attempts to interpret Van in Marin County with the influences of Ramblin' Jack Elliott, and Ronnie Montrose. His muse, Carol Guida, calmed him down until early 1974 and then she was gone. There are still 800,000 plus words in my computer from 1980 to the present. They will arrive. Stay tuned.

A word on the interpretation in this book is necessary. All of the Morrison biographies treat the years in Fairfax and Marin County as a brief interlude. The operative wisdom suggested Van was Irish, Irish, Irish. That is true. What is missing? Plenty! Van had a recording studio a few feet from his Fairfax home. He would call drummer Tony Dey in Sacramento at two in the morning and ask him to be in the studio as soon as possible. Inspiration arrived! Van took advantage of it. The San Francisco Bay Area music venues that Van played perfected the delivery of an at times erratic, unpredictable performer. Maturity on stage was the product.

These years, thanks to the small clubs, the permissive or understanding audiences and the worshipful cooperation of Marin County musicians led to: "Becoming Van Morrison." The business end, with a ukulele playing Sausalito lawyer in charge, emerged to challenge the corporate monoliths threatening Morrison's royalties. The divorce from one muse and the emergence of another sent the Belfast Cowboy's creativity into a refined, intellectual, mature orbit.

Van's morose attitude is a defense of his art. His loneliness has never been addressed. His songs are filled with loneliness. Lost love is a constant theme. Betrayal is the nexus of Van's connection to his writing life. He is pessimistic. He has a sense of solitude. Good humor is foreign to Morrison. That can be temporary. In the next breath he can be a beacon of friendly wisdom. This is a recipe for loneliness. Then the next time you meet Van he can be charming, open, gregarious and entertaining. What "Becoming Van Morrison" suggests is the complexity of the man. It impacts his art. He is brilliant. He is an enigma. This is the key to his success. Why else would Pulitzer Prize winning poets, esteemed authors and select movie producers seek Van's consul? It is his talent. It is his voice. It is his message.

He works alone. He writes alone. He creates alone. He can vanish from one project to the next without explanation. With these limitations why do I continue my biographical journey? There is an answer. It is in Van's life that one sees the limits, the contradictions, the pressures, the rewards and the curse of fame and fortune. The Morrison saga is an insular history of how the music business operates. It is also a story of how those who survive and navigate the entertainment terrain find solace and peace.

Had Van remained washing windows or becoming a veterinarian, he would have had a different life. It was his technique, as a songwriter, that is most important. He is much like a professor in a university painting a picture of life. It is his life in song. It is what the interpreter needs to understand. The six volumes I am writing fulfill that task. Enjoy Van's life. I did!

As Kim Cottrell suggested: "Van's lyrics are so special they cause one to sit up and take notice." Cottrell remarked the "beautiful, poetic" words rush through your soul like a literary hurricane. Cottrell is not alone in the praise for Van's lyrical brilliance. He is a superb writer with surprises in every album. In 2021-2022, the acclaimed black and white movie, "Belfast," featured Morrison's music. The saxophone solos, instrumental breaks and original songs owed their brilliance to Morrison. As Van's voice through the soundtrack the angst and despair of the Troubles brought home the era's heartbreak.

Why did Kenneth Branagh feature so much of Van's music in his nostalgic look at Belfast in the midst of the Troubles? Why, in

1969, did the time period in which the movie is set, emphasize Van's musical connection to Branagh's film? Like Morrison, Branagh's roots were in Belfast. The war between Catholics and Protestants, during the turmoil of the Troubles, was a perfect setting for an in-depth look at Northern Ireland's problems.

Like Greta Garbo, not surprisingly a song Van wrote, he is a contrarian, a mystery, and a virtually unexplainable phenomenon. The Greta Garbo illusion suggests Van's solitude. Later, he sings of disconnecting his telephone. Then he complains of doing business in Los Angeles. As he concluded this song, he talked of being the outside the music business with nowhere to go. When Van writes he feels like "howling at the moon" the angst of being Van Morrison is apparent.

VAN AND THE BARSTOOL BIOGRAPHIES: MARK ISHAM KILLS THOSE STORIES

What is important in this period of Van's life? It is his business. It is his songwriting. It is his performing. It is his continual education. These forces drove his lyrics into unseen dimensions. The problem writing about Van Morrison is he is the product of barstool biographies. Those who complained from a Marin County barstool were unreliable. Those who moved on, after a pleasant experience with Van, had a different biographical tale. One of the most accomplished Morrison co-musical conspirators, Mark Isham, who moved to Marin County where in 1974 he briefly joined the Sons of Champlin, quickly fell into Van's orbit. He was twenty-three years old and as much of a musical genius as Morrison. From 1980-1983 Isham cast a giant influence upon Morrison. From 1974 to 1979 he was a co-conspirator in absentia. Van came to recognize Isham's concert and in studio brilliance. In time the movies came calling for Isham where he has fashioned a legendary presence

Mark Isham had a lengthy interlude with the Belfast Cowboy before heading to Hollywood to write the soundtracks for multi-million dollar blockbuster movies. "For six years I played and arranged for Van Morrison making six records," Isham commented. While in Marin County, he played with the San Francisco and Oakland

Symphonies. He toured constantly with Van. He went from making Van sound great to making movie soundtracks even better.

When Isham talked about connecting with Morrison, he found him easy to work with in the studio. He had the same experience on the concert stage. What was the one word Isham used to describe Morrison? "Precision.

Was working with Morrison a positive? Isham answered that question with a resounding: "Yes." He said it was simple. Van asked for a sound. You played it for him. He was either happy. Or he thanked you. He paid you for your time. He was on to the next audition. Van worked quickly with diligence.

When Isham met with Van they talked about "Troubadours." Van asked Isham if he could improvise a few notes from the Beatles' "Penny Lane." He did! Van was happy. They began working together. As Isham told the story he made it crystal clear, Van was easy to work with. He knew exactly what he wanted. Isham played a trumpet and flugelhorn for Van. Then Morrison asked him if he knew any saxophone players. Isham introduced Pee Wee Ellis to Morrison. "Pee Wee and I became Van's horn section," Isham recalled. Neither recalled Van as difficult.

CAROL GUIDA AND VAN BIOGRAPHIES

As Carol Guida said: "Those who tell stories about Van are not his friends." Van is a songwriter of considerable talent. It is in his lyrics his life explodes with the written word. He has an itch to tell the truth. He provides the biographer with hints to explore his life. He is unique and interesting while living a quiet life. His prodigious output comes from a manic writing schedule emboldened by a voracious reading habit. Bother him! He becomes combative and even more reclusive. Complexity is the key to understanding the Belfast Cowboy.

After almost sixty years of researching his career, I confess I don't understand him. That is the joy of this six volume biography. I am searching for Morrison's Veedon Fleece. It has been one hell of a journey.

To write a proper biography of Van Morrison one must not rely on secondary sources. Interview those close to him. Why? Memory clouds the truth. Interviews years later tend to obfuscate the truth, muddle the facts and provide a forum for grievances. These interviews provide small grains of truth. Combine them and you have a loaf of truth. The small bits of paper Van wrote his song fragments on are lost to history. His thoughts from these bits of paper are not lost. They abound in songs. The people interviewed for this book described Van's literary direction. He remains a memoirist. He explains his life placing it in song context. His intellect! His persona! His joys! His complaints! These factors are the raw material for an in-depth biography. There was no need for written letters, business contracts or public releases from Warner Bros., Van provided a naked view of his life in lyrics. If you examine Van's body of work, he has written the same type of song at least a hundred times explaining his views. For the biographer this is gold.

Remember beauty was born in Van Morrison's lyrics. His muses for "Becoming Van Morrison," at least for this book, were Janet Planet and Carol Guida. They inspired his brilliance. Their caring! Their empathy! Their concern! The forces are buried deeply in his Irish soul. He needed a constant companion to write. Inspiration came from beauty and his surroundings.

Who is the real Van Morrison? His friends say he is mercurial and mystical. When Van emerged as a writer, in the 1970s, he was already a show business veteran. He performed in show bands since he was fifteen. There was nothing banal about Van's writing. He broke new ground with themes of spiritual growth. Morrison's brashness and a tendency to continual reinvent his musical journey made him the poster child for a literary form of rock 'n' roll.

In **Rolling Stone** Jim Miller summed up Van brilliantly: "His vision is hermetic, his energy implosive; yet his vocation is public." This tells it all. Or does it?

ON BIOGRAPHY 3 VAN HAS THE LAST WORD ONCE AGAIN

As this book was ready for publication, Van granted an interview to **The London Times**. He shared his thoughts on his career influences with Will Hodgkinson. With a new album about to arrive the

VAN IN 2023 LOOKING BACK ON THE 1970s (Courtesy Bradley Quinn)

late February 2023 interview said a great deal for the biographer. Van was happy the times, not one of the droll music periodicals or the Fleet Street yellow press, was on hand to interview him.

As Van sat in the lobby of a London Notting Hill Gate hotel, he must have had déjà vu. It was in this neighborhood that he lived with his Them mates beginning his career. He laughed as he recalled: "I would listen to my father's Lead Belly albums and think 'Maybe I can be a folk singer.'" That never happened. Skiffle arrived. Jazz and blues took on a segment of his life in 1960 with the Monarchs. As this interview unfolded the sense of déjà vu hit the **Times** reporter. In March 2023 Van's new album, **Move On Skiffle**, recalled his early days and unwitting influences from Marin County that seeped like breaking ocean waves into this conversation.

Van confessed to the **Times** that his whole life from the 1960s, until he settled in Marin County, was music. He intimated while in his Fairfax home he was finally able to evaluate his life. As Van looked back on Marin County in the 1970s, he smiled as he recalled the power of performing "Caravan" at "The Last Waltz." "Caravan" was in my act at the Maritime Hotel, so I decided to do it," Van continued. "I certainly didn't think anyone would be talking about it 50 years later. In the early days of rock 'n' roll, we thought we would do a couple of years of this and then disappear."

As Van concluded **The London Times** interview, he must have felt good. He didn't have to talk to the acclaimed **Rolling Stone** journalists, he no longer granted interviews to the young music journalists still living with their parents and he was more likely to be profiled by a top level journalist like Fintan O'Toole. The old days were tough but they were gone. He went on to point out he had outgrown interviews with the surreptitious music press. He considers that his greatest achievement.

Bibliographical Sources

Lawrence Ferlinghetti in City Lights Books in 2015 remarked: "Van Morrison's use of language is his forte." Ferlinghetti suggested in some songs Van's words were "bleak but gorgeous." Also, see, a Morrison interview where he discusses his channeling, without mentioning it, and he criticizes Laura Barton's questions. Then he attacks her. Why must he still explain is his complaint. To her credit Barton let Van know her displeasure. She defended her reporting. See, Laura Barton, "A Duel With Van Morrison: Is This A Psychiatric Examination? It Sounds Like One," **London Guardian**, October 31, 2019.

https://www.theguardian.com/music/2019/oct/31/a-duel-with-van-morrison-is-this-a-psychiatric-examination-it-sounds-like-one

See, Steve Turner, **Van Morrison: It's Too Late To Stop Now** (London, 1993) for a Christian author interpreting Van with a beautifully produced coffee table book with memorabilia and prose that is a literary masterpiece. There is also a thoughtful interpretation of how and why Morrison is a seminal figure in the larger picture of rock music. Turner's writing and analysis is in the league of Clinton Heylin and Johnny Rogan without vitriol.

For Van's thirty six examples of "lies" in the Turner bio, see **The London Sunday Times**, July 10, 1994, Dairy-Books, pp. 7-8. Also, see, Martin Wroe "Rock Star Tries To Bring His Unofficial Biographer To Book," **The London Independent**, March 25, 1993, for Turner's response to Morrison. An interview with Art Siegel verified Van's displeasure with the Turner book.

For a reviewer who understood Morrison, see, for example, David Lister, "Profile: Still That Sense Of Wonder: David Lister On The Reclusive Singer-Songwriter Whose Non-Stop Touring Is A Spiritual Quest," **The London Independent**, February 20, 1994. See, Lisa McDonough, "Into The Mystic Soul Of Van Morrison," **The Palm Beach Post**, May 1, 1994, for the comments of Turner and Van concerning the biography.

Stuart Bailie, **75 Songs: Into The Van Morrison Songbook** (Belfast, 2020) is important to understanding why and how Van's songs remain a lasting example of literary bliss. This is a brilliant sleeper book. Bailie offers his analysis of the Morison songs he enjoys. He is a long time music industry critic and reporter. He is also knowledgeable concerning Irish history and how it impacted Van's career.

Peter Mills dissects Morrison's music with the seasoned eye of a professional musician. See, Peter Mills, **Hymns To The Silence: Inside The Words And Music Of Van Morrison** (London, 2010). The Mills volume is not a biography. It is an analysis of the music, the words and Morrison's performances. The purpose, as Mills states, is to demonstrate Van is "the equal of Dylan or Lennon and McCartney." It is a brilliant book. Mills is the architect of how and why Van took rock 'n' roll lyrics into a new creative direction. He does this with a facile pen and the eye of a trained literary critic.

Tony Dey provided insights into Van Morrison in 1975 as his drummer. He allowed me to view the Belfast Cowboy's inner creative soul with tales of various songs. Dey's recounting of Van's early morning phone calls was an important source explaining the period of semi-retirement. These calls prompted Tony to drive from Sacramento to Marin County. This provided a window into Van's working habits.

See, Gavin Martin, "Van Morrison: Dark Knight Of The Soul," **Classic Rock**, December, 2015 for an in-depth interview by Van looking back on his career. With Martin's brilliant questions and a relaxed atmosphere, Van talks about the myths associated with his life. Van gently warns biographers to be aware of the pitfalls analyzing his musical journey. Van went into enormous depth on all aspects of his life, his recordings, his business thoughts, and how and why the media often got it wrong. The interviews, in the decade following the Martin interview, saw Van open up about his past. The biographer had a rare window in his life.

Gavin Martin, who passed away in 2022, at the young age of sixty, was a fan. He didn't like publishing anything negative about Van. Martin was a professional journalist with integrity. The bottom line was he reported accurately and honestly. Van recognized this giving Martin his single best interview.

To understand Morrison see, for example, the Woolhall YouTube interview with Leo Green, "Van Morrison, I Stopped Being An Artist In the 70s, In Conversation, 2007." https://www.youtube.com/watch?v=oCQ4PZQIfLk This was a relaxed interview with Van explaining how the 1970s influenced his songwriting and his perspective on the music industry. This interview, posted on Van Morrison's website, is important. There are also YouTube segments of the interview with Leo Green. The best one is "Van Morrison 'What's The Question?' Part 2." https://www.youtube.com/watch?v=RZZEc95dAXQ is the most revealing. This 13 minutes of reflections on his career, in a no holds barred question period, where Van is comfortable and forthcoming.

For an insight into how Morrison viewed the musical panorama and his past music, see, Ben Greenman, "Van Morrison Discusses How Music Used To Be More Spontaneous And Communal," **The New Yorker**, December 13, 2018. The Greenman article was written to celebrate the release of his recent spate of albums and to look back upon his career.

During this interview, Van spoke at length about Belfast influences. His father's record collection, Ray Charles records, and his love for various forms of music were in the mix. He never mentioned Fairfax. He never mentioned muses. Both of these factors made Van Morrison the man he was at the time of this interview.

Van went into great lengths about American musical influences. He spoke glowingly of the myriad influences from rare 45s, exotic albums and the radio influencing his musical growth. Again no mention of Marin County or the local musical climate. This has caused Van's biographers to ignore the more than decade long influence of this small bucolic area north of San Francisco upon his artistic development.

The problem with a Morrison biography is not the material. His friends, his professional colleagues, his family and his voice form a veritable treasure trove of information. Van is his own archive. He writes with his local environment, his pet peeves, his personal insights into the music, and the result is superior songwriting. In his writing his life comes alive.

Therefore, it is necessary to comb his lyrics for the nooks and crannies of his inner life. He couldn't survive as an artist if he didn't have a different take on songs he has performed hundreds of times. Van's fabulous back up musicians provide the fills allowing him an interpretive depth in showcasing his brilliant songs and vocals. Van's phrasing allows him to cover Frank Sinatra's "That's Life" as easily as Sonny Boy Williamson's "Help Me."

For this chapter phone calls to and breakfast meetings with author, musician, producer and cultural historian Pat Thomas added a great deal to my understanding of Van's music and the process of biography. Numerous conversations with Carol Guida were important and these in-depth interviews added perspective and detail to Marin County's influence. Chris Michie was equally significant by analyzing how and why he believed the Marin County landscape provided the grist, the experiences, the name checking and the inspiration for a dramatic shift in his music by the 1980s. Michie recalled, in half a dozen interviews with me, the spiritual nature of Van's music and life, and these interviews lasted into the late 1990s. Michie was important in suggesting I visit and examine the influence of Allen Ginsberg, Gary Snyder, Allan Watts and Lawrence Ferlinghetti from 1973 through 1974, as their writing infused Van with a writing spirit with quasi-religious overtones. Michie made this observation in 1981 while working with Van in Sausalito for the **Beautiful Vision** album. The best explanation of this phase of Van's career is Clinton Heylin's **Can You Feel The Silence?: Van Morrison, A New Biography** (Chicago, 2002), chapters 21-22 and p. 431, Heylin's brilliant book describes how and why **Common One** was a non-commercial departure. What Heylin fails to point out is Marin County formed the basis of **Common One**. Van spent almost four years of daily discussion with Carol Guida for this new commercial direction. Conversations with Mark Naftalin, Paul Vincent and John Goddard confirmed this conclusion.

The Paul Vincent interview on San Francisco's K-Mel was conducted in their remote studio with no one around. It was reprinted in **BAM-Bay Area Music**. It remains one of the most insightful interviews in rock 'n' roll history. Why? When Van is isolated, the questions are professional. The atmosphere is subdued. Van was at his best. Paul Vincent became personally friendly with Van and together with his then girlfriend, Victoria, he listened to and gave his opinions to Morrison without sharing his celebrity. Vincent was typical of many in the San Francisco Bay Area who befriended Van while keeping the friendship out of the press. A series of in-depth interviews with Vincent further added to his lengthy interview with Morrison.

On the elusive Ulla Munch and Copenhagen, see, for example, Andrew Miller, "How Van The Van Was Once Van of Vanlose," **CPH Post Online**, August 17, 2016 https://cphpost.dk/?p=67254 and Laura Barton, "Hail, Hail, Rock 'n' Roll," **The London Guardian**, March 31, 2011. https://www.theguardian.com/music/2011/mar/31/hail-hail-rock-n-roll The Barton article interpreted "Vanlose Stairway," with a brilliant lyrical touch, suggesting Van's recent intellectual growth. Barton said Van namechecked the Bhagavad Gita, the Bible and Krishna while paying homage to Little Richard, Eddie Cochran and Muddy Waters. She found this lyrically brilliant. If Van read this article he was mystified. When Barton calls "Vanlose Stairway" a "dark horse song," Van's prickly nature erupted. Some years later, he gave her hell in an interview. Van never forgets. When it comes to the press, he is a virulent critic. The Web Sheriff can't cover everything. Van can! For a brilliant look at "Vanlose Stairway" see, for example, Hallgeir Olsen, "Van Morrison's 50 Greatest Songs Countdown-#254 Vanlose Stairway," **Born To Listen.com**, August 24, 2020.

https://borntolisten.com/2020/08/24/van-morrisons-50-greatest-songs-countdown-25-vanlose-stairway/
Bill Janovitz on AllMusic labelled the song one that "offers a glimpse at the soul-the true inspiration of the term soul music."

Molly Fee and Mervyn Solomon helped a great deal with interviews for this chapter. Fee was Van's next door neighbor. Solomon, a wealthy Belfast businessman, helped Van early on his is career with Them. He helped Morrison establish his first blues club and he showed him the way to business success. Phil Solomon added so key information as did his wife Dorothy. Both said they were fond of Van. But he was too difficult for them.

Van's early business success came largely from his association with Mervyn Solomon and Solly Lipsitz. These two Belfast businessman, one an entrepreneur and the other a retail whiz, with a penchant for writing, provided Van with life-long lessons.

For an excellent story on how rock stars react to interviews. How they from time to time get upset, go nuts and confuse the landscape read a Jon Wilde story. He saw Van reading a newspaper in London and walked up to talk to him. Van said: "Fuck off, I am reading the Sunday Times," Van's press agent, Keith Altham, used that brief moment to label Van "deranged" in print. see, Jon Wilde, "Inside Story: Great Rock 'n' Roll Swindles, **London Independent**, August 29, 2005.

https://www.independent.co.uk/news/media/inside-story-great-rock-n-roll-swindles-5347494.html

For Peter Childs' comments on **Hard Nose The Highway**, see Childs, **Van Morrison In The 1970s** (Norwich, 2022), p. 60-72. This is a carefully analyzed book on Van's songs in the 1970s by an academic with a writing flair and a deep understanding of music.

As Van's new album **Moving On Skiffle** was scheduled for a March 10, 2023 release, he sat down for a lengthy interview that was breezy, forthcoming and laced with ironic humor. See Will

Hodgkinson, "Van Morrison: 'I Was At The Bottom. Game Over,'" **The London Times**, February 25, 2023.
https://www.thetimes.co.uk/article/van-morrison-i-was-at-the-bottom-game-over-ccsdjg9td

This interview suggested a joy in Van's words that he had not only survived for more than half a century in the music business, but he no longer had to endure **Rolling Stone** and other music publications that didn't understand his music, his lengthy career and his importance in the industry.

When I went to Belfast to visit where Van grew up, I visited with his neighbor Molly Fee. She was a treasure trove of information over the years prior to her passing. The irony is she was out in the front of her house sweeping and talking with the neighbors on two occasions when I visited Belfast. Her views were much more than on Van's early childhood.

Bill Quarry, a San Francisco Bay Area promoter, who booked Them into a San Leandro Roller Rink, also kept up with Van's career providing important anecdotes. I also talked with Jim Armstrong briefly about Van, and the biographical process with some interesting insights.

When I was doing research for **Van Morrison: The Mystic's Music**, I found the San Francisco Bay Area journalism community open to discussing Van with me. John L. Wasserman and Phil Elwood had the best stories about Van. It was due to them I was able to talk with people inside the Bill Graham Organization. The other person who was important in this scenario was former Paul Butterfield pianist Mark Naftalin who was kind with his time and he filled in many spots in the Morrison biography. As I was finishing this book Carol Guida was unusually helpful concerning how to approach Van's mindset and musical performing life.

FOUR

Warner Brothers And Van: The Good, The Bad And The Ugly

"One of the most powerful tools in the Warner/Reprise strategy was simple patience."

Peter Ames Carlin

"Businessmen, they drink my wine,"

Bob Dylan "All Along The Watchtower"

"I let my artists do my talking for me."

Mo Ostin

"Back in the day Warner Brothers only wanted twenty two minutes a side...."

Van Morrison

WARNER BROS. RECORDS

REPRISE RECORDS

WARNER BROS. RECORDS
VAN
MORRISON
7434
3:02
DOMINO
VAN-JAN MUSIC
WB MUSIC CORP
ASCAP

The subject of Van Morrison and his recording contracts is a tenuous one. The Them contract with the Phil Solomon Organization rankled him. With Bert Berns and Bang Records, Van's contract was owned by mobsters. The management recording deal with Schwaid-Merenstein was his best to date. He came into the Warner Bros. fold expecting something more than he had received from Bert Berns at Bang Records.

Schwaid-Merenstein had control. They were a jazz oriented management-production team. They were musical business pros with a plan for Morrison. They didn't realize he had a plan to free himself from the tentacles of the Warner Bros. corporate structure. Whereas Bert Berns came off like a small time hustler with cigarette breath, Schwaid-Bernstein were cool, conniving, convincing and you would not guess they were mob connected. Van didn't control his commercial destiny until 1973 when **Hard Nose The Highway** was released. He had been under contract for half a decade with Warner Bros. when he figured out what went right and what went wrong in his career.

Hard Nose The Highway was where he had total control. He learned from that experience. Van realized the producer selected the songs. He made the money. He began in 1973 to take control of his career through a double live album **It's Too Late To Stop Now**. Warner was opposed to a double album. "No one that young had taken on a major label," Ray Ruff continued. "Van was the first to make demands, follow up on those requests and convince Warner he would make them more money."

While Warner Bros. was an artist friendly label, the profit margin still mattered. In Marin County Van met, talked with and discussed his royalty situation with a wide variety of music managers, songwriters, industry figures and one hit artists. By 1973 he had a storehouse of knowledge to challenge Warner's edicts.

WHAT WAS VAN WORKING TOWARD IN 1973? THE BEACH BOY CONNECTION, MAYBE! MAYBE NOT!

What was Van working toward in 1973-1974. Plenty! The double live album **It's Too Late To Stop Now** made his point. He taped it. He produced it. He oversaw the final production and release of the album. It was hailed as the best live album to date. He made the point. He was a producer.

He was also tired of Warner Bros. ignoring his vast catalogue of unreleased material. That is one reason he took a few years off. In 1976 at "The Last Waltz," Van's mesmerizing performance brought him back to performing. He realized the silent audience was appreciative of his vocal excellence. He drank in the moment as you could hear a point drop in the cavernous Winterland concert site. That is when he decided to release a new album. That 1977 album, **A Period Of Transition**, arrived with Dr. John as the muse. As always, he needed a muse. The unlikely muse was a piano playing New Orleans hipster with a gravelly voice, a keyboard talent and a production and arranging talent send to none. He was the Hoodoo Voodoo man Dr. John.

At the Last Waltz Van performed two brilliant solos as the crowd sat silently mesmerized. His version of "Tura Lura Lura (An Irish Lullaby)" with The Band's Richard Manuel had the crowd mesmerized. "Caravan" was a fine solo effort. When he joined Bob Dylan and Robbie Robertson, he shared the microphone before an appreciative crowd. He felt the itch to produce an album. Enter Dr. John. They talked. The result was **A Period Of Transition**.

When Van brought in Dr. John, AKA Mac Rebennack, for the 1977 **A Period Of Transition** album, he was looking for new studio musicians. He found them. The studio musicians inspired him as did Dr. John. One song from this album, "You Gotta Make It Through The World" was one Dr. John thought was "listless." Van observed: "It was a survival song." Dr. John viewed it as "a spiritual sound." The mixture of jazz and r and b sounds brought Morrison out of his shell. He was back into the music. He was ready to perform. He was once again reshaping his career. New albums arrived.

In a post in 2021 about Van's **Wavelength** album, Pat Thomas looked back in a discussion from Paul Wexler, son of Atlantic Records Jerry Wexler, stating Van was "artistically lost." This is what I found talking with a wide variety of Morrison's 1970s Marin County friends.

Van was frustrated. Warner's refusal to release some of his recent material irritated him. Paul Wexler took Morrison to the Beach Boy owned Brothers Studio to listen to some tapes. It was a small, one room studio. When it wasn't booked the Beach Boys might show up and record. The ambiance, the equipment, the vibe and the Brothers Studio accessibility pleased Morrison.

Van liked the sound the Brothers Studio emitted for his tapes. He looked for a similar studio. He booked the Manor Studio in the village of Shipton-on-Cherwell in Oxfordshire, England. This would be about the time Van was coming out of his brief retirement. His vision was to make good music as well as great deal of money as an international artist. He realized he needed to move from Marin County. He did that in 1980.

VAN'S EARLY RECORD LABELS AND THE STENCH OF BAD COLOGNE AND CIGAR MANAGEMENT

Van's early record labels, with the exception of those signing and releasing Them material and the abortive Bang Record deal with the King of Bad Cologne, Bert Berns, were ones where the labels were not just unfair to Morrison, the contracts were penury. He had his business dealings under control. Van continued to obsess about the past. He had a long memory. He seldom forgets a slight.

As Van frequently remarked, while with Them, Phil Solomon's management provided barely enough money to pay the rent. A decade later, the images of Solomon's inability to pay a fair wage continued to fester in Van's mind. He intimated this was a dog and pony show to keep the artist in line. He used these past examples when dealing with Warner Bros. and anyone licensing his intellectual property. He continued to protect his intellectual property with the ferocity of a bulldog.

Ivan Little, writing in the **Belfast Telegraph**, concluded "Van Morrison had declared war on Warner Bros. after declaring that this is a not a marvelous night for a **Moondance** re-issue." Surprising? No! Predictable? Yes! Truthful! Who knows!

When Warner Bros. released the **Moondance** box set. Van went ballistic. They owned the rights to it. This was part of the agreement to end the Schwaid-Merenstein deal and to pay Ilene Berns for songs Van included on **Astral Weeks**. It didn't matter. The Belfast Cowboy went to the press making a case he wasn't consulted. Warner spent an inordinate amount of money on the re-issue. Privately, Van told friends he loved the reissue. But complaining over lost royalties continued.

Van's complaint was a solid one. The advertising for the **Moondance** re-issue suggested Van approved of and was involved in the project. He wasn't! That was his point.

The deluxe edition of **Moondance** was superbly packaged. It contained four CDs including bonus tracks and a DVD. The Blue Ray edition featured a remastered version of the original album. The three bonus discs caused collector's, fans, music journalists and rock 'n' roll aficionados to praise the product. It was a magnificent re-release. Van wanted his money. He refused to endorse it. His wife remarked to the **Los Angeles Times**, he was angry he wasn't consulted. Van was a control freak. He was, as Janet Morrison Minto reiterated, "a prickly pear." Let's examine the prickly pear. Van's anger came from Warner Bros. announcing he was re-issuing **Moondance**. It was a corporate gaffe. It was someone in the publicity department making minimum wage who escalated the differences, once again, between Van and Warner Bros.

The press picked up the story. Ivan Little wrote, "...Van Morrison has declared war on Warner Brothers Records...." A lifelong Morrison fan, Little was a reputable journalist and an excellent writer. "I did not endorse this; it is unauthorized and it has happened behind my back." Van continued with a furious tirade. "My management company at the time (Schwaid-Merenstein) gave this music away 42 years ago and now I feel as though it's being stolen from me again." What Van failed to mention is he signed off on the deal to forfeit some of his intellectual property to be released from his Bang

Record Schwaid-Merenstein nightmare. Warner was not the bad guy in this scenario.

Van's criticism of the **Moondance** re-issue came as he was headlining two hundred pound tickets for shows at Belfast's Europa Hotel. It was hard to feel sorry for his loss of control. Janet Morrison Minto posted briefly on the Internet it was time for Van get over it. She pointed out he owned ninety plus percent of his music. None of that was important. What was important was the perception he remained at war with the industry. Maybe! Maybe not! You decide!

THE MYTHS AND REALITIES OF THE RECORD LABELS: TO PAY OR NOT TO PAY, THAT IS THE QUESTION

The music industry was not known for paying its artists fairly. Harry Balk, who produced Del Shannon's million selling debut hit, "Runaway," explained the record labels thinking. "You lost money on most artist. You had to squeeze a few extra nickels out of the hits," Balk commented. Dan Bourgoise, the founder of Bug Music, was the exception to the rule in the music business. He collected royalties. He paid out fairly to the artists. He and Balk were best friends. This juxtaposition tells the observer all they need to know about the record business. Cheating the artist was the norm for the small, independent labels. The exceptions were Lew Chudd at Imperial and Bob Keene at Del-Fi.

The duplicity of the major labels was hidden behind a smoke screen of lawyerese. The one sided contracts favoring the labels, excessive production costs, public relations coups and hidden advertising costs were ignored by young rockers. Payola was no longer the norm. The record labels could still get hype and promotion using their advertising budget. Just ask **Rolling Stone**. As the 1970s rock scene exploded marketing and promotion took on many shapes and forms. The major newspapers, the **New York Times** or the **Los Angeles Times**, began covering the rock scene. The explosion of small fanzines, new specialty rock magazines like **Creem**, **Goldmine**, **Discoveries, Blue Suede News**, **Rock 'N' Blues News** and **Record Profile Magazine** among other amped up sales. In the U. K. **Melody Maker**, the **New Musical Express** and **Disc** were major music magazines. Warner Bros. cultivated, advertised and shipped albums to these outlets. The carefully crafted advertising made Morrison and other artists instant best sellers.

Record stores were another Warner Bros. stroke of genius. In the 1970s Tower Records received one hundred and eighty day credit. Russ Solomon, who founded Tower, said, "I was selling records on consignment. It was a sweet deal." It was the new payola.

Van's complaints about getting paid are legendary. In song he continues to show his disgust with the record companies. In songs like "Professional Jealousy" and "They Sold Me Out," he is on a tirade, years after Warner Bros., screaming about label mistreatment.

Van wasn't alone challenging the industry. The Beatles and **Rolling Stone**s formed their own labels. The Who escaped Shel Talmy's clutches. Van simply funded his recordings and leased them to various labels. Eric Clapton fought for his royalties as early as when he was a member of John Mayall's Bluesbreakers. When Led Zeppelin organized the Swan Song label in 1974, they were doing the same thing Van was at the same time. Van wasn't alone challenging the industry.

By recreating **Astral Weeks**, Van made it clear he was protesting lost royalties while collecting money he saw as his when he was unable to tour behind his legendary album. One of the enduring cries from Morrison, throughout his career, has been getting paid. He has! Often with difficult feelings!

RECREATING ASTRAL WEEKS AND THE FALL OUT

In 2008, when he went on stage to recreate the **Astral Weeks** album in Los Angeles, Van gave a number of interviews about long lost royalties. He was critical of the original Warner Bros. release. Of Warner's efforts to promote **Astral Weeks**, Van said: "It received no promotion, from Warner Bros.—that's why I never got to play it live. I had always wanted to play the record live and fully orchestrated—that is what this is all about. I always liked live recording and I like listening to live records too. I am not too fond of being in a studio. It's too contrived and too confining. I like the freedom of live, in-the-moment sound."

During this time Van was producing a co-directed documentary with Darren Doane in which the filmmaker stated: "It's his film. And the film is about exposing and tearing down all the myths about Van Morrison and the music industry as a whole." Doane was a useful sycophant. As a filmmaker we are still waiting for the final product. No word yet!

In **Irish Central**, Meghan Sweeney observed: "Even this move to revive 'Astral Weeks' could be looked at as a middle finger-laden complaint directed at his old record label. Van feels that Warner Bros. neglected it (**Astral Weeks**) the first time around." Sweeney had other complaints. She could only get one ticket to the Atlantic City Show. "I couldn't even get the live album to review." So maybe Van was pointing a middle finger at her. Then Sweeney went nuts in her article. She complained about the $350 ticket price. "In these tough times, you might want to take in a show by the Cowfast Bellboys, a Van Morrison tribute band from Minneapolis that lends a modern rock stamp on Van's Celtic soul classics."

Things went from bad to worse. Sweeney complained Exile Productions had guidelines for media passes. She didn't meet the requirements. The real reason for her nasty review surfaced. She didn't receive free tickets. The Van Morrison tribute band had to change its website domain name as Exile Productions told them Van owned it. The Web Sheriff was hard at work protecting Van's intellectual property. What in the hell is a reviewer for **Irish Central** doing fighting with Van's management? There needs to be an adult in the room.

THE SEEDS OF MISTRUST: FIGHTING THE CORPORATE MENTALITY

Van remarked the genesis of his hostility to Warner Bros. was not personal. He had a reasoned, often truncated, view of the industry. The labels were born to cheat in Morrison's view.

When Morrison signed with Warner Bros., it looked like the perfect deal. Warner management eagerly sought out singer-songwriters. Warner promised complete artistic freedom. The selection of material was a dream come true for Van. The label treated its artists equitably. They paid a fair royalty. The honest businessmen who were replacing the gangsters proved to be just as ruthless as the gangsters. It was all about the profit margin.

Van lashed out from time to time at Warner's corporate mentality. This impeded his progress with the label. He refused to allow a major label to manipulate his product. Clinton Heylin misrepresented Van's approach to the music business. "It finally dawned on Morrison," Clinton wrote, "how much his lackadaisical attitude to the business end of things had cost him." He was never lackadaisical. He mastered the industry. Heylin's comment obscured Van's complaints about contracts, working conditions and the co-mingling of his intellectual property.

BOB KRASNOW: CAROL GUIDA SAYS HE WAS VAN'S FAVORITE

Van seldom remarked positively about Warner Bros. He did have his favorites. One who receives little, if any, mention, is Bob Krasnow. While at Warner Bros., Krasnow was a 24/7 whirlwind of promotion, planning and finding new talent. He was a Morrison aficionado who argued to Mo Ostin and Joe Smith to give Van more latitude in the studio, leave him alone, and to allow him to produce his material.

What was it about Van that appealed to Krasnow? He went into Mo Ostin's office one day suggesting Van was a black act. Ostin looked at him like he was nuts. Krasnow had been listening to some Van outtakes, demos and unreleased material. He told Ostin they were leaving the best of the Belfast Cowboy's music in the can. Ostin demurred.

Krasnow's short-lived soul label, Loma, was a Warner Bros. imprint. He produced Captain Beefheart's 1967 **Safe As Milk** album. Then he started Blue Thumb Records. He worked with Ike and Tina Turner and then he sold Blue Thumb Records. He came to Warner in 1974 in the midst of Van's **Too Late To Stop Now** album.

What did Morrison value about Krasnow? Carol Guida said: "Krasnow was Van's favorite at Warner." Who was this guy?

Like Van, Krasnow was a high school dropout. He was a self-made record man. When he joined Warner as a Vice President for Talent in 1974, he swung open the doors to some of Warner's premier acts. He was promoted to head Elektra/Asylum/Nonesuch records labels in 1983.

From the time he met Van they bonded in conversation about black music. Krasnow was also known for screaming; "Fuck the industry." Van loved his irreverence. Krasnow told Van he followed a "small but beautiful philosophy" when it came to a record label. He believed in developing talent and nurturing the artist over decades. Van loved that notion. Krasnow was a jazz-soul guy. This was another one of many strengths Van found appealing. Krasnow was a behind the scenes influence promoting Van's music.

DOMINO DEFINES VAN'S PROMOTIONAL GENIUS

When he recorded "Domino," Van's tactics toward Warner Bros. changed. He realized it was a hit. He didn't initially want to release it. That was a ploy. Van wanted more promotional money. He got it. The song charted. "Van was smart as hell when he wanted something," Ray Ruff said. When Joe Smith talked with Van about "Domino," he sensed Van's hard-nosed edge. Van insisted on releasing "Domino" as a single. Some at the label disagreed. Once again Mo Ostin and Joe Smith realized Morrison's genius. With added promotion "Domino" charted at nine on the **Billboard** and on the **Cash Box** Top 100. There was good news and bad news from "Domino." "Van believed the labels could manipulate a hit," Chris Michie continued. "He never varied from that opinion." That made him impossible to deal with when planning promotion. A decade and a half later Warner failed to renew Morrison's contract. He was simply too difficult. As Janet Planet observed he was "a prickly pear."

When he told Tom Kielbania he didn't want to release "Domino" because Warner would make the money, the guitarist was baffled. Graham Blackburn, who was one of Van's staunchest defenders, warned him Warner Bros. would not put up with his attitude. The "Domino" story was typical of Van. He would change his mind without warning.

"Domino" was written several years before its release as single. It was a centerpiece on the **His Band And Street Choir** album. It was a tribute to Fats Domino. When it reached nine on the **Billboard** Singles Chart it became Van's highest charting 45.

MERENSTEIN IS A JAZZ GUY

Lewis Merenstein was a jazz guy. He wanted Van to remain in an **Astral Weeks** mode. Some say the hit records came when Van decided to go as commercial as possible. "Lewis kind of got pushed off the album as **Moondance** went forward," Jef Labes told Clinton Heylin. That wasn't the case. Merenstein was tired of Van. It was time to move on.

When Lewis Merenstein was interviewed, in 2009, by Ryan Walsh, he gave his version of the **Astral Weeks** album. From that lengthy discussion one can see how and why Van learned to deal with Warner Bros. It was Merenstein's careful approach to production, his precise dealings with the label, and his decades of experience that helped Van learn the ins and outs of the business. Merenstein died, seven years after the Walsh interview, Van posted praise for and material on the producer on his website. Van paid tribute to Merenstein. The real story emerged. That story is one where Merenstein allowed Van total studio freedom. He did so for a portion of his early royalties.

Merenstein was an important influence in molding Morrison's career. He was a quiet, reflective person avoiding the media until just a few years before his death. It was in an interview with Ryan H. Walsh that Merenstein made a case for his role in **Astral Weeks**.

WHAT WAS THE REAL LEWIS MERENSTEIN STORY?

The good guy in the early Van Morrison story was Lewis Merenstein. That was the opinion of Ray Ruff. He summed up Merenstein perfectly: "He didn't give a shit about anything but jazz." Others told me when **Astral Weeks** was completed, Merenstein realized he produced a legendary album. Merenstein and Morrison fit like a glove in the studio.

When Merenstein sat in the Warner Bros. offices listening to Van's demos, he contacted jazz bassist Richard Davis. That was the first step in the making of **Astral Weeks**. Then came Connie Kay, Jay Berliner and Warren Smith. They completed the jazz musicians behind Van. The rest was history.

In 2009, Merenstein sat down with Ryan H. Walsh for an in-depth interview. This wasn't surprising. Van was touring with a re-created **Astral Weeks** show. Before he teamed up with Van, Merenstein produced rock, as well as jazz acts. The press described Merenstein solely as a jazz producer. He was more than that. He had completed projects with Miriam Makeba, Gladys Knight and the Pips and a host of other rock acts.

As Merenstein talked with Walsh, he said he selected the songs for **Astral Weeks**. "We'd sit and have dinner together...we'd talk a lot. He had no idea what was going on. He basically didn't have a clue." Why is this quote important? Van put it up on his official website. That tells one all they need to know about his appreciation for Merenstein.

"I heard the lyrics and knew what to do in my mind," Merenstein continued. "I just-not to sound too metaphysical about it, but there was no way of avoiding it." What did Merenstein mean? "I believe that's true of anything that's timeless," Merenstein concluded in his memoir fifty years later. The producer saw the legendary aspects of **Astral Weeks**.

Merenstein told Ryan Walsh it was impossible to recreate **Astral Weeks**. It was a spur of the moment genius. It could not be repeated. "The funniest thing was that Warner Brothers, when they first heard it, didn't know what to make of it." Merenstein reflected only Joe Smith knew what to do with the album. This is one reason it languished for a few years in the cut out bins of local record stores. It is also the reason the angry Van Morrison came to the fore.

Then along came Ben Fong Torres and Greil Marcus writing for a fledgling magazine **Rolling Stone**. They rescued Van. Fong Torres labelled **Astral Weeks** "the album of the year." He was the only one. The rock critics for the fanzines and emerging publications, like **Creem**, faintly praised Morrison and the album. Marcus reviewed his early San Francisco shows. He made comments indicating Van's emerging stardom was a foregone conclusion.

Before he left Morrison, Merenstein produced a portion of **Moondance**. The album and the song hit the charts. Merenstein said Van's first two Warner Bros. albums were never duplicated. "There was a poet that was loose there," Merenstein continued. "It poured out." A sage comment. Merenstein had a point.

As to his personal feelings about Morrison, Merenstein reflected: "Van has never worked for anybody for very long. Van is a very 'I' person. 'I' wrote it. 'I' produced. 'I' sang on it."

When Mary Martin came into the picture, the nightmare began for Merenstein. He wanted out. He couldn't stand Martin. He labelled her a "musically ignorant bully." Her pedigree was that of the old time managers. She had a whiff of Col. Tom Parker. Most people in the industry went running. When Janet Planet told the **Los Angeles Times** Van was having trouble securing management. She didn't mention Martin. One of Janet's friends told me she still had nightmares of being around Martin. Van learned how to deal with the labels from Martin then he fired her.

Van demanded changes in his publishing distribution deal with Warner Bros. Mary Martin stepped in and threatened Warner Bros. stating the **Moondance** album would not be released if they didn't agree to Van's demands. Tired of Van's antics and Martin's bullying, Schwaid and Merenstein took a buyout offer. Later, they acknowledged it was a mammoth mistake.

"I wasn't sure what the hell was going on," Ray Ruff continued. "What I did know is Mary Martin was a tyrant. I thought Van had too many advisers. He realized that and hired people I called toads. They would do what Van wanted."

When **Moondance** was released, Merenstein was credited as executive producer. Van set up a publishing company. The road to protecting his intellectual property began. Once Schwaid-Merenstein ended their business partnership, Van was in control. Now it was time to ferret out back royalties. He did. He sent his lawyers into the Bang catalogue. He sued Ilene Berns. She had an ironclad contract. She won the suit. Warner Bros. had to pay her for Bang material they released on **Astral Weeks**. Van was still learning the business.

RAY RUFF, VAN AND WARNER BROS.

Ray Ruff, who spent a great deal of time at Warner Bros., recalled Van's single minded determination. "He was so fixated on his creativity and battling the label moguls he wouldn't even say hello to you in the elevator or hallway," Ruff said. He was perplexed by Van. He booked Morrison and the group, Them, into the Whiskey A Go Go in 1966. "Van either ignored me or forgot what I did," Ruff concluded. He was mystified by Van's behavior.

Others tell a different story. They claim that Van was not allowed to release singles or 45s of his liking. He was pressured to record other people's material. He refused. Van was an original and wanted no part in promoting other artist's works under his own trademark. He was bombarded with requests to go out on the road and tour. Van understood the business value of live performances and public appearances. He found these requests were acceptable. He was writing. He was producing new material. Van seldom bent to some of these external pressures. He was determined to do it his way.

Van talked about writing songs reflecting his mindset. He yearned to discover the real things in his life. It was from the fragments of his life that he took his songs into a mystical vein. He was among the best rock 'n' roll songwriters. He reconstructed his life experiences and surroundings into song.

MO OSTIN WALKS IN THE ROOM SETTING THE TONE

Mo Ostin walked into a meeting of Warner Bros. producers. He smiled. "Let's stop trying to make hit records," Ostin said. There was dead silence. The producers looked startled. What the hell was going on? Welcome to the new Warner Bros. Ostin made it clear albums, not 45s, were the wave of the future. He held up a newspaper. No one had heard of it. It was the **Los Angeles Free Press**. There was a stone cold silence. Someone mentioned it was a politically left publication with little or no interest in rock music. Ostin screamed: "Wrong! We will change that." The counterculture, he said, needed to be educated on the new music. Advertising dollars flowed to the

Mo Ostin With Dean Martin, Frank Sinatra and Sammy Davis, Jr. (Courtesy Author's collection)

counterculture press. Favorable reviews of Warner albums followed. The hippie media was in bed with the labels.

Ostin's point was the alternative press was a new window for record sales. With advertising and access to Warner artists, the small counterculture weeklies were in a position to influence musical tastes. When the **LA Free Press** was founded in 1964, Warner Bros. was in the process of redefining its approach to rock music.

There were also business changes. In October 1967, Warner Bros records was sold to Seven Artists Productions. creating Warner Bros. Seven Arts. Then they purchased Ahmet Ertegun's Atlantic Records. Suddenly Ray Charles, Aretha Franklin, Otis Redding, Wilson Pickett and Sam & Dave were in the Warner catalogue.

Fledgling artists vied to sign with Warner. Ostin brought acts along slowly. "You didn't need a hit if you had talent," Ostin said. This was his motto. "Everyone believed they had talent." Ostin continued talking to Ray Ruff. "We nurtured that talent for the marketplace. It takes time." Ostin was not enamored with the Tiny Tim's or the Mrs. Miller's. He wanted them gone. When Tiny Tim's first three albums came out on Reprise Records, Ostin was critical of these

Mo Ostin on a Los Angeles billboard

money makers. Ostin sent Capitol Record producer, Lex De Azevedo a note, remarking of Mrs. Miller's album: "How could you?" Over the years Ostin defended rock 'n' roll to Frank Sinatra.

MO OSTIN: FOLLOW THE ARTIST

Some years later, looking back on the 1970s, Ostin recalled: "My feeling was always follow the artist, follow the music. It will lead you to the money." It did! Before Ostin the Warner Bros. roster featured Dean Martin and Allan Sherman. That changed quickly. The youthful prodigies arrived.

The prodigies, Van Dyke Parks and Randy Newman, didn't produce hits. They had a contract guaranteeing the release of a number of albums. Not 45s like the other labels. But long playing albums with a dozen songs. Ostin wanted to embrace the creativity of new, young artists. The old ways of doing business were out the window. This was Ostin's plan, as he assumed the Warner Bros. presidency. When Ostin looked back on his time with Morrison his greatest regret was losing him. In a 1994 interview, with the **Los Angeles Times**, Ostin lamented Warner's financial difficulties. He intimated they gave up on Van because they didn't believe they could meet his fiscal demands. Was that story true? Probably not! At least according to Ray Ruff the decline of sales at Warner Bros., the interference of the other corporate arms in the profit-loss reviews, and the change in music preferences were other factors. Years later, Warner executives said, it was a mistake not to ink a new contract with Morrison in the mid-1980s.

Mo Ostin: "I loved his music, but I just couldn't renew the deal after looking at his sales...you could have no input with the guy at all." This clouded Ostin's view of Warner's future with the Belfast Cowboy. Ostin continued: "He was as difficult as anyone I ever dealt with. He would explode on stage or in your office, having dinner at the house, I remember we almost came to blows because he kept insisting that I guarantee him a number one hit...I kept saying 'Van, who can guarantee you a hit?'"

An examination of Ostin's life and career suggests his importance to the general history of rock music. It is a window into a corporate executive who treated Van well. He did everything he could to further his career. That was to a point. That point was a restructuring of the Warner roster. Ostin may not have had the clout by then to re-sign Morrison. No one has addressed this issue.

WHO WAS MO OSTIN?

Mo Ostin studied economics at UCLA. He graduated in 1951. In the mid-1950s, at twenty-eight, he went to work for Norman Granz's Clef Records. Then Frank Sinatra hired Ostin to head Reprise Records. Then a merger with Warner Bros. took place. In 1963, when Reprise became a part of the Warner stable, the task of taking a label with little success to the next level became Ostin's. Sinatra told Ostin Reprise had a rock singer, Trini Lopez. The education of Sinatra and Warner's out of touch executives began by Ostin when he told Sinatra Lopez was a Latino folk singer. "Don't worry Frank, I went to see the guy at P. J.'s, we'll do a live album." Warner did and this 1963 album, released on Reprise Records, rose to number 2 and remained on the **Billboard** charts for a year. The single "If I Had A Hammer" was Lopez's first hit. When Reprise presented Lopez with a check, Sinatra drove him to Palm Springs.

Mo Ostin at work

He took Trini out to see some homes and with his first royalty check he purchased a home in 1964. This 1961 vintage home at 1139 Abrigo Road sold after Lopez's death for two million ninety thousand dollars. Someone got paid at Warner/Reprise. Shortly after the Beatles arrived, Sinatra changed his mind about rock 'n' roll. It was due to Ostin who convinced Sinatra rock 'n' roll was a goldmine.

When Ostin convinced Sinatra and the corporate management to sing rock acts, he inked the Kinks. For the next thirty-two years, Ostin's brilliant stewardship made Warner Bros. the dream label. Ostin signed Jimi Hendrix after seeing him perform at the Monterey Pop Festival. He brought in lawyers to redefine the corporate structure. Ostin established the Warner Corporation, as the industries major rock label by the late 1960s. Van Morrison observed his every business move. He learned from each one. Ostin was an important father figure for Van.

When Van was in Los Angeles, Mo had him over to the house for dinner. That was when the label head explained his philosophy. To this day no knows what they discussed. What is known is Morrison's business acumen blossomed.

Ostin said Warner nurtured artists regardless of sales. He began a production technique at Warner from 1967 to 1994 that made it not only an artist friendly label, but the commercially most successful one. This benefitted Van Morrison whose debut album, **Astral Weeks**, was a critics favorite but a commercial disaster. In time, it would be one of the most acclaimed albums in rock music history and a certified million seller.

Ostin guided Van through the early 1970s, where his career was built on a solid and lasting foundation. Were they close friends? No! Did Van learn from Ostin? Yes! What made Ostin special? He told the **New York Times** that artists needed time, space and nurturing to fulfill their promise. That quote, taken directly from his interaction with Van, tells one all they need to know about Morrison's genius.

THE EARLIER CASE I MADE AGAINST MO OSTIN: WHY WAS I WRONG?

In my 2020 book, **Van Morrison: From Astral Weeks To Stardom, 1968-1972**, I was adamant Mo Ostin and Warner Bros. treated Van Morrison inequitably. Why did I make that judgement? It was based on Warner Bros. slowly paying Van's royalties and withholding, while allocating some royalties to other places. I didn't realize until I was allowed a look at the inner workings of Warner Bros. that all royalties were paid. Stan Cornyn made a case Van didn't understand miscellaneous or legitimate business expenses. That didn't take away from his art. It made him, as Cornyn told me: "difficult to deal with on all levels." To this day Van remains angry at Warner over royalties. It appears he has no case. That was Cornyn's viewpoint. Then again!

Royalties were withheld from Van because a substantial sum was paid to Ilene Berns and Bang Records. Why? Van used two songs on **Astral Weeks** that Bang Records had under copyright. Ostin, or someone at Warner, taught Van a business lesson paying Ilene with Van's royalties.

After talking with Stan Cornyn and others who were gone, I was shown some letters and documents regarding Warner and corporate policy on charges to recording contracts. I was wrong. So here is the real story in the next paragraph.

When Van was charged for storage of demos and unreleased material, which was a standard industry practice, he complained bitterly. I ignored those at Warner Bros. who told me Van didn't understand the corporate structure. The assignment of an inexperienced house producer, Ted Templeman, to work with Van on his early records was considered a form of punishment.

What I didn't realize in my 2020 book, **Van Morrison: From Astral Weeks To Stardom, 1968-1972** was on some business matters Mo Ostin quietly played hard ball. The corporate structure demanded profit. Ostin gave it to them. Van demurred. In time, Van recognized Ostin's corporate genius. By 1979 Van had a business conglomerate running like a smooth corporate machine. It was thanks to Ostin.

THE RELATIONSHIP BETWEEN VAN AND WARNER BROS.

The relationship between Van Morrison and Warner Brothers was at times a war. There were periods when a truce emerged. It was a relationship lasting for decades fraught with difficulty. When an eventual divorce took place in the 1980s, Van moved on to other labels. The Warner Bros. years were important in "Becoming Van Morrison." Warner was a school for Van's songwriting, recording and management skills.

By 1973, Van was determined to alter his relationship with his label of half a decade. He wanted autonomy in the studio.

Van Morrison

The Warner Bros. public relations department began assigning people to work with him. "That didn't go well," Ray Ruff continued. "Van didn't understand the label lost money on many artists. The operative wisdom was these costs filtered down to those artists making money. Warner charged these acts 'incidental' expenses. That drove Van crazy."

When Warner prepared its advertising campaign for **A Period Of Transition**, a poster showing Van sitting at a table in a blue leisure suit was sent out to record stores, disc jockeys, key industry people

Van Morrison, Capital Theater, Port Chester, Ny

and reviewers. Special promotional 45s were mailed to radio stations. As early 1970 Warner teamed Van with the Kinks for a promotional 45 for disc jockeys only. This highly collectible 45 featured a radio spot for the Kinks album **Lola Versus Powerman And the Moneygoround** with the b-side Morrison's "Domino." A voice over repeated the phrase that Van's album **His Band And Street Choir** was his best work to date. Stan Cornyn told Van the public relations machine never stopped working for him. Van wasn't so sure.

The problems Van had with Warner resulted from their attempts to pigeon hole his music. At least that is how he perceived it. Why? Van didn't always have complete song control. He was uncomfortable with comments about his lyrics. His view was the artist was the creator. The label the facilitator to the public. He never understood Mo Ostin, Joe Smith, Lewis Merenstein, Lenny Waronker and even the kid in the studio, Ted Templeman who was three years older than Van. They all had production ideas. That escaped Morrison. Van was, at times, difficult in the studio. Warner gave up. Templeman was more a minder than a producer.

How did Warner perceive him? Initially, some at Warner, viewed Van as no more than a folk singer. They repeatedly told him he was a cult artist. When Van claims he is not a rock artist maybe it is tongue in cheek criticizing Warner.

Ostin and Joe Smith envisioned him primarily as a singer-songwriter. Other executives told me Warner wanted Van to write songs not sing them. How was Van treated? Warner Bros. treated him very well. From day one Van had complaints and concerns about Warner's commitment. Publicity, public relations, marketing and Warner's feel for the market seldom satisfied him.

There were a small number of Warner executives who envisioned a long term future for Morrison. The problem was his penchant for writing non-commercial songs, his interest in jazz, and his infatuation with country music. Van's early demands for an instrumental album bothered Warner. Ostin, Smith and Lenny Waronker loved his musical breadth. Others, like Stan Cornyn, believed there was too much drama with Morrison. Cornyn argued Van's references to William Blake, and other literary figures, was not a recipe for hits. When Van talked about an instrumental album, Cornyn dissented.

When he heard "Boffyflow and Spike," he loved the Celtic flair. Commercially, he told Van, the song was a disaster. Van ignored him.

Cornyn told Van to stop playing games. He told him to write hits. That may have been the straw that broke the camel's back. For **A Period Of Transition**, Van did everything he could to avoid the hits. He was into name checking. He loved to display his newly enriched intellect. Greil Marcus, who normally praised Van, wrote, of the album, in **Rolling Stone** "a lot of neo R and B huffing and puffing." Marcus continued: "Morrison's performances rarely find a focus, almost never hit a groove...." That is exactly what Van was working on. Continuity in concert with a free song selection. Stan Cornyn loved Van. He thought there was a hint of pomposity. He displayed a bit of career destruction. His attitude was self-centered. His contrarian behavior was over the top. Corny loved Van for all these reasons. Great artist, he observed, often were flawed human beings.

Those inside Warner who were critical of Morrison's name checking artists like the French poet Arthur Rimbaud. They argued Van lacked a continuous commercial instinct. "Tore Down A La Rimbaud" was not a song about the poet. It was a literary illusion. Van began this trend in the late 1980s. He read and wrote furtively. His words evolved into a precocious literary vein. It was off to a new version of the creative races for Van.

When Van talked with Warner executives about "Tore Down A La Rimbaud," he confessed it took years to write. Since the mid-1970s, during his sabbatical from the industry, he wrote and re-wrote the song. The Warner Bros. brain trust wanted songs written quickly with a pop flair. That was no longer Van Morrison. The change in his writing style, his reading, his approach to his craft, and his life, came when Carol Guida became his fiancée. She was as much a literary guide as a songwriting guru.

LENNY WARONKER: THE GENIUS WHO SAW THE FUTURE OF ROCK 'N' ROLL

Lenny Waronker came into a top management position as Van was about to leave Warner. That was unfortunate. Had Morrison remained one can only assume he would have broken new fertile ground.

Waronker was the industry figure who heard Van Dyke Parks, **Song Cycle** and signed Parks to a lucrative Warner Bros. contract. He could care less whether or not Parks had hits. It was about the songwriting, the music, the production and the eventual product. The hits would come. If they didn't, Waronker said: "Fuck it."

He went on to work with Jimi Hendrix, Ricki Lee Jones, Joni Mitchell, Ry Cooder, Neil Young and James Taylor. Waronker was a strong supporter of Van's creativity before he headed the label. In the 1960s and 1970s, Waronker was one of the architects of the artist friendly environment making Warner the industry leader as Morrison's first decade unfolded with the label.

Van Dyke Parks was the first Van Morrison. The difference is Van went on to sell millions of records, while Parks remained a cult figure. His fame largely rests on working with Beach Boy Brian Wilson. When the classically trained twenty-four year old was signed to a lucrative Warner contract in 1967, he appeared to be rock 'n' roll's artistic-literary future. Without Parks, Warner might not have signed Van Morrison.

When Warner Bros. signed Van, they were rebuilding their roster. They were, as Stan Cornyn said, "in it for the music." Mo Ostin, the brains behind the label, worked well with artists with massive egos, who made impossible demands, and had unrealistic expectations. Ostin envisioned future musical trends like no one in the business.

When Lenny Waronker went to work for Warner in 1966, he was a low level A & R employee. "It was always about the artist," Waronker reflected. From day one at Warner, Waronker was committed to the singer-songwriter persona. He said: "Music, not money, was still number one." He became President of Warner Bros. He has never fully articulated his feelings about Van Morrison with the label.

Lenny Waronker was a label head with a unique pedigree. His father was a classical violinist. He performed with the 20th Century Fox Orchestra. Then later with Lionel Newman. He grew up in a privileged home. But, from day one, Waronker had a strong work ethic. He loved music. He loved the industry.

While in school he worked at Liberty Records. He assisted Snuff Garrett at Liberty. He was a producer with a golden touch. In production, Waronker was a quick learner. Soon he was experimenting in the studio and learning the ins and outs of the music business. In 1988, after Waronker took over at Warner, the label had its most profitable year. Waronker came late, but he had an incredible ear for hit records.

The road to Warner Bros. began when Waronker produced demos. Mo Ostin listened to the demos. He hired Waronker. This began his path to the label's presidency.

What did Waronker have to do with Morrison's career? He was president of the label when Van signed elsewhere. Those at Warner Bros., in a number of interviews, said Waronker loved Van's music. His personal contact with the Belfast Cowboy was minimal. But, like Ostin, in retrospect, he believed it was a mistake not to meet Van's contract demands.

While at Warner, Waronker had perspective. He said if they produced good records some would be hits, some would not. Accept it! It was the business. "It's always about the artist's work," Waronker continued. "Let's do something that's real, that really is meaningful."

After serving as Warner's president, Waronker left the label in 1995 with no regrets. He was instrumental in an artist friendly label making hits less significant than his counterparts at other major labels.

JOE SMITH: VAN'S PROTECTOR AND PROMOTER

Joe Smith was important in Van Morrison's Warner Bros. successes. He signed him by going into a Brooklyn garage to give mobsters $20,000 in cash in a brown bag. This ended the Bert Berns-Bang Record connection. Smith's pedigree was outstanding. He grew up near Boston. He attended Yale University. During his freshman year he shared a room with future conservative columnist William F. Buckley. Smith worked on Yale radio. After graduation he thumbed his nose at law school. He ignored multiple Wall Street job offers. He was a jazz aficionado. He was a rock and roll guy. He was intrigued by the music. Smith went to work for a paltry salary for a jazz label. He was consumed with radio.

To the horror of his parents, his classmates and the business community, who came calling, Smith went to work as a disc jockey. By the mid-1950s he was Boston's most recognized Top 40 disc jockey. On Beantown's WMEX, he was a celebrity. Then the roof fell in. Smith was accused of, and he was allegedly guilty of, accepting money to play certain records. This was an accepted norm in the record business until the 1960 payola scandal. Payola wasn't a crime at the time. Smith lost his job.

He packed up and moved to Los Angeles. In October, 1961, Warner Bros. hired him to manage the promotion department. He single handedly turned Peter, Paul and Mary into a top ten hit act. He loaded Peter, Paul and Mary into a station wagon and toured college campuses. In 1961 they played Western Washington State University in Bellingham to a sold out crowd. After the show Smith had them set up downtown at Shakey's Pizza Parlor to play before a hundred drunken college students eating pizza on ten cent beer night. He hawked records for a dollar, from his van, to interested students. This was only one example of his promotional genius. By October 28, 1961, Peter, Paul and Mary's album was number one on **Billboard**. Joe Smith made his bones. He was a label executive who understood how to succeed in the record business.

By 1964 Smith began examining San Francisco's diverse musical acts. He realized there was a bevy of undiscovered talent in the Bay Area. There was a small record label, Autumn, operated by two disc jockeys, Tom Donahue and Bob Mitchell. They had a staff producer, and A & R man, who was a part time performer. His name was Sylvester Stewart. He quickly changed it to Sly Stone. His talent emerged. Another singer-songwriter, Bobby Freeman, had national hits with "Do You Wanna Dance" and "The Swim." The Beau Brummels took a cue from the Beatles adopting their haircut and clothes and "Laugh Laugh" and "Just A Little Bit" were **Billboard** Top 20 chart busters. The money rolled into Autumn Records. But Donahue and Mitchell were drink, drug and ladies men with little business expertise. In time, Joe Smith and Warner owned the Autumn catalogue.

Between the smoking, drinking and occasional drug binges Mitchell and Donahue had the Autumn label in a state of perpetual bankruptcy. They called Los Angeles and talked to Joe Smith who sent them $12,749.30 to cover Autumn's debt. Warner was given the rights to the Autumn roster, all the songs written by its artists and the logo and names associated with all Autumn products, if the loan wasn't repaid in a timely fashion. It wasn't. Donahue and Mitchell were granted the title of executive producer at Warner. Soon Warner owned Autumn Records back catalogue.

HOW MO OSTIN TOOK WARNER TO THE HIP BANK

In the 1970s, Mo Ostin and Joe Smith made sure Warner record executives were the best paid in the industry. Their plan was to create a diverse roster of artists dominating the industry. They did this by signing unknown musicians who were songwriters.

The signing of untested artists drove some at Warner crazy. In late January 1970, when Ostin and Smith took over, they were both Morrison fans. That is of his music. They were less enamored with his demands, his personality and his visits to the label. At times Van was not accorded the best reception. His anger simmered. His rage was beneath the surface. Then he became a best-selling artist. This gave him leverage. He used it to demand heavy promotion and a program of providing not just promotional material, but access to increased freedom in the studio. This made the period from 1970 through 1972 a commercial goldmine for Warner Bros. Van did well financially. The major change Warner brought to the industry was to convince the mainstream press rock 'n' roll was a permanent cultural phenomenon. Serious reviews appeared in the **New York Times**. John Rockwell, the **Times** critic, became a major figure promoting rock 'n' roll. **Rolling Stone** moved to New York becoming the major outlet for rock music coverage. It also became increasingly corporate. Van began distancing himself from the magazine.

By December 1970 **Stereo Review** labeled Warner Bros. the major label for the hip listener. **The New York Times** magazine regularly featured Warner artists. Van Dyke Parks received inordinate publicity for his songwriting and production techniques. While never a hit artist, Parks influenced recording techniques and production experimentation. He also brought a creative intellectual mode to the industry. Parks had the look of a typical teenager and the brain of Einstein. He led the way in the lush instrumental sounds making the 1970s an innovative time. It was perfect for Van's sense of musical innovation.

In 1971, Bob Regehr, a forty-year-old publicist, began working on the Warner Bros. catalogue. He was head of the Artists Relations Department. Regehr was first and foremost a writer. He published a western novel. He sold scripts to the movie studios. He wrote constantly. When he met Van, he was attracted to his writing. He recognized a talent in Van few did. He championed **Tupelo Honey** when it was released in October 1971. He spent hundreds of hours promoting it. Regehr was the hidden factor in bringing Van to the charts from the **Moondance** album through **St. Dominic's Preview**, he oiled the promotional machine.

As Van hit the charts, with his early 1970s albums, Warner Bros. embraced all types of music. When the soul sounds of Charles Wright And The Watts 103rd Street band hit the airwaves, the label was also promoting Gordon Lightfoot. Van was inspired by the Warner roster. He learned from every visit to Los Angeles important industry lessons catapulting his future business successes into catastrophic profits.

What did Morrison learn from Ostin? Plenty! He was there in the Golden Age of Warner Bros. The extravagant nature of Warner was shown on July 14, 1971 when waiters dressed as gorillas served hors d'oeuvres in the Venetian Room of the Los Angeles Ambassador Hotel. This party welcomed Alice Cooper to the label. Van loved the extravagant spending. When he approached Warner to do the same for him, they refused. He was told he was "a cult artist." Mo Ostin told him he was an FM favorite. There was no need for further advertising. Ostin argued the previous year they had broken the **Moondance** album with FM radio play. Van demurred. His representatives said **Moondance**, while playing on FM radio, made him realize how little Warner was doing for his career.

DID MOONDANCE INFLUENCE WHAT VAN THOUGHT OF WARNER?

When **Moondance** was released in 1970 Van saw the road to a royalty bounty. It wasn't from Warner. It was from royalties collected by BMI and delivered straight to Morrison's coffers. He received extensive FM airplay. "I was getting no record royalties, no publishing royalties, no nothing," Van continued. "The only way they couldn't screw me was airplay…that came directly from BMI. "Moondance" and four other songs from the album were featured regularly on FM radio. BMI collected the royalty for airplay and sent the funds directly to Van's management arm. It was a catalyst to his paranoia, not just about Warner, but the music business in general.

The innovative nature at Warner was not lost on Morrison. He embraced it. Stan Cornyn was the go to guy for new sounds. He embraced all forms of experimentation. The patience, the originality, and Cornyn's perseverance made other Warner artists household

MEETING RALPH GLEASON: DID IT CHANGE VAN'S LIFE?

Once he arrived in the San Francisco area, Van met and talked with a number of music critics. In the spring of 1970, Greil Marcus drove the Belfast Cowboy over to Berkeley and back while listening to FM radio. He loved Marcus. Janet sat in the back seat as they talked. Greil and Van were an odd couple. One was a talker. The other a listener. Marcus made Van aware of the role of the critic. Rock journalism was in its early stages. Van wanted to meet a veteran critic.

Marcus drove him over to San Francisco to the **San Francisco Chronicle** building at 5th and Mission. Once inside Van was amazed at the elaborate, high energy newsroom. Ralph Gleason wasn't there. Marcus drove Van back to Berkeley. They found Gleason at his home. They had coffee with him. He was the premier San Francisco jazz critic. He was also a founding member of **Rolling Stone**.

Van was interested in how and why critics analyzed his music. They met and talked for hours. When Gleason reviewed **Moondance**, he raved about Morrison's music. He compared Van's music to that of Irish poets. Gleason said Van was an original like no other in rock music. He predicted an unlimited future for the Belfast Cowboy.

BY 1975 WARNER IS ROLLING AND VAN IS RETIRING

In 1975 Warner Bros. opened a new corporate office. It was a sleek, modern, and located in a non-traditional business space. Suddenly there were new corporate rules. Posters. Crazy blackboard drawings. Funny messages. Crude expressions. They were banned. Warner never wanted to look corporate. Suddenly in 1975 they were ultra-corporate. There was a hip facade. Van wondered what the hell was going on? He was considering reducing his recording and touring. Things were getting to the point of exhaustion. Van remained concerned about his royalties. Or lack of them. Was Warner spending money owed to him? He believed they were. Carol Guida observed in her time with Van, 1974 to very early 1977, he didn't have excessive funds. "He wasn't making that much money," Guida said.

When the new Warner Bros. record building opened in 1975 there was a corporate atmosphere and virtually no security. When I started working on **Van Morrison: The Mystic's Music** in the late 1970s I visited the new building. It was made of wood and glass and looked like a country club not an office building. Once inside a drop dead beautiful secretary met you and asked what you wanted. I explained I was a Professor of History at Ohlone College. I wondered if there was anything in the way of promotional goods. The receptionist smiled. I wasn't sure if I was being escorted out or welcomed. She sent me to another office where I was given ten copies of **The Big Ball**, a two record vinyl sampler with Morrison's "Caravan" on it and a number of promotional pictures. The young lady taking me around asked five or six times if I wanted Fleetwood Mac material? I didn't. I did have a good feel for Warner's promotion. It was real. "Van should be thankful for Warner Bros. helping him to establish his brand," Ray Ruff continued. "Without Warner Bros. there is no Van Morrison." I wasn't sure I agreed.

WITHOUT WARNER BROS. THERE IS NO VAN MORRISON

Rock 'n' roll stardom is not a given. It is a fickle business.

Talented artists get left behind. Just ask Bob Neuwirth! He was an original songwriter. He was a brilliant performer. He remained elusively non-commercial. No matter the talent level there is an element of luck for many rock stars. In Van Morrison's case, he combined luck with talent. It was a group of executives at Warner Bros. who kept him on the label for seventeen years despite his antics.

What did Warner Bros. do for Van Morrison? Their magic was promoting the hits. It was albums like **Moondance** that established his brand. Warner's creative wisdom was maintaining the popularity of albums that didn't sell well. The best examples were **Hard Nose The Highway** and **Veedon Fleece**. They come to mind because Van was doing what he did best. He was expanding his artistic base. In time, Warner Bros. would say they were in on the secret. That secret was an ever evolving and unpredictable Morrison song cycle. By publicizing the albums that didn't initially sell well, as "cult masterpieces," the tepid reviews over time turned into praiseworthy prose. Manipulating the market for corporate profits was the Warner Bros. motto. In time these two albums became examples of Morrison's "hidden talent." That strategy infuriated Van. It was brilliant marketing. In rock music it is not only the artist who excels at drawing a mass audience, it is equally the role of the record label. Van Morrison was lucky to have the backing of the most artist friendly label in the industry. This is not to minimize his talent. He had that. So did Van Dyke Parks. Where is Van today? He is a major cult figure with a legendary following and sold out concerts.

Van cultivated a loyal fan base. Warner Bros. deserved a degree of credit. What did Warner Bros. provide for Van? They created a niche for in in the business. One he grabbed and turned into a legendary career. Thank you Warner Bros.

Bibliographical Sources

The standard history of Warner Bros. is Peter Ames Carlin, **Sonic Boom: The Impossible Rise Of Warner Bros. Records From Hendrix To Fleetwood Mac To Madonna To Prince** (New York 2021). Also, see, Stan Cornyn and Paul Scanlon, **Exploding: The**

Highs, Hits, Hypes Heroes And Hustlers Of the Warner Music Group (New York, 2002). This is a brilliant and studied insiders look at Warner from a key executive who deserves more credit for what Warner did for Van during the 1970s. Also, see, John Gibson, "Stan Cornyn: Free Wheeling With A Purpose," **Record World**, November 25, 1972. Cornyn was a contrarian insider with a penchant for exaggeration, game playing, dirty tricks and hyperbole.

For Van Dyke Parks, see, Elyadeen Anbar, 'The Inimitable Legacy of Van Dyke Parks: A Life's Journey Through Song," **Flypaper.sooundfly.com,** April 25 2017.

https://flypaper.soundfly.com/discover/inimitable-legacy-van-dyke-parks-journey-song/

Van looked back fifty years after **Tupelo Honey** with a sense of nostalgia toward Warner Bros.," see, "The Studio With Redbeard: Van Morrison-Tupelo Honey 50th Anniversary."

https://www.inthestudio.net/online-only-interviews/van-morrison-tupelo-honey/

The importance of Warner Bros. to this period is the corporate types who were a catalyst to Van's business acumen. How he became a savvy businessman remains an untold story. At this writing Van allegedly has nineteen companies protecting his intellectual property and collecting royalties. For a look at the events, the circumstances, and for the business culture as it influenced Van see, for example, Frederic Dannen, **Hit Men: Power Brokers And Fast Money Inside The Music Business** (New York, 2011) and Warren Zanes, **Revolution In Sound: Warner Bros. Records The First 50 Years** (San Francisco, 2009). Zanes was the Warner authorized biographer. His book is one of the best on the label and the industry.

For an insightful, fact filled and revealing interview with Lenny Waronker, see, Robert Wilonsky, "The Music Man," **Dallas Observer**, December 10, 1998.

https://www.dallasobserver.com/music/the-music-man-6401452

There are a number of biographies and memoirs of artists and others important to understanding Warner Bros. and its rise to number one in the record business in the 1960s and 1970s, see, for example, Jimmy Bowen and Jim Jerome, **Rough Mix** (New York, 1997), on James Taylor, see, David Browne, **Fire And Rain** (Cambridge, 2011), and Charles Cross, **Room Full Of Mirrors: A Biography Of Jimi**

Hendrix (New York, 2005). The Cross book is as much as history of the industry as it is a biography.

On the Grateful Dead's lack of a work ethic and how Joe Smith upbraided them for their laziness and failing to deal equitably with Warner, see, Blair Jackson, **Garcia: An America Life** (New York, 2000). There are many other excellent biographies but the ones above have in depth dealings with Warner Bros.

For the Schwaid-Merenstein business agreement with Van, see, for example, Howard A. DeWitt, **Van Morrison: From Astral Weeks To Stardom, 1968 To 1972** (Fremont, 2020), passim.

Lenny Waronker, like Mo Ostin, was a special person in the Warner Bros. management. For Waronker's role, see, for example, Joel Selvin, "A Record Executive's Pride And Joy Warner Bros. Re-Releases Lenny Waronker's Early Masterpieces," **San Francisco Chronicle**, June 4, 1995.

For an insight into Mo Ostin, as Van was leaving Warner Bros., see, for example, Jem Aswad, "Former Warner Bros. CEO Mo Ostin Recalls His Long Relationship With Prince, 'He Was A Fearless Artist,'" **Billboard**, April 26, 2016. https://www.billboard.com/artist/lenny-waronker/ The **Billboard** article is an interesting insight into a corporate music executive who was about the artist, honesty and the integrity of the product. He dealt with Morrison with kid gloves, as he saw the depth of talent inherent in Van's music.

For Bob Regehr's role at Warner Bros., see, for example, "Bob Regehr, Vice President At Warner Bros Records," **The New York Times**, September 19, 1984, Section B, p. 10. Regehr passed away at fifty-two in 1984. His specialty was artist development and publicity. When he became Artists Relations head in 1971, he was instrumental in Morrison's hit records. He was a Van supporter. There are few interviews with Regehr. This is unfortunate. He was an important and respected cog in the Warner Bros. publicity machine. It was Regehr who linked Warner Bros. record sales with levels of touring. He approached Morrison with his data on record sales and concert appearances. How Van reacted is not a matter of public record. In his early years, with Warner Bros., Van was intrigued by Regehr's statistical approach to sales. Like many Warner executives, he recognized and promoted Morrison's burgeoning talent with an eye to Morrison's career longevity.

The impact of Mo Ostin on Van Morrison's career was important to his longevity. For Ostin's role, see, for example, Robert Hilburn and Chuck Philips, "Quotations From Chairman Mo: Mo Ostin Let His Artists Do The Talking For Him His Whole Career. Now The Record-Biz Legend Steps Out Of The Shadows And Takes Us On A Tour From Ol' Blue Eyes To The Red Hot Chili Peppers," **Los Angeles Times**, December 11, 1994.

For a two part interview with Mo Ostin that is a jewel filled with more information than any other source, see, Bud Scoppa "Mo Ostin: The 2017 Interview Part I," **Hits Daily Touble.com**, August 2, 2022 https://hitsdailydouble.com/news&id=332383&title=MO-OSTIN:-THE-2017-INTERVIEW-PART-ONE and Mo Ostin: The 2017 Interview Part 2, August 8, 2022. https://hitsdailydouble.com/news&id=332393&title=MO-OSTIN:-THE-2017-INTERVIEW–PART-TWO

See **Record World**, August 12, 1972 for the dominance of Warner Bros. and its roster in the music business. Much of the sales success was due to Bob Regehr's ability to put together a sophisticated package of records sold. Also, see, R. Serge Denisoff, **Solid Gold: Popular Record Industry** (New York, 1975), chapters 3-4. The Denisoff volume was a brilliant academic analysis of the music business.

The post Mo Ostin Warner label is discussed in Fred Goodman, **Fortune's Fool: Edgar Bronfman, Jr., Warner Music And An Industry In Crisis** (New York, 2014). The Goodman book suggested why Warner had trouble when Napster came on the scene. When Bronfman took over Warner in 2004, he bet his family liquor fortune he would bring the label back to prominence. While this has nothing to do with Morrison, the book suggests the perils and pressures continuing to plague those in the music business.

Van's reaction to the re-release of the **Moondance** album, and why and how it accentuated his war on the record labels is analyzed in Ivan Little, "Van Morrison's Fury At **Moondance** Reissue," **Belfast Telegraph**, July 27, 2013. Over the years, Little was a super Van Morrison fan. He was also a staff writer with the **Belfast Telegraph**. See Ivan Little, "Van Morrison: Van The Man And Me," **Belfast**

Telegraph, August 29, 2020. https://www.belfasttelegraph.co.uk/life/features/van-morrison-van-the-man-and-me-39486664.html

For an academic look at Rimbaud's influence on Morrison, see, for example, M. Dunne, "Tore Down A La Rimbaud: Van Morrison's References And Allusions," **Popular Music And Society**, Winter, issue 24, Number 4, 2000, pp. 15-24. Also, see, Simon Firth, "Why Do Songs Have Words? **Music And Pleasure** (Cambridge, 1988).

"Domino" was more than a song for Van. It was the song he used to pressure Warner Bros. for increased promotional funds. When it charted at nine in 1970-1971 the spate of hits that followed made it impossible for Warner Bros. to deny Van's expertise on how to publicize his 45 releases.

In 1979 Van signed a European distribution deal with another label. Then he gave up on Warner, in the mid-1980s, leaving the label. Warner disputed Van's announcement. They said they couldn't meet his fiscal demands.

There was another factor, Warner Bros as a record label, was too artist friendly and by the mid-1980s there were financial concerns. The corporate structure tightened funds. Had Prince not come along to rescue them financially, they would have had even more difficulty. The key biographies ignore Warner's side of the story. On the "Domino" imbroglio between Van and Warner, see, for example, John Collis, **Inarticulate Speech Of The Heart** (Boston, 1996), pp. 234, Erik Hage, **The Words And Music Of Van Morrison** (Westport, 2009), p. 55, Clinton Heylin, **Can You Feel The Silence?: Van Morrison, A New Biography** (Chicago, 2003), pp. 518-520 and Johnny Rogan, **Van Morrison: No Surrender** (London, 2005), pp. p. 256. Also, see, Gunter Becker's Vanomatic song data base for key information at http://ivan.vanomatic.de

The use of minders, helpers or industry types to help Van was a long held Warner Bros. strategy to keep him happy. It worked. It didn't work. Some of those assigned to Van were Bob Regehr, Paul L. Wexler, Stan Cornyn and Ted Templeman among others.

For a brilliant interpretation of the **Wavelength** album, see, Pat Thomas, "**Wavelength** Tuned In," **Pacific Sound Forever Online Music Magazine**, February 2021.

https://www.furious.com/perfect/vanmorrisonwavelength.html

For one of the strangest reviews of Van Morrison on stage by a journalist of no repute who was pissed she couldn't get free ticket to his shows, see, Megan Sweeney, "Van Morrison's Anger At The Music Biz," **Irish Central.com**. https://www.irishcentral.com/van-morrisons-anger-at-the-music-biz-55112217 Sweeney alleged unfair treatment for her favorite Van Morrison cover band in a vent about his ticket prices, his behavior and Exile Productions unwillingness to give her free tickets. I am with Exile Productions after reading this putrid article, written in purple prose with a broom stick. The only good point is Sweeney can ride her broomstick to her next assignment.

Miriam O'Callaghan's 2018 interview on RTE saw him open up with a vengeance about Warner and his label experiences in general. The reason for Van appearing with O'Callaghan was to express his anger over the re-release of **Moondance**. Van was upset he wasn't consulted. He didn't understand this was an album he didn't control. Or perhaps he did understand and just wanted to complain. The article explaining Van's early years at Warner stated he was paid one hundred dollars a week. Not even close. By 1970-1971 he was making a fair living. Nothing like he would be paid in a few years. "The only way I could get paid, because I wasn't getting any money, was if I joined a union for session singers, if I was a session singer on my own record," Van said. He was correct. But he was referring to the Them sessions and his time with Bang Records. Then Van continued: "So I was the lead singer but I had to get paid as a session singer, not as an artist, because I wasn't getting anything as an artist, so the only way to get money was fill in the forms, send the forms off and then they would get the money from the record company and pay….It was a session fee so that's what I was getting for those records," Van said this is why he funds his recordings, leases his tapes and keep track of every dollar. It is not hard to argue with his logic. For a news story of Van's RTE appearance see, "I Hadn't A Clue What I was Doing: Van Morrison Talks Money And Music In Rare Interview," **Irish Examiner**, December 23, 2018.
https://www.irishexaminer.com/lifestyle/celebrity/arid-30893833.html

Interviews with a number of interns, low level Warner employees, and those who fled to other labels, helped this chapter. Those requesting anonymity were of two mindsets. They either loved or hated Warner Bros. Those opinions were not modified but they were tested against at least two other sources. If the other sources couldn't confirm it, the information did not make it into this chapter. The general tone was Warner did everything they could for Morrison. Even his closest supporters believed he was difficult.

Interviews with Bob Keene at Del-Fi, Dan Bourgoise at Bug Records, John Goddard at Village Music, Russ Solomon at Tower Records and Harry Balk helped to formulate much of the material for this chapter concerning the business activity of Warner.

For Bob Regehr, see, for example, the story of how he used his publicity skills to break Alice Cooper, "Strippers, Drag Queens And Dancing Dogs: The Insane Party That Launched Alice Cooper," **Rolling Stone**, January 22, 2021 and **Billboard**, May 6 1972 for a story on how and why Regehr was able to promote the new Warner acts. A good example of Regehr's use of the newly minted rock 'n' roll press came when he ran an ad in the August 12, 1972 **Record World**. A full page ad on page 97 saw Regehr write: "We have more singles and albums on the charts this week than a lot of our friends have in a year." In 1972, due to Regehr's expertise, Warner signed more artists than at any time in their history. They also made more money that year.

For Van's quotes on not getting paid and not being able to tour with the original **Astral Weeks** album there is a huge body of material. For his thoughts before and after the 2008 Los Angeles recreation, see, for example, David Wild, "Forty Years Later, Van Morrison Returns To Astral Weeks In L. A., **Rolling Stone**, February 14, 2009, Randy Lewis, "Van Morrison Takes Listeners On His Spiritual Journey," **Los Angeles Times**, January 12, 2009, Tim Page, "Van Morrison, Re-Exploring The Mysteries Of His Astral Weeks," **The Washington Post**, December 20, 2008 and Graeme Thomson, "Pop Review, Astral Weeks Live," **London Guardian**, February 15, 2009. These are the best of what was the most reviewed concert of the year.

For Van refusing to release "Domino" as a single, because of the contract with Lewis Merenstein and Web IV, see Erik Hage, **The Words And Music Of Van Morrison** (Westport, 2009), p. 55.

My understanding of the Warner Bros. label was helped by conversations with Cosimo Matassa, Mervyn Solomon, Dorothy Solomon, Phil Solomon, Steve Rowland, Ray Ruff, Chris Michie and Carol Guida.

FIVE

How Can One Escape The Hits In 1973? The Gary Mallaber Influence

"I don't have the fodder to feed the masses. You know why? Because I'm simply not interested. To be a star...I don't even know what that is. I call it ego oriented. You have to want to put your ego up there. I don't need to do that."

Van Morrison in conversation with Chris Salewicz, 1987

"I was just trying to establish how hard it was to do just what I do."

Van Morrison on Hard Nose The Highway.

"Van has lived his songs!"

Gary Mallaber

"The artist today becomes unreal if he remains in his Ivory Tower."

Albert Camus

There were three concerts at the end of 1972 the set the tone for the next seven years of Van Morrison's creative and performing life. He worked 24/7 on controlling his product. He read the reviews. He didn't like what he read at times. He made a concerted attempt to find a formula for his shows. Van hated the concept of a formula. But he invented his own way of performing. It didn't began on Friday, November 17, 1972 at the nearby Bermuda Palms. Alice Stuart believed Van was concerned about his backing musicians. Not critical! Just concerned about his in concert sound. Doug Messenger was with him on guitar and Van was comfortable with his backing. Stuart intimated the seeds to a new band were being formed.

That difference was to begin the lifelong practice of performing songs previously unknown to his concerts. At the Bermuda Palms, he sang Hank Williams "Hey Good Lookin," and although he played on four songs that night Van had a mission. He needed a super band. Whether or not the Caledonia Soul Orchestra was in his thoughts, there was no doubt he wanted more stability in his backing group. Marin County was a veritable hot bed of talented musicians. He began to figure out what would become the Caledonia Soul Orchestra.

Van was surrounded by literary types. It was only natural for him to think about and spend more time on his writing. The last gig of 1972 was a telling one. Van brought jazz piano performed, Vince Guaraldi, and a blues guitarist, Alice Stuart, to open for him at the Berkley Community Theater. These concerts presaged changes in Morrison's career.

In 1973 he eschewed the hits. The Caledonia Soul Orchestra was formed. The It's Too Late To Stop Now tour would be a blockbuster success. Gary Mallaber said it best: "Van has lived his songs."

Mallaber became one of Van's dominant influences. He was more than a drummer. In 1973, he evolved into a co-conspirator. That is Mallaber's studio expertise had a great deal to do with Morrison's growth and success in the music business. Mallaber was an example of how a friendship and musical collaboration expanded Van's commercial appeal.

Van's Fairfax life in 1973 was one of constant creativity despite the pressures of the music business. He had a new album ready for release. Van wanted to make a point. He would remain a working artist without a hit record. He wanted to escape the hits in 1973.

HOW DID HARD NOSE THE HIGHWAY ALTER VAN'S CAREER?

When **Hard Nose The Highway** was released, in August, 1973, it was a time of repositioning for Van's career. He was in a planning stage for permanence. He was cleaning up the loose ends of his business concerns. He established Caledonia Productions, Inc in Sausalito, which the California Corporation Licensing Board identified as a Concert Management firm. Caledonia Productions was incorporated on November 11, 1971. This began Van's corporate structure, which over time, evolved into a sophisticated entity. In a few years, Morrison put together a business management structure guaranteeing his royalties.

He took the embryo seeds of his perfect band concept to create the Caledonia Soul Orchestra and then the Caledonia Soul Express. He dealt with legal problems. He remained agitated by the Bert Berns contract as Ilene Berns shopped his "Brown Eyed Girl" material to re-issue labels. He spent an inordinate amount of time playing local clubs. This was necessary to finalize the Caledonia Soul Orchestra, while continuing to perform in a wide variety of venues. The independence he desired form the industry was on his horizon.

Van would not let anything compromise his musical vision. Not even marriage. Marin County was the saving grace for Van's creative life. It was a death knell for his marriage. It provided a perfect work space. The local clubs allowed him to perform at a moment's notice. The bevy of local musicians spurred his legendary creativity. He was happy. He was relaxed. He was furtively creative. His independence and confidence increased daily.

The Fairfax lifestyle, circa 1973, was a ready-made recipe for taking control of his music, his career and his life. From January through July, 1973 Morrison modified the loose ends in his professional life, while enhancing a career direction making him able to live comfortably from his royalties.

The building of the Caledonia Studio, in late 1972, allowed Van to bring in musicians to work on his mélange of musical ideas. Van converted the garage on the property of his gated home in Fairfax. He had a studio he could work in 24/7. There were a number of locals, as well as Woodstock friends, accentuating his creativity.

One such friend, Gary Mallaber, stepped in to work closely with Van in the post-divorce era before Carol Guida arrived. Collaborators were important. Who was Gary Mallaber? Why was he important? He was a young, but an already seasoned, musician with an unmistakable career drive. His lineage was in New York's Greenwich Village.

THE GARY MALLABER INFLUENCE

In the late 1960s, Gary Mallaber was a Greenwich Village drummer. His band Raven opened for such luminary groups as the Young Rascals, Poco Harem, the Byrds and Led Zeppelin. Hanging out in New York's East Village, Mallaber's drum skills were recognized for his ability to click with other artists.

While in New York, Mallaber discovered the **Astral Weeks** album. Then he went to see Van perform in the East Village at the Gas Light. "He was on stage with a part of the **Moondance** band but…no drummer. I asked the piano player (Jef Labes) if I could sit in tomorrow night, I scrambled my drums into the club and played the entire night. Three months later we were in A & R studio's recording what then became '**Moondance**'." That began a friendship where Morrison depended upon Mallaber for ways to craft his music. A good example was when Gary persuaded Van to overdub the vibraphone's on "Crazy Love." Mallaber was much more than a drummer, he was a producer, a sound person, and he could mix the tracks.

When Van and Janet left Woodstock, Mallaber remarked: "They took me with them." He lived in the garage that became the music studio. He was in the studio making the **Moondance** album. "We were actually rehearsing some of the songs that went into **Moondance** while Woodstock was going on," Mallaber recalled.

Van worked closely with Gary Mallaber. It was a close collaboration. They talked about the lyrics as Van peered into his ragged, little notebook and sporadic pieces of paper. Van was forthcoming. But he talked in fragments. He wrote in fragments. His life was in fragments. Mallaber remarked to Clinton Heylin Van's notebook was titled: "The Jazz And Poetry of Van Morrison." He was never sure what was in it. Van's mysterious ways intrigued Mallaber.

Gary Mallaber told Warner Bros. house producer, Ted Templeman: "You might not get the sound you want....This guy wants to put on headphones and get in there and do takes of songs and really not go through the technical end of it." What was Mallaber's point? He suggested Van channeled his music. He needed a producer.

The interviews Clinton Heylin conducted with Mallaber were puzzling. Mallaber talked of the joy of experiencing Van's creativity. and it seems the ease, of working with the Belfast. Cowboy. Van had a limited attention span. He was precise. He often walked out of the studio angry. A dozen musicians who recorded with Van told me that he was seldom with the engineer or the musicians. Technical aspects of recording didn't interest him.

Ted Templeman, then a young house producer, hung around and learned. He had little to do with the **Tupelo Honey** album. Warner Bros. gave him co-production credit. By the time Van got to **A Period of Transition**, Van had worked all this out. Once again Marin County was the conduit to his perfection.

"Van Morrison was at his best, he was totally open to the band, it was a golden time," Mallaber recalled. "These vocals are not overdubbed" Mallaber said of the **Moondance** vocals. "He allowed free additions....on the slow, soulful song 'Crazy Love'...I said I am going to play brushes like an r and b record." Van said fine. Mallaber stayed in the studio and helped Elliott Scheiner mix **Moondance**.

For the next three years Van and Mallaber worked closely. He recalled how easy Van was to work with, how he incorporated the musician's ideas, and how he worked in close collaboration with the musicians.

WHAT GARY MALLABER TELLS US ABOUT 1972-1974 VAN MORRISON

What does Gary Mallaber tell us about Van Morrison? The friendship suggested Van appreciated his talent. He consulted him for a decade on recording projects. They were only a year apart in age. Mallaber's band, Raven, intrigued the Belfast Cowboy. As a drummer, percussionist, songwriter and singer, Mallaber's multiple talents emboldened Van in the studio. After playing drums and vibraphone on **Moondance**, he continued with Van until the 1982 **Beautiful Vision** album.

Mallaber's reminiscences of working with Van were important to understanding the man. "Van was the kind of artist who really didn't worry about anything," Mallaber continued. "He went at it more like a jazz recording. I figured out the best way the song should be played within the first three or four minutes of his playing the piece on acoustic guitar. There was almost no other way you could do the tune." This quote suggests how well Mallaber worked with Van.

"I don't recall Van ever overdubbing a vocal, so what you're hearing is true performance....We didn't go back and fix anything." Mallaber had a close connection to Van. "I was living with Van in his garage studio in Marin County, and I would float down to Los Angeles. All my work with Van counted for something, and I met a pretty awesome group of people, like Jackson Browne, Bonnie Raitt, Glenn Frey, Don Henley and Linda Ronstadt."

When Mallaber was asked how Van has remained current despite changing themes, styles and fads, he replied: "Van has lived his songs! The renditions were pure and did not reflect any trend." Mallaber went to work with Bruce Springsteen, the Steve Miller Band, Eddie Money and a host of other musical giants. He lives in Los Angeles and continues to make his living as a professional musician. His collaboration with Van helped him enter the mainstream of the recording industry. His multi-talents gave Mallaber a storied career.

VAN'S FAIRFAX LIFE IN 1973

By 1973, Van Morrison's Fairfax recording studio was busy on an almost daily basis. He lived comfortably, if not opulently, in a beautiful home ten miles north of San Francisco. In the rustic town of Fairfax, his home was more attuned to the life of a country gentleman than a rock and roll star. Morrison continued to take offense to the term "rock star." He was twenty-eight years old. He was confident of his place in the music business.

With the time and freedom, as well as the money, the Belfast Cowboy recorded more music than he could place on an album. He held out for double albums. When Van visited Warner Bros., he told them he had almost forty songs finished. Warner demurred. When **Hard Nose The Highway** was released, it included only six Morrison originals. He held out for a double album. The suits at Warner Brothers echoed a hearty: "No!" Did Van have total control? Not really! There were twenty-four tracks archived for future release. Warner wasn't paying attention. Van was setting up an archive leading to the 1998 **The Philosopher's Stone**. It was as if Van was saying "Fuck you," to Warner Bros. He was!

Every day, when Van walked to his home studio next to his house, he was in a creative mood. There was never writer's block. To close friends, he complained about wasting time. They suppressed their laughter. The studio was as much an intellectual-musical playground, as it was a creative space. His obsessive-compulsive drive placed Van in a pleasant mood. This is when the romantic songs emerged.

When Warner listened to his fertile creativity, they had no idea what to do with him. He wrote too many songs in too many styles. Van archived much of the material. Warner's brain trust didn't promote some of his best songs. The rejects included "Madame Joy," "Bulbs," "Spare Me A Little," "Country Fair," "Contemplation Rose" and "The Drumshanbo Hustle." Van was determined to release a double album. His creative juices were at a fever pitch. When he looked back on the **Hard Nose The Highway**, Van observed: "As a concept for the album, I was just trying to establish how hard it was do what I do. Plus there were some lighter things on the other side of it."

One Van insider told me "a jumbled creativity ensued." There were songs Warner Bros. and Van archived. These songs explained his life, his influences and his inner thoughts. Warner believed they weren't commercial. He was increasingly looked at as being quirky. No one asked him what he hoped to accomplish?

One unreleased song stands out. "Not Supposed To Break Down" took its direction, as well as its title, from the Robert Johnson-Sonny Boy Williamson classic "Stop Breaking Down." Warner reacted: "What the fuck is this?" They didn't consult Van as to why he wrote it and what he was doing. Archive it! Joe Smith asked him to write "another Moondance."

Van was frustrated. This is the period in which he threw an ashtray at Mo Ostin while having dinner in his home. The bottom line, Van allegedly said: "profit triumphed artistic integrity."

When Ostin and Smith talked, according to Smith's secretary, they exchanged light hearted banter concerning Morrison's unique creativity. Smith said Van had "a creative duality." The song confusing Smith was "Laughing In The Wind." Was Van lecturing the Warner brass? He was! Warner loved the song. They wondered how he could write such a beautiful song amidst the tunes Smith called "dirges of swill." Van wasn't amused. "Madame Joy" was a song Van loved. Was it a hit? Warner's brain trust said: "No." Ostin said to Smith: "How can Van escape the hits?" He did by writing songs FM radio popularized. Van became a best-selling artist without Top 40 hits.

VAN EVOLVING TO CREATE

As he evolved from his broken marriage into the life of a single man, Van was no longer interested in media interviews. He needed to create. To Van it was simple. Fame robbed him of time, opportunity, inspiration, creativity and solitude.

"Van is often misunderstood," guitarist Chris Michie, continued. "He led a normal and uncomplicated life. If only the press had left leave him alone. The idea he is cantankerous and moody is over blown." Michie stressed Van was a businessman, as much as a committed artist. Van told Michie his past experiences in the record business would not be repeated. He was tough as nails.

His writing and albums provided a steady income. He lived simply. He took charge of his career. He toured when he felt like it. His independence drove the Warner suits crazy.

A myth in Van's early career is he was an erratic performer who had disdain for his audience. This was a false perception. There were a few concert failures. There were more concert gems. Van was shy. He was terrified of going on stage. If there was a less than satisfactory show, he worked even harder on his stage presence. His attitude was that of a consummate professional. He crafted his club shows with skill. He worked hard to develop his stage persona. His disdain was for large venues. He became testy with noisy audiences.

One of Van's training venues was San Francisco's Great American Musical Hall. Van loved this art deco showplace. That was until the night one of his shows attracted a rowdy, obnoxious crowd. It was a few seriously drunk patrons that led to a disastrous show. An afternoon of loud drinking patrons, who entered the club after drinking standing in line in the sun caused a rowdy atmosphere. It prompted Van to end the show. Those who caused the ruckus began drinking in the early afternoon outside the venue. Once inside they were so loud Van couldn't perform. They were thrown out. Van didn't tolerate these types of audiences. Tom Bradshaw, who bought and opened the venue in 1972, told me he calmed Van down. He returned playing the Great American Music Hall for another decade.

The clubs with an inadequate sound system were not given a second chance. Van was, from day one, recognized as a top-level performer who pleased audiences. Early on some shows were erratic. At times it was his mood. The San Francisco audiences often joked about the egg stain on his shirt. He was a blue collar worker creating a lasting career. In time the fancy blues suits, high style hats and ornate shoes arrived. When they did some fans wished for the egg stained shirts.

During the first six weeks of 1973, Van contemplated where to play and when to perform for maximum audience acceptance. He didn't want to travel outside California. Consequently, he sat down and devised a plan to perform while not touring. Chris Michie recalled: "Van was a unique performer; he could go out on the road without being on the road." This strange comment was correct as

Van Morrison: The Road February-June, 1973	
February 15:	Lion's Share, San Anselmo (2 shows)
March 11:	Memorial Auditorium, Marin
April 1:	Berkeley Community Theater
April 14-15:	Fox Theater, Long Beach
April 18:	Shrine Auditorium, Los Angeles
April 22:	Lion's Share, San Anselmo
May 21:	Odyssey Room, Sunnyvale
May 24-27:	Troubadour Club, Los Angeles
June 9-10:	Lion's Share, San Anselmo (2 shows nightly)
June 22:	Orphanage, San Francisco
June 29:	Civic Auditorium, Santa Monica (2 shows)

from February 15 until June 29, 1973. Van played sixteen separate dates close to home.

On February 15, 1973, he premiered his touring show at the Lion's Share. It was his first performance of the year. He felt at home there. He had an audience demanding only his presence. The two sets were broadcast over a local FM radio station. They eventually found their way into a bootleg record. During these two sets versions of "Listen To The Lion," at the first show, and "Saint Dominic's Preview," during the second set, suggested Van would feature these songs in upcoming appearances. A unique version of Sonny Boy Williamson's "Help Me" prompted his fans to scream for more blues. Van responded with a slow blues "I Just Want To Make Love To You." He also performed a version of "Into The Mystic" in a scat style. These were not the songs Warner executives hoped to promote. Van made them the centerpieces of his new act. Van performed "Caravan" and "Hard Nose The Highway," much like they were featured on the album.

Lion's Share, San Anselmo, CA–February 15, 1973
The two sets at the Lion's Share were made into bootleg CDs from an FM broadcast. There is some degree of static on the recordings. These shows were a prelude to the gigs with the Caledonia Soul Orchestra during the next couple of months. Van was relaxed. He displayed jazzy vocals. There is a great deal of musical improvising. The CSO can be heard beginning to take shape with fine contributions from Jack Schroer on saxophone. These shows reflect Van's LP, **St. Dominic's Preview**.
The first set starts off with a nice version of the title song from the recent album and then Van took off with his classic underground instrumental, "Caledonia Soul Music." He performed a unique cover of Hank Williams' "Hey Good Lookin" and a slow rendition of a Lenny Welch influenced "Since I Fell for You." This dramatically changed the mood. The second set opened with Van's cover of (Fred Neil's) "Everybody's Talking." This show included an upbeat "Misty," as well as was a slower version of "White Cliffs of Dover."

Setlist: EARLY SHOW:	Setlist: LATE SHOW:
Saint Dominic's Preview/	Everybody's Talkin'
Caledonia Soul Music	Help Me
Hey Good Looking	I've Been Working
Since I Fell For You	Wild Children
I've Been Working	Saint Dominic's Preview
Instrumental	Listen To The Lion
Caravan	Since I Fell For You
I Just Want To Make Love To You	Misty
Hard Nose The Highway	White Cliffs of Dover
	Caravan
	Hard Nose The Highway
	I Just Want To Make Love to You

Marin Memorial Auditorium, March 11, 1973	
The sound quality on this bootleg CD is terrible. The irony is the performance was a masterpiece. On this CD there are rare, live cuts of "The Great Deception" and "I Wanna Roo You." Jackie De Shannon's backup vocals added a great deal.	
Setlist:	
The Great Deception I Wanna Roo You Snow in San Anselmo Hard Nose The Highway Since I Fell For You Spare Me a Little	Bring It On Home Listen to the Song Caravan, Listen To The Lion And It Stoned Me More and More Come Running

Santa Monica Civic Auditorium, Santa Monica, CA June 29, 1973	
Great, great show and a very high quality audience tape. This performance includes the seldom heard: "I Paid the Price."	
Setlist:	
I've Been Working There There Child Into The Mystic Ain't No Way When You Got A Heartache, Green I Just Want To Make Love To You Hey Good Lookin' Since I Fell For You	Wild Night I Paid The Price I Believe To My Soul Domino, Gloria Buona Sera Moonshine Whiskey Brown Eyed Girl
Lineup:	
Terry Adams – cello Bill Atwood – trumpet Nancy Ellis – viola Tom Halpin – violin David Hayes – bass Tim Kovatch – violin	Jef Labes – keyboards John Platania – guitar Nathan Rubin – violin Jack Schroer – saxophones Dahaud Shaar — drums

Van searched for intimate performing venues to attract a larger audience than in the clubs. He loved the small venues. They weren't money makers. There was one local venue Van coveted. It was the Frank Lloyd Wright architectural masterpiece, the Marin Memorial Auditorium. It had perfect acoustics. It was the scene of a March 11, 1973 concert featuring back-up vocals by Jackie DeShannon. When she joined in as a background vocalist, he was helping her resurrect her career. She hoped that Van's production techniques might bring her back to the charts. He produced four songs for her label Atlantic. They refused to release these songs. Over time they did? What was the reason. Ahmet Ertegun and Jerry Wexler hated anything to do with Bert Berns. They looked at Van as a Berns acolyte. What the hell was going on? Even in death, Berns haunted Van's career.

The thirteen-song set closed with "Come Running." Van didn't encore with "Gloria" or "Brown Eyed Girl." There were cries of anguish from the audience. Van left the stage. He didn't look back. The show's highlight was Jackie DeShannon distinct back-up vocals on "I Wanna Roo You." Van acknowledged her with a smile and a bow.

DeShannon was a brilliant songwriter. Her career never took off. In 1965, she wrote and had a hit, "What The World Needs Now Is Love." It was covered by numerous artists. She was identified as a cult singer. Van believed, like himself, she was disrespected by her label and the industry in general.

The Jackie DeShannon interlude was an example of what Van was up to in the creative department. He was intrigued by her voice, her vocal style and her lack of mainstream stardom. Her in concert brilliance resonated with Morrison. He wanted her to have a hit record. The following year, after appearing with Van, Atlantic released her album **Your Baby Is A Lady**. She said Morrison's creative imprint inspired her. There were no Van Morrison produced songs on the album. Her time working with the Belfast Cowboy helped her career with Atlantic Records.

What did DeShannon learn from working with Morrison? On her future work DeShannon used horns, a string section, and a high powered set of background singers featuring Cissy Houston and Judy Clay. They were right out of the Muscle Shoals playbook with an assist from the Belfast Cowboy. DeShannon used the concept behind the **His Band And The Street Choir** album. This was DeShannon's comeback playbook.

THE PERFECT MORRISON VENUE: THANKS TO FRANK LLOYD WRIGHT

The Frank Lloyd Wright structure, known as the Marin Memorial Auditorium, was the perfect venue for Morrison. Critics described the auditorium as a "journeyman's community theater." Since the opening night in 1971, it served as a two thousand-seat concert hall that included performances by the Vienna Boys choir, Dolly Parton, the Peking Acrobats, James Taylor, Ray Charles and Huey Lewis and the News among others.

The acoustics were marvelous. The Veteran's Marin Memorial Auditorium attracted a laid back audience. Van had no trouble working up an outstanding show. The result was a bootleg catching the Belfast Cowboy in his element with new material, new musicians and a zest for performing. The audience burst forth in continual applause. Van, shy as ever, appreciated, but ignored, the rapturous crowd. There was something else in sight. He was planning a live album.

Bibliographical Sources

For the transition in Van's thinking from late 1972 into 1973, see, for example, Clinton Heylin, **Can You Feel The Silence?: Van Morrison, A New Biography** (Chicago 2002), pp. 250-273, Johnny Rogan **Van Morrison: No Surrender** (London, 2005), chapter 15. A brief conversation with John Platania in Stockholm, when he was touring with Chip Taylor, was important to this chapter.

See Howard A. DeWitt, **Van Morrison: The Mystic's Music** (Fremont, 1983) for an in-depth analysis of why the early 1970s saw Van obsessed with hit records. Then he abruptly changed course. He realized his recording contract with Warner would continue.

There was an angst to Van in his early career. For his concerns about his career direction and fame's burden. See Dean Goodman,

"Van Morrison's Career Almost Ended Before It Began," **Reuters Entertainment News,** June 10, 2009. https://www.reuters.com/article/uk-morrison/van-morrisons-career-almost-ended-before-it-began-idUKTRE5596TU20090610 When the Goodman interview took place Van was only sixty-three looking back to the 1970s and his time in Marin County. Among his evocative quotes, Van observed: "I was practicing songwriting. Each composition is a fictional story I made up to work on my craft as a songwriter. The rest of the stories people say about my music is fiction as well. I do not tend to write about me. I write about the collective, the collective unconscious." During this interview Van claimed the lack of sales for **Astral Weeks** was the determining factor in keeping his concert career afloat. He said he would have retired if the royalties were large. The Goodman article is important for another reason. It contains some of the best comments on why Van was proud of **Astral Weeks**. On performing the album after four decades, Van said: "To me it is very forward-looking and, I am told, iconoclastic to have the guts to take a vintage work and take it somewhere else. Each and every show, I have discovered layers I had not notices in my lyrics and magic from every crowd." In this convoluted explanation, Van said the 40th anniversary shows for **Astral Weeks** brought home the majestic nature of his landmark album. Of his album, Van observed that each song was unique. "Each can tell a story-whatever story one wants to make of it. This is why when people say 'It's about this or that' I just laugh...."

He depended on one person, Jon Gershen, who he flew out from Woodstock for a visit. Gershen was the first person Van talked to about his impending divorce. The tough, gritty, blue collar work ethic Van developed in Belfast came to the fore. He wanted to accomplish three things:

1) Control his product.
2) Make sure royalties were paid.
3) Form a first class touring band, put out a double album and go on a legendary tour.

He accomplished these goals in the next two years. A series of interviews with Happy Traum and Tom Pacheco in Woodstock were important to this chapter.

Chris Michie was important to this chapter. He recalled Marin County, meeting Van and preparing to play and record with him. Michie was an observer of Van in the 1970s, thereby providing a fountain of information for this chapter. Ray Ruff offered anecdotes he heard in Los Angeles as he seldom came to Marin. Carol Guida, was a young twenty year old when she met Van. Since that time she had lived and worked in Marin County. She graciously provided important information on Marin County and her life with Van. She would not share her personal interaction with Van as she has a manuscript in progress. John Goddard, of Village Music was an important source for the musical diversity and his store Village Music was a fountain of information. Mark Naftalin, formerly of the Paul Butterfield Blues Band, was a solo artist living and working in Marin County. In addition to his Blue Monday radio show he was a blues artist in the San Francisco Bay Area. He also performed and recorded with Morrison. His recollections were central to this chapter. Paul Vincent was another key source.

Thanks to Dennis Boegel, Jr., for suggestions on Mallaber's Bruce Springsteen years. Tim Kovatch provided a couple of brief remembrances from working with Van.

See Bud Scoppa, "From Studio To The Board Room-Lenny Waronker's Lost Key, Laissez-Fair Style Pays Off At Warner Bros., **Los Angeles Times**, June 11, 1989. For Joe Smith, see, for example, David Browne, "The Time Joe Smith Sent The Grateful Dead A Letter Complaining About Their Work Ethic," **Rolling Stone**, December 3, 2019.

The influence of Gary Mallaber and how more than a decade of working with Van Morrison helped his career, as well as for his observations on Van, see, for example, "Van And Gary Mallaber," **Sun Coast Van Fans Blog Spot**, January 9, 2020.
https://suncoastvanfans.blogspot.com/2020/01/van-and-gary-mallaber.html?view=magazine

The Library of Congress is the repository for the Joe Smith collection. This is a magnificent source. Smith persuaded two hundred and twenty five artists to be taped for posterity leading to hundred and thirty eight hours of recordings. There is one interview with Van entitled: "Off The Record Interview with Van Morrison, January 12, 1988." https://hdl.loc.gov/loc.mbrsrs/mbrsjoesmith.1836263

Smith's recollections, located in the Library of Congress, Washington D. C ., are invaluable. This collection is one where Smith convinced singers, musicians and industry insiders to discuss their career. Van Morrison was one of the performers providing insights into their careers. The off the record interview with Van from 1988 contains a great deal of useful information for the biographer. https://www.loc.gov/collections/joe-smith/about-this-collection/

Coping with Van's temper tantrums was part of Joe Smith's job. In conversation with Ray Ruff and Chris Michie, including a dozen Warner low level and key employees, none had a negative comment about Morrison. They said it was simply the cost of doing business with the Belfast Cowboy.

The importance of the Lion's Share to Van's advancement as a performer is an often overlooked subject. The Lion's Share, located on San Rafael's Miracle Mile, provided Van in 1973-1974 with the atmosphere, the freedom and the appreciative audiences to perfect his stage presence. For a marvelous article on the Lion's Share, see, "Marin Nightclub Nostalgia: First-Hand Account From Lion's Share," **Marin Independent Journal**, September 20, 2007. https://www.marinij.com/2007/09/20/marins-nightclub-nostalgia-first-hand-account-from-lions-share/

The Jackie DeShannon appearances with Van are intriguing. See the album, **Jackie** (Atlantic reissue 2007) for her versions of Van's "I Wanna Roo You," "Flamingos Fly," and "Santa Fe." DeShannon also recorded Van's "The Wonder Of You" and "Sweet Sixteen." On these cuts Van was not only the songwriter but the producer.

The Marin County music scene and Van's place in it was described by John Goddard, Marie Bainer, Carol Guida, John Dawson and Dan Hicks in varying degrees. The **Marin Independent Journal** was another indispensable source covering not only the music scene but the writers, gurus and itinerant intellectuals populating Marin County.

Alice Stuart provided a great deal of detail from her life in and about Marin County. She was instrumental in providing access to musicians. At Downhome Music Opal Louis Nations and Chris Strachwitz provided further detail on Marin County, the blues and Morrison's life.

For more on Gary Mallaber's influence, see, for example, the Michael Limnios interview "Gary Mallaber: The Wizard Of Rhythm," **Blues GR**, February 24, 2012. https://blues.gr/profiles/blogs/brilliant-drummer-songwriter-gary-mallaber-talks-about-van

SIX

HARD NOSE THE HIGHWAY

"I love 'Astral Weeks' by Van, a great record, one we use to listen to on the road way back."

DAVE CLARK, HOT HOUSE FLOWERS

"Hard Nose The Highway is flabby with words. Blushing blues makes purple prose."

CHARLIE GILLETT

"Well I've got out of the rat-race now I'm tired of the ways of mice and men. And the empires all turning into rust again. Out of everything nothing remains the same. That's why I'm cloud hidden...Whereabouts unknown."

VAN MORRISON

VAN HAD A VISION: WARNER SAID NO! OR DID THEY?

Van had a vision. He planned a double album. The only person who would listen was a recent Warner Bros. hire Bob Krasnow. No one at Warner was interested in a double Van Morrison record. No one in Warner Bros. management has ever commented on why the best songs destined for **Hard Noise The Highway** were relegated to the unreleased bin. There was to be no double album.

When Van went into his home studio, just outside his Fairfax home, he spent between August and October, 1972 on the first solo album of which he had total control. The album contained two non-Morrison originals "Bein' Green" a song made famous by Kermit the Frog on Sesame Street and "Purple Heather," a traditional Irish song. What does this tell us? Van was angry. He placed six original songs from his recording sessions on the album. They were either a love song or a complaint. Eric Hage had the best assessment of the album. **Hard Nose The Highway** seems to have suffered a lot of unnecessary criticism—many commentators consider it his worst and most uninspired album—perhaps because it followed such a remarkable run of LPs, and because two truly forward-thinking albums had come before and after it. The only song everyone loved was "Warm Love." This album demonstrated the critics hadn't figured it out. Every Van album had something new. You might like it. You might hate it. Van didn't care. His creativity triumphed fan or industry demands. That set the template to the present.

DID HARD NOSE THE HIGHWAY SUFFER FROM VAN'S CONTROL?

Some critics concluded **Hard Nose The Highway** suffered from

Van Morrison's total control. They failed to recognize the Belfast Cowboy was heading into new creative directions. Ones accentuated by Marin County's bucolic, leafy countryside. There were new innovations. The traditional ways of writing and recording rock 'n' roll music went through a metamorphosis.

The use of the Oakland Symphony Chorus Chamber in "Snow In San Anselmo" was a songwriting departure. It was a song about a freak snow fall in San Anselmo. This wasn't commercial. Johnny Rogan speculated Van "faced the quandary of considering how much of the publishing might pass to his estranged wife." Had Rogan read the divorce settlement, which is a matter of public record, he would have seen a lack of rancor over royalties. Rogan guessed on many of the issues surrounding this album. The divorce had nothing to do with it.

Concept albums, rock operas and personal journeys into an artist's soul dominated the album charts. Van, ever the contrarian, didn't care what others were doing. He was enjoying his creative freedom.

There was a complex explanation for **Hard Nose The Highway's** initial lack of sales. Some said Van's total control album was a learning experience. He was given an excellent cover designer. Warner did its best in the promotion area. The album didn't register with anyone but the fans. That was enough for average sales. The critic were crying out for "Moondance" or "Domino." "Despite the lack of inspiration," Charlie Gillett wrote, "the record is attractive to listen to."

Some reviewers claimed a lack of focus. There was total focus. The album was Van's view of his life. Muddled! Impersonal! Atmospheric! In search of a calm countenance! "The relaxed rhythms are just lax most of the time, the vocal surprises are mild after "St. Dominic's Preview," Robert Christgau wrote. What did the reviewers miss? Van was tired of the music business. He was making enough money. He had a hard core audience. The important critics loved his music. "When I interviewed Paul Vincent, the K-Mel disc jockey, he said that by the early 1980s Van figured out the music business. He was in charge.

Few reviewers listened to Van's philosophy. Van stated he found his muse. He had his career path. Leave me alone. The lyrics to the title song has Van writing he had seen hard times. As he told Ritchie Yorke about **Hard Nose The Highway**: "No one song in particular stands out." This was Van's way of saying "fuck you" to Warner Bros. They didn't get it.

The title song was an insight into his mindset. He wasn't broke. He was working hard. He was making a living. The lyrics saw Van complaining about difficult times. He mentioned he was so busy he didn't have time for a shoe shine. What is the point? Van was free to create. He loved it. The songs heralded Van's new found freedom. The artist, with total freedom, worked day and night. The result was enough material for a double album. Warner demurred. The battle was on.

Van's lack of a concept or framework was purposeful. It told the listener a great deal about future projects. There were myths and rabbit holes. Why? To make the point he said his songs could not be defined, explained or interpreted.

This was Van's first 1970s album, where the critics chirped and carped about the songwriting, and the lack of theme. These missives, critical or praiseworthy, drove his incessant songwriting. He was on the road to a new level of perfection.

Some reviews were excellent. Some critics were mystified. Van didn't follow past songwriting patterns. Robert Christgau was baffled by **Hard Nose The Highway**. By rating the album a B minus, Christgau labelled the lyrics "mood pieces." The only song he praised, "Warm Love," was for its evocative past. That said it all. Christgau, like many other critics, couldn't accept the new Van Morrison. They wanted the old flavor of the month.

"Van was rarely a great songwriter," Charlie Gillett wrote. Brian Hogg commented: "Van over reached himself." What did these critics miss? The experimental nature of Van's music. Simplistic mood oriented lyrics emerged. Leaves and trees were as important as political-cultural symbolism. The change in themes and the disparate lyrics suggested he was searching for new directions.

JANN WENNER, JACKIE DESHANNON AND THE PRELUDE TO HARD NOSE THE HIGHWAY

As Van wrote songs for and produced **Hard Nose The Highway**, he went to the only source he could trust to cover his career. That source was **Rolling Stone**. He had a special relationship with founder Jann Wenner. They met when Wenner's offices were in the dank, dingy south of Market area in San Francisco. They became solid friends.

At any time of the day or night, Van could drop into the **Rolling Stone** offices. It was hip capitalism on the way to big time commercial journalistic success. When Van appeared on the cover of the July 9, 1970 issue, Wenner's interview went a long way toward making the post **Astral Weeks** releases successful.

When Van confided to Wenner there were ten outtakes from Hard Nose The Highway in Van's Sausalito vault, the **Rolling Stone** founder was intrigued. Then Morrison dropped the bombshell. Van and Jackie DeShannon had unreleased outtakes of "I Wanna Roo You," "Sweet Sixteen," "Flamingos Fly," "Santa Fe" and "The Wonder Of You." This prompted Wenner to push Warner Bros. for a double album. Some years later, DeShannon released the outtakes on Atlantic. "I Wanna Roo You" was a centerpiece to **Jackie** for her 1972 Atlantic album.

Jackie's label, Atlantic, could never get together with Warner until the time of Van's **Wavelength** album. Jann Wenner was in the picture attempting to help Van and Jackie with her album releases. Van never forgave Atlantic Records for not releasing the tracks he cut for DeShannon. He believed Atlantic didn't respect his production skills. They were eventually released with little fanfare and less success. The rub was Ahmet Ertegun. He was the alleged fly in the ointment.

For reasons no one has ever explained why someone in management at Atlantic, which was DeShannon's label, wasn't keen on releasing the material Morrison produced for her. The operative wisdom is Atlantic made a pitch for Van. He turned them down. Ahmet Ertegun never forgave him. Ertegun was close friends with Bert Berns. That was also a contributing factor.

In 2003, Rhino Handmade released **Jackie...Plus** with the twelve songs from the original early 1970s album which included her cover of Van's "I Wanna Roo You." There were twelve bonus songs with four Morrison songs included in the rare five thousand numbered re-issue.

WARNER BROS. CRITICIZED VAN FOR HIS LACK OF PROMOTION

In the irony of all ironies one of the knocks on Van was he didn't do enough promotion. For Hard Nose The Highway he was ready for promotion. San Francisco Bay Area disc jockeys were on board for the promotion. Van complained Warner arranged very few interviews. This became a bone of contention.

Local radio stations played the new album in rotation. College radio was rearing its formidable head as were free form independent radio stations. In the San Francisco Bay Area, Van was played in regular rotation on a wide variety of radio outlets. College radio was new free form style of advertising. It was also a training ground for disc jockeys. In the San Francisco Bay Area virtually every community college had a radio station. Van Morrison was a consummate favorite on these radio stations. He received as much airplay as even local favorites Grateful Dead and the Jefferson Airplane.

THE SINGLE SLEEVE FOR WARM LOVE

When "Warm Love" was released on April 25, 1973, there was a great deal of airplay. John Tobler reviewed it for **Zig Zag**. He concluded it was "the second cousin to 'Crazy Love' and almost as good."

"Warm Love" intrigued the critics. Van said it was a simple song. He claimed it was "just a boy and girl song." He talked of a musical love affair with a young lady bringing her guitar. Maybe Jackie DeShannon!

"Warm Love" had a life beyond **Hard Nose The Highway**. It appeared on the live LP **It's Too Late To Stop Now**. It was a b-side on a German release of "Gloria." Warner Bros. was hedging its bets. If "Warm Love" didn't sell surely "Gloria" would bring in buyers. In

1990, "Warm Love" was included on **The Best Of Van Morrison**. In 2007, it resurfaced on **Still On Top-The Greatest Hits**. The fans couldn't get enough of the song.

When Van cut "Bein' Green" it was a non-original cover. The song came from a Sesame Street program his daughter Shana watched. He recorded it for her. His daughter, Shana, was more important than royalties. It was her favorite song even though she was only three years old at the time. When Kermit the Frog sang it on Sesame Street, Van loved it.

The use of the Oakland Symphony Chorus Chamber on "Snow In San Anselmo" was innovative. The seeds of the Caledonia Soul Orchestra were sown there. Although Van stated for years he had no desire to work with a symphony, he brought in the Oakland Symphony Chorus Chamber Concertmaster, Nathan Rubin, who arranged the strings, while influencing production and mixing. Van had never forgotten how the Rolling Stones sounded on "You Can't Always Get What You Want." He hoped to adopt a similar choral sound. "I think Van had an affinity for the production of Rolling Stone songs," Nathan Rubin observed.

VAN IN THE STUDIO FOR HARD NOSE THE HIGHWAY

Van was an evolving artist. He recorded more songs than needed. He emphasized an avant-garde, experimental mode. From August to November 1972, he cut thirty songs for what he believed to be a double album.

Some of the lyrics centered on Van's co-writing with guitarist John Platania. The themes were often maudlin and sentimental. Clearly, Van's divorce had an impact.

Van was happy many of the first takes were good enough to release on the album. A first take is what he preferred. He believed this vindicated his production skills. "I think Van was frustrated Warner didn't fully recognize his studio genius," Chris Michie recalled.

Michie remembered Van wanted to cover some classic rock and blues, as well as country numbers. Sam Cooke's "Bring It On Home To Me," Leadbelly's "Goodnight Irene," Sonny Terry's "Take This Hammer" and Hank Williams' "Hey Good Looking" were demoed.

These tunes did not make Warner Bros. executives happy. They considered them throw-a-ways. It was the generation of the singer songwriter. Van's original tunes were expected to dominate. He was too eclectic. In conversation with Warner executives, he talked about being honest in his recordings and working with a muse.

VAN ON HARD NOSE THE HIGHWAY

When Van sat down with a Canadian writer, Ritchie Yorke, for a series of interviews, it was for a sanctioned biography. Yorke, a fan, knew the Belfast Cowboy's music inside out. With his long, flowing blonde hair, scruffy jeans and lack of a shirt and shoes, Ritchie was Van's idea of a journalist. He also let Van talk non-stop after answering simple, non-intrusive questions. The Belfast Cowboy went through **Hard Nose The Highway** explaining each song to Yorke.

Van told Yorke side one had a "hard feeling." The other side was "soft." When asked what song stood out, Van said: "Wild Children." Why? He intimated it caught the spirit of the times. His growing songwriting maturity was evident. "For all of the kids born around that time," Van reflected, "I think there was a heavier trip to conform." The images from America were important, as the Belfast Cowboy formed his intellectual personality.

In the Yorke interviews, Van went into excruciating detail about **Hard Nose The Highway**. He told Yorke his life had two directions. One was in the studio. The other was in the bucolic, tree lined Marin County town of Fairfax. Happiness oozed from Morrison. As he compared Marin County to New York, Boston and Woodstock, Van said he was home. He made it clear he was home without the hippie nonsense; the gurus and the trendy causes some Marin residents embraced.

Hard Nose The Highway contained songs defining Morrison's attitude on the corporate world. It emphasized his need for business expertise. The record companies continued to draw Morrison's ire. "Put your money where your mouth is," Van sings in the title song.

SIDE ONE OF HARD NOSE THE HIGHWAY: SOME NEW THEMES AND SOME NASTY ATTITUDES

The Warner Bros. suits ignored him. Van smoldered. He harbored a deep resentment. He believed the industry was taking away portions of his intellectual property.

MARIN COUNTY INFLUENCES VAN IN SONG FORM

The name checking of Marin County incidents are many and varied. At the Marin Veterans Auditorium, he was in front of a friendly crowd. The reception he received was positive. The lyrics were a strange mélange of Marin County influences. He made a reference to the Franciscan Mission in San Rafael. When he throws in a reference to a massage parlor no one realized one of his legs was shorter than the other, Van wore lifts in his shoes and he had back pain. That is why he ordered a professional masseuse. Even his massages showed up in his lyrics. That is also how he met Carol Guida. She was the masseuse sent by the physical therapy company.

As **Hard Nose The Highway** opened with "Snow in San Anselmo," Van finalized its feel. There is a slow, plaintive tone with Jef Planes piano adding a cocktail lounge approbation until the choir bursts in to change the cadence and feel to the song. The pain in his voice is there but as the choir comes in you have the feeling he is taking the listener into ethereal bliss. The Oakland Symphony Chorus Chamber adds an uplifting gospel tone.

"Snow In San Anselmo" stands out as a brilliant example of Morrison's observational genius. Could anyone write a song about a freak snow fall in an area where summer and spring were around for most of the year? As Peter Childs mentioned this is the tune that was "an experimental departure" for Morrison. It was in the use of musicians and the rich history in his environment that Morrison excelled.

This song was performed in an experimental way during a gig at the Marin Veterans Auditorium. In his 1973-1974 shows. Van loved to put "Snow In San Anselmo" into his song list. Why? History excited him. Particularly the history of the moment. He reveled in it.

The locals loved the song when he played it at the Inn of the Beginning or The Lion's Share. He envisioned the tune in a moment of inspiration. "Snow in San Anselmo" was written after Van witnessed a freak snowstorm in the Marin County foothills. It intrigued him. He conjured up poetic images of this unique event. Van mentioned a pancake house, which was the nearby International House of Pancakes. It was an example of his use of environment. He mentioned a massage parlor. A sleepy town seeps into the lyrics, San

Rafael. The tune made moralistic judgments. His comments about the California lifestyle were illuminating. The hip phonies received his private wrath. Van was not above judging the diffident middle class, or the suburban malaise that was Marin County. He saw hypocrisy in the small villages. "Van complained about the trendy folks hanging around Mill Valley," Chris Michie remarked to me in 1983. "I think Van missed Belfast," Ray Ruff continued. "When I talked to him at the Warner Bros. offices, he was preoccupied. With what? I didn't know. Maybe his music." Ruff continued. "He was the most complicated person in the music industry. He was also a God-damned genius."

Ruff's comments provided another biographical window. That window was Van's search for themes. These themes led to discovering serious literature, the arts, symphonic music, philosophy, religion and different intellectual patterns. He drank it all in with a gusto. The time was right for Van to hire and work with symphonic musicians. A local snow storm led to that collaboration.

When Van talked to **Mojo** in November 2012, he remarked: "I was driving and it started to snow and a deer crossed in front of the car on a dark Marin Count road, and there was a drunk who looked like a madman....That's what I saw. That's the song." Maybe Van has a point. Some songs can't be interpreted.

Geoff Brown, in **Melody Maker**, observed "Snow In San Anselmo' was expertly produced and thoroughly enjoyable." Van scratched his head. It was a simple story. What was wrong with the **Melody Maker** scribe?

The album continued with "Warm Love." This love song was replete with images of youthful joy. Many of Van's close friends said this song was written in Woodstock. "Warm Love" is just a boy and a girl song," Van continued. "It's a young song." It was also a modest hit.

"Warm Love" is clearly about his ex-wife Janet. It alludes to how she looked dressed up in lace. Van blanched when the reviewers commented it was a step child to "Crazy Love." He disdained the notion he wrote love songs when he did and one after another had similar themes. Many of them were hits. He sang of "Warm Love" in concert. He never talked about it.

The contradictions in Van's thoughts provide other insights into his thinking. Van is not a fan of pop hits. Yet he had one with "Warm Love." It may have been that his divorce made it among his concert favorites. When the April, 1973 single was released **Cash Box** observed it was "a return to his 'Crazy Love' style."

Van and Warner Bros. believed "Warm Love" was a chart topper. In his early shows, the audience buzzed over this new tune. Warner re-released "Gloria" with the b-side "Warm Love." **Billboard** observed of "Warm Love," it was a testimony to Morrison's "vocal excellence."

The album's signature song, "Hard Nose The Highway," had a multi-purpose. There was an allusion to Frank Sinatra. He walks into a recording studio. He remarks to Nelson Riddle, his arranger and musical conductor, to begin the recording session. The allusion to "Nelson Riddle strings" suggests Van's flirtation with strings. He teamed up in 1996 with Georgie Fame to cut a cover of Sinatra's "That's Life " on a CD single. It featured both a studio and a live version. It was packaged with "Moondance." The 45 cover read: "Van Morrison with Georgie Fame and Friends." Van found Fame and began working with him. Fame assumed the role of Nelson Riddle. In 1995 "That's Life" appeared on **How Long Has This Been Going On**.

Another aspect of the Sinatra fantasy sees Van having Frank take a vacation after completing an album. This was allegorical thinking in the mid-1970s when Van became infatuated with Sinatra. Van was ready to begin a three-year hiatus from recording.

In 2018, in an interview with Ben Greenman, Van revisited his Sinatra phase. When he recorded his album with Joey DeFrancesco, Van remarked his jazz cohort was important in allowing experimentation with some songs on **You're Driving Me Crazy**. Recalling his mid-1970s infatuation with Sinatra, Van explained what his collaboration allowed him: "It let me try different arrangements that I didn't get to do the first time." Then Van discussed how Sinatra, known as a one take artist, like Van, recorded "South of The Border" five times. "When you keep going back to a song you can hear new things," Van concluded. For **You're Driving Me Crazy**, Van didn't select any of Sinatra's favorite recordings. What he did was to use the Sinatra mood in covering Cole Porter's "Miss Otis Regrets," Johnny

Mercer's "Travelin' Light," Pete Chatman's (Memphis Slim) "Every Day I Have The Blues" and Titus Turner's "Stick And Stones." Van imagined he was updating Sinatra. The cocktail lounge feel to the album resulted from Joey DeFrancesco's organ, keyboard and backing vocals.

Howard A. DeWitt and Joey DeFrancesco (Courtesy Author's Collection)

WHAT DOES THE TITLE SONG TELL US? THE LYRICAL BRILIANCE AND FRENETIC ENERGY OF HARD NOSE THE HIGHWAY

How did Morrison write? He produced a stream of consciousness prose often with invective overtones. The musical accompaniment cemented the words like a glove around the music. As he looked back upon **Hard Nose The Highway**, he believed he had arrived as a producer. The critics disagreed. Van said it would take the fans and critics time to catch up with his artistic vision.

The frenetic imagery on side one of **Hard Nose The Highway** continued with a slow jazz infused "Wild Children." Whether or not Van was tiring of the party scene no one knows. His personal behavior suggested his boogie-woogie days were on the decline. In "Wild Children," he was like a hip historian taking stock of the excesses of his day. He used his birth year, 1945, to imagine soldiers coming home from war. Love was their mantra. He name checked Marlon Brando, James Dean and Rod Steiger to evoke his negative view of fame. He mentioned Tennessee Williams as an "inspiration." Van loved Williams' plays because they analyzed how society looked at the outlier, the outcast, the foreigner and the unpopular scribe. In Williams' prose, as he employed themes of love and romance, Morrison envisioned a kindred spirit.

The reference to Tennessee Williams' inspiration on the final tune on the a-side, "The Great Deception" is a nostalgic look to a past that Van believed had long escaped America. When Morrison wrote of "plastic revolutionaries," he criticized their pleas for donations to support liberal causes. Then he skewers the Haight Ashbury with the phrase: "Have you ever been down to Love City?" He disdains hippies. The rise of hippie boutiques, counterculture businesses and licensed tourist goods infuriated him. He responded in lyrics in "The Great Deception." Van wrote of rock musicians with their excesses. He emphasized he was a hard working musician not one with three or four Cadillacs. No one was safe from Van's insightful, if at times, oblique writing.

"The Great Deception" was an example of multiple critical directions in Morrison's songwriting. The song was as much a criticism of the music business as it was the hippie infested San Francisco Bay Area. No one noticed Van's blunt conservatism. It has never varied. He had a one dimensional view of society, music and politics. Conservative to the core.

The Belfast Cowboy was apolitical. He had no interest in political causes. He was consistent concerning his apolitical behavior. As late as 2017, he commented: "I'm apolitical. I've got nothing to say about politics whatsoever. I'm not going to start now." This comment to Catherine Wylie appeared to be a contradiction when the coronavirus pandemic exploded. But he was consistent. He was that way philosophically since his youth. No drugs! Plenty of alcohol! I have my opinions, Van told Mervyn Solomon, and he shares them with us in song form. But don't challenge him. He will explode. Debate is not in his character.

When he moved north of San Francisco, Van achieved an intellectual independence while placing his music in a new perspective. This was evident on the b-side of **Hard Nose The Highway**. On side two his eclectic observations held fast. Van suggested an increasingly, if obtuse, view of American life.

SIDE TWO OF THE HARD NOSE THE HIGHWAY ALBUM

When the second side of the album opened with a cover of "Bein' Green," a Kermit the Frog song without Jim Henson's vocals, there was speculation. Why was Van recording the song? The critics were flummoxed. What was going on? Ray Charles, Frank Sinatra and Lena Horne covered it before Van. To Van, however, "Bein' Green" became an Irish song. That wasn't the reason he recorded it. His daughter, Shana, loved it. Van remarked to Chris Michie he loved the empathy in Kermit the Frog's version.

When the producers of the PBS Muppets Show got in touch Morrison, he wanted to appear on Sesame Street performing the song with Kermit the Frog while Miss Piggy looked on. Van was tied up. He declined regretfully.

Van's cover of "Bein' Green" is a window into how words mattered. As Van listened to the song, he recognized something about himself. The green was not about the Irish. It was about Kermit the

Frog being disrespected. Van had the same feeling. It never left him. The first words of the song Van fixated on were an omen: "It's not easy being green." How many times had Van said what I do it not easy? Hundreds! A kinship with Kermit the Frog was born. In the second line there is a revelation for Van as it recalled bucolic Marin County images. When Kermit the Frog sang "having to spend each day on the floor of leaves" the song caught Van's attention. He allegedly saw it as a wakeup call to take some time off. The last two lines of "Bein' Green" provided a clarion call for Van to reorder his life.

In "Autumn Song" Van spent ten minutes and thirty-seven seconds philosophizing about the change of seasons. A sentimental nostalgia belied his youth. In the leaf falling September, Van sings of hope for the coming year. There is a sense of romanticism missing in Morrison's earlier work. This song was written, as Van sat in his Woodstock backyard unaware of the forces coming to bear changing his life once he moved to Marin County.

The seasonal change inspired Van's songwriting. "Autumn Song" has more in common with Roger Williams than Larry Williams. When he performed it live in 1983, in the Irish RTE studio, the soft sound of Van's voice, and the poetic lyrics, mesmerized the audience. He was much more than a rocker.

Peter Mills speculated John Keats' "The Autumn Song of 1819," "probably provided" the blue print for Morrison's song. Van answered. It did! **Mojo** published an article in 2018 recognizing "Autumn Leaves" as an undiscovered master work. When Lester Bang wrote **Hard Nose The Highway** was an album with "an entire side of songs about falling leaves" he missed the point. The song was personal. Only Van knew its meaning.

Van Morrison: "'Autumn Song' is an ode to autumn." He was flummoxed. The critics attempted to find a deeper meaning. There wasn't one. There was a moody, jazz direction to this song. Charles Gillett, in **Mojo**, observed Van had "flabby lyrics." He concluded there were "boring vocals." Robert Christgau and Dave Marsh accused Van of pandering to the hit record crowd. Christgau rated the album a B minus and Marsh said it was "a failed sidestep." It would take a decade before **Hard Nose The Highway** was praised.

The last tune, "Purple Heather," was a traditional arrangement of an Irish classic by F. McPeake and Robert Tannahill who re-wrote "Wild Mountain Thyme" from "The Braes of Balquhidder." Tannahill, a Scottish poet 1774-1810, was a contemporary of Robert Burns. "Wild Mountain Thyme" was also known as "Purple Heather" and "Will Ye Go, Lassie, Go?" This Scottish folk song was collected by Francis McPeake.

Van retitled it. He rearranged it. He recorded it. Not only had Van met and recorded a home demo with the McPeakes, he grew up with their music. This was a belated tribute to their influence. Chris Michie remarked it was Van's favorite album song. "Purple Heather" challenged his voice. He told Ritchie Yorke he loved his arrangement. He said it was one of his perfect productions.

When Van completed **Hard Nose The Highway**, he felt vindicated. He believed he had to be the producer to record his songs the way he wanted. He incorporated a wide variety of styles into a solid album. This prompted confusion amongst the critics. They were flummoxed by the changes in his musical direction.

On "The Great Deception" references to being ripped off with a smile, living in a world of corporate lies, the famous rock star who is ripped off, and then Van uses Rembrandt as a genius who didn't make enough money to afford paint. This was Van's reference to his earlier poverty in small New York hotels, in depressing apartments in Boston and in a ramshackle Woodstock house owned by a music industry insider. These were less than oblique references to how the record labels treated him. "The Great Deception" makes reference to Hollywood. They weren't licensing his songs. There was one reviewer who got it right. Stephen Holden, in **Rolling Stone**, wrote the album was "lyrically brilliant." That conclusion was tied largely to one song "The Great Deception." Holden praised Morrison's "lyrical depth."

WHAT DID THE CRITICS SAY?

The reviews for **Hard Nose The Highway** were mixed. While some reviews were positive; others were mildly critical to hostile. Why? Van believed the reviewers were stuck in the past. The critics wanted "Gloria," "Brown Eyed Girl" and "Moondance." They said Van didn't develop his rock and roll persona. "Autumn Leaves" was disparaged for its cocktail lounge feel with pop, jazz tunes. The lack of acceptance for Hard Nose The Highway festered in Van's psyche.

Sitting down with Leo Green, in March 2007, Van reminisced on the 1970s. He observed: "I stopped being an artist in the 1970s." What did he mean? Van said: "When I heard rock 'n' roll it didn't have that much of an impact." He said it was the blues, Leadbelly, Ray Charles and rhythm and blues creating his sound.

Why was Van open and transparent with Green? He was first and foremost a friend and a musician. Green performed with the Belfast Cowboy. Green's dad was a legendary London based jazz artist and a respected music journalist. Leo knew how to ask the right questions. He had a laid back non-threatening personality. When early rock journalists came in with their inane questions and bravado, Van cut them to size. The result? A great deal of negative press ensued.

An English critic, Charlie Gillett, concluded the album "didn't have a convincing emotional basis." This review in **Let It Rock** had little impact upon sales. It highlighted the problem reviewers had with Morrison.

Gillett wrote Morrison spent too much time developing an ugly album cover. In an issue of **Creem**, Gillett wrote: "If you can't deal with Van as Van R + B singer yet—well it took me three years to get used to it." One wonders if Gillett had listened to anything since **Astral Weeks**.

In New York, Robert Christgau echoed this sentiment. He called the vocals "too mild." He complained the lyrical quality was disappointing. Stephen Holden's **Rolling Stone** review read like a term paper for an undergraduate literature class. He wrote Van was "musically somewhat uneven and lyrically excellent." The contradiction was he had no idea how and why Van was headed into new thematic directions. He suggested the LP lacked depth. It didn't measure up to his previous work. In convoluted prose, Holden liked and disliked the album. Over time the critics became increasingly laudatory. In 1979, in the **Rolling Stone Record Guide**, the dean of American rock critics, Dave Marsh, offered the opinion the album was "a compromise between the visionary demands of Morrison's work and his desire for a broad-based audience." Marsh was closest to the truth. In a subsequent revision, Paul Evans wrote it was the "vaguest and weakest" of Morrison's early Warner albums. The consensus? There was none.

ERIK HAGE SEES BERNS AS A GOOD GUY AND VAN AS A BLUE COLLAR WORKER

It took some time for Hard Nose The Highway to come full circle. It did with Erik Hage's 2009 book **The Words and Music of Van Morrison**. Hage concluded Van was criticized for not following the trends. In his opinion, the 1972 **Saint Dominic's Preview** LP and the 1974 **Veedon Fleece** albums were unrequited masterpieces. The irony was Van suffered by comparison with himself.

It was his Belfast upbringing transformed Morrison. Belfast created the blue collar manner in which Van approached his career. It was for Hage the reason for his legendary songwriting. Hage doesn't see the mystical side to Van as significant as his other biographers. Hage concluded it was all about songwriting.

Hage views Van's career as one saved by Bert Berns. He argued Berns "plucked Morrison out of obscurity and made him a viable solo artist." The professor believed Berns gave "Morrison reign to explore the extraordinary and dark 'T. B. Sheets'." The smell of cigarettes and bad cologne from Berns' heritage didn't have an impact upon Hage.

Hage was asked why he didn't attempt to interview Van. He replied the song "New Biography" told him it was a waste of time. Van's songwriting defined his legacy.

What does Hage miss? Van's reliance on place names, personal grievances, getting even and suing people. This is minor criticism. Considering the brilliance of Hage's arguments and the clear analytical writing, he sets the tone for brilliant analysis. Hage gave high marks to Van's interpretation of other artists. He cites Don Gibson's "I Can't Stop Loving You" and Ray Charles' country songs as examples.

One of the Hage's strengths is he listened to the bootleg CDs. He found in these rarities a new way to look at Van. "I love how he recreates the songs in concert. The version of '**Saint Dominic's Preview**' is…monumental—it starts really mellow and laid back and then just erupts." The Professor has done his homework. This is a terrific book. Professor Peter Childs is another writer with a clear pen, wonderful insights into Van's music, and a love affair with the 1970s. His book on Van, while he lived in Marin County, got it right and **Hard Nose The Highway** came in for high praise.

PETER CHILDS: THE PROFESSOR CRITIC WHO GOT IT RIGHT ON HARD NOSE THE HIGHWAY

Professor Peter Childs was one of the few critics to get it right on **Hard Nose The Highway**. He got it right in a 2022 book **Van Morrison: In The 1970s**. In thirteen well written and carefully argued chapters, Childs labels the end of 1972 and throughout 1973 as "one of Morrison's most fertile periods." Why and how did he draw this conclusion? Childs believed freedom in the studio and seasoned Marin County musicians made for creativity.

Compromise and interference, Childs reminds us, were no longer in the mix. He urged the listener to pull out **The Philosopher's Stone** to analyze the songs. Childs asked what Warner missed. If you look beyond the released songs to those included on the 1998 **The Philosopher's Stone**, you can understand Morrison's complexity. **The Philosopher's Stone** is a gold mine in viewing how and why Van and Warner Bros. had different career expectations. The songs tell Van's side of the story. They suggest the enormous pressure on his daily life.

Once you have done that, Peter Childs book is important for understanding the brilliance of this period in Van's recording life. In particular one song, "Not Supposed To Break Down," is a paean to his mental strength. Van had to live through and create in this period of his life. The album was about the difficulty of working in the music business.

Name checking for Van, Childs believes, is important. Faron Young's "It's four o'clock in the morning" opens with Van paying homage to American country music. This song, left off the album, tells us why Van was discouraged with Warner Bros. It suggests how hard it was to archive his best material. Once you listen to "Try For Sleep" the eerie image of the Doc Pomus song, "Lonely Avenue," comes to mind. The first line of the Pomus song: "It's four o'clock in the morning and there's a new full moon" is an indication of a songwriting influence upon Morrison. The cadence of the song and the feel reminds one of Ray Charles' version of "Lonely Avenue." It came replete with a soulful Morrison vocal that was like no other he had recorded. The wizards at Warner banned this slow, soulful song to the unreleased storage bin. Van may have had control. But it was not in the final selection process. "Van's falsetto voice caused Warner executives to damn near have a heart attack," Ray Ruff said. They wanted "Brown Eyed Girl."

When Van performed "Try For Sleep" in San Francisco at Winterland on February 2, 1974, there was every indication he wanted it on record. His falsetto gave the song a special tone and only once did the old Van voice come through as the crowd gazed on in mesmerized rapture. The lyrical reference to "family affair" is Van's love letter to Sly And The Family Stone. The soul-jazz influences in "Try For Sleep" was a portent of things to come. Despite his so-called new found artistic freedom at Warner no one wanted this song released. Fortunately, this tune helped give birth to **The Philosopher's Stone**.

Childs asked the question: "Why did it take twenty-five years to release the best songs from what was supposed to be **Hard Nose The Highway**?" He concluded Van was restricted at a time by Warner Bros. when he was most productive. Again, the question. Why? Who knows the answer? Childs speculated Van's album had to have a core feel. A unity. That may have been the reason for leaving off some of his best material.

The reason to spend time with Childs marvelous book is to discover songs you may have skipped. One of these songs, recorded in 1974, is "Tell Me (All About Your Love)" in which Van may be writing about and for Carol Guida. This song was released as a single to promote **Back On Top**. This U. K. import appeared on the three disc bootleg **The Genuine Philosopher's Stone** which speculates it may be from a 1971 recording. There is also a CD single from 1995, with five songs by Brian Kennedy, one which is "Tell Me About Your Love" co-written with Van Morrison. This was an RCA single. The song is identified as a Van Morrison original by some and on the same single Kennedy covers "Crazy Love." This CD single is entitled **Intuition**. The YouTube version by Kennedy is an interesting one. This is an example of the breadth of Morrison's reach.

Childs briefly discussed the bucolic beauty, leafy atmosphere and creative mantra of Marin County. He concluded the local landscape "inspired one suite of gentle songs harnessed together on side two." Van intended a soft and hard side.

SOME THOUGHTS ON HARD NOSE THE HIGHWAY

Hard Nose The Highway didn't have a hit single. It prompted Van to create a personal album. Tony Dey remembered: "Van was a contrarian. He broke up bands. He wrote non-hit songs." Joe Smith observed Van did everything he could to derail his career. Smith said **Hard Nose The Highway** was Van's way of lecturing the industry on his independence. Some critics observed he blew up past successes. The critics didn't realize he would record and tour with a new super group. No one realized a super group was on the horizon. The Caledonia Soul Orchestra was the poster child for Van's experimental nature.

Few people understood Morrison's mercurial moods. These thoughts dominated his songwriting. There is not a book on Van's lyrics. One is in progress by Pat Thomas. He writes: "What Van delivered to Warner Bros. which is a potpourri of stuff that by anyone else's standards was nothing short of amazing....'Warm Love' was equal to 'Tupelo Honey'...." Thomas's blog is soon to be a book. Whatever comes from **Listen To The Lion: Musings on Van, His Band And Street Choir** will be the ultimate word on Morrison's creativity. His lyrical genius. His musical adventures. These themes Thomas will develop with his facile pen and penetrating insights. With the knowledge of a seasoned musician, and a respected record reissue producer, Thomas's analytic writing delves deeply inside

Van's soul. The result is understanding the man and his music. It is about his lyrics not Morrison's personality.

VAN IN THE STUDIO AND CONFESSING TO RITCHIE YORKE

In the studio, adjacent to his Fairfax home, Van put together a brilliant set of songs for **Hard Nose The Highway**; if at times uniquely produced ones. The past haunted Morrison. The images of previously difficult years dominated his lyrics. Van told his friends he needed a few years off.

In conversation with Ritchie Yorke, Van complained he was "just trying to establish how hard it was to do just what I do." This theme remained constant. Van's artistic and creative freedom was a mixed blessing. The critics expected a "Moondance" single on each album. They quickly found out this was not the case. Yorke told Van he thought "Wild Children" stood out. Van went on in great detail giving Yorke his opinions on what he thought his songs accomplished.

There were sub-themes to **Hard Nose The Highway**. They included economic criticism, as well as disdain for the music business. Van described hypocrisy in copious detail. He examined societal problems. Van composed "Warm Love" in a fit of pique. He wanted a song alluding to or describing love. "Warm Love" was an FM radio hit. He didn't perform it regularly he told Chris Michie. Van had a personal angst recalling "Warm Love." It brought back a spate of bad memories. He was uncomfortable with the lyrics. Continual memories populated his prose. It was writing as self-flagellation.

"Warm Love" is an example of how Van molds an old tune, like "Crazy Love" and rewrites and rerecords it into a new version. The other reason for writing and recording it was Van's intention to perform this song on a live album. It didn't take long. The next year on the **It's Too Late To Stop Now** album, it surfaced. Then it was included on the 1990 **The Best Of Van Morrison**. The song was featured on **Still On Top: The Greatest Hits**.

Hard Nose The Highway was an emotional album. Van declared his feelings. He called out role players He criticized pseudo intellectuals. He remarked to Steve Peacock of **Sounds**: "A lot of people in

Hollywood are into their own scene and believe their own publicity." Van wondered why Hollywood movie producers didn't come calling. Van's comments on the lack of movie licensing resulted from Warner Bros. promising movie song placement. It didn't materialize. Van was furious.

DID VAN PAY THE PRICE OR DID HIS LABELS?

The continual difficulties between Morrison and Warner Bros. didn't bode well for the future. He wanted more control. Warner balked. There was a temporary stalemate. There were serious differences over the Morrison advertising dollar. Warner management liked to flex its corporate muscle by not placing advertising in **Rolling Stone**. He was angry. They informed Morrison he was a cult artist.

Hard Nose The Highway contained a number of songs that didn't make the final cut. One in particular was a Van favorite. He fought like hell to have it on the album. Warner refused. Why? The tune, "I Paid The Price," was remainder of his marital difficulties. This song was a harangue about the problems he experienced with his ex-wife.

When Van performed "I Paid The Price," at the London Rainbow Theater, in July 1973, his emotions triumphed. When Van was asked: "Who's the unnamed female sponsor?" He complained he had done everything he could to salvage the relationship with his ex-wife. Then Van denied the song was about his failed marriage. He said it was a literary theme. "That was definitely about his marriage," guitarist John Platania remarked to Clinton Heylin. He co-wrote the song with Van.

On Hard Nose The Highway, Van introduced literary themes. Some critics found these illusions troublesome. Others believed he was a fresh voice. His references to John Keats indicated Van was moving into new writing directions.

He remedied his lack of a formal education with a vigorous reading program. The authors included John Donne, W. B. Yeats, James Joyce, John Keats, J. P. Donleavy and Samuel Beckett. Van felt awkward about his lack of education. "I think he made up for his minimal formal learning," Nathan Rubin continued. "He did so by reading widely and with great taste." Throughout the 1970s, Van was a voracious reader. He evolved into an increasingly critical thinker. His marriage, and subsequent relationships, were important to his writing. He became too reclusive for his socially-minded wife. Carol Guida may have experienced the same sense of isolation. Chris Michie recalled: "Van read so much he ignored other aspects of his life."

HARD NOSE THE HIGHWAY: THE COVER

Warner Bros. informed Van they hired a top-notch album cover artist. They commissioned Rob Springett to complete the **Hard Nose The Highway** cover. He had recently worked with Herbie Hancock. Van was impressed. "Van was a Hancock fan," Carol Guida continued. So was I!

Van balked at Warner's controls. He wasn't sure the cover design reflected his vision. To appease Morrison, Springett took him for a ride in his car. They talked at length about the album cover. After Van discussed his ideas, Springett went home and came up with the LP art. When the album was released, Van loved it. It was exactly what was in his head. Van remarked of Springett: "The cat's incredible." While the critics weren't sure about Hard Nose The Highway, Van loved the music, the concept, the lyrics, and he said the album cover conveyed what he was doing. With a twinkle, a smile and a mischievous look, Van intimated there was a lack of concept. He told one of the musicians in time Hard Nose The Highway would receive its due. Perhaps Van was being the joker. One of his musical sidekicks suggested he watched Bob Dylan's machinations and adopted them. Confuse the critics. Have fun making demands to the record label. That was how many of those close to Van saw it. One band member told me the album heralded another new direction. He smiled. That was the Van Morrison way.

Van would veer off into new and even more obscure musical directions for the next half century with sporadic commercial success that ran like an out of control roller coaster.

VAN TRIES TO EXPLAIN HARD NOSE THE HIGHWAY

It was up to Van to explain how Hard Nose The Highway created new interpretive ground. He declined. That drove the critics crazy. After a string of hit albums, the conclusion was the new LP saw Morrison's decline. There was no decline. Only a change of content, direction and theme.

Van explained what he was up to during an interview with an old Belfast friend and journalist Donal Corvin. This was one of Van's strangest interviews. He appeared on RTE's Talk About Pop with presenter Tony Johnson. For some reason Van didn't take to Johnson. He brought along his friend, Donal Corvin, who took over the interview in a drunken stupor. Van was at ease with Corvin. Carol Guida watched from the wing in amazement. The result was a terrific interview.

In conversation with Donal Corvin, he remarked there were serious themes on the album. Van said: "Take 'Purple Heather'...there's a theme running through that which is pretty similar to the standard rhythm 'n' blues trip and there's a lot of connection to that." Van explained "Snow In San Anselmo" was much like an artist's sketch of a simple event. He abhorred the critical interpretations. Van told Corvin "Snow In San Anselmo" was "nothing more than a tune about a snowstorm."

Donal Corvin commented: "You changed your style an awful lot since **Astral Weeks** and you've come back to it." Van responded: "No not really. I think the style is the whole trip. It's like from that one (Astral Weeks) through all the other ones I do everything. I do the whole, range. You see them as different albums but really it's all the same except it's released at a different time."

Those working with Van said he looked upon his work as a continual opera. Not a rock opera but his observations, his direction and his life. For the biographer that was gold.

Near the conclusion of the interview, Tony Johnson returned to ask questions. He tweaked the Belfast Cowboy with a question on his moods. Johnson suggested he had a chip on his shoulder. Van defended his behavior. "Why would I have a chip on my shoulder? People have a lot of misconceptions about everything," Van retorted to Johnson. Then Johnson said: "We have always had this publicity that for some strange reason Van Morrison doesn't want to play for the Irish people." Van didn't flinch. He looked daggers at Johnson. He answered. "That's the media. The reason you get all that stuff is through the media because people print things without ever talking to the actual people." Then Van went off on rock and roll magazines suggesting reporting was less than professional. All the young rock 'n' roll writers took note. The Shakespeare of Telegraph Avenue, Greil Marcus, read this with glee. Of rock magazines, Van had the last word: "Rock 'n' roll magazines; that's how they make a living, most if it is just rubbish but people love to buy it and read it." Somewhere Dr. Demento was planning a comedy attack on rock music, while Lester Bang was dropping a quaalude. As the interview neared the end Van said: "I feel like taking a long walk off a short pier." Unbelievably, Johnson made what is perhaps the most moronic statement in an interview. "Now at this point, we've got more music." I guess Johnson was saying Van could jump off a pier when the show was over.

This exchange suggests why Van ignored Johnson and brought in Donal Corvin. He was from Belfast. He was a hard drinker. They had fun. "Donal was 100 percent Irish," Carol Guida commented. She said Van was relaxed around him.

THE CRITICS RESPOND AND VAN CONTINUES TO EXPLAIN

Stephen Holden, in **Rolling Stone**, called the album "psychologically complex, musically uneven and lyrically excellent." The yuppiedom **Rolling Stone** experienced was obvious when Holden labeled "The Great Deception," a song that was "a vicious indictment of hip urban culture." The reality is it was a veiled criticism of the Haight Ashbury subculture. Van laughed at the would be posers. He distanced himself from the cool people. He kept his opinions to himself. That is except in song. He told his life in song. The Biographers took note.

When Van talked with Ritchie Yorke about "The Great Deception," he said: "I met this revolutionary guy. I didn't know how well known he was but he came to see me like he was interested in the scene....I just don't like people who write you a friendly letter and the halfway through the letter asked you for a big donation." Fools, ingrates and fake revolutionaries were not tolerated. "That song was for all the phonies. Hollywood is just another one of the illusion trips," Van remarked to Steve Peacock of "The Great Deception."

HARD NOSE THE HIGHWAY: THE CONCEPT OR LACK OF IT AND WRITER'S BLOCK THAT DIDN'T EXIST

From August through November 1972, Van was busy in the recording studio. Unfortunately, of the thirty plus odd tunes not all would make it onto **Hard Nose The Highway**. There were two that would later appear on **Veedon Fleece** and nine more on **The Philosopher's Stone**. Van and Warner were at loggerheads over something. It was never explained. Why did so many of Van's songs go unreleased? Again no answer from Warner Bros. Van didn't need to answer. He created the material for a double album. The controversy over what was on the album and what wasn't led to rumor and innuendo.

The six original Van songs on **Hard Nose The Highway** led to a vicious rumor. It was an unfounded one floating all over Marin County. That rumor was Van had writer's block. Untrue! At the concert sites, in discussions with disc jockeys, like Tom "Big Daddy" Donahue or later K-Mel's Paul Vincent, and then promoters, like Bill Graham and Chet Helms, the question of Van's writer's block was raised. There was no writer's block. The rumor persisted! With only six songs on **Hard Nose The Highway**, there must be writer's block. This is what the critic's speculated. Van loved this unfounded rumor. They left him alone. If he did have writer's block few reporters wanted to talk with the Belfast Cowboy. He started discussing writer's block. Van finally found a way to get the press off his back.

The press has never grown tired of analyzing Van's writing. In 2016 a Nashville writer suggested Van overcame writer's block by recycling old songs. This was a reference to the 2015 album **Duets: Reworking The Catalogue** and later the **You're Driving Me Crazy** release. This well-meaning critic got it wrong at every step of the way.

"This is Morrison when he's not trying too hard, not looking for new ways to express the emotions captured so brilliantly in his earlier work." What is wrong with this description? This critic hadn't listened carefully to the music. Van is known for reworking his material. It is always in new creative ways.

WHAT DID VAN'S FREEDOM PROVIDE HIM?

The freedom Van found during the 1972-1973 **Hard Nose The Highway** sessions was shown when he cut versions of Sonny Terry's "Take This Hammer," Leadbelly's "Goodnight Irene" and Hank Williams' "Hey Good Lookin." He displayed his American influenced musical roots. These songs, and his double album concept, prompted Warner to write a memo to Van suggesting he was not recording a concept album. Van felt creatively strangled. He retaliated by withholding songs from some Warner albums paving the way for the release of **The Philosopher's Stone**.

Warner complained Van didn't include enough commercial material. "Bulbs" was the most commercial song. Van left "Bulbs" off **Hard Nose The Highway**. Why? The musician's recording with Van said he refused to release it as he was dissatisfied with the version he recorded. Van wanted "Bulbs" as the single on his next album. When a Warner executive told Morrison "Bulbs" was not a commercial hit, he re-wrote and re-recorded it. He would show Warner they were wrong.

Hard Nose The Highway provided the freedom Van previously lacked. The themes of love, fate and folksy experiences entered into Van's reading-writing psyche. Descriptions of life dominated the lyrical beauty oozing from Morrison's small slips of paper and his tattered notebooks. The freedom of the mind was the final result. Morrison was finally his own person musically. He took two and a half years off for a relaxed life. There are few writers with Morrison's descriptive skills. Van's bleak vision was often tragic but never depressing. It was driven by an ambition knowing no bounds. The British cultural traditions, English writers of note and Irish literature coalesced in his pen.

VAN IN 1973: WORKING TOWARD A NEW DIRECTION ONCE AGAIN

In 1973, Van formed the Caledonia Soul Orchestra. He molded it in his image. The double live album **It's Too Late To Stop Now** was released. It established Van as a top touring act. Then he spent almost three years playing small clubs. He acted like he was in a period of retirement. The dramatic changes in his work schedule, his life, and his new found business intensity was a contradiction to those writing about him. He left the celebrity goldfish bowl.

Van was eager in 1973 for an extended tour. The resulting tour, It's Too Late To Stop Now, led to the heralded double live album. It vindicated his vison. The tour was successful. But tiresome! The tour took a toll on his writing. He complained he needed more time to himself. What did that mean? He had a psyche full of thoughts, images, reading visions and itinerant concepts of mysticism and religion.

That meant Van was more interested in writing songs. He was composing blue collar lyrical poetry while creating a sense of permanence in the fickle rock and roll world. There were other musical acts taking note of Morrison's songs. As he wrote a bevy of songs, others listened and were covering his style. He labelled them "copycats ripped off my songs." That mantra never ceased. In 1985 Van complained to **The New Age** Bruce Springsteen's "Born In The U. S. A....definitely ripped me off." Van continued "copycats ripped off my words. Copycats ripped off my songs. Copycats ripped off my melody." He had a point. His new music was built on the past. When Van wrote "Have I Told You Lately," it bore a startling similarity to William Bell's 1971 song "I Forgot To Be Your Lover."

The opening line to Van's song is virtually identical to the opening of William Bell's song in both in melody and lyrics. The Bell song "I Forgot To Be Your Lover" begins with the line "Have I told you lately that I love you." That doesn't mean Van plagiarized it. Van built many songs on past ones. "Van doesn't seem to accept the idea he built songs on past tunes," Chris Michie continued. "He wrote for his environment." When the song came out on **Avalon Sunset** in

1989, there is a more plausible explanation. This song was written around the themes and structure of "Someone Like You."

The operative speculation is Van used Bell's song as the model. When the **Vanthology** album was released, William Bell was chosen to cover "Have I Told You Lately." Case closed. Bell's "I Forgot to Be Your Love" was the model.

COMPLAINING ABOUT THE MUSIC THROUGH THE LYRICS TO THE DRUMSHANBO HUSTLE

When Van recorded "The Drumshanbo Hustle," it was excluded from **Hard Nose The Highway**. It was his way of dealing with the concert promoters, the hangers on, and the Warner corporate lackeys. The song was axed from the album for reasons he never explained. Was it Warner? Was it Van? No one has ever explained it.

The lyrics to "The Drumshanbo Hustle" remained in the archives for twenty-five plus years before being released on **The Philosopher's Stone**. It was hyper critical of the music business.

The lyrics to "The Drumshanbo Hustle" draw on Van's experiences. He reflected, years later, "it wasn't the music business." Van writes: "They were trying to muscle in...." The words indicated his displeasure with Warner Brothers. He had just given up some of the rights to his first three Warner albums to settle a legal dispute with Ilene Berns and Bang Records. He was unhappy with Warner. Van's passive-aggressive behavior was reflected in his lyrics.

When Van writes songs about the contracts he signed, he reflects on how he was "puking up his guts" over a business agreement. These songs, his public comments and his legal action opened his soul to the biographer. When a song he believed was uber commercial, and not released, he took his emotions to center stage.

DID THE DRUMSHANBO HUSTLE LEAD TO SUMMERTIME IN ENGLAND AND BECOMING VAN MORRISON?

What did "The Drumshanbo Hustle" really mean? It was Van's declaration of independence. It was an allusion to his Irishness. He was an Irish poet returning to his roots. He was a jazz man turned blues shouter. He brought pop hits out in the early 1970s guaranteeing his commercial future. These songs cemented a legendary career. He reflected on these influences in "The Drumshanbo Hustle." The song made it clear the East Belfast Boy was not backing down. He wanted his money.

By the time "The Drumshanbo Hustle" reached the public, in 1998, some of Van's best work cemented his legend. That creation began in 1980 due to the Marin County influences from 1973 through 1979.

It all began with "Summertime in England." This 1980 tune announced "Becoming Van Morrison." No one got it. Van did! The Belfast Cowboy realized he had to do something unique to announce his newly created presence. What better than to record the lengthiest song of his career "Summertime In England." Then in case the critics didn't get it, he spent the next twenty-five years performing it in concert.

When Morrison performed "The Drumshanbo Hustle," on RTE in 1973, few listeners realized its significance. He announced his independence from the music business. He would not embrace or condone "The Drumshanbo Hustle." He would not be cheated by a business that ate its young.

The puzzling question was: "Why were there only eight songs on Hard Nose the Highway? It was supposed to be a double album. Van had the freedom to record what he wanted. He had some of the best musicians of his career. For unexplainable reasons his best songs were locked away in an unreleased bin. Why? No one has ever explained. why. Speculation is the songs varied from previous styles. When Van tried a falsetto on one song, Ray Ruff told me, Joe Smith asked Van what the hell he was doing? There was no answer from the Belfast Cowboy.

Van wrote six of the eight songs on the album. Why were so many songs left off the album? That has never been explained. This is when the story of writer's block emerged. Those pushing the writer's block myth were San Francisco Bay Area journalists, fans, industry insiders and a select group of radio personalities. The Van Morrison media brigade formed in the San Francisco Bay Area. It has never abated.

EIGHT SONGS ON HARD NOSE THE HIGHWAY: VAN'S AMBIVALANCE

For all the subterranean analysis about **Hard Nose The Highway**, there has been very little attention paid to what Van thought. He was clear. This album was an examination of how difficult it was to survive in the music business. Van complained there was loss and personal freedom. The mental strain from the constant

demands of a rock 'n' roll had him second guessing his lack of a personal life.

Van's adjustment to America was one where he saw Hollywood and the record business eating its young. There was a dark aspect to side one and a light one for the second side. Stephen Holden said it best in his 1973 **Rolling Stone** review: "Van's gift at creating extended meditations that accumulate emotional power as they unfold in modified, impressionistic streams of consciousness...evoking...as few contemporary composers have—the ineffable joys of daily life in attunement to a pleasant environment." If you can get through Holden's rancid prose, he does have a point. Van has a lyrical beauty few singer-songwriters possessed.

BIBLIOGRAPHICAL SOURCES

For Van's comments on stardom, see, Chris Salewicz, "Van Morrison: Quotations From Chairman Van," **Musician**, April 1987, pp. 11-12, 20. See, William Ruhlmann, "Van Morrison: A Look At The Mystic's Career So Far," **Goldmine,** October 23, 1987 for an excellent overview of his career.

Clinton Heylin, **Can You Feel The Silence?: Van Morrison, A New Biography** (London, 2002), chapters 11-16, Brian Hinton, **Celtic Crossroads: The Art of Van Morrison** (London, 1997, revised 2000), chapter 5, Johnny Rogan, **Van Morrison: A Portrait of the Artist** (London, 1984), chapters 10-12, Howard A. DeWitt, **Van Morrison: The Mystic's Music** (Fremont, 1983), pp. 42-49 and Ben Cruikshank, **Into The Sunset: the Music of Van Morrison** (Andover, 1996), pp. 36-38 offer important material for this chapter.

See, Steve Peacock's article in **Sounds**, July 28, p. 15 for some perceptive comments on **Hard Nose The Highway**.

Also, see, Steve Turner, **Van Morrison: Too Late To Stop Now** (London, 1993) for some cogent analysis of this era. Turner comes closest to describing Morrison's irascible nature and contrarian demeanor.

See the Cameron Crowe interview in **Rolling Stone**, August 30, 1973 for material helpful to this chapter.

For Van's concerts see, Simon Gee and Andy Nieurzyla, **The Wavelength Videography, 1962-1999**, volume 2 of the Wavelength Archive Series, 2004, pp. 4-5.2

Also, see, Howard A. DeWitt and Dennis M. DeWitt, **Stranger In Town: The Musical Life of Del Shannon** (Dubuque, 2001), passim for the state of rock touring. Howard A. DeWitt, **Chuck Berry: Rock 'n' Roll Music** (Ann Arbor, 1985) offers an extended analysis of early rock tours.

See Roy Carr's interview in the **New Musical Express**, August 4, 1973, for comments on the changes in Morrison's career. This article is important in discussing Them's influence and Morrison's incredibly piercing lead vocals.

For the Joe Smith interview, see, Bob Sarlin, **Turn It Up (I Can't Hear The Music): The Best of New Singer/Songwriters** (New York, 1973) and on the now defunct website hosted by a Canadian college professor for a wealth of information on Van's life and career, Van Morrison website. http://www.harbour.sfu.ca/—hayward/van/reviews/1973smith.html

See, Donal Corvin, "Van Morrison Interview," **Hot Press,** July 7, 1977. This interview was from 1974. He explains the meanings behind many of the songs on **Hard Nose The Highway**. Corvin was a brilliant observer. He was Van's close friend until his untimely death.

Dan Bourgoise of Bug Music helped me understand the industry and Harry Balk, Del Shannon's producer, schooled me on the production process. A brief conversation with Bob Keene of Del Fi Records in the 1980s helped to understand the industry. Ray Ruff related his tales of Van and Warner Brothers in great detail. Ruff booked Them in 1966 and he got to know Morrison intimately.

See, Barney Hoskyns, **Hotel California: The True Life Adventures of Crosby, Stills, Nash, Young, Mitchell, Taylor, Browne, Ronstadt, Geffen, the Eagles, and Their Many Friends** (New York, 2006), pp. 88-90. For the Southern California rock scene and how Morrison fit into it, see, for example, John Einarson, **The Roots of Country Music** (New York, 2001), John Einarson and Ritchie Furay, **There's Something Happening Here: The Story of the Buffalo Springfield-For What It's Worth** (London, 1997), Anthony Fawcett and Henry Diltz, **California Rock, California Sound: The Music of Los Angeles and Southern California** (Los Angeles, 1978), Art Fein, **The Los Angeles Musical History Tour** (London, 1990), Ben Fong-Torres, **Hickory Wind: The Life And Times of Gram Parsons** (New York, 1991), Jim McDonough, **Shaky: Neil Young's Biography** (London, 2002), Johnny Rogan, **The Byrds Revisited** (London,

1997) and Rich Wiseman, **Jackson Browne: The Story of A Hold Out** (New York, 1982).

On singer-songwriters, see, for example, Mark Brend, **American Troubadours: Groundbreaking Singer-Songwriters of the 60s** (New York, 2001) and Dave DiMartino, **Singer-Songwriters: Pop Music's Performer-Composers, from A to Zevon** (New York, 1994).

A brief interview with Bonnie Raitt helped to highlight some of Morrison's strength and weaknesses in the 1970s as a performer and songwriter. Raitt saw only positive points to Van's talent. She mentioned he needed to do a better job with the media.

A useful bootleg is **Van Morrison: Invocating The Protector of Angels** (Rattle Snake Records, 2 disc, 2004). This bootleg included seven songs from the February 15, 1973 show at San Anselmo's Lion's Share Club. The sound and quality is excellent.

A series of interviews with Chris Michie and Nathan Rubin provided information on Morrison's daily life, as did Mark Naftalin. John Goddard helped with Marin County information. Art Siegel added some useful information, as did Mitch Woods. Carol Guida provided background material. See, "Random Notes," **Rolling Stone**, July 5, 1973, p. 5 for the speculation **Hard Nose The Highway** might be a double album. See, William Ruhlmann, **All Music Guide To Rock: The Definitive Guide To Rock, Pop and Soul** (New York, 2002, 3rd edition) for ratings on Morrison's records. Ruhlmann was an unusually perceptive critic. He wrote **Hard Nose The Highway** "marks a decline from the astonishing run of five great albums Van Morrison had made from 1968 through 1972...." Ruhlmann concluded the album was "still...respectable, if uneven...."

Also, see, Erik Hage, **The Words And Music of Van Morrison** (New York, 2009) p. 69 for some cogent comments on **Hard Nose The Highway**. Also, see, Robert Christgau, "Hard Nose The Highway Review." http://www.robertchristgau.com

An interview with Erik Hage by his home town newspaper provided an in-depth examination of his motives for spending a year writing about the Belfast Cowboy. The article provided some insights that are not in his brilliant book. See, Greg Haynes, "Erik Hage Peels Away The Myth From Van Morrison's Music," **Nippertown**, August

31, 2009. https://nippertown.com/2009/08/31/erik-hage-peels-away-the-myth-from-van-morrisons-music/

For other reviews, see, Dave Marsh and John Swenson, editors, **The Rolling Stone Record Guide** (New York, 1979) and Anthony DeCurtis and James Henke, editors, **The Rolling Stone Album Guide** (New York, 1992).

For the bootleg CD that explains "weasels ripped off my flesh" on the Internet see the following website and enjoy it, the site http://www.bigozine2.com

See Sheila Weller, **Girls Like Us: Carole King, Joni Mitchell, Carly Simon And The Journey Of A Generation** (New York, 2008) for a book that contains some of the same problems that Morrison faced.

See Peter Mills, **Hymns To The Silence: Inside the Words and Music of Van Morrison** (New York, 2010), passim for some of the most illuminating comments on **Hard Nose The Highway**.

A wealth of material is in Ritchie Yorke, **Van Morrison: Into The Music** (London, 1975), pp.97-110. John "Marmaduke" Dawson of the New Riders of the Purple Sage reminisced about seeing Van around Marin County and learning from stories of his independent production techniques.

For a reference to **the Zig Zag** review, see, Ritchie Yorke, **Van Morrison: Into the Music** (London, 1975), p. 102. Also, see a review, "Van Morrison: Hard Nose The Highway," **Let It Rock**, September 1973; Wayne Robins, "Hard Nose the Highway Review," **Zoo World**, January 1973; Tom Nolan, "Review of Hard Nose The Highway," **Phonograph Records**, October, 1973 and a profile by John Tobler, "Morrison: Out Of The Music," **Zig Zag**, November 1973.

The idea that biographer Clinton Heylin pursues is Van wrote two inferior songs "Warm Love" and "Hard Nose The Highway." It is Heylin's opinion these songs should join other rejects such as "Madame Joy," "Bulbs," and "Spare Me A Dime" in the unreleased bin. Van's distaste for Heylin was evident. He believed Heylin had no idea about who he was or, for that matter, what his music proclaimed.

The **Sunshine Coast Van Fans** is an excellent site. On Jackie DeShannon's relationship with Van.

https://suncoastvanfans.blogspot.com/2013/06/van-and-jackie-deshannon.html?view=magazine

For Van's apolitical nature, see, Catherine Wylie, "Van Morrison: I've Got Nothing To Say About Politics And I'm Not Going To Start Now," **The Irish Times**, November 30, 2017.

https://www.irishnews.com/arts/2017/12/01/news/van-morrison-i-ve-got-nothing-to-say-about-politics-and-i-m-not-going-to-start-now-1199647/

For an in-depth book about Warner Bros. and minimal comments about Van's relationship with the label, see, Peter Ames Carlin, **Sonic Boom: The Impossible Rise Of Warner Bros. Records, From Hendrix To Fleetwood Mac To Madonna To Prince** (New York, 2021), pp. 12-13, 87, 93, 109, 132, 149, 177, 223. Carlin had extraordinary inside access to Mo Ostin and Lenny Waronker, as well as the Warner Bros. archives. His book is one of the best on a record label.

Ryan H. Walsh, **Astral Weeks: A Secret History of 1968** (New York, 2019) is an absolute gem. This is the best recent book on Morrison's early years and the legendary **Astral Weeks** album. The long and convoluted road that brought Morrison to Warner Bros. and the early problems he had in concert are examined against the back drop of a music industry unfriendly to many artists. Walsh's primary contribution is in suggesting how and why the industry not only failed to pay a fair royalty but often scoffed at the artist demanding a royalty. The literary sycophants who write about how well record labels treat the artist would do well to read Walsh.

For the in-depth Bob Harris, "Old Grey Whistle Test Interview" in July 1973, see https://www.youtube.com/watch?v=AcoMxC9IYXY. This seven point interview highlights how shy Van remained with the media despite Harris's low key personality and whispering questions. John Platania and David Hays were with Van as he discussed his impending tour.

See Howard A. DeWitt, **Van Morrison: Astral Weeks To Stardom, 1968-1972** (Scottsdale, 2020) for the background to and early planning for **Hard Nose The Highway**. Interviews with Mark Naftalin, Charley Musselwhite, John Goddard, Nick Clainos and Larry Catlin helped to set the stage for the planning behind and the influences necessary to completing Hard Nose The Highway.

Janet Morrison Minto's comments on Ilene Berns came from a Joe Selvin interview, see, Joel Selvin, **Here Comes The Night: The**

Dark Soul Of Bert Berns And The Dirty Business of Rhythm And Blues (New York, 2014).

For Van's quote on why he had to sign with Bang Records, see, Travis M. Edwards, "The Rage of Van Morrison And The Battle Behind His Masterpiece, 'Astral Weeks'," **The Washington Post**, November 30, 2018.

A retrospective look back by Van to his 1970s infatuation with Frank Sinatra is discussed in any interview with Ben Greenbaum, "Van Morrison Discusses How Music Used To Be More Spontaneous And Commercial," **The New Yorker**, December 13, 2018.

https://www.newyorker.com/culture/culture-desk/talking-with-van-morrison

For writer's block and why it doesn't exist for Van, see, for example, Howard A. DeWitt, **Van Morrison: The Mystic's Music** (Fremont, 1983), passim, **Clinton Heylin, Can You Hear The Silence**: **Van Morrison, A New Biography** (Chicago, 2002), pp. 303, 307-308,328, 381,475, 486 and "Review: Van Morrison In Relaxed Groove With Jazzy Reworkings," **Vannews.Com**, April 24, 2018. The writer's block story is traced most persistently to Heylin's book where he writes Van considered leaving the music business due to writer's block. This was the opinion of Van's recently minted manager, Stephen Pillster, or one of his musicians, probably Jack Schroer, but the story was never verified.

When Paul Vincent, the KMEL radio personality, interviewed Morrison in 1981 they talked briefly about Bob Dylan. Van said the concept of being "a joker" was one he learned from Dylan. It allowed Van to ignore the critics questions.

For background on Van in America, see, for example, T. Gleeson, **The Irish In The Atlantic World** (Columbia, 2010) and for Belfast's influence, see, for example, M. McLoone, "From Dublin Up To Sandy Row: Van Morrison And Cultural Identity In Northern Ireland," (Causeway, 1993) and M. McLoone, "Rootedness And Transcendence: Van Morrison's Belfast," **Film, Media And Popular Culture In Ireland** (Dublin, 2008).

The interpretation that Van found meaning for himself in a song by Kermit The Frog on Sesame Street comes from a number of conversations with people close to Van who mentioned he became intrigued by the lyrics. "Van had a connection with words," Chris Michie continued. "He found hidden meaning in song lyrics.

"Autumn Leaves" was a song from **Hard Nose The Highway** that had commercial success as a single. For an excellent summary of why it was an obscured song that was restored by some critics see, Tom Muscarella, "Song Of The Week-Autumn Song, Van Morrison," October 13 2018. https://rockremnants.com/2018/10/13/song-of-the-week-autumn-song-van-morrison/ The original reviews of the song appear in a wide variety of sources, see, for example, Dave Marsh's **Rolling Stone** review, the wit and wisdom of Robert Christgau in his official publication and the scathing remarks of Charlie Gillett. These three are the best writers, the most significant interpreters and the most read critics. Along with Lester Bangs they refused to recognize the new Van Morrison. When Van wrote "close your eyes, clear your mind" they didn't see the next phase of his writing germinating in his 24/7 creative mind.

See Peter Childs' book, **Van Morrison In The 1970s**, for the "experimental nature" quote on "Snow In San Anselmo," p. 64.

BLONDE HAIRED TED TEMPLEMAN: IN THE STUDIO

SEVEN

THE METAMORPHOSIS OF THE NEW VAN: A PERSONAL LOOK, OCTOBER, 1972 TO EARLY 1974

"Van Morrison has enough control and experience to win through where Joe Cocker, perhaps his closest competitor as a white urban blues singer fell away."

ROBIN DENSELOW, THE GUARDIAN, LONDON, 1973

"Perhaps he is a legend largely because he does not wish to be."

MIKE GEE

"That so few dare be eccentric marks the chief danger of our time."

JOHN STUART MILL

In late 1972, Van and his wife Janet appeared to have a perfect marriage. They had an adorable child Shana. They lived in a bucolic town Fairfax. This rustic California countryside was a haven from the hustle and bustle of the music industry. Van's songwriting and touring brought well in excess of a $100,000 a year plus income. A horse, known as Domino, roamed near their property. Van was seen about town in a brand new Mercedes. It was an idyllic life, as his album covers demonstrated. Beneath this seemingly normal living arrangement a wide range of emotions were tearing the marriage apart.

That period of time living in Fairfax and later in the San Geronimo Valley, near Elvin Bishop, was a heightened creative influence. Walking down to the town square Van might see Jerry Garcia and his Grateful Dead friends. A local shopkeeper talked to him like he was no more than a newcomer. Welcome to California! The tourists ignored him. For a time fame and fortune didn't seep into his Marin County life. As Van told Chris Michie years later: "Everyone was famous in Marin County. I was just another bloke," Van's quote was typical of him. He was busy working 24/7 on his career while continuing to finalize a business structure guaranteeing future earnings. It was a full time job with a pressure cooker atmosphere.

The demands of recording for a major label took its toll. Van was caught in a syndrome where a hit record was the priority. The flavor of the day was the singer-songwriter. Van was adamant. He would not be the flavor of the day. He would do it his way. That way, he told Chris Michie, he was guaranteed a lengthy career. How? It was all due to the music. Enough hits bring a long career, Van reasoned, while privately hating the idea. "He was conflicted," Michie said.

Van believed recording live was the best way. Only one cut, he told Michie, or the inspiration, the moment, the feeling was lost.

Van's dream was to record in front of a live audience. He hated studio constraints. After a string of brilliant albums, Van planned for a double live album with an eleven piece band, including backup singers, strings and a sound that was perfect for his growing legion of fans. These thoughts resonated like a creative hurricane. He was doing everything to could to be commercial.

This was one of Morrison's contradictions. He eschewed hit records. He used the phrase he didn't want to be the flavor of the month. In the next breath he told Mo Ostin and Joe Smith realized he needed hits to continue his career. He began talking about a live album like no other in rock 'n' roll music.

The genesis of the **It's Too Late To Stop Now** album percolated in Van's fertile mind. The best way to showcase his talent was with a superior band in a free-wheeling concert atmosphere. He was almost twenty-eight years old. Many Warner executives believed he needed a producer.

Warner selected a house producer, Ted Templeman, who was in the early stages of fashioning a career behind the board creating some of the best 1970s rock and roll with Van Halen, the Doobie Brothers and a host of other platinum acts. He was a blonde haired surfer, who had been in Harper's Bizarre. He was a brilliant producer in training. Templeman later said Van schooled him. Templeman provided little more than advice. Van was in charge. Lewis Merenstein left. Warner gave control to Van with Templeman acting in an advisory role. At least that is what Warner Bros. told Van. It appears they didn't want Van talking about his production skills. This was a tedious time at Warner. Mo Ostin had no idea how to deal with Van. Ted Templeman's involvement has multiple meanings. When his autobiography was published **Ted Templeman: A Platinum Producer's Life In Music**, in 2020, he gave Van credit for helping him refine his production techniques. What was the real story? Templeman reported it accurately. Momentarily, after his early 1970s experiences with Morrison, he was frustrated. As he looked back, he realized Van taught him as much about the industry he did the ways of the recording studio Templeman embraced Van's lessons with productions for the Doobie Brothers, Nicolette Larson, Captain Beefheart and Van Halen among others.

PRODUCER TED TEMPLEMAN: VAN SCHOOLS HIM

Ted Templeman was listed as a Warner Bros. staff producer. He was assigned to Morrison. Templeman was in sync with Van from day one. When Joe Smith took Ted to meet Van, they talked at length. They had a great deal in common. Templeman told Morrison he had been in Woodstock, at the invitation of Albert Grossman, and once there he worked with Robbie Robertson and The Band. While Templeman had little more than a fleeting connection to The Band, it made Morrison comfortable. He could work with this kid. The Band were amongst his best friends.

Van and Ted bonded over jazz. "It turned out he and I owned many of the same records. We clicked over our love for jazz," Templeman continued. "Van asked me to co-produce his next album for Warner Bros.—what became **Tupelo Honey**. Along with being his producer, I was his personal driver."

It took some time for Warner to understand Van. He stayed at times in San Francisco. On some days Templeman drove up to Fairfax to fetch him. It was hard work. Templeman said Van was talkative as they drove to and from San Francisco. This was rare for Van. He felt at ease with the young producer. Templeman got to know him. "Van's way of working made me anxious as hell," Templeman commented. He continued suggesting Van schooled him in matters of production. He observed Van taught him to catch moments of "spontaneous and inspired performances on tape." Templeman remarked: "Van's methods were "unsettling." These observations, in Templeman's autobiography, fail to mention he announced immediately after working with Belfast Cowboy: "Never again." Templeman mellowed over the years recalling he learned a great deal about producing from Van. He also introduced Morrison to new recording studios, a bevy of talented musicians and to new concepts in production.

"Van, invariably, wanted to nail down things on the first take," Templeman continued. "I quickly learned that if I opened my mouth too much, thinking that I could persuade him to do another take or sing something different, I risked unmooring him...." At times, without saying a word, Van would walk out of the studio and go home.

Templeman's patience paid off. He said he coaxed the brilliant **Tupelo Honey** album out of a performer who was uncomfortable in Wally Heider's studio. Van would disagree, according to Chris Michie, as recording studios were his place to finalize the product.

"His singing was always spot on and full of soul," Templeman recalled. The young producer, although he was three years older than Van, was patient. The end product was brilliant. Morrison was the sole producer.

When Templeman told Van he would take him to a "funky studio" in the Haight-Ashbury, known as Funky Jack's, Morrison was intrigued. It was this experience that cemented their working relationship. A short term friendship emerged.

The studio was owned by Jack Leahy. He was a graphic artist who founded Funky Features producing posters and graphics for the Fillmore, the Avalon Ballroom and a host of other rock emporiums. The posters provided the start-up funds to open Funky Jack's Recording studio in 1969. Leahy, a Marin County resident, went on to a legendary career finalizing sound tracks for feature films.

When Van arrived at Funky Jack's, he felt at home. The Edwardian home was laid back, quiet, professional and easy to access. Rod Stewart and Jeff Beck recently had visited. Sammy Hagar was a studio regular.

They cut a few songs. This turn of the century Victorian house converted into a recording studio was perfect for Morrison. "I knew I was making rookie mistakes," Templeman continued. "For the most part though Van was a cool customer."

JACK LEAHY: A SUBTLE AND HIDDEN MARIN COUNTY MORRISON INFLUENCE

How much did Jack Leahy influence Morrison? That question is lost to history. Why include Leahy? He was a pioneer in the San Francisco film and music business. When Van arrived in Fairfax, Leahy had opened a recording studio in his home and later in San Francisco. If not for Leahy the quality of local studios would have been excessively corporate. For Van, a small studio was his thing. He built one. The presence of small, funky, but beautifully equipped, studios blossomed as Van set foot in the San Francisco Bay Area recording community. There was a freedom to local recording studios that the corporate Los Angeles labels could not match.

By 1977 Leahy co-founded Russian Hill Recording, a full service recording studio and audio post production facility for feature films. At Funky Jack's one could see Jimi Hendrix, Country Joe McDonald, Steve Miller and Janis Joplin regularly recording. They were often just hanging out.

Leahy had a video screening room built in his Marin County home. By the 1980s he was working on soundtracks for feature films. I learned about Jack Leahy when I was working on my book **Van Morrison: The Mystic's Music**. I listened to members of the Hoodoo Rhythm Devils talk about Leahy's genius. I didn't connect him to Van. So he didn't make the cut. In retrospect, Leahy was one of many technological, musical and creative forces working in Marin County, while Morrison finalized his recording and production techniques. Van has never mentioned Leahy or his studios. He did record at Funky Jack's. Perhaps one day Morrison will tell us about the subtle and hidden influence from this Marin County recording pioneer.

VAN IN A LOCAL RECORDING STUDIO AND LOOKING BACK ON HIS EDUCATION IN THE RECORD BUSINESS

Van attracted a crowd in the recording studio. While at Wally Heider's, Grace Slick, of the Jefferson Airplane, and blues guitarist Michael Bloomfield watched Van record. As Templeman worked with Van in the studio, he was nervous. Ronnie Montrose, Van's guitarist on the **Tupelo Honey** album, provided his signature guitar on "Listen To The Lion," Saint Dominic's Preview album and "Wonderful Remark" on **The Philosopher's Stone**. That version, as well as "Ordinary People," were examples of an increasingly brilliant maturity in Van's writing. The reading paid off. He had a broader songwriting vision. Montrose also provided background vocals. He helped Templeman finish mixing some sessions. Montrose told him Van was his own producer. Warner Bros. had no clue. Eventually, due to Templeman's comments on Morrison's production skills, Warner agreed to let Van produce his albums. That freedom began with **Hard Nose The Highway**. Van said: "I have always done this because I loved the music." On the 50th anniversary of **Tupelo Honey**, as Van talked with Redbeard's blog, he had fond memories of Marin County. Looking back on the 1970s, he was interviewed in a relaxed manner in a Belfast hotel intimating his debt to Marin's influence.

WARNER BROS. AND HARD NOSE THE HIGHWAY'S FREEDOM

While **Hard Nose The Highway** provided Van with producing freedom, he believed Warner ignored him. He complained publicity behind his records was minimal. He argued Warner chased trends not talent. The Belfast Cowboy was not obsessed with money. He was concerned about those who were attempting to steal his intellectual property. The litigious Van was born as he navigated to Warner and their corporate offices.

In 1973, Van took matters into his own hands. He had riders in his concert agreements on lighting, sound systems, stage management and publicity. He was preparing for the "It's Too Late To Stop Now" tour. When the album was released in 1974, Van's artistry exploded. This took place as he customized his management. The business end of Caledonia Productions kept track of every nickel. Then a complex business structure emerged.

Exile Productions became the evolving business structure maintaining Morrison's independence from the industry. That process began intensely in 1973-1974.Van had his Sausalito lawyer draw up an LLC business. The early 1970s paved the way for a more sophisticated business structure. It wasn't until April 13, 1987 that Exile Productions was registered in Greater London. When the company was incorporated on April 13, 1987, Van had spent a decade and a half finalizing its business direction. There were shifts and changes in the corporate structure. By 1992 when Exile Productions emerged, with a power house organization to accentuate the business lessons, Van learned plenty in the previous two decades. Those close to Van claimed he was in a business mode the minute he arrived in Marin County. Exile Productions Limited is a London based company located at 89-90 Baker Street. It seems fitting the company securing Morrison's royalties is on the same street where Sherlock Holmes operated.

How valuable was Exile Productions? In 2016 the **Irish Times** reported Van's business brought in three million euros that year. The **Times** claimed Van's profits quadrupled from the previous year. The point? The Belfast Cowboy continued to analyze, plan and embolden his fiscal future. His business model was functioning like an economic juggernaut. Something he had been planning since 1973-1974. Van considered **Moondance**, not **Astral Weeks**, his commercial breakthrough. Why? Royalties collected!

Those who worked with Van in 1973-1974 marveled at his business acumen. Not surprisingly, Van planned for the future after only a decade in the perilous record business.

Jef Labes, who initially played with the Belfast Cowboy on **Moondance**, recalled Van's precise planning. He approached Labes one day suggesting: "Let's put together a tour with strings and everything." Labes wasn't sure it would work. The Electric Light Orchestra was the only act touring with strings.

Labes' forte was string arrangements. When Van talked of an eleven piece band with strings and a horn section, Labes was intrigued. "He wanted to create a new show every night," Labes told **Rolling Stones**' David Browne. The planning for the It's Too Late To Stop Now tour was exhaustive. Van wondered if Warner would support it.

VAN WONDERED: WHERE WAS WARNER BROS?

Where was Warner Bros. as Van worked night and day on his career? The label was working on other artists. Warner Bros. signed every known singer-songwriter to a recording contract. They vigorously marketed these performers. This is what Van wanted from the label. He didn't believe they put enough money into his promotional budget. Warner Bros. viewed him as a cult artist. He didn't tour in the larger venues. He loved to play small clubs. He was often inaccessible. He was too private. Van's attitude was "to hell with Warner."

Van realized his producers made all the money. The early producers, like Tommy Scott and Bert Berns, didn't consider the bold nature and originality of his music. They never commented on his lyrics. Lewis Merenstein did. When he realized his couldn't control and manipulate Van in the studio he left. Now Warner had a problem. How to find a producer? That was the question Mo Ostin and Joe Smith debated. They wanted original songs. The direction of his music, and the way he hoped to promote his product was ignored. The pressure was unbearable. The Schwaid-Merenstein production team tied him to a contract that took away a great deal of his intellectual property.

The solution, Ostin and Smith discussed, was to find a producer who was close to Van's age. They wanted a neophyte. Someone learning the production trade. They realized Van had strong studio views. The perfect candidate was someone who had been in a rock band. Someone who was eager to produce. Someone intent on learning the production craft. What they wanted was a baby sitter. Van was understandably furious.

Ted Templeman fit the bill. He co-produced the **Tupelo Honey** album in 1971 and the **St. Dominic's Preview** LP the following year. He received co-producer credit on **It's Too Late To Stop Now**.

The co-production credit on **It's Too Late To Stop Now** for Templeman was outrageous. Van sat in his home study, with Carol Guida, spending hundreds of hours completing the album. I have no idea how much Templeman did. The album finalized Van's production, touring and commercial future.

By the time he was a major star, Morrison was in his late twenties, it was difficult for him to accept fame. As an individualistic person, he had no thoughts of compromising his music. Fame was a corrupting vision.

THE PERSONAL VAN MORRISON

Van Morrison lives a disciplined life. It allows him to create. To understand the man, it is necessary to examine his day-to-day existence. It is in this milieu the seeds of his creativity were sown, blossomed and erupted into a creative hurricane. That creativity was inspired by routine.

In California, he got up to drive out for a morning cup of tea; a scone and some quiet time writing. The coffee shops in Mill Valley. Sausalito, Tiburon and Fairfax were frequent writing homes. He recorded on the spur of the moment. It was in this quiet, bucolic setting he wrote. When he had enough material for a song he was on the phone to his band.

"I would get a call at my Sacramento home at three in the morning," drummer Tony Dey recalled. "The band would meet in Sausalito or somewhere in the Mill Valley area. We would have breakfast and then cut some songs." Dey continued: "To Van it was just another work day, one I think he put in seven days a week."

When in the recording studio, Van was at his creative peak. He was constantly working. Tony Dey remembered the euphoria of working with Van in his home studio and Van's precision in his one take recordings.

Dey worked on the eight minute version of "Not Working For You." He witnessed the angst and depravity in Van's lyrics. When Dey and the others arrived at Sausalito's Record Plant they were struck by Morrison's agitated nature. This may explain a number of 1975 mysteries. The **Mechanical Bliss/ Stiff Upper Lip** album was advertised twice for release. Why was it cancelled? No one knows! Speculation was artistic-label differences. A more plausible explanation was the lyrics to "Not Working For You." Van took his grievances out in Warner in lyrical form.

There was another side to Morrison's personality. When he wasn't writing or recording, he sometimes woke to a day of raging behavior or foul moods. It was these rages that drove a wedge into his marriage and personal relationships. His moods eventually led to a contentious divorce. The constant striving for ultimate perfection, the pressure to produce, and the musician's daily lifestyle were pressures negating his creativity. Van complained continually about a lack of privacy. He cried out for a normal life. He made the decision to step back from the business. This began the metamorphosis of the new Van. What was this new metamorphosis? It was to create a career plan for longevity, personal happiness and a distance from the press.

Chris Michie: "Van worked constantly. He had trouble with free time. The personal Van is one who is constantly creating." In Fairfax another musical friend described Morrison as "well-adjusted and hardworking." Everyone agreed that he possessed a blue-collar persona.

WHAT DID THE REGULAR PATTERNS OF VAN'S LIFE MEAN TO HIS ART?

During the winter of 1972-1973, Morrison established a predictable pattern to his life. He got up each morning. He drank his coffee with a sugarless sweetener. He worried about his weight. A couple of times a week, he tried on his leather vests. He wanted to make sure they fit. Then he walked into his studio, on his Fairfax property, to work on new songs. He spent an inordinate amount of time reading. Van took charge of his intellectual and musical life. He was recharging his batteries. He worried about his health, his intellect and his finances.

Van placed himself under a strict reading regime. Religion, cult figures, Zen Buddhism, a wide variety of religions and numerous philosophical treatises dominated. Morrison's marriage to Janet Planet ended. She complained to friends about enduring his melancholy moods. His drinking, according to Clinton Heylin, was a factor. Those around Van claimed this was nonsense. Van's friends told me they grew apart. The press through innuendo, rumor and happenstance circulated rumors, combined with a dearth of fact on Morrison's private life. Van remained opaquely silent.

According to Nathan Rubin the other side of their marital difficulties centered on Janet Planet's trendy hippie lifestyle. She wanted to make jewelry, meditate and write songs. She was a skilled singer-songwriter. That didn't work in Van's world. She was laid back. She was not happy with meager finances. "I was the muse with no money," Janet told the **Los Angeles Times**. When the money flowed in, she left. It wasn't about the money. She wanted a creative life.

Prior to the divorce there were bills paid out for marriage counseling. This didn't work. It wasn't a union meant for the long term. He loved his daughter Shana. The marriage didn't fail for Van's lack of trying nor was Janet responsible for its demise. They were simply too young. Fame was the culprit. The pressures of the music business eroded the relationship.

The cause of the divorce was not that of the usual rock and roll marriage. Drugs, alcohol or other women did not precipitate the divorce. The problem in their marriage was Janet Planet's creativity. She was a poet, a songwriter, and she had deep knowledge as a new age spiritualist. Van wanted a stay at home wife.

An ambitious person, Janet wanted to start a business. Her intellectual dimensions were similar to Van's. She had the grace, good looks and drive for success in modeling. She displayed musical talent. This didn't make for a workable marriage.

Van spent each day working on his music. He complained when people came over to the house when he was composing or tending to business. Since he was working virtually all the time, there was little time for socializing.

Van's lifestyle was an issue. He depended upon a small coterie of musicians. From time to time, he would abruptly replace those who worked with him. It was never a vicious parting. He searched for a new sound. Van had trouble with lasting friendships. His close friends remarked he often ended close relationships without explanation. This ingrained character trait defined Morrison.

To close friends, he complained he needed a change in atmosphere to write. He would often bring two or three musicians into the studio on the same instrument. Peter Van Hooke complained there were three drummers at an audition. This hurt his pride. Van stared at him. The Belfast Cowboy didn't understand. He needed a specific sound. The best drummer would provide it. Morrison was socially unaware. He didn't realize Van Hooke's feelings were hurt. In the midst of these musical odysseys, his marriage disintegrated. Hints of their marital troubles surfaced in select interviews.

WHAT WERE THE SEEDS OF MARITAL DISSOLUTION?

In June 1972 Janet Planet was interviewed, by an Irish journalist and entertainer, Shay Healy, for **Spotlight** magazine. Van was upset. Why? **Spotlight**, in his opinion, was yellow journalism. Why was an

Irish magazine specializing in folk music interviewing his wife? It was an innocuous article. The seeds of marital dissolution were apparent in her words. She described Van as "incredibly Irish." The translation was he was difficult. She discussed his temper. She reflected on his moody behavior. To close friends, in and around Fairfax, she commented she feared his daily tirades might influence her children. She alleged he was never violent, only sullen and moody.

During the recording of **Tupelo Honey** Janet told **Spotlight**: "Really, he is a recluse. He is quiet. We never go anywhere. We don't go to parties. We never go out. We have an incredibly quiet life and going on the road is the only excitement we have." Janet's monosyllabic answers suggested Van was struggling with his intellectual partner. Her interview was not typical. Chris Michie believed Van thought Janet had fallen into the hippie sewer. "He couldn't understand her," Michie concluded.

Janet moved out of their Fairfax home and into a nearby motel. Eventually, Van purchased her a home in Terra Linda. The divorce wasn't acrimonious. It had a dramatic impact upon his personality. He threw himself into his work. The difficulties Van was having in his marriage were no different than the problems he was having with his managers, booking agents, producers, attorneys, label insiders and concert promoters.

In an interview with **San Francisco Chronicle** writer Joel Selvin, Janet commented she tried to put the best possible face on her marriage. She told Selvin she recognized the pressures on her husband. She tried to alleviate them. Selvin, San Francisco's most accomplished rock journalist, got Janet to open up about their personal life. For weeks, Morrison complained about the interview. He claimed it was a pack of lies.

Many of Van's closest friends did not take the seeds of marital disillusionment seriously. Since Janet wrote liner notes to one of his albums, she was a creative co-partner. She was a poet. She was devoted to his career. Somewhere along the line something went wrong. They appeared to have a perfect marriage. The private pictures taken by Morrison's Marin County friends repeatedly recalled a smiling Van playing with his daughter Shana. Most everyone believed the marriage was on a solid foundation.

Van was a star. He brought in good-sized royalties. He appeared to deal effectively with the capricious whims of the recording industry. As the pressures from the music business accelerated, Morrison became increasingly bitter. The impact of the divorce was a major turning point. It brought on a new creativity. He experienced an even greater disillusionment. Hence, the period of semi-retirement.

As Van's post-divorce burst of creativity ensued, he paid attention to language. Words mattered! Van lost himself in reading. Philosophy, poetry, mysticism and alternate thinking dominated.

DIVORCE IN SAN RAFAEL: A NEW BEGINNING?

Divorce is traumatic. It produces a feeling of emptiness. There is a decline in personal confidence. A sense of loss emerges. A state of confusion follows. The result is self-doubt. These forces took hold of Van's personality. They dominated his songwriting. The path toward divorce drove Van on to monetary success. His life was a simple one. He avoided the trappings of stardom. It was celebrity which was responsible for his divorce. He vowed to rebuild his life. He did with Carol Guida.

He was not caught up in the quagmire of success. It was financial difficulties, not personal achievements, that created a permanent wedge in the marriage. There were too many business decisions, too many nights on the road, too many meetings with musicians and too many distractions from Warner Bros. Van and Janet needed time alone. They had trouble developing their relationship. That was the missing commodity.

Chris Michie speculated Van wanted hit records, money and recognition. "He didn't see the dangers of fame until it was too late," Michie continued. "Ultimately his marriage was the casualty to fame and fortune."

The end came on November 1972, when Janet moved to a nearby motel. In court she said she was without money. Janet Planet had been a wife and mother. Many thought she had no marketable skills. That turned out not to be true. In the shadow of Van, Janet hadn't been able to develop. She was a talented artist. She was an excellent writer. She had musical ability. She developed a custom jewelry business . She became a part of a rock 'n' roll duo.

At first, she wasn't sure if she should retain a lawyer. This quickly changed. She hired Michael Kaiman to represent her. He was a partner in Wiess, Knecht, Shapiro and Kaiman located at 8730 Sunset Blvd. His office was in the Penthouse of this prestigious Los Angeles California firm. His experience and reputation were first rate. Van immediately hired Hadden W. Roth who was a partner in Roth, Thorner and Sherttel. Her lawyer was expensive. Van's was a bargain. It didn't matter. The recent no-contest, no-fault Family Law Act of 1969, which became effective on January 1, 1970 allowed for irreconcilable differences. Despite the law, the divorce was an expensive one. There was little rancor.

Janet didn't formally file for divorce until January 26, 1973. With a son, Peter, and Van's daughter, Shana, the increasingly distraught Janet began a new life. It was Van's professional career, his mercurial personality, and the pressures of show business, which drove the marriage to divorce court.

When Van's attorneys responded to the divorce petition on February 7, 1973, his law firm listed Van's income at $6000 a month with a $3000 net monthly income after expenses. A further declaration of expenses indicated that there was a $600 mortgage payment on the Fairfax home, a bill for $350 a month for marriage counseling and other incidentals, a $200 a month food and household supply allowance, and other incidentals, which added up to $1700 monthly for living expenses. Van also paid $402 toward a deed of trust on the Fairfax home. Van stated his attorney fees at $1000 at a basic rate of $50 an hour. This public information did not make Van happy. His life and his income were out in full view. California law allowed divorce proceedings to be a matter of public record.

Crafting a final divorce agreement was not an easy task. There was property other than the primary residence. The division of assets was a complicated process. The songwriting royalties were a negotiable part of the settlement. Janet could lay claim to a portion of Van's songwriting and publishing. This turned into a major area of disagreement. Eventually, it was worked out. She gave up any interest in song copyrights and publishing in return for a substantial sum of money. It was allegedly $100,000. There were also the usual lawyer disagreements over the division of community property. The local judge was a no-nonsense jurist who quickly forced the opposing lawyers to craft a final divorce agreement.

Divorce is a battle. Van's was no exception. Janet's petition emphasized they had been married for three years, ten months and ten days when she filed for divorce. As was common in these situations, Janet's attorneys filed a restraining order to prevent Morrison from "harassing, annoying or molesting" Janet Elizabeth Morrison. This was outrageous. It was driven by Janet's attorneys. They charged, without evidence, Van was somehow dangerous. It was a petty legal move. There were no incidents of domestic disturbances with local police. Friends remember nothing more than good times at Van's home. Janet's attorney accentuated the differences and intensified an acrimonious atmosphere. It wasn't necessary. Some said Van was baffled by it.

In her divorce petition, Janet Elizabeth Morrison's attorneys listed a savings account in the amount of $40,000, a Volkswagen automobile, a 1972 Mercedes, a Cortina automobile, recording equipment, an interest in Caledonia Productions, an interest in Warner Bros. publishing and recording contracts, an interest in B. M. I., who collected Van's substantial royalties, and an interest in miscellaneous record studio furnishings. All of this was subject to community property, which under California law meant an equitable division of property or a fifty-fifty split. Janet requested attorney fees, spousal support, child support and custody of Shana. Janet expressed a fear her husband would take two year old Shana out of the country. She believed he might go back to Ireland with Shana. This was the furthest thing from Van's mind. The divorce caused irrevocable tension and irretrievable hostile feelings. To this day Van will not license a product with Janet's image on it.

Van's attorney, Hadden W. Roth, responded to Janet on February 7, 1973 by stating George Ivan Morrison "is presently unable to list with sufficient accuracy the nature, extent and character of his property." The legal wars were on. His attorney requested spousal support not be awarded to Janet. It took some time for the lawyers to end the legal wrangling. In time a divorce settlement was crafted. Van and Janet went their separate ways. There was a child custody issue down the road. In California, the divorce procedure, when children are at issue, requires a probation report. This document concluded they were a loving and open family. There were no signs of violence or other problems. On August 15, 1973, a Marital Termination Agreement was filed in the Superior Court of California-County of Marin. It contained a handwritten list of all bills, which included medical, dental, insurance, even a sofa bought from Emporium and listed a debt total of just over $2000. For a man with Van's income this was minimal debt.

The final divorce decree indicated Morrison's income was approximately $100,000 a year. His home in Fairfax was valued at $100,000. He owned other property with an estimated value of $200,000. This included an option to purchase a substantial piece of property in nearby Inverness, California. The agreement allowed him to retain ownership of the hillside house in Fairfax. He had the right to the $40,000 timed savings account. He also was able to retain all of his music properties. The extent of Van's finances were complex. He was given the right to maintain and control the six different savings and checking accounts he maintained. Van was to pay $2250 a month child support for the first year, $2000 the second year, $1750 the third year, $1500 until February 19, 1977 and then he would pay beginning March 10, 1977 the sum of $350 a month until Shana reached the age of eighteen. He paid all attorney fees. He set up separate banking accounts for Janet's son, Peter Gauder, and his daughter Shana Caledonia Morrison. With Van's income and future earning potential, this was a fair divorce agreement. It suggested Janet had little, if any, sense of vengeance. She received a very generous settlement. Van kept working as the settlement cut deeply into his financial reserves. There was no Marin County hippie capitalism for Van. He concentrated upon his future earnings and investments.

The divorce decree contained a provision Van had to place the sum of $50,000 into Janet's personal bank account. In return, he would retain possession of the 1972 Mercedes, license plate number FHA 309. Van had already removed the custom license "R & B." She also received the horse, known as Moondance, and the furniture in the Fairfax home.

There was still the issue of Shana's custody. This brought on a prolonged legal battle. The result? Van had very specified visiting rights.

Van and Janet were young kids when they married. In less than five years, they had a different view of life. This was the single most significant factor in the divorce. The intriguing thing was Van had all of his hits while married to Janet. He was focused on his career. She was his muse. Along the way they took separate paths into a new life.

CAN I HAVE A MANAGER?

There were a large number of managers, tour directors, business people and booking agents who have worked with Van. "I feel that I'm not the type of artist who can have a manager," Van commented in a **Rolling Stone** interview with John Grissim in June 1972. Some six months later, Van mulled over his thoughts. He might have modified his comments to suggest he could not find a new manager who could properly represent him.

As he looked back upon his mangers, Van had trouble finding someone who was independent with integrity. Perhaps the music business didn't create these types. Since his initial management association with Phil Solomon, he had a mercurial record as managers arrived and departed with amazing regularity. Van was difficult and demanding. He remained articulately independent. He demanded management represent him with honesty and integrity.

He fired his Woodstock based manager, Mary Martin, because he feared that she would take over his career like Albert Grossman had Bob Dylan's. Martin was formerly Grossman's secretary. She learned her management techniques from him. It was intimidation, according to people close to Martin, that was her most important asset. Van was angry with the people at Warner. He wanted them to pay for his misery. For a time, Mary Martin was perfect. Not, surprisingly, she was fired.

Joe Smith, Vice President of Warner Bros., put it best when he suggested she represented the typical music manager who asked for too much money, too many concessions and too much promotional money.

It was a difficult situation managing Morrison. He was a star. He was a consistent moneymaker. The managers came and left with increasing regularity. Van was directing his career. He was pulling the managerial strings. "It's ridiculous. If I'm gonna work with somebody, they're going to be working for me and not the other way around," Morrison commented to John Grissim. Van continued: "The word product keeps coming up. And if I'm the product, then these people are supposed to be an extension of how I operate. And if they're not, they're operating against me." Once again Morrison's paranoia ran rampant. Van explained he was not going to be managed by the old time bookers. "I don't want to live by anyone's old philosophies," he concluded. The overweight, old style managers with a pot belly, a combover and a cigar were not on Van's radar. "They would say: "Hey Van baby how's it going?" Carol Guida said. She laughed. "Van ignored them," Guida continued. "These old style managers were a carryover of the rock music business and they were on their way out of the business." Van ignored them.

Carol Guida: "I remember when I was with Van in the U. K. how he walked by these combover types laughing at them, but he was always polite to the old style managers."

CAN I MAKE A CHRISTMAS ALBUM?

There was no stronger indication of how much Van controlled his career than when he approached Warner Bros. about making a Christmas album. They were taken back. A memo was circulated at Warner about potential sales. The response was a tepid one. Van persisted. He did this in the Fall of 1972. He believed it could be completed and released by the following Xmas season. There were preliminary discussions. Warner had little interest in the project.

Despite Van's excellent recent LP sales, they believed there wasn't a market for a Van Morrison Christmas album. Van told the label he would do some traditional Christmas songs. He mentioned "White Christmas" and "Chestnuts Roasting On An Open Fire." Joe

Smith remarked Warner couldn't envision selling this product. This did not sit well with Morrison.

The Christmas Special album controversy tells us a great deal about the strength of Morrison's character. His ability to defend his projects was ongoing. It wasn't a great idea. Warner turned it down. Van remained agitated about it for years.

In 1998, in Dusseldorf, a bootleg, **Van Morrison Christmas Special** without holiday songs was released. The bootlegger had a strange sense of humor. The bootlegger took a live show at the Philipshalle in Dusseldorf on December 19, 1998 and he combined it with tracks from a Waterfront Hall show in Belfast on February 2, 1997. The two disc set was completed with a track from a show at the Spektrum, Oslo, Norway. The title **Van Morrison-Christmas Special** may not have amused Morrison. But it was one hell of an interesting bootleg for the collector. The culprit? Rumor has it the bootlegger worked with someone at Warner.

DID HE RECOVER FROM THE DIVORCE?

By the summer of 1973, Van recovered from the divorce. He was ready for new challenges. For a man who never cared for touring, he had an epiphany. It was time to go out on the road. He was only twenty-eight-years old. He was at the top of his performing game. A small number of negative concert reviews, some cranky album notices, and occasional yapping by the press, on his eccentric behavior, pushed him toward a mainstream tour.

The increased quality and innate professional nature of Morrison's shows was what many critically abrasive reviewers ignored. He decided to go on the road with the Caledonia Soul Orchestra. The result was one of the most professional tours of his career.

For the next few years, his writing, and sometimes quirky performances, suggested the effects of the divorce wore off. He lost himself in his work. Some of Van's best and most personal music came in the divorce's aftermath. However, it wasn't until 1977, that he fully recovered from the trauma. The 1970s was a time reworking his career, his life and his writing. He set the template for the next fifty plus years.

WHAT DID THE SAN FRANCISCO BAY AREA OFFER?

In late 1972, and early 1973, the San Francisco Bay Area offered solace and friendship. He found musical soul mates in former Paul Butterfield Blues Band pianist Mark Naftalin, drummer David Shaw, a. k. a. Dahaud Shaar, keyboardist John Allair, bassist David Hayes, guitarist John Platania, folk legend Ramblin' Jack Elliott, boogie woogie pianist Mitch Woods and local jazzman Jules Broussard. A long and enduring friendship with blues legend John Lee Hooker sustained Van during this difficult period. He would drive down to see Hooker at his home in Gilroy south of San Jose. A few years later, John Lee moved to Redwood City. Van's visits increased in frequency, as Hooker moved closer to Marin County.

Van had known Hooker for seven years. He sought out John Lee. Morrison found out they had a lot in common. Like Van, John Lee preferred to ignore the mandates and requirements of fame. They were both shy. They were also reticent with the media. They didn't care to discuss their careers. Like Hooker, Morrison's style was so distinct it was impossible to categorize.

Van recorded on September 28 and 29, 1971 with Hooker and his band for an album **Never Get Out Of These Blues Alive**. In addition to Morrison, Hooker was supported by a band including Cliff Coulter on piano, Robert Hooker on organ, Ron Beck on drums, Gino Skaggs on fender bass and guest artists Charlie Musselwhite, Mel Brown, Mark Naftalin and Elvin Bishop. Van Morrison was the commercial jewel in the LP. When they talked about the album, Van was excited. "He told me that he wanted to record with me for some time," Hooker smiled. "Sure did make me happy," Hooker remarked of Van's shy nature. Charlie Musselwhite recalled Morrison was so happy with the album. He loved being in the recording studio with Hooker. Even though he was only there for a brief time.

Van was only on one cut "Never Get Out of These Blues Alive." This recording session energized him. By the time the LP was released in 1972 under the title **Never Get Out Of These Blues Alive**, the John Lee Hooker album was Van's favorite side project.

WHAT WAS THE GENESIS OF THE 1973 TOUR? IT WAS THE MAY 23 TROUBADOUR SHOW

When Van was booked into Doug Weston's Troubadour Club on Los Angeles' Santa Monica Boulevard, it was an extended set of dates to test his willingness to survive on the road. The Troubadour gigs were a success. Van was emboldened by the way in which the Caledonia Soul Orchestra followed his every subtle nuance.

The May 24-27, 1973, Troubadour shows were the organizational template for the It's Too Late To Stop Now tour. Van had never experienced a band like the Caledonia Soul Orchestra. The Troubadour, with its diminutive stage, was difficult for an eleven piece band to stand on. The presence of a roomful of celebrities, industry insiders and Frank Zappa with his crew of motley followers made for a festive atmosphere. When the band arrived, they found the street outside the Troubadour filled with celebrity hunters. Nathan Rubin told me: "Van was oblivious to all of it. He asked me: 'What is this book?' I said: 'Bukowski's Post Office.' Van said: 'Hum." He walked into the Troubadour. Nathan Rubin followed him.

That night Rubin experienced the joy of performing with Morrison. He had never witnessed such vocal perfection. When he was playing behind Morrison on "In The Garden," he told me he had a sense of exhilaration. This solo didn't take place until 1974 and by that time he was amazed at how well Van treated and performed with the band. When Van introduced him, Rubin told me: "I had never felt so much a part of something special."

As he prepared for the It's Too Late To Stop Now tour, at the Santa Monica Civic Auditorium, this arena show made Van eager to anticipate the upcoming U. K. shows. This set the stage for the Rainbow Theater appearances on July 23-24. These shows according to a number of musicians, finalized Van's performing brilliance. "He was letting the London audience know he was best blues singer out of the U. K.," Nathan Rubin continued. "He had something to prove.

He did that." These shows created the **It's Too Late To Stop Now** album.

Although he was quiet, and shy by nature, those around Van saw a new confidence. There was a determined direction in concert. It took a great deal of work. At times he showed the strain. It didn't matter.

HOW DID VAN REACT TO HIS EVOLVING CAREER?

"What I do is not easy," Morrison observed. No one who witnessed those shows believed that statement. He made it look easy. The ensuing tour and album was described as the best in rock 'n' roll music. Why? The reason was the rhythm section of Jef Labes on keyboards, John Platania on guitar, David Hayes on bass and Dahaud Shaar on drums followed Van's every subtle nuance. This musical nucleus enabled Van's blues covers.

Van's version of Sonny Boy Williamson's "Take Your Hand Out Of My Pocket" and "Help Me" were flawless. He mixed in Them's "Gloria" and "Here Comes The Night." He finally overcame his disdain for performing these songs.

The musicians could "take the songs anywhere Van wanted to take them," Labes continued. "Van prided himself in performing the songs differently each night." This kept the musicians attuned to his every stage mannerism, vocal direction and interpretive nuance. Labes said it was fun.

John Platania observed the band paid attention. Van would flash signals behind his back for musical changes. He was lost in the intricacy of his performances. Most shows ended with "Caravan." Van was ready for a lengthy tour. The It's Too Late To Stop Now tour percolated. Van's fans extolled his performances.

The May 24-27, 1973 Troubadour shows allowed Van to experiment with a wide variety of songs. At the Troubadour, Morrison blended old and new tunes. This created the template for his in concert genius for the next five decades.

During a spring evening in 1973, Van left the Troubadour thinking of how to finalize the sound, the plan and the implementation of the Caledonia Soul Orchestra. The planning was in place to take the CSO on a series of Canadian and American warm up shows. The tour was to be an extended one. This wasn't Van's usual mantra. He didn't go out on the road for lengthy periods. This tour resulted in a critically acclaimed live double album. Van was making a point to Warner Bros. His one take studio records received criticism. His one take concert clips led to the most acclaimed live album of the 1970s. Van believed there was hypocrisy amongst the reviewers. Van's producing talent was gold. There was also a sense of nostalgia to Van on the It's Too Late To Stop Now tour. He recalled the old days with the showbands and his Belfast blues club.

"I remember how Van glowed years later, as she talked about the tour, with pride," Mervyn Solomon continued. "He said he found his groove. Then he told me the Troubadour show was the inspiration for the tour."

During the Troubadour gig, Van talked with his band about the old days at Belfast's Maritime Hotel. He reminisced the Troubadour was much like Belfast's Maritime club. The shows were frenetic ones. He began thinking about an extended tour. The shows were taped for a live album. Warner Bros. executives embraced the idea.

To perfect his in concert genius, Van booked shows in small Marin County clubs. It was exciting. It was like being back in Belfast's Maritime Hotel. Of all these clubs, the Lion's Share was his favorite. He could stretch out his set list. The club had no rules. The sound person was seen pocketing twenty dollar bills so the bootleggers could record the show. Van's version of "Listen To The Lion" was reproduced on more bootlegs than his hits. A Japanese bootlegger put out a deluxe version of Morrison's Lion's Share shows. A Greek grandfather in his sixties in San Francisco's Mission District, Haik Arakiel, sold a variety of Morrison's bootlegs from his home. He was seen at the Lion's Share with his crew of tapers. Van fans came in all forms.

If there was an argument for releasing Van bootlegs legitimately the 1971 Lion's Share Show was the model. This bootleg included material from three shows which were re-mastered with a brilliant sound. Acoustic versions of "I Wanna Roo You," "Sweet Thing," "Street Choir" and "Tupelo Honey" open the album. There were fifteen songs in the collection. All of them beautifully remastered.

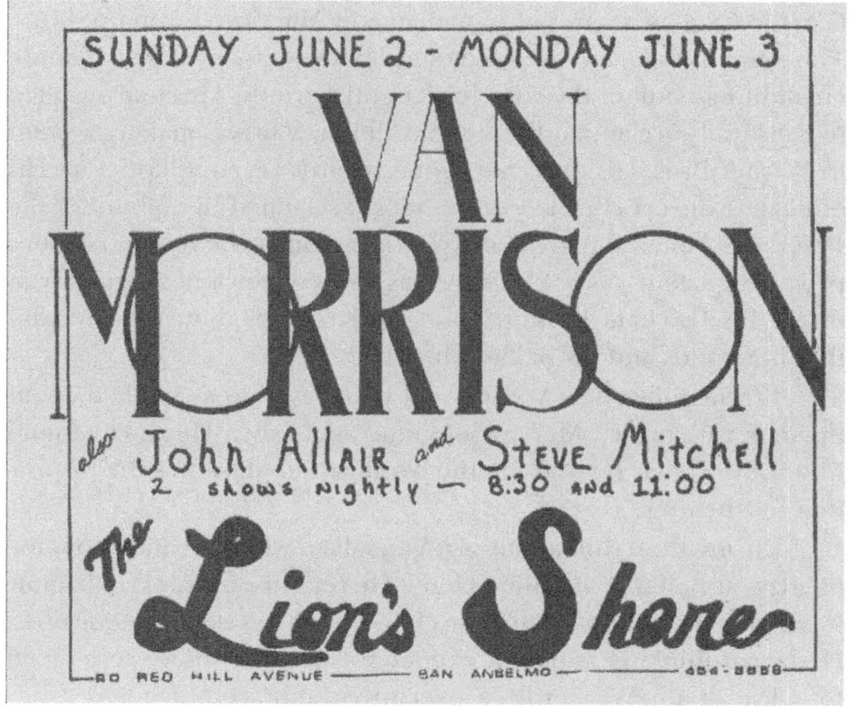

Van Morrison - The Lion's Share in San Anselmo, California

The Van Morrison bootlegs go a long way toward highlighting his in concert genius. They demonstrated how hard he worked to perfect his on stage presence. It was not surprising he doesn't engage in stage patter. He was there to deliver a show of original and cover tunes. His version of Bobby Blue Bland's songs were so original even Bobby Blue Bland praised Van. He delivered surprise songs during every show. An example of a surprise song was Van performing a cover of "The White Cliffs of Dover" at the Keystone Corner on February 15, 1973. Van's version was more like Vera Lynn's than Kate Smith's.

WHY WAS VAN AT THE LION'S SHARE?

The Lion's Share is a small club in San Anselmo. This tree lined California town, north of San Francisco, is sleepy. It is more like a small village. There is little excitement. It was the perfect place for

Van to experiment. He would call the club owner a day before or even on the day he played and a brief radio announcement sold out the premises. The parking lot and streets nearby often had more people than the club.

The 150 seat Lion's Share smelled. The bathroom was filthy. It had bad lighting. The sound system was average. The locals drank too much. For a time, there were also egg cartons on the ceiling to muffle the sound. Chef Jacqueline Clay provided food for Van and the band. One band member told me he would play there for free because of the food. The favorites were the Oyster po boy and the chicken gumbo, which were the best outside of New Orleans.

From 1971 to 1974 the Lion's Share perfected Van's stage presence sending his performances into a euphoric direction. His legion of San Francisco Bay Area fans regularly filled this small club. There were thirteen shows allowing him to craft stage shows true to Marin County. The house band had Mike Finnegan or Bill Champlain on keyboards, Danny Nudalman on guitar, Dave Schallock on bass and Bill Vitt on drums. They were called the Nu Boogaloo Express. The clientele included Ramblin' Jack Elliott, Janis Joplin, Bob Neuwirth and Dino Valenti. Van showed up at times to sing one or two songs.

At the Lion's Share, Van heard Clover who later morphed into Huey Lewis and the News with their pop sound destined for commercial success. The seedy nature of the Lion's Share, combined with the food, drew an eclectic mix of bikers, college students, local businessmen, bored housewives and musicians.

Van's March 22, 1973, appearance came with a surprise. A good-looking young blond walked on stage as a backup vocalist. Her name was Jackie DeShannon. She was a successful folk chanteuse. She had a lengthy recording career. From 1961 to 1980 DeShannon charted twenty-four times on the **Billboard** Hot 200 chart. She continued as a cult artist with more than forty albums. Her songwriting was the stuff of legend. The set list for the Lion's Share show was typical Van Morrison. He covered Muddy Waters, Ray Charles and Sam Cooke while mixing in B. B. King and Hank Williams. The idea was to have fun. An enraptured audience sat spellbound. The shows were superb. Van was in good humor. You could hear a pin drop during the music.

As Jackie DeShannon sang background, she marveled at Morrison's intensity. Backstage she talked at length with various members of the band about her music. This led her to record some Morrison songs. He produced them. Atlantic Records wasn't able to immediately release the four tunes. She was looking to Van to rekindle her sagging career. When DeShannon left Liberty Records in 1970, she signed with Atlantic. She wanted the same team that produced Dusty Springfield's **Dusty In Memphis** album. It didn't happen.

The four Morrison songs produced for DeShannon weren't issued together until 2015 when **All The Love: The Lost Atlantic Recordings** was released. The four bonus tracks were Van's productions of "Sweet Sixteen," "Flamingos Fly," "Santa Fe" and "The Wonder of You." No explanation for the disinterest from Atlantic from the early 1970s until 2015 was ever given.

While at the Lion's Share, she spent a lot of time discussing career moves with Van. She noticed how well the press reviewed the Belfast Cowboy's concerts. DeShannon marveled when she talked to **San Francisco Chronicle** critic, John L. Wasserman, about Morrison's unique singing style.

Wasserman showed up at many of Van's shows. He was in the audience whether or not he reviewed the show. On April 25, 1973, three days after the Lion's Share show, Wasserman gushed over Morrison's talent. "It was kind of old home week on Sunday night at the Lion's Share...when...Van made his regular irregular appearance there." Van did two sets that night. Wasserman circulated amongst the crowd. He went backstage to talk with Van. He hung out with the band. He was ecstatic to see Van drive his performing to the point of perfection.

Wasserman lauded Van for his diverse music. He chatted backstage with folk-blues singer Alice Stuart and bluesman John Lee Hooker, Wasserman realized an emerging Morrison was refining his shows in small clubs. He would have musician he admired open his shows. Over time this became a distinctive part of Morrison's performing strategy. Give credit to his influences. He recognized the talent of others. He paid them well. He had a car at their disposal. He made sure they had first class hotel accommodations. "I loved opening for Van Morrison," Jimmy Witherspoon told me. "I opened for him in 1993, then out of the blue in 1996 he hired me for the New York Supper Club shows. Van is a first class act. I loved the guy." That comment was echoed time and time again. There were also struggling musicians he attempted to help. One was a Berkeley folk chanteuse turned blues performer Alice Stuart.

ALICE STUART AT SEATTLE'S PAMIR HOUSE (photo courtesy Alice Stuart)

Stuart's raven haired good looks, a formidable blues guitar style, and two backing musicians, known as Snake, provided the Berkeley based chanteuse with awesome back up. Stuart was a club favorite. Jimmy McCracklin, who I managed told me: "There would not have been a Bonnie Raitt without Alice Stuart."

The blue greats, notably Lightnin' Hopkins, recognized her performing talent. She was also a songwriter with a wide ranging catalogue. She fronted a male band. She played a monster lead guitar. She handled the business end of her career. She was a stone Van Morrison fan.

A former folkie, Stuart had blues roots. She played a solid and

ALICE STUART in Concert 1975

innovative blues guitar. She learned her sophisticated blues licks from Lightnin' Hopkins. Van loved her devil may care attitude. She said the major labels could kiss her ass.

A decade earlier Stuart burst onto the music scene at the Berkeley Folk Festival. She was at heart a blues singer. Stuart was typical of the musicians Van surrounded himself with in the 1970s. "His so-called period of retirement was in reality an era of revitalization, reinvention and reconceptualizing the Morrison brand," Stuart said.

It was in the small clubs, like the Lion's Share, the Keystone Corner, Ruthie's Inn, Sophies and the Inn of the Beginning Morrison excelled.

Van didn't have to perform his hit songs at the Lion's Share. He could sing anything he wanted. The audiences loved it. John Allair often opened for Van with his Marin County band. Allair ran through a dozen rock standards. They included a strange juxtaposition of Fats Domino's "Blueberry Hill" with the Beatles' "Why Don't We Do It In The Road."

The partnership with Allair is one of the more enduring ones in Van's career. He still plays with Van. Allair's instrumental and vocal talents blended with Van's music. "He has always been on my wavelength," Van remarked. There is a kind personal side to Morrison that goes unnoticed. He treats his musicians very well. He pays them a top wage. He respects their musical talents.

THE JOURNALISTIC SIDE OF VAN

Van Morrison is either the best or the worst interview depending upon his mood. If the person conducting the interview is a professional journalist there is seldom a problem. Well except for Laura Barton and Steven Hyden. An entitled record reviewer or an industry inside can elicit an eruption. A recent example was when a headline in the **London Guardian** in 2019 read: "A Duel With Van Morrison: Is This A Psychiatric Examination? It Sounds Like One." Laura Barton, the **Guardian** journalist, recounted her horror interviewing Van for the **Three Chords And The Truth** album. This was almost fifty years from the 1970s. The Belfast Cowboy could still go off the rails. "I have the feeling that Morrison is curling up into a ball before me and closing his eyes so that I might not see him," Barton said. She admitted her questions were off the beaten path. Barton explained: "His answers took on a hulking and impenetrable flatness."

She paused. She thought. Barton concluded there was a "determined absence of detail." Barton perfectly described the journalistic side of the Belfast Cowboy. From Van's viewpoint the questions were insipid. He said Barton's knowledge was minimal. After more than fifty years of inane questions, he no longer suffered journalists.

Van is at his best while talking with friends. There is one journalist who bonded with Van until he passed. Morrison was warm, open, forthcoming and transparent with the Irish journalist Donal Corvin. They had a long friendship that began in Belfast.

When he performed with Them, Van met Donal Corvin. They bonded over drink, young ladies and a passion for all things Irish. When Ritchie Yorke wrote the first Van Morrison biography, he talked at length with the Belfast journalist. "Van lived in a world of his own," Corvin told Ritchie Yorke. "His dreams were sweet but reality was bitter. He was a cryptic person. Gentle and quiet at the best of times, but given to sudden fits of anger...Everybody kept telling him how big a star he was, but nobody could tell him how to make a living out of it." Corvin described Van's sensitive character in detail.

Of **Astral Weeks**, Van told Corvin the album was about "a lot of various feelings, moods....I didn't write it with an interpretation; that's up to the listener." Over the years, Van gave some of his best interviews to Corvin.

A good example was in 1974. Van sat down with Corvin. He opened up about his life. He described his art. He ruminated on his future. Van concluded his music reflected distinctive Celtic attitudes that brought his surging intellect to the center of his artistic soul. Corvin's thick Irish brogue put Morrison at ease. Van started the interview complaining about managers and record labels. This set the tone for the remainder of his career.

In the 1970s, Van was irritated he had to purchase the reissue Them records. He ranted about the nefarious activity of Bert Berns. Even though Berns was long since dead, Van had bitter feelings. He spoke to Corvin about going into San Francisco's Tower Records to purchase copies of **The World of Them** and another reissue **Backtrackin: Them Featuring Van Morrison Lead Singer**. He loved both albums. For the first time he talked glowingly of Them's successes. He liked the music. He hated the way the story had been told.

He lamented the twenty different versions of Them which were out on tour. "Well after the first two singles the band wasn't even together," Van continued. "But after that it wasn't Them....It got really weird." He was upset journalists writing about the group didn't accurately portray the band. "We were really into blues, like funky," Van paused. "And we had to get into these suits and have make-up put on and all that shit. Ridiculous!" Maybe Van wasn't as cranky as journalists suggested. He was in an impossible situation with Them. He had to go solo. His time with Them continually agitated him.

He returned angrily to the subject of the Them albums. He remarked **The World of Them** had a cover that "looks like a six year old kid did the drawing...." To get out of a situation, where he as artistically strangled, Van left Them. The reissues perpetually tortured him. He wasn't the villain some members of Them suggested. Van had to leave to keep his artistic integrity intact. He recalled the horrors of recording in the studio with Them.

When the subject of producer Tommy Scott came up, Van didn't mince his words. He said Scott was a non-talented opportunist. He selected his songs at the expense of the artist. Scott's songwriting came in for Morrison's virulent tirade. Scott's amateur songwriting and inadequate production made Them less than its parts.

The Scott tunes on the second LP, **Them Again**, came in for Van's most vitriolic criticism. They were pop, bubblegum songs Van detested. He railed on about Scott's condescending manner. His crude production techniques drove Van crazy.

Van was loyal to his Belfast cronies. He had wonderful things to say about Phil Coulter who provided piano accompaniment on the second Them album. Coulter grew up in Derry in Northern Ireland. He attended college in Belfast. He also helped Scott with the production. As Van watched Coulter and Scott work on the Them material, he came to respect the young Coulter who had just graduated from Belfast's Queen's University. One of Morrison's strengths was recognizing musical ability. Coulter had it. Scott was a rank amateur.

When Them recorded the first album with Van Morrison, Coulter was in the studio watching Bert Berns cut "Here Comes The Night." Coulter and Van bonded. He continued to work with Them after Berns returned to New York.

Phil Coulter At Home in 1984 With a Wall of Gold Records

Coulter salvaged Them's second album from the producer. Scott didn't understand how to record Van's voice. Them's musical direction was anathema to Scott. Coulter Coaxed him into producing an acceptable album. This is one of many insights into Morrison's character. He trusts long-time friends or those from Ireland. When Van departed Them, he remarked: "The producer made all the money." That began his road to production.

Coulter was a calming influence. After they met during the Them days, they stayed in touch. Coulter coaxed Sinead O'Connor into a marvelous performance of "You Make Me Feel So Free" for the 1994 Morrison tribute album **No Prima Donna**, which he co-produced. This was thirty years after meeting him. Coulter, like many other long term friends, provided a window who Morrison life-long friends.

When Coulter wrote his autobiography, it was titled aptly, **Bruised, But Not Broken**. The title was evocative. "Happiness is not an ongoing condition," Coulter continued. "It comes in moments." That phrase defined how Morrison viewed happiness.

That moment of magic for Coulter came when he walked into the recording studio and watched Bert Berns record Them's "Here Comes The Night." Van soaring voice caused Coulter to state years later: "It wasn't like hearing a song on the radio. It was my first time to hear a song in its raw state…." He introduced himself to Van. They have been friends since that day.

Although Coulter began his music career in the 1960s it wasn't until his 1980s album, **Tranquility**, that he became a household name. But before that he worked as a staff writer for Phil Solomon for a subsistence wage. He wrote hits for Sandi Shaw, the Bay City Rollers and Cliff Richard. Along with his writing partner, Bill Martin, he composed an award winning Eurovision song in 1968 for Cliff Richard and Cilla Black.

"Music has been a steadying influence on me through those dark hours," Coulter continued. "No doubt about it. It has saved my life on many different levels." This explains his close connection to Van Morrison. Music saved both their lives.

CORVIN PROVIDES INSIGHTS INTO VAN'S PERSONALITY AND CHARACTER

There were also insights from Donal Corvin. His interviews were first rate. He was, at times, in the early years, a drinking partner. During one of the Corvin interviews, Van made brief political remarks. He told Corvin musicians who enter the political arena are out of their depth. For this reason he eschewed the Northern Ireland conflict. Van would not comment on the Troubles. He steered clear of American politics. His parents were concerned for his safety if he returned to Belfast.

By 1974, when the Corvin interview was completed, Van's insights were revealing. He has always been and remains a high character person with integrity. He was gruff. He was grouchy. He has a strong, highly defined character. This makes his personality difficult. His view of life was infinitely defined.

The Haight Ashbury hippie culture that Warner Bros. tried to identify him with was nonsense. "Woodstock did not like hippies," Van remarked. Neither did Van. It was the reason he lived there for only a few years. After the 1969 Woodstock Festival the hippie invasion accelerated his move to California. He took an obsessive interest in his business affairs. Woodstock was not the place to be a music tycoon. Unless you were Albert Grossman.

Elliot Landy, who took pictures of Van in and around the Woodstock, observed it was clear he wasn't happy about the changes in this rural bucolic New York community.

Van believed the music business hurts one's creativity. He didn't socialize or befriend people in the industry. "I know very few people in showbiz," Van continued. "I know more people out of it than in it." This comment was amplified by the gatherings at his home in Fairfax, California. He would have his musician friends came over, but they didn't talk shop. They played in jam sessions from time-to-time. He had an eclectic set of friends. Many had nothing to do with the industry.

The picture of Van as a maladjusted and tormented artist is the fabric of journalistic fiction. He was much like anyone else. The problem was by early 1974, he was famous. He was having difficulty learning to deal with it. Van's privacy was in danger as was his psyche.

Bibliographical Sources

The best statement of the myth of the retirement years and the period is Howard A. DeWitt, **Van Morrison: The Mystic's Music** (Fremont, 1983), pp. 42-46. Also, see, Clinton Heylin, **Can You Feel The Silence?: Van Morrison, A New Biography** (London, 2002), chapters 16-18 and Brian Hinton, **Celtic Crossroads: The Art of Van Morrison** (London, 1997, revised edition, 2000), chapter 6 for important material on this period.

Van is the person emboldening the so-called retirement years. While he was out of the public eye much of 1975 and 1976, he was far from retired. The "retirement myth," as I label it, owes its life to Morrison. He has never stopped talking about it. In the last decade he has pushed it as a fact. Maybe! Maybe not! Here are some quotes from Van buttressing the "retirement myth." He said to **Classic** magazine: "I had people to support-myself and others." To the **London Mirror's** Kim Carr he talked at length about his retirement. He intimated he had so much back product he couldn't retire.

Interviews with Sal Valentino helped to put some of the performing material in San Francisco in perspective. Tom Bradshaw of San Francisco's Great American Music Hall helped with some anecdotes and observations. Bradshaw found Van and his management easy to work with and he was never demanding. Bradshaw's comment was typical of the small club owners, the Keystone Corner management and the bookers who were fortunate enough to come into contact with Van in the 1970s. All that changed in the next decade as corporate Van emerged.

Chris Michie, who played guitar with Van in the 1980s, recalled stories and second hand reminiscences from Morrison about the It's Too Late To Stop Now tour. A brief interview with Bill Graham helped in understanding Van's mindset. Nick Clainos of Bill Graham Presents weighed in with his opinions on working with the Belfast Cowboy as did blue coat Larry Catlin. Clainos, a Stanford trained lawyer, was careful in his comments to me even though he know nothing more than I was a young professor working on my first Van Morrison book.

Clainos was the brains behind signing Van Morrison to a contract with Bill Graham Presents. Neither Graham or Morrison got on with each other. Why did Van sign with BGP? I asked Clainos. His answer was logistics. Van had a self-contained band; he had an excellent road manager and a meager stage crew. Of bands like Van's, Clainos said: "They've got their own lights, their own sound, their own ideas about staging. So this limits the areas of creativity for the concert promoter." This explanation suggests why Van didn't last very long in Graham's management. Van saw BGP for what it was and that was a middle man who took the cut of the proceeds for arranging the gig. Van was also taken back when Clainos said "The satisfaction Graham derives from working directly with an artists' career was important." Van laughed at this comment. Graham wasn't a benevolent despot on the plantation, he was a money grubbing businessman. This was the opinion of Jack Schroer and a half dozen other musicians playing with Van in the Graham interregnum. Clainos was in charge of BGP management side. He had brains and integrity. He couldn't keep Graham and Morrison together.

Also, see, the insightful article with a degree of analysis suggesting Eddie Money was the new BGP favorite, Jack McDonough, "Bill Graham: His Artist Management Division Enters 4 Artists On Market In 6 Weeks," **Billboard**, Septembe4r 13, 1980, p. 32. https://books.google.pt/books?id=jiQEAAAAMBAJ&pg=PT31&lpg=PT31&dq=nick+clainos+and+van+morrison&source=bl&ots=Ay5d9ayxso&sig=ACfU3U0BSC0IKTV6p7sTPe1vlLlzzUo73g&hl=en&sa=X&ved=2ahUKEwio30esytX4AhUSyxoKHQCtA8sQ6AF6BAgeEAM#v=onepage&q=nick%20clainos%20and%20van%20morrison&f=false

This article suggests Graham had something to do with **Common One**. He didn't. Van has never said what he thought of Graham who at this point was promoting Eddie Money. Quotes from Clainos in **Billboard** did little to create love between Van and BGP. "Van Morrison brings another aspect of management into play," Clainos continued. "Van has never played the game in terms of standard career marketing techniques. He wants to be happy with the music. Period. Our job, without compromising the individual, is to help increase the number of his fans." That was horseshit. Van had for a decade worked hard to establish his fan base. Clainos was smart. He liked Van. In his comments to me, he praised his work ethic. Van has never spoken of Clainos. Draw your own conclusions.

See John Grissim Jr's. Interview with Van in the June 22, 1972 issue of **Rolling Stone** and the Shay Healy interview with Janet Planet in the June 25, 1972 issue of **Spotlight** for why Van, at times, reacted indignantly to the press. Van took exception to the Grissim interview. In doing so he gave the biographer insights into how he viewed the writing of rock music critics. Van complained Grissim taped the interview. He made promises. Van insisted the writer told him he would publish it verbatim. He didn't seem to realize a taped interview is the raw material for an interpretive article. Grissim's introduction to the **Rolling Stone** article, one band member told me, sent Van off. Grissim wrote: "This sullen, tweedy-looking little man, light sweater-vest pulled over checkered dress shirt, not saying a word, stood stiffly up there behind the mike, working his magic...." What was Grissim describing? A concert in San Francisco at Winterland. It was excellent writing. Was it Van? Yes! But it was not in his usual manner. The scene Grissim described was simple. Van was getting ready to change his musical direction. He made that clear to those backing him. What Grissim described was a November 1971 show. He made Van appear like a space cadet. The truth was more complicated. When Van changed musicians and reorganized a band, he didn't explain what he was doing. He reasoned it was no one's business. This is what Grissim missed. The **Rolling Stone** writer did get it right concerning Van's stage fright. It was real. "He'd been half paralyzed by stage fright, which strikes just about her time he approaches the stage," Grissim concluded.

Another excellent insight into how Van viewed and dealt with the press is seen in an interview with a small rock magazine. Van told John Tobler, of **Zig Zag**, he was assured of "exactly word for word off the tape" comments and conclusions would be the basis of the article. Van was angry, commenting: "When it came out it was all changed around." Van's complaint was it wasn't so much about him as it was about what Grissim thought. Van didn't like the article. What was the reason for his criticism? No one knows to this day. Grissim's piece was sympathetic with praise and virtually no criticism. Van attempts to maintain control of his music, his career and his life.

The social-intellectual development in Van's career and the manner in which he changed in this period is addressed in Ritchie Yorke, **Van Morrison: A Portrait Of The Artist** (London, 1984), chapters 8-10. In Chapter 10 Van commented extensively to Yorke on the **Hard Nose The Highway** album. Interviews with John Lee Hooker and Alice Stuart were important to this chapter as both recording artists reacted to the album. They were privy to its content prior to commercial release and both said it was a new Van Morrison.

See John L. Wasserman, "Rock Star's Got Feeling For The Blues," **San Francisco Chronicle**, April 25, 1973, p. 48 for a review of a Lion's Share show.

Mark Naftalin, formerly of the Paul Butterfield Blues, now a solo act, was extremely helpful with information on the San Francisco blues scene.

For the paper trail of the Morrison divorce, see, for example, the following public records. Petition (Marriage), Case Number 65668, Filed January 26, 1973, Order To Show Cause, Case Number 65668, Filed January 26, 1973, Superior Court of California, County of Marin, Financial Declaration, Case Number 65668, Filed January 26, 1973, Financial Declaration, Case 65668, Filed February 7, 1973, Response (Marriage), Case Number 65668, Filed February 7, 1973, Interlocutory Judgment of Dissolution of Marriage, Case Number 65668, Filed August 15, 1973, Final Judgment, August 29, 1973. For the child custody dispute see Order To Show Cause, Modification of Child Custody Agreement, Filed January 24, 1974, Stipulation and Order of Child Custody Agreement, Filed May 21, 1974.

For the alleged Van Morrison Christmas LP and other Morrison attempts see, David Chance, "Mechanical Bliss: An Attempt to Reconstruct Van Morrison's Unreleased 1975 Album," **Van Morrison Website**.

http://www.oocities.org/tracybjazz/hayward/van-the-man.info/discography/mechanicalbliss.html

Mitch Woods offered a brief comment on the San Francisco music scene and his admiration for Van Morrison.

The Mill Valley rock and roll scene that Morrison was an integral part of was a complicated and interesting one. Material from Bonnie Raitt and Guitar Mac added a great deal to this chapter.

The key to the Mill Valley scene was the Sweetwater club. John Goddard provided detailed information on this venue. Tony Dey, Van's former drummer, also offered important caveats of information on the Mill Valley rock scene.

An interview with Charlie Musselwhite in 2004 was important to the John Lee Hooker recording sessions.

See Rob O'Connor, "Blue Light Special," for a review of "The Best of Van Morrison," **Spin**, August 1990, pp. 80-81.

One of Van's pet peeves was the media stories he believed were often untrue, exaggerated, self-serving and these "tall tales" had little relationship to the facts. For this viewpoint, see, Ivan Little, "Van

Morrison: Van The Man And Me," **Belfast Telegraph**, August 29, 2020.
https://www.belfasttelegraph.co.uk/life/features/van-morrison-van-the-man-and-me-39486664.html

Ted Templeman's role in leading Van to produce **Hard Nose The Highway** is an important one. He was assigned to Van as a house producer. Templeman was inexperienced. He had all the talent to become an acclaimed producer. He did. Ronnie Montrose was equally important in Van's emergence in the studio. For this period see Ted Templeman and Greg Renoff, **Ted Templeman: A Platinum Producer's Life In Music** (Toronto, 2020), chapter 5. The Templeman book is exceptionally well written and revealing. It is a corrective to his earlier comments when he remarked he would never work with Morrison again. In his memoir Templeman changed his mind. He said "Van schooled him" in the art of production.

An interview with Jimmy Witherspoon, at the Great American Music Hall, provided information on how well Van treated his opening acts. The metamorphosis of Van Morrison took place in a two year period from late 1972 into late 1974. The small clubs in and around the San Francisco Bay Area were like a university training Van for his future. Nick Clainos, of Bill Graham Presents, told me Van was a student of the entertainment business process. Larry Catlin, of Bill Graham Presents, was helpful with material for this chapter regarding Van's shows.

Throughout his career, Van has had interviews where he is explosive, volatile or downright cruel. From his point of view, he believed he was justified due to the type of questions and the atmosphere in which he was interviewed. For an explanation of why Van doesn't like to explain his art, and how some questions set him off, see, for example, Laura Barton, "A Duel With Van Morrison: Is This A Psychiatric Examination? It Sounds Like One," **London Independent**, October 31, 2019. https://www.theguardian.com/music/2019/oct/31/a-duel-with-van-morrison-is-this-a-psychiatric-examination-it-sounds-like-one

For Jef Labes and others commenting on the It's Too Late To Stop Now tour, see, David Browne, "Inside Van Morrison's Legendary 'It's Too Late To Stop Now' Tour," **Rolling Stone**, August, 2017.

https://www.rollingstone.com/music/music-features/inside-van-morrisons-legendary-its-too-late-to-stop-now-tour-202118/

Phil Coulter was a long time influence on Van. For Coulter, see, for example, Patrick Freyne, "Phil Coulter: Music Save My Sanity…And My Life," **The Irish Times**, October 13, 2019, https://www.irishtimes.com/culture/music/phil-coulter-music-saved-my-sanity-and-my-life-1.4046344 and Richard Fitzpatrick, "Culture That Made Me: Phil Coulter On Derry, Van The Man And Swinging London," **The Irish Examiner**, August 16, 20212. https://www.irishexaminer.com/lifestyle/artsandculture/arid-40358894.html

Joanne Savage, "Phil Coulter: When I Was Growing Up In Abercorn Terrace, Did I Ever Think That One Day Elvis Would Sing One Of My Songs," **Derry Journal**, January 18, 2022.
https://www.derryjournal.com/news/people/phil-coulter-on-his-remarkable-life-in-music-and-his-love-of-the-maiden-city-3530853

Phil Coulter, **Bruised, Never Broken** (London, 2019) is his autobiography which goes a long way toward explaining his long time friendship with Morrison. The Coulter story is an important one. He is much like Van in talent but much easier in temperament. Coulter's autobiography has very little in it that was new about Morrison.

Chris Michie provided his insights while not yet playing with Van but living in Marin County and watching Van in the local music scene. Chris's sister, Sarah Pressler, also provided some excellent material on Marin County and its influence. An interview with John Lee Hooker at the Sweetwater in Mill Valley was important to this chapter.

The influence of Marin County was obvious in a number of peripheral interviews. When I talked with Ramblin' Jack Elliott one night where he observed: "Van is so god-damned original it frightens me. A series of brief interviews with Ronnie Montrose helped this chapter.

EIGHT

HAUNTED BY BERT BERNS' GHOST: ILENE BERNS ATTACKS VAN

"Van Morrison acted unprofessionally when my husband, Bert, presented him to the press at the Bitter End."

ILENE BERNS

"At the Bitter End Van walked on stage, he looked at the audience. He walked to the street and caught a taxi to the hotel. Van said the audience was too small, too disinterested and too stiff looking."

CHRIS MICHIE RECOUNTING A STORY VAN TOLD HIM

"It was really hard for him to get representation…to get people to want to work with him…get behind him."

JOEL SELVIN INTERVIEW WITH JANET PLANET

"I don't know where he's buried, but if I did, I would piss on his grave."

JERRY WEXLER COMMENTING ON BERT BERNS TO JOEL SELVIN

The Bang Record contract was like an albatross hanging over Van Morrison's head. No one knows for sure what happened to the Bang agreement once Bert Berns died. His death was unexpected. A heart defect from birth, a life of cigarettes, booze and good times obscured his producing genius. He died while creating the mystique of a legendary producer.

After Berns died his widow, Ilene, took over Bang Records. His December 30, 1967 death left the twenty-four year old Ilene with three children, a mortgaged to the hilt New York Penthouse, and a gaggle of gangsters with interests in Berns' label. His widow, Ilene, solved the gangster problem by learning the ins and outs of the music business. She packed her suitcase and headed to Atlanta. For the next twelve years she became an executive. She was respected by top people in the industry. At least a dozen people told me she was "bright, tough and knowledgeable." She was also broke. Her husband didn't handle business well. There were muddled contracts. A number of artists owed her sessions. She demanded they fulfill their agreements with Bang Records.

One of these was with Van Morrison. He was under contract to her for more than thirty tracks. This led to the "Contractual Obligation" sessions. The result was Ilene had thirty plus worthless recordings. The finished product was unsuitable for commercial release. She is often pictured as someone who hated Van. We don't know for sure. What we do know is she blamed Bert's death on pressures from the Belfast Cowboy.

She never forgave him for not attending her husband's funeral. Van later said it was a mistake. He apologized. The level of her anger escalated. Although Van was under contract to Berns label, he included two songs where Bang had the songwriting right on **Astral Weeks**. Lewis Merenstein, in an interview before his death, claimed to have selected the songs and their order for the album. Van remembers it differently. The truth? Who knows!

Then the story takes on a blurred focus with no one knowing fully what happened. Some people I interviewed said she went after Van to destroy his career. Others said Van was angry with contract inequities. To this day there are no court records. There was proposed legal action. How far that went is not known, and the result is conjecture, innuendo, myths and gangster influences. The truth? Who knows!

These musicians in the Bang Record family claimed Van and Janet moved to Boston because New York clubs would no longer book him. None of these stories are verified nor are they refuted.

Ilene Berns wanted Van deported. He married to Janet Planet thereby escaping deportation. The notion that Van was tied to the mob is neither confirmed or refuted. It is allegedly true. He did live in a mobster's home in Boston for a brief time. "The move to Boston was completely fear based," Ryan W. Walsh wrote.

The presence of a cigar smoking gangster with a spit curl making him look like at Italian enforcer impersonating Bill Haley led to a further mystery. His name was Carmine, the Wassel, DeNoia. He was mob enforcer. His job, according to legend, was to handle Van's contract. When Joe Smith took Warner Bros. money and paid the $20,000 for Van's contract in a Brooklyn garage, Wassel was the contact.

Joe Smith was the fixer. From his days as a Boston disc jockey, fired in a payola scandal, he understood the mob and its influence. When Ilene requested Warner Bros. pay songwriting royalties for using two Bang Record songs on Van's **Astral Weeks** album, Smith was furious. He remarked of Morrison: "He's a hateful little guy, but…I still think he's the best rock 'n' roll voice out there." Smith should have been upset with Warner corporate. They didn't realize the extent of Ilene Berns' business skill. She also had an iron clad contract with Van. She collected her money. She was tired of the fight with Van.

In 1979 Ilene sold catalogue to Columbia Records. She purchased a number of country and Rhythm And Blues radio stations. She relocated Web IV Music Publishing and Sloopy II Publishing to Nashville. In 1993 she revived the Bang imprint. Ilene Berns.

ILENE BERNS: HER SECOND ACT, SHE WAS NOT THE VILLAIN IN THE MORRISON STORY, IT WAS THE INDUSTRY

In Morrison biographies, Ilene Berns is pictured as the villain in the songwriting royalties Van had trouble collecting. "I never made a fucking penny from Bert Berns," Van told Chris Michie. The anger Van spewed in 1974 was demonstrated when Carol Guida took Van to a family celebration. To liven up the evening one family member played "Gloria" to get people dancing. Van looked up angrily complaining: "I never made a dime from that record." The pressure in collecting his royalties prompted angry outbursts. Ironically, Ilene had a similar anger. The people I interviewed took Van's side or agreed with Ilene on the royalties question. But neither Van nor Ilene are villains. It is the predatory story of the recording industry.

It is a complicated story that has more to do with record business contracts, the predatory ways of the industry concerning the payment of royalties, and the constant search for hits sending labels, executives and artist on to war with each other. The story is murky. The main players appear like evil, cartoon characters and in this scenario, no one comes out looking good.

One reissue insider told me: "You don't understand the music business." Another head of a major label commented: "The fucking artists took over in the 1970s due to the assholes at Warner Bros." Harry Balk, a Detroit producer, told me: "When I had Del Shannon and a number one hit producing 'Runaway', I had to hold back some of Del's royalties to keep my business afloat. No one realizes the amount of money you lose on the records that don't sell." That story was repeated by dozens in the business.

For many Morrison biographers, Ilene appears like the devil. She was a hardnosed business woman. She was also smart and accomplished in the ways of the record business. The rumor was she allegedly died broke. What is known is she made a comeback in the business giving her a second act. She launched her comeback a decade after selling the Bang catalogue.

In Nashville, with her husband, Brian Jackson, a former apparel executive, she returned to the business. "To be honest with you,"

Ilene told Beverly Keel, "I just missed the passion of the record business. If I feel like I have a hit song. I get excited about it. If I pitch it to an artist or a label, you never know if they're going to cut it."

As Berns looked back on her career, with pride and insight, she said: "the 1990s were more exciting." She observed the music business was the second time around "a lot harder" to make money in due to changes in the business. That is she had the expertise to handle the new artists, select the songs and produce the music. The business sharks were a concern. Her husband had an MBA from Wake Forest and he took care of the business. Ilene planned a comeback. "We just want to work one artist at a time and be a boutique label," Berns said in the 1990s. Ilene loved Nashville. They returned the favor spanning a re-emergence of his production and marketing skills.

In 1993 she convinced Faith Hill to record "Piece Of My Heart," which was a number one country hit in 1994. Then Miguel Salas charted three country hits and a Monty Holmes single in 1998 "Why'd You Start Looking So Good" hit the charts. When Bert Berns was inducted into the Rock 'N' Roll Hall of Fame in 2016, she was also featured in a documentary "Bang: The Bert Berns Story." A Broadway musical celebrated Bert Berns. Van Morrison made a cameo in the documentary. He rewrote history with nice comments about Berns. The truth was more complicated. Throughout 1973-1974 he complained about the Bang Record deal as reissues arrived like a thunderous cacophony of poorly produced and ill thought of releases. At least this was Van's view of the scenario.

WAS THERE OR WASN'T THERE A LAW SUIT BETWEEN ILENE AND VAN? PROBABLY A LEGAL SETTLEMENT

The final part of the Web IV contract was signed in a specific legal document on September 12, 1968. That agreement released Morrison from the Web IV contract which was an agreement binding Van to record thirty two songs for Berns in exchange for his freedom to begin work on **Astral Weeks**.

Chris Michie: "When I met Van, I was intrigued by his ability to navigate the industry. My take on this was Ilene Berns waited until 1974, when Van was making decent money, to rub his nose in the Them material by licensing it. She let Van know she was getting big money. I don't know that she did." What Michie's comment suggest is Van had a lawyer but brokered out of court agreements. He has done this his entire career. This is why he owns 98% of his songwriting.

She lived until February 2017 when she passed away in Miami, Florida. **Billboard** said she was "one of the leading female independent record label chiefs of her time." As the head of Bang Record and having control of Web IV Music Publishing, she cut a new path for female executives. She not only moved her recording activity to Atlanta. Then to Nashville. When she sold Bang Records catalogue, she retained the rights to the song publishing firms Web IV and Sloopy II for her family. She was a brilliant woman and an industry pioneer. This should not excuse her venality toward Van. Nor should it excuse his behavior.

VAN DECLARES WAR ON THE INDUSTRY

In his long and storied career, Van Morrison is described at war with the music business. His labels have included not just Warner Bros. He has had contracts with Polydor, Virgin, Blue Note, EMI, RCA, Caroline, Parrot and Mercury. His songs slamming the industry and promoters are well known. "Big Time Operators," "The Drumshanbo Hustle," "They Sold Me Out," and "Why Must I Always Explain." They lay out a litany of grievances, some real, some imagined, against the record business.

Van complained about reissues. The Them material and the Bang masters came out in a flurry in 1973-1974 as Van was dealing with divorce, repositioning his Warner Bros. contract and taking control of his production. As he was doing all this a new fiancée, Carol Guida, came into the picture. Van had a full, if complicated, pressure filled life. If he was crabby, angry or simply pissed, there were pressures accentuating that behavior.

There is one experience with Bert Berns and his "Brown Eyed Girl" hit that stuck in Van's craw. When Berns died of a sudden heart attack, his young wife, Ilene, vowed to make Morrison pay. She vowed to destroy the Belfast Cowboy's career. She allegedly told a close friend that Van would be haunted by her legal moves. There was a simmering frustration from Morrison. He viewed Ilene's behavior as "industry hardscrabble."

BERT BERNS AND VAN MORRISON

VAN'S SIMMERING FRUSTRATION WITH THE INDUSTRY

How did Van answer the industry? He didn't answer Berns and the industry publicly until 1991. Privately, his LLCs organized a frontal offensive to secure not just his intellectual property, but to license his songs to the movies, produce videos, and consider book contracts. Business wise he became one of the most sophisticated corporate figures in the industry. As a performer and songwriter, he wasn't corporate. The decade in Marin County was one where Van viewed the music figures who were successful and the dope smoking, let's have fun musicians who were broke once their run ended. Then in the early 1990s, he answered the industry in song.

"Hymns To The Silence" echoed his frustration with labels, industry insiders and the record business. In the title track to this album, Van lamented "hypocrites and parasites." What does he mean? This was a direct mention of Ilene Berns. He claimed her husband, Bert, conned Van with a legal document. In Van's view it wasn't a contract. It was indentured servitude. The Berns story began in the 1960s.

On March 28, 1967, Van Morrison and Bert Berns went into a New York studio for a two day session. Now five decades later, these recordings are the subject of the bad memories persisting with Van.

When "Brown Eyed Girl" peaked at number ten on **Billboard**, Van was owed sizeable royalties. He allegedly didn't receive a penny for songwriting. Van went after Berns and then his estate when he passed away. This is what set his widow, Ilene, off. She vowed publicly to destroy Van's career. He had no choice but to fight. He had to pay her. He had no control over the reissues of the Bang material. While winning his freedom from one set of predators, he lost control of a small portion of his intellectual property.

Van was enraged as the release of his Bang material. He pointed out their little concern for quality. Van said it was all about providing Bang Records with as much money as possible. Berns released material without consulting him. When her husband passed, Ilene waited for the peak of Van's commercial powers in 1973-1974 to pad her bank account. Van's solo album was released with little concern for concept or quality. Bang Records used "Brown Eyed Girl" to sell a Van Morrison album with filler songs. It was an embarrassing LP. He was furious. The album, in Van's view, was an unmitigated disaster.

HOW VAN'S BLOWIN' YOUR MIND ALBUM SET HIM OFF

When Berns released the **Blowin' Your Mind** album in 1967, Van's ire reached new heights. He vowed never to record for Berns again. Ilene Berns sued Van while he was under contract to Warner Bros. He was forced to record the thirty-one nonsense songs for what was referred to as the Contractual Obligation album. In writing these songs in minutes in the studio he made fun of Berns. When Berns wrote "Twist And Shout," this Isley Brothers hit was a song Van loved. When he recorded his criticism of the song Van called it "Twist And

Shake." He did the same thing with "Hang On Sloopy" retitling it "Hang On Groovy." Ilene Berns realized what Van had done. She vowed revenge. She planned her haunting of Van just after his divorce. She was at war with the Belfast Cowboy. The valuable business lessons he learned in this fight provided an education for the remainder of his career.

Why was Van angry? Ilene began to license the Bang material without consulting him. He intimated she licensed the rights to anyone and everyone. At the same time the bootleggers were having a field day taping his shows and the glut of vinyl boots was everywhere. One seller at the Castro Valley Record swap, Lee Cotton, had a special section of Van's bootlegs selling five hundred at each show and when he went down to the Capitol Records parking lot show in Hollywood, he sold almost a thousand Van bootlegs. His supplier and producer, Zaire, ran a mail order business that was international. Whether or not Van knew about the proliferation of bootlegs and the amount of money he was losing is unknown. It seems as though these events coalesced to bring him into the fiscal arena to protect his intellectual property.

Then Ilene Berns made a fatal mistake. She licensed Van's material for no other reason than to piss him off. The gloves were off. The legal wars were on. That war began in 1968 and culminated in 1974 with a legal settlement. A number of people I interviewed, including Carmine "Wassel" DeNoia, believed Ilene and Van were equally intransigent. The issue for Ilene was to be paid. They were both unwilling to compromise. The issue for Van was to be consulted on the sales and marketing of the Them material. Ilene wouldn't consider it.

Whether or not Van had consulting rights is unimportant. He thought he did. He didn't according to the contract. His lawyer's argued he wasn't paid a proper royalty. That abrogated Berns licensing freedom. Ilene Berns had an air tight contract. She went after Van. She won. He reorganized his business. He won in the long run.

Once Berns' widow declared war on Van many New York clubs refused to book him. Or at least that was the rumor. Speculation is Van was working on **Astral Weeks**. He left New York tired of the gangsters, the production criminals, and the intruding and often ignorant journalists. Van had a musical vision. He wanted to record it. That vision was **Astral Weeks**.

When Van moved to Boston, it was due to a quasi-manager of sorts in Boston. He was allegedly a gangster rumored to be laundering money. This unnamed gangster had a factotum in Cambridge who booked rock 'n' roll acts into his club. This mysterious Morrison benefactor managed, owned or had an interest in folk clubs. This mobster provided Van housing. This mysterious person may have been connected to Joe Smith, then a boss on the rise at Warner Bros. The proof of all this is lost to history. Ryan H. Walsh's book told the story not only in great depth, but he escaped the gangsters, the corrupt record executives and the hero, Joe Smith, in this fiasco. If Van is pissed at times, he had good reason. The pressures, the threats and the level of intimidation constantly interrupted Morrison's work. The usual story is Van moved to Woodstock to become friends with Bob Dylan. This is a partially true story. He also moved to Woodstock to write, record and forge a path in the music industry.

There is no proof Ilene Berns was predatory nor is there proof she was intent on destroying his career. Her view was she wanted her money. Van's view was her husband had taken advantage of his naivete. He wanted his fair share of the royalties.

Van put his big boy pants on and met her challenge. The result was he learned to be a hard ass in the industry. That has never changed. The good news was Van organized and finalized much of his business activity. He hired a Sausalito attorney who was an amateur musician playing bar mitzvahs. As Chris Michie told me: "Ilene Berns licensed Van's Bang material to piss him off." In the process she created his first steps to Morrison's corporate entity.

ILENE BERNS VAN BELIEVED LICENSED HIS MATERIAL TO PISS HIM OFF

In 1970 Bang released **The Best Of Van Morrison**. It contained five songs from **Blowin' Your Mind** with five previously unreleased cuts. Van wasn't consulted. He stewed. In 1973, **T. B. Sheets** was released. It was filled with six old songs including earlier versions of "Beside You" and "Madame George." Ironically, Van had redone these songs for **Astral Weeks**. It got worse after she sold the Bang catalogue. In 1990 Columbia reissued **T. B. Sheets**. There wasn't anything Van could do but be angry. The end of the reissues came in 2017 with a three disc set **Van Morrison: The Authorized Bang Collection**. That collection was not only a fine release, the liner notes and the inclusion of unreleased cuts suggested the breadth and width of Van's early talent.

The idea Van engaged in a continual war with the industry is an interesting one. Was it war? Probably not! It is accurate he wanted to be paid. It became an obsession. The tiff with Ilene Berns in 1974 didn't help his career. Or did it? He did learn how to defend his interests. He has done that in toto thanks to his time in Marin County.

The Ilene Berns story is told in depth in Joel Selvin's **Here Comes The Night: The Dark Soul Of Bert Berns And The Dirty Business of Rhythm And Blues**. Selvin makes the point that Ilene Berns had revenge, not business, on her mind when she went after Van. She was loud and clear about destroying Van's career.

THE CONTINUING STORY OF VAN AND THE RECORD LABELS

Travis M. Andrews, writing in the **Washington Post**, observed: "The story of Morrison is of a man constantly at war with the recording establishment." Ryan H. Walsh, in an article for **Pitchfork,** concluded Morrison "harshly scolding a live audience for not listening close enough...." This tells one about Van's temperament. Suggesting Van's erratic behavior. Or was it someone attempting to protect his intellectual property?

Walsh tells the story of Van running up a $2600 bar bill at the Whiskey A Go Go when he performed with the rock group Them with Jim Morrison and the Doors on the bill. That was impossible. The cost of drinks at the Whiskey A Go Go were no more than a dollar. The club never did a $2600 drink night. Walsh's story doesn't meet the fact checking test for other reasons. The bands drank for free at the Whiskey A Go Go. Elmer Valentine told me that the Whiskey was "a cheap ass establishment." He should know, he ran it. Bar bills came later.

These tales perpetrated myths and falsehoods about Van, the industry and the times. The truth? Who the hell knows! The question of Van's behavior rings true in these times. He wasn't as angry as many suggested. He was collecting his royalties while providing oversight to his product. That often took an abrasive personality.

A wife, gangsters and then girlfriends dominated Van's life as he eased into the mid-1970s. Then he had to deal with record industry pros. They were determined to undermine his royalties, and force him to release certain types of songs. He fought the industry. He won. The bad news for Van is he had two storage sheds filled with unreleased material in Marin County when he left to return to the U. K. In a February 2023 interview, Van looked back on these times. Looking back to looking forward has been a Morrison trait. He is his own biographer. In a 2023 interview with Billy Bragg, for **Uncut**, Van complained he had so much material stored he was looking for an alternate means of releasing it. Like Frank Zappa, Van kept an archive. The depth of it remains a mystery. Van is still at war with the industry.

VAN'S BEHAVIOR AND THE TIMES: GIRLFRIENDS AND GANGSTERS MADE HIM A BIT UNEASY

As two of Van's close female friends said: "He is a world class asshole with the voice of a rock 'n' roll Pavarotti." Another female friend took umbrage at the notion Van was difficult. "When I was with Van in Europe, we talked at length about his career problems. He was sensitive to criticism. He was getting over two different female issues in Marin County, he was kind, considerate and never an asshole to me." These two comments were repeated hundreds of times. Van's outbursts with the media never left the front page. His kindness and friendship with a wide variety of people was seldom reported. There was no minimizing Van's rage. In 2023 he sued an Irish political official over differences with the covid pandemic.

What was Van's view as he looked back on these times? "I was totally broke. So I didn't have time to sit around pondering or thinking all this through. It was just done on a basic pure survival level. I did what I had to do." He fought Ilene Berns. He won a battle of sorts despite having to give up some of the rights to his first three Warner Bros. albums.

JOE SMITH, THE BAG OF CASH AND BERNS KEEPS SOME OF VAN'S SONGWRITING, ANDY WICKHAM'S ROLE

Once Joe Smith dropped a bag with $20,000 in cash in front of a group of gangsters in a garage in Brooklyn Van was free to sign with Warner Bros. An Englishman, who went to work as an A & R person, Andy Wickham, was responsible for Van signing with Warner Bros. How? Wickham educated Warner executives on Van's long term commercial success. In London, Wickham was a commercial artist working with Andrew Loog Oldham's Immediate Record label.

Lou Adler brought Wickham to Los Angeles. He became a Warner Bros. talent scout. Mo Ostin paid him $200 a week to find new talent. He did in spades. He was referred to as "the house hippie." Nothing was further from the truth. Wickham was a political conservative. He was more fond of country music than rock. He would eventually head to Nashville turning up as the president of a label.

He may have been the only person to smoke dope in Laurel Canyon with a high class Oxford education and a Savile Row suit. When Wickham met Warner head Mo Ostin, at the Monterey Pop Festival, he recommended signing Jimi Hendrix. That decision alone validated his eye for talent. He was a staunch Morrison fan. His thoughts on the Belfast Cowboy were important in signing him to Warner. Wickham's message? There was gold in Van's songwriting. His performing! Wickham was not sold on it.

The record business is a jungle of deceit, business trickery, contracts for rubes and a systematic short changing of the artist. Fortunately, for Van, this was not the case with Warner Bros. The label was artist friendly.

When Van recorded two songs controlled by her company on **Astral Weeks**, they realized they hadn't done due diligence. These songs were part of the Bang catalogue. Berns had a case for unpaid royalties. She won! She collected!

Why Warner missed these Bang songs and why the royalties were not paid is unknown. Ilene Berns won an open and shut case. Was this due to sloppiness on Warner's part? No one has addressed that question. Warner realized it had a problem. They had to find a way to solve these problems. Van's new contract with Web IV Music brought in two industry insiders Lewis Merenstein and Bob Schwaid. Van worked to get Merenstein-Schwaid out of the way. They were good guys. They got paid. They left by the time **Hard Nose The Highway** was released.

On September 12, 1968, when Van signed a contract with Lewis Merenstein's Web IV Music, this agreement contained a clause he came to regret. This clause was for thirty plus original and publishable songs a year Van had to provide the Bang label. This led to the Contractual Obligation album in which he cut thirty plus songs. Then he was free to negotiate with another label. Except he wasn't free. Berns had borrowed money from gangsters. Joe Smith took a satchel filled with $20,000 and met the gangsters in a Brooklyn garage. He bought Morrison's contract. Then Van was off to Warner Bros. to record **Astral Weeks**.

For a time, the Schwaid-Merenstein management team took over Van's career. Things ran smoothly through the production of **Astral Weeks**. Then the story gets murky. Van was the majority producer for the next three albums. The blonde haired surfer from Harper's Bizarre, Ted Templeman, who hung out with Van, was a producer in training. He was assigned by the label as a producer. This did not sit well with Van. Templeman was learning the craft. Morrison had onerous clauses in his contract. Chris Michie reflected that Templeman was a co-conspirator. Not a producer. I asked Michie: "Did Templeman do some of the producing?" "It's complicated," he said. I asked again. Michie responded: "Yes." Michie had a grin on his face.

On **Astral Weeks** Merenstein was completely in charge. Prior to his death, Merenstein claimed he was the brains behind the album. He said he placed Van in an isolated recording booth and directed the musicians.

Merenstein's role was an important one. He gave birth to **Astral Weeks**. He hired the musicians. He put Van into a soundproof recording booth. He controlled the studio atmosphere. All this led to the perfect album for Van's talent. No one knew it at the time. In 2015, for the first time in almost fifty years, Merenstein looked back on **Astral Weeks** providing his view on the album. He told Randy Lewis: "Thirty seconds into it my whole being was vibrating, because having spent all the time with jazz players…I knew he was being reborn." Lewis asked him what he experienced. Merenstein said: "I got the poetry of it. It was just stunning, and I knew I wanted to work with him...." Merenstein continued explaining how and why he wanted to produce Morrison.

Lewis Merenstein: "Warner Bros. had contacted Bob Schwaid (Morrison's manager)and he contacted me. And they had sent some producers, and they didn't know what he was talking about; people expected to hear 'Brown Eyed Girl." In this explanation, the main Warner Bros. talent scout, the Englishmen, Andy Wickham, with a penchant for eighteen year old Scotch and freshly rolled joints, told Mo Ostin there was a commercial side to Van other than "Brown Eyed Girl." No one bothered to check Van's Bang Record contract. All they could think about was "Brown Eyed Girl" redux. Warner was reluctant to publicize **Astral Weeks**. It vanished. A decade later it went gold.

VAN SUES ILENE BERNS: THE FALLOUT WAS SCARING OFF THE MAJOR LABELS

ILENE BERNS: BERT'S WIFE

In January,1973, Van hired a legal team to pursue lost royalties. When he signed with Warner Bros., the Web IV management contract, with the Schwaid-Merenstein partnership, lasted a few more years. Van not only had to worry about the Bert Berns agreement. He was tied into a management-production deal with Lewis Merenstein's contract. He convinced the Web IV team to allow him a degree of producing and managing freedom. They agreed. Van sweetened the deal by giving up a share of his royalties on the first three Warner albums.

Van told the **Los Angeles Times** the deal "came about when my back was against the wall." He observed: "When success comes 'the sharks in disguise' show up to derail your career." This was a reference to the hardball legal tactics Ilene Berns played with Van after Bert's death. She forced him into a compromise. Van was upset losing out to Bert Berns' widow. He never forgot it.

CLINTON HEYLIN CRITICIZES VAN GETTING OUT OF THE BERT BERNS CONTRACT AND MOVING TO SCHWAID MERENSTEIN

In a strange journalistic twist, Clinton Heylin's biography accused Van of a nefarious plot to end his association with Bert Berns and Bang Records. In dazzling prose, and an attitude dripping with venom, Heylin charged: "Morrison's solution was an original one, though one fraught with potential legal pitfalls, he would record three dozen nonsense songs in a single session." When Van sent the tape to Ilene Berns. She exploded with venom. It was ten hours of asinine songs, veiled threats, silly comments and commercially unacceptable material. Morrison believed he had met the spirit of the contract. It took balls to do it. As Jimmy Page of Led Zeppelin remarked: "Van had big balls." So does Clinton Heylin. His conclusion bore no resemblance to what or why Van recorded a worthless set of songs.

THE MAY 23, 1973 FINAL SOLUTION: BERNS TAKES VAN INTO COURT

When Ilene Berns' lawyers brought Van and Warner into court on May 23, 1973, they filed a lawsuit requesting royalties from **Astral Weeks**. The two songs Van placed on the album that Bang Records had half ownership of were "Madame George" and "Beside You."

They were recorded for Bang in December 1967. Warner wasn't to blame. Neither was Van. The lawyers didn't properly vet Van's contract with Bang Records. Ilene Berns argued Van had not held up his end of the contract. Van countered. He said he was a young innocent. He was outwitted by the music business. The sharks manipulated him.

Warner was unhappy with Van. They had to pay the Berns estate royalties. Ray Ruff told me everyone at Warner thought Van would sound like the "Brown Eyed Girl" singer. "He didn't," Ruff continued. "Had it not been for the so-called 'house hippie', some at Warner wanted to get rid of Van." They didn't. The uncertainty of the early Warner and Morrison relationship was smoothed out by the "house hippie" Andy Wickham.

There was a bad taste in everyone's mouth. Van was unhappy. Warner was incredulous. They couldn't understand why he recorded songs Bang Record's owned. Van contended they were his songs. He could do what he wanted with them. He recorded them in a different manner with unique arrangements. Obviously, Van's education in the intricate nature of copyrights, recording and intellectual property preservation was in its formative stages.

This did not bode well for the Morrison-Warner future. The so-called period of retirement followed and from 1974 to 1977 Carol Guida was there.

To write Van needed a muse. Guida played that role. She was spiritual. She was intelligent. She wasn't concerned with money. Then things got contentious. She left in early 1977. Without a person to listen to his ideas, Van needed someone. For the **A Period of Transition** album, Chris Michie believed Dr. John filled that role. Michie reflected Van was getting his confidence back.

Van and Warner were estranged. At one time things were so bitter between Van and Warner he wasn't talking to his chief Warner Bros. benefactor Joe Smith. The executive reflected his enormous talent kept Van on the industry radar.

ILENE BERNS: DIRECTING BANG RECORDS

When Ilene took over as director of Bang Records, she was

labeled by the press as a former go-go dancer in New York. That was not close to the truth. She was savvy in matters of business. Although only in her twenties, she learned the ins and outs of the business. None of this seemed possible when she married Berns. After Ilene gave birth to three children, she was at Berns' side learning the business. Her husband told her tales of how Ahmet Ertegun, Jerry Wexler and Neshui Ertegun wanted him out of their business deals. They wanted control of Bang Records.

Ilene Berns is a story of persistence, brains and a fight against those in the music business attempting to minimize her husband's talent and steal his intellectual property. Ironically, it is much like Van's tale of industry woes.

Berns liked hanging out with low life characters. The pimps, the prostitutes, the Mafia enforces and those in the record business cheating and manipulating the acts were his friends. He was not a likeable guy. He brought Neil Diamond and Van Morrison to mainstream stardom. The cost? Their copyrights! They fought Berns. They exposed him. Few people in the industry liked Berns.

When Ritchie Yorke interviewed Van, for the first Morrison biography, Yorke told me Van wouldn't stop talking about how Ilene Berns abused his material. Van allegedly intimated Ilene did so for no other reason than to humiliate him. "Van initiated the lawsuit without understanding it might backfire," Yorke observed.

The final court decision was not what Morrison expected. The court affirmed the Bert Berns' estate controlled the Bang material. Ilene Berns won this court battle. She sold the tracks to CBS Records. This led to one disastrous re-release after another. Morrison's Bang Record catalogue was re-released in so many forms it was hard to keep track of it. He complained about the release of the nonsense songs. At first it was in bootleg form.

In 1994 the English label, Charly, issued **Payin' Dues: The Complete Bang Recording Sessions '67**, with an Italian imprint from Fruit Tree records to avoid legal complications. The liner notes were written anonymously by a Los Angeles based record producer, musician and established writer. The reissues multiplied with four more quasi-legal releases. Finally, in 2002, Purple Pyramid released **The Complete Bang Sessions**. Van smoldered. There was nothing he could do about these bootlegs. The bootlegs and the eventual legitimate releases contained thirty one songs. The irony is they sold. The Van fans had to have them in their collection.

The bootleggers and the shifty Charly label paved the way for a beautifully packaged release with copious liner notes, **The Authorized Bang Collection**. It was brought into the market by Legacy, a division of Sony founded in 1990, with the express purpose of producing archive releases. They compiled almost every track Morrison recorded for Bang in a three record release. The first disc contained every track from the first album **Blowin' Your Mind**. The second CD "Bang Sessions And Rarities" collected alternate takes from the Bang archives. The final CD was what became known as the Contractual Obligation Session, which contained the throw away songs. Some critics labelled them the "revenge songs."

ILENE BERNS EXITS THE BUSINESS

In 1979, after Ilene Berns sold her company to Columbia, she left the business. This meant future Bang releases would be packaged in a more professional manner. In 1990, when Columbia re-released a CD version of **T. B. Sheets**, it didn't appease Morrison. The controversy made for renewed interest in Morrison's earlier material. The packaging was eloquent. His fan base made the album a best seller.

Van was pissed. He was receiving royalties. He didn't have control. That was the issue not the Bang re-releases. To this day, the Bang Record fiasco festers in Morrison's psyche. He can't stop complaining about it. "He had good reason to be pissed, Chris Michie continued. "Bang made a fortune from Van due to his 1970s hits.".

The Ilene Berns law suit, the divorce, and the ensuing the legal difficulties led Van to write "The Drumshanbo Hustle." This was his view of the 1973 difficulties that threatened to derail his career. His contract with Lewis Merenstein and Web IV, as well as the disastrous Bang Record fiasco, was the catalyst to regaining control of his career. He achieved that goal.

Van Morrison commented on the unfriendly artist contract he signed with Bert Berns: "I was totally broke. ... I did what I had to do."

As the lost royalties from the Them records simmered, Decca released a flurry of Them albums. The repackaging drove Morrison crazy. He protested the accuracy of the liner notes. He didn't care for the album covers.

In 1974 London Records marketed the album **Backtrackin': Them Featuring Lead Singer Van Morrison** (London Records PS 639). This ten song American repackaging was Them material from the mid-1960s. The selections included "All For Myself," "Mighty Like A Rose" and "Hey Girl." With the inclusion of "Just A Little Bit," London Records placed a song on the LP that was a rarity. This became a highly collectible album. In a small pressing of 30,000, it sold out.

Two years later, the English Decca label released the album **Rock Roots: Them**. This thirteen-track LP collection of Them's earliest tracks included "Don't Start Crying Now," as well as the saccharine "The Story of Them, Parts 1 and 2." On this LP there were five tracks not previously issued in the United Kingdom. The liner notes and the album cover radiated an expensive production. The overall sound quality was outstanding. For the British fans this album filled in many holes in the serious record collections. "Mighty Like A Rose" was not an easy song to acquire in 1976. Chris Poole's liner notes, while brief, were informative.

Bibliographical Sources

See Joel Selvin, **Here Comes The Night: The Dark Soul Of Bert Berns And The Dirty Business of Rhythm and Blues** (New York, 2014) for the story of Bert Berns and Van, as well as the contracts Morrison signed. Selvin's book is a brilliant recreation of the time. He is fair minded and even handed with his conclusions. That said the smell of cigarettes, alcohol and bad cologne in Berns' life pollutes the story.

The Selvin book was a major reinterpretation of Bert Berns and his relationship with Van Morrison. He shows that his work producing Solomon Burke was a window into Van's world. By bringing the heart of mambo into rock 'n' roll he influenced records by Jerry Leiber and Mike Stoller, as well as Burt Bacharach. This caught Morrison's attention. Van wanted to know how Berns produced. By introducing the mainstream careers of Morrison and Neil Diamond, Berns production genius was evident. Berns was told he would not have lived past twenty-one due to a heart condition. He entered the music business at thirty one and he was a one man hit production machine. Selvin documents the gangsters, the con men and the nefarious industry insiders that Berns existed with in the shadow of the rock 'n' roll world. How did this impact Van Morrison? He has never said in detail. The murky story of their relationship is buried under a pile of industry secrets. Berns made fifty-one pop singles in seven years. In 1964, his first year at Atlantic, he produced nineteen records.

See the Shannon Vale book for the songs Bert Berns had the copyright on and why Van didn't perform them, Shannon Vale, **Astral Weeks Live: A Fan's Notes** (Londonderry, 2011). The Vale book is a brilliant sleeper. The inside of Van's life. His thoughts! His nascent career! His struggles! These elements populate Selvin's well researched and cogently written book. It is a brilliant inside look at the Morrison phenomenon. Berns worked when independent producers thrived. By the time he died, corporations controlled rock 'n' roll. Berns was there at the right time. A single recorded by Russell Byrd is actually Bert Berns. The producer? Phil Spector! It was a different time in the record business. Van learned many of his early business lessons in this environment. Also, see, Jesse Kornbluth, "Astral Weeks: Live At The Hollywood Bowl (Did You Guess That Was By Van Morrison?)," **The Good Men Project**, May 16, 2023 https://goodmenproject.com/featured-content/astral-weeks-live-at-the-hollywood-bowl-did-you-guess-that-was-by-van-morrison/

Clinton Heylin, **Can You Feel The Silence?: Van Morrison, A New Biography** (Chicago, 2002), pp. 155-167, 176-180, 221-233, 266-267. Also, see, Joel Selvin unpublished interview with Janet Planet quoted in Heylin. During my extensive interviews with Mervyn Solomon in Belfast in 1981, 2002 and 2003, he discussed in detail Van's antipathy to Ilene Berns. The problems with Bert Berns and the Bang Record contract is detailed in Howard A. DeWitt, **Van Morrison: Astral Weeks To Stardom, 1968-1972** (Scottsdale, 2020), chapter 8.

See Ryan H. Walsh, **Astral Weeks: A Secret History of 1968** (New York, 2018), pp. 4, 13-15, 268-288 for Van Morrison in Boston and how the city influenced the eventual album. The Walsh helps to set the stage for Van's eventual break from Bert Berns suggested some of the circumstances by which Van extricated himself from the jaws of the criminals surrounding him. Joey Bebo was important for this chapter. Bebo's **In The Back Of The Van: The Story of One Unforgettable Summer** (Hudson, 2016) is a marvelous account of his time drumming with Morrison in Boston. The book is detailed, well written and presents a side of the Belfast Cowboy that is personal. It shows how some excellent, if unheralded, musicians were important in Morrison's rise to fame and stardom. Bebo is a professional musician. After attending the prestigious Berklee College of Music, he graduated with a degree in Arranging and Music Composition in 1971. His story with Morrison and his subsequent career, after playing the summer of 1968 with Van, is a tour de force in what is right and what is wrong with the music industry. Bebo's book deserves careful attention. There are a number of Janet Morrison Minto interviews regarding living in Boston and Van's contract with Bang Records. The role of Joe Smith is alluded to in much of this material. See, for example, Louis Sahagun, "Janet Planet: Van Morrison's 'Brown Eyed Girl' The Clouds Have Lifted, Those Tumultuous Years Behind Her, The Astral Angel Lives A Quiet Life And Still Writes Music," **Los Angeles Times**, November 17, 1998 and the hit piece by Barry Egan, "Love Lost In The Myths of Time," **London Independent**, January 30, 2000.

The Egan article is an attempt to curry favor with Van and his take on Janet Morrison Minto to closer to fiction than the truth. For interpretations of "T. B. Sheets," see, for example, John Collis, **Van Morrison: Inarticulate Speech Of The Heart** (New York, 1996), pp. 84-85 and Brian Hinton, **Celtic Crossroads: The Art Of Van Morrison** (London, 1997), pp. 80-82. Ritchie Yorke after interviewing Van a number of times was convinced **Blowin' Your Mind** was an illegal album. Morrison made a strong case to him that the contract did not specify an album. Van was incorrect. He was tied into a one-sided contract. See Ritchie Yorke, **Van Morrison: Into The Music** (London, 1975), p. 188.

Phil and Dorothy Solomon talked at length about their relationship with Morrison and their interaction with Bert Berns whom they despised. The Solomon's were not just music managers, they were at the heart of signing new acts. Phil reminisced about what a talent Van was while telling one irascible story after another of what he did while with the Solomon Organization. Not only was Phil fond of Van, he understood his moods, and his feelings. The **Blowin' Your Mind** album was Morrison's first solo LP. He was unhappy with it. The Bert Berns experience was a roadmap for his future career. That roadmap was never to allow the producer, the label or the industry to control the product. Of all the songs on the album "T. B. Sheets" has drawn the most attention. In numerous interviews Janet Planet stated "T. B. Sheets" was based on a real-life experience. Violet Morrison said her son's song came from a nightmare. The operative wisdom is "T. B. Sheets" was about his cousin Gloria Gordon. Van said the song was fictional. From his youth Van was told of the dangers of T. B. This was a memory he could not escape.

Andrew Male, "It's About Time: Who Kidnapped Van Morrison And Replaced Him With this Guy," **Uncut**, January, 2019, pp. 60-65 is a reflective look back by Van in and open and friendly manner with a surprising candor. He corrected many myths about his music, those who influenced him and those who didn't have much of a say but claim a degree of inspiration. This is a brilliant, introspective interview. When the critics reviewed the re-release of **Blowin' Your Mind** there was universal praise for the album. For the best review see, Bob Cannon, "Blowin' Your Mind," **Entertainment**, February 10, 1995. https://www.ew.com/article/1995/02/10/blowin-your-mind/ He gave it a B rating but the comments overall were praiseworthy. Van said it best when he commented his initial view of the album which he said caused him to "throw up." For the critics response to the release of the Bang material, see, for example, Daniel Kreps, "Van Morrison Details 'Authorized Bang Collection'," **Rolling Stone**, March 30, 2017. https://www.rollingstone.com/music/music-news/van-morrison-details-authorized-bang-collection-117565/

The best review of the Bang material is Doug Collette, "Van Morrison: The Authorized Bang Collection," **All About Jazz**, April 29, 2017 https://www.allaboutjazz.com/the-authorized-bang-collection-by-doug-collette.php The Collette review concentrates on Van's growth as an artist between the Bang recordings and the release of **Astral Weeks**. The journey for Van was from incipient creativity to a level of jazz genius seldom seen in a few years. Collette analyzed Van's developing music with the observation that the first three tracks into this Cadillac release were the earliest signs of Van's creativity. Collette said that conclusion came from repeatedly listening to "Brown Eyed Girl," "He Ain't Give You None" and "T. B . Sheets." Collette recognized the historic importance of the sixty-three songs on the reissue **The Authorized Bang Collection**. He argued the authorized reissue was a road map toward analyzing how and why Van was able to survive Bert Berns, Bang Records and the gangsters like the Wassel. Collette argued some of the songs the fans ignored had a systematic quality of excellence. Such a tune was "Who Drove The Red Sports Car." He described as "almost cinematic in the mysterious unfolding of events Van describes with a delivery as wide-eyed in wonder as it is guttural." It is "feeling the soul in the singing," Collette wrote the three reissue CDs were more than a one off release of left overs. Legacy hired Grammy winning producer Andrew Sandoval who provided a meticulous time frame for the songs. The emotional vocal tones in "Joe Harper Saturday Morning" brought Collette to write this "galvanizing performance is framed with terse and savvy accompaniment by a wealth of experienced studios musicians including keyboardist Paul Griffin (who took part in Bob Dylan's early electric work two years before)." The Legacy three CD reissue was the best-selling Bang release. Did that make anyone happy? No! Well, maybe the fans. See, Johnny Rogan, **Van Morrison: No Surrender** (London, 2006), pp. 212-222 for the best account of this by one of Van's biographers. Also, see, Randy Fairman, "Standing In The Sunlight: Legacy Preps Authorized Reissue Of Van Morrison's Bang Recordings Including Infamous 'Contractual Obligations Recordings,'" **The Second Disc**, March 30, 2017 https://theseconddisc.com/2017/03/30/standing-in-the-sunlight-legacy-preps-authorized-reissue-of-van-morrisons-bang-recordings-including-infamous-contractual-obligation-recordings/

For Andy Wickham, see, Howard A. DeWitt, **Van Morrison: From Astral Weeks To Stardom, 1968-1972** (Fremont, 1983). Also, see, Jerry Hopkins, "Inside The Los Angeles Scene," **Rolling Stone**, June 22, 1968 and "Andy Wickham Obituary," **London Times**, April 5, 2022. Wickham, often referred to as "the house hippie" was in fact a key executive for Warner Bros. signing new acts. He was a serious record person who went on to head Warner's country music section in Nashville. He was an Englishman who loved to smoke dope, listen to music and to analyze trends and acts. He was good at it. The English music scene formed Van's attitudes. He brought these thoughts to America. When Van settled in Marin County it was a new experience. It was the first time he saw musicians controlling their destiny. Van watched. He learned.

For an extended review of how **Astral Weeks** made and influenced Van, see, Andy Gill, "Van Morrison-Astral Weeks And His Band And The Street Choir," **Uncut**, December 1, 2015 https://www.uncut.co.uk/reviews/van-morrison-astral-weekshis-band-and-the-street-choir-71910/

Also, see, Michael Bonner, "Expanded Editions Of Van Morrison's Astral Weeks And His Band And Street Choir Announced," **Uncut**, August 27, 2015 https://www.uncut.co.uk/news/expanded-editions-of-van-morrisons-astral-weeks-and-his-band-and-street-choir-announced-70490/

For Lewis Merenstein's comments, almost fifty years after **Astral Weeks**, see, for example, Hank Shteamer, "In Full: Lewis Merenstein, Producer Of **Astral Weeks**, **Dark Forces Swing Blind Punches**," March 1, 2009. This is a complete transcript of an interview with Lewis Merenstein on October 29, 2008 at an Upper West Side New York restaurant. The revelations from this interview helps one understand how important Merenstein was in conceiving **Astral Weeks**. Of the first time he heard Van, Merenstein said: "My first thought was when I heard him, I heard Richard Davis, because I used to use Richard in a lot of sessions." What did Merenstein mean? He believed, like Davis, Van was a subtle jazz performer. After working in a practice studio with Van, Merenstein said: "I culled through it and chose what tunes I thought-in my mind, I'm very conceptual, and I never asked him to discuss the meaning of any of his tunes." Then Merenstein said he contacted Larry Fallon. Why? Merenstein said: "He's a jazz player, and he came in and wrote out the chord sheets and got Richard involved." The beauty of this interview is that it demonstrated how easily Van worked with others on the **Astral Weeks** concept. Who did Merenstein believe was most important of the musicians? It was Richard Davis. "Richard was the soul of the album...the heart and beat of it," Merenstein reflected. "The funniest thing was that Warner Brothers, when they first heard it, didn't know what to make of it." Of **Astral Weeks**, Merenstein concluded: "It's a very jazz feel in a traditional way."

The differences between Van and the record labels is a long, complicated, blame ridden, story with peaks and valleys. The amount of inside information is minimal and often incomplete, in error or one sided. To overcome this problem, I haunted the various Warner Bros. locations to find out what I could. I talked with a number of employees, managements folks at all levels, year-long interns, UCLA students on summer internships and a few people close to Van. No one had the same story.

In my previous book, I was much too hard on Warner Bros. and I believe while not getting the story entirely wrong, I didn't recognize how much time and trouble Mo Ostin and Joe Smith took to maintain Van's Warner Bros. career. I never interviewed Ostin. I had two very brief discussions with Smith. I came to admire Smith's persistence, intelligence and what I call man up intensity in dealing with the Belfast Cowboy business dealings. Van had to fight the first dozen years with Warner Bros. to maintain his place in the music business. He fought. He won. It cost him two marriages. He has been described by Pat Daly, a brilliant writer on the **Van Morrison: New York Sessions, 1967** as having "a special kind of hate to write 31 songs for the sole purpose of torching your record label." That conclusion misses the point. Why? Daly writes: "Van Morrison has always hated the record industry." Not necessarily incorrect. While recording, releasing, leasing and negotiating with almost ten major labels, Van has learned the ins and outs of the business. He knew how to beat the labels at their own game. He did!

Now for the assholes. In Van's view, as I have been told by everyone close to him other than Morrison, the list includes: Phil Solomon, Bert Berns, Ahmet Ertegun, Ilene Bern and Carmine DeNoia (the Wassel). There were plenty of good guys. Van has seldom praised them. But you can see glimmers of respect in Van's words for Joe Smith, Mo Ostin, Mervyn Solomon and a host of others in the Warner Bros. family.

For a beautifully written and deeply researched article on Van and the record business that despite its title is not unfriendly to the Belfast Cowboy, see, Pat Daly, "Van Morrison's Fifty-Year-Old War On The Music Business," **Rock & Roll Globe**, April 30, 2018 https://rockandrollglobe.com/rock/van-morrisons-fifty-year-old-war-on-the-music-business/

The Daly article is essential to understanding Van's so-called war with the industry. The article is a brilliant review of the nonsense songs with an interpretation for each tune. Where is goes wrong is when Daly writes: "Morrison Appears To Troll Bert Berns In The Afterlife." Maybe! Maybe not! While Daly may not be wrong, I think he misses the essence of Van's thought process. The Belfast Cowboy was so attuned to his songwriting, the progression of his career, and to protect his intellectual property. The feelings of others and the decorum of good manners seldom enters Van's thought process. He is not mean. He is not a bully. Van is not like most people. It is all about him. That is a part of the problem in analyzing him and writing about his professional life. No wonder he doesn't want his private life discussed. It is no one's business. I have ignored it.

The Blue Note label has shown undying love for Van's music. Their biography describes Van as: "Equal parts blue-eyed soul shouter and wild-eyed poet sorcerer, Van Morrison is among popular music's true innovators." Why is this important? Blue Note is the only label to understand Morrison as a jazz artist. For their bio see, https://www.bluenote.com/artist/van-morrison/ Blue Note is America's best jazz label.

Van's war with the record business remains an ongoing one. For an example of how he never forgets what he believes the industry has done to him that hurts his royalties, his fan base and his incipient creativity, see, the following article, "Van Morrison Has A 'Mountain Of Material' He Wants To Release," **Longview News-Journal**, February 16, 2023. This article is a recap of the interview Van did with Billy Bragg for the April 2023 issue of **Uncut**. This interview was to promote his 44th studio album **Moving On Skiffle**. The irony to this review was the hidden anger in Van over the ways of the industry and how that has persisted for more than half a century. His complaints are many but the nub of his argument is he is losing money by not having more product released.

I found an old Carmine "Wassel" DeNoia in New York and a brief interview added some anecdotes. It has been widely reported, even by me, that he broke a guitar over Van's head and threw him into the water on the cruise celebrating "Brown Eyed Girls" and its Top 10 hit status. Why is this important? It goes to Van's state of mind. He goes off the radar when confronted with news that is less than accurate.

The material on Carmine "Wassel" DeNoia surfaced in 2000 when the **New York Times** found him. See Ralph Blumenthal, "Some Retired Runyon Guys Are Still Handing Out Dolls," **The New York Times**, December 18, 2000. This article glamorizes the ruthless nature of DeNoia in the record business. Thanks to this article, I looked up DeNoia at his apartment in the Franconia, 20 West 72nd Street, New York. He didn't tell me anything useful except that Bert Berns was a great guy and he couldn't understand a damned thing Van said because of his thick Irish accent. He did point out many false stories about Van and Berns. In the studio DeNoia said: "They were like bothers." The irony is after he retired as a record business enforcer, DeNoia led a charity collecting toys and distributing them to needy children. He got a pass from the local media for his past behavior hanging people out of a window at the Brill Building until they singed over their songwriting and publishing rights.

Van's use of the term "industry hardscrabble" came from a conversation with Jack Schroer. Elmer Valentine of the Whiskey A Go Go provided some important anecdotal material as did legendary producer Steve Rowland. The record business insiders who helped ferret out the subtle nuances of Van at Warner Bros. included Los Angeles disc jockey Jim Pewter, Bug Music founder Dan Bourgoise, label head Bob Keene and promoter-recording artist Ray Ruff.

An interesting article suggesting Morrison had more sway or power over Bang Records which helped, not hurt, his career is Margaret Jones, "The Turbulent Brilliance of Van Morrison's Bang Years," November 91,1 2021 https://www.ubisoft.com/en-gb/game/rocksmith/plus/news-updates/mjwy07dBxcjQy8SZdJOM7/the-turbulent-brilliance-of-van-morrisons-bang-records-years Jones is a University of California, Berkeley, PhD with a working band and a musical career. She has taught at the San Francisco conservatory of Music. She documents 1967 and without drawing conclusions suggest it was more than a turbulent year. She make the point this began Van's war on the music business. Or more appropriately it began an eight year ordeal for Van fighting for his intellectual property. She concluded, by 1973, he was getting his career trajectory in order.

See Sam Kemp, "Why Did Van Morrison Deliberately Write And Record 31 Terrible Songs?" **Faroutmagazine.co.uk**, April 2, 2023 https://faroutmagazine.co.uk/why-van-morrison-write-31-terrible-songs/ This is a thoughtful article detailing the improper contract Van signed with Bert Berns. Kemp claims Van was banned from performing in New York. This was not true. Despite that faux pas he does a nice job setting the tone for the contract dispute between Van and Ilene Berns.

For a sympathetic view of Ilene Berns from a Nashville perspective, see, for example, Beverly Keel, "In With A Bang," **Nashville Scene**, May 7, 1998 https://www.nashvillescene.com/arts_culture/in-with-a-bang/article_2102199e-6e80-5a6a-99a5-cc77231733e2.html

NINE

Van And The Writing Process: Lit Up Inside, Selected Lyrics And Keep 'Er Lit: New Selected Lyrics

"The singing is only a part of Van Morrison's music. He is an artist who Has gradually achieved control over all the components of his material—he writes the songs, orchestrates and produces them."

Gerald Dawe

"Some of my songs are just straight poetry."

Van Morrison

"To find a form that accommodates the mess, that is the task of the artist now."

Samuel Beckett

"Van Morrison is interested, obsessed with how much musical or verbal information he can compress into a small space...."

Lester Bangs

VAN MORRISON
Lit Up Inside
Van Morrison Keep 'Er Lit
New Selected Lyrics
with a Foreword by Paul Muldoon
Van Morrison Keep 'Er Lit
New Selected Lyrics

When Van Morrison published his two books of lyrics, he opened up his life to biographers. He selected the songs. He hand-picked those who wrote introductions, prefaces and other forms of praise and recognition for his writing talent. The forward to the second volume, written by Paul Muldoon, with an introduction by Eamonn Hughes, brought together two literary heavyweights to praise Van's lyrics. By personally selecting one hundred twenty one songs for the second volume, with a top tier London publisher Faber and Faber, Van ascended into the literary limelight.

Van's songs combine blue collar, childhood, spiritual, personal, mystical, love and historical themes into a potpourri of influences upon his life and career. By looking back, Van has said many times, he can look forward. His spiritual quest resonates in all parts of his life, as does his romantic side.

Although Van selected songs from his entire career, there are specific themes. His childhood memories. His name calling. His memory of his life. His preponderance of Marin County images dominate these two volumes. They provide a window into his life. There is also a paean to his future. As he writes about falling leaves, evening shadows and joyous moments, there is a wisdom to his words. He is more than a rock 'n' roll performer who writes songs. He is a now Sir Van Morrison with a lineage and accomplishments so far removed from his Hyndford Street home that he appears like a different person. He is. Van is an international star with a legend so vast it is difficult to describe.

When the first volume, **Lit Up Inside**, was published by Lawrence Ferlinghetti's City Lights Books in 2014 it was released with a modest party. Ferlinghetti told the press the notoriously shy and private Morrison preferred to let his lyrics do the talking. The creative consciousness that is Van Morrison shone through in his brilliant writing.

The second volume, **Keep 'Er Lit**, released in 2020, was a more extensive companion. The British publisher, Faber and Faber, commissioned a literary introduction. The two volumes provide a half century of Morrison's haunting lyrics, warm love songs and biting criticism. The mysticism that is Van Morrison translates to Socratic observations for the common person.

These volumes provide an insight into Van's creative process allowing the biographer to let Van tell his story.

VAN'S LYRICAL BOOKS REFLECT THE 1970s

In 2014, after more than fifty years in the music business, Van Morrison published the first of two lyric books. Since his youth, Van was intrigued with and worked on his writing. He read voraciously. In school he wrote poetry. He thought. He analyzed. He wondered how and why writers crafted their lines. He was inordinately private about his writing. It was something he had to do. He was consumed with writing. He believed his writing was preordained. Hence, the channeling claim.

He writes in a stream of consciousness. He writes when inspired by small events, seemingly insignificant instances, personal visions or contentious points. Getting even in lyrical prose was constant. Van differs with record labels, musical colleagues, journalists and those who deign to disagree with him. He is the ultimate contrarian. He remains a brilliant, if a diffident, writer.

How does Van write? A local event can inspire him. "Snow in San Anselmo" was an example of this influence. When a deer ran in front of his car, when a drunk was hollering while he was driving, while he was eating in Marin County's International House of Pancakes, he was inspired by these seemingly insignificant events to furtively write a song. He would read the newspaper, an obscure book, or watch an advertisement on a billboard, these sightings could turn into a song. The 1970s was the period in which he worked the 10,000 hours to perfect his songwriting. Perfection ensued. Somewhere Malcolm Gladwell is smiling.

As this book demonstrates, Van came of age as a lyrical poet in Marin County. Poets like Allen Ginsberg, philosophers like Alan Watts, musicians like Mark Isham, writers like Gina Berriault and gurus like Ali Akbar Khan combined to influence Morrison. As he looked back from the vantage point of a brilliant career, Marin County's influenced seeped into his writing. He recalled the San Francisco Bay Area in the 1970s with a nostalgia and an appreciation for finalizing his art.

One of the most intriguing comments concerning Van's lyrics came when Northern Irish poet Paul Muldoon quipped: "There is no need for a song lyric to stand up on the page....What it has to do is work with the music." Muldoon explained Van's gift poetically.

When the two volumes of songwriting entered the marketplace as hard cover books, they provided insights into his facile pen. The selections were from the breadth and range of his career. These songs defined his creativity. The lyrics formed a biographical overview.

The biographer was compelled to re-think long held opinions. The titles of these two books tells one all they need to know about Van's lack of pomposity. He writes for the everyday reader. When City Lights published the first book, the title, "**Lit Up Inside**," told the story. Van was euphoric composing these songs. It was not just the song lyrics. The book was special. He personally selected the songs. A microcosm of his thoughts thundered onto the pages. It was typical Van. No explanation! No indication of how and why he selected the material. No interpretive essays. He wanted the words to stand on their own. The second volume included praise from literary types suggesting Van's writing reached a broader audience.

The attraction of top level literary figures, on the second volume, highlighted the level of Van's prose. That talent included Professor Eamonn Hughes, who wrote the introduction, David Meltzer who wrote a forward, and Ian Rankin, a populist novelist, who contributed another forward. All are major cultural icons. They stand out in the literary community.

Professor Hughes' literary excellence, as well as his teaching of Irish literature at Queen's University, Belfast, made him a natural to interpret Van's prose with local color and landmarks. He helped select and introduce Van's songs. When asked his goal, Hughes responded: "To offer a map to the world of Van Morrison's lyrics. The past, present and future of Van's birthplace, Belfast, dominated the songs. The name checking for Belfast is unlimited." Hughes provided insights into the Belfast Cowboy's spiritual, romantic and literary side. In "Mr. Thomas," Van explained Dylan Thomas in his world with his neuroses. That might as well as have been a Morrison confessional. Hughes sees him as a Dylan Thomas influenced writer. Ian Rankin's contribution suggests you will believe you have a deeper understanding of Van after reading the lyrics.

The songs from the 1970s suggests Van's literary maturity. He understood the words. He interpreted his life. He was his own biographer. He was his own professor. The songwriting process matured as he turned twenty-five in 1970. "When I started writing songs it was totally unconscious. I didn't start writing consciously, or shall we say observing it…until I was twenty eight years old. Before that everything I wrote was completely unconscious; I hadn't a clue what it was about," Van remarked. That was 1973. Hence, the thesis of this book: "Becoming Van Morrison."

Van's musical vision created the lyrics. He became a literary stylist whose daily life was his laboratory. He is the unique personification of a recording artist with a literary bent. The contradictions of life emerge in Morrison's lyrics. He doesn't invite the listener to interpret. The reader can decided for his or her self. With two volumes of lyrics, there is plenty of room to analyze Van's prose. The road to his books originated in San Francisco's bustling North Beach. It is an Italian neighborhood. It is a home to poets, fiction writers, a wide variety of performers and near do wells with talent. It is also home to Lawrence Ferlinghetti's City Lights Bookstore.

SAN FRANCISCO'S NORTH BEACH PROMPTS VAN'S BOOKS

In the early 1970s, Van Morrison stood at Broadway and Columbus in San Francisco. He lived across the Golden Gate Bridge in Marin County. The trips to San Francisco intensified his songwriting fever. Many of his literary heroes lived there. Some artists still performed in local poetry circles. It was North Beach. This area was filled with Italian restaurants, memories of Jack Kerouac walking up Grant Avenue to the Coexistence Bagel Shop or the Coffee Gallery for a glass of wine, and the Beats engaging in conversation at

Vesuvio's Café or City Lights Books. These landmarks inspired him. When Van walked into City Lights, he noticed the display of Beat books. The owner, famed poet Lawrence Ferlinghetti, often worked behind the counter. On Grant Street the Coffee Gallery turned into the Lost And Found Saloon. It was a former Beat poetry outlet. The legacy of beatnik culture continued in North Beach. Van was intrigued. He examined the area. He drank in the cultural milieu.

The Belfast Cowboy was seen in City Lights going through the philosophy, religion and fiction sections. He was often alone. No one bothered him. He loved the Beats. He read everything he could. It was City Lights and San Francisco that provided the roadmap for the literary Van Morrison.

"In Tiburon," written years later, was a song where Van name checks beat-jazz culture in the San Francisco Bay Area. He pays tribute to jazz musician Vince Guaraldi, comedian Lenny Bruce, the No Name bar in Sausalito, a jazz trumpeter Chet Baker lived there, Lawrence Ferlinghetti, Allen Ginsberg, Gregory Corso and Neal Cassady were name checked. There was more as Van mentioned the famous San Francisco Cliff House with its spectacular bar and gourmet food. The Seal Rock Hotel is another reminder of how Van mined the local area for his lyrical brilliance with a historical-literary bent.

The image of driving down Geary Street when he was headed for an Irish bar and the mention of his house on the Fairfax hillside nostalgically recalled Van's time in Marin County. His personal images were those of a sharp eyed historian. He contrasted the normal with the bizarre. After all it was San Francisco. He provided the grist for his creative persona. This obvious reference to his home, high on a bluff overlooking Marin County, made for a wistful reminder of what he left behind when he exited Marin County. These reminiscences came in 2016 in the **Keep Me Singing** album. Marin County was never far from Van's mind. For tax reasons, Van returned to live in Belfast.

VAN: THE BEAT MUSEUM CONNECTION TO HIS WRITING

In 2013, Van wandered into San Francisco's Beat Museum. Jack

Kerouac's **On The Road** and the **Dharma Bums** were among Morrison's favorite books. After Van toured the museum, it was over to City Lights Books, and then an Irish coffee at Vesuvio's. The person telling me this story said Van's Irish coffee came sans liquor.

Van decided City Lights should publish a book of his lyrics. Ferlinghetti was still alive. Van loved to watch him work in the bookstore in his nineties. Ferlinghetti's work ethic was much like Van's.

What prompted Van to approach Ferlinghetti and City Lights to publish his first book? No one knows! What is known is he believed he had a kinship with Jack Kerouac and Allen Ginsberg. They were City Lights regulars back in the day. They were also published by Ferlinghetti. This made City Lights the place for **Lit Up Inside: Selected Lyrics**. After the book appeared, Van regularly came by the bookstore to sign copies.

The October 2, 2014, publication date was a special day for City Lights, Van fans, as well as a group of literary luminaries to celebrate. They were there to launch Van's book with bottles of Irish whiskey. The irony was Van no longer drank Irish whiskey. City Lights thanked Van. Lawrence Ferlinghetti said Van approached City Lights "based on his admiration for their publishing program." City Lights was ecstatic. Van was looking forward to promoting the book. This publication was followed by a second volume in 2020, **Keep 'Er Lit: New Selected Lyrics**, with a Pulitzer Prize winning Irish poet, Paul Muldoon, contributing the foreword. Eamonn Hughes edited both volumes. For Van's lyrics to be edited by a distinguished poet was a tribute to his lyrical achievements.

BAD MEMORIES OF THE YORKE BIOGRAPHY SURFACE AS CITY LIGHTS PUBLISHED VAN'S BOOK: TURNER AND ROGAN TOO

After City Lights agreed to publish his book, Van selected 200 pages of songs. He believed these songs reflected his best writing. He seldom discussed his writing. In the early 1970s, as he sat down with a Canadian journalist, Ritchie Yorke, to discuss his writing, he was forthcoming about his early albums. Van's interviews with Yorke were revealing, insightful and illuminating. They were often rambling. They elicited deep thoughts. Mainly on what was right and what was wrong with his career. Yorke finished the first Morrison biography. Now forty years later, Van finally had his own book. He could answer the critics. But the Yorke book remained a yoke around Morrison's writing reputation. He thought of it as unedited prose attributed to him. In 2014 as Van's book sat prominently in the window of San Francisco's City Lights Books, he thought back with horror on the 1975 biography came out under Yorke's pen.

Van hated the Yorke book. He claimed he was misquoted. He vowed never to work with a writer on a biography. That was until a Christian writer showed up. His name was Steve Turner. He was a superb literary stylist. He was a diligent researcher. He was analytical. His conclusions were reasoned. Turner interviewed him. A book resulted. Was Van happy? No! Why? The Belfast Cowboy claimed he was continually misquoted. Clinton Heylin's biography made extensive use of Turner's book. "When Steve Turner published an extensive essay on the man in a 1993 Bloomsbury coffee-table sized book, **Van Morrison: Too Late To Stop Now**, he managed to interview double the number of people who had written Morrison biographies. Then Turner was passed by supreme researcher with a golden pen Johnny Rogan who talked to over two hundred people for his two Morrison biographies. Rogan was so anal he interviewed every member of one of Van's school classes. I asked Rogan why? He replied: "Why not!" Like Heylin, Rogan had to have a new angle.

ROGAN GETS LOST IN THE VAN MORRISON FOG WITH THE TROUBLES AND CUTE WRITING

For Rogan's second book **the Troubles** dominated. As one of Van Morrison's fans living in the English countryside remarked: "Bollocks." "Irish folk influences were often present in Morrison's work but he had seldom explained them," Rogan wrote "This was a low blow. It got worse. Rogan said Van was a "surface philosopher." Nasty! Nasty! What Rogan suggested is that Morrison didn't attend college. Another low blow. For all the acclaim accorded Rogan's research, which is justified, he was a nasty little bitch. I personally loved the guy the one time I met him. But he could hold a grudge as much as Morrison.

It was Van's collaboration with the Chieftains that caused the venom to roll from Rogan's pen. The venom manufactured history with the skill of a university professor. When Van sat down with Paddy Molony for breakfast in the late Notting Hill Gate restaurant, Rogan claims only music was on his mind. What Rogan suggested is Van created the partnership with the Chieftains for an album and a tour. That is a part of the story. The other part is the Chieftains had concerns and input. Rogan makes it appear like Van was the King-maker. Maybe! Maybe not!

The Troubles is the most troublesome aspect of Rogan's book. He has no idea what Van thought of the problems in and around Belfast. Yet, he dissects them with the skill of a surgeon. The patient died from malpractice. That is literary malpractice. It is in Rogan's chapter 21 titled "Are You A Proddy" that his cute writing and insipid wit raises the question of the role being a Protestant played in Van's life. What this had to do with his career remains a mystery.

Johnny Rogan for all his brilliance as a researcher and clarity as a writer gets lost in the Morrison fog. He attributes influences to Van that are non-existent. Here is the irony. The person who got it right among the biographers was Clinton Heylin. Why? Heylin used the framework, the intelligence, the diligence, the point of view, the overall picture and the knowledge that made Steve Turner's book so valuable.

HEYLIN GETS TURNER'S BOOK RIGHT: VAN DOESN'T

Clinton Heylin provided an accurate assessment of Turner's book: "He also maintained a thoroughly respectful tone throughout, having drawn on his personal experiences with the man culled from their arm-length friendship in the mid-1980s." What was Heylin referencing? Apparently, in the 1980s, as Van delved deeply into Christianity, he made Turner's acquaintance. They became quasi-friends. Then Bloomsbury showed up with a book contract for Turner. It has nothing to do with Van. The contract was to complete a Christian rock book. Van, somewhat reluctantly, agreed to talk with

Turner. The outcome was a brilliant book on Christian rock. Van's comments embraced the project.

This was followed by Turner's coffee table biography which was a serious, analytical interpretation of the Belfast Cowboy's career. Van was furious. He believed he was set up by Turner to get a lucrative book deal. This was, of course, nonsense. Van proved he could never work with a biographer. His view on his life was one dimensional.

What Van failed to understand is Turner admired his uncompromising stand toward the music industry. Van took umbrage with Turner's notion he wrote from "the stuff of his life." The Belfast Cowboy took exception to the characterization of his mother as a "door step evangelist."

Turner got most everything right about Van. He possessed sharp insights. Quotes used in the book were extraordinary. They explained Morrison. Van said: "It's very hard for me to relate to people asking questions that are not only boring but don't have anything to do with my life...it drains me from doing what I really want to do, which is just play music." Touché!

Turner's detractors criticized the books coffee table format. The brilliant photo lay out, blended with exquisite prose, provided rare insights into Van. Turner didn't deserve the nasty criticism. The reviewers were mild compared to Van's criticism. It bordered on a lack of manners. The criticism descended into crass and petty areas. The Belfast Cowboy's vitriolic behavior frightened Turner. Earlier Van had willingly worked with him. These interviews were for a Christian rock music book. Van believed he was used. The Turner book set the stage for Van's lawyers to pounce on Clinton Heylin the moment the Morrison biography was announced. They not only pounced. They threatened. They cajoled. They intimidated. To his credit, Heylin stood firm as did his publisher. Van has a habit of demanding rights for himself, but those of others he often ignored. Heylin won the battle. It took its toll. He announced no more Van Morrison books. The mantle was passed to Johnny Rogan. Now Rogan is dead. There is no one with the mantle.

Whatever one thinks of Heylin's books, he is a diligent researcher, an analytical writer, a careful person with undisputable facts, and his writing evoked a fair minded interpretation. He is a brilliant biographer. He is also combative. The result was his 2002 book **Can You Feel The Silence?: Van Morrison, A New Biography**. It remains the best book on the Belfast Cowboy. It is also the most contentious one. What does this have to do with Van's writing? Plenty! It caused Van to begin thinking about writing an authorized memoir. His management contacted a German publisher to secure a contract for his autobiography. They were interested. Nothing came of it. To this day there has been very little in the press. When contacted Van's management has no comment.

Van's book was announced at a Frankfurt Book Festival. This upset Van. Not much had been written. Finally, in 2014, the City Lights Books **Lit Up Inside: Selected Lyrics** appeared. A selection of Van's songs, with introductions and commentary, was received with warm enthusiasm. Van had Steve Turner to thank for this book.

The Frankfurt Book Festival was not happy with the announcement of a Morrison biography. One official told me it wasn't Van who created the problem, it was a low level employee. Somewhere the ghost of Stephen Pillster resonated.

Why will Van not write an autobiography? It is simple! He is private. He believes he can write just about the music. His personal life remains sacrosanct. That will never change. You can examine interviews that are fifty years apart. Van has the same comments, the same ideas, the same reluctance to commit his life to paper and the result is his autobiography is in song form. Enjoy the lyrics. They highlight his life.

VAN TALKS WITH STEVE TURNER AND CLINTON HEYLIN CLAIMS HE IS REWRITING HISTORY

As Morrison talked with Steve Turner the idea germinated for his books. Van's book highlighted his writing style with a penchant for blue collar in your face prose. A second Morrison selected lyrics volume was even better. The literary Van Morrison was established.

One of Morrison's writing traits is to spend years on a project. The irony is he can also write a song in minutes. This was generally not the norm. His books of lyrics took time. He worked laboriously to select the proper tunes. He told close friend he would bring the "memoir songs" quickly to fruition. He did! The first book of lyrics began when he walked into City Lights Books, sometime after 2010, when he was in the San Francisco Bay Area. One of his musical cohorts said he had been thinking about it for a long time. The Steve Turner book festered with Morrison. Once he had a complaint it gnawed within his psyche. He often referred to Turner's book with a rage over what he got wrong. There are stories of Van marking up mistakes in the book. Turner drove him to publish his literary lyrics. City Lights gave him carte blanche to select the songs.

Turner's oversized, coffee table book was a major biography. Why? Turner's incisive and analytical prose was the best among Morrison biographers. He was a deep researcher. He presented an accurate and even handed picture of the Belfast Cowboy. There were some minor mistakes. Some years later, Van was at a party in San Francisco's Mission District, there was a copy of the book on a coffee table. He spent the evening writing in the book. He scribbled "wrong," or "mis-quoted" on numerous pages. The women who owns the book still has it. Rumor has it she wants to sell it.

Clinton Heylin accused Van of attempting to rewrite history. Is he correct? Yes! Is it over substantial facts that Morrison quibbles? No! "Morrison has always threatened to put the record straight," Heylin continued. "He just never has—and it is doubtful if he could. He has burnt too many bridges, and when interviewed, displays too foggy a notion of his own past." Not true! In 1995,when he sat down with Michelle Rocca for a lengthy interview. Van was unusually reflective. He was insightful and honest. His opinions were strong and forthcoming. His view of history was precise.

For the biographer this was gold. The treasure trove of information Van delivered over the years was due to Clinton Heylin, Johnny Rogan, S. Bailie, Greil Marcus and Steve Turner. One can also thank Erik Hage, Peter Mills, John Collis, Brian Hinton and Peter Childs for their contributions in understanding the gifts Morrison brought to the music business. Van tells his story. Just not in a conventional manner. After he married Michelle Rocca, he sat down with her for four interviews looking back on his life. He was casual. He was open. He was friendly. He was forthcoming. The

FRIENDS OF LIBRARIES U.S.A.
LITERARY LANDMARKS REGISTER
This site where in 1953
Lawrence Ferlinghetti and
Peter D. Martin founded the
Nation's first all-paperback bookstore
is designated a Literary Landmark
by Friends of Libraries U.S.A.
Designated June 26, 1992

Rocca interviews provide a rare insight into his psyche.

VAN WITH MICHELLE ROCCA: HE TALKS HIS WRITING AND OTHER FACTORS IN 1995 LOOKING BACK

"I've gone out of my way not to be a rock star. I write songs, I do gigs. I work for a living," Van told Michelle Rocca, as he began a four part interview in 1995. As he opened up in conversation, Van looked back upon his career. What did he value? His writing! The discussion of his lyrics dominated the conversation. He looked back upon his life with a beneficent sense of his past.

As she began the interview, Rocca asked him about getting into big band music. Van said he had come full circle. The Monarchs were a show band he never forgot. He suggested he was looking back to his early solo career in the 1970s.The Rocca questions, in 1995, recalled the bucolic images of Marin County. Van's frenetic writing and the relaxed atmosphere in and around the San Francisco Bay Area created "Becoming Van Morrison."

"Do you see yourself as a blues singer?" Rocca asked. Van responded soul music and his writing came out of Sam Cooke. He paid tribute to John Lee Hooker and Leadbelly as major influences. One gets the feeling blues is soul music to Van. He listed another series of influences. They included Muddy Waters and Dallas, Texas saxophonist popular in the U. K. Jimmy Giuffre. This conversation suggested the breadth of Morrison's early influences.

Van told Gavin Martin in 2015 of Jimmy Giuffre's Trio and their influence on him from a television show. When Van comes out on stage with his saxophone, it is due to Giuffre. The cool, detached manner in which Giuffre performed had an impact upon the Belfast Cowboy. So did a host of other unknown performers. They all had something to offer. The Jimmy Compton Jazz Band performed at Van's school. A more popular and pronounced rock act, Emile Ford and the Checkmates, appeared in Belfast's King's Hall. Van saw his future. In his conversation with Michelle Rocca, Van continued paying tribute to the wide ranging Belfast influences. He never mentioned Marin County. This picturesque California settlement allowed Morrison to form his words, modify his lyrics, take the small scraps of paper with his thoughts and work them into brilliant songs. Van did this while bellowing he wasn't a rock artist.

Van bemoaned the changes in rock 'n' roll when he said of rock: "It lost its beat. There's always been an element of bad music selling. People can get away with more," Van continued. "The real rock and roll...these people can't get much work now." This is why Van hired Jimmy Witherspoon, George Benson, Taj Mahal, Sam Butera, Bobby Blue Bland or Charlie Gracie to open for him. He paid them well. He made sure they had first class accommodations and a car with a driver. He treated them with class, dignity and respect. He paid a high wage. Van paid tribute to these artists. He didn't want any publicity. It was about thanking those before him for providing the road he followed.

When Rocca asked Van if he had periods where he dried up, he thought for a moment. This was a question harkening to his past. He said he never had writer's block. "I think I just lost interest," Van continued. "I just got fed up with the whole scene, making records, I didn't feel like doing anything." He intimated it was a couple of years before he started writing again. Van needed a muse. After his divorce from Janet Planet he floundered until Carol Guida entered his life. She was his second muse. He said he started writing from a different place. "I just keep writing...If I stopped, I would get blocked."

VAN ON UNRELEASED SONGS, WRITING AND HIS LITERARY LIFE

When Van was questioned about his unreleased songs, he said there were only a few he hoped to release. He was never asked how large his archive was or why he maintained it. One suspects that when he lived in Marin County it was at a time when the bootleggers were almost like record companies. They released thousands of bootlegs. It wasn't until the 1980s that the RIAA and the industry went after the bootleggers. My book with Lee Cotton, **Jailhouse Rock**, published by Pierian Press in 1983, was an in-depth examination of Elvis Presley bootlegs. During this time we talked with Richard Minor, Vic Colona, and Paul Dowling about Van Morrison bootlegs. To a man they laughed and said that Van's fans were furious with the bootleggers, but they bought whatever bootleg came out. Whether or not Van was aware of the level of bootlegging is unknown.

The bootlegger's success allegedly angered Van or someone in his management. He found out about the bootlegging phenomenon. He hasn't commented on it. The operative wisdom is this was another example of Warner Bros. not knowing what to release. The bootleggers released it.

Van said many songs deserved to be unreleased. He reflected he could only write a couple of lines to a song. Then he might complete it five years later. At other times he finished a song in one sitting. There was no schedule, no plan, only inspiration. In other words no guru, no method, no teacher. This suggests why Van talked of channeling songs. This interview demonstrated, as Van said, that there were no rules to writing.

"Do you think cynicism is the death of imagination?" Rocca asked. "It could be," Van continued. "Cynicism has taken me into another jumping off place." Van was asked if he had songs he wished he could fix. Van thought for a moment. He hated this question. Van didn't answer. Why? He reinterprets songs. He doesn't rewrite them. When the critics suggested he didn't necessarily believe in what he was writing, it made him angry. He learned, in the 1970s, to accept the hyper-interpretive nature of writers whom he believed practiced fiction in looking at his body of work.

That was the appellation the critics suggested when they dubbed him "Van The Man" or "The Belfast Cowboy." He hated categorization. He was forced from day one to endure titles, categories and branding. He screamed out in protest. It was to no avail. "Years later that was thrown back at me," Van said. He remarked when he wrote of religion, particularly of Scientology or Buddhism, his words were "criticized or misunderstood." He glowered. A fuck the critics pale came over his face. "It was just research," Van said of his writing. It wasn't about his life. The biographers, the critics, the professors, the fanzines and the mainstream media set Van off. He angrily inferred they spent too much time on what his songs meant. Van remarked they were just songs. They might not have a meaning.

When you are a public figure, you need to get used to the acclaim, the criticism and the interpretation.

"I always like to move on," Van said of his creative process. "The thing I do live is really where I am at." In his down time, he remains a furtive writer. "I can understand nostalgia," Van continued. "I don't think nostalgia has to be negative." He remarked he remembered something Roy Orbison said about his old recordings. Roy said they were "pure songs" not nostalgic ones. That is how Van sees himself.

"Do you play to record? Or do you record to play?" Rocca asked. Van looked at her quizzically. You could see the disbelief in his face. This was his wife. She should know. He recorded. He played. Why was she asking him these inane questions? She knew the answers. He couldn't escape the fools. Even when he was married to them.

Van talked about times when he didn't record and just played live. That brought back memories of Marin County in the 1970s. These were sweet images of an innocent past. He treasured them.

He explained there were no rules on recording or touring. He was in charge. He suggested if he had something to say he would write it quickly. "Songs are just ideas you work with at the time," Van said.

Concerning "Brown Eyed Girl" and "Gloria," Van said, he didn't necessarily dislike performing the songs. "I am just not there; I have moved on." Times have changed. These songs often close a show. Van understands show business and performing. "If I go see Ray Charles I want to hear 'What'd I Say,' but he is probably sick of it," Van concluded. Ditto with Van for "Gloria."

Van remarked his songs kept on evolving in concert. "It's the nature of the environment. You either go forward or backward." He continued. "Songs are just ideas you are working with at the time, I tend to go with what I am doing at the time."

He noticed his audience was getting younger. The younger fans hadn't heard of some of the old songs. "You change consciousness at certain stages of your life," Van said. He explained he didn't write at forty what he wrote when he was twenty-three. Van said when he was younger there was very little editing. As he grew older, his songs were tighter. They were more philosophical. He was more concerned about language. He was editing. He grew as a writer.

"I can remember writing things in notebooks when I was at school," Van said. When Rocca asked him if he was a poet. Van said emphatically: "No." He was a songwriter. "There were so many games going on," Van complained. He said the professors and pundits played the interpretive game. He abhorred being labeled a poet "There is no benefit to me for saying I am a poet," Van concluded.

Van described how music on Hyndford Street, his dad's record collection, and his mother's singing formed his early musical persona. In "On Hyndford Street," he reflected on his neighborhood. He remarked his father's collection was no longer intact. When asked about the first singer influencing him, Van paused and reflected: "I remember Bing Crosby, then Mahalia Jackson." "I was singing from when I was three," Van said. He remarked no one believed he would become a musician.

The Belfast he grew up in, Van observed, is no longer the city it once was due to the Troubles. He called the Troubles, in response to Rocca's questions, the "separate thing." He intimated it changed everything. "I miss the people I used to know," Van said of his Belfast years. It was difficult for him to keep in touch. "My privacy is cut down a lot. I can't go out and observe people," Van continued. "You can't go back. You grow and you change."

WHEN IT'S TIME FOR ME TO DO THAT, I'LL SIT DOWN MYSELF: VAN TO HIS BIOGRAPHERS

Van was asked about writing a memoir. He answered the question dozens of times. During the coronavirus pandemic the **Irish Times**, "Sunday Life" section, featured a story where Van talked of releasing his memoir. In an interview with David O'Dornan, Van said of a memoir: "I'm writing it, but it's a long process. I've been writing it on and off for a while, so it's about finding the time." Van lamented the ease of writing songs: "When I'm writing songs, everything is condensed into 16 or 20 lines, but doing a book is much more difficult for me." Van said he writes in notebooks. They are scattered. "I have to compile it," he confessed. His commitment to a memoir began in

Marin County. He would sit in a coffee shop. He watched local authors write in note books. He wrote on scraps of paper, as others pounded on antiquated typewriters. Van realized a memoir would set the record straight. Gina Berriault recalled the furtive concentration as Van sat at a nearby table writing alternately on small scraps of paper and in a tattered notebook.

Who was Gina Berriault? She was an acclaimed short story writer who lived with Leonard Gardner, the author of **Fat City**, in Marin County. They both were amazed seeing Van in the 1970s writing with intensity in coffee shops. Berriault, an award winning short story writer, listened to and was influenced by Morrison's grasp of language. The Marin County influences were dominant. The area where Van lived was home to Muir Woods, redwood trees, Mount Tamalpais and more noted writers than nine to five workers. Berriault, an award winning author, said of Van Morrison: "He was a quiet scribe. Few people talked to him. I thought of him more as a writer than a musician." Praise from serious literary figures suggested Van arrived in Marin County as a writer.

VAN'S THEME OF BEING TAKEN ADVANTAGE OF BY THE MEDIA ERUPTED IN 2021: LOOKING BACK ON 1973-1974

The theme of Van being taken advantage of his entire career erupted constantly since the 1960s. In June, 2021, in an interview for the **Belfast Telegraph**, Van discussed with David O'Dornan how and why he fought to maintain his artistic freedom. There was a paranoid note to his past. He complained Robin Swann, a public health official, took advantage of him by denying live concerts. The cause of this was the coronavirus pandemic. It didn't matter to Van. He took legal action. In doing so he looked back on the 1970s.

The rants since the Them days coalesced in the O'Dornan interview. "Most of the mainstream media don't really know anything about what I do. They don't care and so what?" Van's anger in this 2021 interview suggested his demand for intellectual freedom. He saw no danger in the coronavirus pandemic. Van said he "studied psychology" to interpret how he was being treated. O'Dornan asked Van when he was initially aware of being taken advantage of. This rambling interview, marked with frustration, Van said he "wondered if he had been taken advantage of in the past after going over his life." He told O'Dornan he was writing his memoir. He commented this was more difficult than composing lyrics.

Van said he found it strange looking back on his life. He talked of Jim Morrison and the mishandling of the Doors lead singer in the press. "Hanging out with Jim Morrison. He was just a normal guy....I was a friend and how he's portrayed now is not him." Van suggested he worried about his portrait. This is why he doesn't talk with biographers.

"When it's time for me to do that, I'll do it myself. I'll sit down and I'll write a book and I'll backtrack and I'll go through everything. I'll say the song was about this....it won't be somebody else's opinion." Van wrote these words in 1979.

The theme of being taken advantage of has never left Morrison's mental framework. He is manic about respect, being treated fairly, while learning and controlling the publishing game.

THE PUBLISHING GAME AND VAN

Van decided to move forward to secure a publisher for his lyrics book. He said his words provided the window into his life. He analyzed publishers. Not surprisingly, he selected a non-traditional San Francisco house. That was Lawrence Ferlinghetti's City Lights Books. He published the first of two lyric books with this esteemed San Francisco publisher. A second volume, a few years later, was from a major London publisher Faber and Faber. With increased promotion and author events, the second volume sold much better. But Lawrence Ferlinghetti's volume was a best seller for City Lights. The two books were reviewed ecstatically. Why? For their mellifluous prose. That is Van's lyrics were recognized for their depth, their cogent reasoning, and their insights into a life fraught with love, pain and heartbreak.

The writing and selection process began with Van mentioning an autobiography. Then along came the coronavirus pandemic. Suddenly, Van had time on his hands. Then rumors circulated he was writing a memoir. Those close to him gave it little credence.

On June 21, 2021, the **Irish Times** reported Van was working on a book "he has been penning for ages." As the Belfast Cowboy screamed about the coronavirus pandemic, he teamed up with Eric Clapton to deny vaccinations. He was busy writing. Or was he? We have no idea. My guess is Van will continue writing songs. A memoir? I would hope so. I won't hold my breath.

VAN'S RELUCTANCE TO TALK ABOUT THE WRITING PROCESS: TWO BOOKS DO IT FOR HIM: NOW HE TALKS

Why was Van Morrison reluctant to talk about his writing process? He seldom discussed it. That was until 2020. Then Van suggested coyly his writing was under siege. He couldn't perform. The coronavirus pandemic shut down live concerts. He was stuck in lockdown in Belfast. Bored beyond recognition, Van talked with the **London Independent's** Roisin O'Connor. He discussed his lyrical books. The writing process was on his mind. In this free form interview, Van opened up about his intellectual development. He said it was the catalyst to his writing. He alluded to the 1970s. It was the period in which his voracious reading finalized the beauty of his prodigious prose. Marin County was on his mind.

After he spoke at some length to Martin Chilton, of the **London Independent**, he intensified and discussed his writing process. The Chilton interview, via the telephone, was a productive one. "I want to write, but I am kind of getting a bit low at the moment," Van remarked. Van recalled his songs were essentially poetry. He didn't see this comment as a contradiction. Van accepted the plaudits and accolades. He was now comfortable described as a poet. If only reluctantly. He said he had a book of Cole Porter lyrics. He saw them as poetry. "As I start writing the song and putting the music to it, I get more pictures and more impressions mainly impressions. It's never exactly the same twice. It's on a subliminal level. A lot of it I don't really understand myself," he said. Chilton asked him about "Mechanical Bliss," Van responded: "It's probably one of the only tracks where I played that many chords on piano…It was just a take-off of British comedy, the Goons and such." Chilton was knowledgeable about Morrison's music. He knew what questions to ask. Van was forthcoming. He loved talking to Chilton.

Van talked about a wide range of subjects from jazz, blues, key books influencing him, his childhood fascination with soccer, and the pressure of writing a memoir. Van's interest in explaining his writing was due to **Lit Up Inside: Selected Lyrics**. This book, was released in 2014, by City Lights Books, to critical acclaim. That Jack Kerouac, Allan Ginsberg and Lawrence Ferlinghetti were published by this prestigious press prompted Van to smile. Forwards by David Meltzer and Ian Rankin, with an introduction by Eamonn Hughes, provided Van the recognition his writing deserved. The second volume, **Keep 'Er Lit: New Selected Lyrics**, published by Faber and Faber, with a forward from Paul Muldoon, a major literary figure, was released with more publicity. There were also more author events.

These books sealed Morrison's reputation as a writer. What was his literary direction? What was his writing process? Why was this a gift? The answers were simple ones. His writing matured. The themes, while remaining simple, had a literary complexity. Van's voracious reading melded into his writing. Maturity brought depth. There was a degree of clarification to his lyrical genius.

The forward to **Lit Up Inside: Selected Lyrics**, by Beat Generation poet David Meltzer, evoked appreciation from a writer who came of age with Miles Davis. Then he surreptitiously evolved listening to Morrison's music. Meltzer was a jazz guitarist. He recorded an album on a jazz label, Vaja, with Bob Dorough and Jim Dickson. **No Eyes**, one of more than fifty of Meltzer's poetry books was about Lester Young's music. He was briefly a professor at the New College. He lived most of his life in the San Francisco Bay Area. With this literary background, Meltzer had insights into the Belfast Cowboy. He explained Van's lyrics with consummate skill. He developed an eye to their interpretive mania. After haunting book and record stores in California and New York, Meltzer was a stone Morrison aficionado. He knew every subtle nuance of the Belfast Cowboy's persona. He knew every lyric.

He initially listened to Van with Them. He recalled "Gloria" and "Here Comes The Night." These were the first Morrison records he

David Meltzer's 50th Birthday Party, 1987

heard as Van's voice struck him like a bolt of lightning. "This collection of lyrics," Meltzer wrote, "offers a major insight into his experience." Meltzer argued there was a "purity" to the Belfast Cowboy's style. He said the threads of Morrison's life emerged in song form. This prompted Meltzer to suggest this was a window into Van's soul. "Indeed, his songs often reflect an ongoing struggle with fame's deceptions and reductions," Meltzer observed.

VAN'S JAZZ VOICE, A POET AND HIS PROSE

There was another connection from Van. It was his jazz voice. "Morrison is an improviser in performance, like a jazz musician, or those blues singers who improvise songs on the spot." Meltzer said. Van was "like a Beat poet." Like the Beats, the Belfast Cowboy rejected pop and mainstream culture. Van was, as Meltzer observed, "a dissident, poet and outsider." This is why it was fitting he was published by San Francisco's City Lights Books. Lawrence Ferlinghetti was one of his favorite poets. The City Lights founder was a Morrison fan. It was a marriage made in heaven.

Van didn't consider himself a poet until his lyric books appeared. Finally, he accepted the accolades., the pundits, the journalists and the serious biographers accorded his words his praise.

One of the ironies in Meltzer's foreword was his description of Morrison's prolific nature. As a working poet with numerous volumes of poetry, Meltzer knew something about the time required and the rewriting necessary to bring his lyrical-vocal magic to the public. In his later years, the bespeckled, balding, glasses wearing Meltzer was a familiar figure travelling from his Oakland home to Berkeley while reading at Moe's Books or shopping at Amoeba Records. He was the consummate jazz collector. He was a public figure without fame impeding his daily journey.

Our celebrity culture is bone crushing. It leads to inane interviews. There is a fish bowl existence. To survive Van identified with writers who either ignored fame or skirted its boundaries. In his remarks on Van's book, Meltzer speculated on writers who served as role models for the Belfast Cowboy. Among them William Blake and Jack Kerouac. Why? They inspired Van's esoteric reading.

Richard Meltzer was also a rock and roll critic. He wrote in that genre. Unlike the Shakespeare of Telegraph Avenue, Greil Marcus, his writing resonated with the fans. He didn't live in on Ivory Tower on a hill overlooking the peasants in Berkeley. Meltzer was one of the peasants. For that reason he understood Van as a writer. Meltzer said he came late to Jack Kerouac. Why did he make that comment? Meltzer intimated Morrison's lyrics were Kerouacian influenced. Literature and poetry, Meltzer said, made the writer. Those comments were a perfect description of what made Morrison a superb lyricist. He had a penchant for blue collar themes. They were drawn directly from his life. Van said to **Rolling Stone's**, David Wild: "I don't talk about my music. I don't talk about my private life." He has since 1985 talked at length about his life, his music and his personal concerns. Where? During interviews! Why? To air grievances. To explain his new musical path. To complain about misinterpretations of his life. Van is an open book talking about his life. Since 1985, in interviews and on social media platforms, Van has told us a great deal about what makes him creative. He does not tell you where he lives. He does not talk about his collaborators. His backing musicians or his concerts are seldom mentioned. What he does is to share how he thinks, what he believes, and why this is important to his writing and performing. While many writing about him describe Van as egocentric. He is not. He remains humble. His version of Van Morrison is a blue collar worker who toils daily. He sees himself as a worker carrying his own lunch.

The print and YouTube interviews run well over two hundred and ninety different versions. These discussions, with the Belfast Cowboy, opened up avenues of previously unknown information. For that that biographer is grateful. But some observers are more important than others. Richard Meltzer is example of a key figure in Morrison's life. He is a shrewd analyst of intellect, talent and determination.

Why is Richard Meltzer important to the Van Morrison writing legend? He was one of the initial critics recognizing what Van was reading, thinking and writing, while proclaiming his greatness. No one listened. Meltzer recognized and highlighted Van's intellectual maturity, thanks to Marin County influences. He labelled Morrison a "forgotten hero" in the rock 'n' roll jungle.

Morrison's private side intrigued him. Van was a reclusive intellectual. Meltzer said this perfectly described him. When he asked who were the writers influencing Morrison, Meltzer got it right.

Meltzer identified Eliot, Rimbaud, Coleridge, Yeats and Donne as seminal figures in Morrison's evolution. Of Morrison, Meltzer wrote: "He is a genuine original." Meltzer intimated he had the habits of a seasoned writer at a youthful age. He was influenced by great literature. He had his own take on these writers. It was original. Van interpreted what he read. He transformed it into his own brand of poetic brilliance. When Ian Rankin was struggling as a writer, Van Morrison was an influence. Not surprisingly, he was asked to write a forward suggesting why Van's writing was important.

Ian Rankin's forward, recalled his days as a record reviewer. He struggled with a writing career. He described it as going nowhere. Rankin connected with Morrison in a different way. He viewed Van as a poet of everyday life. While listening to "Cleaning Windows," Rankin tried to think of another lyricist who could make a mundane chore like cleaning windows into a beautiful song. The beautiful visions! The passion! The observational brilliance! These images defined Morrison's creative life. Rankin believed listening to Van's music enriched his writing. He said it provided a path to his genesis as a literary crime writer. Rankin observed there was one dominating influence. That was the alchemy of spiritualism.

Rankin analyzed the spiritual nature of Van's lyrics. He concluded these words spoke to the Belfast Cowboy's mystical persona. He posited Van was not as grumpy as the critics suggested. That was until he came into contact with those needlessly analyzing, obtusely criticizing or falsely praising him that he erupted. Rankin described Van's reactions as the heart of a dedicated writer. He applauded Van for lashing out at critics. In the 1995 tune, "Songwriter," Van discouraged his fans from labelling him a legend. He was just a working man. He said he was a scribe. That remains his path. Just another Irishman going to work. That is how he sees himself. The Sir Van Morrison moniker makes him uncomfortable. Privately, he loves it. Respect! That is what resonates with the Belfast Cowboy.

EAMONN HUGHES: THE FROSTING ON VAN'S CAKE

Eamonn Hughes' introduction to **Lit Up Inside: Selected Lyrics** is the frosting on Morrison's writing cake. Hughes, an English professor at Queen's University, Belfast, is an Irish literary and cultural specialist. He is a brilliant observer. He is a lyrically sophisticated writer. His view of Van and his music emphasized Belfast's influence. He worked closely with Morrison for **Lit Up Inside**. His nine page essay is a landmark of interpretive brilliance. It is from the pen of an English professor writing like a novelist. "Van," Hughes writes, "has created a world through his words." The beauty, the hard work, the contradictions, the warmth of Belfast's parks and city streets stream through Morrison's lyrics. They provide an indelible history of Belfast and Northern Ireland.

As Professor Hughes described Belfast, the reader can understand his Irish nature and comprehend the influences from 1973 into mid-1974 in his writing. How his time in Marin County helped Van develop his spiritual quest is evident when he met writers who searched for personal awareness. Those insights, combined with his Irish heritage, were the formative foundation stones in his evolution as a writer.

Images of jazz and blues drove Van to Marin County, where these musical styles dominated. Van was an Irish exile living in California's rich musical and cultural heritage. It was an influence he imbibed. He developed and articulated his personal soul translating it into exquisite, often opaque, lyrics with a musical paean to his surroundings. From **Hard Nose The Highway** through **Into The Music** he moved into interpreting his Irish roots via the Golden State. His Irish heritage, with an assist from Marin County, became the force driving Van's songwriting. Why are the Irish literary heavyweights? The Irish have a gift for words which is oral and calls out local landmarks. The Irish have their own way of telling a story. Van is at the apex of that talent.

Another type of literary Irish foundation was built in America for a half century career of creative excellence. To understand Van a brief examination of his relationship with English journalist Martin Chilton is necessary. A March, 2020, interview saw Van reflect on his literary style, his lyrics and his life. It was the ultimate transparent interview. The Belfast Cowboy was eager to discuss his writing. That was not the norm. In conversation with Chilton, Van's lyrics and music move forward and backward. That was the basis of an open discussion. Transparency was a Van trait under the right circumstances. Van made references to his time in Marin County. Martin Chilton pulled answers from Van that no previous journalist did.

MARTIN CHILTON PULLS WRITING ANSWERS FROM VAN: WILL THE PRESS LET HIM BE THE BELFAST COWBOY?

Van's adventures with the press are well documented. His tirades are often followed by cooperation and a butter will not melt in his mouth demeanor. This is not a contradiction It is Van being Van. He has become increasingly transparent. After Chilton interviewed Van, he went on Twitter speculating that the press should reconsider the Belfast Cowboy's demeanor with more forgiveness. Chilton described him as a normal, hard-working guy. He interviewed him a number of times. They became friendly. Chilton remarked of the passion with which Van discussed his music. They also discussed his second book with Faber and Faber.

"We talked jazz, football, books and I even asked him what he sings while washing his hands...." Chilton said. Over the years, as Van talked with Chilton, he became at ease. The reporter with a balding head, a cherubic smile and ill-fitting suit looks more like a high school English teacher than a first rate reporter. Chilton was knowledgeable about Van's music. He recalled every nook and cranny of the Belfast Cowboy's career. Van may have felt like taking notes.

Chilton intrigued Van. He wanted to know more about him. The reporter wrote his first letter to **Melody Maker** when he was thirteen. He immersed himself in rock 'n' roll. A number of rockers called Chilton to seek information on their careers. Chilton talked with Van at high points and low parts in his career. When Chilton died unexpectedly at sixty, Van graciously paid tribute to him. What did Chilton elicit from Van?

Van confessed he was "trying to get back to writing." There was a slow, burning anger over the coronavirus pandemic. Van discussed his writing. "I notice things or I might hear a phrase I like, but I won't necessarily think that's a good idea at the time. Then it will come out later from the subconscious...." Van continued. "I get more pictures and more impressions-mainly impressions. It's never exactly the same twice. It's on a subliminal level. A lot of it I don't really understand myself...."

During the lockdown, Van gave out numerous interviews discussing how he writes. His life is in his lyrics. He told Chilton he was proud of his two books. Some critics suggested when Professor Hughes began and concluded **Lit Up Inside**, he presented two different versions of Belfast. He suggested "The Story of Them" and the 2012 song "Mystic of The East" from the **Born To Sing: No Plan B** album are complex examples of Morrison's East Belfast roots with multi-faceting meanings. Mystery is what was suggested.

As Chilton left Van he wrote in his notebook "a complex man" but "a good man." Transparency is now a Morrison trait. It took fifty years. He still agonizes over the press. The **London Guardian** treated him badly during the pandemic. They were also lukewarm toward the lyric books.

THE LONDON GUARDIAN ARGUES VAN'S CONSPIRACY THEORIES OBSCURE HIS POETRY

The **London Guardian** didn't understand the lyrics when they accused Van of having conspiracy feelings against the press. The Belfast Cowboy's complaint was not about their coverage. He was concerned about their interpretive excesses. The **Guardian**, Van intoned, didn't research, didn't write and didn't present, with clarity, his daily life. He said his life was no one's business. He was a blue collar kid feeling disrespected. By 1995, he was a multi-millionaire and a legend. It was time to answer the petty criticism. Van was critical of the **Guardian's** coverage. He said he had a legitimate beef. The press won't let him be Van Morrison. The truth was more complicated. In 2023 Van took on **Rolling Stone** complaining they ignored such giant American artists as Bobby Blue Bland and Sam Cooke when they rated the Top 200 singers. He said **Rolling Stone** was no longer a cutting edge publication.

To answer the critics, Van published the first lyric book in 2014.The second volume, **Keep 'Er Lit: New Selected Lyrics**, arrived in 2020. It was even more prestigious and well received. The one hundred-twenty songs in this follow up tome combined Morrison's themes of pain, healing and reconciliation with lyrical moments of joy and romance. On his website, Van described this volume as "Songs of Memory And Childhood," he reconnected to a time where he wrote of "falling leaves and evening shadows." The praise for Van's romantic side was ignored by the mainstream press. Whether or not that exclusion festered in Van's psyche is unknown. His two lyrical books addressed musical, business and personal issues.

Somewhere along the line the poetry in Morrison's lyrics was lost in media arguments. There were tendentious and audacious reviews, as well as petty fights over his career direction. Fortunately, Professor Hughes provided the clarion call for recognizing Morrison's writing skills. What and why Morrison was writing attracted interest outside the confines of the rock 'n' roll world. Obscuring Van's poetry ended. His poetry highlighted how common, blue collar words made him the voice of the working class with a rock 'n' roll bent. Years earlier, in a **Rolling Stone** article, Jonathan Cott made that point. In 1978 Cott asked Morrison, who he identified with as his most important early musical influence. Van replied: "Leadbelly." From that quote, Cott made the point the Belfast Cowboy was "a blue collar worker." Professor Hughes took that quote, and he built around it using Van's 1982 song "Cleaning Windows." Once again looking back to looking forward was a means of interpreting the Belfast Cowboy.

Hughes' commentary described Van's poetic view of Belfast. His descriptions of the clubs, the proliferation of musicians, the venues, and how Morrison connected these images with visions of Howlin' Wolf, John Lee Hooker, Bobby Blue Bland, Jimmy Witherspoon and a host of American musical influences cemented his legendary career. He brought diverse musical interests into the package. He became an acclaimed singer-songwriter. Belfast was his muse. Marin County influences provided the formula for the finished product.

In making use of Belfast place names, Van embraced being Irish. Belfast provided a foundation for his writing. The everyday events. The local pleasures. The landmarks. They worked their way into his songs. Van's memories and experiences stretched his lyrics. Professor Hughes added an air of legitimacy. There was an interpretive recognition of Van's talents.

Van opened "Cleaning Windows" with the line: "I heard Lead Belly and Blind Lemon, on the street where I was born." This line explains Belfast. Van paid tribute to Jack Kerouac. Of Kerouac, he told Fintan O'Toole: "Well, three important books for me...one was **Dharma Bums** by Jack Kerouac...." Morrison found that wanderlust was a Kerouac trait. One assumes his early wanderlust was a Kerouac creation. Of the **Dharma Bums**, Van observed: "The spontaneity of the writing and just the way that it was unfolding" is what drove the Belfast Cowboy. Kerouac's inspiration was immediate. The Zen Buddhism Kerouac introduced influenced Morrison's psyche. The Belfast Cowboy's sense of Zen was reflected in his voracious religious spiritual reading. The impact was upon his songwriting. Zen was a small part of Morrison's intellectual package. Carol Guida said Van read about Zen but he never practiced it. He read deeply concerning mysticism, historical religions and how and why spirituality was necessary to his life. Self-education was a necessity to finalizing Van's prose.

When he reflected on Kerouac's influence, Van told Gavin Martin: "(The) rhythm of the language" in Kerouac's writing inspired him. Van felt like he knew Kerouac. He identified with him. Visions of Kerouac percolated as he went through his mammoth song catalogue. He spent many hours making sure the songs, for the City Lights selections, reflected his best writing. He searched for language similar to Kerouac's.

In "Rave On, John Donne/Rave On, Part Two," Van claimed he channeled the song. The radio was increasingly a conduit to Van's observations. His love for Belfast. His cerebral loyalty to Ireland. These factors came to the surface. They were more pronounced in the 1980s.

Living in bucolic Marin County, with a short drive to a coffee shop, was not conducive to Irish or English subjects. John Lee Hooker was more of an influence than William Butler Yeats. When Van relocated to the U. K. and Ireland, it intensified the Irish influences, the literary themes and the spirituality enveloping his prose.

Van's poetic voice and name checking characterized his songwriting. By the 1970s, there was a new found lyrical sophistication. He displayed a developed poetic maturity. This growth was due to his spiritual journey. Initially, Van's innocence led him to experience disillusionment. Then, as the "fame game" crept into his songwriting, he exploded in a creative manner to take his life back. He envisioned songwriting as the road to maintaining a private life. Unwittingly, fame and fortune compromised his privacy.

Name checking is a Morrison writing trait. It is a window into his soul. The simplicity of "Summertime in England" reminds us in 1980 how Marin County fermented his lyrics into a fine brew.

As a fifteen minute song, Van used his American experiences to rekindle his English-Irish memories. He began rehearsing the song in 1979 along with "Haunts of Ancient Peace." This song had a line

"Can you feel the silence?" What did it mean? To some it was a phrase breaking with his Marin County past. Morrison remarked of "Summertime In England: "It was actually part of a poem I was writing, and the poem and the song sorta merged...I'd read several articles about this particular group of poets who were writing this particular thing, which I couldn't find in the framework I was in." Clinton Heylin paid attention. He took his book title from this song.

WHAT IS LIT UP INSIDE? AND THE MORE ELABORATE KEEP 'ER LIT: NEW SELECTED LYRICS

Lit Up Inside is not a mini-history of Van's songwriting. It is a smorgasbord of diverse writing styles. One song, "Why Must I Always Explain," suggested how and why Van complained of the inane interviews. It explains his angst over fame. His concern for privacy escalated. No matter what he says. No one seems to get it. Like Van has said his fans and the critics need to catch with him. They did in the reviews for **Lit Up Inside**.

The reviewers were ecstatic for Van's first book of lyrics. "Very few rock and roll poets would survive artistically if their songs appeared on the printed page without the music...a thoughtful and brilliant poet stands for all the world to see," Dick Weissman wrote. That comment was echoed by Dennis Sullivan who concluded "the combination of deep personal content and universal humanity...was largely lost on me until reading the verses...the story of Morrison's life unfolds." Jon Landau in **Rolling Stone** wrote: "One of the few originals left in rock." Greil Marcus labelled Van as pop music's richest and most expressive voice since Elvis Presley. "When a brilliant, reclusive musical icon peeks his head out to make a statement about his life's work, you can only sit up, listen and be grateful," Joanne Moreno wrote. The reviews were universally laudatory and the sales made Morrison's tome the best-selling City Lights book.

MORRISON'S SECOND LYRIC BOOK: HIGH END LITERARY APPPEAL

The second volume **Keep 'Er Lit: New Selected Lyrics** was

graced by Paul Muldoon's literary foreword. It was edited with an introduction by Eamonn Hughes. The erudition and insights Muldoon's foreword provided further understanding for Morrison's writing. His prize winning insights into the Belfast Cowboy are unique. He is a chairholder in the Princeton University English faculty. He was Oxford Professor of Poetry from 1999 to 2004. He also served as the **New Yorker's** poetry editor. Heady praise from an erudite scholar finalized Van's writing reputation.

What did Muldoon's words add to Morrison's lyrics? Legitimacy! Scholarly praise! Critical comments! Formidable insights! Van's literary influence was apparent. In 2012, when Steve Dickson's novel, **These Dreams of You**, lifted its title from a Morrison song the word was out amongst young fiction writers that Van was a source and inspiration. Why? It was his exquisite use of words.

For more than half a century, Van has paid attention to his craft. Enter Paul Muldoon and Eamonn Hughes. Why would two English professors at the top of their game be concerned with Morrison's lyrics more than his music? The answer is a simple one. Van's lyrics are transformable. They provide a window into his creative process.

Van is reluctant to discuss his writing. He claims: "A lot of it is below the surface." That combination of humility and hubris explains the Belfast Cowboy. His references from William Blake to Seamus Heaney intrigues the biographers. Another intriguing trait is Van's use of book titles for his songs and interviewers show their literary skill when they question Van on how and why he uses a book title for a song title. Haunts of Ancient Peace is an example. That phrase was used by Alfred Tennyson in the 1840s. Van is aware of that. He corrected the interviewer. "I took that from a book title by Alfred Austin, but he must have got it from Tennyson." Van knows literature. Austin was appointed the English Poet Laureate in 1896 after Tennyson's death.

As a literary stylist how does Van fit into the rock 'n' roll milieu? He doesn't. He rants on about not being a rock performer. Morrison solidified his legend with denial. That denial leads to a flurry of beautiful words describing his life. Lester Bangs said the heart and the soul of Van's writing was a female muse. He said it was dependent upon the ladies surrounding him. Bangs' essay concluded, with a nod to Van's poetry, comparing him to Federico Garcia Lorca. While suggesting female muses were essential. Janet Morrison Minto, Carol Guida and Ulla Munch would agree. This explains why the professors, Paul Muldoon, and Eamonn Hughes, drank from the fountain of Morrison's poetic nature.

Paul Muldoon, a New York based Irish poet, brought his literary skills to analyzing Morrison's songwriting. It is easy to see why he is Morrison's friend. Muldoon writes about a connection between poetry and jazz. He says it is a marriage "not without some issues." Muldoon, who looks like an unmade bed, influenced Van's writing. He is a writer who sees little difference between writing poetry and songwriting. Muldoon is described as an "eclectic poet" with a penchant for breaking the rules.

PAUL MULDOON: IRISH PULITZER PRIZE POET AND VAN ACOLYTE

Paul Muldoon's sense of and feel for the Belfast Cowboy's writing is munificent. In his foreword to **Keep 'Er Lit: New Selected Lyrics**: he observed: "Van Morrison seems to lend credibility to the notion of the 10,000 hours of limbering up they put in before reaching their full potential and coming into their own." Muldoon recognized the blue collar work ethic leading Morrison to the Rock and Roll Hall of Fame. From the age of twelve, Van created his word world. By 1963, he had played in at least a dozen small bands with the Monarchs making history. Van's toil in showbands led to his professional career. It was from this often rocky road his creativity accelerated.

Muldoon is a brilliant observer. The poetry professor said Van straddled genres. He was the blue collar kid who went on become a songwriter with a performing genius. "It's been a dream of mine for forty years to try to do something with Van," Muldoon remarked to the **Belfast Telegraph**. That wish came to fruition when he was selected to write the foreword to the second book. Since that time he has bonded with Morrison. On the occasion of Van's seventy-fifth birthday, Muldoon performed "Coney Island" for Van's birthday celebration. During the covid lockdown, he told the **Irish Times** Van was "one of the world's most gifted poets...."

When the second volume, **Keep 'Er Lit: New Selected Lyrics**, was published by Faber and Faber, it was a coup for the London based firm. The one hundred and twenty one songs included in this volume covered every aspect of his career. **The Irish Times** noted of Van's songs: "These trance-like, free forming lyrics are amazing—Van Morrison's glorious art, for which these lyrics are the score, comes close to perfection." Morrison's Grammy Award winning career came full circle. His poetry was recognized.

Paul Muldoon's foreword was from the pen of a professor who had a personal relationship with the Belfast Cowboy. When Muldoon read from his eleventh collection of poems in a New York performance, he paused at the reading stating: "Ah, that music must be Jackson Browne next door. Is it?" The quizzical audience was stunned. What the hell was going on? A smiling Muldoon remarked: "I can't imagine they're having more fun than we are." Rock 'n' roll was as much a part of Muldoon's life as was poetry.

When Muldoon moved to Belfast in 1969, Morrison's early legend was blossoming with **Astral Weeks**. Like Van, Muldoon lived in dilapidated student housing. He had a view of a blue collar street much like Van had in Belfast. As he read Van's lyrics, they resonated with Muldoon's student life. The Irishness of Van's work, he suggested, is a facet critics never fully understood. As Muldoon described the Belfast Cowboy's infatuation with blues, he recognized all things Irish. "It's the blues line typified from 'Goin' Down To Monte Carlo," Muldoon continued: "That's the most common driving force in Morrison's music."

Van's lyrical touch with religion, mysticism, the occult and Celtic images intrigued Muldoon. This created a picture not just of Ireland but of a wandering minstrel attempting to define his life in lyrical form. There were many others recognizing the literary muse inside Van.

The notion of Tobias Carroll Van was the "Unlikeliest of Literary Muses" was a reminder rock 'n' roll is not considered literary. Carroll described Van in the light of an undiscovered poet with literary originality. The notion of a professor arguing Morrison's writing takes one "in unexpected directions" was not a staple of the rock 'n' roll community. His writing, as Carroll, a novelist and Managing Editor of **Words Without Borders**, suggested, is one where Van takes people into "places where writers can push their own prose toward the heartfelt and ecstatic...." Carroll viewed Morrison as less prolific than Bob Dylan. But Carroll concluded, he is equally important. "There's something about Van Morrison's music that pushes writers...." Carroll continued: "Morrison's music... (was) vital for a certain strain of writer."

Who does Carroll believe Morrison influenced? He cites Jessica Hopper's, **The First Collection Of Criticism By A Living Female Rock Critic** (Chicago, 2015) as an example of a writer influenced by Morrison's mellifluous prose. Carroll views Morrison as an artist "infamously oblique." What does this mean? It is simple. He is an enigma.

EAMONN HUGHES: VAN MORRISON'S SONGWRITING

After working with Morrison on two books, Eamonn Hughes believed his music represented a unique side of Belfast. "Van Morrison's status as an original is assured," Hughes wrote in the introduction to **Keep 'Er Lit**. The originality was in his independence. His use of local place names. His blending of Irish history. His Belfast rural and urban images. His blue collar view of Belfast. These factors created Van's literary independence. He embrace trendy styles, current fashions and artistic restraints. This made Morrison a voice in the musical wilderness. Then two years after **Astral Weeks** he became a commercial success.

"Just flicking through the book and noticing the different shapes of the songs gives an immediate sense of the many different ways that Morrison has approached the art of songwriting from tightly controlled early lyrics to through more free flowing songs or even spoken word pieces into what look like more conventional song structures," Hughes concluded. Van's fifty year overview, in two volumes, is a sacred window into a creative mind with few restrictions. A poet's touch is evident on every page.

His songwriting dissected spiritual matters. Hughes says he writes of "pain and anxiety," while on a private spiritual quest. "There are songs of falling leaves and evening shadows, of joyous sounds," Hughes observed. That Van can write a ballad or a love song as easily as "Whatever Happened to P. J. Proby" is a mystery to everyone but Morrison.

Gardens, autumn leaves, love, nature, close relationships as in "If You And I Could Be As Two" occupy another aspect of Morrison's songwriting. He writes of the world as he sees it. When the coronavirus pandemic shut down live performing in 2020, Van wrote "Born To Be Free." He was accused by the London press of being a conspiracy advocate. Even worse a Covid denier. Van said Covid-19 was a means of limiting his concerts. He sued demanding Covid-19 restrictions be lifted. He withdrew the legal action. At the end of 2020, Morrison had written three anti-lockdown protest songs. He made his point. He hated bureaucracy. Government bureaucracy reminded him of the record business. This was typical Van Morrison. No one can predict his mind set. That is what makes his songwriting unique. It is evolutionary but never boring.

The use of literary references is a Morrison trait. He can quote from Walt Whitman, as he did in "Rave On John Donne." Then he will include Omar Khayyam, Kahlil Gibran and conclude with a brief reference to John Donne. Van writes through history, literature and his evocative past. His songs include visions of how he views the world. Why does he use name dropping devices? He believes poets, critics and novelists have a more accurate view of history than the professors, the journalists and the politicians.

In "Goldfish Bowl" Van provided a window into his life. He complained fame accelerated into a howling wind of discontent. When he writes about wanting to be left alone, it is not without anger. He evokes his frustrations. He writes of "parasites" and "psychic vampires." What does Van mean? He charges those around him lack empathy. He is critical of the "newspaper barons." He writes of publishers: "They are the scum of the earth." If you asked Van to name a half dozen newspaper barons, he couldn't name one.

Van crafted Irish influences into his Marin County writing. Some years later "Goldfish Bowl" was a plaintive cry from Van, along with his co-writer, Joey DeFrancesco, to be left alone. This song was released in 2003 on **What's Wrong With This Picture**? Van made it clear he wouldn't live in a goldfish bowl. That theme began in earnest in Marin County.

As Van wailed on about "doin' my gigs," his words harkened back to the 1970s. His comments resound like a loud, out of control bass drum, as the pressures of the music business brought out his contrarian nature. Marin provided the atmosphere, the sanity and the inspiration for "Becoming Van Morrison."

Van grouses if he doesn't have a hit record. He will blame the label. He has done this from the days of Them, when he complained of Phil Solomon and his management techniques. Van may have had a point in the Solomon criticism. Even his brother, Mervyn Solomon, was a bit critical. At late as 2018, Van continued grumbling about the past. In an interview aired on RTE Radio, Van demonstrated a consistency since 1973-1974 about his attitude toward the media. He was grumpy toward Miriam O'Callaghan during an interview, but, for the biographer, he presented penetrating insights. That is Van being Van. He will follow it with heartfelt insights.

In the O'Callaghan interview, Van said: "Anyone who's successful in this, we all feel the same way, it's not just me saying this like I'm a voice in the wilderness and I'm complaining about the music business." Convoluted? You bet! Insightful! Of course. What Van emphasized was his distaste for the music business. That distaste made him a multi-millionaire. But he is still the blue collar guy, in his own mind, struggling to survive.

If Morrison was so hostile to the business side of the record business, why did he talk to O'Callaghan? The answer is a simple one. He needed to sell his latest release **The Prophet Speaks**. He detests the business. He loves his product. This conundrum bothers Morrison. The compromise? Interview where he is alternately grumpy and even at times forthcoming and happy. That is not a mystery. It is Van being Van. It is all about record sales.

Van perceived successful record sales were in the record label's domain. Van believed hit records were orchestrated by the labels. He has not bent to this dictum since the Them days. If he writes a song about fame, a lack of hits, or the evils of the record business, there is invariably a narcissist flashback to his earlier life.

As he wrote and then performed "Goldfish Bowl," in 2003, there were eerie flashbacks to the 1970s. The song was a fitting reminder of his complaints. Van continually, in song form, lists the litany of wrong doings he has experienced. He writes of "myth people" in sparkling prose. Who are the "myth people?" Only Van knows for sure. He doesn't share his secrets with us. What is known is he vents, in brilliant lyrical form, what he views as those compromising his intellectual property. Biographers are near the top of the list.

When ends "Goldfish Bowl," he asks: "Why he had to live in a goldfish bowl?" Poetic? Yes! Confusing? Yes! Why twenty-five years after leaving Marin County does Van continue to write similar themes? It is about his demand for respect and recognition. This is what drives him.

THE QUESTION OF LITERARY INFLUENCES

T. S. Eliot, William Blake and W. B. Yeats are Morrison's literary favorites. They bucked tradition. They were angry. They were in the shadow of other writers. Think of Van's complaint "weasels ripped off my soul." Van identified Bob Seger, John Cougar Mellencamp and Bruce Springsteen who built their careers on the foundation stones of his songwriting. That is the nature of the music business. His manic desire to protect every inch of his intellectual property is a laudable goal. To recognize others, with a similar creativity, is difficult for him. They became the "weasels" and "parasites."

Professor Hughes argued Morrison's songs were a "conversation with himself." It is hard to disagree. Or perhaps it is the genius of his self-expression. A facile pen and extraordinary mind makes for a different kind of songwriting.

The second lyric book ends with "**The Prophet Speaks**." This is the title of his fortieth album. It peaked at number two on the **Billboard** jazz chart and fifteen on the rock listing. What did the lyrics suggest? Only Van knows! Many Morrison songs remain a mystery. As he has said numerous times, only he, not the critics, know what the songs mean. Van's mention of W. B. Yeats and Robert

Johnson is typical of his ability to employ literary and blues themes in the same song. The similarities between Morrison and Yeats intensified after the 1970s. Both were interested in mysticism, the occult and theosophy.

MORRISON IS THE W. B. YEATS OF THE MUSIC WORLD

In 2015, when Van received the MBE and became Sir Van Morrison, he received the respect he had worked for since the 1970s. Queen Elizabeth recognized his "service to the music industry." That was a sweet moment. In three weeks, Van turned seventy.

Van's backup vocalist, Brian Kennedy, commented: "His contribution has been so extraordinary. They broke the mold when they made Van." A BBC Radio Ulster DJ, Ralph McLean, observed: "In the pantheon of great Irish artists, he is right up there with the W. B. Yeats and the James Joyce's of the world." Everyone agreed he brought Belfast place names to international acclaim. It wasn't until the 1993 album **Too Long In Exile** that Van paid the ultimate tribute through an adaptation of Yeats' "Before The World Was Made." Van took Yeats 1933 poem, and he gave it a second life. It became a legitimate blues song.

VAN'S INFATUATION WITH T. S. ELIOT: DEFINING HIS LIFE AND NEW YORK TIMES CRITIC JOHN ROCKWELL BLASTING IT

Why was Van infatuated with T. S. Eliot? He saw a kindred soul. Eliot viewed poetry as an art. Songwriting for Morrison was on a similar level. Like Eliot, style and content dominated the Belfast Cowboy's literary output. Wisdom and drama, Van believed, were centerpieces to his songs. In using language Van was a master. He embraced Irish history. He wrote of the Emerald Island's long held traditions. He had a sense of their place in the world. T. S. Eliot had similar thoughts.

Whereas T. S. Eliot was slow and careful with his poems, Van's blue collar writing turned out albums regularly. Some critics concluded he glutted the market. At least that was the view of the **New**

York Times' critic John Rockwell. In a 1977 article. Rockwell pontificated: "Quite apart from his only intermittent commercial success or even from what you may think of his music, Van Morrison remains one of the great innovators and influences of rock-and-roll." Damning Van with faint praise was constant by the late 1970s. The result? He backed off from interviews. His in-depth conversations were carefully selected. Why? Rockwell spent a paragraph telling **New York Times** readers, Morrison has "hardly a trace of his original Irish brogue...." The logical step is to ask: "Why?" Marin County was the answer.

Rockwell goes on to praise **A Period of Transition**, while pondering Van's retirement and recognizing his creativity. What does Rockwell miss? He failed to recognize the consistent themes in Van's writing and how these themes mirrored his life in song form. The blue collar ethic of "Becoming Van Morrison" was not apparent in Rockwell's review. What was apparent was Van had a defined intellect seeping over into his writing.

Like T. S. Eliot, Van remained rigid in his thinking. His work habits were structured with a frenetic base embracing his life experiences. His commitment to his craft was continuous. Compromise was impossible. Conflict was inevitable. Eliot evolved from a radical modernist writer into an arch conservative. Van took the same path thanks to the Covid pandemic. Eliot's poem, "The Waste Land," influenced Van as well as David Bowie, King Crimson and P. J. Harvey. Eliot gave songwriters a new lyrical freedom. When Bob Dylan's 1985 "Desolation Row" wrote "Ezra Pound and T. S. Eliot/Fightin' In The Captain's Tower," there is a new language the Hibbing Bard learned from English literature. Van took these lessons to heart. He did so quietly, while obliquely mentioning Eliot in his lyrics. He didn't want to talk about the English poet. For Van "The Waste Land" was a paean to the oblique, often obscure, references he loved to drop into his songs. When Eliot refers to show tunes, operas, ballads, folk songs and ragtime tunes, he gave Van and other rock songwriters a freedom previously unknown. Lyrics for Van became biography. Eliot wrote: "Genuine poetry can communicate before it is understood." Van lyrics follow that quotation.

VAN ON FAME, BOX SETS AND MORE T. S. ELIOT INFLUENCES

Van has lived his life large. He abhors fame. He has fame. That drives his writing. Like Eliot, whose collected works ran over seven thousand pages, Van has written furtively for almost sixty years. The result was albums that are a quasi-biography. The unreleased demos, the alternate cuts, the live cassettes and the unreleased master tapes, as well as the sketches, notepads, all of which have coalesced to provide a Morrison archive. It is a hidden one. No one knows what is in the Morrison archive. It has unlimited potential. Box sets are in the works. Whatever else Van writes remains in his storage facilities. The future is bright with an eye to rarities. When released these tapes will tell Van's full, unbridled story with a panache.

The hint of box sets is an indication of the breath, scope and depth of the Belfast Cowboy's creative life. It is a treasure trove not yet unveiled. The items not previously seen in print offer a panoply of Morrison's life leading to a broader interpretation of what his thinking, his observations, and what his writing meant.

Like T. S. Eliot, Van's life experienced its share of obstacles. With two failed marriages, a history of jumping to and from record labels, a cranky nature, and an at times abrasive personality, Van works at a feverish pace to maintain his literary-musical excellence. While never publicly apologizing for his egregious remarks, temper tantrums or ill thought out dictums, he is seldom personally threatening. His one dimensional drive to success derails interaction with people. He demands respect. It comes with enemies. Like T. S. Eliot, he is complicated. Van believes a culture without religion, philosophy and critical writers is not a life worth living.

There is a morality to Van's songwriting. He lectures the reader and the listener with his music. He tells them what is right and what is wrong with society. He skewers fame with the barbed criticism of a literary scholar. The public fascination with Van Morrison remains high with a bit of mystical uncertainty from the critics. The contradictions in his character fuels a wide variety of writers. Van complains he is an impersonal writer. The individualist and personality oriented curmudgeon from Belfast contradicts his self-analysis. He is a powerful critic. He is a brilliant writer. He remains a continual contradiction. He continues to occupy a central place in our culture with more to come from his facile pen. The themes may not vary, but they are increasingly deep with a penchant for self-analysis, visual wisdom and interpretive excesses.

Professor Eamonn Hughes gave Van an academic, as well as a popular cultural legitimacy. It all began to come together in Marin County in 1973 when Van's serious reading, evolved into heady writing and an intellectual growth prompting academics, serious scholars, and those with an interpretive eye to scan the daily events influencing his life and art. The result was "Becoming Van Morrison."

VAN HAS THE LAST WORD ON HIS WRITING

It is only fitting that Van has the last word on his writing. "When You're writing a song there's no audience....So there is no set thing where a song is....Some songs might be all about me or my life, most of them aren't, most of them are bits from here and there, different people's lives..." Van made this remark to Candy Dulfer on a Dutch Public Service program, April 14, 2007 recorded in Cardiff and broadcast October 28 and November 11, 2007.

During numerous interview Van remarked romantic songs were easy to write. Why? Van sees himself as "a minstrel...singing songs of love on the road." "Troubadour" suggests this direction. While he has never experienced writer's block, Van has talked about it in detail. It is his worst fear. For that reason he is driven to write.

Bibliographical Sources

See Lester Bangs, Greil Marcus, editor, **Psychotic Reactions And Carburetor Dung: The Work Of A Legendary Critic: Rock 'N' Roll As Literature and Literature As Rock 'N' Roll,** (New York, 1988, reprint) for a penetrating analysis of Van's songwriting and albums. See Ryan H. Walsh, **Astral Weeks: A Secret History** (New York, 2019) for the material in and around the creations of the **Astral Weeks** album. This is an unusually brilliant book, with a penchant for superb analysis in and around the Boston area, as Van escaped the New York gangsters.

Van Morrison, **Lit Up Inside: Selected Lyrics** (San Francisco, 2014) and **Keep 'Er Lit" New Selected Lyrics** (London, 2020) are selections of his songwriting. Both volumes were edited by Professor Eamonn Hughes with brilliant introductions.

For the argument Van Morrison is an unlikely literary influence, but still an important one, see, Tobias Carroll, "Van Morrison, Unlikeliest Of Literary Muses," **Lit Hub**, April 26, 2018. https://lithub.com/van-morrison-unlikeliest-of-literary-muses/

For Van's remarks on his writing in the 1970s, see, Clinton Heylin, **Can You Feel The Silence?: Van Morrison, A New Biography** (Chicago, 2002), pp. 349-352. From his earliest days in Marin County, Van recounted his debt to American rhythm and blues, soul music and the pioneer like Leadbelly. Sonny Terry and Brownie McGhee were another act he credited with finalizing his musical direction. In "Cleaning Window" Van writes he grew up listening to Terry and McGhee. In that song he name checks Muddy Waters and the British author of Buddhism books Christmas Humphreys then he goes to mention Jack Kerouac. Blind Lemon Jefferson is in the mix in this tune and these references suggest the critical potpourri influencing Morrison.

For "Irish folk influences were often present in Morrison's work", see, Johnny Rogan, **Van Morrison: No Surrender** (London, 2005), pp, 372.

An interesting look at Morrison's writing and music, very briefly is in Jessica Hopper, **The First Collection of Criticism By A Living Female Rock Critic**, (Chicago, 2015).

During the coronavirus pandemic lockdown, Van discussed his writing, his thoughts on an autobiography and his future music. For this interview, see, Roisin O'Connor, "Van Morrison Is A Toxic Menace-Glastonbury Shouldn't Be Hosting Him," **London Independent**, June 16, 2021.
https://www.independent.co.uk/arts-entertainment/music/features/van-morrison-glastonbury-abbey-extravaganza-b1865613.html
O'Connor attacks Van as a delusional conspiracy theorist regarding Covid.

On Van writing his autobiography see, David O'Dornan, "Van The Man To Chronicle His Precious Time With The Release Of Memoirs," **The Irish Times**, June 21, 2021.

https://www.belfasttelegraph.co.uk/sunday-life/news/van-the-man-to-chronicle-his-precious-time-with-the-release-of-memoirs-40558251.html

Another interesting interview where Van discusses his writing, while complaining about lockdown, is Martin Chilton, "Van Morrison In Lockdown: I'm Trying To Get Back Into Writing Songs," **The London Independent**, March 30, 2020. Also, see, "Portadown's Pulitzer-Winner On Van Morrison, MLA Pay And Donald Trump," **Belfast Telegraph**, October 20, 2018.

https://www.belfasttelegraph.co.uk/life/features/portadowns-pulitzer-prize-winner-on-van-morrison-mla-pay-and-donald-trump-37438811.html

When Van's first book came out Muldoon read some of his lyrics at a celebration for the City Lights volume at the Culloden Hotel in Hollywood, Northern Ireland. He had for a long time been a Morrison fan.

In the aftermath of the release of his first book of lyrics, Van was interviewed about his City Lights book and his legendary career by a number of journalists, celebrities, authors and friend from Belfast. Paul Brady, a working musician who had a guest spot form Van on his album **The Vicar Street Sessions, Vol. 1**, brought together a series of interviews, observations and suggestions as to how and why Van was such a writing force. Brady had met Morrison the first time in 1980 when the singer was living in a house in Oxfordshire. Brady's observations and those of others close to Van appeared in 2015 in an article for **The Irish Times**. Brady was a songwriter, fledgling punk musician and sometimes musical artist. When he initial interviewed or talked with Van it was in 1980 in Oxfordshire where Morrison had relocated. They talked about his 1979 album **Into The Music**. Brady played Van some songs he had recently produced for his own solo album. Brady was a fan. He wrote: "What is it about Van that appeals to musician and fans, whether they are new to the game or 40 years in the business? Brady continued: "He's force of nature....When it comes to Van's music, I guess people pick up on that life force." Brady was an unadorned Van fan.

See, Paul Brady, "Blowin' Your Mind: What Van Morrison Means To Us," **The Irish Times**, August 29, 2015.
https://www.irishtimes.com/culture/music/van/blowin-our-mind-what-van-morrison-means-to-us-1.2332194

Brady surmised by 1980 Van was a seasoned producer. Becoming Van Morrison is this book's theme. The Brady interview validated it. On Paul Muldoon, see, for example, Siobhán Brett, "Eclectic Picnic: Paul Muldoon's Feast Of Poetry And Prose," **London Independent**, August 6, 2017.
https://www.independent.ie/entertainment/theatre-arts/eclectic-picnic-paul-muldoons-feast-of-poetry-and-prose-35999159.html

Muldoon was an important force in Van's life. He was a famed Irish poet with a Pulitzer Prize. He had not lived in Ireland for more than thirty years. Like Van, Muldoon was dominantly Irish, while living in an American setting for financial and artistic reasons. Whatever concerns Van had about the Marin County years, if any, they were alleviated when talking with Muldoon. In an interview with **Poetry Northwest**, Muldoon said of Morrison: "Poetry is indistinguishable from songs."

Muldoon is a Paul McCartney fan, friend and writer. As a Pulitzer prize winning author, Muldoon, added credibility to Morrison's career. He placed him in the pantheon of rock gods the professors and New York critics lionized. Not even Van can deny a portion of the media has a soft spot for his enormous talent. Muldoon's editing of McCartney's lyrics volume is a tribute to the former Beatle. See Paul McCartney and Paul Muldoon, editor, **Paul McCartney: The Lyrics, 1956 To the Present**, published in 2021. The important point is Muldoon in a surreptitious manner compares McCartney and Morrison. That in itself is a major interpretive point. In his writing, Muldoon considered Van a major poet. See https://www.poetrynw.org/paul-muldoon-between-rail-end-and-rail-end/

The celebrated Irish writer, Edna O'Brien, said of Van's songs: "In my novel **Girls In The Married Bliss**, from 1964 the bleakness of burial was partially redeemed by "the Wreaths and the Roses and Mozart and Van Morrison." That was heady praise. O'Brien said Morrison's lyrics were "the crux of last mankind."

The literature on the Steve Turner book goes on forever. Why? Van's comments were negative. He urged his fans not to purchase it.

See Thomas C. Palmer, Jr., "A Poet's Appreciation of Van Morrison, Man And Music," **The Boston Globe**, December 10, 1993. https://en.wikipedia.org/wiki/Van_Morrison:_Too_Late_to_Stop_Now

For a great deal of peripheral information and some looking backward on Van from the Turner book. See, for example, Jonathan Rennie, "Van The Man Takes Life In His Stride," **The Evening Times**, August 2, 2002, for the reaction of book reviewers and industry insiders to the Turner volume. See the Editor's Choice selection in the **Sunday Age**, which praised Turner's scrupulous biographical work. The article by Michael Gordon, John Schauble, Gary Tippel and Gervase Greene, "Top Shelf,' Editor's Choice," **Sunday Age**, January 2, 1994, p. 8, Section, Top Shelf was high praise for Morrison's work. See **Publisher's Weekly**, November 11, 1993 for complimentary comments on Turner's work. One of the ironies of Turner's book is it was appreciated in 2005 when critics compared it to Johnny Rogan's second book. Bernard Perusse, in the **Gazette,** echoed the opinion of many critics when he looked back positively on Turner's book. The term, "coffee table book," was the kiss of death for Turner who turned in a brilliant volume.

John Boland, an Irish critic, was the snobbiest reviewer, but he did provide excellent criticism and some degree of truth. What Boland didn't consider the broader scope of Morrison's songwriting and career path to stardom. He praised Turner's photographs, which was a low blow, as Boland attempted to curry favor with Morrison. **Publisher's Weekly** wrote the book was a requirement for fans due to his discography. For this review see, Publisher's Weekly Staff, "Van Morrison: Too Late To Stop Now," **Publisher's Weekly**, November 1, 1993.

For Van writing "Summertime In England, see, Clinton Heylin, **Can You Feel The Silence?: Van Morrison, A New Biography** (Chicago, 2002), pp, 358-362 and Brian Hinton, **Celtic Crossroads: The Art Of Van Morrison** (London, 1997), p. 229, 379. For an excellent performance of "Summertime In England," see the DVD **Van Morrison: Live At Montreux, 1980/1974**, which suggests how and why Morrison evolved as a performer. He was distinct on stage by 1980 due to the years in small California clubs, working with seasoned musicians who were still in their twenties and observing first hand what his audiences wanted. He took these lessons to larger stages while continuing to play for intimate audiences in small, often seedy, clubs. Seedy with good food in Marin County or Berkeley.

The subject of a memoir has been on Van's mind since the late 1970s. When he lived with Carol Guida, from 1974 into 1977, they spent a great deal of time reading, talking about the books and suggesting how and why famous people survived in a world in which fame intrudes upon one's live. There are many interviews with Van where he talked of writing a memoir. Those around him remarked to me he has fragments, slips of observations, little notebooks and a personal memory which is a storage point for his life. Most of his friends doubt that there will be an autobiography.

For a coronavirus pandemic interview, where Van discusses a memoir in depth, see, David O'Dornan, "Van The Man To Chronicle His Precious Time With Release of Memoirs," **Belfast Telegraph**, June 21 2021. https://www.belfasttelegraph.co.uk/sunday-life/news/van-the-man-to-chronicle-his-precious-time-with-the-release-of-memoirs-40558251.html The O'Dornan article, featured in the "Sunday Life" section, was particularly forthcoming with a great deal of personal insight into what Van thought was important in his early life. Equally important concerning Van's writing was another coronavirus pandemic interview, see, Martin Chilton "Van Morrison In Lockdown: I'm Trying To Get Back Into Writing Songs," **London Independent**, March 30, 2020.

https://www.belfasttelegraph.co.uk/sunday-life/news/van-the-man-to-chronicle-his-precious-time-with-the-release-of-memoirs-40558251.html

The Chilton interview is one of the best looking back on his writing, his life and his future. Chilton's hour telephone interview was a window into the Belfast Cowboy's soul. Chilton wrote: "I find him friendly and happy to share anecdotes, his voice a mixture of low drawl interspersed with sudden moments of lightness." When Chilton asked what Van was currently writing there was a lull in the conversation. Van thought and answered. "I want to write, but I am kind of getting a bit lazy at this moment," Van said with a slight chuckle. He lamented his appearance at the Hay-on-Wye Literary Hay Festival was cancelled due to Covid restrictions. He told Chilton he was observing the lock down protocols. With rare candor and tremendous insight Van discussed his songwriting. "A lot of it is below the surface," Van remarked of his songwriting. "I get an initial idea and then paint a picture of that idea. As I start writing the song and outing music to it. I get more pictures and more impressions—mainly impressions. It's never exactly the same twice. It's on a subliminal level. A lot if it I don't really understand myself. In the 1970s, people were taking everything I wrote personally and seeing every song as personal, but it can't be—that impossible." One of Van's songwriting traits, that has never subsided, is to look at and explain his environment. It is what he writes about much of the time providing the biographer a window into his soul. Most of his songs are personal. He denies. As Van has said: "Some are just songs."

The Chilton interview contained other firsts. Van talked of playing soccer. "I was quite good at the time…." As Van discussed soccer, and his cousin who tried out for Manchester United, he paid tribute to Belfast. He also discussed Louis Armstrong and how on the 2003 Blue Note album **What's Wrong With This Picture**, he paid tribute to Armstrong by recording "St. James Infirmary." In a moment of unmitigated candor, Van explained of the song: "That was based on the trumpeter's All Stars version with Jack Teagarden." In 1979, while still under the influence of Marin County, Van did a brief vocal impersonation of Armstrong on his 1979 hit "Bright Side Of The Road." Van went on to discuss how he took saxophone lessons from Belfast's George Cassidy, who also lived on Hyndford Street. "Morrison is undeniably a complex man…at heart he seems to be all about the music," Chilton concluded. On writing a book, Morrison concluded: "It's a slog, writing a book….Sometimes I get going when I feel like I have a certain part I want to write, and then it dries up for a while. I'm very disorganized." Van writes in longhand. Stay tuned a memoir is in the works.

For Eamonn Hughes and his role in **Lit Up Inside** see, for example, "Eamonn Hughes On Memory And Place In Van Morrison," **Writing, Books & Music**, December 25, 2014.

https://writingbooksandmusic.wordpress.com/2014/12/25/eamonn-hughes-on-memory-and-place-in-van-morrison/

This is a helpful article explaining how and why Professor Hughes selected and introduced a wide variety of Morrison's songs. Hughes said he was offering "a map of the world of Van Morrison" in lyrical form. What Hughes did, wittingly or unwittingly, was to provide deep insights into the lyrical selections from Van's Belfast days. The professor allegedly believes myth and spirituality haunt Van. He sees the years of exile, particularly in Marin County, as influencing, nurturing and finalizing Van's talent. "Becoming Van Morrison" is the explanation through his lyrics. The image of the Welsh poet, Dylan Thomas, in "Mr. Thomas" is a literary masterpiece that Hughes and other literary heavyweights have praised.

For an insightful commentary on Dr. Eamonn Hughes and what it meant to work with Van Morrison and how and why it is important to Belfast, see, a brief explanation, "Eamonn Hughes-The Train And The River-Van Morrison's Belfast," Liverpool Irish Festival.com.

https://writingbooksandmusic.wordpress.com/2014/12/25/eamonn-hughes-on-memory-and-place-in-van-morrison/

This is an explanation of an October 21, 2018 seventy five minute lecture explaining the name checking from Belfast in Van's songs.

For a review by one of America's best known rock critics damning Van with faint praise and curious comments on **A Period of Transition**, see, John Rockwell, "The Pop Life," **The New York Times**, April 22, 1977, p. 79.

https://www.nytimes.com/1977/04/22/archives/the-pop-life.html

The announcement of **Lit Up Inside** from the rock music press indicated a new awareness for Morrison as a writer, see, for example, Kory Grow, "Van Morrison To Release Lyric Book 'Lit Up Inside' This Fall," **Rolling Stone**, August 8, 2014.

https://www.rollingstone.com/music/music-news/van-morrison-to-release-lyric-book-lit-up-inside-this-fall-77254/

G. Smyth, "Hymns To The Silence: Inside The Words And Music Of Van Morrison," **Irish Studies Review**, volume 19, issue 2, pp. 243-244. This is a literary review placing Van's music into an academic perspective. Also, see, L. Onkey, "Ray Charles On Hyndford Street: Caledonia Soul," in D. Negra, editor, **The Irish In Us: Irishness, Performativity And Popular Culture** (Durham, 2012). This is a marvelous collection of essays reflecting on the "Irish condition."

R. Elliott, "My Tongue Gets T-T-T: Words, Sense And Vocal Presence In Van Morrison's It's Too Late To Stop Now," **Twentieth Century Music**, volume 13, issue 1, pp. 53-76.

Nigel Hunter, "The Poet In Van Morrison," Paper Presented to the First Symposium of Irish Studies in South America (Readings of Contemporary Irish Studies, September 2006), pp. 28-30. Also, see, Peter Mills, "Into The Mystic: The Aural Poetry Of Van Morrison," **Popular Music**, volume 13, issue, November 11, 2008.

Discussions with Steve Turner, at a Beatlefest in Los Angeles, helped me understand Morrison's personality, his writing and his working habits. The literary and Christian influences upon Van's music were evident in Turner's writing and conversation.

Gina Berriault, an award winning short story writer and novelist, and her partner, Leonard Gardner, author of **Fat City**, were witnesses to Van's furtive writing in local coffee shops. They discussed their impressions. Both concluded Van was more than a singer-songwriter.

See Jonathan Cott, "Van Morrison: The Poet," **Rolling Stone**, November 30, 1978 for the best explanation of his growth as a writer in the 1970s. Also, see, Randy Lewis, " Why Van Morrison Keeps On Singing: Irish Troubadour Touring With Songs From His New Album," **Los Angeles Times**, October 7, 2016. The Lewis article is an important one for Van's reflections on his past life.

For an understanding of Van as a writer, there is an excellent chapter in Peter Mills, **Hymns To The Silence: Inside The Words And Music Of Van Morrison** (London, 2010). Professor Mills entitled his chapter "Get The Words On The Page: Van Morrison As Writer." Mills does this by beginning with "Gloria," in which he provides a mini-history of this signature song on Van's writing, performing and dynamic style. By the time that Van revisits this hit on **It's Too Late To Stop Now** it was, as Mills pointed out, "already locked in its classic, authentic status...."(p. 86). That fact alone made Morrison nervous. He was too young for fame.

As Mills analyzed "Brown Eyed Girl," he employs a brilliant Morrison quote. "Let's do 'Brown Eyed Girl' and get it over with," Van Morrison, Chester Race Track Concert, June 21, 2001. The subtle nuances and meaningful changes Van brought to "Brown Eyed

Girl" in concert are analyzed by Mills. He points out how Van fought producer Bert Berns "every step of the way" in the recording process.

When Mills writes of "Jackie Wilson Said (I'm In Heaven When You Smile)," he dissects the essence of 1972. Not only did Van use this song as a tribute to a soul-rock pioneer, Jackie Wilson, he also wittingly paid tribute to another influence, Louis Jordan. When Van reissued the song in 2007 on the **Still On Top** album, he recalling Jackie Wilson's influence. Why? Van never stops praising, bringing back and highlighting those who made his music work.

When Mills introduced romantic songs, he quoted Morrison extensively. "It's easy to write romantic songs," Van remarked in Cardiff in 2007. Mill intuits the Belfast Cowboy's "love songs frequently make a connection between his more esoteric vocabularies and the tradition of the well-made romantic song." (p.96) Of all the types of songs Mills analyzed the romantic ones take up the bulk of this chapter. Why? Van's love songs convey personal emotion allowing the biographer to delve deeply into his psyche. He says he doesn't discuss his personal life. He does repeatedly and, in depth, in love songs.

A conversation between Candy Dulfer and Van for Dutch Television in Cardiff on April 7, 2007 was important in analyzing Van's writing. Peter Mills uses this material in his book with great skill.

For the biographer the personal insights are a cornucopia of tales leading one into Morrison's soul. The handpicked songs are a window into the jazz, blues and rhythm and blues tunes impacting Morrison. Peter Mills chapter seven, "Down The Road: Exile Place And The Idea of Eternal Movement," in **Hymns To The Silence: Inside The Words And Music Of Van Morrison** (London, 2010) asks the question: "When Van sings about exile, what does it mean?" (p. 251) While Mills' chapter examines the 1990s and "Too Long In Exile," Van talked with friends about being in "exile due to the Troubles." Also, see, Peter Childs, **Van Morrison In The 1970s** (Sonicbond, 2022), for the manner in which the 1970s music was influenced by Morrison's geographical background i.e., Marin County.

The two volumes of lyrics are an important tool for the biographer. They have elicited in depth studies of Van Morrison's songwriting and intellectual development. Like T. S. Eliot, Van remained rigid in his thinking. His work habits were consistent. His commitment to his craft was continuous. Compromise was impossible. Conflict was inevitable. Eliot evolved from a radical modernist writer into an arch conservative. Van took the same path thanks to the Covid pandemic. Eliot's poem, "The Waste Land," influenced Van was well as David Bowie, King Crimson, P. J. Harvey and dozens of others. The reason? Eliot gave songwriters a new lyrical freedom. When Bob Dylan's 1985 "Desolation Row" wrote "Ezra Pound and T. S. Eliot/Fightin' In The Captain's Tower," there is a new language the Hibbing Bard learned from English literature. Van took these lessons to heart. He did so quietly while obliquely mentioning Eliot in his lyrics. He didn't want to talk about the English poet. For Van "The Waste Land" was a paean to the oblique, often obscure, references he loved to drop into his songs. When Eliot refers to show tunes, operas, ballads, folk songs and ragtime tunes he gave Van and other rock songwriters a freedom previously unknown. Lyrics for Van became biography.

For a doctoral dissertation delving deeply into Van's creative process see, Geoff Munns, **The Places Of Van Morrison's Songwriting** (London, 2022). This 1972 page book is from an Australian author with a PhD. By selecting some key Songs, Munns provides what he considers a way of looking into Morrison's creativity. The songs are placed in chapters where streets, Hyndford, the local sights and influences from foreign lands coalesce to explain Morrison's creativity. An excellent piece of literature if a bit quirky.

Discussion with David Meltzer at the Castro Valley Record saw in the 1980s helped me to understand the literary-poetic side of the Belfast Cowboy. When Meltzer passed at 79 his fifty plus poetry books and his writing on rock music allowed him an understanding of Morrison few possessed. In 2014, when the City Lights book came out, Meltzer smiled. He realized Van finally got his due as a poet Meltzer died two years later at seventy nine a stone cold Van Morrison fan to the end.

TEN

VAN MORRISON: THE MAKING OF A LEGEND, 1973-1974, INTO THE MID-1970S

"Anyone who cannot cope with life while he is alive needs one hand to ward off a little of his despair over fate...but with his other hand he can jot down what he sees among the ruins."

FRANZ KAFKA, DIARIES, ENTRY OF OCTOBER 19, 1921

"What I do is not easy."

VAN MORRISON

"It's been a dream of mine for 40 years to try to do something with Van. I was reared on rock 'n' roll."

PAUL MULDOON, PULITZER PRIZE POET, NEW YORKER POETRY EDITOR AND PRINCETON UNIVERSITY PROFESSOR

In the mid-1970s, Van Morrison experienced the power of the media. As he reordered his life, finalized his career plans, organized his business activity and focused on his reading and writing habits, the press speculated on his future. That drove Van crazy. Hence, the retirement myth. He was lauded by a friendly San Francisco press. His experimental writing and performing fit into the California cultural milieu. He had freedom in Marin County to experiment. He had top flight musicians. He had a major label contract. He had Carol Guida on his arm. What could go wrong? Plenty! There was the so-called period of retirement. There were unfounded rumors he had writer's block. Van was so private no one realized he was working 24/7 on his career.

Van's experimental music was shown when he sang in a falsetto in "Try For Sleep." Warner Bros. flipped out. They wanted "Moondance." Joe Smith screamed: "What the fuck." Warner had no idea as to the extent of the Belfast Cowboy's experimental nature.

Van had a long term career plan. He didn't ignore his personal life. He took control of it with Carol Guida by his side. He did everything he could to maintain his privacy.

The media speculation he was semi-retired. Privately, Van said this was the stuff of massive misinformation. He was avoiding the limelight. He was concentrating on his fan base. How? His small club shows were a paean to his willingness to make less money to have his music connect with his audience. His lyrical sophistication was built in Marin County. He wasn't interested in a batch of hit records.

In March 1975, at San Francisco's Great American Music Hall, Van told a **San Francisco Chronicle** reporter: "I'm getting into something different." That was a horn based sound. He was creating longer instrumental flourishes. He was increasingly writing instrumental music.

His half dozen, but furtive, writing years in the 1970s produced new musical directions. **Veedon Fleece** was that direction. It wasn't, as the critics suggested, a blatant return to **Astral Weeks**. It was a writing direction combining Marin County influences with those of his Belfast past. The new Van Morrison was being created in the leafy suburb north of San Francisco. It came with new music and a renewed lease on life. Van was happy. He looked forward to solitude and frenetic creativity. These factors caused the press to portray him as a mysterious, elusive character. He wasn't. He was simply a hard-working, blue collar musician planning his future.

The press wasn't paying attention as he worked daily. As least this is how Carol Guida remembered her time with Morrison. If the media had scrutinized his shows, if they had listened to what he performed. If they understood the way he interpreted his songs, they would have realized Van's intellectual soul.

A blue collar guy with a Protestant work ethic doesn't go into semi-retirement. It was complicated. No one wants to question you when you are retired. It was a perfect excuse for Van not to have to explain himself. The biographers, the top level rock writers, the mainstream press, the fanzines and the casual writers ignored Van. Why? Because he said he was retired. He wasn't.

Van performed thirty-two shows in 1975. Many were two sets a night. They were all in California except the year's first appearance in Buffalo. Three of the shows were in a recording studio with guests. The favored venue, the Great American Music Hall, was home to fourteen shows in a seven day period. Van was fine tuning his music. He was systematically planning for the remainder of the 1970s.

Clinton Heylin claimed Van retired after the Great American Music Hall shows. Heylin wrote "The GAMH shows were to be his last concert appearances for three and a half years." The truth was more complicated. He wrote. He recorded. He held hundreds of auditions for new musicians. He archived his work product. He established a complicated business structure. He protected his intellectual property. Retirement! Van couldn't spell the word.

"The sheer weight of his productivity," drummer Tony Dey remarked, "didn't seem to make any difference to the ever persistent critics."

Clinton Heylin observed Van "reached a point where it all seemed, well, pointless." This comment enraged the Belfast Cowboy.

He was working night and day to further his career. "What I do is not easy," Van remarked in numerous interviews. Apparently, Heylin ignored Van's blue collar roots. His attention to detail and his obsessive devotion to detail established a full, rich life. He stepped away from the limelight. The work never stopped.

Carol Guida led the way from late 1973 into early 1977 with a 24/7 partnership healing the wounds of his divorce, battling a contentious atmosphere with his label and evolving into a level of musical genius with an unprecedented impact upon his concerts and songwriting. I asked Guida if Van was retired in the mid-1970s. She laughed. I had my answer.

VAN'S LEGEND BY THE MID-1970s

The Van Morrison legend loomed large by the mid-1970s. As he turned thirty, Van was famous. He told Carol Guida, and others, the praise and acclaim for his music was a double edged sword. It made him publicly accessible. His private life! Forget it! It vanished! He was building a formidable repository of literary references. He did this through a program of self-education. Cult status? He denied it.

A portion of Van's cult status was the mystery surrounding his professional life. He didn't maintain a predictable touring schedule. He was increasingly professional in concert. The ensuing publicity he was retired spurred his legendary work ethic. This unpredictable creativity intrigued some while confusing others. There was an aura or mystique to Morrison.

As he explored his creative life in Marin County, Van's newly minted lyrics and over the top New Age remarks intrigued the media. What the hell was going on with Van. John L. Wasserman, the **San Francisco Chronicle** critics, asked Van what he was doing. Wasserman told me that Van looked at him blankly. He clearly didn't understand the question. Wasserman knew the answer. Don't interpret Van. Don't ask him rational questions. Wasserman saw Van as the product of Marin County's creative influences as they meshed with the artist's talent.

What did the press miss? He was working hard while enjoying life with Carol Guida. They didn't see this side of his life. He was belligerently private. It was as if he was attending a college of expanded musical awareness. As he continued to explore new lyrical themes, his eclectic approach brought surprises in theme and content. Contrasting styles emerged. There was no predictable Van Morrison.

Clinton Heylin labels the 1973-1974 period "a commercial cul-de-sac." The reality is it was a period of spectacular growth. It brought a new sophistication to Morrison's music. "I think Van took the challenge to separate his music from that of his contemporaries," Chris Michie remarked.

A NEW VAN AND HIS MARIN CONTEMPORARIES

Van was a constant source of inspiration to musicians around him. Ramblin' Jack Elliott, the Youngbloods, Elvin Bishop, the New Riders of the Purple Sage, Stoneground, Jerry Garcia, Commander Cody And The Lost Planet Airmen and a bevy of lesser known, but talented, musicians were Marin County neighbors. They watched him evolve. They had their own musical directions. He remained a creative inspiration to their developing musical journey.

Alice Stuart, who opened for Morrison during this period, remembered his inordinate interest in reading. She observed most of what he read was philosophy, Irish history and religious studies. A continual program of reeducation impressed those around Morrison. He was private, quiet and non-demonstrative.

After Van played small clubs, he had an occasional mini-tour in larger venues to keep the money rolling into the coffers. These shows were profitable enough to pay the band. He could also craft his more popular songs to please his audiences. He increasingly added "Brown Eyed Girl", "Gloria" and "Here Comes The Night" to his shows. The audiences loved it. Van saw it as an obligation. The songs brought back unpleasant memories. There was enough money from his LPs, after **Astral Weeks**, to allow Van to live comfortably.

ALICE STUART IN THE ZAPPA MOTHER OF INVENTION DAYS (photo courtesy Alice Stuart)

From 1973 into the summer of 1974 Van developed his art. The tangled links between the world of local events and his imagination collided in his lyrical quest.

THE FLAVOR OF THE MONTH: A COMMENT ON STARDOM AND ITS PITFALLS

Van despised recording artists who were the "the flavor of the day." They could easily be forgotten. He worried he was too productive. He might be repeating his musical self. There was one new album theme after another. Van hit a dry period in the mid-1970s. He didn't experience extreme writer's block. He had theme concerns. At least this is how he described his difficulties to drummer Tony Dey. He told Dey he was increasingly retrospective. Van informed Dey he needed time to read, to write and to plan his future. He hesitated to use the term writer's block.

The fear of writer's block prompted Van's increased productivity. That fear still drives him. By recycling songs in concert, rewriting his gigantic oeuvre and working with new musicians, he has remained fresh. **Duets: Re-Working The Catalogue** is an example of this approach. When he was working with Joey DeFrancesco, Van brought back a song from the **Astral Weeks** album "The Way Young Lovers Do." This is typical Van. He looked back to move forward artistically. He will take a rock 'n' roll tune and turned it into a jazz gem.

The more he feared failure, the greater his successes. During the period from 1973 into mid-1974, Van loved seclusion. He lived a sheltered life. One that saw him thrive in the bucolic wilderness around Marin County. When D. H. Lawrence, in **Women In Love**, speculated on living "in a world of empty people," he unwittingly reflected on Van's life in the mid-1970s. Van was a blue collar worker living in another world.

It was from the rock stars, the movie people, the businessmen, the common folk and the counterculture, Van found themes to craft his music. To some observers he had taken a step backward. He hadn't experienced the large arenas.

THE MILL VALLEY CULTURAL SCENE

There has been very little attention paid to the Mill Valley cultural scene and its impact. This small town, north of San Francisco and west of Sausalito, was a mecca for writers, artists, musicians and poets. The local film festival was so pompous they turned out an advertisement suggesting that if someone drove a Ford or Chevrolet into Mill Valley it was déclassé.

Van loved Mill Valley's ambiance. The offerings in Mill Valley included the Depot Book Store. It was one of his favorite haunts as was John Goddard's Village Music. There were other attractions. The Sweetwater Café featured Jules Broussard, a jazz saxophonist of immense talent, in a Sunday brunch concert. There were often more musicians in the audience than on the stage.

The foreign films in Mill Valley were excellent. There were so many famous people living there, Van looked like just another anonymous resident. John Goddard recalls Morrison wandering into Sausalito's Upstart Crow Book Store for coffee and a scone. He was left alone to read at a table. By the late 1970s, this was no longer an option. Herb Gold, the San Francisco novelist, was sitting one day in the coffee shop. He noticed Van. He walked over. He said hello.

They exchanged small talk. In Mill Valley, Van was approachable and happy. That didn't last long. Fame soon intruded.

The restaurants were a means of entertaining friends. The small venues he loved to play were nearby. Mill Valley offered peace and solitude. He was a wandering gypsy. This accelerated his creativity. Productivity was the key to his restless nature. His biographers have wondered if he was productive enough in the mid-1970s. He was!

In October, 2021, Mill Valley officials organized a shuttle bus to Van Morrison's concert at Berkeley's Greek Theater. As a gaggle of middle aged, entitled, gray haired seniors and well-dressed aristocrats showed up a young woman hollered: "Mom, hurray, you don't need to go back to the car for the brie and the prosecco." Her mother turned screaming: "Gerald is driving the bus. He will wait." As the bus rolled out for the hour plus drive to Van's concert the mother passed out cheese plates and poured the bubbly alcoholic drink. This was Van Morrison's Mill Valley cultural scene more than forty years after he left it.

Van wrote of his San Francisco Bay Area experiences in Mill Valley coffee shops. He composed songs using local imagery. "Warner Bros. has given me complete artistic freedom," Van told **Rolling Stone**. He enhanced that freedom in the Mill Valley coffee shops. A half decade of productivity created a body of work defining his legacy.

Bob Gordon, an entertainment lawyer since 1960, represented the Kingston Trio, Janis Joplin, Bobby Darin and the Doobie Brothers among others. He was also an amateur ukulele performer with his All Star Review. Morrison couldn't believe his good fortune when he found him in his Sausalito office. Gordon organized the early stages of Van's fledgling business empire.

Despite Van's quirky nature, his productivity took a strange turn. He refused to release certain material. Or conversely, Warner would not release some songs. It was not until **The Philosopher's Stone** that the full extent of Morrison's workaholic ways became apparent. He viewed unreleased tracks as foundation stones. It was his art, not commercial sales, that drove him. His business was in order. His writing flourished. The royalties were invested, sheltered from taxes and the royalties funded his career expansion.

His songs were literary garnish to his psyche. He was virtually two people. The private George Ivan Morrison, who drank coffee in Mill Valley, Sausalito or Fairfax, and the more public Belfast Cowboy seen in Tom Donahue's Orphanage Club in San Francisco, Bill Graham's Old Waldorf or Jack's Blues Club on Fillmore Street. The idea he wasn't making new music was laid to rest by his appearances in small clubs like the Keystone Corner in Berkeley, Sophie's in Palo Alto or the Odyssey Room in Sunnyvale. He loved playing small clubs. The myth Morrison wasn't cognizant of his audience was laid to rest in these stunning shows.

THE CHANGING NATURE OF VAN'S MUSICAL AND PERSONAL DIRECTION

What made the period from 1973 into mid-1974 significant? It was Morrison's lyrics. They developed a distinct literary direction. These lyrics, combined with the music, created a unique performer. Van's use of language is the key to understanding his lyrical precision. He continually rewrote his life in song form. Insights into how he viewed the world, the direction of his life, his friends, his foes and the music business abound in his songwriting. He was never the flavor of the month. He took his lyrics continually into new directions.

The critics took note. Van was never predictable. Language was a tool for change. He used it to define his life. He constantly experimented. How many singers could write and then perform "Listen To The Lion?" It was a personal plea to be left alone. That level of musical sophistication surfaced in 1973.

It was in the lyrics to **Hard Nose The Highway**, Van hinted at things to come in the 1970s. The album's cover was an indication his intellectual growth was coming full circle. He approved of the cover concept. This was the first time he had control. There was no mystery to the cover. That is unless you were a reviewer. Some spent as much time complaining about the cover as they did discussing the music. Rob Springett designed the cover. It was after multiple conversations with Van that the imagery appeared on **Hard Nose The Highway**.

The elderly Chinese man who looks up at the birds suggests Van was looking for philosophical salvation. The lyrics took strange turns.

There was the localized song "Snow in San Anselmo." Van wrote this song after a freak snowfall in this small Marin town north of Fairfax. A story in the **San Francisco Chronicle** was the inspiration. It was a unique and interesting way to open an album. It was a commentary on his life. His personality was tranquil. He was searching for contentment, calm and peace. He had no trouble finding it in his private life. This is why his so-called period retirement is largely a myth. His musical life took over. The ensuing privacy fed his creative soul. He achieved a quiet and contemplative life. One allowing his rough edges to surface to blend with his artistry. That took place in August, 1973 when Carol Guida entered his life. She quickly became his muse.

Few people in and around Marin County found Morrison tempestuous. He wasn't. He was quiet. He was reflective. He was shy. At times he erupted. All his life Van's one dimensional drive for artistic perfection impacted his personal life.

When Morrison believed his space was invaded or his privacy violated, he could be a devilish rascal. He was naturally a contrarian. He was a dedicated curmudgeon. If at times a loveable one. Van had little regard for famous people, or industry big wigs. Fame allowed him the freedom to explode in contrarian ways. It was his way or the highway. Had he not been that way he would have been the next Gary Puckett going out on the road with an Oldies But Goodies show. He was determined to avoid that trap. He crafted a varied musical catalogue in the 1970s guaranteeing relevance.

IS TEMPESTUOUS REALLY THE WORD? IT IS!

No life, unless it is overtly simple, can be analyzed in a single word. The Belfast Cowboy is the exception. There is one word, Van said repeatedly, that identifies him. That word is consciousness. Van sees channeling of songs coming through his consciousness. His inner mind is the conduit to his creative process.

Van's life can be described as a tempestuous one. His early drinking sprees. His frequent temper tantrums. His love-hate relationship with the media. His spats with record labels. His obsessive demand for privacy. These factors tell us a great deal. His attack on those he believed slighted him often created disturbing scenarios.

"Anyone turned biographer," Sigmund Freud wrote "has committed himself to lies, to concealment, to hypocrisy, to flattery, and even to his own lack of understanding for biographical truth is not to be had, and even if it were, it couldn't be useful." Freud's quotation described Morrison's sometimes tempestuous behavior, as well as highlighting his disdain for the biographical process.

There were a number of compulsive factors in Van's life. One was music. Another his home in Fairfax. He loved Marin's solitude. He enjoyed serious musicians. The media constantly judged his lifestyle. This made him uncomfortable.

Some of his albums would not be as strong as others. He agonized over what he would be and what he would not be as a performer. He was an Irish citizen. He found fame in England. He moved to America. By the mid-1970s, the Marin County hippie lifestyle, near his Fairfax home, was wearing thin. He was divorced, dating and then he was engaged to Carol Guida.

VAN MORRISON'S EVOLUTION OR IS IT DEVOLUTION?

Van envisioned life in ways others missed. He was seldom secure in his work. This drove him to lyrical and musical perfection. Reading! Discussions! Listening to music! These were the means to a healthy life. His pursuit of a vinyl record collection was a personal joy.

He loved to search out blues albums. He haunted the second hand record stores. He frequently drove down to Village Music in Mill Valley, where John Goddard would try to meet his blues music needs. Van was seen wandering around the used record section in Rasputin's in Berkeley or at Let It Be Records in San Francisco. He remained an inveterate record collector.

Some saw him as prickly. The "prickly pear" quote was from Janet Planet. His friends described him as kind, supportive and inordinately shy. Because he was generally considerate to close friends, Morrison had a small coterie of followers who isolated him. The inner circle didn't speak to the press. His road manager from the

1970s has never spoken to the press. He lives, retired in Northern California, on a goat farm. He has changed his name. Ed's most profound quote was: "Van was not comfortable in his own skin in the 1970s." Maybe Marin County made that skin mature. Then again, his whole life has been a battle to maintain a personal life in light of industry pressures.

CONCLUSION: THE BALANCE IN VAN'S LIFE

Van's balance between writing, performing and living made for a normal life. He reordered his life. Music dominated it. He developed a private, defined personal life. He created a serene lifestyle and a reborn confidence in his daily life. No outsiders were allowed into his kingdom.

There was a book of magic in Van. It came in song form. He was determined not to let his musical career get in the way of his daily life. He kept himself mentally and spiritually healthy. He refused to limit himself for the sake of his art.

As W. B. Yeats wrote: "The intellect of man is forced to choose. ... Perfection of the life, of the work." Van wisely selected a course bringing both elements into play. It was Yeats who remarked verse was meant to be heard not read. Van used this statement. It was an axiom for his career. "Write for the ear," Yeats continued. "So that you may be instantly understood."

In Marin County, Morrison inaugurated his towering achievements, eccentricities and pretensions. A career was underway blossoming into many directions. There is an eloquence and a permanence to Morrison's art.

As the pundits and critics speculated on the course of his career, Van pursued his art. He didn't listen to or care what the critics thought. He was too busy "Becoming Van Morrison."

Bibliographical Sources

Interviews about Van's life, concerts, moods and charisma came from Alice Stuart, the Barsotti brothers, Tony Dey, Mark Naftalin, Elvin Bishop, Chris Michie, Mitch Woods, Marie Bainer, Bill

Graham, Nick Clainos, Carol Guida, Larry Catlin and John Goddard. They were all important to this chapter. Also, see, the conclusions for this period in Morrison's life in Clinton Heylin, **Can You Feel The Silence?: Van Morrison, A New Biography** (London, 2002) chapters 18-19 and p. 302, Johnny Rogan, **Van Morrison: No Surrender** (London, 2005) and Howard A. DeWitt, **Van Morrison: The Mystic's Music** (Fremont, 1983).

See Vincent Powers, **Send 'Em Home Sweating: The Showband Story** (Dublin, 1990), for some of the early musical aggregations influencing Morrison and how they shaped his career in the mid-1970s. The Powers book is unusually helpful in understanding how the multi-instrumental showbands helped Morrison form his musical persona.

For his aversion to a regular recording studio, see, for example, Ian Birch, "Morrison Interview," **Melody Maker**, June 25, 1977.

The San Francisco Bay Area music scene was important to Morrison. Those who helped fill in the concert influences include, Bill Quarry, Art Siegel, Ron Sexton, Chris Bradford, Paul Vincent, and Charlie Musselwhite. Jimmy Witherspoon was interviewed on Van's career at a solo show he did at the Great American Music Hall.

For Van reflecting on what influenced his writing in and around the San Francisco Bay Area, see, John Grissim, Jr. "Van Morrison: The 1972 Rolling Stone Interview," **Rolling Stone**, June 22, 1972. Also see, Erik Hage, **The Words And Music Of Van Morrison** (Westport, 2009), passim.

Tony Dey was Van's drummer in 1975. His recollections were important to this chapter. For Van's total freedom at Warner Bros., see, for example, David Wild, "A Conversation With Van Morrison," **Rolling Stone**, August 9, 1990 for an interview where Van reflects on fame, the music business and MTV. Beginning about this time, Van is reflective, open, less hostile and transparent about his musical life. His personal life remained a no no. But the Wild piece is important. It suggests the Belfast Cowboy's continual dissatisfaction with aspects of his career. Not surprisingly, Wild concluded: "Van Morrison is the real thing." That is on his own terms when he controls the narrative. Also, see, Travis M. Edwards, "The Rage Of Van Morrison And The Battle Behind His Astral Weeks," **The Washington Post**, November

23, 2018. https://www.washingtonpost.com/lifestyle/the-rage-of-van-morrison-and-the-battle-behind-his-masterpiece/2018/11/29/38d67a88-f32e-11e8-bc79-68604ed88993_story.html

For a penetrating insight on Jimmy Giuffre's influence on Van Morrison and how his early jazz provided a roadmap for Morrison's future music, and its impact upon his writing, recording and performing, see, Gavin Martin, "Van Morrison: Dark Knight Of The Soul," **Classic Rock**, December 1, 2015. https://www.loudersound.com/features/van-morrison-dark-knight-of-the-soul The Giuffre influence is also covered in Howard A. DeWitt, **Van Morrison: Them And The Bang Era, 1945-1968** (Fremont, 2005). Van's jazz roots remain a largely untapped resource for biographers. There is a jazz story running through his career from the Monarch days to the present. There are numerous interviews where he discusses jazz influences.

The retirement myth Van perpetuated in the mid-1970s served him well. As late as 2016, the press repeated this story. The source? Van himself. Why would Morrison use this onerous tale? Probably because he believed it was true. Half a dozen people close to Van in the 1970s reflected he loved the period of retirement story. Why? It was another way to rant against the music industry. The issue? Always royalties! In 2016 Van wrote the **London Mirror** reporter, Kim Carr, he quit the business because he didn't have enough money to "cover his outings." What this comment suggests is that the large number of small gigs Van played in 1973-1974 led to his so-called "period of retirement." Carr didn't interview Van, she simply took an article from **Classic Rock** to report Van stating he returned to performing because, as Van said, "I had people to support-myself and others." This is an example of Morrison's legitimate bitching about the myopic and falsely reporting press. **The London Mirror** reported Van remarking: "I'm trapped. I've got so much product that even if I stopped public appearances, I'd still have to manage my catalogue, so I'd still be working." I am not sure there is an insight there. It may be bragging. But it is true. The operative wisdom is Van will never stop performing. So why not use a curious press to publicize his career. These comments came as Van released his 36th album **Keep Me Singing** in September 2020. See Kim Carr, "Van Morrison Says He Returned To Music After Quitting For Two Years Because He Ran Out Of Money," **The London Mirror**, November 25, 2106.

https://www.mirror.co.uk/3am/celebrity-news/van-morrison-says-returned-music-9336023

The retirement myth is also alluded to in Randy Lewis, "At 73, Van Morrison Is No Longer Doing Things 'For Survival'," **The Los Angeles Times**, February 1, 2019. https://www.latimes.com/entertainment/music/la-et-ms-van-morrison-las-vegas-residency-wiltern-20190201-story.html The Lewis article is one where Van uses "Into The Mystic" to reflect almost half a century later on the period that made him a seasoned performer. Van looked back on his career to the 1970s when "Becoming Van Morrison" was so carefully plotted he has had to deny it. He told Randy Lewis in Las Vegas, while preparing for a lengthy residence at the Colosseum that he had come to terms with his past successes and failures. He continued to move his career forward. Mentally healthy, emotionally sound and rich as hell, Van was relaxed talking with Lewis who has worked with Van in a public relations capacity. Lewis asked Van about his loyal audience and if they might expect "Gloria" or "Brown Eyed Girl." Lewis was curious if the fans wanted more of the old days. "Did they look back?" Lewis asked Van. "It's not like looking back," Morrison continued. "There's not really pressure…It's a workout. And if it's a musical workout…they'll fit in." Van has looked back during interviews since 1985 when he turned the ripe old age of forty. Now Van does it his way. "I paid my dues," he told Lewis, "that's what they call it."

By the time he returned from Ireland, with Carol Guida, Van imagined his life was in a "cul-de-sac." Hence, the title to a song on **Veedon Fleece**. He lived in Fairfax and San Geronimo Valley in homes with a cul-de-sac. The title for a song resulted. This is one of hundreds of examples of Van using the setting he lived in and the environment around him to craft new songs.

For a well written, carefully researched and thorough biography of Leon Russell, which helped me understand Warner Bros., Lenny Waronker, the Southern California music scene, the problems artists had with labels and the 1970s rock 'n' roll subculture, see, Bill Janovitz, **Leon Russell: The Master Of Space And Time's Journey Through Rock 'n' Roll History** (New York, 2023). There are numerous references to Morrison in the Janovitz biography that helped to focus attention on Morrison's approach to the business.

ELEVEN

THE BIRTH OF VAN'S MUSICAL FREEDOM: THE ROAD TO THE CALEDONIA SOUL ORCHESTRA, 1973-1974

"But to look back from the stony plain along the road which led one to that place is not at all the same thing as walking on the road; the perspective...changes only with the journey; only when the road has, all abruptly and treacherously, and with an absoluteness that permits no argument, turned or dropped or risen is one able to see all that one could not have seen from any other place."

JAMES BALDWIN, GO TELL IT TO THE MOUNTAIN

"For me, performing requires a tremendous amount of concentration."

VAN MORRISON

"Caravan will be played at my funeral."

NICK HORNBY

Nathan Rubin

David Hayes Jeff Labes

Dahaud Shaar

Van Morrison

The Caledonia Soul Orchestra

John Platania

Tim Kovatch

Nancy Ellis Jack Schroer

Terry Adams

Bill Atwood

James Trumbo

Tom Halpin

In the early weeks of 1973, Van Morrison finalized a master plan he had been working on for years. Van has never said exactly when the Caledonia Soul Orchestra idea emerged. His band mates have their thoughts. One told me he at the **His Band And Street Choir** sessions that was the genesis of the CSO. Another said it was a last minute decision after some failed 1972 club appearances. Still another said after Van worked with Sound Hole, he decided to form a band that would be a permanent fixture but with a horn section and strings. One musician suggested it was the appearance on Don Kirshner's Rock Concert in April, 1973. Van has never said.

The San Francisco Bay Area was replete with excellent musicians. Why did Van form a super band? He needed perfection in concert. He got it by assembling a core of musicians who followed his every move, whether in the studio, or in concert. Some said the super group was to combat stage fright. John Platania, David Hayes, Jack Schroer and Dahaud Shaar fit that description. The other seven musicians had a specific role in backing Morrison. The CSO was formed with a precision unseen in the rock 'n' roll music world. In some early 1970s San Francisco Bay Area appearances, he walked off the stage and out of local clubs a few times. This was due to raucous audiences. I saw him do it once. It was at San Francisco's Boarding House. It didn't seem to matter the audience loved what they heard even it was only a few songs.

The Boarding House appearance was a strange one. A college newspaper, **The Stanford Daily** covered it with a quizzical conclusion. "Why would anyone go to see Van Morrison in concert?" **The Stanford Daily** story was quizzical. The reporter wondered why Van left the Boarding House? That quote didn't resonate beyond the Palo Alto campus where Stanford University was located in the midst of conspicuous wealth. When Van exited the stage, it was due to audience noise. By 1974, he conquered that peccadillo with carefully crafted shows. The Marin County inherent ambiance mixed with the counterculture as the dope smokers, the suburban music fans, the college students and the hard core musicians made Van's club crowd was a raucous one.

Chris Michie told me he thought the Boarding House show was the gestation of the Caledonia Soul Orchestra. Michie said, as Van walked off the stage, he vowed to form a band bringing the audience to its feet. He did that with the CSO. At the time Chris Michie was a decade away from playing and recording with Van. But he was an interested observer. He watched as Van puta together his ideas on a premium backing band.

That extraneous thought from Van lead to the **It's Too Late To Stop Now** double album and **Veedon Fleece**. The ebullient creativity, the blue collar work ethic and the ferocious attention to detail meant that since the Bert Berns' album **Blowin' Your Mind**, Van had released eight albums by 1974. It is not hard to see that 1974 was the apex of his early career.

WHAT WAS THE FORERUNNER TO THE CALEDONIA SOUL ORCHESTRA?

Van's backing groups in 1972 became the forerunner of the Caledonia Soul Orchestra. He was formulating his perfect band. Why? He was not satisfied with his small club shows. What was his vision? It was to blend jazz and rock using classical trained symphony musicians.

Sometime in the early 1970s, Van recorded a sixteen minute plus largely instrumental with a few chord changes, a number of meaningless phrases and it was just having fun in the studio. It could have been recorded for the **His Band And Street Choir** album but the music and Van's few small mutterings are absolutely brilliant. Listen to it on the Internet at https://soundcloud.com/lex_borskyi/van-morrison-caledonia-soul-music The person who posted it called it "Caledonia Soul Music." The clip stands as another attachment to Van's embryo originality.

The birth of Van's musical freedom came slowly in 1972 in concert. He concluded he needed a tighter band. He believed he could form a band backing him flawlessly. The idea was he would lead the musicians with a flick of his hand didn't seem plausible. Van had no doubts about his vision. He made it work.

THE ACCIDENTIAL SIDEMEN SHOWING UP IN THE SAN FRANCISCO BAY AREA

Where did the remainder of the Caledonia Soul Orchestra originate? James Trumbo was a disc jockey on New York's WMFU. He was a horn driven rock and roller who could play piano, organ and kazoo. Trumbo left the CSO after two months. He was replaced by Jef Labes who was an organist, arranger, band leader, producer and singer-songwriter. With classical training, Terry Adams was a San Francisco based cellist who was an experienced session musician. Van believed she was perfect to introduce a string quartet to rock music. In addition to Van, she performed or recorded with John Mitchell, Linda Ronstadt, Grootna and Mad River among others. Her cello was featured on Chad and Jeremy's "In The Attic" and "The Ark." Nancy Ellis, a classical viola performed on **Hard Nose The Highway**. Tom Halpin, a violinist, was a teacher who left the group due to a classical violin contest. He was replaced by Tim Kovatch who was in the midst of a thirty-seven year career with the San Jose Symphony. Kovatch's casual life in the Santa Cruz mountain town of Dunsmuir caused him to reflect. He had a relaxed lifestyle. He decided to concentrate on symphony music. Kovatch retired in 2019. The jewel in the Caledonia Soul Orchestra, Nathan Rubin, was a professor and Oakland Symphony Orchestra legend. These additions made for a classically trained group of musicians.

Tim Kovatch was playing a show at San Francisco's Curran Theater with Terry Adams. She invited him to become a member of the string quartet. Van agreed after hearing Kovatch play. The string quartet practiced by themselves at the San Francisco Opera House. When they were ready, they went up to Van's house. He loved their sound. On the tour Kovatch had many fond memories. Topping the list was one night in the Green Room when Van started singing accompanied by an acoustic guitar. Suddenly Van said: "Tim play. I was startled. He told me to improvise." Van and Kovatch made the band loose with this magic musical moment. "Never happened during the show…which was more structured," Kovatch recalled. On the tour, Kovatch roomed with Nathan Rubin. They became good friends. "Tim was so talented, we were in awe of him," Rubin told me in his CSU, East Bay office.

Warner Bros. sent along a roadie who was first rate. The band recalled everyone had a drink set up for them. The hotel and travel facilities, while shared, were first rate. Rubin told me the Warner roadie would pop up by the piano with two long necked beers during the set. Warner also helped with tour logistics.

Van's String Quartet

What song on the album did the CSO blow up into epic proportions? It was "Caravan." Nick Hornby said it best: "Caravan isn't a song about life or death…it's a song about merry gypsies and campfires and turning up your radio…."

There were other musicians, not in the CSO, who caught Van's eye. One of them was Pee Wee Ellis. Mark Isham introduced Van to Pee Wee and in time he became Morrison's band leader, a close friend, a musical ally and a connection to James Brown.

When Ellis, who was James Brown's saxophonist, relocated to San Francisco it was to work in the local clubs. He met Mark Isham who asked him to arrange a track for Morrison. Mark Naftalin, the Paul Butterfield Blues band pianist, moved with his wife to Marin County. He began a solo career. Ellis, Isham and Naftalin were uncredited influences on Morrison's evolution in Marin County into a musician with increased creativity which led to more productive studio time. Which created commercial releases carrying Van into a legendary solo career. The Shakespeare of Telegraph Avenue, Greil Marcus, lurked in the background providing feedback, soft criticism and friendship to the young Morrison. But there were other musicians with an exploding creativity who befriended Van while working with him.

No one early on was more important than David Hayes. He was a crackerjack bass player. He refused to talk to the press. He was loyal to Van and he worked with every musician of note in Marin County. He played with Jesse Colin Young, Southside Johnny and the Asbury Jukes, and Country Joe and the Fish among others. Marin County was filled with musicians of unrequited talent. Van had his pick of them. What did they all have in common? At one time or another they recorded with, or performed with Morrison in the studio. They talked of writing music with him. Marin County's creative juggernaut was in full swing. "Becoming Van Morrison" was in full swing.

WHY VAN NEEDED TO FORM THE CSO

Van was unhappy with some of his supporting musicians. Mark Isham had the best description of working with Van. It was a simple explanation. Van asked Isham to play a part of the Beatles "Penny Lane," which Van would use on "Troubadour." Van asked Isham what else he played. Isham said he played the fluegelhorn. Van hired him. At that point Isham introduced Van to Pee Wee Ellis. Isham said Van was the easiest person he ever worked with, as long as you played it the way Morrison wanted it.

Isham's opinion was Van knew what he wanted. Not only in the studio. But on the concert stage. "If You played it right, he was fine," Isham continued. "If you didn't, he paid you for your time. He wasn't difficult."

Van, at times, was mystifying. He was occasionally an erratic solo act. This occurred when he selected songs no one knew. It was a trait the fans accepted. Many loved it. The critics labelled it genius. At one of his 1970s shows, at the Berkeley Community Theater, there was a sparse crowd. It was due to little advertising. None of this bothered him. He played series of other shows in the dozen local clubs to hone his in concert persona to a new level of sophistication. Van was learning in the San Francisco Bay Area how to attract and maintain an audience.

Everyone who knew Van in Marin County in the 1973-1974 period remarked on how hard he worked in the studio. He worked even harder on the concert stage. Van was and is a contrarian. There was no predicting his mood, his performance level or the next step in his career. That remains a constant.

Some said Van imposed his will on the musicians. He would tell the drummer what to play. How loud! How soft! There was no improvisation. Van would stop a recording session, a concert or a rehearsal making it clear he wanted a clean, simple sound. That master plan had its roots in 1972. As he found the right musicians, with requisite skills, a mellower Van emerged.

Many musicians who swear by Van on record with the media. Jack Schroer told anyone who would listen Van provided saxophone solos for him. John Platania's lead guitar and co-writing received rave reviews. Before he went to Hollywood to score soundtracks, Mark Isham said: "It you please Van there is not a problem." Pee Wee Ellis remarked: "Van knew what he wanted. If you could do it. Fine! If not, you were gone." David Hayes, John Platania and John Allair fit into this mold.

After a 1972 Sacramento show, Mark Naftalin asked Van: "Am I in the band?" Van never answered him. This was typically Van. He didn't mean anything disrespectful. He was searching for a sound. Personal relationships weren't in the mix.

Chris Michie, who played with Van in the 1980s, said that a number of Marin County musicians told him Van was taking a page out of Bob Dylan's documentary **Don't Look Back**. Van has never mentioned it. A number of journalists, as late as 2007, reported Van was looking for a director like D. A. Pennebaker to direct a documentary.

Van was intrigued by what Pennebaker caught on film. Dylan's iconic stage presence mesmerized the Belfast Cowboy. The intensely private Morrison has never discussed a documentary. That project is still in the works.

Many musicians in Marin County believed Van's large band concept was unwieldy. His Fairfax home studio was a constant source of frenetic creativity. By May, 1972 he had a crack ten piece band. It was the proto type of the CSO. There was still a need for some fine tuning.

Van has spent a great deal of time with female muses and session, touring players who collaborated with him. He doesn't like to mix his material. Van favors a first take recording. He attempts to select the best in concert song and not perform any studio tricks to clean it up. So Van needs talented, multi-instrumentalists who can mix and produce. No overdubbing. That is a Morrison no no.

There is an often overlooked source when writing about the Caledonia Soul Orchestra. That source is Van Morrison in conversation with Ritchie Yorke. As the Canadian author ,with the long blonde hair and no shoes, worked on his Morrison biography he had unfettered access to the Belfast Cowboy.

Van told Yorke an audience inspired him. Yorke's chapter 11, "Unlocking The Myths Of A Timid, Tipsy Gypsy Of Sorts And A Real Live Triumph, It's Too Late To Stop Now, 1973-1974" begins with Yorke charging disrespect for not understanding why Van doesn't want a spotlight. One bitch after another about promoters for the first few pages was the reason, Yorke maintained, for the at times poor to average to excellent shows. It was as if Van was writing the chapter. When he read it. He hated it. That was 1975. He didn't want a biographer. In 2023 that thought persisted. For years Van has

PP
VAN MORRISON
SPECIAL GUEST STAR
JOHN FAHEY
LAMB
ALBUQUERQUE CIVIC AUDITORIUM
SATURDAY MAY 13 8PM
TICKETS: $4.50 BALCONY $5.00 MAIN FLOOR
AVAILABLE: RIEDLINGS—DOWNTOWN, GOLD STREET
CIRCUS RECORDS, BEAU BRITCHES, MR. CASUAL—
EASTDALE AND NORTHDALE SHOPPING CENTERS,
AND AT THE DOOR
PACIFIC PRESENTATIONS

threatened to finish his autobiography. So far, no word from Van. But the interviews provide fodder of the biographers. They continue to arrive in droves.

As Van sat for extensive interviews with Yorke, there was a window into his creative psyche. Van believed some of his songs were better live. "They're different anyway, when done live...." Van said. He mentioned "Wild Children" was more dynamic live than on **Hard Nose The Highway**.

Van told Yorke the 1973 shows brought him rewards. He said he finally mastered the art of the live performance. He said he left "Moondance" off the album because of one wrong note.

DOUG MESSENGER TO THE RESCUE: A MUSICAL MUSE

The muses necessary to Van's creativity weren't all beautiful women like Janet Planet, Carol Guida and Ulla Munch. Some were musical cohorts. Doug Messenger was one of the unrecognized musicians helping Van to form and finalize his musical persona. Neither Heylin or Rogan analyze Messenger's seminal role in forming the Caledonia Soul Orchestra or formalizing the concerts necessary to the CSO's legacy. Heylin doesn't mention him. Rogan has one brief entry.

Who was Doug Messenger? Why did Van employee his talents? One reason for Van's infatuation with Messenger was the level of talent he could spot. After working with Van he alerted producer Ted Templeman to a band he said would make Warner Bros. millions. That band, Van Halen, turned into a mega million selling act. "My main thing was to tell Warner Bros., you got to see this guy Eddie Van Halen...." Messenger said.

As a guitar player and producer, Messenger was as good as he was as a talent scout. Before he worked with Van, Messner was a producer and engineer on eight albums in 1964. He produced Joe Pass and two other Jazz albums **Lights Out** and **Hipster Jazz**. In 1972 he wrote songs for Jackie DeShannon. He was conduit for Van and Jackie recording, and her singing back up in some concerts may be due to Messenger.

MESSENGER TALKS OF LIVING WITH VAN TO UNCUT

Doug Messenger was a staple in Morrison's life. When he performed in the studio with Van, he talked song ideas. He had instrumental, arranging and production influences. Messenger paved the way for John Platania to be the Caledonia Soul Orchestra guitarist. He was friends with Platania. His advice to Van on how his friend performed in the studio and in concert led to a career where he remains Morrison's longest employed guitarist.

In January, 1972, Messenger said he was living with Van at a hotel. "He and Janet were fighting and she'd thrown him out. Van talked to Messenger about two songs. "Listen To The Lion" and "Almost Independence Day" and that set the tone for Morrison's mood as the early to mid-1970s saw Van accelerate his career.

There were tunes the Belfast Cowboy loved. But Van was unhappy with one song "Jackie Wilson Said." With Messenger's guitar, Van was able to cut the song in one take. In sharp contrast, it was difficult to finish "Saint Dominic's Preview." Van had serious doubts about how the guitar blended with his voice. "Van had five guitar players come up from LA and he hated all of them," Messenger continued. "Eventually I did the guitar overdub and Van ran out of the studio." He was happy. When Messenger talked to him, Van observed: "Now it's starting to sound like a song, but my vocal isn't good enough." Messenger loved the song. He wondered why Van was unhappy with it. "He changed stuff around to make it fresh," Messenger continued. "He was so happy, he hugged me. Once Van got the vocal he wanted on a song, that was it. He didn't care if the band screwed up."

"I'll Be There" was the song Messenger rescued for Morrison. In April, 1972, at Wally Heider's San Francisco studio, Messenger helped to flush out the song. That was Messenger's gift, it was to help Van finalize songs that were stuck into a creative limbo.

THE BACKGROUND TO AND THE ACCOMPLISHMENTS OF THE ROAD TO THE CALEDONIA SOUL ORCHESTRA

In retrospect the Caledonia Soul Orchestra appears to be no more than a band that went on a brief three months tour with Van, recording a live album, and then being disassembled by Morrison. Everyone was surprised when the CSO was disbanded. It was legendary. The band focused on backing Morrison by embracing his every subtle stage cue while in concert.

When the CSO began performing in Marin County at the Lion's Share, no one in the Marin County crowd realized the depth, breadth and scope of the band's creativity. John Platania remarked of the It's Too Late To Stop Now tour: "I would say that that tour represented the height of his confidence as a performer."

This tour convinced Van to edit the concert tapes from the It's Too Late to Stop Now tour. The resulting double album remains one of the best live rock concerts ever recorded. But when he got home, he wasn't sure. When he met Carol Guida, she fired up his creative imagination.

When he looked back on the tour, Van had positive thoughts about it. He talked to a number of reporters about what he accomplished in the lengthy It's Too Late to Stop Now tour. "I figured that we'd done that show so much that it should be captured," Van remarked to John Tobler, who wrote for **Zig Zag** magazine, in 1979. "We were using strings on the tour, so I figured if I'm going to do a live album, I'll put this string section on it, because it's really nice and it freshens the songs for us."

When John Tobler asked Van why did he disband the CSO, Van answered without hesitation. "I wanted to keep the band together, but it had got to a certain point where it had peaked...." Van concluded. After the Caledonia Soul Orchestra, Van was tired. Burnt out was more like it. He explained to Tobler: "I took actually a year or so off, when I didn't even play. I mean a whole year went by, and I didn't even touch a guitar or anything, because I just needed a break." What he leaves out is the planning, the events and the pressures from his divorce to pay the bills for all involved. The tour was artistic. It was also financially lucrative.

If you take Van at his word, and there is no beginning or end for the CSO. That is contrary to the facts. Van doesn't give himself enough credit for more than a year conceptualizing the band, helping plan the tour spending long hours on rehearsal and finalizing the CSO's brilliance. Chris Michie told me that when his group,

Lamb, travelled to Santa Fe to open for Morrison, the Belfast Cowboy discussed the need for new touring group.

A GIG IN NEW MEXICO WITH LAMB FINALIZED THE CALEDONIA SOUL ORCHESTRA CONCEPT 1972: DOUG MESSENGER RECALLS

A Morrison show at the Albuquerque Civic Auditorium finalized the Caledonia Soul Orchestra concept. The Saturday May 1, 1972 show featured the Marin County group, Lamb, opened the show, followed by guitar virtuoso John Fahey with Van was the headliner.

With three back up vocalists Janet Planet, Mark Springer and Ellen Schroer, Van had his Street Choir now turned into a proper stage act. He wasn't sure it worked. How could he tell his wife he needed a different back up sound?

The key to the sound came from the electric, the acoustic and the twelve string guitar Doug Messenger brought to the band. He had been working with Morrison for only a few months. When he appeared with him in Albuquerque. Messenger added the various guitar instrumentals Van favored. He would continue until mid-April 1973 performing on twenty-five shows. He was a part of the **Saint Dominic's Preview** album. What was Messenger's contribution to the eventual formation of the Caledonia Soul Orchestra? It was to create a free form innovative guitar sound. That is exactly how John Platania played.

When Messenger met Van during Christmas 1971 in Woodstock, he remembered walking up the hill carrying his amp and guitar where Van lived. He knocked on the door. The door swung open. Van stood there silently. "He looked at me for ten minutes," Messenger continued. "Van pointed to the kitchen. I walked in the kitchen. I got to stop drinking," Van said. He looked at Messenger. Then Van went back in the bedroom and Messenger sat in the kitchen.

When Messenger brought his guitar to Morrison's music, he established the sound that the Belfast Cowboy would use for the Caledonia Soul Orchestra. He didn't make the cut for the CSO.

Messenger was a creator with a footnote. While playing and recording with Van, he brought out the sound characterizing how Van wanted to emulate on an album.

HOW CARNEGIE HALL CHANGED VAN'S PERCEPTION: HE NEEDED THE CSO

Song selection has always been a mystery with Van. The Carnegie Hall show was no exception. He reached back into the Bang years for a short medley of "Little Girl" and "He Ain't Give You None." He also introduced an early in concert version of "Listen To The Lion." One of Van's band members told me: "Van's in concert choices were perplexing."

Van was unsure about the musicians behind him, he worked on refining his back-up band by searching out and auditioning classically trained symphony musicians. He talked about new instruments, like the viola and violin. He needed professional back-up singers. Using his wife and Dahaud Shaar's spouse as back-up singers, it didn't work. There was something missing. He worked on it. Viola! The plan for the Caledonia Soul Orchestra slowly emerged.

"A lot of times in the past I've done gigs and it was rough to get through them," Van said. That said it all. As the concept for the Caledonia Soul Orchestra blossomed Van was perplexed. He had the CSO idea. He couldn't refine it. Why? At Carnegie Hall Van brought in a ten piece group with seven band members and three back up vocalists. The musicians were excellent. The sound on stage not so much. But something was missing. Van wanted to redo his plan for an eleven piece backing band. But how? Something was missing. Then he recalled **Astral Weeks**. He hired Boots Hughston. Why? His flute was instrumental in the search for a new sound. He was the right flautist. Van momentarily harkened back to **Astral Weeks**. The realization was a classical sound, with a jazz tinge, was needed. He formalized an eleven piece super band. It included a string quartet. That band would take some time to come together.

Why did Carnegie Hall have an impact? As Van came out on stage the bright tinged décor, the red seats and the air of opulence struck him this was a perfect concert venue. The magnificent sound system created Van's final vision. He was ready for the Caledonia Soul Orchestra.

At Carnegie Hall, Van experimented. He opened the show with "Astral Weeks." This was only the fourth time he played the song live. Van introduced a new medley "Little Girl/He Ain't Give You None," harkening back to the early Belfast days. Why did he perform these songs? Morrison has never explained. One can only guess. The operative wisdom was they were difficult live. Van was demonstrating to Warner Bros. the depth of his skill in concert.

With Janet Planet singing back up at this show, Van had no idea his life was about to be turned upside down. The divorce was a surprise. That was a catalyst to Van's furtive burst of creativity.

AS VAN CREATES HIS LEGEND JANET MORRISOON MINTO RE-EMERGES IN PRINT

Janet Morrison Minto is a sincere, compassionate person. Like Van, she doesn't like the limelight. Like Van, she is enormously talented. She is an artist and jewelry designer. She has sporadically written and performed in the music industry. She has had a solid marriage of four decades with sound engineer Chris Minto. Now he is in bad health. She is there to take care of him. She refused interviews on her life with Van for twenty years. The she broke her silence. Why? She has a creative journey. She explained it.

His wife began a creative burst of songwriting. She recorded an album two decades after her marriage ended. Those close to Van alleged she didn't share her career ambitions with Van. She had her own intellectual goals. Songwriting was one of them. Then twenty-five years later, she shared her thoughts with a Los Angeles reporter. She recalled the early 1970s, from her perspective, with little rancor and no bitterness. It was their youth and the music business that drove Van and Janet apart.

As his career evolved, Van looked to Janet as a creative muse. He had her design an album. She sang back up with the Street Choir. "I think Janet believed she would have a music career," Chris Michie continued. "I joked Van fired his wife as a backup singer. Then I realized it wasn't a joke." In Van's view, he wasn't firing his wife. He was improving his sound.

Looking back upon her life with Van, Janet Morrison Minto gave an extensive, open and heartfelt interview with the **Los Angeles Times**. She had a record coming out. She was a thriving artist. She was happily remarried. She followed her daughter's life. Shana graduated from Pepperdine. Janet had a full life. Her interview was honest. She harbored no ill will toward Van. Her reflections helped biographers understand the extremely complicated and often mysterious Belfast Cowboy. Janet looked back fondly without regret.

She said Van was afraid to take the stage. Living in Woodstock, she feared stage fright could derail his career. It didn't. He conquered it. This was largely due to the Caledonia Soul Orchestra. This backing band gave him hope for freedom on stage. The CSO eventually conquered all transgressions making Van's live shows among the best in the business.

As Janet looked back, on her marriage, in the **Los Angeles Times** interview, she said: "I was confusing the music with the man. The music was everything you could hope for as a romantic. The man was a prickly pear." Janet had good things to say about Van as a father. Van wouldn't go out on a tour without Janet and his daughter. She would pack up Shana's diaper bag and head out on the road. The rock 'n' roll lifestyle broke up the marriage. She left. Her explanation was he raged daily against the music business. She worried it would be a detriment to her family.

VAN: AN EVOLVING PERFORMER

In a 1972 interview, Van said: "I get into playing live in a different way than a lot of people. Like I dig singing the songs, but there are times when it's pretty agonizing for me to be out there." This suggested the depth of his stage fright. The depravity of the business infected his soul. Van's musicians said it was his disdain for noisy audiences, inadequate sound systems, brain dead sound people inept club employees and journalists who impeded his shows drove his anger. He worked diligently on his stage presence. By 1974, Van's shows reached an uber threshold of professionalism. His on stage brilliance was not always apparent in reviews. His tantrums were more often reported.

Van evolved into a unique ninety minute performer. He varied his sets nightly. His concerts improved. It was hard work. There was the occasional rant. A few times he ran off stage for a smoke break. He would have a brief meltdown due to the musicians, the audience or his mood. "Becoming Van Morrison" was the result. Van prided himself on being a professional musician. From 1973 into mid-1974 he developed an outstanding concert persona. Why? He read the reviews. Music was the main focus of his life. Nothing else mattered. He was 24/7 building a career.

This was the long term plan. Create the perfect backing band. Change the sets nightly. Develop a stage persona. He worked hard attracting a fan base tied to his lyrical brilliance. His performing genius was on its way to perfection. The hard work paid off. This led to the It's Too Late To Stop Now tour. The subsequent double album resulted. It all began in Marin County with a fertile field of local musicians.

In the year after Van's May 18, 1972, Carnegie Hall show was one of constant exploration. He discovered what worked and what didn't. By the May 23, 1973 Los Angeles Troubadour show, Van honed his band into a well-oiled machine. They became the Caledonia Soul Orchestra. This intimate club convinced Morrison to take his eleven piece CSO on the road.

The formation of the Caledonia Soul Orchestra indicated Van's producing genius. It was also a paean to his Belfast roots. The CSO was assembled to tour the United States and Europe in support of a proposed double album The It's Too Late To Stop Now tour band was an unknown aggregation. When the group played a few small San Francisco Bay Area shows to test their mettle in concert, Van introduced each member proudly, and many commented this experience was the highlight of their professional careers.

The It's Too Late To Stop Now tour was the quintessential rock and roll show. The performances were crowd-pleasing. It was carefully crafted. It was superbly produced. The result ? It was one of the finest live rock 'n' roll albums of the 1970s. Sales were tepid initially as the album didn't make the Top 40. That changed! As Van said:

"My audience has to catch up with me." They did! The album went gold. It has endured achieving a mythic legend among live albums.

Van believed live was the best way to record. When he went into the studio, he wanted a concert vibe. He commented the first take was the best. This gave him inspiration. Warner Bros. demurred. He decided to show them. They didn't understand how to produce him. By 1973, Van told everyone he was the producer. When asked: "Why?" He said: "The producer makes all the money."

A double album from the tour, Van believed, would showcase the depth and breadth of his in concert vocal talents. When the songs for **It's Too Late To Stop Now** were selected, few realized it set a new standard for live performances. There was talk at Warner Bros. about a triple album. This idea was nixed. This was due to the cost factor. The reception for **It's Too Late To Stop Now** surprised Warner management. Ray Ruff told me an internal memo suggested they lost some profits by not releasing a triple album.

In the midst of the It's Too Late To Stop Now tour, Van and Warner Bros. continued a dialogue over promotion. Warner Bros. was the best label for advertising in the industry. This was largely due to two in-house publications, Waxpaper and Circular, which allowed those in the A & R offices to use these printed handouts to make any claim they wanted about an artist or a song. These publications were irreverent and fun to read. They often got it wrong. When they did it was in good faith. Or perhaps in good fun. "Along the way Circular and Waxpaper irritated Van," Ray Ruff commented.

WAXPAPER AND CIRCULAR: WARNER'S FAILURE TO PUBLICIZE VAN, WARNER DISPUTES HIS CLAIM

The problems between Van and Warner were long standing. Their differences were over promotion. Morrison's primary grievance was the Warner Bros. tip sheets didn't do enough for his career. The label sent out an elaborate weekly report ubiquitously called "Waxpaper." An earlier tip sheet, "Circular," which was launched in 1969, was not as effective. Neither one was as serious or as effective as Van demanded.

In 1969 Warner Bros. released seventeen tip sheets with the ubiquitous title "Circular." Not one Circular mentioned Van in detail. He was pissed. Fleetwood Mac and Frank Zappa were regularly featured. Van wondered what the hell was going on? Despite Van's hits the publicity people ignored him. He simmered. The March 30, 1970 in the volume 2, number 7 issue there was a small story on Van. No one talked to him. He was flummoxed it appeared.

The Warner/Reprise tip sheet continued into 1973. When it ended no one was more relieved than Morrison. Anyone who signed up could receive a free tip sheet. It was to quote Stan Cornyn: "tongue in cheek promotion." Van wasn't amused. Cornyn said Circular was meant to be "rebellious." Cornyn concluded Circular was "the anti-corporate arm of Warner Bros."

Van complained Warner released bizarre advertising. The stories had little to do with his music, his career and his vision. Was it effective, publicity? Cronyn said yes. Van said no. You decide! that did little for his career. Van met frequently with Mo Ostin. He complained the label ignored him. When they did publicize his albums, Van said the publicity department didn't understand his creative direction. One Warner ad editorialized of Van: "This man wants to get laid." Van didn't find this funny. The Belfast Cowboy never complained publicly. He was trying to play Warner's corporate game. Privately, he groused to friends. Publicly, Warner Bros. was paying him well. Or were they? That question has never been answered.

Warner Bros. spent more money publicizing other artists. Van was left behind. He smoldered. In the late 1960s, and into the early 1970s, Warner executives were almost too artist friendly. Warner Bros. placed ads in **Rolling Stone** and the underground media with little, if any, reference to Van. This helped the commercial growth of James Taylor, Joni Mitchell, Randy Newman and Neil Young. In London, Peter Asher, working for Apple Records, was amazed at Warner's friendly artist approach. They let many acts record two or three albums before giving up on them. Randy Newman was an example of a singer-songwriter who needed time to develop. Warner stuck with him. Eric Anderson recorded two albums, and two singles released with songs written by Carole King. Warner booked him for an appearance on the Johnny Cash Show. Warner envisioned

Anderson as a cult artist with a folk following. One executive told me they lost money on him. Anderson went on to release more than thirty albums. He remains one of the best singer-songwriters still recording and performing while living in Amsterdam.

Van continually complained about being categorized. In private moments he told Jack Schroer he needed a few hit records to bring in the money to further his career. He did that from 1970 through 1972.

The string of albums he released beginning from **Moondance** and concluding with **St. Dominic's Preview** set the template for the Van-Warner Bros. differences. These albums were chart friendly. Van balked at continually chart oriented album releases.

Warner demanded more chart friendly releases. Van balked. When he responded with **Hard Nose The Highway**, the best songs were left off the album. They appeared later in **the Philosopher's Stone.** Warner was nonplussed.

Joe Smith endorsed the Belfast Cowboy's talent. Smith said the label give him appropriate Marin County to Los Angeles to complain about lack of promotion. Can disagreed.

There were other concerns from those advising Morrison. The Warner tip sheet, Circular spoofed artists. The fans had trouble with the tall tales like the one where Van and John Lennon were having dinner. Not true! It was a joke!

Van's sense of humor precluded tall tales. When Warner surreptitiously connected Morrison with John Lennon he became contentious. What the hell was going on? Van couldn't believe it.

Stan Cornyn was the catalyst to these fun stories. They didn't have to be true. They had to be interesting. They sold records. Cornyn worked out of the original Warner Bros. office. He said of his writing: "absurdist humor!" That was the charm of Waxpaper as a tip sheet. It poked fun at the industry. He did this with venom in Circular and Waxpaper. He devoted one issue of Circular to angry fan letters. Cornyn recognized musical tastes were changing. He figured out 45s, album sales and promotion were vehicles for increasing sales. He envisioned Van as the Warner Bros. artist whose music

STAN CORNYN

changed from release to release. In publicizing Morrison this is the tactic he wanted to take. Cornyn was anti-corporate. Van appreciated him.

Circular was the first Warner tip sheet. No expense was spared in putting it out. This magazine emerged in the summer of 1969 to advertise the vast Warner singer-songwriter catalogue. Circular was shaped like a 45 record. Circular's first issue featured a spoof ad asking for "Qualified Girls" to file lawsuits to help poorly selling artists merchandise their product. The second issue featured the Fugs describing them as "bathless thugs."

When fans wrote into Warner Bros. requesting a copy of Circular, one was sent to their home. The loyalty Warner built with the record buying audience was unprecedented.

The Van Morrison Circular entries were often ribald. These were tall tales to sell records. A sample of a Circular comment was: "Groovy Tuesday spotted John Lennon chomping with Van Morrison in LA's tiny, but well known for good food, Lost on Larrabee restaurant. Could it be the Walrus will be assisting on Van's forthcoming two or three-record set?" There was no truth to this egregious statement. The irony was Van was discussing a three disc album release with Warner executives. This entry was from a Circular on October 29, 1973. It was designed to test the market. The eight page handout was fully of nothing more than creative nonsense. It bore no relationship to Van's music or to the **It's Too Late To Stop Now** album. When Van visited Warner Bros., he raised hell. Stan Cornyn loved it. He never took umbrage with his comments.

Lost on Larrabee was a West Hollywood restaurant favored by David Bowie, the Beatles and Jim Morrison. Van didn't dine there. It was not his thing. What did Van think of Warner Bros. fictionalizing a meeting with John Lennon? He has never said. Those at Warner thought it was good fun. Van wasn't laughing. He was trying to fit into the Warner culture. It wasn't happening.

The publicity behind Warner Bros. artists from the pen of Stan Cornyn drew attention from the mainstream press. He was what the **New York Times** described as "an offbeat recording industry executive known both for his unusual promotions and for his album notes two of which won Grammy Awards."

Cornyn praised Warner for providing its artists creative freedom. Every fledgling musician wanted to sign with the label. The company was viewed as cool. The quirky advertising, freedom in the studio, and understanding the artist was important to Warner executives. Cornyn was a publicity genius. He was funny and passionate. He was driven to make Warner Bros. noticed. Circular, Cornyn told his staff, had to appear like an insider's view of Warner Bros. This would establish fan loyalty.

Cornyn realized musical tastes were headed into uncharted waters. He urged Warner recording artists to take all the time they needed. He told them to sound like themselves. This was a salve to Morrison's ego. Cornyn with his finger in the air, his dark colored glasses, his ill kept beard and his disinterest in dressing like a recording executive, was not typical of record executives. He used irreverence and a hipster persona to sell Warner's artists. One headline read: "Once you get used to it, his voice is really something." This described Randy Newman's debut album. It sold poorly.

THE CASE OF VAN DYKE PARKS: CORNYN AND WAXPAPER EXPLAIN WARNER'S BENEVOLENCE ON ASTRAL WEEKS

When Warner Bros. signed Van Dyke Parks, they believed they had the future of rock 'n' roll. Parks' album **Song Cycle**, released in November, 1967, combined bluegrass, ragtime and shows tunes into a classical musical context. The critics loved it. No one bought it. What did this have to do with Van Morrison? Plenty. When Van completed **Astral Weeks**, key Warner executives listened and said: "Van Dyke Parks!" That didn't make Van happy. He pondered the question. How could he make Warner Bros. understand his music? He decided he couldn't. That did not bode well for future interactions.

When Warner Bros. signed Parks, the contract was influenced by his work with Beach Boy Brian Wilson. Again there was a Morrison connection. Stan Cornyn believed that Van, like Wilson and Parks, had a unique studio approach. He predicted continued gold for the Belfast Cowboy.

Van Dyke Parks album **Song Cycle** was praised by critics. That was due to Cornyn's promotion. The album was a colossal flop. In a hilarious piece Cornyn wrote: "How We Lost $35,509.50. The Album of The Year (Dammit)." He described the dismal sales. Cornyn suggested Warner Bros. did this to show other artists that they would stick with a sound, a concept or with a performer no matter the commercial consequences.

WHAT DID THE TIP SHEETS REALLY DO?

These beautifully produced, tip sheets sold Warner records in large quantities. On January 1, 1977, Judy Rhodes edited volume 2 of Waxpaper with interviews, album reviews and commentary. It was collected in a beautifully produced book of 390 pages. It contained very little about Van Morrison. Dr. Demento wrote in-depth artist spotlights. Van was relieved. He wasn't featured. He thanked Cornyn.

One issue was entitled: "Rutlemania." No comment from Van. Asinine insanity prevailed. But it was served with Stan Cornyn's viewpoint. He told Mo Ostin and Joe Smith stick with Van. "He has a career coming you won't believe," Cornyn said.

Waxpaper came out weekly. Ashford & Simpson, Slade, Robin Trower and Maria Muldaur were featured more frequently than the Belfast Cowboy. Why? The Warner corporate heads believed Van was no more than a cult artist. He would sell the same number of albums no matter the advertising.

Van believed Warner Bros. failed to adequately promote his albums. He looked elsewhere to sell his music. Television was a natural outlet. The Caledonia Soul Orchestra was in its formative stage. The possibility of exposure on television blossomed as the 1970s brought a late night In Concert show from Don Kirshner.

AMERICAN TELEVISION MADE ME A STAR: DON KIRSHNER'S IN CONCERT WAS WITHOUT THE CALEDONIA SOUL ORCHESTRA BUT THE CONCEPT WAS COMING TOGETHER

In 1973, Don Kirshner's In Concert television show weekly highlighted rock and roll artists. Kirshner's early shows were originally taped at Hofstra University. This ABC television program was broadcast on the weekend giving Dick Cavett a night off. It was usually a Friday night. The shows had a dramatic impact upon record sales. By 1973 In concert was a bi-weekly show with a mammoth TV audience.

Who was Don Kirshner? He was an executive producer for ABC. He convinced the network to run Friday night concerts at 11:30 when ABC's ratings were in the toilet. Kirshner's In Concert was another venue for Van to develop his stage show beyond California's small clubs.

In early 1973, the Caledonia Soul Orchestra, then in its embryo stage, when Morrison was booked on Kirshner's program. Van's eight piece backing band, featured Tim Kovatch's violin. It was a preview of the Caledonia Soul Orchestra.

Nathan Rubin: "Van wasn't sure he wanted to do television. He was a shrewd businessman. He realized the importance of the television audience."

On April 18, 1973, as Van appeared on In Concert, "he performed five numbers beginning with a hard driving version of 'I've Been Working'." The egg stained shirt and the wrinkled pants were long gone. Van even wore a stylish hat. His stage presence was beyond energetic. Jack Schroer's saxophone was featured with gusto. The call and response Van brought to "I've Been Working" made it sound like a new song. At times a gospel dirge with soul resonated. Then Van followed with "Caravan." The horns blended behind Van's vocals. The brief violin interludes made the sound luminary. During "Caravan," Van kicked his leg into the air. Then came a ten minute version of "Gloria." A thirteen minute "Flamingos Fly" and a nineteen minute "Cyprus Avenue" concluded a stunning performance. It was a brilliant performance. Van was slim and handsome. He was at the top of his performing game. The band blended behind him with precision. The back-up vocals added to the munificent sound. The shaping, the formation, the thought behind and the concept for the Caledonia Soul Orchestra took shape. There was one instrument Van loved. It was the violin.

The violin on every song was another innovation. Van may have heard It's A Beautiful Day, a group who lived in Marin County. The use of the violin was Van's way of accentuating his vocals.

No one knows for sure but, Eric Isralow, aka Dr. Rock, told me Lester Bangs may have watched this In Concert appearance. When he wrote his much praised review of **Astral Weeks**, it was due to watching a re-run of Don Kirshner's In-Concert. Bangs discussed Morrison's concert brilliance. It almost didn't happen as planning for the It's Too Late To Stop Now tour was grueling.

PLANNING FOR THE TOUR IN THE MIDST OF BUSINESS PROBLEMS

The It's Too Late To Stop Now tour almost didn't take place. There are enough reasons to fill a book. Van wasn't sure he was physically up to a lengthy concert in the U. S., Canada, Europe and the U. K. Big venues were not his thing. He only performed at a few. So, then, why did he go out on tour, with Alice Stuart sitting in the wings, and the band percolating on stage like they had played together for a decade? He had a master plan. That was to guarantee performing stardom.

Those close to Van said the initial idea was a series of concerts to produce the raw material for a live album. There was talk of a double live album. Warner reluctantly agreed. The careful planning for new instruments took place. The violin and the viola became an integral part of Van's musical concepts.

The logistical problems were enormous. Van hired a veteran New York road manager Stephen Cohen. At the time Cohen was managing Alice Stuart. "I couldn't figure out why Van wanted my manager to become his road manager. He had one already. That was the Belfast Cowboy. You never knew what he would do," Stuart said.

Things went smoothly after that. Many close to Van wondered why Pillster remained in the mix. Alice Stuart, who opened for

Morrison, had high praise for the road manager. "He really took care of me," Stuart remarked.

As Stuart negotiated to bring her band to Europe and the U. K., they were told they wouldn't be paid. All expenses would be covered. She also had to put up a $5000 bond. It was dicey but everything worked out.

Stuart claimed Morrison had little contact with his band or with the supporting act. She believed he needed isolation to perform. "I was opening with my band for Van. I never talked to him," Stuart told me. This was one reason these shows were among the best of his career. The genesis of the It's Too Late To Stop Now tour tells us a great deal about the difficulty of keeping this mammoth undertaking on the road.

Others like Tim Kovatch remember Van interacting with him before they went on stage. Nathan Rubin said he talked at length about changes in each performance. Van was complicated. He planned! He thought! He crafted! He took the first steps into a legendary performing career.

THE CALEDONIA SOUL ORCHESTRA AND THE GENESIS OF THE IT'S TOO LATE TO STOP NOW TOUR

In the spring of 1973, when he appeared at Doug Weston's Troubadour, Van didn't know what to expect from a lengthy tour. The last minute planning was the reason for the tour's spectacular success. Van hired two road mangers.

Van told Nathan Rubin: "Let's just try to have fun." That attitude kept the band loose. He created the atmosphere making the album special. It was a triumph. Van confessed the It's Too Late To Stop Now tour made him nervous. He didn't want to become a perennial touring act. Contradictions! This is how one understands the Belfast Cowboy.

While Van's performances were inherently excellent, there were shows where he faltered. The band filled in instrumentally when the Belfast Cowboy was not in top performing meddle. Did Morrison enjoy the It's Too Late To Stop Now tour? He did! That is until the last few shows when he was exhausted. He cancelled the last two dates. "We were given a check and told Van didn't want to do it anymore," Tim Kovatch said with a puzzled expression. Nathan Rubin told me he was equally puzzled and his roommate on the tour, Kovatch, seldom shoed an expression. "Tim was caught by surprise," Rubin told me. Even the band was shocked at the abrupt end to the tour.

Nathan Rubin: "The operative wisdom is Van loved the It's Too Late To Stop Now tour. He was consumed with logistics. It drove him nuts." Rubin observed that he had never worked with a musician who had more experimental musical ideas. I asked Rubin why Van disbanded the CSO so quickly? "That is Van being Van. Who knows!" Rubin concluded.

A dozen people close to him claimed the tour turned only a small profit. It was not about the money. That didn't matter. Van's goal was translating his music and lyrics to the stage with precision.

STEPHEN PILLSTER, VAN'S BUSINESS STRUCTURE AND CALEDONIA PRODUCTIONS

Van needed management. Danny Cowan, Alice Stuart's manager, recommended his next door neighbor Stephen Pillster. For a time Pillster managed Dan Hicks and the Hot Licks. When Hicks broke through with the **Striking It Rich** album on Blue Thump in 1972, he seemed like a good fit to manage Morrison. The results varied as Pillster was a step away from being a top fight manager. On March 31, 1973, Pillster announced he was leaving Hicks to pursue other opportunities.

Pillster founded a management firm, Guideposts of California and he looked like the perfect person to run Morrison's business. He wasn't. He had too many outside business interests. He didn't possess the experience to guide Morrison's business. Surprisingly, he lasted on and off until 1990. Van paid him well. He even had a phone in his car. He didn't need it. Ego dominated over loyalty to Morrison. But Pillster was a music professional. He knew how to promote, manage and address some issues. Why did he fail? Van simply became too big for him.

Initially, Van was impressed. Pillster's experience was as the road manager for Charlie Daniels. He worked with former Youngblood musician Jerry Corbett then going solo. The key music management people in and around Marin County and Berkeley musical had high praise for Pillster. His time managing Dan Hicks was a trial by fire he handled it with professional skill.

As a general manager for Caledonia Productions, Pillster had pluses and minuses. He was knowledgeable. He was efficient. He was a music insider with connections. That was the good news. As the music business changed, Pillster was not at adept at the larger business matters. There was a need for corporate lawyers, tax experts, CPA's and a money manager. Van's recording contracts, intellectual property and public relations became too complicated for Pillster.

The bad news was Pillster recalled events in Van's life with an alleged fictional flair for Clinton Heylin and Johnny Rogan. It was to enhance his importance in the Van Morrison story. He told tall tales of Carol Guida. He resented her. Guida's role in Van's life was too vast. He wanted her out of Van's life. She informed the Belfast Cowboy, Pillster was an entitled wannabe.

On the October-November, 1973 trip to Ireland, Pillster recalled it in great detail. The problem was he was only there for a couple of days. He was at Sutton Place after enjoying the luxurious surroundings for two days he returned home. Then Van and Carol Guida left with Van driving for almost three weeks around the Irish countryside. Pillster spent only a few days in Ireland. Yet, he continued to describe the trip. Van sent him home to tie up some business matters.

Johnny Rogan interviewed Pillster for **Van Morrison: No Surrender** where upon Pillster inflated his role in Morrison's life. The fictional narrative Pillster spun ignored Van's business brilliance and Carol Guida's role as the Belfast Cowboy's muse.

Pillster was important in the early stages of Van's business organization. Why? He gave Van time to write. He kept the media away. The privacy Van desired important after Janet left. The one off gigs at The Lion's Share or The Inn of the Beginning were arranged by Van not Pillster. He was a manager in name only.

What was Pillster's fiction? He told Clinton Heylin that Van didn't take "particular pride in authorship," Pillster continued. "He thinks of himself more as a channel." Did Van tell Pillster this? No! He read it in interviews. If Van had a fault, it was being too loyal to those who didn't deserve it. It wasn't until 1990 that Van wised up. Until then Pillster took him for an alleged financial ride. He was paid well. Did Van receive proper representation? Only Morrison knows the answer.

The October 1973 trip to Dublin and throughout the Irish countryside was a watershed moment. That trip, with Carol Guida's presence, has never been fully explained. Guida's manuscript on her reminiscences, and the photos taken of their engagement, present another side to Van. It is a compassionate, tender picture with a developing literary intellect.

Bibliographical Sources

For background on the Caledonia Soul Orchestra see, for example, Clinton Heylin, **Can You Feel The Silence?: Van Morrison, A New Biography** (Chicago, 2002), pp. 271-272, 285, 328, Johnny Rogan, **Van Morrison: No Surrender** (London, 2005), pp. 282-294, 338-334, 482, Steve Turner, **Van Morrison: Too Late To Stop Now** (London, 1993), p. 115, John Collis, **Van Morrison: Inarticulate Speech Of The Heart** (Boston, 1996), pp. 132-136 and David Burke, **A Sense of Wonder: Van Morrison's Ireland** (London, 2013), chapter 6.

Interviews with Ronnie Montrose, Tony Dey, Chris Michie, Paul Vincent, Tom Bradshaw, Mark Naftalin and Nick Clainos were important to this chapter. The Barsotti Brothers and Larry Catlin at Bill Graham Presents helped in defining and explaining the local San Francisco music scene. See **Q** magazine for ratings by readers of live albums and Van comes into the top 100 equation. Carol Guida provided information on Marin County in the period before she met Van. This helped to figure out the time line why, when and how he formed the Caledonia Soul Orchestra.

For the notion Van was searching for a director to support a documentary on his career, see, for example, Mary Wogan, "He's An Artist, He Don't Look Back," **Visions Bob Dylan**, February 26, 2007. https://visionsbobdylan.wordpress.com/2007/02/27/hes-an-artist-he-dont-look-back/

For Janet Morrison Minto looking back on the early 1970s almost thirty years later, see, for example, Barry Egan, "Love Lost In The Myths Of Time," **Marin Independent**, January 30, 2000. https://www.independent.ie/woman/celeb-news/love-lost-in-the-myths-of-time-26253156.html

Louis Sahagun, "The Clouds Have Lifted," **Los Angeles Times**, November 17, 1998. https://www.latimes.com/archives/la-xpm-1998-nov-17-cl-43498-story.html These two article are revealing with Janet discussing the difficulty of living in the pressure cooker of fame with a volatile artist. Her time meeting Van in a San Leandro roller rink, to New York, to Boston, to Woodstock, to Fairfax and, finally, to a life of her own is revealing. Janet Morrison Minto is a lovely person. She has never broken the code of silence. When she did in these two interviews, it wasn't mean spirited. She was a songwriter. She released an album. She was happily married. Her third husband was a sound engineer. She lived a quiet life in a middle class Los Angeles suburb. Her creativity continued. She operates a thriving jewelry business. She has worked in the music industry. She has lived a rewarding life. The muse without money was happy. It showed in these interviews. Janet commented her marriage was "an emotional rollercoaster." She said she fled the marriage as a desperate gesture of independence. "I would have done anything for the man who wrote those songs, who whispered in the night that they were true," Janet continued. "I wanted more than anything to make him happy. But I just couldn't do it. When I left, everybody got really mad at me because I had become an important cog in a music industry machine that was starting to make so much money. On the other hand, I just had to find peace and my own voice." Why did Janet Morrison Minto break her long held silence? She had a product. A German record company, MTM Music, marketed her CD **Dreaming Ezekiel** with a studio musical aggregation Fake I. D. This was a CD that sounded much like 1980s arena rock 'n' roll. But Janet wasn't a one trick pony. She wrote songs for movies, including "The Blob" and "Roxanne." A Levi's 501 jeans commercial provided a nice payday. The muse with little money was now living in a 1950s Orange County bungalow with her husband. She was happy. She was accomplished. As she finished a series of interviews, Janet's calm angelic demeanor was shown when she concluded her time with Van was a "fabled love lived...." She sighed and recalled: "I couldn't reconcile the fragile dream with the emotional chaos which kept intruding and crashing everything down." The rock 'n' roll life is an unforgiving bitch.

For the issues of Circular and Waxpaper, and how Warner Bros. used these advertising devices to support their artists 24/7, see, Stan Cornyn and Paul Scanlon, **Exploding: The Highs, Hits, Hype, Heroes And Hustlers Of The Warner Music Group** (New York, 2002), pp.72, 117, 137186-187,207-212,235, m254, 264-265, 288, 399. This is one of the best books on the music business. It suggests how and why Warner Bros. created an artist friendly label at a time gangsters, low level criminals and shlocky business types dominated the record business.

For Van Dyke Parks, see, Elyadeen Anbar, "The Inimitable Legacy Of Van Dyke Parks: A Life's Journey Through Song," **Flypaper**, April 25 2017. https://flypaper.soundfly.com/discover/inimitable-legacy-van-dyke-parks-journey-song/

For Van's appearance on April 18, 1973 on Don Kirshner's In Concert, see https://rvm.pm/tv-today-van-morrison-don-kirshners-rock-concert-1973/#arve-youtube-jlyoq7l2gkq62db374206e14367661489

A **YouTube** interview with Mark Isham goes a long way toward explaining how musicians who auditioned for Van's band could please him. See. "Penny Lane Sound, Playing With Van Morrison, And My Piccolo Memories: Behind The Notes, Episode 1," **YouTube**, December 16, 2021. https://www.youtube.com/watch?v=JiViQPR6vfE

See Nick Hornby, **31 Songs** (London, 2011) for his comments on "Caravan." The Hornby chapter is a brilliant analysis of how and why authors see in Morrison's lyrics and music a path to their personal accomplishments. With a literary flair, Hornby makes a case for Morrison's use of a string quartet on a live rock and roll album with pop overtones. Van would take issue. But Hornby's eloquent prose makes the point. "Caravan" is the perfect live song.

See Peter Mills, **Hymns To The Silence: Inside The Words And Music Of Van Morrison** (New York, 2010) pp. 12-15 for the best explanation in print of how Van wrote. Professor Mills employs sections of Van's lyrics to make the case for his songwriting prowess. As a wordsmith Mills suggests that Van favors certain songs in concert. He concluded that these songs have an "enduring presence in his live sets...." (p. 13) The idea that Van thinks there is "a world to be explored within the song...." (p. 13) Another interesting conclusion is Mills sees some songs as not being re-recorded in the same vein or re-done in concerts. An example is "I Will Be There" from **A Period of Transition**.

A brief interview with Jack Schroer added a great deal to this chapter. Also, see, Peter Wrench, **Saint Dominic's Flashback: Van Morrison's Classic Album, Forty Years On** (London, 2012), passim.

There is no mention of David LaFlamme and his band It's A Beautiful Day or Dan Hicks And The Hot Licks, but the band members loved Van Morrison's music. Sid Page, who was in the Hot Licks, played with Van Morrison four times from October 5, 1973 through December 1, 1973. He is now a feature film soundtrack producer and has a high end movie career. Chris Michie believed Van was intrigued by It's A Beautiful Days use of the electric violin and Pattie Santos' vocals impressed him. Michie believed these were influences upon Van's 1970s musical development. Ruff wasn't so sure.

TWELVE

The Caledonia Soul Orchestra On The Road And Alice Stuart And Snake

"Caledonia is just a tag I came up with…I am not sure what it Means."

Van Morrison in conversation with Ritchie Yorke

"The Caledonia Soul Orchestra was so different from everything else that's going on…Van knows the showband sound, and he had found a way of setting it inside contemporary music."

Paul Charles

The Caledonia Soul Orchestra was one of the great touring bands. What is ignored? The string quartet! The symphony musicians! The precision with which Van put the CSO together was stupendous. Van planned and navigated a brilliant and lengthy tour. What has been overlooked or not reported. Plenty!

Alice Stuart and Snake opened for Van on many, not all, of the It's Too Late To Stop Now shows. Why is Alice Stuart important? As a folk-blues performer, Stuart had a niche in the San Francisco Bay Area music culture. She and her band weren't paid. Their hotel, food and expenses were covered.

The logistics of the tour, the financial demands, the planning and the need to perfect the Caledonia Soul Orchestra rested in Morrison's hands. He worked 24/7 on his stage appearances. The Caledonia Soul Orchestra was professional, and was not a huge moneymaker.

In the months prior to the official launching of the It's Too Late To Stop Now tour, Van put the Caledonia Soul Orchestra together with precision. He spent hundreds of hours auditioning local musicians. He brainstormed with close Woodstock friends, like Jack Schroer, who advised Van to look at the training, the experience and the desire to perform in his super band. As a graduate of the prestigious Berklee School of Music, Schroer was the eyes and ears for many of Van's new band mates. The selection process for the CSO took months.

ENTER CHRIS MICHIE: THE FRIENDSHIP YEARS

In 1969 Chris Michie left the University of Wisconsin. He moved to San Francisco with the Mendelbaum Blues Band. He would lend his blues oriented guitar to Van's sound in the 1980s. After meeting Van in the 1970s, he was a friend and witness to his Marin County artistic evolution. As a witness to Van's evolving career, Michie was

ALICE STUART

KARL SEVAREID AND SNAKE BOB JONES

inspired by Van to pursue his dreams. He did for a decade before joining Van in 1981 recording with Van on the **Beautiful Vision** album. Then he performed with Morrison until 1987 while adding his signature guitar sounds to **Inarticulate Speech Of The Heart**, **Live At The Grand Opera House, Belfast**, **A Sense Of Wonder** and **No Guru, No Method, No Teacher**.

He was a life time guitarist whose final project was the soundtrack for the documentary "The Wild Parrots Of Telegraph Hill." He also toured, recorded or played lead guitar with Boz Scaggs, the Pointer Sisters, Link Wray, Maria Muldaur and Jerry Garcia. When TV actor David Soul toured, Michie was his musical director.

His San Francisco Bay Area legend was enhanced by working with Barbara Mauritz for her 1973 album **Music Box** for Columbia Records. This is when Van discovered him. Michie's guitar work was outstanding.

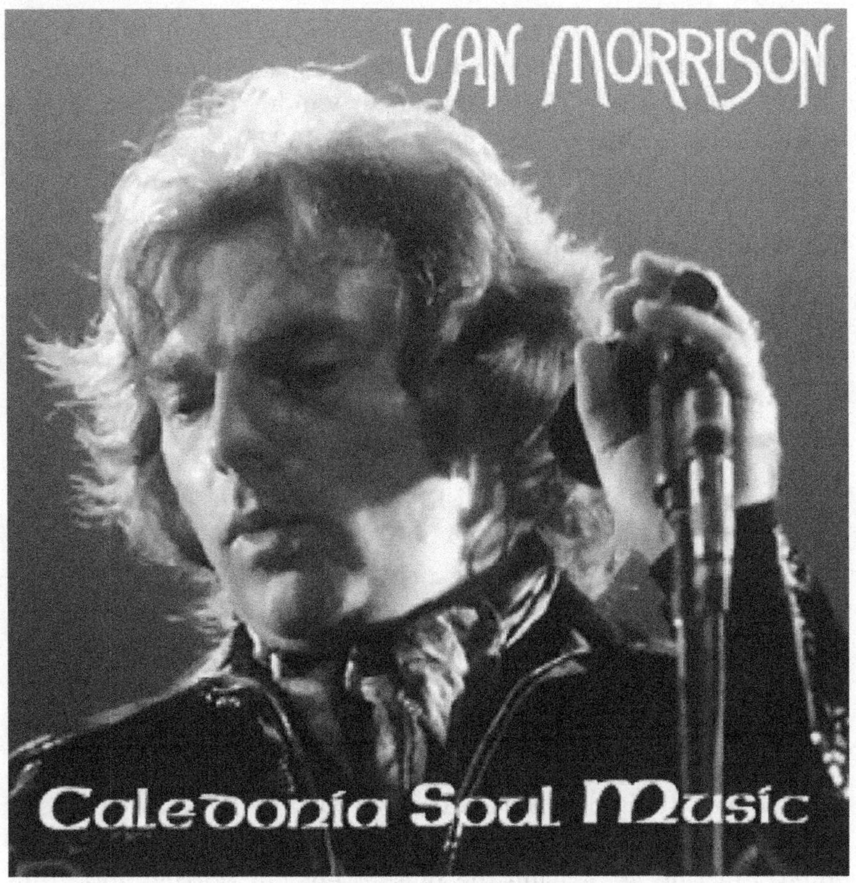

A Bootleg Record Cover

For a decade he talked music with Van. Then, he boarded a plane for Hawaii with his family, a call came from Van to join him to cut an album. This began almost a decade of work with Morrison. Michie's book **Name Dropping: It's All About Me, Isn't It?,** (Xlibris, 2001) is a brilliant look at his life and legacy.

For the **Beautiful Vision** album, Van couldn't get the proper guitar sound out of Herbie Armstrong or Mark Knopfler. Jim Stern, Van's engineer, called and Michie came into the studio. For two decades Michie provided a window into Morrison's life.

Van and the Caledonia Soul Orchestra embarked on a three-month tour. The result was the **It's Too Late To Stop Now** album.

The CSO was Van's answer to backing problems in small clubs. Chris Michie, a decade later, said he thought Van was working hard on the CSO concept in 1972. Michie lived near Van in Fairfax. As a witness to Morrison's creativity from 1981 through 1987, he marveled at how Marin County sired his musical growth and development. It was Marin musicians and local studios that did a great deal for Van's artistry. Others said he retained the concept since **Astral Weeks**. No one in Marin County agreed on how Van created. They all agreed he was a creative genius in the studio or on stage.

THE WARM UP SHOWS GETTTING THE CSO READY

As an ultimate perfectionist, Van readied the CSO with some small club gigs. By May 12, 1973, the Caledonia Soul Orchestra was firmly implanted in Van's psyche. The musicians were in place. Van was finalizing his concept. "I played with Van for the first time at Diablo Valley College near my home in Concord. He was in the final stage of putting together the Caledonia Soul Orchestra. We weren't there yet," Nathan Rubin said. Then two weeks later, Rubin was on stage with Van at the Troubadour.

Nathan Rubin and Alice Stuart speculated the warm up shows in late April, 1973 at San Anselmo Lion's Share were precision oriented. But who was paying the bills? Even Van worried about the financial end of the tour.

It was not until May 1973 that the CSO was announced as his official backing band. They didn't just come together. It took a great deal of experimentation. The practice necessary to formulate the CSO sound jelled at the Lion's Share shows.

Van agreed to allow Tom "Big Daddy" Donahue to broadcast two of his Lion's Share shows. Donahue did so over Berkeley's public radio station KPFA-FM. It was during these shows Van performed a cover of a Fred Neil inspired "Everybody's Talking." The band was surprised. Why? Fred Neil didn't appear to be a fellow artist. Harry Nilsson's "Everybody's Talkin" in 1970 won the Best Contemporary Vocal Male Performance. It wasn't considered Morrison's style. It was pure pop. Van hated pure pop. How did he discover the song?

Estrella Berosini, a Neil protege, allegedly alerted Van to the song. She was at a party with Bob Neuwirth and others with Van in Marin County a couple of years after Nilsson had the hit. Berosini performed a version of "Everybody's Talkin" acapella. "Van loved the song," Chris Michie recalled. Like most Marin County residents, Van was a Neil aficionado. Neil's last appearance in California was in the early 1970s in Sacramento. It appears Van did not know him. He loved his signature song.

John L. Wasserman, the **San Francisco Chronic** critic, reviewed the late April Lion's Share show. His article headlined: "Rock Star's Got Feeling For The Blues." Wasserman loved the performance. He raved about Jackie DeShannon's backup vocals. With a legal capacity of 150 Wasserman didn't mention more than 200 people were crowded into the Lion's Share. The parking lot was full of Van fans. Fillmore Slim, a pimp turned blues singer, showed up with his Cadillac and bevy of young girls. With folk-blues singer Alice Stuart and blues legend John Lee Hooker in the audience, Van's set included covers of Muddy Waters' "I Wanna Make Love To You" and "I've Got My Mojo Working," as well as Ray Charles' "What'd I Say," Sam Cooke's "Bring It On Home To Me," and Hank Williams' "Jambalaya." Wasserman suggested Morrison had few peers when it came to singing the blues or country. Warner Bros. ignored this review.

Then the March 18, 1973 CSO show in the cavernous Marin Memorial Auditorium, produced two sets finalizing the CSO sound. There was a considerable amount of preparation for a lengthy tour, these gigs helped Van sort out his vocals while figuring out the rigors of the road. The critics wondered: "What was the Caledonia Soul Orchestra?" No one knew. Was it a Morrison concept? The press didn't report on it in detail. Van worked 24/7 to perfect the group.

RICHARD WILLIAMS: A JOURNALIST ON THE CSO AND 40 YEARS LATER REFLECTING ON CELLIST TERRY ADAMS AND VAN

Richard Williams, a **New Musical Express** reporter, covered the Birmingham and London shows. The **NME** reporter was impressed with the string quartet. He praised Jef Labes for his innovative sounds. The ease with which he backed the Belfast Cowboy impressed the critics. Van's press was excellent. The CSO was praised. For Williams, the blonde cellist, Terry Adams, was a vision of beauty with unparalleled musical excellence. Then forty years, after covering Van and the Caledonia Soul Orchestra, Williams went to a film, **A Late Quartet**, and the image of Adams' cello came roaring back into his imagination.

Williams wrote, in 2013 of **A Late Quartet**, it was a film with "a wonderful performance by Christopher Walken as an aging cellist…." This movie prompted Williams to reflect on the It's Too Late To Stop Now tour. He reviewed it at London's Rainbow Theater. He called it "the gig of the year." He believed Van was returning from an American exile. A bit dramatic! It was also positive. Van's exile would not end until the 1980s. But Williams comment made the point of Morrison's significance to the rock concert stage in the U. K. On a song near the end of the Rainbow show, as Van performed "Caravan," he recalled forty years later, he was transfixed and in awe of Terry Adams cello. When the concert was over, he remarked this was the first time he experienced a string quartet in a rock concert. "This was the night we all fell in love with the blonde cellist," Williams wrote.

Williams pointed out Terry Adams continued to work for George Lucas at his Skywalker Ranch on film music while performing with the Oakland Symphony. Her Nob Hill String Ensemble was busy at a wide variety of San Francisco functions. The point? Van hired musicians with so much talent most still work. He was the guru putting it together. He had an eye for talent second to none.

HOW DID WARNER BROS. REACT TO THE CALEDONIA SOUL ORCHESTRA?

The executives at Warner Bros. were ecstatic with the CSO. Van's touring plans guaranteed increased record sales. An internal Warner Bros. memo reported Van's product needed increased advertising. The memo observed this was necessary for the tour to succeed financially. By supporting his tour while allowing Van complete creative control, the live double album exploded in sales. The public acclaim was stupendous. Warner didn't want an unhappy Van Morrison.

Since the singer-songwriter was still a big part of the industry, Warner spent a considerable sum advertising **It's Too Late To Stop Now**. The label worried Van's reclusive ways would hamper sales. It didn't. If anything the mysterious and elusive Morrison image spurred sales.

Warner Bros. was happy. Van was back on the road. They helped with tour logistics. Advertising flourished. It was key executives, like Joe Smith and Mo Ostin, who realized the Caledonia Soul Orchestra was Van's commercial summit. The It's Too Late To Stop Now tour was never guaranteed a long life. It had a longer life than even Van intended. This was due to the Caledonia Soul Orchestra's brilliance on stage.

VAN'S INFLUENCE OF THE CALEDONIA SOUL ORCHESTRA

The Caledonia Soul Orchestra was one of rock and roll's most accomplished touring bands. It was the first time Van had complete confidence in his backing band. He selected musicians who were familiar with artists like Sam Cooke, Sonny Boy Williamson or Bobby Blue Bland. This was to stretch his shows into a pronounced blues direction. He also expanded his repertoire. By perfecting his smooth in concert vocal nuances the Belfast Cowboy unwittingly was preparing his future legacy.

Few performers have had such a tight backing unit. The name came from an eighteen-minute instrumental outtake from the **His Band And Street Choir** album. When the band came together the group understood his musical direction. The Morrison playbook was born. The band learned a hundred songs.

John Platania remembered the tour with glee. He called Van's performances "impassioned." He suggested the tour increased his "confidence as a performer." He discussed how the musicians enjoyed it.

ON THE ROAD WITH THE CALEDONIA SOUL ORCHESTRA

The Caledonia Soul Orchestra began the lengthy tour on May 8, 1973 at the Performing Arts Center in Milwaukee Wisconsin. The audio bootleg from this show was a reminder of how much better Van was with the group. Van remained critical and skeptical of his performances. He was unsure if he could maintain the stamina for a lengthy tour.

Van contracted for three nights at Los Angeles' intimate Troubadour Club. To prepare for these shows, he booked a San Francisco Bay Area club with a cocktail lounge. This one night practice gig at Sunnyvale's Odyssey Room was designed to perfect CSO's sound. Located just north of San Jose, on the San Francisco peninsula, the Odyssey Room was a campy club with leopard skin wall adornments and a cheesy look. The sound system, the crowd and the management were Morrison aficionados. It was one of Morrison's favorite venues.

The Odyssey Room allowed Van to premiere songs he had written but not recorded. He also reworked unreleased material. The Odyssey Room attracted a college crowd. Stanford University was nearby. There was so much success the club remodeled. It became a venue where Tower of Power, Santana, and the New Riders Of The Purple Sage perfected their shows. With a first class sound system, a bouncer at the door and an ownership that was hip and paid whatever the door charged. The five hundred and seven hundred dollars meant Van lost money. He never complained. Van loved the place. The bootleggers showed up to document the performance. A one hundred dollar bill to the guy running the sound system guaranteed a board tape. This led to a perfect bootleg.

It was at the Odyssey Room where Van sang "Warm Love" for the first time. This song became a staple of his 1973-1974 concerts. A band member told me the song was played when "Van was morose over a woman." Guess who?

At the Odyssey Room, the Caledonia Soul Orchestra was in full swing as they played a set designed for a larger arena. Van performed an abbreviated version of "T. B. Sheets." When the show was bootlegged, it included great cover versions of Hank Williams' "Hey

Good Lookin" and Webb Pierce's "More And More." Van had enough material for a country album. Warner wasn't interested. This was one of Van's unique shows. He covered Sonny Boy Williamson's "Help Me," Sam Cooke's "Bring It On Home To Me" and Fleetwood Mac's "Spare Me A Little of Your Love." He ended the show with a cover of Willie Dixon's "I Just Wanna Make Love To You." Van's set list intrigued the crowd. This was a warm up show for what would become the **It's Too Late To Stop Now** album. The CSO was so tight at the Odyssey Room, Van abandoned the usual hand gestures to the band to signal a musical change. They were on the same page with him.

For three nights at Doug Weston's Troubadour Club, the Caledonia Soul Orchestra was near perfection. The May 24-27, 1973, Troubadour shows continued Van's intimate connection with his band. He mixed as many as forty songs into his sets. After these shows he green lighted extensive touring. "No one could believe his commitment to touring," Nathan Rubin continued. "I wasn't sure he would add shows. He did." When Mo Ostin showed up at the Troubadour, he was pleasantly surprised by the nascent professional sound. The CSO put a smile on Ostin's face. Morrison's magnificent stage presence indicated he worked hard on his live appearances. Ostin told Joe Smith the band was the best Van played with in his career. Warner Bros. pressured him to lengthen the tour. Ostin smelled heavy record sales. Van wasn't sure. His perfectionist nature demanded a little more tweaking with the band.

On June 22, 1973, another warm up show at Tom Donahue's San Francisco club, the Orphanage, was an unmitigated success. Van was eager to continue the Caledonia Soul Orchestra's perfection. Van loved the Orphanage. Donahue was privy to Morrison's every need. The sound system was first rate. The band was fed. The audience was attentive. Van was spectacular.

The Orphanage, at 807 Montgomery Street, located in the heart of the Financial District, was an after work pick up place for young singles. Donahue advertised fifty cent cocktails from 5 to 6 and on week-ends there was a free, extensive buffet with ribs, chicken wings, meatballs, celery, carrots and a host of dips.

The Orphanage audience for Van's shows looked like a bunch of business executives. They wore suits. The women had on office dresses and high heels. There were a few leisure suits. Van was happy with the rapt attention. There were no cries for "Gloria" and "Brown Eyed Girl." Donahue hovered nearby serving the band's needs. He was a great promoter. He was a lousy businessman. Joe Smith lent Donahue money. Then Warner Bros. foreclosed on his Autumn label.

VAN MORRISON FOR RAINBOW

24 JULY 1973 LONDON

VAN MORRISON — former Them leader and now a superstar in his own right — returns to Britain next month.

He will play six major concert dates in this country, including two at London's Rainbow Theatre. And NME readers are today given an exclusive opportunity to book seats for the two London shows ONE WEEK before the box-office opens to the public.

Details page 2.

THE MOST COMPLETE AUDIO & VIDEO REMASTER BOX

ALICE STUART: THE FORMATIVE YEARS

Donahue paid the bands well. One week in October, Redwing, Lydia Pense and Cold Blood and the Average White Band played the

Orphanage. As many musicians, as interested patrons, showed up for these shows. When members of Tower of Power walked into the club, Donahue had two tables up front to let Lydia Pense sit with Stephen "Doc" Kupka and Emilio Castillo. They drank and ate for free.

On Thursday night ladies were free. As he was putting together Sly and the Family Stone, Sylvester Stewart played the club to showcase his new music. The Jerry Garcia Band, the Charlatans and the Tubes were regularly featured. Dan Hicks said: "I would play it for the food and drink and Donahue always had something to smoke, snort or drink." After a hard year of being away from the Orphanage, Van returned for another show. He was now a full-fledged star. He played the venue to help Donahue get out of debt. That didn't happen.

Who was Alice Stuart? She grew up in Eastern Washington. In the small town of Chelan, she was the only person playing a Martin D18 guitar. "I had grown up loving Elvis Presley, Jerry Lee Lewis, Buddy Holly, Roy Orbison and Chuck Berry," Stuart recalled. She played piano and drums in high school. She was part of the marching band. She decided the guitar was her instrument. Her vocals were a throaty, folk influenced mélange of traditional blues tunes. She was searching for a different sound from the classic rockers. She found it with a blues direction. Her mellifluous voice stood out in the clubs. She played a scintillating lead guitar which was unheard of for ladies on folk stages. When Lightnin' Hopkins heard her perform in Berkeley, he provided tutoring. The result? Her lead guitar parts soared. Early on Alice was a full blown folkie. Then the blues followed. She became Bonnie Raitt before Bonnie Raitt. Her early folk education and training led to Seattle and eventually to California.

Stuart fell in love with Burl Ives' music. She purchased one of his songbooks. She learned a play a baritone ukulele. She quickly developed a ten folk song set. That allowed her to relocate to Seattle. A nascent folk scene burgeoned near the University of Washington.

She completed high school. She left to frequent Seattle's folk music scene. She was a regular performer at a folk coffee venue, the Pamir House. The excited crowds, who frequented this venue, enhanced a burgeoning folk scene. In the University district, as students, from the University of Washington, came to listen to the folk singers, she became a popular folk performer. There was a strong folk scene with a national charting hit act from a nearby University fraternity, the Brothers Four.

Stuart realized her folk act needed updating. She began to experiment with blues songs. Alice also began a career long tutorial in American roots music. She blended her folk roots with blues and a touch of rock 'n' roll. She loved rhythm and blues, as well as jazz. It was folk music that began her transition into the blues. Her guitar riffs were as prominent as her vocals.

As Stuart incorporated blues riffs into her folk performances, she moved beyond the genre. Seattle venues came calling with booking requests. There was a proliferation of sounds in Seattle. Stuart was in the forefront of the developing musical revolution freeing up venues for all sorts of musical acts leading to a rock and roll scene.

The Pamir house, at 4111 University Avenue, brought in Seattle's finest folk music performer. It was a meeting place for folkies. The blues and rock and roll acts increasingly influenced her as she drifted full-time into the blues. It was there she learned of the Berkeley Folk Festival and the musical innovations in and around the San Francisco Bay Area. This began her long road to playing, living and meeting Van Morrison in Marin County. When Van heard her play, he was mesmerized by her talent.

But it was in Seattle that she learned not only folk music but it was in the Pacific Northwest that the burgeoning bar bands and teen dance halls influenced her. The Frantics, Little Bill And The Blue Notes, the Ventures, the Wailers and the Night People inaugurated the 1950s rock 'n' scene. Soon they gave way to the Sonics, Don and the Good Times and Paul Revere and the Raiders. There were dozens of the local rock bands who placed folk music in the grave. But it was at Seattle's folk clubs Stuart saw her initial future.

The Place Next Door, the Edge, the Eigerwand Kaffeehaus and the Café Corrobboree were other University district haunts providing an open stage for Stuart's guitar wizardry. There was little money. In Tacoma, the End was the only real folk music opportunity. With almost a one hundred thousand alcoholics, Tacoma was a rock 'n' roll mad town. That influence turned Stuart toward a blues-rock direction.

The Ventures were a local band. They were playing the biker bars while working day jobs and perfecting their first monster national hit "Walk Don't Run." The Wailers kept the teen dance scene alive at the Spanish Castle. The Wailers "Tall Cool One" was one the Pacific Northwest's early national rock hits. Little Bill And The Bluenotes were another rock 'n' roll favorite. Little Bill's "I Love An Angel" was a number one Pacific Northwest hit and peaked on **Billboard** at sixty-six in the summer of 1959. "The Seattle rock scene changed my act," Stuart told me.

"Tacoma was a blue collar music town dominated by the Wailers," Don Wilson of the Ventures remarked: "There wasn't much truck with folk singers." When I asked Wilson about Alice Stuart, he said: "A calm blues lady with a folk pedigree." That boded well for Stuart's commercial future. Musicians embraced her talent.

Stuart realized Seattle's folk scene had limited commercial possibilities. She left for California. She moved to Berkeley. The folk music scene boomed for a decade when Stuart arrived. The annual Berkeley Folk Festival filled this college town with huge crowds. The local clubs had slots for musicians and forgotten blues artists like Son House and Mississippi John Hurt. They were brought in by Arhoolie Records to play the local venues. With students from the University of California crowding the clubs nightly, there was a musical vibrance to the San Francisco Bay Area music scene.

Stuart received a musical education hanging out with Country Joe McDonald, meeting Lightnin' Hopkins while finalizing her act thanks to the money to perform in the Berkeley folk-blues scene. She made friends with a bevy of talented musician. She exhausted the Berkeley scene.

She drifted to Los Angeles playing the coffee house circuit. She discovered the blues clubs. By hanging out in seedy blues venues, she perfected that sound. After hearing Lightnin' Hopkins, Stuart had all the tools for stardom. Then she met Frank Zappa at Kantor's in Los Angeles.

"I drove down to Los Angeles to meet with a guitar playing friend of mine, Steve Mann." Stuart continued. "I started to talk with another person....Turned out it was Frank Zappa." When her friend didn't show up, Stuart left with Zappa.

For a time she was a member of the Mothers of Invention. Ray Collins of the Mothers of Invention recalled: "We brought her in to share vocals with me but she never recorded with us." Ray thought for a moment and continued: "She had a blues voice like no other."

It was Stuart's time with Frank Zappa and the Mothers of Invention that turned her music into a solid blues direction with a rock and roll tinge. Her musical style did not mesh with Zappa's. They were close personally. They were far apart musically. She left the Mothers of Invention to pursue a blues direction returning to Berkeley.

She signed a contract with Chris Strachwitz's Arhoolie label. The problem was her debut LP, **All The Good Times,** released in 1964. She didn't fit into the burgeoning rock and roll market. The cover of the Arhoolie album displayed an Angelic Stuart. The songs were traditional folk. She continually drew the ire of critic Phil Elwood. He was a traditionalist. The manner in which Stuart mixed folk with blues brought praise from blues legend Mississippi John Hurt. The condemnation from critic Phil Elwood hurt her career. Stuart was frustrated. She was a hybrid performer with roots in three genres folk, blues and rock.

She caught the attention of Barry Olivier who signed her to appear at the 1964 Berkeley Folk Festival. It was not the time for a folk singer who loved the blues to go mainstream. Then it was off to Los Angeles to pursue her blues-rock career.

When she appeared in Berkeley, California on May 6, 1965 at the Jabberwock, Stuart followed Son House. He loved her music. The Jabberwock was a folk club at 2901 Telegraph Avenue in Berkeley. It was a place that brought in Bukka White, Ian and Sylvia and Country Joe McDonald for regular performances. Stuart stood out much like she had in Seattle. It was Country Joe and the Fish who encouraged Stuart to take her blues act on the road. She never forgot her Seattle roots. She returned there to perform regularly.

In 1971 Fantasy released her cult album **Full Time Woman** (Fantasy 8403). It didn't sell. A follow up LP **Believing** (Fantasy 9412) sold a bit better. "Without the **Full Time Woman** album," Chris

Michie continued. "There would not have been a Bonnie Raitt." Both LPs were met with excellent reviews. But sales were tepid. Alice Stuart's albums sold well in Europe. Fantasy sent her on a six-week tour in 1971 with Redwing. "We had a London apartment and played all over the U. K. and Europe." Stuart recalled: "It was great." In London's Camden Town, Stuart brought the house down with strong performances at the Dublin Castle and Dingwall's. The only thing she lacked was a paycheck. After the Van Morrison tour, her early records with Arhoolie and Fantasy she didn't make a living wage. She was tired. She was burnt out. She married. She raised a family. She completed a community college degree. She continued to perform when she could.

The responsibility of kids and a husband drew her temporarily from the music scene. She decided to play the Marin County clubs while attending the College of Marin. It was during this time, 1972-1973, that her band Snake became a local favorite. This is when Morrison discovered her.

The irony was Alice Stuart lived in Fairfax. So did Van Morrison. She heard through the grapevine that her band Snake was one of Van's favorites.

The Alice Stuart and Snake story is one that is typical of the San Francisco Bay Area. It was a great band, with an over the top singer, which never achieved commercial success. The critical acclaim for Stuart's voice resonated in the press. Money never followed. She became disillusioned. She took a sabbatical from the music business. She continued to write and perform while balancing a husband and children. What did Alice Stuart bring to Van Morrison's It's Too Late To Stop Now tour? She brought the pedigree of a great two piece band and her blues tinged vocals.

ALICE STUART AND SNAKE WITH VAN MORRISON

Her California appearances were highlighted by a scorching version of "Full Time Woman." This is what sold Morrison on her talent. She took her band into Marin County. She continued to rehearse for the European tour. Stuart and Snake were excited about touring with Van. They saw it as an opportunity to take their blues sound to a larger audience. It guaranteed record sales. Some degree of financial stability was necessary for Stuart to continue her career. That fiscal push never materialized.

Before Stuart and Snake left for the European leg of the It's Too Late To Stop Now tour, they flew to Toronto, Canada to open for Morrison at the Convocation Hall. This July 7, 1973, show was a warm up for the larger tour. It began with a series of dates on the East Coast. Stuart and Snake also appeared at the Lenox Arts Center in Tanglewood, Massachusetts. Alice Stuart and Snake flew into Amsterdam. They were greeted by a tour bus and taken into the city. "I was met by a Marin County waitress, Norma Gutierrez, she was watching Shana who was along on the tour." Stuart was impressed by what a great father Van amidst the chaos of organizing a major tour.

As Van prepared for the It's Too Late To Stop Now Tour, his life was in turmoil. John Platania remembered he was alternately distraught and happy. He was distraught over fighting with Janet over visitation rights with Shana. Platania said Janet contested Van's requests. "He was a great father," Platania mentioned casually in a conversation with me in Sweden, while he was touring with Chips Taylor. He said Van was "family oriented." Platania said that working while dealing with the record business. Van was inordinately shy in the 1970s. Earlier in conversations with Steve Turner, Platania remarked of the atmosphere surrounding Van. There was continual turmoil over his visiting rights with Shana. Platania said Van was a devoted father. "We went to the house where Shana was with her baby sitter. It was a place that Van had rented for Janet after they split. He took Shana to be with him but it didn't last long. There was a big battle over that though because I don't think he was supposed to be seeing her at that time," Platania concluded to Steve Turner.

The personal drama in Van's life was one her never took into the public forum. He does hold grudges. But they are private and exasperated by events in his life. His focus in 1973-1974 was solely on his career. A failed marriage with Janet was one result. The other was the relationship with Carol Guida that lasted three plus years and, finally, when he moved out to San Geronimo Valley, he could work 24/7 without hinderance.

Those around Van said the planning, the logistics, the practices, the early local shows, prior to the tour, and the need for attention to business kept Van going 24/7. Music saved his professional life. It made him a superstar. His personal life. That is his own business.

Bibliographical Sources

For Alice Stuart, see, Michael Limnios, "Alice Stuart: An American Treasure," **Blues GR**, September 20, 2012.
http://blues.gr/profiles/blogs/amazon-of-music-alice-stuart-talks-about-her-respect-and?override_MobileRedirect=1

Also, see, "Alice Stuart Interview," **Guitarhoo!** May 14, 2004 for a lengthy interview on her career. Of working with Van Morrison, Stuart said: "My most memorable gig was opening for Van Morrison at the Rainbow Theater in London. I toured with him in the It's Too Late To Stop Now tour in the U. S., Canada and Europe." A **Seattle Times** article "Seattle Blues Women Itching To Get Back On The Road," January, 2008 has illusions to Stuart and important material on the difficulty of women singing the blues. For Stuart becoming a blues musician Bill White, "Stuart Makes The Shift From Sweet Folk Singer To Blues Guitarist," **Seattle Post-Intelligencer**, January 2006.
https://www.seattlepi.com/ae/music/article/Stuart-makes-the-shift-from-sweet-folk-singer-to-1192807.php

The Alice Stuart story is the prototype for what Bonnie Raitt became as a blues singer. After a very successful tour of Australia she returned to the U. S. hoping to make a transition to a mainstream blues act. Her two piece band, Snake, was terrific but the critics and reviewers were hostile to her. She found his difficult to please San Francisco Bay Area critics. In March, 1974 an **Oakland Tribune** review of her show headlined: "The Mediocrity Predicament: Alice Stuart And Snake." That review wasn't a nail in the coffin of her career but she left the industry for a dozen years to raise a family.

Also, see, Interviews with Ray Collins of the Mothers Of Invention, George Palmerton of the Frantics, Night People and the Highlighters, Ron Peterson of the Frantics, Don Wilson of the Ventures and Little Bill Englehart were important in placing Alice Stuart's Seattle story into perspective. Numerous interviews with Alice Stuart were important to this chapter. She detailed her career calling the time touring with Van the most important of her career. She continues to perform. Her observations on preforming with Van during the It's Too Late To Stop Now tour added depth, new information and analysis. Alice also provided detailed information on the complicated logistics of the tour and how and why the road manager was a key to the successes that Morrison experienced on stage. Chris Strachwitz and Opal Louis Nations provided material on the Berkeley folk scene and Stuart's role in it. Interviews with Snooky Flowers and Gino Landry were important on the Oakland blues and club scene and how it influenced artists like Van Morrison. Steve Gannon, an English guitarist with the Jimmy McCracklin Band, provided information on Stuart's blues guitar playing as did another McCracklin guitarist Pee Wee Thomas. San Francisco Bay Area saxophone blues legend Bobbie Webb went with me to three Van Morrison concerts to judge his sax skills. Webb said; "A sax player who fits the playing to his vocals. Top notch for a self-taught musician."

For John Platania's conversations with Steve Turner, see, Steve Turner, **Van Morrison: Too Late To Stop Now** (New York, 1993). Also, see, John Collis, **Van Morrison: Inarticulate Speech Of The Heart** (London, 1996), pp.126-127 and a brief conversation with Turner at a Beatlefest helped my focus on Van in the 1970s. I talked briefly with John Platania in Stockholm, Sweden where he was providing guitar support for Chip Taylor while the "Wild Thing" songwriter

The website **Van Morrison News** was instrumental to this book. The material is amazing and the unofficial blog spot does ten times the job that Morrison's official website does. The key to this website is the reaction from fans and friends of Morrison.

A lengthy conversation with John Platania at a Chips Taylor show in Stockholm helped to sort out the impact of the divorce on Van's musical journey.

Clinton Heylin, **Can You Feel The Silence?: Van Morrison, A New Biography** (Chicago, 2002), pp. 285-287, 293-297 provided information important to this chapter. An in-depth interview with David Hayes by Truls Meland in **Wavelength** number 14 was instrumental to this chapter.

John Collis, Van Morrison: Inarticulate Speech Of Heart (London and New York, 1996), pp. 122-129. Howard A. DeWitt, **Van Morrison: The Mystic's Music** (Fremont, 1983), pp.45-48. Steve Turner, **Van Morrison: Too Late To Stop Now** (London, 1993), chapter 6. The Turner book is valuable for his insights, research and cogent comments on Van's life. It was released as a coffee table book with many photos and illustrations, but it is also a serious look, with in-depth analysis of Van's musical journey.

For Janet Morrison Minto's comments on her husband see, Barry Egan, "Love Lost In The Myths Of Time," **London Independent**, January 30, 2020.
https://www.independent.ie/woman/celeb-news/love-lost-in-the-myths-of-time-26253156.html
and Louis Sahagun, "The Clouds Have Lifted," **Los Angeles Times**, November 17, 1998. https://www.latimes.com/archives/la-xpm-1998-nov-17-cl-43498-story.html

The Circular and Waxpaper Warner Bros. advertising campaign is described in Peter Ames Carlin, **Sonic Boom: The Impossible Rise of Warner Bros. Records From Hendrix to Fleetwood Mac To Madonna To Prince** (New York, 2021) pp. 105-108, 122-123, 130, 152-158, 170, 211. On Warner Bros., see, Jo Bergman, **The Book Of The Road** (Burbank, 1975), Stan Cornyn and Paul Scanlon, **Exploding** (New York, 20020, Fredric Dannen, **Hit Men: Power Brokers And Fast Money Inside the Music Business** (New York, 1990) and Warren Zanes, **Revolution In Sound: Warner Bros. Records, The First Fifty Years** (San Francisco, 2009).

A top notch assessment of Morrison's writing is Jonathan Cott, "Van Morrison: The Poet," **Rolling Stone**, November 30, 1978.
https://www.rollingstone.com/music/music-news/van-morrison-the-poet-245962/
This article suggests that Van was one of the "few originals in rock."

An excellent Stuart interview with Stuart looking back on her lengthy career and private life as well as her time with Van Morrison is Mike Plumbley, "Gold From California: Alice Stuart Is Back," email interview July 1998.
https://wiki.killuglyradio.com/wiki/Gold_From_California:_Alice_Stuart_Is_Back
On Stuart also se, Colin Larkin, editor, **the Guinness Encyclopedia Of Popular Music** (London, 1992). For a review of her Fantasy CD see, **Rolling Stone**, 1971.

Stan Cornyn joined Warner in 1958. He was a cornerstone of the corporate publicity arm in the 1970s making Van Morrison a legendary act with mammoth record sales. For his career, see, Sam Roberts, "Stan Cornyn, Creative Record Executive, Is Dead At 81," **The New York Times**, My 14, 2015 and Stan Cornyn and Paul Scanlon, **Exploding: The Highs, Hits, Hype, Heroes And Hustlers**

Of The Warner Music Group, (New York, 2002). Cornyn was also a minor source for this book. In two interviews he suggested how and why Warner Bros. and Van didn't always get on. But Cornyn concluded the partnership was much stronger than previous writers indicated. "Van was respected at Warner," Cornyn continued. "He returned that respect."

For the Circular Warner Bros. handouts promoting Van records, see, for example, Matt McCue, "How To Cultivate A Culture Where Creative Freedom Rules," **The Creative Factor**, n. d., Warner Archives.

Chuck Schoning of the Frantics, later known as Chuck Steaks, of the Quicksilver Messenger Service added material on Stuart and the Seattle rock scene as did Don Fulton and Bob Hosko of the original Frantics.

For material on Stephen Pillster, see the announcement of him being named general manager of Caledonia Productions in **Billboard**, October 20, 1973 and conversations with Carol Guida clarified much of what Pillster did and didn't do in Morrison's business structure.

TERRY ADAMS

For Richard Williams' blog, where he recalls the Caledonia Soul Orchestra and Terry Adams forty years after the 1973 London Rainbow show, see, Richard Williams, "Terry Adams On The Cello," **The Blue Moment.com A Blog About Music By Richard Williams**, April 15, 2013. https://thebluemoment.com/2013/04/15/terry-adams-on-the-cello/ This blog is literate insightful and provides a view of the contributions of Terry Kovatch and Nate Rubin, violins who worked with Adams. This article is important in recognizing Jef Labes and his contribution to the CSO.

Another important blog on Van and the CSO is "Watchin'….

Van Morrison," **Learning To Say Nothing: Music. Sport. Life. It's All In Here Somewhere**," January 29, 2010.
https://agentcoop.wordpress.com/2010/01/29/watching-van-morrison/ This is a marvelous eye-witness account with great writing and observational skills beyond most journalists.

For the July 24, 1974 Van Morrison interview with Tom Donahue at the Orphanage see, Van Morrison Interview 7/29/1974 Orphanage, San Francisco, Ca. (Official).
https://www.youtube.com/watch?v=Cchja88Rn5w&t=79s

THIRTEEN

The Philosophical Pathology Of The It's Too Late To Stop Now Tour: Jef Labes, The Cso, Recovery, Performing Excellence, Rediscovering Ireland

"I am getting more into performing. It's incredible. When I played Carnegie Hall in the Fall something just happened."

Van Morrison on his 1972 Carnegie Hall show

"I seldom play the same thing twice."

Van Morrison commenting to Rick McGrath, February 24, 1971

"I noticed he had a t-shirt with his picture on it during my first massage with him. The next time he had another t-shirt with his picture on it. I wondered who was this guy?"

Carol Guida

The It's Too Late To Stop Now tour offers a philosophical path to analyzing Morrison's career. How did the tour benefit Van? The operative wisdom is he performed and produced one of the best live rock 'n' roll albums. He also returned to larger performing venues. The template was set for "Becoming Van Morrison."

There is much more to the tour than a live album. The musicians performing with Van created the next half century of his performing genius. The show bands and his Belfast roots were all over the material.

There were many people who were a key to understanding the depth, breadth and brilliance of the It's Too Late To Stop Now tour. They have nothing in common, but they provide a window into how and why this tour revolutionized the rock music world. Jef Labes is the first person essential to analyzing the tour and album. He was a musician, who as I will show, helped Van conceptualize the It's Too Late To Stop Now tour. Labes worked in the studio with Van and convinced the Belfast Cowboy the studio one take recording technique he favored could be translated into the concert arena. Viola! Van had his path of producing a live album. The second key player was Ritchie Yorke. He had nothing to do with the tour or album. But he was a key player. Why? In researching the first Morrison biography, Yorke interviewed Van many times. Van's comments on the It's Too Late To Stop Now tour and the subsequent album explained why it was a watershed event in his career's evolution. Van was open, transparent and thoughtful responding to Yorke's questions.

Like Yorke, Alice Stuart, the blues guitar virtuoso, kept copious notes on the tour. She was enthralled with discovering how and why Van could mesmerize an audience. When she opened for Morrison, she was a studious observer. With the eyes of a poet and a knowledge of the blues she saw change. Van's dramatic, unprecedented concert genius sprung out and grew each night. He communicated with his audience. Stuart observed it was "a love fest every night with the audience." It was also hard work. Van had to cancel the last two shows. He was exhausted. "I couldn't believe how much Van put into each show," Stuart continued. "When he cancelled the last two shows it was due to pure exhaustion."

JEF LABES: A KEY INGREDIENT IN BECOMING VAN MORRISON

Jef Labes was one of the key ingredients in "Becoming Van Morrison." Why? Labes was a force in the evolution and brilliance of the Caledonia Soul Orchestra. He also worked behind the scenes on the live album.

They key to Labes' influence came during the **Hard Nose The Highway** album. He had worked with Van on the **Moondance** album. The he took some time off to live in Israel.

When he returned to the Morrison fold it was to work on **Hard Nose The Highway**. His influence was evident when Van credited him as a co-producer. What did Labes possess? His studio expertise prompted Morrison to acknowledge his production skill? It was Labes' ability to arrange strings and woodwind instruments that made him essential to Morrison's future albums.

Labes was independent minded. Van discussed the Caledonia Soul Orchestra concept with him. Initially, Labes didn't appear interested. When the CSO was organized he wasn't in the band. He came in quickly replacing James Trumbo.

When Labes sat down for an interview for the Jake Feinberg Show, he spoke of his experiences with Van Morrison. What did Labes possess in the area of talent Van needed to complete his artistic transition to legendary status? Many things! Studio expertise! Jazz insights! These were Labes' forte.

As a working New York musician in the late 1960s, Labes delved into jazz while playing in rock 'n' roll bands. In doing so he learned to do everything in the studio. He also lived in Woodstock where he was close to the Belfast Cowboy. Like Van, Labes was learning the business. They were developing their studio skills. By the time that the Caledonia Soul Orchestra came together, Labes was an integral component in the planning. His contribution as a keyboardist, arranger, sound engineer and producer helped to solidify the CSO.

That attracted Morrison. On stage, Labes knew how to work an audience. By the time he played with Van, he had a career plan. Working in the studio was Labes' strength. Van recognized it. He used his talents.

THE TALE OF THE CALEDONIA SOUL ORCHESTRA: DID HE CONNECT WITH HIS BELFAST ROOTS?

The tale of the Caledonia Soul Orchestra defined Morrison's concert legacy. He morphed from a shy, at times uncertain, concert artist, in the late 1960s and early 1970s, into a virtual lion on stage. He toured and performed with the CSO to universal acclaim. That super band liberated Van. He developed an in concert persona of ninety minutes of pure blues featuring his growing catalogue of personal songs.

"The Caledonia Soul Orchestra," Van told a number of people was "recovery" for him. What did he mean? The CSO, the tour, the resulting double album and the public acclaim was a roadmap to another life. That life was as a permanent fixture on the trendy music scene that swallowed artists.

How did Van envision the Caledonia Soul Orchestra? When you saw him in concert, he blurted out the CSO's name at appropriate moments while praising a solo. "I loved Van for the way he took my solos and called them out," Labes said.

The warm up concerts in the San Francisco Bay Area, Los Angeles, Canada and the East Coast were important to the CSO's U. K. success. The genesis of the band was in Van's head. The early signs of it coming together took place in a series of non-descript San Francisco Bay Area clubs, a community college auditorium, and a few venues ripe for experimentation.

What was the first Caledonia Soul Orchestra shows? Hard to say! It was probably at Tom "Big Daddy" Donahue's Orphanage. This was, at the time, a premier performing venue. The ambiance was cocktail lounge casual with an audience in suits and ties. There was excellent food. Tom Donahue, the owner, was a local disc jockey with immense reach into the San Francisco record community. He became a friend and promoter of Van's music.

On May 15, 1973, Van brought in eleven musicians in what appeared to be the origins, as far as public performances were concerned, of the Caledonia Soul Orchestra. What was new in this group. Tim Kovatch was a San Jose Symphony musician as was Nathan Rubin from the Oakland Symphony. The beautiful cellist, Teresa Adams, was classically trained. The CSO was intact.

What was Van doing? No one seemed to know. The concept was a new one. Symphony musicians, an eclectic set of songs and mystical experimentation made for a new majestic, orchestral-rock sound. This was not the norm in rock 'n' roll music.

VAN AND WHAT THE CSO MEANT TO HIS SHOW BAND DAYS

In 1973, as Van Morrison spent months organizing a new band, he auditioned musicians non-stop. In his private time, while listening to his record collection and thinking about the old Belfast days, he had an epiphany. He would go back and re-create the show band days with the Caledonia Soul Orchestra.

As Van recalled the six to eight sets a night with the Monarchs, he longed for the showband atmosphere. It was a distant memory. Now, with commercial success, he had the resources to pursue his dream. Van had a nostalgic feel for what had once been a performing nightmare.

His idea was to put together a big band. The old days, when he was in the Monarchs, resonated in his psyche. Van either forgot or sublimated the six to seven sets a night, the low pay, the seedy working conditions, the inadequate hotel rooms and the brusque promoters.

ENTER JEF LABES AGAIN

Why was Jef Labes one of Van's confidants? It was to enable the formulating of the Caledonia Soul Orchestra. Why Labes? His piano on "Moondance" was one of the best keyboard accompaniments in rock 'n' roll history. Labes was a jazz guy who played rock like no other. Like Van his jazz education was a late blooming interest. Van was intrigued by his ability to pick up jazz idioms and define them with the grace of a seasoned scholar.

Jef Labes provided an interpretive window into how Van blended his musical talents with others in his quest for commercial success.

The musical pedigree bringing Labes to Van's attention was an impressive one. At the tender age of thirteen, he became a professional musician. He worked in and around Boston. In 1964 an obscure 45 "Put The Clock Back On The Wall," for the Cori label, began Labes' recording career.

After relocating to New York, he joined the Sacred Mushroom, a psychedelic band. Then he became an integral part of the Apple Pie Motherhood Band. This group was a cult favorite with two albums in 1968-1969.

For eight albums, Labe's signature piano sound was a key to Morrison's music. They talked music. They talked concepts. He was a constant companion. He witnessed the evolution of Morrison as a performer, writer and producer.

He was only twenty-five when Van connected with him. While living in Woodstock, Labes was not a member, but he played at times with the Colwell-Winfield Blues band. "We first got together with Van for the **Moondance** album," Labes said. "I played piano on it. We talked a lot about how the album should sound. Van said it sounded too much like **Astral Weeks**," Labes continued. "I told him I agreed." According to Labes, **Moondance** was pure pop so Van could continue to record for Warner Bros. if he had a series of hit albums.

As Labes talked about Van he remarked: "He was a complicated guy." Labes believed Van was misjudged. "Van looks at music as a job, he was a local hero with Them, he was famous since sixteen," Labes continued. "He was fed up with the fame aspect." From 1970 into 1973 Labes at times lived with Morrison. They were close musically and personally.

A reason for Labes initially not joining the Caledonia Soul Orchestra was he left Marin County for a time to study in New York at Julliard. When he moved back to Fairfax in 1972, Dahaud Shaar told Van Labes was back. Van was on the phone to him. They worked together on **Hard Nose The Highway**.

In 1975-1976 Labes worked on the first season of Saturday Night Live doing musical arrangements. He also worked in Hollywood in the cartoon industry and as a solo artist. Arranging was Labes' key skill of many musical talents.

The irony was Labes didn't join the Caledonia Soul Orchestra until May 8, 1973. He replaced James Trumbo the piano player on **Veedon Fleece**. Van told Labes he was reconnecting with his Celtic roots. **Rolling Stone** labelled the CSO "a pinnacle for Morrison...." Jef Labes told **Rolling Stone** that Van "wanted to create a new show every night."

WAS IT'S TOO LATE TO STOP NOW A RECOVERY TOUR?

Van prized musical innovation. He will complete a project to great acclaim. If a project was praised, he often abandoned it. No flavor of the month for Morrison. Every album has to have a different sound. He feared compromising his musical magic. There was no part two to the Caledonia Soul Orchestra. Van disbanded it. The Caledonia Soul Express was a different group. It emerged to give Van a new life.

Did **Veedon Fleece** amplify **Astral Weeks**? The critics said: "Yes." Van wasn't so sure. Some days he said "Yes!" Other days he said; "No." After thinking about it over many years, he debunked the idea. **Veedon Fleece**, said Van, stood on its own. He said this was true of all his music.

Chris Michie said of **Veedon Fleece**: "It was a modified Astral Weeks with love." Van said he was reinventing himself. He did this to achieve continued creativity. The critics agreed. Van was at a creative peak. Why, then, did he form the Caledonia Soul Orchestra? It was simple. He would mold the band to follow his every musical nuance. In concert, Van believed this led to performing perfection. It did!

The Caledonia Soul Orchestra, and the subsequent tour, kept Van busy. He minimized the heartbreak of his wife leaving him. He could answer the critics who carped at his often erratic concert performances.

The house on a hill in Fairfax, with the ominous gate, shouted security. Van was lonely there. When Janet and Shana were there to assuage Van's personal and creative needs, he was ready to produce. When they left his production accelerated. He put a failed marriage in the rear view mirror. He worked 24/7 on "Becoming Van Morrison."

"He called in friends from Woodstock. He was in touch with a few Irish friends. I was there. I wasn't sure what the hell was going on," Jack Schroer continued. He was amazed at how easily Van reached out to people. A member of the Caledonia Soul Orchestra argued there was one song illuminating his failed marriage.

He wrote "I Paid The Price" reflecting on his failed marriage. He would lose himself in the It's Too Late To Stop Now tour. As a member of the Caledonia Soul Orchestra observed: "It was a very exciting time…it was also hard on him since his marriage was breaking up."

What would become the It's Too Late to Stop Now tour began inauspiciously in Los Angeles at Doug Weston's Troubadour? Why this venue? The industry big wigs hung out there. The Troubadour was known for breaking new artists. It was the launching pad for record releases, smoothing out touring bands and receiving positive publicity. Van wanted to showcase his strings, while Jef Labes fine-tuned the arrangements. The road manager, Stephen Cohen was new, but he skillfully helped organize the legendary tour. No one realized any of this as the Troubadour shows commenced.

Experimentation at the Troubadour was Van's goal. He wanted to stretch out some songs with new arrangements. This explains the changes in "The Way Young Lovers Do." Van became more soulful and the musicians were playful behind his vocals. Nathan Rubin's violin stood out. "Cyprus Avenue" became a ten minute version. The instrumental solos were important as Van showcased his musicians. "We could take the songs anywhere Van wanted to take them," John Platania observed.

Most band members believed Van was a jazz performer. "His vocal on 'Moondance' rarely repeated the recorded version," Platania said. "Van was having fun," Nathan Rubin remarked to me. The high kicks on stage were not a Morrison trait until this tour. Van smiled. He continually looked at the beautifully blonde cellist, Terry Adams, as he carefully planned each song. "It was a recovery tour," Rubin continued. "Van was recovering from domestic fragility."

As an incipient contrarian, with an eye for perfection, Van realized he couldn't be on the mark each night. He told friends the Caledonia Soul Orchestra was the closest he had come to perfection. They bailed him out when he was not up to it on stage. He loved the freedom the CSO gave him. Van said it best to **Rolling Stone's** David Browne: "You can't be on every night. But I can honestly say that with this group of people, it's mostly on."

IT'S TOO LATE TO STOP NOW RECONNECTS VAN TO HIS BELFAST ROOTS

The It's Too Late To Stop Now tour began a journey for Van. That was to reconnect with his Belfast roots. This tour remains a legendary moment in rock concerts. For three months the eleven piece Caledonia Soul Orchestra produced the best live concert of the decade. They didn't go near Belfast. But Van's psyche had never left his home town.

His biographers pass over the It's Too Late To Stop Now tour like it was a minor blip. Clinton Heylin has seven pages describing it. Johnny Rogan pays short shrift to it with two pages.

What did the biographers miss? For starters the band. The Caledonia Soul Orchestra was made up of classical, jazz, concert trained, blues and rock musicians. With the exception of Leonard Cohen's backing musicians, no one assembled such a diverse group. The result was Van's vocal brilliance. The tight nature of the Caledonia Soul Orchestra, the fawning London press, and the influence of Marin County musicians highlighted a once in a lifetime concert experience.

On the eve of the tour, Van remarked: "When I played Carnegie Hall in the Fall something just happened. All of a sudden, I felt like you're back into performing and it just happened like that...A lot of times in the past I've done gig and it was rough to get through them." Van's comment set the tone for the tour.

CONTROVERSIES: REAL AND IMAGINED FOR THE IT'S TOO LATE TO STOP NOW TOUR

There were inane controversies. It was rumored Van would perform in Belfast. It was strictly a rumor. It was reported as fact. Stephen Pillster was the source. When Pillster promised a return to perform in Belfast, Van never agreed to it. Pillster should have been sacked. Van kept him on.

The rumor of Van's return to Northern Ireland took on a mythical character. It prompted some drunken concertgoers, who traveled from Belfast to see Van perform, to act up. Drink and stupidity was a tough combination. Violent drunks! Fools! Poseurs! Van ignored them. It was simple! Van was a Protestant. He feared potential violence. He would not return to Belfast. The Troubles remained an issue.

Van's volatile behavior was controlled during the It's Too Late To Stop Now tour. He was not shielded from the media. He was cooperative. He did his best to avoid the Troubles. He ignored inquiries concerning his personal life. He met and talked with the press. It was controlled. So were the performances. It was grueling. There was enough time off to keep Van fresh. The band never got tired.

When the double album was released, it represented Van's best shows. The Troubadour appearance, May 24-27, 1973, set the standard for his small venue genius. This was followed by the cavernous Santa Monica Civic Auditorium show on June 29, 1973. Then came the triumphant return to London for two nights at the Rainbow Theater on July 23-24, 1973. From these shows the double album was assembled from cassette tapes; Carol Guida sat next to Van in the studio. They worked on the cassette tapes together. "Someone told me I should get co-producers credit," Guida said with a twinkle in her eye.

Van needed a muse. There is no way of knowing how much Guida's support added to the finished product. There is no question she calmed him down. She accentuated his creativity. The box of tapes for the double live album was a daunting task.

The tapes from the tour were crystal clear. Although little more than cassette tapes, they were extraordinary in sound. When Van finished a ten minute plus version of "Cyprus Avenue," a concert goer shouted: "Turn it on!" Van said: "It's turned on already." This was not typical of Van. He seldom responded to the audience. When the concert's ended, Van screamed: "It's Too Late To Stop Now." The album had its title.

An Irish journalist demonstrated his hostility. Jack Lynch criticized Van's vocal delivery. Everyone scratched their head. Clinton Heylin picked up Lynch's criticism. He wrote: "Morrison's singing style cloaks the immediate understanding of many of the words and phrases by a smooth and vocal slurring." This was nonsense. Van's vocals no longer contained his Irish brogue. He sounded more like Ramblin' Jack Elliott than Shamus Heaney.

When the tour ended, in March-April. 1974, Van disbanded the California Soul Orchestra. It was too expensive. The eleven piece group proved he could front a big band. He wanted a more intimate sound. This led to the stripped down Caledonia Soul Express. This group altered his performances. The Caledonia Soul Express was as tight as the CSO. This was typical Van Morrison. What was he doing? He was doing what the classic blues men did. They performed their songs a different way every night. In this way they grew artistically.

The Caledonia Soul Orchestra had more than a musical influence. It was as much a group of friends as a band. The CSO encouraged Van to experiment. They followed his every nuance. When he closed a show with these musicians, Van would perform an extended version of "Cyprus Avenue." When he finished the song he would scream: "It's Too Late To Stop Now." This was an exclamation of liberation. Not just from Warner Bros. Not just from a fragile marriage. Not just from the sharks, the wannabes and the ne'er do wells populating his world. It was an announcement of his independence. It highlighted the finishing school of intellectual depth in his psyche. Suddenly, Van had a vibrant stage persona. His level of professionalism exploded in an aura of personal liberation. That level of in concert excitement was due to Marin County and the surging creativity from this small, bucolic settlement filled with rock 'n' roll royalty intensified his stage show.

Knebworth Park Bucolic Frolic Concert Poster, 1974

There was another change in Van due to the CSO. He dressed for the first time like a stage performer. That is he wore a Lord Byron designed coat and a stylish ascot. He had a confident stage manner. He was coming of age as a performer. That was a compliment to the Caledonia Soul Orchestra. The showmanship during the It's Too Late To Stop Now tour was part of "Becoming Van Morrison."

The model for Van's next fifty years was planned, executed and finalized during the first phase of the It's Too Late To Stop Now tour. The live songs were unlike anything he recorded in the studio. Morrison's concert brilliance was established. He never stopped building on his live performances.

When the live album was released, it comprised three shows. The Troubadour in Los Angeles, the Santa Monica Civic Auditorium and London's Rainbow Theater appearance. The eighteen songs set a new standard for live performances, as Van worked the group into a groove seldom seen on a live recording.

Van praised the CSO. He said they allowed him to stretch his songs beyond the original concept. An example was "Wild Children," which was on **Hard Nose The Highway**. Van told Ritchie Yorke "Wild Children' was "much better live." He intimated he held back in the studio. Van's creative agenda was like a freight train hurling through the rock 'n' roll jungle.

There was another contribution from Van during the tour and album. He brought renewed attention to the work of Ray Charles, Sam Cooke, Sonny Boy Williamson and Bobby Blue Bland. He said his goal was to make the general public aware of these enormously talented, but often forgotten, artists. In his lengthy career, Van has never stopped showcasing his intricately developed blues voice. It is the bread and butter of his creativity.

THE FIRST PHASE OF IT'S TOO LATE TO STOP NOW: A JOURNEY TO PERFORMING EXCELLENCE AND REDISCOVERING IRELAND

Before the It's Too Late To Stop Now tour traveled to Europe and England there was a honing of musical talent. The Canadian journalist, Ritchie Yorke, told a member of the Caledonia Soul

Orchestra the American shows were so finetuned that when the group reached the U. K. Van's blockbuster shows would be praised. Van was concerned about the reception. After the Los Angeles shows, Van realized he had something special. The Caledonia Soul Orchestra worked hard on the East Coast to make sure the stage shows were perfect. They were ready for Europe and the U. K.

There was a level of personal trepidation with Van. He wasn't sure what the reception would be in London. He had not been back to perform in almost a decade. The planning, because of Van's concerns, was finite.

It wasn't until mid-July 1973, that Van and the fifty plus entourage flew to Amsterdam. There were two concerts on the continent before the group headed to the U. K. These were well planned warm up shows. Members of the Caledonia Soul Orchestra exhibited a level of stage precision emboldening the Belfast Cowboy's shows. Hard work, perseverance and planning paid off.

After his eleven piece band landed in Amsterdam, there was time for rehearsals. There was also a day to enjoy the local Amsterdam sites. Smoking a dube. Seeing the Anne Frank house. Or simply sitting by the canals drinking was therapeutic. Van and the band toured the Royal Theatre Carré. They were impressed. The Neo-Renaissance look appealed to the symphony musicians traveling with him. The building, located near the Amstel river, was originally a circus venue. By 1973 it was for pop music or cabaret acts.

The atmosphere was relaxing. Van appeared on stage in a casual sweater with a cigarette hanging from his right hand. He was in a dreamy mood. He attacked his vocals holding the microphone in his left hand. With a full head of red hair, and, at times, a tan sport coat, there was a new Van Morrison. The years of hard work paid off as he mastered the stage and controlled the audience. The joy he exhibited on stage was infectious.

By the middle of 1973, Van Morrison completed the first phase of his journey to performing excellence. He did this with the planning, the formulation and the execution of the Caledonia Soul Orchestra. The May 24, through July 24, 1973 select live shows were released as a double album on February 24, 1974 as **It's Too Late To Stop Now**.

He accomplished this with a three month tour dubbed It's Too Late To Stop Now. The temperamental nature he previously exhibited in San Francisco's Boarding House or the Great American Music Hall, when he stormed off stage, was a thing of the past. The tight eleven piece group, created a new standard for live shows.

Van recognized the necessity of working the larger venues. They paid the bills. The smaller clubs refined his stage presence. It was time to take it to the larger stages. He was a seasoned performer realizing he had to take another step. He did thanks to the It's Too Late To Stop Now tour.

As Van finalized the Caledonia Soul Orchestra, it was an evolutionary group. With stupendous creativity, they became a well-oiled machine. Of his new band, Van remarked: "Now the combination seems to be right and it's been clicking a lot." Van's shows were triumphant. They received the best press of his career.

Van's guitarist, John Platania, remarked the tour was "a funeral for a lot of his old songs." What did Platania mean? He emphasized like the old bluesmen; Van reinvented his music. By "a funeral for some songs," Platania made a statement. Van improved his music in concert.

The family atmosphere, the fawning media, and the over the top fan reception made the tour successful. The shows were taped for a live album. The eight set of tapes in 1973 provided the material for Van's double live album. Then in 2016, a re-release three CD set of **It's Too Late To Stop Now, Volumes II, III, IV & DVD,** added unreleased material. There were no overdubs, no studio fixes and the shows stood as a monument to his performing skill.

The tour and material for the double album began in Southern California. The positive press encouraged Van. He decided to book more shows. Whether or not he was going on an extended tour early on wasn't decided. The reviews accentuated his thirst to perform. After railing for years about journalists and their miscreant misdeeds, it was ironic the flattering reviews brought Van on the road like a ferocious hurricane. As he performed "Listen To The Lion," Van realized he had a song defining his career direction. In 1973, "Listen To the Lion" was his second most played concert song. Only "Caravan" was performed more times. Why? As Johnny Rogan observed: "During the 11-minute voyage, he sings, shouts, improvises lines, delays and omits them, until he symbolically recreates the sound of an unleashed lion within himself." That said it all. The Caledonia Soul Orchestra and the It's Too Late To Stop Now tour featured the song. Jay Cocks remarked: "You can hear Van Morrison courting this muse in the Pentecostal growls...." While Andy Whitman observed the song was that of a man "casting off all earthly bounds and battering down the gates of heaven." The frenetic zeal with which Van performed "Listen To The Lion" broke his shackles of shyness.

With shows at the Troubadour and the Santa Monica Civic Auditorium, the band and Van achieved a groove seldom seen on the concert stage. The May 24-27 Troubadour shows, the June 29, Santa Monica Civic Auditorium appearance and the July 23-24,1973 Rainbow shows were the essence of the new Van Morrison. The cranky Los Angeles critics loved the Belfast Cowboy. It was time to conquer Europe and the U. K.

No sooner had Van landed in London than he was interviewed for the Old Grey Whistle Test. The host, Bob Harris, was perfect to talk to Van. His low key, whispering, friendly questions put the Belfast Cowboy at ease. Van was shy. He was soft spoken. When asked about the shows Van remarked: "Just digging the scene." Van talked about "some movie things." What movies they were remained a mystery. He was welcomed to London with adulation.

BEGINNING THE TOUR: OFF TO THE EAST COAST

After the flight to Toronto Canada, where the band performed on July 7, 1973, at the Convocation Hall, the schedule became more hectic. The work of Van's stage managers, Ed Fletcher and Stephen Cohen, made the tour run with an unseen precision. The opening shows in New York were a harbinger of things to come.

The shows in New York were at the Philharmonic Hall on July 12-13. These dates were performed without Alice Stuart and Snake. Then, on July 16, in Tanglewood, Massachusetts, Stuart rejoined the tour. She was the perfect opening act. Blues with Stuart's brilliant guitar riffs.

At the New York Philharmonic Hall, Arthur, Hurley and Gottlieb opened for Van. They were a Tampa Bay Florida garage band Columbia Records signed. Their self-titled album didn't sell and after two LPs with Columbia they moved on to A & M Records releasing **Sunshine Ship** in 1975. Their career ended. Their high point was opening for Van.

On July 17, the musicians boarded a plane for London. On the flight Van talked with John Platania at length about returning to the U. K. He discussed rekindling his Irish roots. He lamented to one band member; he missed Ireland. The Troubles kept him away.

The Old Grey Whistle Test interview was the most important one. It was a barometer for record sales. Van's show at the Rainbow Theater was a ten-song set that began with Sonny Boy Williamson's "Keep Your Hand Out of My Pocket." The set included a cover of Willie Dixon's "I Just Want To Make Love To You," as well as

Williamson's "Help Me." Van performed "Brown Eyed Girl," "Moondance," "Domino" and "Caravan." The commercial Gods were with him. The show was widely praised. There was another first from this performance. The Old Grey Whistle Test show broadcast the first FM stereo simulcast on U. K. radio and television.

Van was happy with the Old Grey Whistle Test interview. He decided to tape the show at London's Rainbow Theater. He took four songs from the July 23-24 shows to be broadcast in Ireland. They included: "I Paid The Price," "Wild Night," "Saint Dominic's Preview" and "Gloria." During the Rainbow Theater shows, he stretched his songs into new creative directions. He performed "Cyprus Avenue" and "Into The Mystic" with new arrangements. The raucous audience approval signaled their delight.

The Rainbow Theater shows were special. The press concentrated on describing Van's vocals. He left the U. K. as the lead singer of Them. He returned as a lauded solo performer. His talent and stage appearance had matured. As Van told Mervyn Solomon, one day in his Belfast home: "I want my audience to learn my music and I want to do it my way and not to just please my fans." This happened at the Rainbow.

Melody Maker anticipated Morrison's arrival. The fanfare was that of a returning hero. Michael Watts, writing in the July 21, 1973, edition called Morrison: "The best white blues singer of them all." Watts, who hadn't done his homework, wrote of Morrison: "It's a pity he's never performed in Britain." Van read these words with trepidation. He didn't respond. Watts was an ill-informed critic. A wanker without knowledge.

ALICE STUART RECALLS GETTING READY FOR THE U. K. IN AMSTERDAM

Alice Stuart was a witness to history. Sitting ten feet from Van to the side of the stage she watched every performance. "I had never seen anything like Van in concert. I learned plenty," Stuart told me.

The first night at Amsterdam's Carré Theater, Stuart was intrigued by the crowd. "All the theaters were wonderful, I marveled

at the tour. I was pretty excited," she continued. "I didn't think Van gets enough credit for inspiring others; I mean the white boys who sing the blues. Kind of what I had to do."

The second concert in Rotterdam, in the South of Holland, at the De Doelen Theater was a formal theater with white walls and a minimalist ambiance. As the opening act, Stuart recalled: "I was stoned with rotten vegetables at that place before I even started singing." She continued: "I did my set, at that time I was doing 'Golden Rocket, Golden Women,' a lot of stuff from the first Fantasy album." The crowd's response prompted her to take on a more pronounced blue-rock persona. England's blues aficionados were aware of her guitar playing and bluesy vocals. "I performed but I knew everyone anticipated Van. I did too," Stuart concluded.

The crowd welcomed Van with a standing ovation. "They loved him," Stuart concluded. Richard Williams, in **Melody Maker**, reviewed the Birmingham show in the July 28, 1973 issue. In a poorly written review, Williams praised Morrison's performance but wondered why it had taken him so long to return to the U. K? Van politely answered all his questions. He wondered if Williams was a high school dropout. He didn't seem to know anything about him or his music. The questions were asinine. Morrison's cryptic answers were polite. There were bigger journalistic fish to fry. The Birmingham concert was a portent of things to come. The Town Hall show was the first in England after a lengthy absence. The audience was rapturous.

One of the persistent myths of Van's early career was that he was always cranky with the press. Not true! He was at times. On other occasions he was cooperative. A reality was you never knew what you were going to get in a Van Morrison interview. Alice Stuart recalled: "Van tried to cooperate with the press....they went after him at times." With his James Brown swagger, Van was at the top of his performing game. Thanks to Marin County and the small San Francisco Bay Area clubs he was "Becoming Van Morrison."

In London, at the Rainbow Theater, Van's performance made a lasting impression on Stuart. "It was big, wooden and old, and I was so impressed with it. One of Van's roadies, who is now in Hawaii, recalled: "I loved it as it was the night we played the Rainbow." The band got him a bottle of Tequila for his birthday. They walked up into the back of the Rainbow and had a tequila party. This took place while Van took some time with extra preparation. What was going on? He was finalizing an elegant stage appearance. With a stylish Edwardian jacket, an ascot an, shined shoes, Van was looking good. He was in fine performing mettle. He worked the stage with a fervor. Stuart watched in awe from the wings. She was amazed at the consistency of his shows.

Alice Stuart received excellent press. Van was treated like a returning hero. **Melody Maker**, the **New Musical Express** and **Disc** labeled the tour 1973's rock event. One reviewer remarked there was a James Brown swagger to Van's shows. Another critic concluded: "Prepare to be astonished." The critics saw the manner in which Morrison connected with his audience.

Bibliographical Sources

Much of this chapter came from interviews. Alice Stuart provided in-depth information in a number of important interviews. The encyclopedic knowledge of John Goddard of Village Music seeped into this chapter. The pages of **Melody Maker**, the **New Musical Express** and **Disc** provided background information and some praiseworthy articles. Conversations with Nathan Rubin at California State University, East Bay provided anecdotes from the tour. A series of interviews with Carol Guida helped to formulate the influences on Van after the It's Too Late To Stop Now tour concluded and what it did for his creativity. Guida sat with Van as he produced the cassette tapes that became the acclaimed double album. She has a manuscript of her life dealing with this time with Morrison as well as dozens of her other accomplishments.

For **Mojo's** ranking the **It's Too Late To Stop Now** album the sixteenth best of all time, see, **Mojo**, https://www.muziekliijstjes.nl/MojoBestLiveAlbums.htm

The major Morrison biographies pay scant attention to the Caledonia Soul Orchestra and the It's Too Late To Stop Now tour. For these references, see, for example, Johnny Rogan, **Van Morrison: No Surrender** (London, 2005), p. 282-292, John Collis, **Van Morrison: Inarticulate Speech Of The Heart** (London, 1996), p. 136-137 and Clinton Heylin, **Can You Feel The Silence?: Van Morrison, A New Biography** (Chicago 2002), passim.

The Jef Labes interview-podcast on the Jake Feinberg Show was important to this chapter. See, "The Jeffrey Labes Interview", https://podtail.com/en/podcast/the-jake-feinberg-show/the-jeffrey-labes-interview/

A number of Marin County residents helped this chapter, they include Mark Naftalin, Chris Michie, Carol Guida and Marie Bainer. In Sacramento Tony Dey discussed his time with Van and Marin County in general. Paul Vincent, a KMel disc jockey, spoke at length about his interaction with Morrison. Russ Solomon at Tower Records added a great deal of information.

VAN MORRISON: 1970s

FOURTEEN

Revisiting The U. K. Shows, The Triumphs Of The Caledonia Soul Orchestra And The Emergence Of The Caledonia Soul Express

"Hearing the blues changed my life."

Van Morrison

"You have to understand a bit about the poetry of the blues to know where the references are coming from."

Van Morrison

"I understood jazz, I understood how it works. That's what I apply to everything"

Van Morrison

VAN MORRISON

AND THE CALEDONIA SOUL EXPRESS

CALEDONIA

What was the It's Too Late To Stop Now tour designed to accomplish? A portion of each show highlighted songs influential in Morrison's career. That explains the Ray Charles, Bobby Blue Bland, Sonny Boy Williamson and Sam Cooke covers. Soul, blues, jazz and rock were mixed throughout Van's extraordinary performances. He developed a distinct performing style during the tour. He called up his blues and r and b influences with the passion of a preacher converting his flock. The magnetism of these covers brought gasps of recognition, when he arrived in the U. K., from a press looking to be overtly critical. Van insiders said he was surprised by the praise.

The U. K. reception allowed Van to make peace with the past. While he had intermittently performed Them's "Gloria" and "Here Comes The Night," as well the Bert Berns produced "Brown Eyed Girl," he only recently showcased these past hits. They conjured up dark images. He overcame those memories.

In 1973-1974 Van performed "Here Comes The Night" for the first time since 1965. Then, not surprisingly, he didn't perform this tune again until 1979. He performed "Gloria" from 1973 through 1974. In sharp contrast "Brown Eyed Girl" was a concert favorite throughout the 1970s. The reception for cover songs was always a part of Morrison's appeal.

THE IT'S TOO LATE TO STOP NOW TOUR WAS A TEMPLATE FOR THE NEXT 50 YEARS OF VAN'S SHOWS

The It's Too Late To Stop Now tour was much more than highly acclaimed concerts. The shows at the Troubadour, the Santa Monica Civic Auditorium and the Rainbow Theater produced a double LP masterpiece.

When the album arrived there was no post production. It was as you heard the music in concert. Van arrived as a producer! He had been one since **Moondance**. Finally, recognition arrived. It was a long time coming.

One critic observed the album was "an engaging, warm portrait of the man at the peak of his powers." The peak of Morrison's powers arrived in Marin County. Another reviewer suggested the shows highlighted Van's "blue eyed soul." By revisiting the triumphs of the Caledonia Soul Orchestra and the Caledonia Soul Express the reader was taken on a journey where Morrison takes firm hold of his music.

The glue holding Morrison's music together came from Marin County. The local recording studios were an added bonus, as was his Fairfax home recording studio. There were a number of musicians in the San Francisco Bay Area Van found to accentuate his sound. Many were not traditional rock musicians. Some, like Mark Isham and Doug Messenger, went on to Los Angeles movie and studio production careers. Others were symphony musicians. Van even found a University Professor of Music who carried around Charles Bukowski books. There were many seasoned symphony musicians. "Some of us in Marin County," Charlie Musselwhite continued. "Thought Van was a bit too far out. We were wrong." The use of symphony music was nothing new.

No one was more important than a balding, sensitive, introverted college professor who happened to be a classical musician. It turned out he was a widely read, classically trained musician with a penchant for more than rock music. Nathan Rubin was charming, self-effacing and the smartest man in the room. Van loved his understated personality.

Rubin read Jack Kerouac and Charles Bukowski. He was a brilliant classical music concertmaster. He mixed classical music influences with Dave Brubeck's jazz standard "Blue Rondo a la Turk." He was as experimental as Van. He was the glue holding the Caledonia Soul Orchestra together.

NATHAN RUBIN: THE UNSEEN GLUE IN THE CSO

How long did the Caledonia Soul Orchestra last? I went in search of a founding member with a musical pedigree. Nathan

Rubin, sitting in his office at California State University, East Bay, greeted me warmly. He was a thirty-one year career professor at this blue collar university just south of Oakland. I taught at Ohlone College in nearby Fremont. He consented to lengthy interviews. I wasn't sure what to ask or how to approach him. Rubin turned out to be an open book with firm opinions on the genius he said was Van Morrison.

As a young man, Nathan Rubin was destined for classical music acclaim. He gave his first recital at the age of eight at Berkeley's Claremont Hotel. He was a soloist with the Oakland Symphony at fifteen. He picked up a musical instrument at three. He never looked back. At seven Rubin won a major violin contest. He attended the Julliard School of Music.

Nathan Rubin was a first chair violinist with the Oakland Symphony Orchestra. He was the Oakland Symphony Concertmaster. He played Bach, Mozart and Beethoven with concertmaster Luciano Berio. He also performed with the San Francisco Symphony and Opera Orchestras. On April 8, 1993, Oakland celebrated Nathan Rubin Day.

My first question was: "How did you get into the Caledonia Soul Orchestra?"

"I auditioned for Van. He loved what I did."

I didn't know how to ask a classical violinist about rock music. Rubin sensed my indecision. He began talking.

"Let me explain a bit about myself. I grew up in a non-musical, but loving family, and my parents saw something in me so I had musical lessons from age five. They bought me a quarter-size violin," Rubin said. As I talked with him, he looked more like an Englishman than an American. I imagined him in Downton Abbey.

"What was your favorite course to teach?" I hope he wasn't prissy. This is like asking: "What is your favorite color?" He smiled.

"I loved teaching a course in the evolution of rock 'n' roll. I heard about your two courses at Ohlone College, and we modeled one after your 1960s course." Flattery will get you everywhere.

"How was the It's Too Late To Stop Now tour?" I realized it was a less than professorial question. Rubin smiled. He answered.

"I loved it. In Amsterdam I bought Charles Bukowski's **Post Office** in Dutch. I don't read Dutch but I wanted the Bukowski book as a reminder of his fame. I also purchased a great deal of poetry in London. Van was on his game every night," Rubin continued. "He cancelled the last two dates of the tour. Pure exhaustion was the reason."

Then Rubin looked back at the concerts that made up the **It's Too Late To Stop Now** album. "Pure magic," he continued. "I couldn't believe the sound quality. Van edited from the tapes we recorded in concert." Rubin said. The Rainbow Theater was his favorite show. "I think people began to appreciate **Hard Nose The Highway** after we played some album songs live but quite differently." I asked how Van reacted to the lukewarm reception for **Hard Nose The Highway**? "Van had few negative feelings about the album or the tour, when I read some of the music press, I wondered if they were at the shows they reviewed," Rubin continued. "Van had no negative feelings about his personal life. He was intent on performing excellence."

Rubin was embarrassed. He commented on what he said was the "romantic side of Morrison." I asked Rubin what he meant by "romantic side?" He replied: "Van was complicated. He could turn out a sweet lyric, the next moment he would settle a score in a lyric. 'The Way Young Lovers Do' and 'Sweet Thing' were songs revealing Van's inner soul." The gentle lyrical nature Morrison wrote about was in contrast to his volatile personality. I was curious about the strings.

"When you hooked up with Van on the strings for **Hard Nose The Highway** what did you think?" Rubin responded: "I couldn't believe it, Van has a writing palate like no other, we cut most songs in one take and others did the mixing. He is a no-nonsense genius." Rubin also worked with Link Wray and the following year with Bola Sete and Jerry Garcia. When Van brought him aboard, for **Veedon Fleece**, his connection to the Belfast Cowboy's music was instant.

Rubin went on to accompany Coke Escovedo, Ron Carter, Hubert Laws, Patti LaBelle, the Pointer Sisters, Herbie Hancock, Todd Rundgren and Al Green. I asked the obvious question. "What about Van and jazz?"

"Van is a jazz man," Rubin continued. "He sees jazz through another prism. He is much like Herbie Hancock."

As he reminisced a twinkle came to his eye. He mentioned Linda Ronstadt. "I worked with her. I can say she was as soulful as two other young ladies I played behind." I asked: "Who were these young ladies?" Rubin responded: "Aretha Franklin and Patti LaBelle."

Then we discussed Rubin's books. He was the author of **Rock And Roll: Art And Anti-Art** and **John Cage And The Twenty-Six Pianos of Mills College**. He also contributed articles regularly to **Strings**. This was a magazine for music professionals and those interested in string instrumentation.

Rubin's 1993 **Rock And Roll: Art And Anti-Art** is a textbook that he used in his course on rock music. In 242 pages Rubin defined art and anti-art. Then he described Bill Haley, Elvis Presley and rockabilly, he did this to introduce what he labeled crossovers. Those artist included Chuck Berry, Little Richard, Bo Diddley, Fats Domino, Sam Cooke, James Brown and Aretha Franklin. In seventeen chapters he took the material of Bob Dylan, the Beatles, the San Francisco, the Who and virtually everyone else right up to avant-garde, punk, reggae, New Wave and what he called "counter currents," which was his description of rap music. For Van and the band, Rubin was a veritable encyclopedia. Quiet! Shy! Vulnerable! Knowledgeable! Brilliant! Innovative! Introverted! These were the words used by those close to Rubin.

The tour de force of Rubin's books came in 1994 with a 227 page examination of John Cage. This was a quirky, but brilliant, book. It was a collection of loosely based essays on composers who were associated with Mills College. For years Rubin taught courses at Mills. He was a regular contributor to their award winning music program. What made the Cage book unique? It was when Rubin discussed how Cage, and other Mills composers, developed contemporary music. This was one of Morrison's interests. Rubin said they didn't talk often. When they did it was about composing and writing.

Nathan Rubin: "Van was interested in how those who composed music and also wrote books. He told me James Joyce was intriguing.

I asked: "Why?" "Van was surprised Joyce liked classical music," Rubin concluded.

"Did you ask Van about his interest in classical music?"

"No," Rubin continued. "You didn't have those kinds of conversations with Van."

Rubin sent me a copy of his John Cage book with the inscription. "Howard, with my compliments." This was vintage Nate Rubin. A gentleman to the end. When he passed there was a sadness on the California State University, East Bay campus. There was an equally shocked reaction in the rock and classical music worlds. There was only one Nathan Rubin. He was a genius who taught thousands of students. He was also a musician hired by dozens of rock stars.

At forty-four, when he toured with Van, Rubin was older. "Did your violin concertmaster training, beatnik novels and poetry interests confuse anyone?" Rubin smiled. "It did. No one seemed to know Bukowski. They all knew Jack Kerouac and Allen Ginsberg. I turned everyone on to Gary Snyder and Lew Welch. Van know all of this. Maybe that was why I was hired." With that I left Rubin's neat, but dingy, office for the Mission Bell Tavern. I needed a beer.

As I looked back on my interviews with Rubin, I recalled his shy demeanor. He talked with his violin. He played in concert with Van from May 12 until July 27, 1973. He was the hidden backbone of the Caledonia Soul Orchestra. The thirty-nine shows Rubin performed with Morrison were amongst the best of Van's career. That tells one all they need to know about Nathan Rubin. It also tells one all they need to know about Van Morrison's ability to search out and work with brilliant talent.

Van contemplated his future. He realized he was sitting on gold. The tapes from the It's Too Late To Stop Now tour would make up the double album a blockbuster. He was happy with every show. Now he had to go over the tapes. in detail. There would be no overdubbing. He reinterpreted every song. He loved making them over in his unique vocal manner.

In August, 1973, Van returned to the San Francisco Bay Area. His final show in the U. K. at the Newcastle City Hall on July 27, 1973, was a blockbuster. The local promoter, Geoff Docherty, made sure tickets were reasonably priced. The Hall was filled to uber capacity.

Many critics, notably John Collis, said Van came of age as a performer on this tour.

ON THE FAIRFAX: THE CSO DISBANDED AND SOME GIGS WITH SOUND HOLE

After three weeks of rest in Fairfax, Van made plans. He took a new Marin County band, Sound Hole, into small clubs. He wanted to stretch out his It's Too Late To Stop Now band concept with a smaller backing group. Van's ever evolving creative process continued.

From August 20 through September 22, 1973 Van played twelve shows with San Francisco's Great American Music Hall and the suburban Circle Star Theater accounting for eight of the shows. He also performed at Marine World. This small amusement park south of San Francisco was populated by Dolphins and Sea Lions. Carol Guida was at his side. Her drop dead good looks. A sultry personality. The ability to talk to and make anyone around Van feel comfortable was an asset to Van's career.

On August 20, 1973, he played San Francisco's Orphanage. It was a warm, seasonably sunny and wonderful night. The crowd was half business types. The Orphanage was in the financial district. The diehard Van fans took up half of the audience. The remainder were business types n suits and a gaggle of young ladies in secretarial dresses. Take your choice a Martini or smoking a joint in the bathroom. The club was subdued with Tom "Big Daddy" Donahue's two bouncers smiling like they wanted to break your arms and legs. Van loved the club because he could perform an experimental set list. He did with ten songs. For the fans it was incredible as "Brown Eyed Girl," "Here Comes the Night" and "Moondance" brought down rapturous applause. Versions of "Domino," "Caravan" and "Cyprus Avenue" had the diehard fans standing and applauding. The business types went over to the free hors d'oeuvre table for chicken wings and carrot sticks. For Van it was a strange sight. It was a great place to stretch out his music.

Van was back at the Orphanage the next night. It was a Tuesday in San Francisco and it brought out the same crowd. There were more carrots and chicken wings. Donahue expected a bigger crowd. For this show they were standing around the room.

Then Van took ten days off before returning on September 2-3 in San Francisco at the Great American Music Hall. The band loved the Great American Music Hall. It had a sort of class that was déclassé with great food in the dark, cold basement before the show.

There was one venue that made Van uncomfortable. It was in a suburb south of San Francisco. Belmont's Circle Star Theater. It was a theater in the round. There were only about twenty rows of seats with the audience too close to the band. The band and Van had to walk down from the dressing room through the crowd to walk up on the revolving stage. Van was noticeable uncomfortable. The sold out crowd stared at him. Once on stage the band began playing as the stage started evolving. As a spotlight hit the stage evolved faster. Van looked blankly at the audience. It wasn't his kind of place. Halfway through the show, he stopped. He sat down. He got up. He walked to the side of the revolving stage. A few minutes later the stage stopped revolving. His show improved from that point.

During the month long San Francisco Bay Area shows, Van added new songs. "Harmonica Boogie Chillen," a John Lee Hooker inspired tune, that was a reworking of "Boogie Chillen." Van showcased his harmonica talent.

Then he headed to Los Angeles with a stripped down six piece band that became the prototype for his new band. It included Sid Page's violin and Bill Atwood's trumpet blending effortlessly with David Hayes' bass, John Platania's guitar, Jack Schroer's saxophone and Dahaud Shaar's drums.

Morrison pulled out a song, "Try For Sleep," which he debuted at the Los Angeles Shrine Auditorium October 5, 1973. He wouldn't release "Try For Sleep" until 1998 on **The Philosopher's Stone**. New songs Van introduced at the Shrine included "Hard Times," "Harmonica Boogie Chillen" and "You Done Me Wrong." Why the new songs? This was another way of letting Warner know some of his best songs went unreleased. He continued writing instrumentals. Van was flirting with an instrumental album. Warner Bros. didn't want to hear about it. He continued to bring in one or two new songs in his shows. The making of **The Philosopher's Stone** was taking place.

By late 1973, Van's schedule was like a pogo stick hopping from one venue to another. It was a brisk set of appearances that had little order or unity. A member of Van's band told me he felt at home in the greater Los Angeles area. He enjoyed dropping in unannounced at Warner Bros. He loved the local record stores. He wasn't recognized as much in Hollywood.

Van returned to the Los Angeles area for shows at the Shrine Auditorium and later at the nearby Swing Auditorium in San Bernardino. Its vibe was different from Marin County.

He returned twice to Los Angeles for pre-Christmas shows. After the concerts at the Shrine Auditorium, on October 5-6, Van talked at length with Joe Smith about the coming **It's Too Late To Stop Now** album.

On December 1, 1973, he appeared at San Diego's Sports Arena. The location was in a cavernous auditorium. It was not Van's kind of place. After two opening instrumentals, he delivered a stunning show. He closed with four fan favorites, "Domino," "Caravan," "Gloria" and "Brown Eyed Girl." This set became the template for his arena shows. He would mix in Them's "Here Comes the Night" and close with "Brown Eyed Girl."

On the Swing Auditorium, and the San Diego Sports Arena shows a fill in guitarist, Bill Bridges, played the two shows. Then a blues guitarist, Ralph Walsh, replaced him. He had worked with the Paul Butterfield Blues band. Walsh was a vocalist as well as a superb guitarist. On "Streets of Arklow" his guitar work stood out.

WHY DIDN'T THE IT'S TOO LATE TO STOP NOW TOUR CONTINUE?

Everyone was shocked the It's Too Late To Stop Now tour concluded and the aggregation was disbanded. On July 27, 1973 the Caledonia Soul Orchestra gave its last performance. Why was this shocking? There were more dates booked. "Van was tired and bored," Nathan Rubin continued. "We were all shocked." Van's back hurt. He was tired of performing. He was lonely. The road wasn't his thing. When he returned home, he needed medical treatment for his back. That led him to call for a professional message. The masseuse showed up. It was Carol Guida. His life was about to take another creative turn.

Filmore North Ticket Stub July 27, 1973

It was time to head home to Fairfax. The divorce was over. His professional career was in full bloom. His writing called. He would not let Warner Bros. or the music business dictate his life. A new day dawned. It was one of relaxation, creative isolation, and a burst of spiritual music unseen in the rock 'n' roll world. **Veedon Fleece** was coming.

The last two shows of the It's Too Late To Stop Now were scheduled for the Carlton Cinema in Dublin. No one ever explained why Van was ready to go home. He flew to New York on Monday, July 30. The musicians were surprised.

Tim Kovatch: "Sadly and inexplicably, the tour ended several weeks early, when management came to us and said 'Van does not want to do anymore.'"

Bibliographical Sources

A series of interviews with Nathan Rubin, 1982, 1985, 1999 and 2002 were important to this chapter. Mark Naftalin and Tom Bradshaw of the Great America Music Hall were important sources.

Also, see, Cameron Crowe, "Van Morrison: I'm Not A Rock & Roll Performer," **Rolling Stone**, August 30, 1973. For Nathan Rubin. See Joshua Kosman, "Nathan Rubin—Concertmaster For Decades In Oakland," **SFgate.com**, October15, 2005
https://www.sfgate.com/bayarea/article/Nathan-Rubin-concertmaster-for-decades-in-2601869.php
and "Remembering Nathan Rubin-Master Violinist And Populist," **East Bay Times**, January 27, 2006.

https://www.eastbaytimes.com/2006/01/27/remembering-nathan-rubin-master-violinist-and-populist/

On the Caledonia Soul Express, see, for example, Robert Christgau, "Another Moving Van," **Robertchristgau.com** March, 1974 for a post on the Felt Forum show in New York where the Caledonia Soul Express backed Morrison. The Christgau short piece was an interesting one. He wondered if Van was "an unprecedented original" or "an undisciplined weirdo." As one of my favorite early rock critics, Christgau told it like he saw it. He was an original critic who ignored the fawning reviewers. Christgau wrote that **Astral Weeks** "is still considered unlistenable obscure by many astute observers...." But Christgau wasn't through with the cute criticism. He used faint praise in describing the Belfast Cowboy. "Morrison has written some of the greatest lyrics in contemporary music, but his verbal attack, is often oblique." The point is this criticism had little, if anything, to do with Van's shows.

Clinton Heylin, **Can You Feel The Silence?: Van Morrison, A New Biography** (Chicago, 2002), chapter 17 and Johnny Rogan, **Van Morrison: No Surrender** (London, 2005), chapter 16 were important for background material. The website for Van concerts, musicians and general knowledge operated by Gunter Becker was instrumental in this chapter and helped to correct many errors. http://ivan.vanomatic.de/shows/1973-12-19_regular.shtml

On Morrison's music, see, the brilliant study by Peter Mills, **Hymns To The Silence: Inside the Word And Music of Van Morrison** (London, 2010), pp. 209-216. Mills, a Professor at Leeds Metropolitan University, is not only a seasoned scholar, he has insights few possess into Morrison's creative mantra. His book is a sophisticated analysis of Morrison's writing genius.

Professor Mills asked the key question: "What is the point of a live album." (p. 209). Why does he ask this question? Mills makes the point live rock 'n' roll albums were souvenirs or left overs. Few people took them seriously. They were a symbol or suggestion you were at a live show. They were dreadful pieces of music. Without directly making the point, Mills suggests Van's difficulty, considering the technology, in producing the perfect album. But Mills concluded he did.

A few exchanges with Tim Kovatch helped this chapter as did conversations with a number of musicians requesting anonymity. Alice Stuart was an observant musician who, not only opened Van's shows, sat by the side of the stage drinking in every moment of his performances, but she shared the joy of performing with Van in half a dozen interviews.

See the **New Spotlight**, August 9, 1973, volume 7, issue 7 for a brief reference to the mystery surrounding the cancellation of the last two tour shows.

Van was tired. Ray Ruff theorized he was ready to mix the live double album. Mervyn Solomon believed Van wanted to avoid Ireland, as the fans who came down from Belfast to see him were drunk, rowdy and unpredictable. Solomon blamed the end of the It's Too Late To Stop Now tour on Van's quasi manager, Stephen Pillster, who Solomon called "a rank amateur."

Ritchie Yorke, **Van Morrison: Into The Music** (London, 1975), chapter 11 detailed Van's approach to the back breaking series of concerts that was the It's Too Late To Stop Now tour. The extensive interviews Van sat for with Yorke were ones he came to regret. Yorke, whom Van liked and remained friends with until his death, sat for interviews in which Yorke failed to interpret the key aspects of Van's career to 1975. In writing the book Yorke sought Van's approval. At least this was Van's view. Yorke begins his chapter on the tour by suggesting Van did it for a live album. That was only a part of the reason. Another reason was Van was determined to polish his concert act. Yorke never dealt with this issue. In fawning prose, with hints of hagiography, Yorke's long, detailed description of what he called "the mound of myths" surrounding Van's stage presence was a disaster. Van a Vancouver British Columbia show and he wasn't able to explain Van's stage magic. Yorke didn't research his Marin County shows. He writing was sophomoric and, frankly at times, embarrassing. A good example was when Yorke wrote: "It was widely believed Van was an alcoholic, a dope addict (this was particularly claim since it was felt that no artist could create such powerfully emotional music without drugs), given to falling off stages in his drunken stupor, a timid tipsy gypsy of sorts." (p. 113) Van was mystified. This quote was meant to curry favor with Morrison. It infuriated him. The seeds of media dissatisfaction were sown by a journalist Van considered a friend. There was some acceptable reporting in Yorke's book. Van told him he was tired of the managers, the promoters, the stage managers and the press.

Carol Guida provided background on Marin County, as well as Van's interactions in the mid-1970s with everyone from music insiders, label moguls, bookers, musicians and close friends. Guida helped me to understand Morrison's complexity. Charlie Musselwhite provided some anecdotes as did Barbara Mauritz concerning Marin County's fertile creative atmosphere.

FIFTEEN

IRELAND CAME CALLING: CAROL GUIDA AND A DEFINED CREATIVITY

"Van Morrison is singing 'Cyprus Avenue' On the car stereo system when we turns into Mourneview Car Park."

LEONTIA FLYNN

VAN'S 75th BIRTHDAY SETS THE TONE FOR HIS LITERARY INFLUENCE

On Van Morrison's 75rth birthday, Gerald Dawe observed Van's prose was linked to Belfast writers. That link, Dawes emphasized, was one where Van inspired a bevy of fledgling local writers. His songs were an inspiration to a generation of Irish literary types. Dawes was an aspiring musician. It was the Belfast Cowboy's lyrics which opened the road for Dawes to evolve into a man of letters, a University professor, an outstanding poet and a literary critic with enormous skills. Dawes suggested that Van was the foundation point or the progenitor for a generation of Irish writers with Belfast themes.

Why was Van's 75th birthday special? It was a time when Belfast intellectuals, musicians, aspiring writers, local historians and literary types celebrated his lyrics. Invariably, many of the images adopted were from the 1970s. All decades of Van's career inspired him. The earliest defining decade, the 1970s, produced songs like "Moondance," "Caravan," "Domino," "Come Running," "Warm Love," "Into The Mystic," and dozens more defining Van. On his 75th birthday Raven Eye recorded a version of "Into The Mystic." This band, with its roots in garage rock and the blues, paid Morrison the ultimate comment. The lead singer and guitarist Oli Brown credits Van's influence for his career.

What did emerging Belfast writers have in common with Van? Lucy Caldwell's love story "Here We Are," is filled with images, lyrics and a feel for Belfast right out of the Morrison playbook. The image of Cyprus Avenue stands out with young Belfast writers.

Van's literary influence was all over Northern Ireland. Chris Michie recalled: "Ireland came calling for Van, Belfast defined his creativity."

Leontia Flynn is an Irish poet reflecting Van's music. The Bangles, Neil Young, Karen Carpenter and Patsy Cline among others are name checked in her poetry. Van Morrison is one of her favorite writer. Not musician! Flynn name checks Belfast much like Van. She said she learned this from Van's lyrics.

David Ireland is another Belfast playwright feeding on the fountain of Van's lyrical brilliance. Ireland told the **London Guardian** "as a writer I want to be socially irresponsible." He names checks Van's influence as has Wendy Erskine. The norm is Belfast writers, due to the Troubles, as well as what they perceive as a misunderstood or disrespected history, lash out with social challenges and contrarian viewpoints.

Van's inner creative soul was formed from the same influences fledgling writers experienced. That is he read Jack Kerouac, wrote in a similar vein, and in time he found his unique literary voice.

Belfast never left Morrison's psyche. East Belfast remained a boost to his creativity. Morrison's name checking influenced a younger generation of writers.

Leontia Flynn wrote:

"And Old song splays on the radio
I am captured in a car seat.
On the points of summer and youth."

That said it all. Flynn's evocative poetry was straight out of the Van Morrison songbook. Van's territory was Hyndford Street, Abetta Parade, Grand Parade, the North Road and Orangefield. Belfast provided a continual boost to Van's creativity. For six decades he name checked his birth city. Cyprus Avenue remains the street in which the locals walk down to recall their nascent past. Everyone who writes in Belfast has a Cyprus Avenue tale.

CREATIVITY & CAROL GUIDA: RECALLING VAN

While living in Fairfax, Van missed Belfast. His parents warned him the Troubles were not a place for Protestants. They moved to Marin County. After his divorce, and the success of the It's Too Late Stop Now tour, he needed a vacation. His back hurt. He had a congenital back problem. He needed a rest. He had few thoughts his future. until he called a Marin County professional registered massage company. He needed a licensed masseuse. His back was killing him.

Van had back problems from his youth. One leg was shorter than the other. He wore lifts in his shoes to alleviate the pain. Corrective shoes didn't help Van's back pain. He found relief through professional massages. The medical profession had no answers for Morrison's pain. Massage alleviated it. Enter Carol Guida.

As they worked together medically, Van said: "I am going to write a song for you." Carol was impressed. "This guy was getting to me," Guida continued. There were other concerns. Van's manager was an obstacle. "Stephen Pillster wanted to get rid of me," Carol continued. "'You Don't Pull No Punches, but You Don't Push The River' is all about me. It was one of the first songs Van wrote when we arrived at Sutton Place." The trip to Dublin in October, 1973 was a window into Morrison's songwriting.

Carol discussed Vans' use of autobiographical and environmental influences on his writing. As I interviewed her, she loved recalling the songs on **Veedon Fleece**. "We were also really into Meher Baba," Guida recalled.

Being positive remains to this day one of Guida's strengths. "I was always positive around him….'Comfort You' was written for me."

When Guida met Van, she wasn't a rock and roll aficionado. She thought the **Tupelo Honey** album was overrated. She was educating herself in the ways of classical Indian music.

Carol Guida: "I met him when I was a licensed massage therapist." Then Van and Carol fell in love. He wrote songs for her. He intimated she was his muse. "People who have written that he was broken up by the divorce don't understand Van," Guida continued. "He thought the world was against him."

After two massage treatments, Van said: "I have a proposal for you. I want to hire you as my personal massage therapist." Carol was taken back. He was a client. She reluctantly agreed. After a while Carol thought, this guy is getting to me. Then out of the blue Van asked her to go with him up to California's north coast for the weekend. "We became soul mates," Guida told a close friend. That was it. She became his fiancée. They planned a trip to Sutton Place, a luxury hotel outside of Dublin. That was followed by a leisurely drive around Ireland.

While in Ireland, Van proposed. After taking the pictures for the **Veedon Fleece** album, the photographer shot a large number of engagement photos. Carol has a large cache of pictures. She described the scene in her in-progress memoir.

Van Morrison

BACK IN IRELAND AND RETHINKING THE FUTURE

When they returned from Ireland, it was late October, 1973. The vacation prompted Van to privately reassess his Irish heritage. It re-charged his creative batteries. It would be almost a decade before he moved permanently back to the U. K.

Chris Michie: "One day out of the blue, Van reminisced about his trip to Sutton Place. He said he channeled songs. He couldn't believe it. Something came over him. He couldn't explain it." Sutton Place inspired Van. It was a romantic Irish setting. A good friend, Donal Corvin, was there. Carol Guida loved the place. Van relaxed.

According to close friends, Van ruled out a return to Belfast. The Troubles remained. He loved Northern Ireland. He realized he couldn't return. Van considered other living options. London and the English countryside entered his psyche. When he was Them's lead singer, Van lived in London's Notting Hill Gate. With its numerous record store, university oriented coffee shops and small eateries, it was a creative mecca. It was the perfect setting to write and develop his music.

The Notting Hill area of London continued to intrigue him. In lyrics, Van mentioned Notting Hill Gate in Them's "Friday's Child." Ladbroke Grove was another landmark he immortalized in song. By the 1980s, Van was living at times in or near Notting Hill Gate. His autobiographical lyrics tell a story of his time in West London. The local record stores was where he searched out Bobby Blue Bland, John Lee Hooker, B. B. King and Sonny Terry and Brownie McGhee records were abundant in nearby shops. He intimated it was not as rewarding as perusing records in Mill Valley at John Goddard's Village Music. The lure of Marin County never left Van. He returned regularly. He purchased a home in Mill Valley on Laverne Avenue. It was his temporary residence. He still owns it. Shana lives there.

VAN'S WANDERLUST: LOOKING FOR MARIN COUNTY IN ENGLAND'S COUNTRYSIDE ON INTO THE 1980s AND VAN'S INFLUENCE ON LITERARY TYPES

The frenetic relocation was a lifelong trait necessary to finding new writing sources. After he lived in Marin County, for most of the 1970s, he relocated to a London suburb Oxfordshire, then to a land-locked county in South East England. Oxfordshire is located near Oxford University. Ironically, unbeknownst to Van, he lived in a setting providing inspiration for a novel.

A Morrison fan, Andrea Kayne Kaufman, wrote a novel, **Oxford Messed Up**, featuring an older Rhodes scholar and an underachieving musician who became friends. They shared a college bathroom and Van Morrison's music. This 2011 novel suggested Van's influence on the literary community. Kaufman's novel won the Gold For Best Adult Fiction E-Book. The academic world and Morrison's music collided.

Andrea Kayne Kaufman is a lawyer-college professor heading the Doctoral and Master's Program in Educational leadership in Chicago at DePaul University. She has a Harvard pedigree. She is a brilliant scholar celebrating Van's music in a fictional form. Her book is a tribute to his musical performing style. Her novel centered around a romantic relationship fueled by Morrison's music. One critic remarked: "There is no reason to include the words of Van Morrison on every page." That is unless your writing is fueled by his lyrics. Van's trademark was paramount.

The majority of novels influenced by Morrison's songs are set in the countryside. Van purchased a county home in the late 1980s.

It was in the bucolic, tree lined village of Little Somerford in the English countryside near Alsbury. The area bore an eerie resemblance to Marin County.

In the English countryside, Van's evolutionary intellectual growth continued. In "Summertime In England" Van pays tribute to the influence of William Wordsworth and Samuel Taylor Coleridge. He name checks the voice of Mahalia Jackson. Stream of consciousness writing by James Joyce is echoed in Van's words. He said of "Summertime In England," "it isn't a song it is an epic poem." The intellectual aura of Marin County wafted through the air. Van's business office in Somerford brought a new found expertise to controlling his intellectual property. He set up Exile Productions in 1987. While he worked out of Bath, he created a complex business structure. Exile Productions became a sophisticated arm of his business empire. This influence came from Marin County. A local lawyer, Bob Gordon, as well as the wisdom in business Bill Graham imparted and what Van observed navigating the waters of the music industry led to the first steps to corporate expertise. These influences created "Becoming Van Morrison."

Van operated efficiently in a quiet, and a rural setting. The coffee shops, fellow musicians, a girl friend and business associates accentuated his productivity. His search for seclusion, isolation and environmental impulses made his songwriting successful. Pat Corley labeled Van "a country poet." He was right. Marin's tree lined streets, the small town pubs, the tea and the coffee shops and a quiet countryside provided isolation for blissful creation. He needed to have people around who understood his music. The surroundings enhanced his songwriting. In the U. K., Van looked for a Marin County setting. Whether it was intentional or not Somerford was closest to this environment. What he experienced, in and around Fairfax, intensified what Van needed to create in the U. K. Van learned intellectual lessons in California he carried to the U. K. Equally important were the business lessons. Van was a quick learner when it came to protecting his intellectual property.

Initially, when Van returned to the U. K., it was to Notting Hill Gate. He found temporary peace and solace there. Then he relocated to Oxfordshire and Somerford. It was as much for business as personal reasons. These were temporary stops. Before relocating to Ireland, Bath provided the atmosphere for Van's writing.

VAN IN BATH: IS IT THE NEW MARIN COUNTY?

While living in Bath, Van discovered the Woolhall Studio near Beckington. It was a stately English building dating back to the 16th Century. In the 1980s it was converted into a recording studio by the pop group Tears For Fears. After recording five albums there, Van purchased the studio in 1994. How does this relate to the 1970s? Woolhall provided a similar atmosphere to that he was used to while recording in Marin County. This small, home studio was perfect. He would enter it any time. It was a respite from the rigors, distractions and bothersome intrusions from the music business. The lessons he learned in Marin County continued to direct him as a writer and producer in the Woolhall Studio.

Bath was a marvelous town. It was quiet, rural and frightfully conservative. There was an air of English indifference. Van purchased a five bedroom townhouse in St. James Square. This is one of Bath's more beautiful, prestigious and expensive neighborhoods. It is a short walking distance from the downtown coffee shops. It was perfect for Van's daily writing. It is Bath's only residential square. Privacy ruled!

Van's home had a walled garden providing security. The view was on the park side of the square. The walled garden led to a gate where he could walk into a communal garden. Quiet! Reflective! Comfortable! A ten minute walk to a coffee shop for a cup of tea and to read the newspaper was an integral part of his day. Morrison loved it. Charles Dickens lived here. This was a fact not lost on Van.

Van was trying to relax. This surprised his close friends. His blue-collar work ethic had gotten in the way of his daily life. The early 1970s creative output exhausted him. He was on a mission to songwriting perfection. For almost twenty years, Van created in and around Bath. What did Bath do for his creativity? Was it the new Marin County?

As Pat Corley observed of Morrison: "He was a nature poet." Bath's beauty was its hidden urban atmosphere with nature nearby.

The business offices in Bath were a short walk from where he set up Exile Productions.

While living in Bath, Van had anonymity. A record store, Raves From The Grave, in nearby Frome, was a place for Van to purchase blues records. When this record store opened in 1997, it was popular with collectors. Van also found a similar shop in Trowbridge where he purchased **Melody Maker** and the **New Musical Express**.

Bath was home to some of Morrison's investments. He allegedly had a small share in a restaurant, a wine shop, Raincheck, and the sightings of Van in and around Bath were many. He loved the calm, relaxed pace of life.

It was through tension, adversity, a driving blue collar work ethic and an anger to prove his detractors wrong that he wrote with bursting creativity. His friends had no idea the level of his intellectual depth. Those who knew him saw it bloom daily.

VAN ON THE NEED TO RELAX

"I got to the point where music just wasn't doing it for me anymore, a point I never thought I'd reach. I hadn't taken time off before and something was telling me to knock it off a bit. I caught up on years of sleep...when you're committed to a series of concerts you lose all the spontaneity...."

VAN MORRISON IN CONVERSATION WITH ROBIN DENSELOW, LONDON GUARDIAN, JUNE 21, 1977.

WHAT DID THE IRISH VACATION DO FOR VAN?: CAROL GUIDA'S INFLUENCE

The strange part of the October 1973 Irish vacation, with Carol Guida, was he had no desire to visit Belfast. Northern Ireland was off limits. It was the Troubles. He was apolitical. It was dangerous. He needed to rest. He hoped to recharge his life. To write songs for a new album was his top priority.

After stops at Cork, Cashel, Killarney, Arklow and Galway, Van returned to California. His parents were living in Fairfax. His dad was about to open a Fairfax record store. The record store sold classical and jazz vinyl. No rock 'n' roll. There was one exception. Van Morrison records were sold.

The Irish vacation evolved into a writing spree. Due to the local countryside the seeds of **Veedon Fleece** were sown. Van had a habit of pulling up songs from the past, rewriting them, and then recasting the images. He has never said if he did that for **Veedon Fleece**.

Once he returned to Ireland, he wrote a batch of new songs. He was seen working in coffee shops. **Veedon Fleece** was the album he wrote to recall his Irish past. There was an emptiness to Van when he wasn't writing. When Carol Guida entered his life that changed. They talked about what they read. The new songs reflected Ireland. There was a bit of Marin County in the songs. The twist of Ireland dominated.

"Country Fair" highlighted his Irish visit. Van wrote he "watched the river flow," he reflected on youth, love and lost opportunities. The soft, acoustic feel to "Country Fair," with its Celtic flair, announced a new songwriting direction. Erik Hage suggested Van demonstrated "renewed poetical confidence and a direct nod to actual literary influences." This was in part due to Carol Guida. Morrison read and thought along literary lines. He wrote fervently of things Irish.

Because of his wide range of his reading, his interest in spiritual matters, his need to be a centered writer, he devoured books on personal growth. One writer, Barry Stevens, introduced Van to Gestalt Therapy. She developed her own brand, known as Go Gestalt. Her voluminous writings intrigued Van. She was self-educated. Her work was linked to Fritz Perls, Bertrand Russell and Aldous Huxley.

HOW DID BARRY STEVENS INFLUENCE VAN?

How did Barry Stevens inspire Van's writing? It was not only as a writer, but as a Gestalt therapist. Her publications were highlighted in a 1970 autobiographical journey through Gestalt Therapy. Her 1970 book **Don't Push the River (It Flows By Itself)** was a description of her education in Gestalt Therapy. She urged anyone who was anxious, uptight and tense to consider ways "to deepen and expand" personal growth. Van heard the message. He immersed himself in it. He subscribed, according to Carol Guida, to Stevens' philosophy.

Stevens immersed herself in Zen Buddhism. The philosophy of Jiddu Krishnamurti, and the study of Native American religious rituals completed her education. She became a cult figure in the 1970s. The Human Potential Movement was a counterculture spinoff with a message. It was a simple one The HPM's claimed undiscovered talent could be developed for a life of fulfillment, happiness and creativity.

The Beatles' George Harrison was a HPM advocate. For Morrison HPM's refusal to accept mainstream psychology and organized religion drew his attention. Aldous Huxley was an HPM advocate. The Esalen Institute became a well-known human potential educator. What attracted Van to the HPM? It was the message that you controlled your intellectual destiny.

It was Barry Stevens who provided the answers to his self-education intellect. She was deemed a guru. She was uncomfortable with fame. She was shy. Van recognized a kindred spirit. Morrison read deeply in Gestalt Therapy. He found answers to many things personal and professional.

After reading Barry Stevens and William Blake's **the Book Of Urizen**, Van decided on the October 1973 trip to Dublin to write songs for a new album. With Carol Guida by his side, he drove around the Irish countryside. It was there, with Carol Guida's inspiration, he took charge. He needed to write songs to recall the bucolic Irish setting. He was in the midst of forming his intellect. He found it by reshaping Steven's book into a lyrical tribute to his life with songs influenced by her writing.

"You Don't Pull No Punches, but You Don't Push The River," opened up his psyche. In a nine-minute plus song, Steven's book was an inspiration for Van's journey to Ireland. As Morrison wrote the song, his Celtic heritage rushed into his psyche. He made his initial reference to William Blake. "We read William Blake together. We talked about it," Carol Guida recalled. Literature was a point of departure. Inclusion, references and name checking followed.

As Van drove with Guida, along the west coast of Ireland, he imagined the "**Veedon Fleece**." What was it? Van has never said.

Steve Turner argued it was Van's version of the Holy Grail. Johnny Rogan saw it as a love song. Barry Stevens wrote a book, **Don't Push The River (It Flows By Itself)**. It was an inspirational moment. Van read her book. He conceived a song. Viola! The title was a tribute to her book. Clinton Heylin quoted Van as "channeling" the song. Van told Chris Michie; he was channeling her philosophy. Michie believed "You' Don't Pull No Punches, but You Don't Push The River" was written for Carol Guida. The evidence supports his comment.

BARRY STEVENS: VAN'S GURU

Barry Stevens wrote: "We must turn ourselves upside down and reverse our approach to life." Van remarked of Barry Stevens that her writing, her use of Gestalt theory, and her thoughts on self-education emboldened him. When he picked up her book **Don't Push The River**, he found his guru. Van was not about a guru. His interest was in her writing. "I was also reading a couple of books at the time...there's a bit of Gestalt theory in it, too...." The part about the Gestalt theory was Steven's way of drawing Van into her theories. He wrote a song about her using a portion of her book title.

On "You Don't Pull No Punches, but You Don't Push The River," he credits Stevens as the inspiration for the song. What makes "You Don't Pull No Punches, but You Don't Push The River" special? It is the collaboration with studio musicians who were new faces in the warm confines of his Fairfax home studio. The guitar player, Ralph Walsh, added a different touch. He was a seasoned blues artist. Walsh was also a vocalist. His work with the Paul Butterfield Band was outstanding. He was more than just a traditional blues guitarist. The tune was dominated by Walsh's acoustic guitar. The understated bass by David Hayes became a staple of Morrison's 1973-1974 sound. The drums by Dahaud Shaar provided Van a steady stage presence. The understated piano from James Trumbo completed the sound. After the initial recording, Jef Labes added the string section and a flute which included Nathan Rubin, James Rothermel, Teresa Adams and himself. The reviewers labeled this song the "nine minute masterpiece on Veedon Fleece."

DON'T PUSH THE
RIVER
Barry Stevens

Who was Barry Stevens? She did more than inspire Van's song? She was an early guru to his expanded creativity. He never met her. He never hung out with her followers. Her ideas nurtured him. She was a guru in absentia.

Stevens lived to be eighty-three. When she died in 1985 her work as a Gestalt Therapy was hailed as one that helped her develop a unique form of Gestalt. This intrigued Van. Stevens was a guru to the Human Potential Movement. She transformed Gestalt in the 1970s into a babble of psychotherapy. Why would Van follow her? He recognized a fellow traveler.

Stevens was shy. She was a contrarian. She seldom accepted praise. She was cranky. She was aloof. She was egotistical. She was difficult. Stevens was also a high school dropout. This intrigued Van. Fritz Perls, the noted German born psychiatrist, described Stevens as "a natural born therapist." Van was intrigued by Stevens first person writing. Her books reminded Morrison of how he composed. He constructed his lyrics with a detached personal touch. Stevens was a woman asserting herself in a male dominated profession. Van loved this aspect of her character. She was a contrarian with a different view of the world. Van's disdain for journalists was legendary. Stevens had the same feeling. Need anymore be said?

IRISH TELEVISION AND VAN

After the October 1973 Irish vacation Van and Carol Guida flew home. The vacation invigorated him. He wrote furtively. She was the literary muse who discussed in-depth philosophy. Their travels provided the name checking necessary to Van' songwriting. Dublin, Cork, Cashel, Killarney, Arklow and Galway completed the visual imagery running through **Veedon Fleece**.

After returning to rest in Marin County, Van and Carol Guida flew back to Dublin to appear on an RTE show on November 2, 1973. The twelve days at home were restful ones. "Van was never happier than when Carol Guida was around," Nathan Rubin noted. He was contacted by Talk About Pop, a show that ran briefly on RTE.

Van's Talk About Pop appearance was a solo acoustic performance. What was Van's motive? He told everyone it was to increase record sales. Or was it about Ireland? Or was it about an acoustic show?" It was about all these things.

Van's apprehension increased due to the RTE host, Tony Johnson. He was known to put guests on the spot. He upstaged them. Van asked his friend, Donal Corvin, to show up for the taping. The Irish setting was a perfect one. A friendly welcome. A positive reception from friends. A culpable press. Still Van had misgivings. Those thoughts centered around the presenter, Tony Johnson, who asked inane questions. Van watched as Johnson spent more time getting his hair done rather than concentrating on the questions he would ask Van.

After Van met RTE host Tony Johnson, his uneasy feeling intensified. He was in a Dublin studio for a taping. The host was too eager to make an impression. Van was on another short holiday. But work was always a consideration. He brought along a Belfast friend, well-known journalist Donal Corvin. That helped Van control the RTE interview. Morrison and Corvin took over the interview.

On November 2, 1973, as Van recorded the Irish television program, Talk About Pop, he was happy, relaxed and in love. His fiancée, Carol Guida, was smart, philosophical and drop dead gorgeous. She sat where Van could see her as the show unfolded. "We were never apart," Carol Guida continued. "If he couldn't see me, he would stop the show."

As a returning hero, Van sat in the RTE Studios in Dublin smiling. He was at ease. Carol Guida was an important reason for Van's calm nature. She worked her magic on the RTE hosts. His factotum, Donal Corvin, sat nearby smoking, a drink in his hand, while he eye balled the ladies. RTE asked for a set list. They wanted some latitude in selecting what to broadcast.

Van prepared a lengthy set. He performed thirteen tunes, only five "Wild Children," "Slim Slow Slider," "Warm Love," "The Drumshanbo Hustle" and "Autumn Song" were broadcast. The other eight songs, included a marvelous version of "The Wild Side of Life," were not on the air waves. There is a bootleg of the concert. These songs would be heard shortly on another Irish TV show. Van's relaxed countenance was a stark contrast to media reports of a contentious soul with a chip on his shoulder.

To reward his audience, he performed new material. "Autumn Song" was introduced. He seldom performed "Slim Slow Slider." It was in the set for only the third time. Another new song, "Wild Side of Life," bewildered the audience. Few knew it was a Hank Thompson tune from 1951.

When Tony Johnson jumped in, with his puerile smile, there was tension. Johnson suggested there were rumors Van didn't like playing in Ireland. Morrison looked at the presenter with a scowl. Then Corvin took over the interview. Van had fun with the press. He was in a comfortable setting. He didn't waste his time. Corvin asked him about the insidious press reports. They shared a moment of quiet mirth. Johnson was sent to the wings. He fluffed his hair and angrily departed. Later he would return to the show with frightfully nasty questions. The press report reported Van was difficult.

"That's the media," Van continued. "The reason you get all that stuff is through the media because people print things without ever talking to the actual person." Touché! Someone in Van's management agreed to a Dublin concert without talking with him. It was allegedly Stephen Pillster who booked the concert on his own. He never asked Van. Rather than throw Pillster under the bus, Van said he hadn't agreed to a series of Belfast concerts. Pillster remained on the payroll. He should have been fired. More than half a dozen people in Van's inner circle remarked Pillster's job was over his head.

WHAT DID TALK ABOUT POP DO FOR VAN?

The Talk About Pop appearance was a turning point in Van's U. K. career. Why? Van was alone in the studio. The Caledonia Soul Orchestra was at home. His audio performance, with an acoustic guitar, was brilliant. "Becoming Van Morrison" was the result.

The show began with "Wild Children." He quickly segued into "Slim Slow Slider." Then Donal Corvin inquired of Van: "You changed your style an awful lot since **Astral Weeks**." Van looked dumbfounded. He answered: "No, not really. I think the style is the whole trip. It's a lie, from that one (Astral Weeks) through all the other ones I do everything…it's all the same except it's released at a different time." Corvin looked confused.

Then Tony Johnson jumped in requesting "Warm Love." Van played it. Corvin took over. Van looked at Johnson like he was a pretty boy presenter. He was! Corvin asked about the soon to be released double album. Van mentioned Ray Charles, Sam Cooke and Sonny Boy Williamson cover songs on the album. He explained the importance of these artists. Then the interview took a strange turn. The last thing Van talked about was Bang Records, Bert Berns and the lack of royalties from "Brown Eyed Girl."

Corvin said: "Good old Bert," in reference to the Bang Record impresario. Donal elicited a critical response from Morrison as he discussed "The Drumshanbo Hustle." Van said: "I got the title from a town we played when I was with a showband one time. We were being ripped off in those days…like they do if you're a musician." As Van paid tribute to his showband days suggesting his professional nature was nurtured there.

During the Talk About Pop taping, Tony Johnson set Van off by intimating he was difficult. "Why would I have a chip on my shoulder? People have a lot of misconceptions about everything. We have always had this publicity that for some strange reason Van Morrison doesn't want to play to the Irish people." Morrison continued. "That's the media. The reason you get all that stuff is through the media because people print things without ever talking to the actual people. They make money out of that, columns in papers and stories in papers, they sell. Especially rock 'n' roll magazines-that's how they make a living, most of it is just rubbish but people love to buy it and read it." It was hard to argue Van was wrong.

The solo acoustic performance Van delivered for Talk About Pop was his quest for exposure through television. He could appear without his backing band. When Van performed "I Shall Sing," it was previously with a big band with horns. The Talk About Pop selection made it a new version. That became Van's mantra. Redo old songs in a new, legitimately reinterpreted manner with a new creative direction.

MARK JORDAN ON WORKING WITH VAN: EASY OR NOT? AND FREEBO'S LEGACY

Van's collaborators were extremely important to his personal development. He writing became more sophisticated. Many were educated in a traditional University setting. Others learned on the job. They were professional musicians writing songs from an early age. There was one Morrison musical cohort with a degree in English literature, an appreciation for good music, and a studio expertise he expanded in many directions. His name was Mark Jordan. He was the prototype of the University graduate with musical expertise. Literature and music poured from every portion of his creative persona. He was the perfect Morrison musical collaborator.

MARK JORDAN

Mark Jordan was not your typical Marin County musician. How did he break the mold? It began with a B. A. in English literature from the University of Pennsylvania. At Penn, he was in the Men's Glee Club. Then he co-founded Philadelphia's Edison Electric Band. As a composer and keyboardist Jordan had few peers. It was on the Hammond B-3 organ that Jordan stood out for Morrison. Rock and rollers loved the Hammond B -3. He remained with Van until 1979.

What was it that attracted Morrison to Jordan? It was the 1970 Edison Electric Band album **Bless You Dr. Woodward**. This album featured covers of Percy Mayfield's "Please Send Me" and Doc Pomus's "Lonely Avenue." The majority of the album songs were originals, which Jordan co-wrote with Joshua Rice and Daniel Friedberg, known as Freebo. He was a member of the band. Freebo went on to work with Bonnie Raitt from 1971 through 1979, as well as performing with Ringo Starr, John Mayall, Aaron Neville, Dr. John and Crosby, Stills and Nash among others. Freebo's bass line on Maria Muldaur's "Midnight At The Oasis" attests to his studio creativity. He continues as a creative force in the music industry.

Jordan played keyboards with Bonnie Raitt. He wrote for her. In the 1970s, Jordan lived and worked in Marin County. He played on the **Moondance** album. In 1979 Jordan was a key member of the **Into The Music** recording unit. Jordan, along with guitarist Herbie Armstrong and bassist David Hayes, were mainstays in Morrison's 1970s Marin County musical evolution.

Warner signed Jordan to a record deal and his 1978 album **Mannequin** was brilliant. It featured a cast of high end session musicians as well as future stars including Jeff Porcaro, David Foster, Donald Fagan, Tom Scott and Larry Carlton. The operative wisdom was Jordan had a brilliant future. He achieved it as a writer, a session musician and as a producer.

Everyone I interviewed concerning the 1970s recalled Jordan and Freebo. They were described as the quintessential creative types populating Marin County. "Van benefitted from them as I did," Chris Michie said. The well-educated musicians, with new ideas for song structure, populated the area around Fairfax.

When Jordan looked back on his time recording, performing and working closely with Van, he was proudest of his barrelhouse piano on the early 1970s recordings. The versatility with Jordan demonstrated came when he worked with Lyle Lovett, Taj Mahal, Big Al Downing, Buddy Guy, the Judds and Link Wray. It doesn't get more eclectic than that.

The shuffling of new musicians, along with the old standbys, was a key to Morrison's musical evolution. Morrison was not easy to work with in the studio. That is unless you hit the right notes. Then he was a prince. There were a few of the old standbys remaining in the band. Mark Jordan, recorded for the 1970 **Moondance** album, as well as the 1971 **Tupelo Honey**. Then on **St. Dominic's Preview** where he had an even closer working relationship with Van. These early years defined his worth to Van's productivity.

What was Jordan's contribution to Morrison's music? It was in production. He knew sound. He knew how to make it perfect. On **Tupelo Honey**, his piano provided the album with a barrel house boogie tone. Throughout the 1970s Jordan was with Van every step of the way. He was influential on "Listen To The Lion." He remarked there was no need to worry about "Listen To The Lion's" length. That may have been the push Van needed to record a longer eleven minute version for **Saint Dominic's Preview**.

In the San Francisco Bay Area, Jordan was a mainstay in Van's bands. His genius was shown in Van's cover of Louis Prima's "Buena Sera, Senorita." It appeared like a Morrison original thanks to Jordan's interpretive excellence and production clarity.

Throughout the years, Jordan has spoken of the ease of working in the studio with Van. He explained it. The majority of sessions musicians had no trouble with Van in the studio. He selected them. They did the job. The creative latitude Van accorded his musical cohorts in the 1970s was one reason for his evolution. They had unstinting praise for working for him. Van, said Jordan, was idiosyncratic. That was a small price to pay for working with him.

Jordan suggested you defined Van's mood and creativity by his idiosyncratic methods. "It is a kind of challenge to your musical abilities," Jordan continued. "Van expects you to run through a new song once and get it." Jordan loved that about Van.

Like many musicians, Jordan had problems because Morrison does not read or write music. The problem was while the lyrics were brilliant, there was difficulty recording some songs without charts.

"I gigged with him many times but I think the highest I ever got was when I jammed with him at his home one night," Jordan continued. "Just he and Doug Messenger on guitar. He ad-libbed both lyrics and melody and just totally blew us way. He's a genius."

This description suggested how Morrison operated in the studio. Those who worked with him described him as a musician, arranger, producer and songwriter who was the entire package. His inability to read music is a minor problem. It is only the mixing the Belfast Cowboy's disliked.

When Jordan played piano in 1979 on **Into the Music**, he was an eye witness to Van's studio growth and maturity. Jordan provided once again a barrelhouse boogie direction. This was important for Van in the 1970s.

Bibliographical Sources

This is a reflective chapter on how and why the Caledonia Soul Orchestra, Mark Jordan, and a myriad of influences brought Van's career into a new popular direction. His commercial success was guaranteed. The sources for this chapter were largely interviews.

For Mark Jordan, and his role in Van Morrison's early 1970s music, see, for example, Bill Holl, "The Musical Sparks of Van Morrison," **The Washington Post**, September 5, 1979.
https://www.washingtonpost.com/archive/lifestyle/1979/09/05/the-musical-sparks-of-van-morrison/f6a16d96-6a03-4aaf-b05d-e562a3ca08fa/
The Holl article is a review of the **Into The Music** album.

For Barry Stevens' influence, see, for example, **Don't Push The River (It Flows By Itself)** (n. p. 1970), passim and D. Kranz, **Barry Stevens: Leben Gestalten** (bibliographical article in German, 2011). Carl Rogers and Barry Stevens **Person To Person** (Lafayette, California, 1967). The Real People Press was founded by Stevens and Connirae Andreas to promote Gestalt Therapy. See, Clinton Heylin, **Can You Feel The Silence?: Van Morrison, A New Biography** (Chicago, 2002), pp. 279-281 for the period in which Barry Stevens' influences led to Van's early 1974 concert brilliance. Heylin neglects to show her impact upon his writing, his continual intellectual development, and how her Marin County popularity, as well as her Gestalt Theory contributions, were a major influence on Van's writing, his career and his personal life. Carol Guida's influence as Van's muse is another significant fact missing from Heylin's otherwise brilliant analysis of the **Veedon Fleece** interlude.

Also, see, Pat Corley, "Van Morrison & Literature," March 3, 2021, http://patrickmaginty.blogspot.com/2021/03/van-morrison-literature.html

For Irish writers influenced by Van see, for example, Gerald Dawe, "Van Morrison And 'The Power Of Naming': How He influenced Belfast Writers," **The Irish Times**, August 31, 2020. https://www.irishtimes.com/culture/books/van-morrison-and-the-power-of-naming-how-he-influenced-belfast-writers-1.4324800

Chris Michie is known more for Van's music in the 1980s than in the 1970s. But he spent hours telling me about Van reminiscing about the mid-1970s. Michie was very favorably impressed by Carol Guida and her lack of interest in Van's money, Michie said: "She was truly a soul mate." Michie also spent a great deal of time describing how Van thought and how this influenced his music. Because he lived for a time as a very young man in London, Van felt close to Michie. Michie played briefly in a cult Marin County band, Lamb, which had a major record deal. He got to know Van when Lamb opened for him on a brief Pacific Northwest tour. As a free-lance guitarist he played with Boz Scaggs, Maria Muldaur, Jerry Garcia and Link Wray among others. He also toured with and was the musical director for David Soul when the "Starsky and Hutch" TV star attempted an abortive pop music career.

Michie hooked up with Van almost accidentally. He was a last minute replacement for Chris Hayes of the Huey Lewis band when Van recorded "Cleaning Windows." Van was impressed. They remained musically and personally in touch until Michie's untimely death of melanoma in early 2003. Michie lived in Fairfax near Van and they were frequently in touch. Michie's uncle, Professor Jerry Pressler, was big help with the material for this chapter.

See Andrea Kayne, **Oxford Messed Up** (Chicago, 2011) for references to Van Morrison's music in a novel. Of Morrison, Professor Kayne writes: "Van Morrison's lyrics were poetic genius as well, but his bluesy, soulful, and often improvised melodies not only calmed but inspired." (p. 5). Then Kayne goes on to quote Greil Marcus. Remember this is a novel. It attests to the breadth of Van's musical influences.

This chapter was aided by the extensive reminiscences of Nathan Rubin and a brief comment from his on tour roommate Tim Kovatch. On the It's Too Late To Stop Now tour, Joe Smith and Stan Cornyn told me about Van and Warner Bros. in brief interviews. A few conversations with Mark Naftalin about performing with Van and Tony Dey's description of him in the studio helped to formulate key portions of this chapter. The Ivanvanomatic website provided a treasure trove of information. http://ivan.vanomatic.de Art Siegel over the years provided anecdotes and many were used in this chapter.

John Collis, **Van Morrison: Inarticulate Speech Of The Heart** (New York, 1998) is the best book on Van's maturity in the studio and his growth as a songwriter. Collis also presents evidence of Morrison's concert growth.

For Van in Bath there is an unusually well-written, carefully researched, filled with inside information and poignantly observed article by Pat Corley, "Van Morrison And The City of Bath," **Quiet Days Just A Hobby On The Internet**, May 29, 2019.

http://patrickmaginty.blogspot.com/2019/05/van-and-city-of-bath.html

For Van's attraction to the Human Potential Movement, see, for example, Jessica Grogan, **Encountering America: Humanistic Psychology, Sixties Culture And The Shaping Of The Modern Self** (New York, 20913. Also, see, Christopher Lasch, **The Culture Of Narcissism: American Life In An Age of Diminishing Expectations** (New York, 1979).

For a tribute to Van's 75th birthday and his influence on local Belfast writers see, Gerald Dawe, "Van Morrison And 'The Power of Naming': How He Influenced Belfast Writers," **The Irish Times**, August 31, 2020. https://www.irishtimes.com/culture/books/van-morrison-and-the-power-of-naming-how-he-influenced-belfast-writers-1.4324800 One of the relevant points of the Dawe article is how he connects Van to Stewart Parker's **Dramatis Personae** in which insights into Van's early East Belfast roots are explained. Parker was a pet, a pop columnist, a playwright and a devotee of popular music emboldened by Van Morrison's lyrics and music.

SIXTEEN

THE CALEDONIA SOUL EXPRESS AND VAN RETOOLING THE SOUND: NAPPY BROWN, FAIRFAX AND CAROL GUIDA: A 19 MONTH TRANSFORMATION

"When Van played Nappy Brown's 'The Right Time' he was honoring a pioneer Black songwriter while paying tribute to Ray Charles' cover"

CHRIS MICHIE

"I sat next to Van as he took cassette tapes and turned them into an album. We talked. He worked. It was unbelievable."

CAROL GUIDA

"If you don't like it. Go fuck yourself."

VAN MORRISON REMARKING TO THE MONTREUX AUDIENCE, 1974

WINTERLAND
Bill Graham's
WINTERLAND
FEB 2
VAN MORRISON
INTO THE MYSTIC
TICKETS FOR ALL SHOWS AT
BILL GRAHAM'S
COLUMBUS

What was Christmas 1973 like for Van Morrison? It was a time of happiness. He was sitting with the love of his life, Carol Guida, in a new home in the San Geronimo Valley. His visitation rights brought his daughter Shana regularly to stay. The wholesome family atmosphere calmed Morrison. He was putting the finishing touches on the **It's Too Late To Stop Now** double album with Carol Guida sitting next to him in his Fairfax home studio.

Van was organizing cassettes from the It's Too Late To Stop Now tour. Warner Bros. was listening to some of his suggestions. Joe Smith told Mo Ostin; he saw Van's new commercial direction. It was a positive one with steady sales. "He was happy," Joe Smith continued. "He was easier to work with." Van was also in love. Carol Guida was a constant companion. She was a muse to his creative direction.

Long before the holiday season, Van finalized the album. He was planning his future. The plans for a new backing group percolated. He was emboldened by the It's Too Late To Stop Now tour. Careful planning took over. He had an epiphany. That is he didn't want the music business to dictate his life. He also didn't to become, what he termed, the flavor of the month.

From Christmas 1973, until he appeared on July 29, 1974, at the Knebworth Music Festival, Van intensified his songwriting. He refined his performing. He solidified his place in the music business. The hard work paid off. He was "Becoming Van Morrison."

The last few weeks of 1973 were idyllic ones for Van. The tapes for the new double live album **It's Too Late To Stop Now** were being produced for an early 1974 release. Van's idea of relaxing was to play locals shows. After a brief show at Berkley's Keystone Corner, Van appeared for two shows on December 21, 1973, at San Francisco's Great American Music Hall. He couldn't resist introducing a new song that fit his life. "Don't Look Back" was played for the time as a reflection of his post-divorce life.

WHAT DOES WONDERFUL REMARK TELL US ABOUT VAN MORRISON?

Time, place and environment created many of Van's songs. Many of these songs were unreleased. They provide a window into his psyche. In 1973-1974 Van had too many things modifying his career. His personal life was uneven. When he wrote "Wonderful Renmark," in 1973 it wasn't released until 1983 on **The King Of Comedy** soundtrack album.

The lyrics are another window into his thoughts. He wrote the lyrics in his comfortable Fairfax hilltop home. The lyrics, as Van said. were about a difficult financial time. This took place as he and Janet were living in New York. "It was about people who were supposed to be helping you and they weren't there. It was about the business I'm in and the world in general. A lot of times you can't count on anybody."

The future Van Morrison was shown when "Wonderful Remark" was recorded with Bill Church, Ronnie Montrose, Boots Hughston and Lee Charlton. The song was included on **The Philosopher's Stone**. Later, Van re-recorded it with Robbie Robertson, David Hayes, Richard Tee, Jim Keltner and Nicky Hopkins. "Wonderful Remark" was first recorded during the "Moondance" sessions. The August 1969 cut languished. This was typical Van.

Once again, Van was looking to the past to re-imagine his future. The melody for this song was based on a Bang 1967 song "Joe Harper Saturday Morning."

VAN: JANUARY 1974: STILL WORKING ON THE STAGE SHOWS

In January 1974, as Van's growth as a songwriter and performer accelerated, his increasingly on stage independence led to brilliant small venue shows. What that meant was simple. The hours spend redoing his stage act at the Inn of the Beginning, the Lion's Share and one show at the Church in 1973 honed his craft for the first six months of 1974.

From January 11 through May 24, 1974 Van was on the road constantly. In addition to numerous American shows, he performed in the U. K. and Europe. When he returned to Marin County Van took only eleven days off before he took the band into nearby San Anselmo for two nights at the Lion's Share. What was going on? Van was crafting his stage act to ultimate perfection. That mania for performing perfection came from the musical jungle that was Marin County. You could find more successful musicians living there than bankers or businessmen.

Marin County influences dominated. All around Van musicians were honing their craft. He watched. He was inspired. That creative atmosphere increased his writing confidence. These were traits apparent to close friends. Marin County was a laboratory for his future.

Whether Van consciously planned his future career direction, or simply followed his intellectual muse, is unimportant. What is significant is he continued to experiment with backing groups because he needed a specific sound. When those who passed Van's audition, and either recorded or toured with him, they invariably commented they were hired due to a specific sound Van needed. This was more important to him in the studio than while touring.

He worked hard in the studio. He returned from the It's Too Late To Stop Now tour to finalize the live album immortalizing his on the road genius. With Carol Guida by his side he produced the **It's Too Late To Stop Now** album.

He looked to scale down the eleven piece Caledonia Soul Orchestra. The five piece Caledonia Soul Express emerged. The growth of his live performing was evident when he headlined the 1974 Montreux Jazz Festival without his own band. Claude Nobs at Montreux cobbled together a makeshift band. Van was brilliant. Nobs didn't take credit. He said it was Morrison's ability to connect with first class musicians. This was followed by a brilliant show at the Knebworth Music Festival.

In roughly nineteen months from January 1973 through July 1974 the frenetic pace of Van's creative growth highlighted his blue collar work ethic. This established his permanent stardom. That was Marin County's influence.

ONCE AGAIN, THE RETURN TO FAIRFAX: PHASE TWO, THE CALEDONIA SOUL EXPRESS

When Van returned to Fairfax to spend Christmas 1973, with his daughter, Shana, and Carol Guida, he had a plan. It was to put together a small backing band. Marin County was a fertile creative field. The extraordinary musicians allowed him to seek out new musical directions. Van decided to go back on the road with a five piece band. The Caledonia Soul Express was born in this moment of inspiration.

After he listened to the tapes from the It's Too Late To Stop Now tour, he sat with Carol Guida in his home studio, it was cold, Van was excited. He knew he had a set of special analog tapes. They highlighted the hard work he put into the tour. The extensive performing and the brilliant selection of musicians made for a live sound that didn't need overdubbing or other studio tricks. When the album was released, Van produced a double vinyl masterpiece.

The fiscal and logistical nightmare of the Caledonia Soul Orchestra ended in a flurry of publicity. Van was bone tired. The CSO was shocked when he ended the tour cancelling the last two dates. "He didn't want to do it anymore. We got checks and went home," Tim Kovatch said. Everyone didn't believe it when Van dissolved the Caledonia Soul Orchestra.

THE CALEDONIA SOUL EXPRESS

The Caledonia Soul Express was a streamlined version of the CSO. With the new band, he went into the studio recording a 45 "Caledonia" backed with "What's Up Crazy Pup," which Warner Bros. released in Germany in 1974. No one has ever explained the release of Caledonia without the E. Ray Ruff, Chris Michie, Tony Dey and a host of others said: "It was Van being Van." It was a cover of the Louis Jordan song.

"What's Up Crazy Pup" is an example of how the historical awareness of the American West crept into Van's psyche. As Van told those around him "sometimes a song is just a song." A compressed, chanting vocal makes it hard to disagree with the Belfast Cowboy. He also wanted to give the Caledonia Soul Express a chance to record.

The question of why a slimmed down version of the Caledonia Soul Orchestra was formed was never answered. It didn't matter. The Caledonia Soul Express was in Van's grove. What is known is musicians were eager to play or record with Van due to his sumptuous creativity. There were other reasons. Van's creative nature demanded change. He continued to redo his musical backing. He looked to write in new directions.

BACK IN FAIRFAX PLANNING

In Fairfax the Belfast Cowboy turned his critical attention to business matters at Warner Bros. His album sales had fallen off since the early 1970s. He believed there was an inconsistency to Warner advertising. Mo Ostin told Van, a few months earlier, they had spent an inordinate amount of money promoting his material. There was an internal Warner Bros. shake up in the advertising department.

Industry insiders claimed Warner believed Van was a cult artist. Some at the Warner public relations office were not receptive to his repeated requests for increased advertising. This was a part of the corporate structure he disdained. Ray Ruff said top Warner executives, Joe Smith and Mo Ostin, viewed Van as erratic. They couldn't believe he sacked the Caledonia Soul Orchestra. The strain at Warner between Van and the label, Ray Ruff said, was a continuous one. "It was a soap opera drama."

The quick formation of the Caledonia Soul Express was the antidote to the successes of the Caledonia Soul Orchestra. That was Morrison. Anytime he had success he broke it down. Those in the industry, in the media, and in and around Marin County counseled, Van to keep the CSO together. They didn't understand his quirky creative nature. He wasn't blowing up success, as some critics charged. He followed his intellectual mantra.

BACK ON THE ROAD: THE CALEDONIA SOUL EXPRESS

On January 11, 1974, after two shows at the University of Houston, Van introduced the Caledonia Soul Express. This lean five-piece group brought a stripped down sound that lost little in concert.

The Caledonia Soul Express backed him perfectly on "Mystic Eyes," "Brown Eyed Girl" and "Gloria." Reaching into his catalogue, Van optimized his concert box office. He made his point. He could tour with either an eleven or a five piece band.

On January 16, 1974, as Van appeared at the Armadillo World Headquarters in Austin, Texas, he was performing before a new audience. This alternative musical center welcomed him with open arms. This venue was famous for breaking the 13th Floor Elevator.

Then the band flew to the Cowtown Ballroom in Kansas City, Missouri, where Van experimented with covers including Harry Nilsson's "Everybody's Talking." Local roadies were not above providing a board tape for the bootleggers. The $100 they received was a nice bonus that made Morrison one of the 1970s most bootlegged concert acts.

Cowtown Ballroom, Kansas City, Mo.–January 17, 1974: BOOTLEG CD Description

The quality of this bootleg CD is very average. The band was reduced in size and is more reminiscent of the Caledonia Soul Orchestra. "Don't Look Back" is a cover of the classic John Lee Hooker song. The fans loved a Them inspired version of "Mystic Eyes."

Setlist: Ballerina, Friday's Child, It's All Over Now Baby Blue, Don't Look Back, These Dreams Of You, Heathrow Shuffle, Into The Mystic, Ain't Nothin' You Can Do, I've Been Working, Take Your Hand Out Of My Pocket, Warm Love, Mystic Eyes, Brown Eyed Girl, Domino, Gloria, Cyprus Avenue, Caravan.

The Lineup: James Rothermel – saxophone, Dahaud Shaar – drums, James Trumbo keyboards, Ralph Walsh – guitar, David Hayes — bass

Van brought along Carol Guida. He introduced her as his fiancée. While in Austin, Van went out the see Yurt Town. It was a settlement that attracted a motley group of philosophers, teachers, designers, artists and ne'er do wells. He was asked what he thought of it? Van didn't comment. His silence told it all. He couldn't stand phonies and poseurs. Van remarked: "If something is going to save the world, that something has to pass several tests. One of those tests is, it's got to work in New York City."

WHAT WAS THE CALEDONIA SOUL EXPRESS? INSOUSIANT CREATIVITY!

The Caledonia Soul Express was a tight backing band who were more of a traditional rock 'n' roll unit with a blues tinge. Johnny Rogan failed to describe or analyze the CSE. Instead he argues that Van disrespected former flutist John Payne at a show in Boston. Why did Rogan ignore the Caledonia Soul Express. The answer is a simple one. He never envisioned or interpreted Van's musical changes while he was living in Marin County.

The major biographies pay scant attention to the Caledonia Soul Express. This was a mistake. Despite the death of recording with the CSE, Van benefitted from the free flowing in concert backing and the experimental nature he was accorded when performing with the group. Clinton Heylin dismissed the group in three pages and Johnny Rogan has four pages on the CSE. They treated it like a temporary aberration. It was another example of Van's insouciant creativity. Insouciance is a relaxed happy state of mind with no feelings of worry or guilt. That described Van in Marin County.

While not receiving the critical acclaim of the Caledonia Soul Orchestra this five piece aggregation was dynamite. They had a jazz-blues direction Morrison loved.

Ralph Walsh was a blues guitarist. He displayed jazz overtones. He played with and recorded with the Paul Butterfield Blues Band. He had a contract with Elektra Records. When he signed on with Van, he gave his name as Wash because he had an exclusive deal with Butterfield. He was so versatile he even worked with Todd Rundgren.

Walsh was more than a sideman. He wrote. He produced. He mixed songs. In the studio and on stage in his interaction with Van, he was a creative force. Walsh, who for some unexplainable reason in the recording studio, listed himself as Ralph Wash, teamed up with Morrison's rhythm section of bassist David Hayes and drummer Dahaud Shaar. James Trumbo came in on keyboards. James Rothermel on saxophone completed the group.

Why the Caledonia Soul Express? Van never said. The operative wisdom, according to Chris Michie, was Morrison was interested in a different recording unit. It was not just about concerts.

Walsh was the key to the new sound. He performed with Van from December 13, 1973 until May 21, 1974. On the fifty one shows with Van his guitar stretched the shows into new directions. Walsh provided a pedigree from the Paul Butterfield Band that accentuated Van's sound into a more pronounced blues direction.

The first performance of the Caledonia Soul Orchestra was a radio spot in December, 1973, on KZEW, in Arlington Texas. This was a college station operating from the University of Texas, Arlington. This promo spot publicized Van's forthcoming appearances in the Lone Star State. The first real gig came on January 11, 1974 at the Houston Room on the University of Houston campus.

The Caledonia Soul Express continued until May 21, 1974, when they played their final show with Van at Pittsburgh's Syria Mosque. They backed Van effortlessly.

There were many highlight shows with the Caledonia Soul Express. The ones Van enjoyed were on college campuses. He felt the student vibe. The venues were intimate. When he appeared in the Ballroom of the Student Center at Kent State, it was his only Ohio appearance. There were only two thousand seats available. The five dollar tickets sold out quickly.

THE RETURN TO SAN FRANCISCO: EARLY 1974

Before the Caledonia Soul Express disbanded, they played legendary shows. Their best ones were in the San Francisco Bay Area. By this time Bill Graham was attempting to manage Van. The five

ACPB Presents

VAN MORRISON

with the Caledonia Soul Express

In Concert: Thursday, May 16

Ballroom - Student Center

Tickets :
Available only at the Student Center Box Office
for $5.00
Only 2000 tickets available on sale starting today
Buy early or you won't get one

THIS IS VAN MORRISON'S ONLY OHIO
APPEARANCE THIS YEAR!!!

piece Caledonia Soul Express headlined a San Francisco show at Bill Graham's Winterland Auditorium. The bootleg CD suggested how much Van admired Bob Dylan. Van performed an excellent cover of "Just Like A Woman." This bootleg CD caught everyone's attention. For the first time, he performed "The Streets of Arklow" with Ralph Walsh's brilliant guitar. He yearned for Ireland. The capacity crowd gave Van two standing ovations. There were calls for "Brown Eyed Girl." There was a smile as Van left the stage.

Located near the Fillmore district of San Francisco, Winterland was one of Morrison's favorite venues. It was cavernous, but comfortable, with a stage apart from the audience and plenty of room for the crowd. It had great acoustics. Bill Graham Presents managed the shows with precision.

The balcony seldom had people. Van loved the audiences. He was able to craft the shows anyway he desired. At Winterland Van performed more cover records. The stoned out audiences were so mellow they often thought it was his song.

The nearby Fillmore nightclubs, restaurants and coffee shops were a mecca for musicians, late night intellectuals and a bohemian crowd. The Fillmore was an African American section of San Francisco experiencing gentrification. The remnants of the rib joints; the nightclubs, the blues taverns and the street people remained. Van was often seen walking along Fillmore Street after a Winterland show. He was just another guy looking for good music, some barbecue and a beer. Van's anonymity didn't last. Van realized too many tourists, too many new clubs, and the luster, vigor and musical vibration of the Fillmore turned from blues and jazz morphed into rock and roll. He was a jazz-blues guy who still found these venues in the Fillmore.

His fans were also some of the San Francisco Bay Area's most noted bootleggers. When I completed my book, with Lee Cotton, **Jailhouse Rock: The Bootlegs of Elvis Presley**, for Pierian Press in 1983, I visited legendary Zaire and Haik Arakiel to look over their Van Morrison bootlegs. The result was a collection of some of the best club concerts in and around the San Francisco Bay Area.

Winterland, San Francisco, CA–February 2, 1974: BOOTLEG CD Description

This is a unique bootleg with atypical songs including "Streets of Arklow." There is also a brilliant version of Bob Dylan's "Just Like a Woman" and a bluesy "Try for Sleep" (released on **The Philosopher's Stone**) with Van singing in a high falsetto.

Setlist: Ballerina, Streets of Arklow, Just Like A Woman, Try For Sleep, Into The Mystic, I Just Want To Make Love To You, Moondance, These Dreams Of You, Listen To The Lion, Wonderful Remark, Warm Love, Help Me, Here Comes The Night, Gloria, Caravan/You Don t Pull No Punches, Cyprus Avenue.

The Lineup: James Rothermel – saxophone, Dahaud Shaar – drums, James Trumbo keyboards, Ralph Walsh – guitar, David Hayes – bass, backing vocals: Dorothy Morrison, Bill Combs

After an appearance in Southern California, Van flew to Boston where he appeared in two shows at the Harvard Square Theater. The bootleg CD of the Harvard March 14 show included interesting new songs "What's Up Crazy Pup," a cover of Ray Charles' "I Believe To My Soul," and a raucous closing version of "Cyprus Avenue" were highlights.

There was a provincial Irish feeling to Van's set. Like San Francisco, the Boston audience was familiar with his music. The Irish hollering out in the audience drove Van's show to new heights. He pulled out versions of "Domino," "Brown Eyed Girl" and "Moondance" prompting an uproarious audience response.

The time in Boston was special for Van. He loved the city. The old days on Green Street provided fond memories. His friend, Peter Wolf, of J. Geils fame, showed up to recall the magic of the late 1960s. The restaurants and clubs were another drawing card. Much like the Fillmore district in San Francisco, the area in Cambridge surrounding Green Street had a nostalgic feel to it.

Before he left for the U. K., Morrison appeared at New York's Felt Forum. The mid-March show was reviewed by John Rockwell in the **New York Times**. Rockwell concluded the cappella quintet, the

Harvard Square, Cambridge, MA–March 14, 1974: BOOTLEG CD Description

Once again there was an excellent version of "Streets of Arklow," as well as a unique performance of a song that he seldom performed live "What's Up Crazy Pup?"

Setlist: Ballerina, **Astral Weeks**, Streets of Arklow, Madame George, Brown Eyed Girl, Ain't Nothin' You Can Do, These Dreams Of You, Warm Love, I Believe To My Soul, What's Up Crazy Pup, I've Been Working, Moondance, Domino, Caledonia Soul Music, Caravan, Gloria, Cyprus Avenue, You've Got The Power, Caledonia

The Lineup: James Rothermel – saxophone, Dahaud Shaar – drums, James Trumbo- keyboards, Ralph Walsh – guitar, David Hayes — bass.

Persuasions, who opened the show for Van were an "opening act (that) doesn't matter so much." He had no idea who the Persuasions were or why they were on the bill. One of America's premier rock critics had not done his homework.

Then Rockwell observed Van who was known to be "an on-and-off performer...was quite remarkably on." Rockwell continued: "His work has a calculation to it that earns enormous respect." At the time Rockwell was the dean of American music critics. Dave Marsh was working for a small outlet **Creem**. Robert Christgau was establishing his legend. Greil Marcus, the Shakespeare of Telegraph Avenue, was working on his magnum opus. Praise from Rockwell in the prestigious **New York Times** was the supreme compliment.

On March 16, 1974, Van appeared at The Capitol Theater in Passaic, New Jersey. Terry Reid followed by the Persuasions opened the show. Van brought out an eclectic set. He stunned the crowd with "Moondance" and "Brown Eyed Girl."

After this show he boarded a plane an flew to London. Then five days later to inaugurated a lengthy U. K. tour and eventually was off to Paris. He was exhausted. It was a shaky tour once he arrived in the U. K. Van was by all accounts exhausted. His 24/7 work ethic was bringing the legend out front for all to view.

THE SHAKY U. K TOUR AND ON TO PARIS

He flew to London for a series of shows. He contracted pneumonia. The tour was supposed to kick off on March 21, 1974. This led to the cancellation of six shows. From March 21 through March 27, Van rested. Then it was off to Ireland for four shows in two nights. Dublin's Olympia Theater was one of Van's favorites for its acoustics and audience friendly ambiance.

While in Dublin, he performed "Street Theory," which was destined in 1998 for **The Philosopher's Stone**. This song was performed for only the second time. Van proposed an instrumental album to Warner Bros. They promptly rejected the idea.

The late show on March 29, 1974, was one where Van's health acted up. He had to remain in the dressing room longer than normal. The band played more than a half an hour of instrumental music. Then Van walked out on stage performing "These Dreams of You." A medley of "I Believe To My Soul" and "I've Been Working" was a new offering. The audience cheered with abandon. When Van closed with "Gloria" he had made it through a difficult night.

In Dublin, on March 30, 1974, a twenty-seven minute introduction with instrumentals caused concern. As the crowd grew increasingly restive, rowdy Belfast revelers threw bottles on the stage. Ed Fletcher, the tour manager was arrested for jumping into the crowd, shouting at drunken revelers and swinging at anyone who got near him. He began to beat up those who were trying to storm the stage. When the police arrived, Fletcher was adamant, Van did not deserve this type of behavior. Fletcher was arrested.

The weird part was a train load of Van fans arriving from Belfast with the idea he would soon perform there. No one knew where this asinine rumor originated. It was allegedly due to Stephen Pillster's interviews and his presumptuous behavior.

As Morrison's health acted up, he cancelled shows in Germany before appearing on stage in Munich followed by shows in other parts of Europe where he struggled with a cold or the flu. Or both!

When he arrived in Copenhagen on April 6, his health returned. Van checked into the Trafalgar Hotel. That afternoon he gathered the band to go over the set. The Caledonia Soul Express

assembled for a practice session. Everybody was ready to go. The practice session was at a small bar, the Tre Falke, where the locals watched in awe. Van and the group practiced for a bar of silent but startled, listeners.

A young journalist, Truls Eland, hung out with the band. He was commissioned to write a story. He was training to be a journalist. He was readily accepted by Van and the band. Eland stood in awe during the rehearsal as Van belted out three rhythm and blues numbers during an aborted sound check.

On April 6, as Van appeared at the Falcon Center in Copenhagen, Denmark. it was a cool Saturday night. The crowd arrived early. They were unusually quiet. Van peeked out from backstage. He was amazed at the attentive audience. After Van performed for almost two hours in a twenty-song set, he smiled, acknowledging the crowd. After the show he gave a lengthy interview to Eland. The set included some surprises. There was a cover of Sonny Boy Williamson's, "Take Your Hands Out of My Pocket," a Louis Jordan inspired "Caldonia (What Makes Your Big Head Hard?)" and a medley "Street Theory/Don't Look Back/Since I Fell For You." He closed the show with covers of Louis Prima's "Buona Sera" followed by Little Walter's "My Babe." The audience left ecstatic.

Morrison was in a rare performing mood. He had rested. He was dynamite on stage. With his bushy red hair, a smart looking sport jacket and a fashionable scarf, he conquered Copenhagen.

After a day off, Van performed at the Carré Theater in Amsterdam. The next day Morrison went into the Intertone Studios in Heemstede Holland to cut two songs "Caldonia (What Makes Your Big Head Hard?)" and "What's Up Crazy Pup" for Dutch television.

Then a few days later, Van ended this tour on April 11-12, 1974, with sold out shows at London's Hammersmith Odeon. He opened the first show with an instrumental "Mr. Clean." This was followed by another, instrumental "Song Of The New World," which Van never played again in concert. There was a stunned silence. No one knew the songs. That was because they had never been performed in concert.

Van pulled out one of the most unique, eclectic sets of his career for the next two nights. He performed "Bulbs" and "Caldonia" with new arrangements. The surprise was both nights brought out a stunning version of "Gloria."

The Belfast Cowboy was touched by the admiration for and attention to his music. At the Hammersmith, Van's fans were treated to a rousing cover of Nappy Brown's "Night Time Is The Right Time." When Van realized Ray Charles didn't write the song, he paid tribute to Nappy Brown. With his in-depth knowledge of America's obscure jazz-blues songs, he pulled out a tune from a rhythm and blues pioneer who wrote songs others took to the top of the **Billboard** Pop chart. Van discovered Brown through Marin County musicians.

John Goddard's Village Music in Mill Valley stocked used records from Brown's early careers. The blues purists searched for his records while Van was living in Marin County. There were requests for Nappy Brown to re-enter the music world. He finally did in the 1980s appearing in blues festivals, touring Europe and answering the call from the blues scholars who wanted to share his career. The creative juices that flowed in Marin County attempted to bring Nappy Brown back to performing prominence. He was working a day job and no longer concerned with music.

As Marin County musicians talked of Nappy Brown's return, Village Music ordered what was available of his back catalogue. John Goddard was the catalyst to the Nappy Brown San Francisco Bay Area renaissance. He didn't have an American label. His Savoy records were long out of print. The Nappy Brown renaissance tells us a great deal about the energy in Marin County furthering Van's appreciation of little known artists who deserved to be once again recognized.

Van began hiring those like Jimmy Witherspoon or Charlie Gracie to open for him.

WHAT DID THE NAPPY BROWN'S CAREER AND VAN'S INSTRUMENTALS TELL US?

How deep is Van's knowledge of songwriting? Deep! He loved Ray Charles version of "The Night Time Is The Right Time." The Belfast Cowboy allegedly assumed Ray Charles wrote it. "I told Van that Nappy Brown wrote it," Chris Michie continued. "He looked at me like I was nuts." In his quest to learn more about Brown and the song, Van spent hours looking through books, magazines and talking to people. John Goddard's Village Music populated by a gaggle of record collectors was the center of the Nappy Brown renaissance. Goddard was a record store owner who brought in artists like blues singer Jimmy McCracklin so Ry Cooder could play "The Walk" with him at the Sweetwater. This is what Van loved about Mill Valley. If there was an obscure blues story Goddard was after the truth about that tale. So it was only natural for Village Music to be the center of the Nappy Brown second act.

Brown re-emerged in the late 1970s as a solo artist, when his back catalogue on Savoy Records was bootlegged by record collectors. It would not be until the 1980s that he once again was out on the concert trail. That is when Morrison discovered him.

Van must have had empathy with Nappy Brown. Everyone believed Ray Charles wrote the song. In time, Van knew better. Bob Corritore, a brilliant harmonica player and the owner of Phoenix's Rhythm Room, said it best when he wrote in **Living Blues** that Brown was "singing better than just about any other bluesman currently recording."

Brown, an African American soul artist, with a gospel background, wrote hits others covered. "The reason I went beyond the blues was money," Brown explained. When he started recording in 1954, Brown sounded like an African American Louis Prima. He wrote "Don't Be Angry," covered by the Crewcuts. It peaked at two on the **Billboard** Rhythm and Blues listing and twenty-five on the pop listing. The Crewcuts covered it and it reached fourteen on the

Billboard Pop chart. Brown didn't receive royalties. Brown also had R & B hits with "Little By Little" and "The Night Time." When Ray Charles rechristened it "The Night Time Is The Right Time," he took the song to white record buyers.

NAPPY BROWN (Courtesy Tahoe Tribune)

Brown's pop-gospel voice made him a club favorite. He was never able to maintain a lengthy career due to a label owner stealing his intellectual property. Van's goal was to highlight how badly the industry treated Nappy Brown.

Nappy Brown was a victim of record mogul, Herman Lubinsky. He was never paid his songwriting or publishing royalties. Lubinsky brought in the best New York session musicians with Mickey Baker's guitar featured on his records. At the recording sessions, Lubinsky screamed "Go white." What he meant was for Brown to write and record a cross over hit. Brown was on the road 24/7 to support his family. Nappy was arrested numerous times on domestic abuse charges. He realized he was out of control. He left music and went to work as a maintenance man at John Smith University. He re-emerged in 1972 in with a gospel hit on Jewel Records "Do You Know The Man From Galilee?".

In the 1980s, Brown made a major comeback thanks to European and U. K. audiences. Brown returned to music in 1983 with a brilliant album for the Landslide label. The LP, **Tore Up**, with the Heartbreakers led to a successful tour of Scandinavia and appearances at American blues shows. His Savoy hit, "Piddily Patty" was featured in John Waters film "Cry Baby."

The acclaim Brown missed was highlighted in 2007 when Blind Pig released the **Long Time Coming** album; a reprised Brown's greatest songs featuring Junior Watson, Bob Margolin and other guests. He was on the cover of **Living Blues** in September, 2007. He died the following year. In June 2020 a Google commercial featured Brown's "Open Up That Door." In death he achieved the acclaim denied him in life. A person close to Van told me he identified with Brown.

Why did Van identify with Nappy Brown? Morrison has never commented on Nappy Brown. The operative wisdom is Van loved to perform Ray Charles' "The Night Time Is The Right Time." Brown had his intellectual property stolen. Van has never remarked whether or not he know the Nappy Brown. Since the tale was a part of the record collector mythology, John Goddard's support for Brown and the local bootleggers bringing in his material, it seems likely Van know about Nappy Brown.

In his own way, Van rectified that wrong by performing a version of "The Night Time Is The Right Time" that was much like Brown's. The story of Brown's song drew eerie parallels with Van's experiences.

When Brown wrote and recorded "The Night Time," he sold the rights to Savoy Records owner Lubinsky who sold the rights to Ray Charles. It was alleged a gangster held Brown outside a New York hotel window on the 6th floor until he signed over the rights to the song. Van Morrison could have identified. The Wassel came in many forms.

Taking advantage of Brown, the Savoy label legally compromised his intellectual property. Van not only identified with the story, Chris Michie thought he performed "The Night Time," in the manner Brown did. He was giving Nappy Brown his due. "Van never stopped honoring the pioneers," Chris Michie said.

Throughout his career, Van championed African American artists whose intellectual property was stolen. He hired them as opening acts. He paid them well. He provided first class accommodations, and a car with a driver. He often came on stage for a duet with these legends. Van viewed this as payback for their contributions to his artistic side.

RETURNING TO FAIRFAX BUT STILL PLAYING

When Van came home to Fairfax, he mulled over another brief European tour. Should he go on tour? With the right band, he loved to tour. He formed the slimed down Caledonia Soul Express. There were two members of the Caledonia Soul Orchestra that carried over into Van's future musical plans with band. David Hayes on bass and Dahaud Shaar (David Shaw) on drums. They provided the backbone to the new musical aggregation. They were sympathetic ears to Van's creativity. The Caledonia Soul Express played with Van in a series of successful American dates.

From April 18 through June 3 the Caledonia Soul Express backed Morrison with a frenetic precision. These concerts were important ones. They demonstrated Morrison was happy to be on the road. His appearances increasingly garnered a positive press. His confidence soared. Van needed to periodically alter his band. It was to keep him from getting stale. The creative mantra was helped with Carol Guida on his arm.

After the It's Too Late To Stop Now tour, Morrison's performances were perfection. The nightly changes in his demeanor were positive ones. He caught the nuances the audiences loved. His eclectic approach to live shows saw him vary his sets nightly. That trait remains.

This musical mix created crowd pleasing shows. It was hard work. "Becoming Van Morrison" was not easy.

BACK IN MARIN COUNTY PERFORMING: I LOVE THE LITTLE CLUBS

When he returned to Marin County, Van booked new local shows. He had an idea for a hit song. That song was "Bulbs." He had written, re-written and recorded this song. Never to his satisfaction. He decided to record a jazz version of it. Warner was on board. The minute he talked to Joe Smith; Van was given the green light.

What song did he want to feature? He brought "Bulbs" into the mix. He had high hopes for "Bulbs," as a Top 40 hit, when he went into New York's Mercury Studios in March, 1974 to record it. Carol Guida was by his side. The night before recording it, Van and Carol stayed with drummer Dahaud Shaar and his wife in their New York apartment. Smith brought in two jazz musicians guitarist John Tropea and bass player Jerome Rimson. The session was, according to Smith, reminiscent of the **Astral Weeks** recordings minus the enclosed recording booth. Smith went to a lot of trouble to record the single.

The single wasn't released until November, 1974. This was one example of Van's planning for the growth of his career. "Bulbs" was left off the **Hard Nose The Highway** album. Warner Bros. was there to help promote a potential hit single on **Veedon Fleece**.

"Bulbs" was performed the first time on April 11, 1974, in what was a test run for a chart hit. For the next forty years Van sang it only five times. When it premiered at London's Hammersmith Odeon, Van couldn't tell if the crowd loved it or not. Van had other thoughts don his mind. He looked into his past as he tuned up a new sound in the clubs near his Fairfax home.

The April 18 through June 3, 1974 San Francisco Bay Area training ground was a fertile field for experimentation. He was bringing back old songs. These songs were brought back with new arrangements. The idea was to update the masters and pay tribute to them. Looking back on his career in the 1980s, Van blurted out one day to Chris Michie: "I love the little clubs." As he talked with Michie, Van said the small clubs were intimate with a sense of artistic freedom. He could perform covers of the artists who influenced him.

He loved the call and response in this song. He listened to and emulated Ivory Joe Hunter's "Since I Fell For You." Van found it was a way of using a piano or organ to accentuate his vocals. Ivory Joe Hunter played for years in small cocktail lounges. He performed with a two or three piece back-up band. In later years, it was Hunter and his solo organ lighting up the small, out of the way, clubs he played. Van read about Hunter. He was intrigued how a middle aged African American playing a solo organ most of the time in dead end cocktail lounges could hit the charts so often. With fifteen **Billboard** chart songs over a thirteen year period, Hunter was another American artist intriguing Morrison. The cadence of Van's version and that of Hunter's were similar in some songs Van performed in this period.

A cover of Bob Dylan's "It's All Over Now Baby Blue" honored the Hibbing bard. Van's version of "Caldonia" was one without an "e," it paid tribute to the musical genius and influence of Louis Jordan. Van remained upset with a lack of **Billboard** hits. He shouldn't have worried. The 45 was going the way of the dinosaur.

Just six days after leaving Europe, he performed at Sophie's in Palo Alto. It was an unseasonable windy night when he and the band entered Sophie's. This club at 260 S. California Avenue opened as a Top 40 dance bar. The owners was a music aficionado. He loved Van Morrison. The place was small and the owner never made any money on live music, but he booked it for the college students.

It was April 18, 1974, with Stanford students were everywhere, Sophie's intimate atmosphere energized Van. There was no raucous drinking. Van's fans filled this small restaurant turned night club

with a quiet and serious countenance. This is why Van loved the San Francisco Bay Area.

Sophie's was an upscale venue. It was purchased in the mid-1970s and morphed into the Keystone Palo Alto. It was a mile from downtown Palo Alto. When the Keystone Corner purchased it there was a remodel. It became elegant and corporate. The funky ended. So did Morrison's shows.

Van loved Sophie's for its laid back atmosphere. There was a full bar in the back room with a Stanford coed in a mini skirt serving unlimited drinks. There was plentiful food and there was something to smoke for an illegal smile.

Once it became the Keystone Palo Alto, it lost its charm. The music got broader. The club struggled until 1986. The Keystone Palo Alto was kept alive by the Jerry Garcia Band, with Merle Saunders, and the many nights of the week Garcia played there. Some shows were advertised others weren't and you never knew who would show up to play with the band. Drinks were cheap and the bar was always full. After a series of renovations with a fancy night club look replacing the previously funky décor, Van moved on. So did most of the music fans.

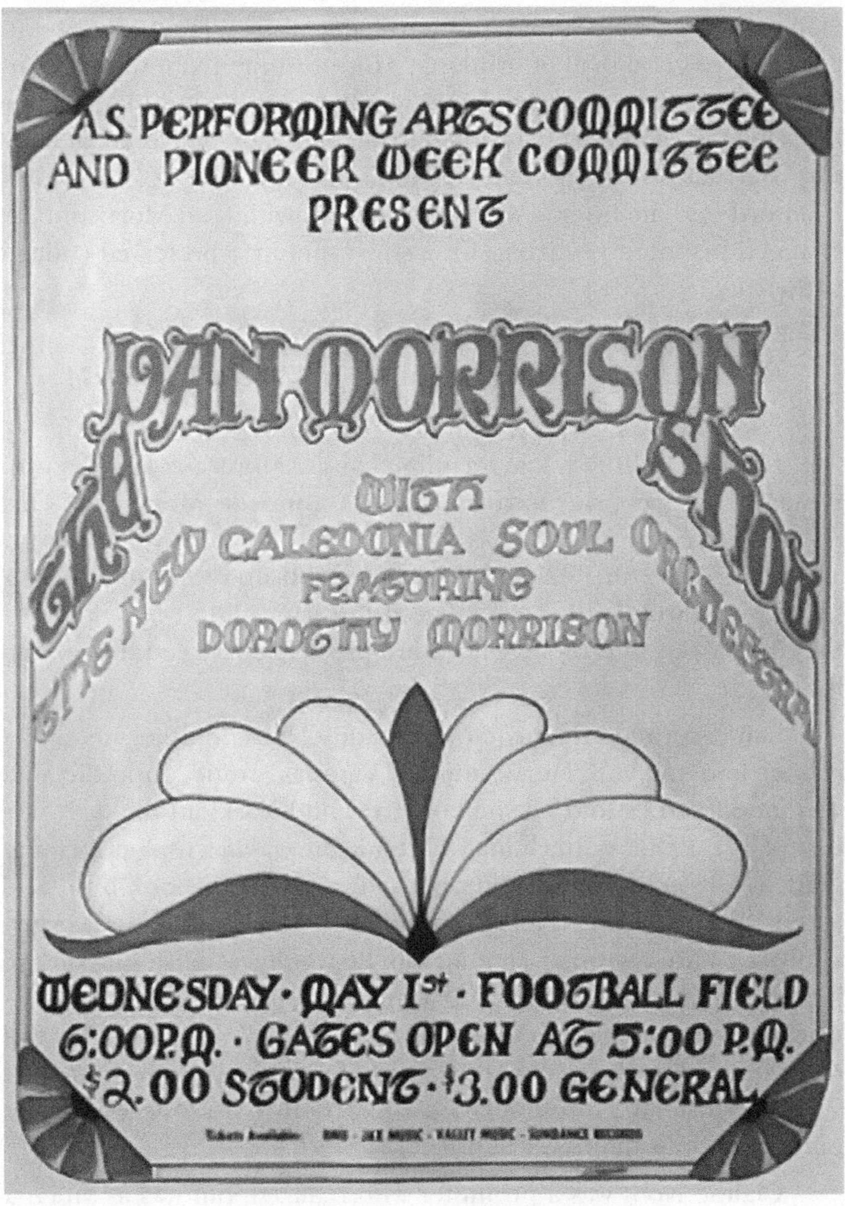

Poster for Van at Chico State College, May 1, 1974

After the Palo Alto shows, which were a two hour plus drive from Fairfax, Van looked for another club his perfect his stage act. He found this venue in San Francisco. The Great American Music

Hall was an art deco venue with perfect acoustics. The fans loved it. There was a great deal of drinking. This prompted Van to quit playing the club when a group drinking all afternoon, waiting to enter the club, became virtually uncontrollable. Van delivered a brief show. He was no longer interested in performing at the GAMH. John Bradford told me no one was easier to work with than Morrison. He changed his mind returning for a short time. He preferred college audiences.

HEADLINING THE MONTREUX JAZZ FESTIVAL, 1974

On June 30, 1974, Van headlined at the Montreux Jazz Festival. It was an elegant site located in the Casino de Montreux. This Switzerland concert venue was a prestigious one. It provided Van an audience of jazz aficionados. He wondered if they were discovering his music. Carol Guida remembered the band didn't practice with Van. He talked with them. They were pros. They backed him effortlessly.

Guida recalled the promoter, Claude Nobs, told her he took a chance booking Van. He was warned Van was erratic, unpredictable and moody. Nobs told her he know it would work out due to Van's love of jazz. It did! With Guida by his side, he was in a top performing mode. Nobs told Carol Guida he had a reason to book him. She asked: "Why did you?" Nobs responded: "I knew Van was a jazz guy at heart. I wasn't wrong." He told Van he would establish him on the jazz circuit. Nobs had a plan. He would book rock 'n' roll acts. Van's brilliant performance brought him back in 1980 and the door was open for a wide variety of rock artists to woo the jazz crowd. In 1974 Van's performance brought rock and jazz into a venue where the purists said it would never happen.

Claude Nobs was a promoter who realized Van was as much a jazz performer as a rocker. In a phone call to Van, he convinced him to fly without musicians, a sound man, a roadie or anyone else and to perform with a pick up band instead. Nobs said his 1974 appearance would establish him on the jazz circuit. Nobs had a long term plan. He would convince Van to return to Montreux. Morrison's plan

- VAN MORRISON -

IF YOU DON'T LIKE IT, GO FUCK YOURSELF

MONTEUX 30.06.74

1.IT'S NOT THE TWILIGHT ZONE
2.I LIKE IT LIKE THAT
3.T FOR TEXAS
4.BULBS
5.BUFFY FLOW
6.HEATHROW SHUFFLE
7.NAKED IN THE JUNGLE
8.STREET CHOIR
9.INSTRUMENTAL
10.SINCE I FELL FOR YOU

ALL COMPOSITIONS BY VAN MORRISON, EXCEPT
" SINCE I FELL FOR YOU " BY LENNY WELCH
BAND : PETER WINGFIELD / keyboards, vocal
DALLAS TAYLOR / drums JEROME RIMSON / bass
VAN MORRISON / lead vocal, guitar harmonica, sax.

Produced and published by LIFE LIVE L - 5801 Hesperange

LIFE LIVE

LL CD 9101

worked as the Belfast Cowboy and has performed there more than twenty times.

Nobs surprised Morrison by requesting he not perform "Gloria" or "Brown Eyed Girl." Nobs didn't share his intention to open up Montreux to a wide variety of blues and rock acts which included a 1977 Muddy Waters show. It was Waters' last Montreux show. An album **Muddy Waters: The Montreux Years** highlighted his legendary blues performances. Waters appeared at Montreux in 1972. Nobs went so far as to have Deep Purple performing alongside Herbie Hancock, Chick Correa and Billy Cobham.

The initial audience reaction to Van was not a positive one. There some cat calls he was a rocker. There were cries of "jazz." Finally, Van screamed: "If you don't like it, go Fuck yourself." He smiled at the vocal young lady with too much alcohol. Then the Belfast Cowboy settled into a performing groove silencing the critics. "The Montreux 1974 show," Chris Michie said, "was proof of Van's versatility. He could perform anywhere on his stage." Carol Guida recalled how well the concert went over. She also had eyes for bass player Jerome Rimson. That didn't make Van happy. He pulled out a set that no one believed. It was Van at his best.

Van performed "Bulbs" at Montreux which preceded a single release scheduled for later in the year in tandem with the **Veedon Fleece** album. Montreux convinced Van his wide ranging writing, his diversity of theme, and his name checking of environment created hit singles for new audiences. That audience, Van imagined, was a jazz one.

He believed there were three songs "Twilight Zone," "Foggy Mountain Top" and "Naked In The Jungle" that were previously unreleased which had unmitigated commercial appeal. Van loved the Montreux experience. He treated the audience with new songs to see how a jazz audience would respond was his goal. These songs did not appear until the 1998 compilation of rarities and outtakes on **The Philosopher's Stone**.

The Montreux appearance was particularly pleasing, as he performed to a traditional, often snooty, jazz audience. While he abhorred the notion of being labeled, he made an exception for the jazz definition. The comments of critics who saw him as a one-dimensional artist were ignored. They were the minority critics. The audience and the press praised Morrison's show. The Montreux show expanded his credentials and after he told a woman to "fuck off," as the crowd listened intently.

The jazz critics loved the show. "The way he altered his phrasing of the lyrics on 'Street Choir' is the kind of ingenuity that made him one of the most remarkable singers of our time," Doug Collette wrote.

THE AFTERMATH TO MONTREUX: CREATIVITY CONTINUES

A week later the band appeared at the Kongresshalle in Frankfurt. The German audience was highly receptive. Van loved the setting. The venue was located in a historical estate. The promoter Freddy Bannister was an eclectic booker and a person of privilege. He was also a fan. Bannister remarked he booked Van because, he told a friend, he needed to make his personal dreams come true.

It was a strange, if wonderful, place to hold an open-air rock concert. The 60,000 who attended the show weren't disappointed. It was one of the best of the early rock festivals.

As the festival opened, it was a perfect Saturday. The English weather cooperated. The musicians were in fine form. On July 20, 1974 the Knebworth show, thanks to Van's performance, was the stuff of legend. Van's seventeen-song set was a festival highlight. The admission price was two pounds seventy five. That was roughly six dollars. This festival also featured the Doobie Brothers, the Allman Brothers, Tim Buckley, The Sensational Alex Harvey Band and the Mahavishnu Orchestra.

Van's first Knebworth show was an attempt to duplicate the American rock festivals. It was five years after Woodstock and promoters were making a great deal of money with open air rock concerts. There was a corporate atmosphere. To pull off a twelve hour show with 60,000 people attending put Knebworth on the rock and roll map. When Tim Buckley opened the show there was an explosion of applause. Van followed him and the promoter made the disclaimer the Caledonia Soul Orchestra would not be appearing. The

VAN MORRISON AT KONGRESSHALLE, 1974

New Musical Express was the only press outlet to criticize Van's performance. "Van looked like a probationary teacher on his first day in the science department of an East End Comprehensive," the **NME** wrote. There was no comment on the songs or the musicians backing Morrison, This was the Van said he wouldn't discuss his music or private life.

WHAT CHANGED DUE TO THE KNEBWORTH SHOW?

For the Knebworth show, Van as dressed in a satin shirt with stylish trousers. He had a confident stage manner. He arrived as a performer. He had the appearance of a stylish performer. That was not the Van of the past. He was "Becoming Van Morrison." He had a new group of backing musicians.

The new band followed Van with ease despite little pre-show preparation. Because of Pete Wingfield's boogie woogie piano, and

Jerome Rimson's Detroit style funky bass, Van never sounded better. Peter Van Hooke joined the group on drums as Dallas Taylor left for other assignments. Rimson, who previously played with the Detroit Emeralds, added a funky bass line. This was previously unknown in Morrison's music. Rimson was a Detroit based African American musician with a jazz pedigree.

Carol Guida loved this show. She was intrigued with Jerome Rimson. After she spent a great deal of time talking with Rimson about jazz. Van sat her in the front row for the show. "He always wanted to see me while he was on stage, if I wasn't backstage, I was in the first row. Once I went to the bathroom and Van wouldn't go on stage until I took my seat."

There was one strange occurrence during the Knebworth Festival. The promoters were worried Van would leave the stage early. He had a rider in his contract allowing him to end his performance if he didn't like the looks, the actions or the demeanor of the audience. Bannister joked he had to pull Van off-stage. He played longer than his contract stipulated. There were a number of British journalists who asked to talk to him about songwriting. "I don't talk about my songwriting. I don't talk about my private life," Van said with a surreptitious smile. He was polite. He was pleasantly cooperative. But the interviews had to be on his terms.

What changed, due to Knebworth? The media recognized, if a bit late, Van's ability to write and perform in an effortless manner regardless of the band. When he closed the show with "Brown Eyed Girl," it was a gracious gesture to a crowd hollering for the song. The eighty-three minute show featured a version of "Bulbs" that drew bursts of applause. A reinterpretation of "Into The Mystic" was another highlight.

In his trailer backstage, Van was besieged by journalists. The press had a renewed interest. Van ignored them. He was angry over past U. K. coverage.

As belated recognition for his songwriting skills accelerated Van felt vindicated. While the press in the past mentioned his prowess as a writer, there was now virtually universal acclaim for his themes. The complexity of Morrison's writing received recognition. It was a sweet time for Morrison. He believed he was getting long overdue recognition.

The bootleg album from Knebworth Bucolic Frolic is a paean to the Belfast Cowboy's artistry. Pete Wingfield's unique piano styling and had an upbeat instrumental tone with a strong boogie woogie beat. The key to Van's performance was that he was not the headliner, it was the Allman Brothers. He answered the call with a sterling set.

Bibliographical Sources

For Van's comments on how and why the appearance at Carnegie Hall, led to the formation of the Caledonia Soul Orchestra and the need to refine his stage act, see, John Collis, **Van Morrison: Inarticulate Speech Of The Heart** (London, 1996), p. 136-137. For

Van's comment on recording "Wild Children" live, and why it was better with the Caledonia Soul Orchestra, than in the studio, see, Ritchie Yorke, **Van Morrison: Into The Music** (London, 1975), p. 11.

Clinton Heylin argues: "'The Great Deception,' 'Wild Children' and 'Snow In San Anselmo' are equally nostalgic...." (p. 265) Heylin concluded these songs were part of Van's plan to make the album more commercial. The truth is more complicated. There were disparate parts to the song. "The Great Deception," which criticized Bert Berns and Bang Records, was filled with other comments indicating what was on his mind while living in Fairfax. Van skewers the Haight Ashbury, Hollywood, Sly Stone and a bevy of artists who irritated him. Getting even in song is a Morrison trait. In "Wild Children," he name checked Rod Steiger, Marlon Brando, Tennessee Williams and James Dean. Why? Only Van can tell us. The operative wisdom is fame impeded their lives as it did his life. After Van observed teens in Boston, Woodstock and Marin County, he wrote his version of young people adjusting to rock music in the lyrics to "Wild Children." He was not yet thirty when he wrote the song. A conservative sage at an early age, according to those around him, wrote songs with a historical eye. Van's ability to describe the unusual, the quirky and the myriad changes in pop culture remained consistent. "Snow In San Anselmo" resulted from driving his car and reading the newspaper. Since he was a teen, Van poured over the daily newspapers. His quest for knowledge was, from an early age, the force driving his songwriting. Van's surroundings and reading dictated his lyrics.

For a brief description of this period, see, Howard A. DeWitt, **Van Morrison: The Mystic's Music** (Fremont, 1983), passim. This book was one where I saw the majority of the American concerts with the Caledonia Soul Orchestra and later the Caledonia Soul Express. Both bands were excellent. The CSO delivered every night due to the symphony trained musicians. The California Soul Express allowed for a more sporadic or momentary experimentation in concert.

Some of the early reporting on the It's Too Late To Stop Now Tour comes from Ritchie Yorke. He had access to Van and to the musicians. See Yorke's, **Van Morrison: Into The Music** (London, 1975), p. 283 for John Platania's remarks on the tour.

For the critics commenting on the 1974 Montreux show and a ravingly positive review, see, Doug Collette, "Van Morrison And Rory Gallagher Live At Montreux," **all about jazz.com**
https://en.wikipedia.org/wiki/Live_at_Montreux_1980/1974

Clinton Heylin, **Can You Feel The Silence?: Van Morrison, A New Biography** (Chicago, 2002), pp.285-287, 291-295, 368, 378 and Erik Hage, **The Words And Music Of Van Morrison** (Newport, 2009) pp. 79-81 provide a setting for and some important information on the 1974 Montreux Festival.

"Wonderful Remark" is a Morrison song with its own creative history. The number of times he reflected on it, after reworking it, is an insight into how he worked in the studio. Van wrote this song recalling his early days in the record business. Chris Michie provided extensive observations, as well as personal insights, in this song.

For the manner in which the It's Too Late To Stop Now tour and album altered Van's stage show, his manner of recording, and his music model, see, Peter **Mills, Hymns To The Silence: Inside The Words And Music of Van Morrison** (London, 2010), chapter 6. When he finished a series of concert dates on July 20, 1974 at the Bucolic Frolic, Knebworth Fayre, Knebworth Park, which is near Steven age, England, Van finalized his on stage persona. The mid-1974 performances were amongst the best of the career. Montreux's joy was reflected in his stellar performance rendering "Brown Eyed Girl" and a new song "Naked In The Jungle" to a rapturous, attentive audience.

Why did Van perform in Knebworth? It was more than the money. "Van told me that Knebworth had a sense of history and a mission and he loved drinking with the promoter," Chris Michie recalled.

Claude Nobs told Carol Guida he was taking a chance booking Van. After the show Nobs sidled up to Guida stating he never doubted Van could win over a jazz audience. When Van arrived at Montreux, he was asked about the Caledonia Soul Orchestra. "I'm experimenting with other things," Van replied tersely. This comment was a window into his interactive soul. As Van's road manager,

Ed Fletcher, told Clinton Heylin: "Van called me up and said: "Eh, we're gonna go to Montreux." Fletcher said: "I will call the guys." Van said: "No!" He would use pick up musicians. Fletcher was flummoxed. Fletcher, Morrison, Guida and for a brief few days Stephen Pillster joined them.

An interview where Van discusses his love for jazz and how he would rather play it than talk about it, see, Giovanni Russonello, "Van Morrison Would Rather Play Jazz Than Talk About It," **The New York Times**, April 24, 2018.
https://www.nytimes.com/2018/04/24/arts/music/van-morrison-youre-driving-me-crazy-jazz.html

A series of interviews with Keystone Corner's management helped to shed light on Morrison's performances. They found him easy to work with and they were amazed he would play for the small guarantees. Keystone employees and management told me he was "a prince."

For a rave review of Van in New York in 1974, see, John Rockwell, "Van Morrison Sings At The Felt Forum," **The New York Times**, March 17, 1974. Rockwell wrote: "Mr. Morrison has produced some of rock's finest songs since he began with the Irish group Them in the early nineteen sixties." This was heady praise from a newspaper not keen on covering rock concerts.

A number of bootleg CDs were instrumental to this chapter. **Van Morrison-1974-04-06 Copenhagen DK (SBD/FLAC)** is a gem helping to recreate that seminal concert. See http://theultimatebootlegexperience7.blogspot.com/2020/12/van-morrison-1974-04-06-copenhagen-dk.html for information on this CD.

The tricky business of putting together concerts for this chapter was helped by Simon Gee's brilliant magazine **Wavelength** and the equally inclusive and reliable German site for Morrison run by Gunter Becker.

For insights into the tour, see, David Browne, "Van Morrison's Legendary 'It's Too Late To Stop Now' Tour," **Rolling Stone**, August 31, 2017. https://www.rollingstone.com/music/music-features/inside-van-morrisons-legendary-its-too-late-to-stop-now-tour-202118/ The Browne article saw Van open up about the Caledonia Soul Orchestra with effusive praise.

For Jay Cocks comments on "Listen to The Lion," see, **Time**, October 28, 1991. The Cocks review compared Van's lyrics to Mose

Allison's, and he concluded in the next song Van could sound like John Lee Hooker. "The sheer force of spirit," Cocks wrote, "is what made it work." Morrison's lyrics, Cocks argued, combined Yeats, Kerouac and Chuck Berry. Like the Shakespeare of Telegraph Avenue, Greil Marcus, Cocks concluded Van had "the yarrrrragh." This is "a mythic inclination." The Irish tenor John McCormack said this identified the great voice from the common ones. Van used the "yarrrrragh" effectively. "Van seems to be sustained by some spiritual essence," Cocks continued. "Van had no time for superficial cool." That said it all.

See, Andy Whitman, "Listening To Old Voices: The Lion In Winter," **Paste**, November 14, 2005 for a summary of Van's career and this period in it. This review was written as Van turned sixty. Whitman speculated why Morrison released three new albums in three years. The article spends time analyzing and discussing 1970s albums calling Van's voice "almost feral in its intensity." Whitman remarks "Listen To The Lion" was "an impossibly idiosyncratic track from Van's 1972 album **St. Dominic's Preview**...." He wrote Van "wrestles his lyrics like a dog worrying a bone...." In convoluted prose and insipid analysis, he makes the point there is no easy way to categorize Morrison. But Whitman does categorize. "Morrison's willful obstinacy and refusal to conform to commercial trends is legendary, and at the peak of his popularity he took a left turn into mysticism, poetry and the power of childhood memory." That is great writing. Since **Astral Weeks** there are many themes Morrison embraced. They are more varied than Whitman described. He continues to mine them. There is no left turn. Whitman praised Van's continued creativity into the 21st century when he observed that three albums, **Down The Road, What's Wrong With This Picture** and **Magic Time** indicated Van's talent continued to accelerate.

For the song "You Don't Pull No Punches, but You Don't Push The River," see, for example, Clinton Heylin, **Can You Feel the Silence?: Van Morrison, A New Biography** (Chicago, 2002), pp. 277-283, Steve Turner, **Van Morrison: Too Late To Stop Now** (New York, 1993), pp. 123, Johnny Rogan, **Van Morrison: No Surrender** (London, 2006), pp, 299-300 and Brian Hinton, **Celtic Crossroads: The Art of Van Morrison** (London, 1997), p. 179. Interviews with session and concert musicians performing and recording with Van helped me to understand this song.

Carol Guida's reminiscences about meeting Van were helpful to this chapter as was her vast knowledge of Marin County. She has a manuscript on her life. She does not discuss any part of her personal intimate life with Van nor does she discuss his private life.

For Van's comment on "Wonderful Remark," see, for example, John McCarthy, "Did Ye Get Healed—How Van Morrison's Music Helped Me Recover My Life," **BBC News**, January 21, 2017. The McCarthy article is a poignant reminder of the aura of Van's music. In his case it was a healing power. McCarthy was held captive for five years in Beirut with Irish writer Brian Keenan. To keep their sanity they talked about Morrison and his music. These conversations kept them sane. They were released. Keenan went to work for the **BBC**. Van knew the story of his horror in Lebanon. When Keenan attended a Van concert years later, he dedicated "Motherless Child" to the BBC documentary filmmaker. Keenan never forgot the humanity Van displayed.

John McCarthy was released from a Beirut prison in 1991. He settled in Oxfordshire. Ironically, Van lived there for a time. As he attempted to put his life back together, after five years in prison, he listened intently to Van's music. One song, "Wonderful Remark" resonated with him. This story has another happy ending when Van Morrison agreed to meet with McCarthy at the Culloden Hotel after a charity event. These types of stories are not rare. He meets with average people, celebrities and those needing a lift in life. He doesn't publicize it. Those I talked with requested anonymity. There is one exception. Van helped a psychotherapist, Bart Hendriks, with his book. Neither Hendriks or Van are interested in publicizing this fact suggesting why Van worked with him.

Van has a soft spot for people who have had a bad experience. His music has gotten them through it. He honors them.

Also, see, David Browne, "#50 Greatest Concerts: Van Morrison, 1973, **Rolling Stone**, July 21, 2017. https://rollingstoneindia.com/50greatestconcerts-van-morrison-1973/

SEVENTEEN

THE IT'S TOO LATE TO STOP NOW ALBUM AND VAN MATURES AS A PERFORMER: MARIN COUNTY PUTS IT IN PERSPECTIVE

"Morrison was in the midst of what was arguable his greatest phase as a performer on vinyl."

JOHNNY ROGAN

"Songs that were poorly performed or were just lame in the first place have more force and tightness here than in their studio versions."

ROBERT CHRISTGAU

"This is soul music in a very real sense."

CHRIS JONES, BBC ON MORRISON'S VOCALS

"I do music from an introverted space...in an extrovert business."

VAN MORRISON

". . . IT'S TOO LATE TO STOP NOW. . ."

In the nineteen months from January 1973 until July 1974, Van solved the problem of concert inconsistency. He worked laboriously on his stage presence in small Marin County clubs. He was determined to play what he wanted in concert. To do this he needed a proper backing band. He formed two stellar groups the Caledonia Soul Orchestra, perhaps the greatest live touring band, and the Caledonia Soul Express. Both aggregations took his shows to stellar heights.

"I'm getting more into performing," Morrison continued. "It's incredible….A lot times in the past I've done gigs and it was rough to get through them. But now the combination seems to be right and it's been clicking a lot."

When he returned home from the It's Too Late To Stop Now tour, Van sat in his Fairfax home studio for months with the analog tapes figuring out what he wanted on the album. The final product changed how music aficionados viewed live albums.

HOW VAN CHANGED THE LIVE ALBUM CONCEPT

Van Morrison single handedly altered how the consumer viewed live albums. Before the double vinyl masterpiece, **It's Too Late To Stop Now,** the in concert album was viewed as a promotional gimmick. For some artists it was a place for leftovers. **The Beatles - Live At The Hollywood Bowl**, recorded in 1964-1965, was not released until 1977. The sound quality was so poor even the bootleggers were embarrassed. Prior to Morrison's double live vinyl classic, there were only a few best-selling live albums. The best example of albums emptying an artist's unreleased material was the Jimi Hendrix's releases. They were dreary left overs form his catalogue.

There were some excellent live albums. The Rolling Stones' **Got Live If You Want It** and their 1970 album **Get Yer Ya-Ya's Out!** were best sellers, and exceptional in quality. The Who's **Live At**

Leed's was brilliant.

The idea for a double live album percolated with Van. He realized his old hits were moneymakers. With versions of "Gloria" and "Brown Eyed Girl," he believed it was important to emphasize his past. These two hits defined him. He was over having a snit at playing these tunes.

Van loved the thought of re-recording songs. Why? He didn't always feel he got it right the first time. He believed a song was better when it was live. So, not surprisingly, in the studio, he would rewrite and re-record songs before their commercial release. "The 'Wild Children' track that we recorded…it's much better than the version on **Hard Nose The Highway**…." Van said. That comment to Ritchie Yorke suggested the interpretive nature of Morrison regarding his recordings.

"Wild Children" was the end result of Morrison's reading. His movie-television interests and his observations on the world were formative influences. Van wrote of his Belfast memories. When he sings "Born 1945" it is a paean to his youth. The phrase "when the river flows" comes from reading the New Age philosophers. The spirituality in Van's life exploded. This took place during the final production phases of **It's Too Late To Stop Now**.

A few examples of the spiritual-religious nature that appeared were "Whenever God Shines His Light," "When Will I Ever Learn To Live In God" and "Dweller On The Threshold." Spiritual songs never abated. What was Van doing? Where was he headed? His later albums **Beautiful Vision**, **Inarticulate Speech of the Heart**, **No Guru, No Method, No Teacher**, **Enlightenment**, **Poetic Champions Compose** and **A Sense Of Wonder**, suggest his unrelenting search for spiritual truth.

WARNER BROS. COMMITS TO VAN'S DOUBLE LIVE ALBUM WITH PLENTY OF TOUR SUPPORT WHILE FINANCIALLY UNDERWRITING THE PROJECT

Warner Bros. pulled out the advertising dollars for the **It's Too Late To Stop Now** tour and subsequent album. "When you listened to the album," Ruff continued. "You felt like you were sitting with Van and the band."

The question everyone asked Van: "Where did Van get the idea for a live album?" He didn't answer. There was a model album. It was B. B. King's **Live At The Regal**. The answer was in his record collection. This is where Van found his model for a live album. Ruff said he talked with Van about the King album. This 1965 release, a classic blues album, was obscured in the larger pop-rock market. It was not a chart hit. The album peaked at fifty six on **Billboard**. It was strictly for blues fans.

When Van Morrison selected the eighteen songs for the **It's Too Late To Stop Now** album, did he have a purpose? He has never said. He floated the suggestion of a triple album. Warner demurred.

VAN'S HARD WORK OBSCURED AS THE IT'S TOO LATE TO STOP NEW ALBUM EMERGES

The It's Too Late To Stop Now tour ranked amongst the best in rock history. The album consisted of songs selected from the Los Angeles Troubadour, the cavernous Santa Monica Civic Auditorium, and the more intimate London Rainbow Theater. They were perfectly recorded on analog tapes.

As Van uttered the closing stanza from "In The Mystic," the album title was born. The diligence he took to recharge his chart success, keep his business affairs in order and to please the often cranky, fussy audiences was a tribute to his talent.

When the Caledonia Soul Orchestra was announced there was skepticism. An eleven piece band, with classical musicians, appeared to be a recipe for disaster. Van carried it off with aplomb. The CSO was carefully planned and crafted to perfection.

One band member told me the concept for the Caledonia Soul Orchestra was traced to 1972. He said Van was consumed with perfection in concert. "It's like watching a tiger. The tiger isn't thinking about where he's going to put his paws or how he's going to kill…the same thing with Van. He's just so there that you're completely drawn to it," Jim Rothermel continued. "He wanted to create a new show every night," Another band member, Jef Labes, observed there was a constant reworking of songs. This led to a ten minute version of "Cyprus Avenue." The band, according to John Platania, "could take the stage anywhere Van wanted to take them."

When Van appeared in Los Angeles at Doug Weston's Troubadour, the stage was barely big enough for the band. The audience, the critics, the industry insiders, the corporate heads, assorted artists, producers, hangers on and the foreign press mixed with the crowd enjoying an intimate show. "Van loved the Troubadour," Chris Michie continued. "He told me the band was even more than he anticipated."

Then it was off to the cavernous Santa Monica Auditorium, where another version of Van's concert delighted a sold out house. The large arenas were not his favorites. The memory of Doug Weston's Troubadour spurred him into the larger venues. He needed to do this to pay the musicians. At the time Van paid amongst the highest wage to his touring group.

When the tour arrived in London, it had been six years since he performed there. He was welcomed like a returning hero. When Whispering Bob Smith interviewed him, Van took along John Platania and David Hayes for support. He didn't need it. Smith's questions were a love fest. Once again Van looked back to Marin County for the inspiration.

WHAT THE SHOWS MEANT MAKING UP THE IT'S TOO LATE TO STOP NOW ALBUM

The shows at the Troubadour, the Santa Monica Civic Auditorium and London's Rainbow Theater provided the tapes for the album. He put nine together in his Fairfax home. He dipped back into the 1950s and 1960s covering Bobby Blue Bland, Sam Cooke and Ray Charles. Even further back he acknowledged Sonny Boy Williamson and Willie Dixon.

The London press anointed Van's Rainbow shows as "the rock event of the year." The press was laudatory. The BBC provided the first simulcast of a concert on BBC 2 television and Radio 2 stereo. The result was an explosion in record sales. It was shortly after these shows **Astral Weeks** went gold.

In London Van waxed nostalgically about his time in Notting Hill Gate when he was Them's lead singer.

VAN ON MAKING AN ALBUM EVERY YEAR: IT IS LIKE BEING PREGNANT

How did the tour and album influence Morrison's career? In the decade following the It's Too Late To Stop Now tour the pressure to release an album a year became a burden. In a 1982 **Rolling Stone** interview, he equated recording an album every year with being pregnant. "Because when you're working in the studio and you're making an album, you have to be pregnant every year and give birth to material." Van addressed the drudgery of the recording studio. He said he needed an audience to create. He was a songwriter searching for an outlet.

The double live album was that creative spark taking his career to perfection. Once he had the songs recorded, he validated his creative process with careful production. The double album made his point. Van was a seasoned producer. Van's point was creativity wasn't turned off and on like a water faucet. Some of his best material was archived. Why? Only Van can tell us. The operative wisdom was he had plans for future releases. Now rumors of impending box sets circulate.

In early 1974 Van realized he had an archive of future releases. Some were hits. Some weren't. **The Philosopher's Stone** germinated. The tracks for this CD covered the years 1969 into 1988.

When he reflected on the music business, Van was morose. "It's not much different from other jobs. I mean, a recording studio is not different from a factory. It's just a factory for music. And sometimes there are moments when you get off....The rest of it is very hard work. And the environment is not a creative environment," Van concluded. In a January, 2023, YouTube interview, Van looked back on the music business in the 1970s. He mentioned if you had a hit or two it would "make mincemeat out of you." His lyrics suggested show business sucked "the life blood out of you." He wrote it took you away from your family. It destroyed your life. He wrote of drugs and booze as an epidemic. Neither was a problem for Van. His lyrics emphasized he just wanted to be alive in the music business. He was recalling his time in Marin County in the 1970s. It was there he made a plan to survive.

Van Morrison: "When I started it wasn't called the music business...it was show business." He observed the show bands were about entertainment. Everyone sang. Everyone played an instrument. He intimated he was training to entertain people. All of this was prior to Them. Once he became a defined rock 'n' roll singer everything changed. At least this was his perception. Van said early in his career he didn't care for performing. He viewed writing as redemption. On **The Philosopher's Stone**, Van commented on the phony nature of show business. He wrote of "a phony smile" reflecting on an interview with Dick Clark. He said his song "Showbusiness" was written as a paean to the 1970s.

VAN LOVED THE LIVE RECORDINGS: WHAT IT MEANT

Van loved recording live. He said it captured the essence of his sound. He suggested a second take was a declining moment. Van wanted to stretch out past songs. He believed they became new versions. He said he captured the essence of the old classics.

Why did Van Morrison favor live recordings? It is part and parcel of his perfectionist nature. He believed the initial inspiration was the best. Isolation, Van intimated, brought out his soul. He set the template for this approach to recording albums was when he went into a soundproof booth to record **Astral Weeks**. The best statement about first takes are from the live **It's Too Late To Stop Now** album. Why? Van believed he was proving something to Warner Bros. Privately, he was unhappy with Ted Templeman listed as a co-producer. Templeman did little more than drive Morrison to the studio. He listened quietly to Van's contrarian views. He put up with his eccentric behavior. In some ways Van's first take argument is him saying: "Fuck you I am doing it my way."

Van's recordings are a testimony to his tried and true formula. It brought success. That formula is one where he carefully plans, precisely executes, and he fulfills a vision. Looking back to looking forward has always been a Morrison trait. In the 1991 **Hymns To The**

Silence album, he observed he wanted to be taken back: "To when the world made more sense." That world was the one take recording studio and the simple, bucolic Marin County life.

VAN ON VAN: WHAT WERE THE CHANGES?

With the It's Too Late To Stop Now tour and album, Van experienced a musical rebirth. His spiritual life accelerated. He received inordinately positive publicity. Warner Bros pulled out a vigorous advertising campaign.

The critics loved the album, with the exception of Robert Christgau, who wrote: "Songs that wore poorly or were just lame in the first place have more than...rightness on this exemplary live album, than in their studio versions...." Later Christgau would change his mind. It appears Christgau imagined blues and oldies taking over **It's Too Late To Stop Now**. That wasn't hip. Christgau certainly had to be hip. He was after all the self-proclaimed dean of American rock critics.

Once Christgau's review came out, Warner built on his duplicitous comments. Stan Cornyn publicized Van's deep connection to the blues. He embarrassed a critic who allegedly didn't listen to the album. Christgau crept off like a wounded tiger. Not even the Shakespeare of Telegraph Avenue, Greil Marcus, agreed with him. Professor Christgau was put in his place.

Stan Cornyn was responsible for much of Warner's positive publicity. He called the album "a revolution." Cornyn created a Warner Bros. culture combining creativity, while meshing complicated personalities. For Cornyn, Van Morrison was the apex of what the label sought to do with an artist.

Cornyn did everything he could to promote Morrison. He loved Van. It was the Belfast Cowboy's "fuck you" attitude he admired. Once in the hallway at Warner, Cornyn hollered: "Hey Van, great album." Van looked at him like he was nuts. The Belfast Cowboy walked away. Cornyn said: "This is why I love this guy." Cornyn continued: "He has no idea who I am and he doesn't give a shit about anything. This is why I love Van Morrison."

Van's complicated inner life intrigued Warner Bros. executives. The publicity people looked to the alternative press to publicize his albums. In counterculture publications, like the **Berkeley Barb**, the San Francisco based **Oracle**, the **Los Angeles Free Press** and the **San Diego Door**, Warner spent appropriately to guarantee sales.

Van produced more material than Warner could release. He had the blue collar work ethic of a construction worker. He told a story in a magical way. He connected with his audience. Never predictable! Always volatile! Van was back with a vengeance. He had a business plan for long term success.

During interviews, he recalled the 1970s vividly. In copious detail, with a slanted autobiographical penchant, he opened up about the difficulty of securing and protecting his intellectual property. Convincing Warner Bros. he had a better idea about his record releases than they did, he secured the advertising and publicity necessary to maintaining his career.

This period of whirlwind planning witnessed concerts that were perfection. He was not always happy with his shows. He was his most volatile critic. Alice Stuart recalled during the European dates, he kept to himself. To those who knew him well, this was not surprising. He had to concentrate to perform. He contemplated new musical directions. He needed privacy to create. He demanded isolation to perform.

Van was tantalized by his new life. He no longer worried about royalties. His lawyers solved that problem. He knew how to collect his money. The business model Van built was impressive.

While he was alternately happy, and, at times, less than joyous with Warner Bros., he was on top of his business. Warner was good to him. They paid royalties. They maintained a publicity machine to further his career.

He believed by his fourth or fifth Warner album, he might be repeating himself. In numerous interviews, Van shuttered when he described becoming the flavor of the month. He blew up his bands to freshen his shows. Ray Ruff said he constantly demanded more publicity from Warner Bros. Chris Michie observed the daily quest for perfection.

It was the little stories that made Van's songs work. On **Veedon Fleece,** there were new, reinvigorated tales of past experiences. Most of them involved his trip to Ireland. They were Irish experiences with a rural Marin County flavor.

The muse, that went not entirely unnoticed, Carol Guida, was the inspiration for many of the **Veedon Fleece** tunes. As Van worked his songwriting magic, visual images abounded. These images combined with spiritual friends, and writing led to brilliant songs.

Van did not consider himself a writer. He believed he was first and foremost a storyteller. He claimed he channeled songs. He described how his subconscious wrote telepathically. Some Irish critics suggested he was a seanchaí. That was he composed his songs in the tradition of the major Irish fiction writers.

He wrote best under stress. In the aftermath of the divorce he crafted a cache of songs unrivalled in the history of rock 'n' roll music. Turmoil defined him.

VAN'S SUCCESSES AND PROBLEMS, 1973-1974

Although Van experienced enormous success in 1973-1974, with highly profitable concerts, a double live album, and unmitigated praise from the London press, he faced the constant demand of paying his musicians, send out monthly alimony payments, while maintaining his California lifestyle. He paid a high wage. In his private life Van took time for visitations with his daughter, Shana. His ex-wife challenged the initial custody agreement in 1974. She alleged, in court documents, there was an unsavory atmosphere. Whether it was Janet or her attorneys it created problems. Shana's visits to her father were ones where he was a doting father. He remains that to the present day. The court ruled there was no evidence to support the allegations. These spurious allegations wore heavily on Van. He cancelled many well-paying concerts. This guaranteed his time with Shana.

John Platania recalled Van's difficulty with the divorce. The mood swings in Morrison's life were agonizing. He worked hard to put his life in order. He worked even harder for monetary success. Once the It's Too Late To Stop Now tour made money, Van was nervous and unhappy. He despised fame. He tolerated the money. He plotted his future.

When Van wrote "I Paid The Price," he reflected on his life with his ex-wife Janet Planet. A divorce ensued. This led to one of the most intense periods in his artistic growth. Then abruptly he slowed down. He lived a normal life. By 1974, he was mentally exhausted. He found it difficult to share his thoughts. He did in song form. The tunes he crafted were a testimonial to his intellectual rigor. His life emerged in lyrical profundity. When Ritchie Yorke interviewed Van for his 1975 book, he was amazed at how forthcoming the Belfast Cowboy was about his creative journey. Van detested the fawning nature of Yorke's book. It was hagiography. There would be fewer intensive interviews. The Yorke book reads like an archive of Van's private thoughts.

THE IT'S TOO LATE TO STOP NOW ALBUM

In February, 1974, when Warner Bros. released the double album, **It's Too Late To Stop Now**, there was immediate acclaim. Predictably, Van said he didn't care for the LP. Ever the contrarian Van used the album's success to incentivize his criticism of Warner's publicity department. This was a strange comment. Warner embraced the live double album.

It's Too Late To Stop Now transcended earlier LPs. Van's remarkable in concert vigor added a new dimension to his legacy. Warner complained Morrison spent too much time talking about **Veedon Fleece**. This wasn't a surprise. Warner Bros. was used to Morrison's unpredictable nature.

When Warner released **It's Too Late To Stop Now**, Van complained there was a predictability to the album. He intimated it lacked an avant-garde appeal. He believed a live product needed more of an edge. The laudatory reviews ended Van's momentary criticism of his album. Warner was flummoxed.

It's Too Late To Stop Now was a masterpiece. The cover photo showed him at his performing peak. The eighteen tunes displayed Morrison's pure on stage genius. The album began with the Caledonia Soul Orchestra backing him on a cover version of Bobby

Blue Bland's "Ain't Nothin' You Can Do." In this song, as he paid tribute to one of his early influences. The blues and the sounds pioneers were on his performing palate.

Van discovered Bobby Blue Bland's music in 1960. He toured Germany with a showband, the Monarchs, and he heard African American GI's singing along to Bland's songs. Van became a lifelong fan. "I can't put into words the phrasing and the way he interprets a song," Morrison remarked of Bobby Blue Bland.

The next three songs were Morrison originals "Warm Love," "Into The Mystic" and "These Dreams Of You." Side one closed with a cover of Ray Charles' "I Believe To My Soul." On side two "I've Been Working" is followed by a cover of Sonny Boy Williamson's "Help Me." Then Van launched into upbeat versions of "Wild Children," followed by "Domino." Willie Dixon's "I Just Wanna Make Love To You" which closed out side two. It created perfection.

The most adventurous songs on side three of the vinyl album included a soulful cover of Sam Cooke's "Bring It On Home To Me," a re-interpreted "St. Dominic's Preview," a cover of Sonny Boy Williamson's "Take Your Hand Out of My Pocket" and this vinyl side concluded with Van's unique version of "Listen to The Lion." The last side of this two disc vinyl masterpiece opens with the Them's "Here Comes The Night." This was followed by "Gloria." Then Van moved on to "Caravan." He concluded with the mysterious and eerie "Cyprus Avenue." For Van "Caravan" was the album's centerpiece.

The CD reissue, with three discs and a DVD, included a bonus live cut of "Brown Eyed Girl." The five blues and rhythm and blues covers suggested what Van's direction was in the mid-1970s. He enjoyed performing his roots mentor's songs.

Sitting with Carol Guida he took cassette tapes and edited them into a formidable two disc album. Then he left the cassettes with Warner Bros. They outdid themselves with the beautiful, remastered brilliant notes highlighting Morrison's production skills. Did the **It's Too Late To Stop Now** album have a meaning? It did. Van would say no. It was a tribute to Van's mentors. An examination of what it was and what it meant to his career suggests the album was an epic turning point. One of many in his illustrious career.

THE MEANING OF IT'S TOO LATE TO STOP NOW

Van established rules for **It's Too Late To Stop Now**. There was no overdubbing. Ted Templeman, the co-producer, complained this was unheard of amongst live albums. Van believed artistic authenticity could not be achieved with overdubbing. By selecting songs by Ray Charles, Bobby Blue Bland and Willie Dixon, Van stamped it as an excursion into the blues.

Van Morrison: "People cut live albums and they take it to the studio and play with it for about a year, but this one is just as it happened." The band concurred. David Hayes remarked: "It's one of best ever."

He told Yorke he wanted a flawless live album. That concept came from Van believing that his 1973 show at New York's Carnegie Hall was a harbinger of things to come concerning his live shows. He looked back on the album, in a 2016 interview, celebrating the reissue of **It's Too Late To Stop** Now. Van commented he loved the phrase he used: "Turn it up." Why? The band followed him so closely he screamed as they played on: "Just one more time."

Morrison lost himself on many tracks. His soulful wail on "Cyprus Avenue" recalled **Astral Weeks**. It was a reminder why the public embraced his shows. His fluid high kicks in the shows suggested the fun and flair he had on tour.

Geoff Barron, in **Melody Maker**, labeled the album a "paint box in words." Nick Kent, in the **New Musical Express**, concentrated on the LPs soul sound. Another London critic, Brian Hogg, countered Morrison's live album "overreached himself, unable to see his limitations." Most London based journalists knocked themselves out with unmitigated praise. Hogg was the exception.

One of the deans of British rock criticism, Charlie Gillett, pontificated Morrison was convincing in his musical approach. Van's earliest biographer, Ritchie Yorke, didn't care for the LP.

A number of biographers got it right. John Collis' **Van Morrison: Immaculate Speech of the Heart** offered the most perspective appraisal when he wrote "with the magnificent Caledonia Soul Orchestra...Morrison came of age as a magnetic stage performer. His concerts were an act of perfection."

When Van performed in the U.K., he was praised to the sky. "I don't know about the critics," Alice Stuart continued. "The fans loved him on stage. The critics fawned over him backstage. That is when they could talk to him which wasn't often." Stuart said he was at times ill at ease with certain reporters from the **New Musical Express** and **Melody Maker**. "The London based music press," Stuart continued, "were a different breed. They were entitled."

The chart positions for **It's Too Late To Stop Now** reflected his international appeal. In the U. S. **Billboard 200** the album peaked at fifty-three. In Australia, Austria, Belgium, Holland, Germany, Ireland, Italy and Spain it hit the charts. Warner Bros. realized they had an artist with a multi-international appeal. When the 2016 reissue emerged, the album peaked at fifteen on the **Billboard Top Pop Albums** while charting in Italy, Scotland, Sweden and Switzerland.

WHY IT'S TOO LATE TO STOP NOW WAS A DEPARTURE

Why was **It's Too Late To Stop Now** a departure? It wasn't! The critics failed to mention it was a natural progression. He had been working on the concept of a live album, without overdubs, since the Them days. Chris Michie said in retrospect, "Van was surprised Warner was with him. They didn't realize the extent of the genius behind his double vinyl masterpiece."

The blue eyed soul passion Morrison crafted was noted by select critics. He became the Van Morrison in concert he is to the present day. That is a performer unrivaled in showcasing his original and cover songs. He continues to honor those who influenced him. The phrase: "It's too late to stop now" was a cry for the next half century.

Van selected the closing line to the 1970 song "Into The Mystic" to title the album. He used past material "Gloria" and "Brown Eyed Girl" to appeal to those who loved his hits. Van wanted to redo some of his tunes. He believed he could improve upon them. He would recreate is in concert shows. This was the essence of Morrison's professionalism. He never stopped innovating. Improving his on stage persona was constant. He followed the same pattern in writing lyrics. He looked to live shows to improvise.

"Wild Children" was, Van remarked to Ritchie Yorke, a song he was never comfortable with on stage or in the studio. He mentioned to Yorke he wanted to record it live. He said that was the only way to improve upon it. What did Van mean by improve? He often judged his songs by the fan reaction during his shows.

By including "Wild Children" on the live album, Van delved into a past that conflicted him. To this day Van has never been clear why he wrote the song. The operative wisdom was he was searching for meaning in the post-war malaise by name checking actors from a by gone era. "Wild Children" was autobiographical. Van lamented his difficulty in fitting into the post-World War II era. Even to the Belfast Cowboy "Wild Children" was an enigma. He wrote it. He said repeatedly he couldn't figure out what he was saying. Channeling became his operative explanation.

Van lamented "Wild Children" lacked something. What? He couldn't put it in words. On stage, Van could gauge the depth and breadth of his writing. In the studio, he was lost in the milieu of production. His confidence faded into a morass of self-criticism.

Van remarked: "You put it on tape and you think it's as close as you can get it, then you move on." He never looked back. This was part of his recording genius. He mastered the nuances and subtle nature of the concert stage. Then he abandoned it for two and a half years. Why? "Becoming Van Morrison" was his mantra. He achieved it. It would take critics and fans decades to catch up with his personal picadilloes.

THE CRITICS RAVED: WHY THE ALBUM WAS A BLOCKBUSTER: KEN EMERSON GOT IT RIGHT IN ROLLING STONE

Ken Emerson's **Rolling Stone** review argued: "Van Morrison…for whom the American music tradition is passionate and alive, loves this tradition with the insight and fervor of a foreigner." Emerson complained of oldies and revival concerts. "Morrison's music," Emerson wrote, "is not diverted by faddish ephemera…." The **It's Too Late To Stop Now** album, Emerson said: "shows where Van came from…." **Rolling Stone** concluded the album was by "a great traditionalist" who was an "original talent." Emerson concluded Van was "a jazz singer."

What mattered to Van was the **Pop And Jazz** poll of American critics. This was the **Village Voice** praising Morrison. This poll rated Van's album as the twentieth best of the year. In this poll, Greil Marcus, Robert Christgau and Ellen Willis had the album in the Top Twenty. Christgau was the critic record buyers looked to for wisdom. He noted that eighteen of the Top Thirty albums were Warner Bros. releases.

Once the hoopla died down, Jason Akeny in **All Music** looked back fondly. He mentioned Morrison was an "erratic and temperamental live performer." He didn't realize this wasn't the case during the It's Too Late To Stop Now tour. Akeny recognized the power of the double album. He concluded it was "an engaging, warm portrait of the man at the peak of his powers."

Chris Jones, of the BBC, was the most perceptive critic regarding the album's relationship to Van's future. He saw it as blending Van's life through song. Jones argued Van was the progenitor for turning Celtic visions into a rock 'n' roll format. That became Van's future.

Morrison continued to play small venues. In the midst of the publicity for **It's Too Late To Stop Now**, he appeared on March 14, 1974, at a small venue, the Harvard Square, in Cambridge Massachusetts. Not surprisingly, it was a tune up for bigger concerts. This prestigious club, just a short distance from his former Green Street apartment, provided a sense of the past. This inspired Van.

While in Cambridge, Van visited his old neighborhood. He was amazed at how little had changed. He had fond memories of the area. He was inspired by his early life there. It showed in concert. When he took the stage for his Cambridge show, Van was in fine form. He used it to showcase new tunes. It was as if he was saying: "I am productive, still working and loving it."

The nineteen-song set featured unique versions of "What's Up Crazy Pup" and "Streets of Arklow." In Boston he had fond memories of creating parts of **Astral Weeks.** The band performed an instrumental version of "Brown Eyed Girl." He closed the show with "Gloria." It was hard for him to accept the accolades. He was only twenty-eight when **It's Too Late To Stop Now** came out to rave reviews. Fame was bothersome.

While in Boston, Van had a sense of his past. He loved talking with Peter Wolf of J. Geils fame. The Green Street neighborhood reminded him of how far his career had progressed.

The next day Van flew to New York, where he headlined at the Felt Forum. He was testy. He abhorred venues like the Felt Forum. The mammoth 20,000 plus seating capacity made him uncomfortable. He needed to play this venue for the money. It was a necessary sacrifice to pay the band for the smaller gigs he loved to play.

When Van disbanded the Caledonia Soul Orchestra, he rechristened his next band the Caledonia Soul Express. Then later in 1974, with his fiancée Carol Guida on his arm, he flew to the Montreux Jazz Festival without a band. Van was about to take his performing genius into a new venue and win over a jazz audience. This was lesson he learned on the It's Too Late To Stop Now tour.

WHAT IT'S TOO LATE TO STOP NOW TELLS US

By using three live venues the Troubadour, the Santa Monica Civic Auditorium and London's Rainbow Theater, Van captured his live essence. The other important aspect of this LP was the influence of Bobby "Blue" Bland and Ray Charles. He performed their songs flawlessly. He recognized blues and soul were influential on his artistry.

When the **It's Too Late To Stop Now** album was reissued the two disc set contained a live cut of "Brown Eyed Girl." Morrison wanted to perform his early hit in a more imaginative manner. The second time around for a song was the best for Van. Thanks to what was arguably the greatest live rock 'n' roll album to date, the Belfast Cowboy reached a creative peak with another half century of performing in front of him.

TO BE COMMERCIAL OR NOT TO BE COMMERCIAL THAT IS THE QUESTION

The **It's Too Late To Stop Now** album raised unnecessary questions concerning the Belfast Cowboy's commercial future. When he disbanded the Caledonia Soul Orchestra there were cries Van dismantled his creative success. The opposite was true. He was enabling a new level of creativity. Phil Coulter observed Van had a "restless creativity." That was a nice way of saying each period of Van's life led to another that was musically different, intellectually filled period with new ideas. His commercial considerations as Coulter said "were spot on."

Some say Van's lack of concern with commercial success was a problem. It wasn't. He had commercial success on his radar. If you expected a certain product from Van, you would be disappointed. He did it his way. Warner Bros., his audiences and even his friends didn't understand this personality quirk. Van believed longevity in the music business resulted from constant change. His wide ranging experimental songs and concert performances drove his career.

Mainstream success was the source of Van's constant experimental nature. He believed his ninety minute show with one or two words to thank the band was what the fans wanted. The in concert perfection was rooted in Marin County in the 1970s.

Bibliographical Sources

For descriptions of the It's Too Late To Stop Now tour, see, for example, Johnny Rogan, **Van Morrison: The Portrait of The Artist** (London, 1984), Chapter 11 , Clinton Heylin, **Can You Feel The Silence?: Van Morrison, A New Biography** (London, 2002), pp. 270-283, 285-287, 294-295, 368, 378, Brian Hinton, **Celtic Crossroads: The Art of Van Morrison** (London, 1997), chapter 5 and Howard A. DeWitt, **Van Morrison: The Mystic's Music** (Fremont, 1985), pp. 44-46, 96-97. For an updated and highly interpretive look at this period see Johnny Rogan, **Van Morrison: No Surrender** (London, 2005), passim. Rogan called the double album a concept carried out so well it might be considered "his greatest phase as a performer." (p. 282).

See Nathan Wirth, "The Road Goes On Forever: Van Morrison on Stage, 1967-1984," **Wavelength**, number 16, June 1998, pp. 15-16 for the It's Too Late To Stop Now tour. Simon Gee also provided supplemental information.

For Van in Copenhagen, see, Truls Meland, "Who Was That Masked Man? The Story of Van's Visit to Copenhagen in 1974," **Wavelength**, number 14, 1997, pp. 8-10. This is an unusually brilliant piece of journalism.

See John L. Wasserman, "Rock Star's Got Feeling For The Blues," **San Francisco Chronicle**, April 1973, p. 48 for a review of a Lion's Share show. Wasserman was San Francisco's best known critic. He loved talking with Morrison about jazz. Like Phil Elwood, Wasserman was a fan, as well as a critic. He never let his friendship get in the way of his reviews. Elwood, due to health concerns, was often crabby and impetuous, but he praised Van.

The rigors of touring and the logistics were explained in several interviews with Larry Catlin a veteran of the Bill Graham Organization. An interview with Dorothy Morrison helped to put much of this chapter in perspective.

A great deal of information about Marin County musicians came from interviews with Mark Naftalin who spent much of his life after the Paul Butterfield Band living in Marin County with a radio show, playing as a sideman to Van, and others, while pursuing a highly successful solo blues career.

Nathan Rubin provided information about life on the road with Morrison. He also suggested the importance of the rehearsals. He was a Professor of Music at California State University, Hayward and a seasoned symphony musician.

For bootleg CD descriptions, with copious liner notes, key information and set lists, see the excellent site, which is invaluable for some bits of information on the bootleg phenomenon http://www.themusicarchive.com/intothemusic/concerts/vanbest-1c.htm

See the London based **Q** magazine for a listing of top concerts and at times reactions to Van's shows.

Mervyn and Phil Solomon added a great deal to this chapter in numerous interviews. Mervyn was a distinguished Belfast businessman with a record label, Emerald, and other business interests. He had tapes of the Maritime Club, which he played for me. He was a friend to Van until Mervyn died prematurely in an auto accident.

A conversation with Tom Bradshaw in 1982 at the Great American Music Hall was important on Van's concert appearances. Articles on rock music in the **San Francisco Chronicle**, the **San Francisco Examiner**, the **Los Angeles Times** and the **Oakland Tribune** reinforced the mid-1970s atmosphere and key facts.

A great deal of the material in this chapter came from Sacramento blues legend Guitar Mac. The comments of Oakland blues guitar legend Steve Gannon helped in evaluating the musicians performing with Morrison.

See Ritchie Yorke, **Van Morrison: Into The Music** (London, 1975), pp. 11-12, 61, 97, 114 for this period. A telephone conversation with Ritchie Yorke in 1982 helped my first book, **Van Morrison: The Mystic's Music** to come together. He spoke in great detail about interviewing Van.

For coffee houses in Seattle that influenced Alice Stuart and for the folk scene in general, see, for example, Stewart Hendrickson, "Musical Traditions: Pacific Northwest Folklore Society-Concert Review" http://stewarthendrickson.com/VictoryMusic/December-MusicalTrad_FirthNelsonConcert.html

This chapter was helped by material from Phil Hardy and Dave Lang, eds., **Encyclopedia of Rock, 1955-1975** (London, 1977) and Irwin Stambler, **Encyclopedia of Pop, Rock & Soul** (New York, 1974).

For Van's summer 1973 trip to Europe and the U.K., see, Michael Watts, "Van The Best Blues Singer Of Them All," **Melody Maker**, July 21, 1973, p. 9. On the return to the U. K., see Richard Williams, "Van Morrison: Gonna Rock Your Gypsy Soul," **Melody Maker**, July 28, 1973.

See John Collis, **Van Morrison: Immaculate Speech of the Heart** (Boston, 1996), p. 136-137 for the Caledonia Soul Orchestra comment. Collis does a brilliant job with this part of Morrison's career.

Erik Hage, **The Words And Music of Van Morrison** (London, 2009), pp.71-75 is important for Morrison's songwriting maturity and quotes about how the tour and album influenced his future musical direction. Hage's brief book is an excellent analysis of why and how Van redefined his personal and professional life in the 1970s.

See the Michelle Rocca interview with Morrison in **Vox**, January, 1995, for some interesting insights into the double album. In an open and transparent set of conversations, Van talks at length about his writing and why the **It's Too Late To Stop Now** album was important to his career.

For the Armadillo headquarters show, see, Eddie Wilson, Frank Zappa, Van Morrison and the Yurts, 1973 and 1974.

The website **Van Morrison News** was instrumental to this chapter. The material is amazing and the unofficial blog spot contains excellent information. The key to this website is the reaction from Morrison's fans and friends.

For the Tony Johnson interview for Irish television RTE, see, Michael Walsh, "1973 Talk About Pop Interview," **Into The Music**, issue 8 (1992). Art Siegel transcribed this article from the original show. This is a particular revealing interview suggesting Van was having fun with his music. This was a strange show as Van took it over. There was a new and playful Morrison during this show. Tony Johnson didn't feel that way. There is a marvelous bootleg of this show. It may be the only bootleg in history where the bootlegger was in a rage because he couldn't find versions of the last two songs "Snow In San Anselmo" and "Beside You."

See Mike Jurkovic, "Van Morrison," **Elmore Magazine**, June 10, 2016 for a look back suggesting how early critics may not have appreciated the beauty of Van's double album. **Mojo** listed the album as number sixteen on the best live albums of all time. The 2016 re-release brought a new level of acclaim, Van believed the double album deserved. For a review arguing Van and the band may have progressed further than the reviewers suggested, as an in concert act, see, Jason Akeny, "Van Morrison: It's Too Late To Stop Now," **All Music.com**, https://www.allmusic.com/album/its-too-late-to-stop-now-mw0000193616 Akeny does a nice job positing the pros and cons of an album that went on to legendary status.

David Browne, "Inside Van Morrison's Legendary 'It's Too Late To Stop Now' Tour," **Rolling Stone**, August 31, 2017 https://www.rollingstone.com/music/music-features/inside-van-morrisons-legendary-its-too-late-to-stop-now-tour-202118/ The Browne article is important to understanding the difficulty, the planning, the precision and the attention to detail that was part and parcel of Morrison's skill in taking more than fifty people on the road with an eleven piece band and the necessary support system.

See the brilliant academic article by Richard Elliott, "My Tongue Gets t-t-t: Words, Sense, And Vocal Presence In Van Morrison's It's Too Late To Stop Now," **Twentieth Century Music**, March 2016, Volume 13, Issue 1 pp. 53-76. This is a strange, but useful, article on Van's live version of "Cyprus Avenue" on the **It's Too Late To Stop Now** album. Elliott's thesis is the song is an example of how Van's voice has so much authority it sends the musicians into submission. The professor realized Van crafted the production of the song. He trained the backing band, and then the legendary Caledonia Soul Orchestra Professor. Elliott concluded the article suggesting there is a stutter at the conclusion of the song which is intended as an "aesthetic stutter." What does Elliott mean? He argues Van's voice connects with the musicians via the so-called stutter. Then Elliott observed Van connected with the audience and, finally, the rock critics. Also, see, Martin Buzacott and Andrew Ford, **Speaking In Tongues: The Songs of Van Morrison** (Sydney, 2005) for interesting thoughts on Van's songs and albums. This is an overlooked book that is excellent.

This chapter owes a debt to Peter Mills, **Hymns To The Silence: Inside The Words And Music Of Van Morrison** (London, 2010), Chapter 6. Mills provided the setting for the live album. He also switched back and forth between Irish and American themes while highlighting how and why Morrison selected the material for the album. He also analyzed how and why Van recorded a live album every decade after this with references to **Live At The Grand Opera House, Belfast** (1984), **A Night In San Francisco** (1994) and **Live At Austin City Limits** (2006). Mills concluded, using the wisdom of Phil Coulter, Van achieved creative, artistic and financial success with his seminal live album.

For the "Wild Children" quote by Van see, Ritchie Yorke, **Van Morrison: Into The Music** (London, 1975), p. 11.

For Van's comments on Bobby Blue Bland's influence, see, for example, Ray Padgett, "Van Morrison Covers Bobby Blue Bland Classic On New Album," **Covermesongs.com**, October 6, 2014 https://www.covermesongs.com/2016/10/van-morrison-covers-bobby-blue-bland.html See Van Morrison's website for further comments on Bland's influence https://www.facebook.com/vanmorrisonofficial/posts/bobby-bland-was-an-inspiration-to-me-from-the-start-from-covering-his-song-turn-/546064308764617/

Pierre Perrone, "Bobby Blue Bland: Blues And Soul Singer Whose Work Inspired Van Morrison And Eric Clapton," **London Independent**, June 24, 2013 https://www.independent.co.uk/news/obituaries/bobby-bland-blues-and-soul-singer-whose-work-inspired-van-morrison-and-eric-clapton-8672090.html

The best tribute to Bobby Blue Bland's influence on the Belfast Cowboy is Ben Greenman, "Promised Bland," **The New Yorker**, January 23, 2011 https://www.newyorker.com/magazine/2011/01/31/promised-bland One of the most significant influences Bland provided was the theme for "Goin' Down Geneva." This song on the **Back On Top** album was not a tribute to Bland. This song was written and performed in Bland's style. He never mentions Bobby Blue Bland in the song. Instead Van inserts a phantom rocker, Vince Taylor, and the oblique nature of the song virtually hides Bland's influence. But it is there in Van's mind body and soul. The lyrics to "Goin' Down Geneva" are a window into Van's psyche. When he sings "Vince Taylor used to live here, nobody ever heard of him." Van writes of an American who traveled to England for rock 'n' roll fame. That was Vince Taylor. He didn't find it. He did in France. Then Taylor vanished from the music business. He died in Paris while working as a baggage handler at a local airport. This song was a paean to Morrison's dictum he didn't want to be the flavor of the month. Taylor had one quasi hit and vanished into the cesspool of forgotten rock 'n' rollers. Van was fond of Taylor's "Brand New Cadillac." He loved the Clash's version on **London Calling**. David Bowie also acknowledged Taylor's influence. "Just who was he and where did he fit in?" Morrison said of Taylor. Van didn't know. No one knows!

Barney Hoskyns, **Small Town Talk: Bob Dylan, The Band, Van Morrison, Janis Joplin, Jimi Hendrix & Friends In The Wild Years Of Woodstock** (New York, 2016 reprint) is a book essentially about Bob Dylan, the Band and Woodstock. How this small town rural community north of New York influenced Bob Dylan and the Band. For the Van Morrison story it is a road map to his early 1970s hit albums. Many songs, like "Moondance," were conceived in this rural community. Van's friendship with the Band was the reason he preferred first take, live recordings. While not about Morrison, the book in reality, was a peek into his creative life. Woodstock was like a girlfriend to Morrison. It fed his creative ego. The story is Van moved to Woodstock to meet Bob Dylan. Privately, to friends, Van has said this story is another journalistic fabrication. Van was moved by a mysterious Boston management entity, allegedly owned by the mob, to Woodstock. Nothing in the Boston era made sense for Van, except for finalizing **Astral Weeks.** During interviews with Artie Traum, he didn't believe the Dylan story. Neither did Sally Grossman, Tom Pacheco, Happy Traum and dozens of others in Woodstock.

Barney Hoskyns remarked of Morrison: "he was terrified of meeting Dylan, but desperate to do so...." This is not close to what happened. The prologue to Hoskyns' book leads off with a quote from Morrison's "Old Old Woodstock." This use of Van's lyrics is poignant. "Listen, oh don't it get you. Get you in your throat," are words setting the tone for what Hoskyns termed: "Into the mystic." If Van has reason to complain about someone stealing his intellectual property, he should read Hoskyns book. It sounds like it was written by Van. Hoskyns writes of the symbolism of Woodstock suggesting its importance to the rock music subculture. "I was always hearing Dylan, Hendrix, the Band, Van Morrison. You can feel it in the air." Great writing. What is the point? Hoskyns uses the Belfast Cowboy's imagery stating: "There's a mystical quality to these hills," (p. 5).

The praise for the **It's Too Late To Stop Now** album has never ceased. For some insights, after the 2016 reissue, and the criticism of a critic who sees a sameness in Morrison's live show, see, for example, Tom Hull, "Rhapsody Streamnotes," **Tom Hull.com**, June 2016 http://www.tomhull.com/ocston/blog/archives/2399-Rhapsody-Streamnotes-June-2016.html For a less nuanced review, see, Mike Jurkovic, "Van Morrison...It's Too Late to Stop Now...Volumes II, II, IV," **Elmore Magazine**, June 10, 2016 http://www.elmoremagazine.com/2016/06/reviews/albums/van-morrison-2 The Jurkovic reviews pays tribute to Guy Massey who mixed the reissue giving the listener a CD with exquisite sound. Jurkovic prefers the audio over the video.

An excellent review of the album of "It's Too Late To Stop Now," is Ken Emerson, "Van Makes A Present Of The Past," **Rolling Stone**, April 25, 1974, p. 61 In this review Emerson who understood Morrison accurately described why and how the album was a ground-breaking piece of music at a time of sameness in the industry. "Van Morrison, one of the few...for whom the American musical tradition is passionate and alive, loves this tradition with the insight and fervor of a foreigner." Emerson suggested there was a "lack of a living history" in American music. It took a migrant from Belfast, Ireland to discover roots music and place it into a new perspective. Van did that Emerson suggested in the double live album with a look back to his heroes while supplying his music grounded in American themes and Marin County's subculture.

EIGHTEEN

Van Evolves: What 1973-1974 Tells Us, Carol Guida's Role, Chris Michie's Recollections And A Change Is Coming, With Continual Pissing And Moaning About Hard Nose The Highway

"Van had a way with words no one understood. Then he added the music, it was pure magic."

Chris Michie

"Van would write on bank slips as I stood in line to make a deposit on my account."

Carol Guida

"Going away and coming back are the themes of all Irish writing."

Van Morrison

Rolling Stone magazine caricature of Morrison 1978 (Courtesy Bruce McGillivray)

What did the years 1973-1974 accomplish for Van Morrison? As a writer he came of age. He was already critically acclaimed for **Astral Weeks**. There was a new Van emerging. A writer! A musical innovator! An improved in concert performer! These were the descriptions of the newly emerging Morrison persona.

"By Van evolving," Chris Michie said, "it meant he was planning a long term career. He had a vision. He didn't share it." That was typical Van. He was not only reclusive. He was private. What accelerated this careful planning? It was his divorce. It was the anxiety from the music business. It was a muddled personal life. Chris Michie continued: "I wasn't performing with Van until the 1980s. What I saw in the mid-1970s was a performer at the top of his game. Change was coming. I wasn't sure what it is and I found out when I played with him."

The gnawing criticism of **Hard Nose The Highway** from a bevy of confused critics frustrated Van. Or did it? He has never said. What he found strange, according to Chris Michie, and half a dozen other people around Van is his artistic vision was never addressed. Van didn't understand why his songs weren't appreciated. The rejection for an album where he had total control led to his exit from the commercial stage. He didn't exit from his career. He spent 1973-1977 planning future albums.

How does one understand the myriad influences of 1973-1974? It is not an easy task. A good starting place is to examine Van's lyrics. They provide a road map to his musical growth. It is what Peter Childs characterizes as "a fertile musical period."

PETER CHILDS WINDOW: A FERTILE MUSICAL PERIOD

What did "fertile musical period" mean? No one answered the question until 2022 when Peter Childs' book **Van Morrison In The 1970s** appeared with eloquent descriptions of how and why the decade was the period of "Becoming Van Morrison."

Peter Childs labelled the 1973-1974 era one of Van's "most fertile musical periods." That seemed improbable. He released one album and a double live vinyl masterpiece. What was Childs referring to as "fertile." He discussed the songs that went into the 1998 **The Philosopher's Stone**. Many of those songs were amongst Van's best of the decade.

For some reason, never explained, Warner Bros., or perhaps Van, placed at least nine and maybe ten songs into the unreleased bin. None were released on **Hard Nose The Highway**. Van wanted a double album. Warner said no. The culprit? No one knows! What we do know is the unreleased songs were superior to those on **Hard Nose The Highway**.

What do the unreleased songs tell us? Plenty! "Not Supposed To Break Down" has a telling lyric: "Swallow the dirt. Keep listening to the hurt." This is allegedly what Van felt about the problems of the music business, his personal life and this lyric foreshadowed elegant prose. The trauma it induced accelerated his writing with vehement observations. It wasn't necessarily Warner Bros. he believed mistreated him. It was from the days with the showbands to Them to Bert Berns and Bang Records that he recalled. Throughout his life Van never forgave bad treatment. "The Great Deception" was an even more pointed criticism of the music moguls, the "plastic revolutionaries" and what he termed "love city." That was the Haight Ashbury. Van realized he was "living in this world of lies." These phrased appeared in his songs. Some were direct. A reference to Sly Stone has Van writing a song lyric quoting Stone. The quote "saying power to the people, dance to the music" was one Van believed pointed to the arrogant hypocrisy of a lyricism with little to say and nowhere to go with his music. The Van obliquely compares himself to Rembrandt, when he writes of the painter: "He didn't have enough money for his brushes." This is an illusion to Van's years of poverty in New York, Boston and Woodstock. These words tell more about Van's 1973 as **Hard Nose The Highway** confused the critics. Warner Bros. wanted Van to work on new musical avenues.

Warner Bros. promised Van movie soundtracks. It never happened. He wrote "Madame Joy," a song which Chris Michie said was "the PG version of Madame George." Piano based songs were attractive to place on movie soundtracks. Van had a vast supply of such songs. No one at Warner attempted to place them with movie producers.

As Van said the twenty two minutes Warner wanted on each side of each record left him with hundreds of minutes of unreleased songs. When a Warner executive labelled them "leftovers," Van blanched.

What Childs' book tells us is Van was in transition. A creativity that was never predictable brought Morrison another half century plus of musical creativity. The highs and lows of his future writing was ignored. The view of Van's Irish heritage grew stronger every year in his writing.

The fierce dedication to business, during and in the aftermath of his divorce, righted the financial ship. By refurbishing his stage act and while performing at small venues, he introduced new elements.

THE THREADS IN BECOMING VAN MORRISON: BUSINESS ONES

There are many threads in the Morrison story. In this year and a half examination of his life, it is difficult to place them properly into the narrative. What was the most important element in this period? It was the money question. It was redoing Caledonia Productions while setting the legal framework to control his intellectual property. To some of his friends this seemed strange. Van had little interest in money. He spent as little as possible. He was playing local clubs and paying the band well. To continue to develop his career money was a concern to support the small club appearances. Why, then, was the money question an important one?

The money question evolved around his intellectual property. He fought a phase of that battle in 1973-1974 establishing a business framework. He was paid. He continued to pursue back royalties. Righting the fiscal ship became an obsessive priority. Van invested wisely if privately.

He finalized a settlement with Ilene Berns. The law suits from using two Berns songs on **Astral Weeks** was settled out of court. The settlement? It has never been made public. Van established a production company. He was in control of his Warner contract. He paid his musicians an excellent wage. The business plan was well organized. This sophisticated business plan guaranteed his long term future. Financial freedom prompted his creativity to flow. Money and muse connected in 1974 making productivity for Van a driving force The relationship between the money and the muse drove him 24/7 in the 1970s.

THE MONEY AND THE MUSE: THEY GO HAND IN HAND

"Van didn't have the money he had later," Carol Guida remarked. The divorce agreement, which is a matter of public record, demonstrated Van was frugal. He invested wisely. He kept careful track of his royalties. Protecting his intellectual property was a constant concern. There have never been tax issues. This was due to his financial wizardry.

The cash flow into Morrison's coffers began after the slow selling **Astral Weeks.** Where were the royalties? They were minimal for **Astral Weeks**. When his management people began checking there was a dribble of income from his first Warner album. He has never said but the people who worked with Van told he me set out to make a string of albums with pop friendly songs. He did this to guarantee his career longevity.

The **Astral Weeks** masterpiece was followed by hit albums through 1972. They included **Moondance**, **His Band And Street Choir**, **Tupelo Honey** and **St. Dominic's Preview**. This established Morrison's brand. Van slowly moved away into a brief periods of pop hits into serious literary themes. He was heading into a more esoteric writing direction. Creativity, not money, continued to drive his career direction.

Van addressed the 1970s money issue in a 2016 interview with the **London Mirror**. He told Kim Carr he secretly quit the music business in the mid-1970s. The operative wisdom was this 1974 to 1977 slowdown was merely Van reorienting his career. Van says: "No." He is emphatic that he returned to the music business, as he told Carr, "to pay his bills." Otherwise he intimated he would have remained retired. Why remain retired? Van loved reading. He discovered Samuel Beckett. What did he learn from Beckett. One word: "Exile." When Beckett surfaced in 1979 on the **Wavelength** album, it was an indication of his intense reading. The previous year a November 16, 1978 an illustration by Bruce McGillivray showed Van with a pen in hand writing like Beethoven. It appeared in **Rolling Stone**. This was tacit recognition for his writing. The romantic image of a writer was a refutation of his taciturn image.

WHEN DID VAN DISCOVER SAMUEL BECKETT AND CAROL GUIDA?

How did Van discover Samuel Beckett's **Waiting For Godot**. How did it influence Van? Like Beckett's prose, Van's writing was different from anything else in rock music. The critics took note. They were impressed. He intensified the intellectual direction of his songwriting. A new muse showed up to put a literary flair into his pen. Her name was Carol Guida.

When Van called a Marin County medical office for a masseuse it changed his life. A beautiful young lady showed up with medical and spiritual credentials. While working on Van her magic hands and casual conversation displayed her scientific training and, as she talked, a never ending intellect searching for spiritual truth emerged. Van saw it was a sign that she showed up in his life at a time of personal crisis.

The muse, Carol Guida, was spiritual. She loved literature. She had a commitment to Buddhism. Here calm relaxed personality never exploded. This made her a woman Van pursued. She was centered and bright. That is how those close to Morrison described Guida. Van couldn't believe his good fortune. She was a breath of fresh air. In a life filled with tension and sycophants, she had no baggage. Inspiration followed. So did a few years of Van minimizing his performances. He didn't need interviews. He didn't have an album to promote. But Van wasn't retired. He was "Becoming Van Morrison."

Guida's personality was warm, non-threatening and happy. She was a reader. She was a thinker. She wasn't a brain dead rocker. She was Van's perfect partner. "We became soulmates," Guida mentioned shortly after meeting Morrison. "He said he would write a song for me. I told a friend this guy was getting to me."

As Van's songwriting headed into new directions, the debate over the meaning of his lyrics intensified. Van began extensively archiving his recordings. He had a vision for his future. It included box sets, alternate cuts, rarities and live albums. To do this he needed to find an alternate storage facility other than the Warner archives. He quickly found two storage units. Rumor has it they were in Sausalito. By 1974 the Morrison archive was in full bloom. It didn't take long before he began complaining he had too much product.

In 2016, looking back Van said he will never be able to retire, "I'm trapped. I've got so much product that even if I stopped public appearances, I'd still have to manage my catalogue, so I'd still be working." Van may be right. Looking back to look forward is a lifelong trait.

HOW IT'S TOO LATE TO STOP NOW AND VEEDON FLEECE CHANGED

The next two albums **Van Morrison: It's Too Late To Stop Now** and **Veedon Fleece** bore Carol Guida's unmistakable influence. After living in Marin County for four years, Van's creative mantra swung into new directions. He had been working on a live album since **Astral Weeks**. The double live album was not surprising. What changed was the direction in **Veedon Fleece**. The critics saw it as the progenitor of **Astral Weeks**. It wasn't, Van said, it stood on its own.

There was a problem emanating from the **It's Too Late To Stop Now** album. Van put together one of the greatest touring bands. Then he dismantled it. The critics wondered what was wrong with Van. He disbanded the greatest live band in touring history. That was van being Van.

When Van landed in Dublin, with Carol Guida, in late 1973, he was thinking of writing a book. As Van drove from Wicklow to Cork to Killarney songs popped into his head. His dormant Celtic flair led to **Veedon Fleece**. At least the vison for the album. He still had to finish editing the **It's Too Late to Stop Now** album. With Carol Guida by his side his vision of the tour was edited into a double vinyl masterpiece.

Neil McCormick, of the **London Daily Telegraph**, remarked of the live album "Van climbs right out of these songs and onto another plane." What song portended Van's change? "Streets of Arklow" had the phrase "God's green land" telling anyone listening that the poetry in Van's pen had Emerald Island influences. Ireland cleansed his soul. He had to return to it.

WHAT THE CRITICS MISSED ON HARD NOSE THE HIGHWAY? CHANGE IS COMING, SO QUIT PISSING AND MOANING

There was very little on **Hard Nose The Highway** to attract the critics. To friends, those around Van at Warner, and in conversation amongst musicians there was no consensus why the critics were so hostile. Van was done with the "sha la las" in "Brown Eyed Girl," and the rollicking vocal thunder of "Here Comes The Night." No more formula hits were in his writing. He would write and record his way. It was as if Van wanted to tell the critics to quit "pissing and moaning."

Van dismissed the criticism of **Hard Nose The Highway**. He never complained Warner Bros. allegedly forced him to archive three dozen songs. Or Van may have purposely withheld them. No one clarified this problem. One hint is the album was the first since his Bang debut LP to have cover songs by another artist. That is if Kermit the Frog was a recording artist. The traditional Irish song, "Purple Heather," was an indication Warner Bros. was the song selection culprit.

Why did Van complain about not having a hit single? Why was he not able to point the album into a more commercial direction? Van believed there was little input from the Warner Bros. brass for this release. That wasn't true. There were two singles "Warm Love" backed with "I Will Be There" and "Bein' Green" backed with "Wild Children." "Warm Love" charted at sixty-six in Canada. One Warner executive commented on Van's input. "We listened. We tried to accommodate him. He wasn't writing pop hits."

When he took an Irish vacation with Carol Guida a new album came together. Morrison rediscovered his Irish roots. He combined Celtic themes with Marin County influences to produce an album as close to **Astral Weeks** as the original. Van needed wisdom from his environment.

That wisdom was a Dublin hotel, which was a comfortable mansion. It became the inspiration for Van to write. The Sutton House mansion was a call to the Dublin area. Once he toured Ireland, he was home. The writing intensified. The production blossomed into **Veedon Fleece**.

He had a home studio in his Fairfax home high on a hill with a beautiful view. He was with a gorgeous women. He was inspired. The amount of work Van put in daily was an indication of the breadth and depth of his blue collar work ethic. "I had absolutely nothing" Van remarked of his days leaving Them. By the 1970s, while living in Marin County, he recalled the days of living in Boston. "I was sleeping on a friend's couch," Van continued. "I was at the bottom. Game over. Total Oppression." In this discussion with **The London Times**, Van opened up about the music business. "You work through the moment. There is a book called **The Business Of Music** and the advice is: don't rely on anybody, trust nobody. Understand the business, the contracts. Does the producer or manager own the recordings? That's why you end up getting nothing because someone else owns it all. I was forced to learn this stuff." Van became the producer. He, in time, funded his recordings, controlled the production and worked on label placement of his product. This explains why Van is at times a bit cranky. Business was an all-consuming passion. He did it well.

Veedon Fleece suggested Van's evolution as a writer. The intensified serious in Van's work was due to the criticism of and lack of understanding for **Hard Nose The Highway**. A new muse. A literary giant. A view of Ireland. These forces led to his reinvigorated Irish themes.

Album Cover: HARD NOSE THE HIGHWAY

THE MUSE, THE LITERARY GIANT AND VAN'S RETURN TO IRISH THEMES

He finally had someone to read the same books. He discussed literature with the intelligence of a recent convert. The ignorance of the banal assholes in and around the music business surfaced. He ignored them.

There were three literary figures defining Van, T. S. Eliot, William Butler Yeats and William Blake. They came into the picture influencing Van's lyrics, his themes and at times his esoteric writing. In 2001 Tom Paulin, a Northern Irish poet, included Morrison in his lectures on Blake at Hertford College in Oxford. Paulin argued Van

Morrison "invoked Blake's presence" and he concluded the result was the "extraordinary ferment which was Belfast of the 1960s." In Paulin's lectures he concluded Van made recordings of Blake's poetry "in America." The Professor intimated Blake's poetry may have resulted from Van's Marin County residency.

What is not in the biographical realm is the influence of his new muse Carol Guida. How did she influence him? They read the same books. They came to conclusions about how and why these literary giants were important. They debated, analyzed and formulated the literary references increasingly surfacing in his lyrics. Along the way Van evolved as a writer. Guida's role was as a quiet inspiration.

The role of Marin County in Van's voracious reading remains an undiscovered factor. "Becoming Van Morrison" was the inauguration of a writer. Tony Dey recalled his cryptic writing. So did Carol Guida. She saw the small pieces of paper on their way to becoming magnificent songs. Van was an Irish writer in America. He unwittingly blended his San Francisco Bay Area experiences into a lyrical Celtic beauty. Years later in writing "In Tiburon," he commented on his San Francisco experiences.

Van was diligently learning his craft. He saw the fruit of his labors in **Veedon Fleece's** lyrics. When Van was gloomy it was not because writing was difficult. The gloom set in when he didn't have time to write due to concert commitments, business concerns or his daily life. Being a writer became an integral part of his life.

The flashes of Ireland in **Veedon Fleece** indicated Morrison's literary independence. Those insights provide windows into Carol

Guida. The recurring visons of Belfast surfaced before the divorce, before Carol came into the picture and before Van's business plan was in order, those visions were few and far between. She inspired him. Her role? Intellectual stimulation! An ordered life! A reading partner!

Bibliographical Sources

For Van discussing why he can't retire, see, Kim Carr. "Van Morrison Says He Returned To Music After Quitting For Two Years Because He Ran Out Of Money," **London Mirror**, November 25, 2016. https://www.mirror.co.uk/3am/celebrity-news/van-morrison-says-returned-music-9336023

For some intriguing comments on **Hard Nose The Highway**, see, for example, Tony Thompson, "51 Disappointing Albums—Van Morrison, Hard Nose The Highway," **Daily Review.com**, July 31, 2020. https://dailyreview.com.au/51-disappointing-albums-van-morrison-hard-nose-the-highway/

Ritchie Yorke, **Van Morrison: Into The Music** (London, 1975), chapter 16. This is the part of the book where Van talks at length about his music and Yorke interprets it in dulcet tones. Also, see, "Van Morrison on an Introduction to Music," on YouTube. https://www.youtube.com/watch?v=EYwksFQTOOo This interview is one where Van discusses the importance of the radio on his songwriting and career. Leo Green pulls some great comments from Van with some interesting asides about Solly Lipsitz's record store. This interview took place as the album **Three Chords And The Truth** was released.

See Peter Childs, **Van Morrison In The 1970s: Decades** (2022). For a local Marin County writer looking back on Morrison's years in the area from the vantage point of when he left in the 1980s to 2006 with fond memories of how the area influenced the Belfast Cowboy, see, for example, Paul Liberatore, "Van Morrison Wows Them Any Time," **Marin Independent Journal**, March 3, 2006. https://www.marinij.com/2006/03/03/van-morrison-wows-them-any-time/ The Liberatore article an unannounced concert Van gave at Rancho Nicasio, West Marin County roadhouse, for a friend who owned the place facing financial ruin. The four o'clock in the afternoon show was Van's way of helping Bob Brown pay the bills. It was also his love letter to Marin County a quarter of a century after leaving California.

Throughout much of the mid-1970s Tony Dey, a Sacramento based drummer, was on Morrison's payroll. In interviews with Dey he recalled his time playing with Van and the influence of Marin County.

John Goddard of Village Music provided background information on how Marin County influenced his music. A dozen phone interviews with Carol Guida were important to this chapter.

One of the best interviews with Van was published in a 1972 **Rolling Stone** article. For the clues from the **Saint Dominic's Preview** album showing how Marin County influenced Morrison, see Peter Wrench, **Saint Dominic's Flashback** (San Francisco, 2012). Also, see, Howard A. Dewitt, **Van Morrison: The Mystic's Music** (Fremont, 1983), passim.

Of the major biographers only Johnny Rogan believes that Van extensively mined the local Marin County landscape for his songs. His prime example is the 1972 single "Redwood Trees." See Johnny Rogan, **Van Morrison: No Surrender** (London, 2005) p. 275. For others who wrote of this song see, John Collis, **Inarticulate Speech Of The Heart** (Boston, 1996), p. 126, 132, Eric Hage, **The Words And Wisdom of Van Morrison** (Westport, 2009), p. 57, Brian Hinton, **Celtic Crossroads** (London, 1998), p. 143. The critics agreed that "Redwood Tree" was as close as was possible to a love letter from Morrison to California. If it was, Van has never acknowledged it.

For the Neil McCormick quote, see, Pat Carty, "Van Morrison: Looking For The Veedon Fleece, **Hot Press**," September 17, 2022. https://www.hotpress.com/opinion/van-morrison-looking-for-the-veedon-fleece-22828010

One of the most poignant interviews with Morrison, where he looks back aghast at the 1970s is "I Had Absolutely Nothing! Van Morrison Recalls Struggles Of Early Career," **News-Graphic, Georgetown, Kentucky**, February 26, 2023 https://www.news-graphic.com The original article appeared in **The London Times**. What this brief interview does is to put into perspective the overall bitterness in Van's soul over the Them and Bert Berns years. While he can act like an entitled person at times these memories continue to haunt him. Or perhaps they continue to warn him the music business can turn on you at any moment.

The mea culpa moments in Van's life described in this chapter came from a wide range of interviews. They included on the music conversations with Tony Dey, Mark Naftalin, John Goddard, Chris Michie and a brief interview at a Morrison show with Jack Schroer.

See Gerry Smyth, "Gardens All Wet With Rain': Pastoralism In The Music Of Van Morrison," **Irish University Review**, May, 2019, volume 49, number , pp. 171-187. This is a very useful article concentrating on the environment and Morrison's writing. Professor Smyth is an erudite scholar with a penchant for name checking. Hence, his attraction to Van's songs for an academic article. He argues Van created a form of mystical Celtic Music which led to the career of Enya. He employs the "ecomusicology" field which explores the relationship between modern-eco theory and historical and contemporary musical influences.

Tom Paulin was a University lecturer who connected Van to Irish history, English poetry and the influence of William Blake. For the comments of the Oxford Professor on how Van Morrison was influenced by William Blake, and how Van's lyrics reflected the turmoil in and around Belfast in the 1960s, see, Niall Delaney, "The Influence Of The Poet William Blake On The Work Of W. B. Yeats," **The Irish Times**, August 9, 2001.
https://www.irishtimes.com/news/paulin-links-blake-and-van-morrison-1.321692

NINETEEN

Carol Guida: A Hidden Muse To Van's Creative Process

"One must be a living man and a posthumous artist."

Jean Cocteau

"Morrison works intuitively and is a searcher for meaning...."

Bart Hendriks

"Johnny Rogan said I was the waitress in 'Snow In San Anselmo.' I wasn't."

Carol Guida in conversation with the author

"Johnny Rogan got the stuff wrong; I didn't chase Van."

Carol Guida in conversation with the author

"To be a man of letters is an incurable disease."

Goethe

Carol Guida is mentioned in most Morrison biographies. She is introduced as Van's fiancée. She was. Van asked her to marry him. That didn't happen. She remained in his life until just after The Last Waltz. She watched the show from the audience with Van's parents. She held Shana's hand. Carol had a sense of déjà vu. By this time Carol and Van had been in a relationship for three years. Things were not going well. Her whirlwind romance with the Belfast Cowboy provided her with a creative window into his life. When she looked back on her time with Van, she realized she was a muse to his creative process.

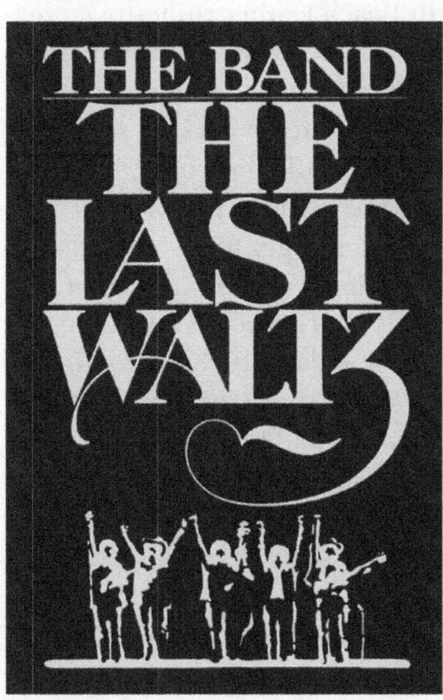

While Guida was his partner, Van continued to play his shows with more gusto and energy. Guida had a special seat at his shows. Van would look out to see her. If she wasn't there, he wouldn't go on stage. "In Europe I would be backstage, one night at the Olympia Theater in Paris, it took me a long time to get to my seat, the crowd was getting restive," Carol continued. "My job when I was backstage was to tell Van to turn on his amp and go back on the stage for an encore," Guida laughed. I asked her why are you laughing. "Van didn't want to assume there was an encore. He felt it was arrogant to assume there would be an encore." Carol said David Hayes always had the same comment.

David Hayes said: "If Carol would get to her seat we could go on stage."

When Bill Graham Presents announced a 1976 Thanksgiving farewell concert, with a turkey dinner, to celebrate The Band's last show, Van was an invited guest. He accepted. Martin Scorsese arrived to film the show. A surprise guest was announced. It was Bob Dylan. The twenty five dollar ticket was pricey for Thanksgiving 1976. The best turkey dinner in town went for ten dollars.

Scorsese's presence interested Morrison. Why? Warner Bros. promised him movie soundtrack deals. That never materialized. Van was interested in meeting with Scorsese. Movie soundtracks were on his radar.

Van was picked up by a limousine. He went to the Miyako Hotel. He brought along a change of clothing. He talked to the musicians. Robbie Robertson came up and asked if he was going to wear the maroon two piece hand made North Beach leather rhinestone creation with sparkles with bell bottoms. Van said: "Yes." The anticipation surrounding the event, the special guests and the electric atmosphere emboldened Van. It made him eager to go back on stage.

When he talked with his biographer, Ritchie Yorke, after the show, he mentioned he wasn't sure he was going to perform. He told Yorke the presence of The Band made him eager to go on stage. His old buddies from Woodstock caused him to rethink his career. He didn't perform for the remainder of 1976. He was all but retired in 1977. Van was still living the good life into early 1978, when, finally, he got back in concert on September 30, 1978 at Santa Clara's Meyer Theater. By that time Morrison and Guida had been apart for more than a year and a half. The operative wisdom was Van refined his song catalogue, reconfigured his business interests and formed a recording-touring plan for the future.

WHAT DID THE LAST WALTZ DO FOR MORRISON?

The Last Waltz was therapeutic. That is he saw the excesses of the rock 'n' roll life. He looked at his friends, The Band, realizing they were burnt out from less than a decade of rock 'n' roll stardom. Did he want that? No! One thing is certain about Van. He is crafty about his product. The Last Waltz unwittingly brought the inspiration for the 1977 album **A Period Of Transition**. He witnessed some listless performances at the Last Waltz.

Peter Barsotti recalled Van wanted to turn up the musical temperature due to an average set by Joni Mitchell. Her soft, dull vocal spot spurred Van on. He entered the stage with a manic frenzy. His performance mesmerized the audience.

As Van recalled the night, for Yorke, he said: "If you're with a good band and everybody's from the old school it's different....You don't have to drag or force things out...." That comment suggested how Van critiqued his live performances.

The crowd's energy, the acclaim he felt from the other musicians, and the audience reception for his versions of "Tura Lura Lura (an Irish Lullaby)" and "Caravan" prompted Van to begin writing a new album. He found a new muse. It was Dr. John. He would co-produce **A Period Of Transition**. The concert stage was Van's home. The music his muse.

When "The Last Waltz" was release, as a concert film, in 1978 there were rave reviews. Bookers, record labels and the general public were interested in Morrison's future shows. Looking back on The Last Waltz, in a conversation with Ritchie Yorke, Van said there was a five minute rehearsal where "we jammed on some Bobby Blue Bland tunes for a while to get the groove...." That did it. Van was back. The period of semi-retirement was in the past.

WHAT WAS GUIDA'S ROLE IN VAN'S LIFE?

To understand Guida, it is necessary to examine her influence on Morrison. She grew up in the Peninsula south of San Francisco. It was as close to a Leave It To Beaver childhood as possible. Family was the key. Education was mandated. Nature! Spirituality! Literature! These were early influences. She was a typical high school teenager in Redwood City. She was in the Sequoia High class of 1971. Then less than two and a half years later she was Van's fiancée.

What changed in Morrison's life when Guida arrived? He

Pelé and Carol Guida

developed a literary direction. Carol was able to introduce Van to philosophers, writers, poets, gurus and intellectual miscreants who populated Marin County.

In over a dozen interviews, she discussed her role with Van concerning his writing, his concerts, his reading habits, his intellectual pursuits, his business interests and their daily life. She made no mention of his private life. Carol is private, thoughtful, spiritual and quiet. Van had never met anyone like her.

Those around Van said she intensified his productivity. Together Van and Carol furtively read William Blake. Shortly after she came into his life Van talked at length about Blake's influence.

When Blake wrote: "Wisdom is sold in the desolate market where none come to buy," Van was mesmerized. As he read on Van discovered the caveat linking Blake to him. That caveat was the power in Blake's writing concerning women, love and jealousy. Van envisioned his writing future.

Blake, like Van, was a voracious reader. Van was also influenced by the mystic Emmanuel Swedenborg. Ditto for Blake! W. B. Yeats influenced Blake. Van on cue read Yeats. Blake's Protestant prose appealed to Morrison. In a post on Van Morrison's website five tracks are listed as Blake influenced: "You Don't Pull No Punches, but You Don't Push The River," "Summertime In England," "Let The Slave" which employs Blake's poem "The Price Of Experience," "Will I Ever Learn To Live In God" and "Golden Autumn Day." What do these songs have in common? Nothing! That is the beauty of Van's writing. Disparate word pieces! They melded together to create music that has endured.

Once Van and Carol discovered each other, he found a path to a more creative life. This was his first in-depth female partner with a sense of his intellect. Carol had a personality drawing people to her. His ex-wife, Janet, was beautiful, bright, independent, talented, and a marvelous person. She had musical ability. She went on to make an album. She opened and has a thriving jewelry design business. Janet was as intellectual as Carol. The time wasn't right for her to be with Van. Fame intruded. Carol came along at the right time. These two remarkable women blended their talents to make the Belfast Cowboy's life a personal joy. Janet has spoken of the beauty of Van's songs. Carol offered vignettes of how he sourced his words.

Charlie Musselwhite and Carol Guida in January 2020 at The Sweetwater Music Hall

THE MYTH AND REALITY: CAROL GUIDA AND VEEDON FLEECE

There is little understanding of Carol Guida as Van's fiancée. She is to the present day a free spirit living in Marin County. She is not accurately described in the various Morrison biographies. Her life with Van was simple. They were in love. He bought her an engagement ring. When they traveled to Sutton Place in Dublin, a photographer came along to take pictures for the **Veedon Fleece** album. The photographer spent hours on engagement photos. Carol has an album of those pictures. They spent a great deal of time getting to know each other. Van drove her around the Emerald Island. She was open minded, flexible and enjoyed a wide range of interests. She was infinitely more social than Morrison. He reveled in her social abilities.

Van is private. So is Carol. She loved Van. It didn't work out. She has nothing derogatory to comment about him. She is in the process of completing her autobiography. There will be a few chapters on Van. Her life has been a full one with many accomplishments. I asked Carol: "Why are you writing your autobiography?" She replied: "I want to set the record straight. I was more than an inspiration to **Veedon Fleece**."

Carol Guida: A High School Picture In Her Bedroom With Her Cousin

Growing up in an suburb between San Francisco and Palo Alto, Carol's childhood was normal, warm and loving. She has an existential personality. The Carol Guida story began in the mid-1960s in a small suburb south of San Francisco-Redwood City.

HOW SEQUOIA HIGH SCHOOL FORMED CAROL'S PERSONA

While attending Sequoia High School, Carol was a typical student. Sequoia was a preparatory school for Stanford University. The faculty was liberal. The courses were advanced. As San Mateo County's oldest high school, Sequoia had a reputation for academic excellence. Guida excelled. "I was really blessed to be exposed to worldly thinkers. My history teacher was a twenty three year old Stanford student, who spoke fluent French. I wound up leaving to study in North Africa and France. I loved living in the French countryside," Guida continued. "I learned more living in Africa and Europe than I would have in Redwood City."

She returned to California and moved to Marin County. She worked as a licensed massage therapist. She studied classical Indian music at the Ali Akbar College. She was prepared for this by her years at Sequoia High. The curriculum there resembled a college more than a high school.

"Sequoia was an enlightened high school teaching yoga." Guida continued. "The emphasis on foreign languages included French, Latin, Spanish and Swahili." Carol combined a liberal education with an innate feel for things musical.

In Redwood City, Carol lived next door to David Harris, Joan Baez's future husband. He attended Stanford where he was the Student Body president. She watched as Harris protested against the Vietnam war. While not an active peacenik, Carol was intrigued by Harris. Sequoia High was an anti-Vietnam hot bed. Carol protested against the war in Vietnam. "We were peaceniks, we were influenced by the music. I loved John Lennon's "Give Peace A Chance." She loved music. "I loved Jessie Colin Young and the Youngbloods and his song "Get Together."

With drop dead good looks, a brilliant and an inquisitive mind, she had a strong work ethic. Traditional college seemed like a waste of time. Calm! Regal! Stately! This is how Van's friends described her.

As she looked back on her life Carol commented: "I was fortunate to grow up in these times. I was a Brownie and a typical girl growing up in a wonderful home. Then it was off to North Africa and France to being my life journey." Carol thought for a moment. She said: "I was from a big, warm, loving close Italian family. I have twenty-one cousins and only two were girls. We were more than a family. We were like a sports franchise."

From the time she left high school until she met Van, Carol finished her high school studies, worked on one profession and began another as an CMT. By the time she met Van she was twenty, self-sufficient, adventurous and working on her literary-spirituality personality.

THE ROAD TO MARIN

In Marin County Carol developed a wide circle of friends interested in poetry, literature and mystical religions. She went to school with Gretchen Hayden, the actor Sterling Hayden's daughter at the Ali Akbar College of Music. Like Gretchen, Carol studied Indian dance. Rock 'n' roll wasn't Carol's first musical love. She studied the sarod and performing Indian classical music. She came to know and was mentored by Ali Akbar Khan. Her search for spiritual and personal enlightenment led her to settle in Marin County. She lived an organic life with a philosophical bent.

Guida's spiritualism cascaded when she met Ali Akbar Khan. He was a pioneer responsible for popularizing Indian classical music in the San Francisco Bay Area. At twenty, Carol sat in his home listening to his spiritual wisdom. Her study of Indian classical music melded with Eastern philosophy.

Van Morrison was attracted to her intellect. Her beauty was obvious. She was the first young lady of intellectual depth in his life. After a number of massages, coffees with Guida, and some philosophical conversations, the Belfast Cowboy was in love. He offered her a job as his personal masseuse with a monthly salary. She refused. Then one day he said he would write a song for her. That did it. She was smitten. Along the way they developed a relationship. How? Spiritualism! Literature! The result? Love!

VAN'S FRIENDS AND BIOGRAPHERS ASKED WHO WAS CAROL GUIDA? HER BUDDHIST INFLUENCE

The question of how long Carol Guida was with Van Morrison is a constant one. She met him in the Fall of 1973, and after moving in with him, she remained until the first few months of 1977. What did this relationship offer? She was swept off her feet by a rock star. The irony was she had little interest in Van's music. She had even less interest in money. Her continued study of classical Indian music, at the college level, was her main interest. "In terms of music, when I first met Van, I asked my boyfriend what his records were like? My boyfriend, Michael Bancas, said we should listen to a record. We lived in this cool compound in an old dairy with cottages. It was full of hippies and we found **Tupelo Honey**. We laughed derisively because Van was pop, we were music snobs."

Carol Guida thought for a moment: "When I went to Los Angeles in 2008 to see the 2008 **Astral Weeks** Live it was as if every note was encased in a golden bubble that floated from his mouth and above the crowd. He absolutely nailed it."

I asked Guida how she thought his voice was recently? "As a singer he improved dramatically. He became a better singer."

The degree to which Guida influenced Van's reading on Buddhism is unknown. Carol remarked of her "Buddhist influence." Van discovered and read the books of Christmas Humphreys, a British lawyer, who spent much of his life writing about Buddhism. What Van received, intellectually, is not known. Nor is the extent of his reading on Buddhist literature.

The role of Buddhism in Van's life remains a mystery. He has never explained it. What did Buddhism bring to Van's songs? When he wrote "Satisfied," Van used "Karma" in the lyrics. Karma is what an individual has achieved and is currently pursuing in a creative life. "Satisfied" name checked **Catcher In The Rye**. Why? Probably due to the constant demand to turn out albums. Van envisioned himself much like J. D. Salinger. A loner! Misundertood1 A genius without respect and recognition. Another song "Daring Night" has the phrase "Lord of the Dance." This is a clear Buddhist reference. The phrase "the burning ground" is a Hindu symbol for death purification by fire and the eventual rebirth.

Van Morrison addressed his interest in Buddhist philosophy. "I've also investigated Buddhism, Hinduism...various forms of Christianity, esoteric Christianity...I don't believe in myths anymore. If I could find a relation that worked..." He didn't elaborate. These quotes came from an interview with B. P. Fallon.

"I was interested to Buddhism in 1980 by Herbie Hancock. It was the Buddhism of Nichiren Daishonin which is a Japanese sect of Buddhism." I asked Carol: "Do you still practice?" She said: "Yes." I asked why: "Because it works, it gives me the ability to go through life. It works. This Buddhist practice is powerful. I lead a life full of appreciation for relationships and nature."

Van in front of Hungry I Club in San Francisco, California

As I left my interview with Guida, I wondered what Van's life would have been like had he practiced Buddhism since 1980.

HANGING OUT WITH VAN IN ALI AKBAR KHAN'S HOME: THE ROOTS OF SPIRITUALISM IS PLANTED WITH CAROL GUIDA

Van read and thought along spiritual lines. When he met Guida she took him to Ali Akbar Khan's home. Of Khan, Guida said: "He was our teacher. He wasn't my guru. He was an educational source." That said it all about Guida. She was not a star chaser. Her intellectual journey was personal, private and tuned to spirituality.

This is what Van loved about her. She was independent minded. Van was intrigued by Ali Akbar Khan. Guida explained how Khan increased her spirituality. "We called him Khan Sahib," Guida continued. "We would sit on the carpet at his feet. He would tell stories of India." Van was present at some of these discussion. In the month before he died, the poet Alan Watts discussed philosophy with Ali Akbar Khan. Van was there. When Carol and Van connected with Watts their philosophical world was enlightened by Eastern thought. Discussions on cultural musicology, through poetry, intrigued Morrison. It was one of many examples of how Marin County nurtured the Belfast Cowboy. "I can't take credit for Van's spiritualism, I added to it," Guida said.

ALAN WATTS BLUES: AN INFLUENCE ON VAN

One day Van came to pick up Carol at Ali Akbar Khan's home. He waited in the driveway. She coaxed him into the house. After some moments of shyness, Van entered the conversation. He had never had this experience with a previous woman. He had never been possessed by a female intellect. He had never met a guru. Nor a poet like Alan Watts. That brought a new intellectual aura to Morrison's life.

What did Ali Akbar Khan offer Guida? He enhanced her developing spiritual life. He was a brilliant classical Indian musician. Khan was nominated for five Grammys. He received a prestigious McArthur grant. He was the first Indian musician to record an album of Indian classical music in the United States. His diversity was shown when the Grateful Dead embraced his music.

When Alan Watts was at Ali Akbar Khan's home the group discussed the poet's ideas, philosophy and approach to life. How this influenced Van is unknown. He did write "Alan Watts Blues." That song is a window into Van's evening with Watts. Van's lyrics tell us a great deal about this brief period hanging out with Watts. As the song opens, Van mentions his "quiet friend" influenced him. That was

Guida. He talked at length with Watts. What did Watts provide Morrison? A window into Eastern philosophy.

Watts' last book, **Cloud-Hidden, Where Abouts Unknown: A Mountain Journal**, published in 1973, influenced Morrison. This collection of essays examined Eastern philosophy. Watts' influence was shown in the 1987 song "Alan Watts Blues." Van's lyrics were influenced by the poet. He employed some of the same language as Watts. "I'm makin' some plans for my getaway" was a window into Van's writing. Another line from the song: "I'm waiting in the clearing with my motor on" indicated he was rethinking his life. Planning his career and preparing to leave Marin County was on his mind. Ulla Munch and Copenhagen, a decade later, continued the influence of young, dark haired ladies influencing his creativity.

Van wrote he loved "takin' some time on my own." That lyrical fragment suggested his relaxed mindset. Van writes of "blue skies" then remarks he is "cloud hidden." The Watts meeting convinced him to "get out of this rat race." These lyrics provide a road map into Van. The only happy note on "Alan Watts Blues" was the joy Van felt getting up in the morning and "sittin' up on the mountain-top in my solitude." That was his time to contemplate. It was easier to do that with Carol Guida by his side.

Van listened and absorbed Watts' writing. The influence of his philosophy? Van has never commented other than in "Alan Watts Blues." Ironically, Watts died a few weeks after talking with Morrison and Guida.

Van saw a kindred spirit in Watts. He was English. He settled in the U. S. Watts was prominent as a Zen practitioner. He moved to San Francisco establishing the American Academy Of Asian Arts, which attracted the 1950s Beats and the 1960s counterculture. Watts believed in non-traditional schools. He was a self-educated guru.

As Watts lectured in the San Francisco Bay Area, he was an influence upon a generation of poets, fiction enthusiasts, Zen practitioners and personal philosophers. Van never stated his indebtedness to Watts. This impressive philosopher, who lit a joint and talked of spiritual fulfillment, was outside of traditional religion. But he was on Van's wavelength.

Watts suggested most people were enlightened. They didn't need to work on it. I asked Chris Michie about Watts influence, he responded: "Who knows! Van was private." The meaning of Watts philosophy was simple. One person was as good as another. Watts said one person had the same talent as a Harvard graduate or a mail man. Van thought of the talent of a person washing windows. He felt good about his past and Watts fit into his philosophical mode.

Van heard the message from Alan Watts. He embraced it. It wasn't until 1987 that Van wrote a song reflecting those times on **Poetic Champions Compose**.

That song, "Alan Watts Blues," was as close as Van got to acknowledging the Zen poet's influence. "They were talking about philosophy and Van was enjoying it," Guida said of Morrison sitting in Khan's home. He found a level of spiritual calm previously unknown.

ON TO MARIN COUNTY FOR GUIDA

For a time in Marin County, Guida lived in Michael Bloomfield's former Mill Valley home. The Bloomfield home high on a hill top overlooking Mill Valley was on Reed Street. It was walking distance to the restaurants, the music outlets and the shopping unique to the city.

By 1971-1972 she was an independent young lady with a love of Indian music, a grasp of literature and a deep knowledge of mystical religions. She was independent financially.

CAROL GUIDA'S INFLUENCE ON VAN AND THE RETURN TO IRISH THEMES

As a writer and performer in Marin County, Van Morrison depended upon the environment for inspiration. The local geography, the tension in the San Francisco Bay Area music community, and the joy in his life guaranteed the breadth and depth of his prose. There was constant writing. Guida understood his creativity. She could talk about literary themes. There was a duality to Morrison's writing. He could pen a love song. The next tune might be a complaint against the industry. He was in lyrical form rebelling against rock 'n' roll's restrictions.

When Guida arrived, there was a new, more mature Morrison. For the next decade his personal life grew daily. By the mid-1980s a few reviewers complained Van had left the building. That is his best known songs: "Moondance," "Domino," "Bluer Money," "Come Running," "Tupelo Honey," "Wild Night" and "Jackie Wilson Said (I'm In Heaven When You Smile)," were hits from 1970 to 1972. It made him feel like an oldies act. Van was flabbergasted. It was less than a decade later. The cry was for hits like those from the early 1970s. Van moved into new lyrical directions. The reviewers didn't understand. Van's albums created new song cycles.

When Van left Warner Bros., one reviewer remarked, **A Sense of Wonder** demonstrated Van's "creative juices" were evident in a new directions only on the opening track. "Tore Down A La Rimbaud" was the only acceptable song according to one critic. The reviewer concluded the remainder of the album was leftovers. This assessment missed the point. Van's creativity was rolling in new directions. Nicholas Jennings wrote: "Van Morrison seems now to have found his peace, but in the process, he has lost his muse."

While Guida was with Van, she inspired him. He wrote furtively. One day at the Bank of Marin, Van had to wait in line to make a deposit. He grabbed a few deposit slips. He began jotting down song lyrics. When they bought a house in San Geronimo, Van name checked the valley using Geronimo as a reference in "Fair Play."

INTERPRETING VAN THROUGH YOU DON'T PULL NO PUNCHES, BUT YOU DON'T PUSH THE RIVER

When Van and Carol walked on Shady Lane, in Ross, the street was featured in a song. That song "You Don't Pull No Punches, but You Don't Push The River" came partially from reading and discussion with Carol Guida. "It was about we were experiencing at the time," Guida continued. Van made references to Meher Baba who was an Indian mystic. "Meher Baba was an early influence," Carol continued. I asked her: "I don't understand, what do you mean an early influence?" Carol replied: "In high school I had his picture up on my bedroom. I was influenced by him before I met Van." Pete Townshend, of the Who, was obsessed with Baba and much of his work from 1966 to 1980 showed his influence. Meher Baba was name checked on **Wavelength**.

After his period of retirement, Van mentioned California influences. What were these influences Here is a list of local San Francisco Bay Area people influencing Van as he prepared to exit the Golden State. Werner Erhard's EST intrigued him as did Richard Alpert, who went by the name Baba Ram Dass. The operative wisdom was Guida influenced the Ram Dass infatuation. He preached everyone was divine. These influences are only a small number of the smattering of California's culture Van imbibed. In time, Scientology and other mystical-religious forces crept into Morrison's life.

"You Don't Pull No Punches, but You Don't Push The River" was autobiographical. After reading Barry Stevens, **Don't Push The River (It Flows By Itself)**, Van used her comments to focus on Gestalt therapy. He wrote about his life. When he and Guida motored on the West Coast of Ireland, he looked for inspiration in what he termed "the Veedon Fleece." What it was remains a mystery. The operative wisdom was Van searched for a spiritual direction. What that was remains unknown. Steve Turner believed it was the Irish equivalent of the Holy Grail. Van Morrison solved the mystery stating: "I haven't a clue what the title means. It's actually a person's name. I have a whole set of characters in my head that I'm trying to fit into things." What is known is for twenty years after reading Barry Stevens, her work brought Van headlong into a frenetic study of Gestalt Therapy.

Guida was a partner with Van who shared the same feckless fascination with William Blake. He was as he wrote: "looking for the Veedon Fleece." When the song appeared on **Veedon Fleece** there was no consensus on what it meant. There is no question Gestalt therapy influenced how Van composed the song. Blake's **The Book Of Urizen** was the source for much of his thinking. The mention of the Eternals was a references to a religious organization founded in Dublin. The song was Irish. Van's trip to a Dublin suburb, Sutton Place, and the subsequent automobile vacation around Ireland accelerated his songwriting.

"We were really into William Blake," Guida continued. "Meher Baba was another source of happiness for us." She attempted to make Van comfortable after his songwriting, attention shifted to business and contract negotiations with Warner Bros.

At this time Van and Carol were together the Belfast was in a contentious legal argument with Ilene Berns over the Bang Record material. "He would rant endlessly about ripped him of by Bang Records or Bert Berns," Carol continued. "Van would go to family gatherings and when her cousin Nick attempted to make Van happy, he told Van the one song that would get them on the dance floor was to play 'Gloria'," Much to Nick's chagrin Van angrily retorted almost spitting out the comment: "I never made a God damned dime off the record I don't care I ever hear it again."

Her memories of Morrison were positive. The song "Comfort You" was explained to me by half a dozen of Van's musicians. They all said the song was a beautiful testimony to Van and Carol's relationship. Jack Schroer told me he credited Guida with what he termed "the stabilized Van." When Van wrote "Comfort You," he expressed the tender side of his writing. This was something he had difficulty doing in his public life. He could write things on paper he would not utter publicly.

The musicians around Van used the term BC. I asked John Platania what BC meant? He said it meant before Carol Guida. What does this mean? To me it suggests the burst of creativity around the **Veedon Fleece** album was more than the trip to Sutton Place. Carol brought a source of contentment to Van that hadn't been witnessed for many years. Much to the relief to his sidemen, Van was happy and eager to work in the studio or on the concert stage.

CAROL GUIDA: LIFE WITH VAN: FROM FAIRFAX TO SAN GERONIMO VALLEY

After meeting Van, Carol spent time with him in his Fairfax

home at 89 Spring Lane. This six bedroom, four bath home 3038 square foot home was perfect for a reclusive personality. The redwood bark around the property gave it a rural ambiance. The view from high on a hill was of a florid, inspiring landscape. There was a massive hot tub inside the home. Carol purchased plants. She spent hundreds of hours making it look like someone lived there. The inside of the home was stark. It was primitive but frighteningly beautiful. The house was 1970s California.

Van decided to tear down a wall to make the home warmer. He and Carol heard about a church in the South that was being razed but had beautiful stained glass including one massive piece of an old meriting ship. They bought the stained glass and had it shipped and installed in a spot where at certain times of the day the sun came through and hit the massive crystal and the entire room would swim in rainbows. "One room swam in blues when we installed the window," Guida recalled. The Fairfax home had a lovely inner décor with a blue and yellow tile floor with a fleur de lye on it. The walls in the kitchen were a brilliant mosaic. A huge matching table with twin mosaics on the top added to the unique kitchen. The kitchen table from the Fairfax home was taken by Van to the Mill Valley.

Van and Carol spent a year in the Fairfax home. Then they moved to San Geronimo. After looking around for a suitable home, Van found an estate sale. The home at 404 Meadow Way was located on a small street with vegetation on both sides of the road. The isolated large home was perfect for Van. "He didn't want to be in Fairfax," Guida continued. "He kept the Fairfax house because it had a recording studio."

The San Geronimo home was a unique property. It was gigantic. This old one story home was on twenty acres. "It was off the beaten path," Guida continued. "We loved it." The estate sale made the house a shrewd business decision.

He loved the burnished walls giving the place an old fashioned look. The interior was unique. The silk wallpaper gave off an opulent feel. A gardener lived on the premises.

Van Morrison and Carol Guida with an Irish Wolfhound (photograph taken by photographer, Tom Collins)

CAROL GUIDA AND VAN'S PARENTS

A highpoint in Guida's years with Morrison was her friendship with Van's parents. Violet and George Morrison were easy going people. They loved living in Fairfax. Carol had an excellent relationship with them. Guida said: "Violet was the de facto Mayor of Fairfax. She rode in convertibles in the parades, she was the Grand Marshall.

Violet wore her white karate outfit in the parades. Years later when I ran into Violet, she would whisper in my ear; you were the favorite of all Van's girl friends. She knew everyone on a first name basis. She never met a microphone she couldn't grab and put on an instant song fest. I loved Violet."

Van's father, George, was the opposite. He was taciturn. He was shy. He dressed well. He smoked a pipe. He carried himself like a college professor. His record store primarily carried classical and jazz records. He refused to sell Grateful Dead records. "He was drop dead handsome," Guida continued. "He had an air of quiet authority. He was much like Van." George, according to store customers, was often grumpy. When John Goddard delivered records as a distributor to George, he told me "like father, like son."

CAROL GUIDA RECALLS INFLUENCES FOR VEEDON FLEECE

The October 1973 trip to Sutton Place, outside Dublin brought Van out of his songwriting funk. This trip set the stage for **Veedon Fleece**. What was Guida's role and influence?

"When we landed in Ireland, Van wrote some songs," Carol Guida continued. "He wrote 'Who Was That Masked Man'." She recalled he name checked Marin County. When he wrote of Shady Lane, it was a tribute to a street in the bucolic Marin County town of Ross. "I was proud to be the muse of that song," Guida recalled. As I walked down Shady Lane, with Carol, I could visualize her beauty as Van wrote these poignant lyrics.

The three weeks Van and Carol spent in Ireland led to **Veedon Fleece**. When Van wrote "Linden Arden Stole The Highlights," it was as Johnny Rogan explained: "The tale of an Irish expatriate in San Francisco." Van said the song was a simple one. It was the tale of an Irish American living in San Francisco.

In "Bulbs" and "Cul de Sac," he lamented moving from one's home. He was relocating from Fairfax north into the San Geronimo Valley. He found kindred spirits there. Kate Wolfe, Elvin Bishop, Janis Joplin and Jerry Garcia lived there briefly.

"We were never happier than when he was working on **Veedon Fleece**," Guida recalled. Jack Schroer told me Carol was "a tonic" for

Van. Schroer said **Veedon Fleece** "was magic." Chris Michie said the period was "immersion into an Ireland he had left but did not forget."

Warner Bros. was solidly behind the album. The label produced a sophisticated marketing plan. The album cover was truncated with a picture of a dog being petted with a description of the album from Van Morrison. It was tasteful. The ad meant to emphasize Van's writing. This ad was the first Warner Bros. piece to have his input.

When Van wrote "Come Here My Love," he looked to Carol's personality for the lyrics. "I was always positive around him," she recalled. The use of his environment and a muse accelerated Morrison's productivity. The analysis for this album is fifty pages in the next book.

There were many highpoints in her time with Van. She witnessed his interaction with many who helped his career. One memory was of the way a local San Francisco disc jockey, turned night club owner, with a record label, Tom Donahue, who treated Morrison with dignity and class. He respected Van's talent.

On the July 29, 1974, show at the Orphanage show, Carol recalled: "I loved 'Big Daddy.' I took a madras bed spread from Cost Plus and made it into a long skirt with a leotard." Van loved her sense of fashion. She watched as Donahue and Van shot a video.

"The video of Van at the Orphanage was an example of how well connected Donahue was and how he loved Van," Guida continued. "The film was shot by two CBS cameramen who were delayed from covering a CIA event in Latin America." The cameramen never forgot Guida's kindness. Van's calm demeanor was due to Guida. She encouraging him to pursue video shots. Guida pursued a television career.

In 1981 Carol was to appear on Entertainment Tonight, when there was an entertainment industry strike. "I interviewed Marsha Mason," Guida continued. "I met Dusty Street about this time and I became a disc jockey. That led to high paying gigs."

Carol shared to a great deal of music with the Belfast Cowboy. He had a habit of going back to the 1960s while listening to other artists. "At this time, Van loved Junior Walker's 'Cleo's Gone,' he loved this record, listening to it constantly."

While in Montreux with Guida, Van met blues guitarist Ralph Walsh. "Walsh was there to meet with one of the Rolling Stones," Guida recalled. She was a steadying influence on Van as he globe trotted the world re-organizing his career.

CAROL GUIDA: EARLY IN VAN'S LIFE

Carol Guida, 2013

By July 1974 Van was settling into a new phase of his life. With Carol Guida by his side, he slowly withdrew from the spot light. When **Veedon Fleece** was released on October 5, 1974 Van felt a sense of déjà vu. He had two hit albums in a year. The earlier release of the double live album **Van Morrison: It's Too Late To Stop Now** began a year that brought the Belfast Cowboy to the pinnacle of the record business. Like he always did, when success arrived abundantly, he went into a new direction. This time it was a period of semi-retirement where he worked like a blue collar musician—worried he might never have another payday. Whether or not Van had a long term plan for his career, he has never discussed it. What emerged was a new writing direction involving spiritualism, various forms of religion and personal reflections on Ireland's bucolic countryside. Guida's beauty, calm personality and under the radar demeanor calmed the Belfast Cowboy's surging intellect. When **Veedon Fleece** was issued, it was not just a departure, the album brought an increased sophistication and maturity to Morrison's songwriting. The next volume, **Van Morrison: The Marin County Subculture Transformation Period, 1974-1979** will discuss how **Veedon Fleece** inaugurated the new Morrison.

The irony was Van retreated to his San Geronimo home with Carol Guida. It was three years before he released another album. What did Van do in those three years. Clinton Heylin claimed he had writer's block. No one around Van recalled he slowed down his writing. He accelerated it in isolation. The large product catalogue of unreleased material that he talks about is what I term "the storage years." Those years are still going on.

When I completed this chapter I called my sources in Belfast, Bath and Marin County and I asked about Van's storage of materials. This May 23, 2023 phone call had my sources alert me to three storage areas and enough unreleased material to fill, as one Belfast Denizen said, "ten box sets."

Carol Guida and Van had a magic time. They parted. The results were two great albums, a bucolic retirement for the Belfast Cowboy, and they both enjoyed their time together. Carol will continue the story in her autobiography. Stay tuned!

Bibliographical Sources

In addition to the Carol Guida interviews, which I cite later in in this list of bibliographical sources, Dan Hicks one night when we had too much to drink took me up to Morrison's Fairfax home. It was Hicks who described the interior of the home on the hill.

The material for this chapter came from interviews with Mark Naftalin, Chris Michie, Jack Schroer, John Goddard, Dan Hicks, Tony Dey, Marie Bainer, Gina Berriault, Leonard Gardner, members of Van's band anonymously, Peter Barsotti, friends of Dahaud Shaar, a group of former students including former Bill Graham Presents employee, Larry Catlin, as well as Ed Diaz and Ronald Vega. A number of school administrators in the Redwood City public school system, as well as band members from other Marin County groups, provided helpful information.

For the importance of a muse to Van's music and its importance in his songwriting process and intellectual development, see, Nicholas Jennings, "A Sense of Wonder," **McLean's**, February 25, 1985.

Also, see, David Burke, **A Sense Of Wonder** (London, 2013), Chapter 7, Brian Hinton, **Celtic Crossroads: The Art of Van Morrison** (London, 1997), chapter 6, Clinton Heylin, **Can You Feel The Silence?: Van Morrison, A New Biography** (Chicago, 2002), p. 277 and Johnny Rogan, **Van Morrison: No Surrender** (London, 2005).

For Alan Watts and Ali Akbar Khan, see, for example, the essay by Samuel B. Cushman, **Alan Watts**, Ali Akbar Khan And Hindustani "Music In The Psychedelic Sixties" in **The Relevance Of Alan Watts In Contemporary Culture** (London, 2021).

See, Gary Suarez, "Looking For The Veedon Fleece, Van Morrison's Elusive Treasure," **Vinylmeplese.com**, January 29, 2019. https://www.vinylmeplease.com/blogs/magazine/van-morrison-liner-notes Suarez compares Carol Guida's influence to that of Janet Planet. In reality, the opposite is true as Guida had a more pronounces intellectual and spiritual influence. Janet was a pragmatist and a talented artist. Carol was spiritual, a reader and she had a strong work ethic.

See Ali Akbar Khan, **The Rough Guide to Ali Akbar Khan** which is an hour and nine minutes of his music. The Ali Akbar College of Music was established in San Rafael. It celebrated his one hundredth birthday in 2022. Along with Ravi Shankar, with whom he played, Khan was more than a musician. He was a spiritual force in Marin County. After founding the Ali Akbar College of Music in Berkeley Khan moved it to Fairfax in 1968 and then to San Rafael.

This chapter benefitted from interviews with Carol Guida on December 30, 2020, January 22 and 27, 2021, December 20-21 2021, February 21, 2022, April 8, 19, and 22, 2022, August 4, 2022 as well as a dozen 2023 interviews.

For Alan Watts influence on Van, and how it impacted his lyrics is debated in florid tones of whether or not Van is a solid Christian. This article is an exercise in intellectual blabbering, but interesting, see, for example, Dennis Lund, "Behind The Mystic Music: Van The Man," **Benicia Herald**, April 28, 2012. http://beniciaheraldonline.com/behind-the-mystic-music-van-the-man/

On the importance of "You Don't Pull No Punches, but You Don't Push The River," there is a systematic body of literature with enough conclusions for a new book. For the conclusion it is a love song, see, Johnny Rogan, **Van Morrison: No Surrender** (London, 2005), pp. 298-300. For the notion it is a spiritual song see, Steve Turner, **Van Morrison: Too Late To Stop Now** (London, 1993), p. 122. Turner briefly discusses Van's search for the Veedon Fleece.

Another great source is Clinton Heylin, **Can You Feel The Silence?: Van Morrison, A New Biography** (Chicago, 2003), pp. 277-283. For Van's comment on the song see, Brian Hinton, **Celtic Crossroads** (London, 1997) p.179.

The quotes from Van about The Last Waltz, which Ritchie Yorke taped and played over a Vancouver B. C. radio station, are taken from Peter Viney, "Van Morrison At The Last Waltz." https://theband.hiof.no/articles/van_at_tlw_viney.html Also, see Howard A. DeWitt, **Van Morrison: The Mystic's Music** (Fremont, 1983). Van's purple sequined jump suit received as much media play as the music.

The Carol Guida influence fostered a William Blake sense of romanticism. Van experienced the euphoria of talking about the Irish Saints and the mystics. He longed for Belfast. Without Guida this would have been impossible. She was an enabler to his dreams. Chris Michie told me: "Van listened to Lou Reed's 'Berlin,' it influenced him. How? I have no idea."

This chapter benefitted from interviews with a number of Marin County residents close to the music scene. They included Dan Hicks, John Goddard, Mark Naftalin, Chris Michie and Marie Bainer. Guitar Mac and John Lee Hooker provided some reminiscences as did Jimmy McCracklin, who I managed in the 1980s.

Carol Guida was a columnist for the **Ross Living**. She wrote intensely of the Ross and Fairfax and Marin County in general.

For a view of Van's spiritual nature, see, for example, Jerry Mooney, "The Spirituality Of Van Morrison," **Sivana East**, n. d.

VAN MORRISON: PERSONALITY AND THE BIOGRAPHICAL PROCESS, GOOD LUCK INTERPRETING HIM

"Is it okay if I go to sleep?"

VAN MORRISON IN AN INTERVIEW WITH LIAM MACKEY

"I'm not a nice person. I don't expect anyone to say I'm a nice guy. If somebody says I'm grumpy....I think I'm a loner."

JOHNNY ROGAN CLAIMS VAN SAID THIS

"He is not a genius. He is just completely hooked on what he does."

JANET PLANET

"I always thought he would commit suicide because he seemed so unhappy."

A BELFAST MUSICAL COLLEAGUE

A proper Van Morrison biography would be incomplete without a short chapter on his personality. How did it influence the biographical process? That is an easy question to answer. His personality drives his writing. His personality has been the same since he arrived in Marin County. But can the biographer interpret him? Probably not! Erik Hage said it best when he described Van as personally elusive. He is unpredictable. The tendency is to concentrate on his tirades, his songs seeking revenge, and his quixotic examination of events surrounding his life.

Clinton Heylin and Johnny Rogan analyzed all aspects of Van's life. They were vilified for their efforts. Justified? Perhaps! Dangerous to the biographical process? Yes! You need a balanced chapter on Van's personal life. No one agrees on his life. That includes Van who has different interpretations of how he has lived.

Johnny Rogan remarked to me: "Van Morrison is a world class asshole." I never talked to Clinton Heylin. There was no need as Heylin's prose dripped with venom but also with honesty and careful analysis. Erik Hage, Peter Mills, John Collis and Brian Hinton view Van's life primarily through his music and art. The Shakespeare of Telegraph Avenue, Greil Marcus, is Van's most perceptive, academic reviewer with stilted references to his musical genius. Steve Turner sees Christian seeds in Van's music. Van, in a drunken stupor, criticized Turner from the stage for writing about his personal life. Ryan H. Walsh's book was a brilliant look at **Astral Weeks** and Van's difficult life. I have a deep and heartfelt respect for these superb authors. They all have contributed to the mountain of material written on the Belfast Cowboy.

The problem with a Van biography is the fear of legal action. The web Sheriff and the barristers break down the doors. Van has a bumptious fear of personal interaction. Those from Belfast, or from the bucolic grove of academic life, notably Gerald Dawe, Peter Mills and Peter Childs, have been given a pass.

Morrison in 1972
(photograph taken by photographer, Michael Maggid)

A book entitled "Van Morrison And Journalists" would be a fascinating foray into his mind and the depth of his hostility to some of those who write about him. David Wild, of **Rolling Stone**, tells the story of Van running away from him in New York and later Boston. Why? Van consented to an interview. He changed his mind. He ran away. Sounds crazy? It isn't! What does it tell us? Van can change his mind in seconds. That is an undeniable character trait. Another of Van's phobias is a paranoia people are attempting to take advantage of him.

Morrison is difficult. He has been since the 1960s. Why discuss it? If you want to understand the man, it is necessary to examine what sets him off, what he appreciates, and why he has been described by the press in recent interviews as "the pettiest musical genius" or as Laura Barton, wrote in the **London Guardian**; she felt like her interview with Van was "a psychiatric examination."

The Barton interview received extraordinary publicity? The media reaction suggested Morrison was suddenly difficult. Those comments neglect how cooperative he is at times. The simple fact is that from time to time Van goes off during an interview. This is a positive. He provides insights into a personality with a gulf as big as the Grand Canyon. He has little consistency during interviews. This is what makes Van a transparent subject. He gets complaints off his chest.

Since 1985, there have been honest, open, transparent and heartfelt interview. Van is not always difficult. He is often forthcoming. When he is nasty all hell breaks out. Those who interact with Morrison socially find him charming. He loves to discuss literature, art and popular culture. These topics reflect his wide ranging reading.

The problem with biography is many writers attempt to curry favor with him. That truncates the biographical process. To understand the man it is necessary to examine when he is difficult, and when he is a prince. You never know which Morrison you will get.

WHY VAN IS DIFFICULT AND WHEN HE IS NOT: YOU NEVER KNOW

After marrying Michelle Rocca, Van was on his best behavior. He completed four interviews with her in the mid-1990s in which he looked back on his life. In select interviews he was charming, well dressed, articulate and never over the top. That behavior could vanish.

There was not a new Van Morrison. The 1995 interviews with his wife, Michelle, Rocca, were placed on YouTube on the Internet in 2020. Social media became a research tool for Morrison biographers. Courtesy of Woolhall, Morrison and Rocca offered a slice of his life in four distinct interviews.

As many times as he has said: "I don't talk about my personal life, I don't talk about my music," he will continue and discuss his rich life. Then along came YouTube in 2005. It became a veritable Morrison archive.

The Leo Green are a set of interviews that are friendly, open, informative and above all Green asked excellent questions. Not everyone got it. Just ask Laura Barton. Just ask David Wild. Just ask Clinton Heylin. Just ask Johnny Rogan. Just ask Steve Turner. What do they all have in common? Van's tirades.

There is abundant evidence he can be a little cranky bastard. There is statistical evidence he gives warm, often lengthy, open interviews. If you quantify the interviews, you will find Van can sit with a cup of tea giving his version of the future. This is easy to do since he has had a legendary songwriting-performing career. When David Wild interviewed him in 1990 for **Rolling Stone**, the writer concluded: "He sits there mostly scowling, shooting down some topics..." That is an accurate description. Van often remarks: "I don't need to explain what I do."

To ask Van to speculate on the past or predict the future is a recipe for disaster. He considers these questions inane. Barton's questions, Van believed, were insulting. This is not to excuse his behavior. It is simply Van being Van.

In 2019, after the interview with Laura Barton, she wrote a scathing article. The headline for this interview was: "A Duel With Van Morrison: Is This A Psychiatric Examination?" It was a title titillating the reader.

On Twitter in August, 2021, Barton wished Van a Happy Birthday. She tweeted: "Happy Birthday, Van Morrison. Let's all listen to this and remember how goddamn sublime the man can be when he's not being a curmudgeon or a covid-denier or spoiling for a fight." Then she posted a YouTube video of Van singing "Linden Arden Stole The Highlights." Van didn't respond.

The Laura Barton interview appeared in the **London Guardian** and the **Irish Times**. The headlines suggested Van's difficult nature. Van's interview tirades sell a lot of newspapers. His interviews in the same time frame, with Leo Green, were open, honest, revelatory and interesting. Those interviews, on Van's website and YouTube, didn't generate the same media interest. Why? No sensational headlines! The best way to understand why and how Van reacts with the media is to examine his personality.

Van Morrison Cutting His Birthday Cake

In 1990, David Wild in **Rolling Stone** wrote: "He doesn't smile. He does not charm. He does not offer anecdotes freely." Van is tough minded during interviews. He is outspoken. He is committed to his ways. His personality drives his art. But can you understand it? In one of the more bizarre recollections in journalism, Wild appeared in November 2015 on a podcast entitled: "My Bad Moondance With Van Morrison," in which he recounted his experience with Van twenty five years after the abortive New York and Boston interviews. The twenty-seven year old Wild was now fifty two with two Emmy's and a legendary writing career had a horror filled story of that encounter with Van.

VAN MORRISON: THE PERSONALITY TRAITS

There are rules for understanding Van's personality. First, he doesn't suffer fools. Second, he is 24/7 promoting his career. Third, any sign of disrespect leads to a volatile exchange. Fourth, he is absolutely anti-pop and anti-hit record. Fifth, he remains critical of and suspicious of record labels. Sixth, he protects his intellectual property. Seventh, he has a black and white personality. Compromise is not a part of his personality. Eighth, he is spiritual, self-educated with a penchant toward brilliant thought. He is an esoterically intellectual writer. Ninth, he has a blue collar personality with a vision of his creativity and a constant window into his fiscal future. Perseverance, integrity, honesty and vision define him. Tenth, an unpredictably mercurial personality dominates his life. He was born with a chip on his shoulder. That trait defines his personality.

The interview with Laura Barton, for the **London Guardian,** received an inordinate amount of negative publicity. She is a seasoned journalist. Van flared! Why? It was the nature of her questions. He was enraged. The broad and imprecise questions upset him. This is a character trait. He goes off the rails. It is simply Van being Van. Nothing personal! The reporter looked forward to the interview. Her 2019 experience contradicts my conclusion Van has mellowed. But Barton's view is quite different. She believed she experienced Van's wrath for no discernible reason. A look inside this contentious interview suggests the complexity of the celebrity interview.

LAURA BARTON EXPERIENCING VAN'S WRATH, 2019

"The singer-songwriter is releasing his sixth album in three years—his best since 1997. Would he like to expand on how he made it, or why he chose his collaborators? He would not."

LAURA BARTON

As Barton anticipated the interview she recalled a Van song, "Why Must I Always Explain?" It was an omen for what she was about to experience. The interview was rushed and uncomfortable. She would not agree to a set of pre-determined questions. She was a pro. Van loves to control the narrative. She was a professional journalist. Barton would not agree to hagiography.

He rails at most books. It was not a surprise. Why did he have trouble with the October 2019 interview with Laura Barton? It was a matter of interpretation. On Twitter, Barton wrote: "I spent sixteen minutes and twenty-eight seconds in the company of Van Morrison and then I wrote about it here." She was not happy. His behavior irritated her. Van felt the same way. This was a recipe for a contentious conversation. To Barton's credit she handled it well. She stood up to him.

As Barton walked into a Cardiff hotel, she was excited. Van was one of her favorite singers. She spotted Van sitting by a window in a fourth floor hotel looking nervous. "It is a peculiar setting for a conversation," Barton wrote. "Let's see if I need to make some notes here," Van remarked. Barton looked dumbfounded. What the hell was going on? "Before me, my favorite singer in the world, a man I wanted to interview for two decades, holding a notepad. A sour air settles over the room."

The interview was for the release of Van's new album **Three Chords And The Truth**. Barton was about to discover Van Morrison's truth or perception or personality. Take your choice! She discovered these disparate personality traits. That is the truth of how he views journalists. Barton noted it was the sixth album Van released in a little more than three years. She remarked it was the best since the 1997 **The Healing Game**. She had listened to all his albums. She knew a great deal about his career. Barton thought she might be able to get inside Van's head. Help! Little did she realize the man had an attitude.

Barton asked good questions. They talked about Jay Berliner's guitar genius. Van loosened up. When discussing Bill Medley's vocal back up on one song from the album, he was euphoric. He described the unique nature of Medley's vocal style. Of Berliner, Van observed: "Well, he's just a genius." On former Righteous Brother Bill Medley, who appeared on one track singing back up, Van said: "I've just always liked him as a singer."

When Barton asked Van what he looks for in a duet partner, he became cantankerous. "I don't need to explain what I do or how I do it.... To me it's OK if it's a mystery." Barton wrote: "I have the feeling that Morrison is curling up in a ball before me and closing his eyes so that I might not see him."

Barton asked him what he liked to listen to in quiet moments. Van responded: "Jazz or classical music." She asked: "Why?" He looked at her with disdain. "Cos that's what I like." After she asked a few more questions, Van said: "Is this a psychiatric examination?" She said it wasn't. Van responded: "It sounds like one." He tells her he sings, he writes, he plays. Things are not going well. "For a moment I consider telling him to grow up," Barton continued. "I look him in the eye and tell him that I am not trying to psychoanalyze him, that his music has simply meant more to me than any other throughout my life." This is a defining moment. Barton stood up to

Morrison. They agreed to end the interview. Van comes across less than charitable in select interviews. You figure it out. I can't.

When Van knows the interviewer, everything is fine. Donal Corvin, Sam Smyth or Leo Green make him at ease. When Van ended the Barton interview, she noticed on his note pad an angry drawing. Barton thinks back to a 1979 song. She believes it explains his mercurial temperament. This song, "You Know What They're Writing About," was the final tune on **Into The Music**. What is the point? From day one Van has had issues with journalists. His biographers, and those who interpret his music, have experienced his ire. Rather than seeing interviews and books as a sign of respect for his writing and performing brilliance, Van sees it a challenge. Genius is the result in his lyrical and performing life. He gets a pass for personal peccadillos. He was exactly this personality type in 1973-1974 in Marin County. The Laura Barton interview is a window into the consistency of Morrison's personality. Obstinate behavior drives his creativity. Brilliant but frustrating.

This attitude was Van's in 2019. He hadn't changed an iota since the 1970s. It was more than a half a century this behavior helped, not hurt, his rise to fame as a major solo artist.

There was a reason. Van feared people taking advantage of him. He is slightly paranoid. He has a loner persona. He has a short attention span. That remains a personality trait. He changes his mind by the minute. These traits were in place when he lived high on a hill in Fairfax.

THE OTHER SIDE OF VAN MORRISON: THE OLD GREY WHISTLE TEST INTERVIEW 1973

In 1973 when Van arrived in London on the It's Too Late To Stop Now tour, he was media friendly. He cooperated with every journalist. His first stop was an interview for the Old Grey Whistle Test. Whispering Bob Harris conducted this brief interview. Van had fun with Harris. When Harris asked him when the tour was planned. Van responded with a straight face. "About two minutes ago." This dour media personality asked how British audiences had changed. He wondered what Van and the band were expecting. He turned to

John Platania and David Hayes. They said nothing. They smiled. The interview continued. In a monosyllabic tone, Harris asked Van how he was? Van said: "Great." When Harris went on about how he was going to perform, Van looked perplexed. John Platania suggested Van should stay: "Uninhibited." Then Van talked about the Bert Berns album and recording "Brown Eyed Girl" in New York. Harris asked for more information on Berns and New York. Van was evasive. "I was just digging the scene," Van said of the Big Apple. He talked about a few gigs, some promotion and some recording. Van remarked he was struck by how well the studio engineers worked on his sessions. Then he described the **Astral Weeks** sessions. Harris wasn't interested. The questions were stilted and inane. They made Harris look good. Van was a prince. If a nervous one.

Harris asked about studio work. Did it take more or less time? "If you are looking for something extra, you zone in. Generally…I prefer the production," Van said. "Hard Nose The Highway seems to be more complex….How much time did you spend on this album," Harris asked. Clearly, uncomfortable, but very cooperative, Van turned to David Hayes. "We started in November…we did about thirty tracks," Van said as Hayes and John Platania talked a little bit.

The Laura Barton and Whispering Bob Harris interviews suggested the differences between the 1973-1974 and 2019 interviews. Van had grown. He was a different person in 2019. He was confident. There are different sides to the Belfast Cowboy. He has never been predictable. That is the joy, as well as the detriment, in interpreting the Belfast Cowboy. Paul Vincent, the San Francisco KMEL disc jockey, told me a revealing story. As Paul sat with Van in the radio station's remote control room. It was just Van and Paul. When Vincent played a record or an ad, Van remarked how he loved the quiet and the isolation of the interview. It was as if Van didn't realize that a San Francisco audience was tuned in to his every word. Paul Vincent remarked: "Van is not worldly. That is he lives in an alternate universe." What did Vincent mean? He suggested the creative process was constant with Van. It was never interrupted. Carol Guida agreed. She talked of Van writing 24/7 during their intense four year relationship.

CODA: A PERSONAL LIFE WITHOUT A PUBLIC PERSONALITY

The major contradiction in Van Morrison's life is he pursues a personal life without a public personality. Van is open and honest with the faults and successes of his life. He is always working on a new album. As he was in his seventy-seventh year as I completed this book, Van was at the top of his fame. He had just released a double CD **Moving On Skiffle** which debuted at number one on the **Billboard** jazz chart. He was getting ready to announce a blues albums for the Fall of 2023. There were no signs of slowing down. Age wasn't a factor. He had the freedom to write and record whatever he wanted. **Moving On Skiffle** was Van's forty-fourth studio album. The **Irish Times** noted "it was good to hear Van Morrison happy." His two previous albums were views as political ranting over Covid. This is the charm of Morrison. He can be a contrarian. In the next breath he will release a beautiful album.

When **Hard Nose The Highway** was released, it reflected his mood. That mood matured, grew intellectually and fifty years later Morrison was as relevant as ever in the music business. His personality didn't matter. It was his music. His writing. His artistic growth. These were the factors keeping Morrison at the top of the music business.

Bibliographical Sources

For Van erupting while being interviewed, during an album release discussion, there is interpretive gold for the biographer. One of these incidents took on a life of this own. If Van has a legitimate complaint about the media, it is for a 2019 interview with Laura Barton. If you Barton she has the same complaint. He believed he was ambushed by her questions. She argued he didn't respect journalists. Things did not go well. I stand neural. Read the interview. You decide.

For this interview that went viral with a volcanic Internet thrust, see, Laura Barton, "A Duel With Van Morrison: 'Is this a Psychiatric

Examination? It Sounds Like One'," **The London Guardian**, October 31, 2019.

https://www.theguardian.com/music/2019/oct/31/a-duel-with-van-morrison-is-this-a-psychiatric-examination-it-sounds-like-one The Barton interview is a prime example of the salacious interest in what I term "Morrison eruptions." I don't excuse Van for his, at times, contentious behavior. It is fair to point out when he acts up there is more publicity than when he is the calm Morrison. Bad publicity is better than no publicity at all.

On Morrison's difficulty with interviews, see, for example, David Wild, "A Conversation With Van Morrison," **Rolling Stone**, August 9, 1990. In this interview Morrison stated: "What people write about you is not real. I just want to be left alone and live my life." Van ended the interview lamenting fame's burdens.

In 2015 Wild appeared on a podcast recounting how he was bewildered by the 1990 interview with Morrison, After twenty-five years he was still attempting to figure out the Belfast Cowboy's behavior. See "My Bad Moondance With Van Morrison With Writer David Wild," **Story Worthy**, 2015. https://www.imdb.com/title/tt24922838/ This is an intriguing podcast suggesting the difficulty in interviewing Morrison. Wild, a brilliant **Rolling Stone** writer, has no rancor concerning Morrison. He reflects twenty-five years later on understanding the man. His music! Wild loves it! The man? Wild is not so sure.

For the Old Grey Whistle Test interview with Bob Harris, see, "Exclusive Van Morrison In Conversation," London, July 1973. https://www.youtube.com/watch?v=AcoMxC9lYXY

Leo Green's YouTube Interviews included lengthy descriptions from Van about working with home grown artists. Invariably, Marin County crops up in this interviews. As Van looked back on the 1970s, he paid tribute to Marin County's enormous creativity.

The poster child interview for positively analyzing Van's personality is Paul Vincent. The KMEL disc jockey provided six separate interviews for **Van Morrison: The Mystic's Music** (Fremont, 1983). The Vincent-Morrison interview was published when Blair Jackson was managing editor of **BAM**. This was a free magazine providing wonderful coverage of the San Francisco music scene. Blair Jackson edited this piece. He was a brilliant writer with unique insights into the local music scene. He lived in Oakland and covered the blues. He was the San Francisco Bay Area Grateful Dead specialist.

Those interviewed with in-depth knowledge of Marin County included Jack Schroer, Mark Naftalin, Tony Dey, Carol Guida, John Goddard, Marie Bainer and dozens of anonymous Van friends.

One of the most penetrating, if brief, insights into Van's personality comes from Martha Wainwright who opened for him in a Montreal show. She spent time in Woodstock and while not knowing Van intimately she talked of his musical genius and feral personality. In her memoir she writes: "Around that time, someone had given me Van Morrison's old **Veedon Fleece** album, and I turned it up as I drove, his voice and poetry reverberating in me with added meaningfulness as he sang about laying it down for a while and taking a rest, hidden away from world. (I still love that goddamn record, even though the man himself is a real schmuck who once, after I opened a show for him in Toronto came on to me in a way that was not only sexist and boorish but uninteresting and sad. So different from his music)." For this quote see, Martha Wainwright, **Stories I Might Regret Telling You: A Memoir** (New York, 2022), p. 230. Wainwright, the daughter of Kate McGarrigle and Loudon Wainwright III, described the duality of Morrison's personality. You can define him. You will never know him. For Wainwright, Van's music helped her get through a divorce.

The Leo Green interviews, with Van Morrison, on YouTube provide special insights. A relaxed Morrison spent a great deal of time looking back on the 1970s. For the best of these conversations, see, for example, "Van Morrison-On Getting It Right," October 29, 2018, and "Van Morrison-on Keeping It Simple," October 28, 2019 and "Van Getting It Right," October 29, 2019 on YouTube. This last YouTube interview was posted on Van Morrison's Official Website indicating his approval.

Also, see, the Leo Green four episodes on "Too Late To Stop Now-The Van Morrison Story," **RadioTimes.com.**

https://www.radiotimes.com/programme/b-5u4ss4/too-late-to-stop-now-the-van-morrison-story/

The amount of material from Van on the Internet is a bonus. He talked in depth to certain people. When he married Michelle Rocca, he opened up about his life. On Rocca's relationship with

Van, see, for example, Tanya Sweeney, "Van Morrison and Michelle Rocca: How Their Stormy Relationship Came To A Bitter End," **Belfast Telegraph**, March 27, 2018. This is an interesting article by a reputable journalist. Tanya Sweeney wrote of "secrecy and controversy in Van's marriage." Predictably, he was furious. Why? The divorce took almost a decade. He was of the opinion it was private. It wasn't. It got worse. Sweeney reported the couple had a "lupine hunger for privacy." Not exactly rocket science reporting but good writing. The author concluded: "They were a prominent couple socially." This was a new Van. The ferocity of Sweeney's prose, which, in Van's opinion, was what agitated him. He told a friend there was insidious reporting. He didn't care for it. His marriage to Michelle Rocca was no one's business. He moved out in 2012. This article came six years later and Van believed it was an attack on his credibility. Those who knew Van told me the article "took enormous liberties with the facts." After Van moved out Michelle Rocca sued the neighbors for cutting a hedge she said Van wanted for privacy. When Rocca made that claim, Morrison was not living in the Dalkey home. The Sweeney article described, in copious detail, food fights in the Dublin's La Stampa restaurant. The stories of Van having drinks with Mick Jagger at the Shelbourne Hotel was another revelation into Van's private life. When one enters his private life there is war.

Van with Michelle Rocca
(photo courtesy Belfast Telegraph)

TWENTY-ONE

Clinton Heylin's Chapters 17-19: 1973-1974, A Commercial Cul-De-Sac, It Didn't Exist, Here Is What Heylin Missed And Why It Is Important, Johnny Rogan To The Rescue

" I don't get credit for my time as Van's muse."

Carol Guida

"There is not enough space in this article to convey how disappointing a book this is."

Kevin Mitchell on Clinton Heylin's biography

"We read all the time. We discussed literary, philosophical, religious themes."

Carol Guida

"This is a person uncomfortable in his own skin."

Ed Fletcher

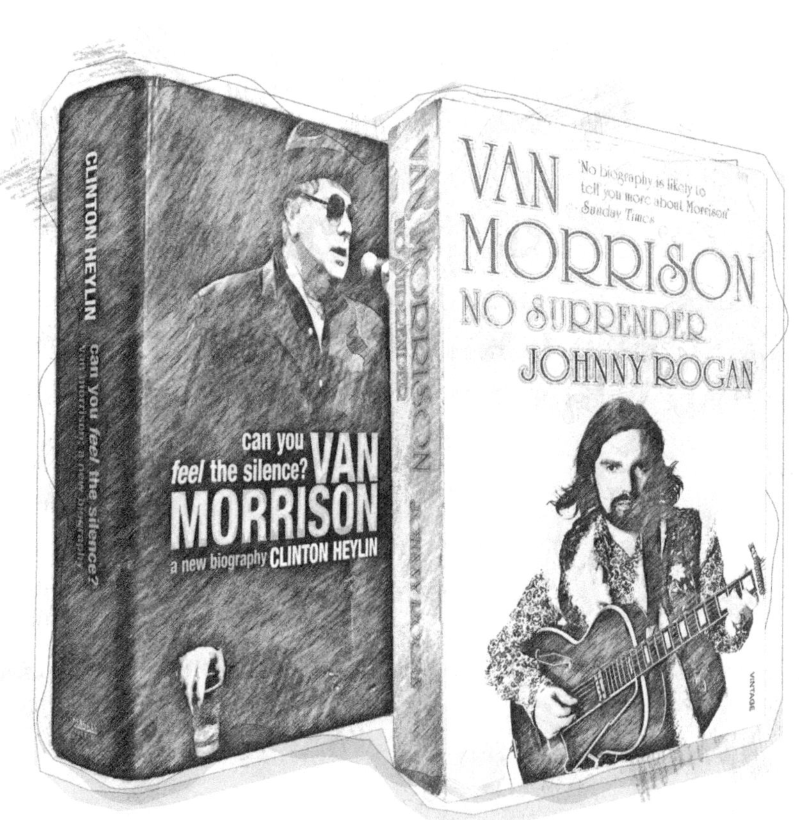
CLINTON HEYLIN
can you feel the silence?
can you
feel the silence? VAN
MORRISON
a new biography CLINTON HEYLIN
VAN MORRISON
VAN
MORRISON
'No biography is likely to
tell you more about Morrison'
Sunday Times
NO SURRENDER
JOHNNY ROGAN
VINTAGE

Clinton Heylin is a brilliant researcher. He is a gifted writer. He has a penchant for analysis that makes Johnny Rogan blush with embarrassment. Rogan, like Heylin, has two of the best biographies of Morrison and he unearthed material no one had previously discovered. Rogan went so far as to interview everyone he could find in Belfast who had known Van in the 1950. Considering Van was born in 1945 these early years were deemed by many to be insignificant. What Rogan found it that the early teen age Van was no different than the Van we all know and love. That is as a performing and recording artist.

Why have a chapter discussing Morrison's two most prominent biographers? It is to understand the enigma that is Van Morrison. How did Heylin and Rogan differ. Heylin is about how Van's divorce, his home studio and his fights with Warner Bros. shaped his career. Rogan, for some unexplainable reason, suggested that the Troubles kept Van from returning to Belfast. As a Protestant, Rogan reasoned, he was in danger. That belief was partially true. What did they miss? Plenty! Marin County shaped Morrison. Neither biography pays attention to the whirlwind influences from the bevy of talented musicians, producers, music industry figures and creative gurus living in small California County. Van drank in the influences, he drank in the coffee, he drank in the booze, he drank in the business lessons. "Becoming Van Morrison" resulted.

CLINTON HEYLIN: ARGUABLY THE BEST MORRISON BIOGRAPHER

Clinton Heylin is arguably the best Van Morrison biography. He has interviewed more people close to Morrison than any other author. His work is authoritative. So why a chapter in my book on Clinton Heylin's brilliant biography?

To praise Heylin is my goal. But to criticize Heylin opens new interpretive doors. The **London Guardian** unfairly criticized Heylin's book using the headline in their review: "How To Make Van Ordinaire?" Kevin Mitchell concluded of Heylin's biography: "Like its subject, it is riddled with contradictions." Charles Shaar Murray was closer to the truth. In **The London Independent**, Murray argued Van didn't look like a rock star, he didn't want to be one. He writes Heylin's book is "a thorough biography." The two reviews tell us a great deal about the press.

Whereas the **London Guardian** gives Van an excuse for his eccentric behavior, the **London Independent** review attempts to understand his personality. That is what Heylin has done in his pathbreaking biography. Why is it pathbreaking? Heylin talked to everyone inside the Van camp. He had a level of cooperation from some in Van's management circle, notably Paul Charles. He searched out every musician who would consent to an interview. Along the way Heylin revealed the inner Van. It wasn't pretty. Warner Bros. gave Heylin a company desk, carte blanche to examine sessions sheets. He was allegedly not allowed in the area where the masters were stored. Why did the management provide hours of research material for Heylin's brilliant tome? I asked that question to a number of people at Warner. No one responded.

The conclusions to Heylin's book? You decide! Heylin vows never to go down that path again. Murray's review suggests Van was part of the "awkward squad." What does that mean? He argues Neil Young, Bob Dylan, Elvis Costello and Lous Reed were musicians "we might call the 'Awkward Squad." Great writing. Even better analysis. "They set their faces against the demands of the marketplace, the media and sometimes their own audiences," Murray in scintillating Oxford-Cambridge prose. Heylin places Van in this rarified company. Of Van, Murray wrote: "He's indubitably the most awkward of them all."

Heylin has three brief chapters on this period. Is my six hundred plus page book necessary to explain a year and a half of Van's life? It is! Why! Marin County, Carol Guida, the Caledonia Soul, the Caledonia Soul Express, the It's Too Late To Stop Now tour and album, the San Francisco Bay Area clubs and dozens of local musicians created "Becoming Van Morrison." These influences have been mentioned, but never analyzed or interpreted in depth. This is why a six hundred page book is just enough to examine the renaissance of a young Irish kid turning twenty-eight in 1973 as he evolved into a world class performer and increasingly sophisticated songwriter.

Heylin is a remarkable writer. He is more than a successful journalist, biographer and observer of the rock 'n' roll music scene. He is an analytical cultural historian. As such he was able to select Van's words as a means of understanding the Belfast Cowboy. When Morrison wrote: "The fact that I may be successful at what I do does not mean that I accept that anyone can come along and publish details of my life, for other people to read, purely for their own personal enjoyment," Morrison remarked in 1993.

One of Van's failings is he doesn't understand biography, rules of government and law, the literary process (even though he is steeped in literature) and he has a Protestant tough nature of never backing down. A fan, known as the Dude, remarked: "Van is a world class asshole." Maybe! Maybe not! He is more aptly described as someone who goes to great length to protect and ensure his privacy. Clinton Heylin wrote: "Even if Morrison believes he holds the copyright in his own life, the question of whether his wishes should be respected remains."

JOHNNY ROGAN COMES CLOSEST TO EXPLAINING MORRISON'S CHARACTER VIS-À-VIS BELFAST

In 2005 Johnny Rogan's **Van Morrison: No Surrender** was a brilliant analysis of Van's character. He described how Protestant influences making him the underdog, and the difficulty East Belfast, where Van lived, had with the Troubles created a personality so erratic defining him was impossible. He also developed a blue collar work ethic making Van a lunch pail worker in the music business. There are dozens of friends who socialized with Van who described him as animated concerning literature. He has a strong interest in the arts and he is consumed by religion.

Rogan emphasized Belfast was "no Protestant picnic." When he described the squalor in which Morrison lived, he misses the point.

That squalor made the Belfast Cowboy an unmitigated blues man. It also formed his erratic character. Respect! This is what Van demanded from day one.

When Van arrived with Carol Guida in Sutton Place in October, 1973, his life changed dramatically. She was the conduit to a new sanity and an emboldened creativity.

WHAT DOES BECOMING VAN MORRISON: IT'S TOO LATE TO STOP NOW, 1973-1974 DO FOR BIOGRAPHY?

Becoming Van Morrison: It's Too Late To Stop Now, 1973-1974 is a maximalist biography. What did Clinton Heylin and Johnny Rogan miss in their brilliant biographies? By analyzing chapters seventeen through eighteen of Heylin's book where he concluded Van rediscovered his Irish roots, there was no consideration of forces in and around his California Fairfax based home. What did Heylin miss? The San Francisco Irish pubs. The local landmarks in Marin County reminding him of Belfast. These influences melded with Marin County to create Morrison's musical legacy.

It is about interpretation. It is about the interviews. It is about the facts. He is not wrong. I am not right. So what am I doing? I believe in his brief look at this period Heylin ignored the essence of Van Morrison. That is when Morrison took his career into stratospheric heights. A five year career vaulting him to stardom emerged in 1974, when this book concludes, and at that point he was no longer a singer-songwriter looking for his place in the music business. He had found it. Marin County gave birth to his writing and performing genius.

When he began chapter seventeen "1973-1974: A Commercial Cul-de-Sac," one of Heylin's major source was Stephen Pillster. He was unreliable. Why was Pillster unreliable? He described Morrison and Carol Guida in their romantic getaway to Sutton Place in October 1973, and he outlined the trip in great detail to Heylin. Carol Guida told me Pillster was with them for only two days. Then Van sent him on his way home. If Pillster was there for two days and returned home to Marin County, he had little idea what Van and Carol did or how or why the trip inspired the Belfast Cowboy. Van was loyal to Pillster. Why? Who knows! He may have believed he had business expertise. He didn't. One of the Barsotti brothers told me, Pillster was a "babe in the woods" in terms of the concert business and management in general. The Barsotti brothers and Bill Graham were in the process of educating Van as where a number of people inside Bill Graham Presents including Nick Clainos.

When Heylin writes of Van; "an older, gentler Ireland was assuredly on his mind." he ignores Marin County. The influences from Van's Fairfax home, to his outpost of love with Carol Guida in San Geronimo and his endless small club Marin County appearance honing his talent has been ignored by his biographers. In 1973-1974 Van Morrison was the James Brown of Marin County. He was the hardest working man putting his career into orbit for the next half century. That year and a half was the well thought out template for a career about to explode in the music business stratosphere.

Van in A TV Concert with Etta James
(Courtesy of the Midnight Special)

THE NEW VAN ON TALK ABOUT POP

Heylin's description of Van's RTE solo show in early November 1973 is well written and instructive. What does it miss? Plenty! The playful way Van and his journalistic cohort, Donald Corvin, took over the show was a glimpse into Van as a show business elf. It was also an early indication he was learning to deal with the media. With Carol Guida by his side he had an eclectic confidence previously lacking. The shy nature that was Van Morrison was giving way to a fully developed personality. That is he was learning to deal with the press in a more sophisticated manner.

This November 2, 1973 interview was the earliest sign of "Becoming Van Morrison." After brief introductory remarks by mc Tony Johnson, Van sent him off stage. Donal Corvin took over the interview with light banter that turned serious. Van was comfortable and forthcoming.

Or perhaps on outlier in training. Van is accused of being sullen, uncooperative and at times down-right nasty. He is! But on Talk of Pop he was impish. It was RTE's most watched show of 1973. Why? Van's solo acoustic versions of his songs were stunning. Not just outstanding. They were unbelievable. He was Becoming Van Morrison. Heylin ignores Morrison's personal growth and hard work.

The bootleg album of the November 2, 1973 RTE show **Live At Talk About Pop** is a rare window into Van's burgeoning creativity. With his acoustic guitar Van presents a laid back set of songs beginning with "Wild Children" before he goes into "Slim Slow Slider," continues with "Warm Love" and by the time he finished with "And It Stoned Me" this bootleg demonstrates he can perform a marvelous show with no more than an acoustic guitar.

When Heylin hinted at writer's block, he failed to realize how productive Van was in his Fairfax home studio. As Carol Guida observed he wrote constantly. Once again, the brilliant researcher who is never wrong—that is how I see Heylin—turns to Stephen Pillster for the truth. "Morrison has never taken particular pride in authorship…." Pillster said. That comment is antithetical to everyone who has worked with or been around Morrison. He is fiercely protective of his product and more than proud of his lyrical beauty.

VEEDON FLEECE IS NOT ASTRAL WEEKS

The notion that **Veedon Fleece** is the bastard stepchild of **Astral Weeks** is overblown. **Veedon Fleece** stands on its own with Marin County influences mixing with Irish themes from the October 1973 trip with Carol Guida to Sutton Place and on to an Irish tour. This trip receives more credence for **Veedon Fleece** that it deserves.

When Heylin concludes that "Bulbs" and "Cul de Sac" were recorded in New York because "he didn't feel they had the right feeling," he misses the point. Joe Smith had Van recut "Bulbs" promising to release eleven separate releases in the world market. To placate Van, Smith hired three jazz musicians. The Belfast

Cowboy readily agreed. This suggests Van's relationship with Warner was not fraught with the difficulty Heylin described.

In concert, Van paid Joe Smith back for the favor of promoting "Bulbs" by making it the most played song from the album. Van told everyone it would be a massive hit. It didn't happen. Not only was Morrison praiseworthy and kind about Smith, he realized Warner Bros. was doing their best to promote his albums. Van didn't view **Veedon Fleece** as an extension of **Astral Weeks**. He abhorred the notion. The critics demurred.

Heylin argued **Veedon Fleece** "closed what could be designated the Warner era by delivering on much of the promise of **Astral Weeks**." The truth was Mo Ostin didn't want any more hippie music. He described **Astral Weeks** as "a non-commercial interlude forcing Van to the pop charts." The puzzling conclusion Heylin provided for **Veedon Fleece** was: "The critics' sense of dislocation would not be theirs alone." Good writing! Incorrect analysis!

What, then, was **Veedon Fleece**? It was no more and no less than Van's 1973 Irish vacation with Carol Guida. But Sutton Place and the lovely lady on his arm changed his world.

HEYLIN'S COMMERCIAL CUL-DE-SAC: IT NEVER EXISTED, WHY SUTTON PLACE AND BEYOND WITH CAROL GUIDA CHANGED VAN'S WORLD

In his best-selling breakthrough biography Clinton Heylin devoted an eleven and a half page chapter covering what this book examines. In those pages, Heylin summarized a period of transition in Morrison's life. A divorce, a new fiancée, a new musical direction, a new band, a best-selling life album and a need for down time with a private life made for complications. Heylin did a magnificent job covering this period. Why, then, did it take me six hundred pages to analyze the same time frame? The answer is a simple one. This period defined "Becoming Van Morrison."

Clinton Heylin deserves respect, admiration and praise for his biography. He still has the best Van Morrison biography. In some instances it is not that he is short sighted, but he failed to recognize the quirks, the contrarian nature and the unexplainable behavior that is Van Morrison. Those traits made Van the great artist he evolved into by the 1980s. The training ground that was the 1970s in Marin County created an artist with a half century of brilliance ahead of him.

When, in chapter 17, Heylin labels the years 1973-1974 as a commercial cul-de-sac, he depends upon oral interviews bearing little resemblance to what occurred. As this book has shown 1973-1974 emboldened Van's creativity into a whirl wind of writing, reading, thinking, discussing and hanging out with musicians, poets, literary types, entrepreneurs and dead end hippies. Van attempted to find a life. He did!

THIS WAS NOT A COMMERCIAL CUL-DE-SAC: IT WAS SUSTAINING CREATIVITY WITH PRIVACY

After Van, Carol Guida and Stephen Pillster landed in Dublin and checked in at Sutton Place, Pillster talked negatively about Guida. Van sent Pillster home. Heylin wrote: "After checking into a Dublin hotel, they took off in a hired car, visiting Cork, Cashel, Killarney and Arklow." The purpose of the trip was, Heylin correctly stated, was to rest and relax. The inner working of Van's mind made that difficult and Heylin is brilliant in pointing out Ireland's boost to the Belfast Cowboy's creativity.

The song that began **Veedon Fleece**, "Fair Play," Heylin nails it with the ferocity of a seasoned scholar who has discovered a major literary vein. He sees "Fair Play" as Van's "finest post **Astral Weeks**" song. Heylin in just a few sentences provided one of the best explanation of Van's artistic angst. He was angry with Ilene Berns for suing him. In a complete contradiction to what he termed "never playing Bang Record cuts he appeared on RTE's Talk About Pop performing "Madame George." That was Van being Van. Always the contrarian.

In 1987, when Van looked back on 1973-1974, he told Chris Salewicz: "By the fourth or fifth album you're writing more songs but you write from the point of view that you are searching—but you're actually not...in fact you're just telling little stories." Heylin used this quote suggesting Van had a method that even he had trouble accepting. Genuine inspiration, Heylin wrote, didn't come easily to Van. It did in 1973-1974 with Carol Guida at his side.

One of take aways from 1973-1974 came when Van said: "I had to start being responsible for me." He made that observation a decade later, in 1985, as he complained about that: "Everything was just pulled out from under me." With the turmoil in his life it was not easy for Van to consider love. He did! The romantic writer inside Van intensified in 1973-1974 thanks to Carol Guida.

One of Heylin's most important contributions was suggesting Van began to define himself as a writer in 1973-1974. While he had written plenty of songs prior to his period, Van had never thought of or questioned his writing. He talked to family and friends about writing for the first time. "I think Marin County in the 1970s forced Van to look at himself as a writer," Chris Michie continued. "Van said he channeled songs so he didn't have to answer questions about how he wrote."

NASTY AND NAKED TO THE WORLD: HEYLIN INTERPRETS VAN: USING INTERVIEWS WITH THE SKILL OF A SURGEON

In chapter 18: "1974-1975: Naked To The World," Clinton Heylin has a surfeit of material. So what did he do? He used the "F" word to describe Morrison. It was actually Van using the "F" word at Montreux.

By the end of 1974 Van was done for a time as a performer. "I've managed to please a lot of audience; when it gets to that point, then it's time for me to be myself..." Van hated the record business. It showed. He was not easy to deal with as fame took his life into a cauldron of despair. Carol Guida assuaged those feelings. She was a light in his life he had never experienced. That is she was a happy go lucky person with intelligence and integrity. Van had never experienced that with a woman.

In the first few pages of Heylin's book he employs quotes about Van setting the tone. The quotes Heylin employs from his extensive interviews are employed with the skill of a surgeon. That is he cuts up, while defining, the Van Morrison legacy into a biographical framework attuned to understanding the man. His music? That question is left to conjecture.

Keith Altham, Van's English public relations specialist, wrote a book on his clients. For Van, Altham labelled him an "arse." "I think he's been fairly consistently difficult. The most disturbing thing about Van is that he's disturbed," Altham continued. "I think he's a man who's gonna be searching all his life for something he'll never find...he hops from one spiritual idea to another with alarming dexterity." Altham was correct. Every manager that Van has worked with has been shown the door for reasons no one understood. When super Van fan Michael Seltzer took John Rodgers wife to lunch in 2023, he mentioned to a friend that the late Rodgers had a following out with Van. Seltzer observed: "That is Van." The point is Morrison is excused for this behavior. The reality is he is all about his career. Nothing else. Like it or not this is Clinton Heylin's contribution. His contribution is Heylin has made Morrison naked to the world.

John Savannah is another source Heylin employs to make the case for Van's social interaction, or more precisely, the lack of it. "He doesn't have a good social interaction with people," Savannah continued. "I don't think he ever had. And it could be because of this thin-skinned nature...." One wonders if those quoted on Van were happy with how they were presented depicting Morrison in Heylin's biography. Clive Culbertson is quoted on Van. I never interviewed Culbertson. From my research he appears to be a long-time friend of the Belfast Cowboy. That said a Culbertson conversation with Morrison was a strange one. "We were talking about what we were doing and why we were doing it," Culbertson continued. "You've got everything." Van said of his success: "You know something, in twenty years, I've only ever owned a house, a car and a studio." This remark was made in 1988. It was an example of Van rewriting history. By that time he owned multiple homes, a number of recording studios, investment property and one can only speculate on his investment strategy when he returned to live in Ireland. The tax on artists there is negligible. He had somewhere between seventeen and nineteen companies. Morrison's business remains private. He is a consummate businessman. That skill came with tension and a personality busting attitude toward the record business. Van won the battle with the industry.

Heylin's razor sharp research concludes with the number of times Van has threatened to set the record straight. He has announced numerous times that his autobiography is in the works. The first mention was in 1974 when he worked with Ritchie Yorke. Then in 1979 Marin County inspired another rumor, fueled by Van, of a prescient tome on his life. In 1983 and again in 1990 the press dutifully reported Van hard at work on his life. Nothing materialized. In 1997 the Frankfurt Book Fair publicized a Van Morrison book. Silence ensued. The two books of lyrics 2014 and 2020 were as close to autobiographical gold as we got.

In 1979, Heylin reported Van said: "When it's time for me to do that, I'll do it myself. I'll sit down and I'll write a book and I'll backtrack and I'll go through everything." We are still waiting.

Bibliographical Sources

The problem with interpreting Van Morrison lies in the interviews with those close to him, those who deal with him at the various record labels, those who have interaction with him in the recording studio, those who have interviewed him and those who have had difficulty with Morrison. The outcome is a varied and at times confusing biographical record. Matt Holland, a trumpet player with Van since the early 1990s, sees how problems working with Van as does long departed Mark Isham. While others, like one time close friend David Shaw, aka, Dahaud Shaar told me in a moment of pique: "Van stayed in my house in New York, we were best friends, I was his drummer and then one day he auditioned three drummers. I wondered what the hell was going on,' Shaar concluded.

Alice Stuart: "Shaar and Jef Labes had had it with Van. Shaar told me he didn't want to play with him anymore. Too much drama." Stuart's comment echoed many others who talked of the emotional balm in Morrison's personality. His personality and character traits made it difficult to deal with him, Stuart told me in numerous interviews. "He was a brilliant, but strange, little curmudgeon," she said. She also believed he lived in the moment and he was extremely thin skinned. Grievances and settling those open wounds drove him mercilessly. He never forgot a criticism, real and imagined, and he continually complained about those he believed were after him. Stuart said his "self-destructive streak was dangerous but she understood it because of his treatment by industry power brokers."

This comment is as close to the truth as any about Morrison. He doesn't think like other people. Van wanted a sound. He auditioned the three drummers. End of story. He couldn't understand why Shaar was upset. While not excusing Morrison's behavior, he does have his own vision. Often it is not friendly to others. He can be spiteful. Clinton Heylin, for whom I have great respect, highlights Van's moments of egregious behavior in his brilliant work. Everyone agreed his narcissism influenced his. His personality contained a fragile ego that often spelled trouble for people. There is the good Van capable of generosity and humor. There is the bad Van who is insecure and abusive. You never know which one will show up. Carol Guida experienced living with and dealing with a creative artist. She has never opened up, even to me in a dozen interviews. When Carol left Van in early 1977, after less than four years, she had no rancor and no ill feelings toward the Belfast Cowboy. Her book? Who knows! She holds the key to explaining Van. In interviews with her she refuses to talk about his private life. Her book length manuscript explains the Belfast Cowboy in depth.

See Chris Salewicz in **Q** magazine, # 4 in January 1987 for some revealing Morrison quotes on his song selection. The rock and roll press continually speculates on and examines what Van's songs may or may not mean. He is unusually tight lipped about what his writing means.

The book reviews for Clinton Heylin's biography often turn into interpretive piece that have little to do with the book and more to do with what the reviewers believes. For a well written review of Heylin's book that is less than complimentary and for many reasons, some real and some imagined, calls many of his conclusions into question, see, Kevin Mitchell, "How To Make Van Ordinaire," **The London Guardian**, December 7, 2002

https://www.theguardian.com/books/2002/dec/08/biography.vanmorrison

Mitchell wrote: "It is not a biography; it is a quibble, a long-far too long- and humorless snarl of a book." This is over the top criticism but correct to a point.

Another great source is Clinton Heylin, **Can You Feel The Silence?: Van Morrison, A New Biography** (Chicago, 2003), pp. 277-283 and Johnny Rogan's **Van Morrison: No Surrender** (London 2005),p. 283.

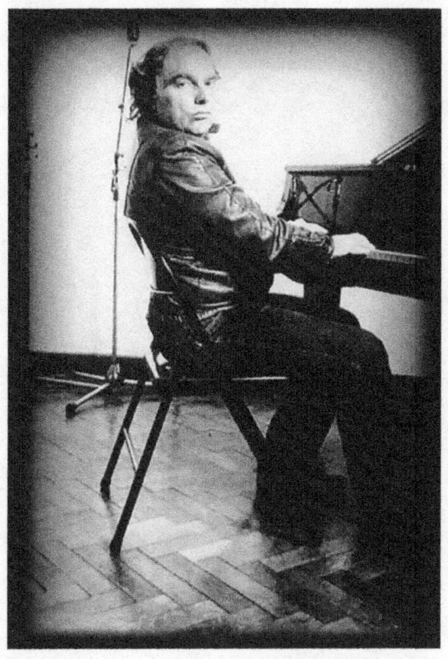

EPILOGUE

"A man's work is nothing but this slow trek to discover through the detours of art, those two or three great and simple images in whose presence his heart first opened."

ALBERT CAMUS

"Did you ever hear about Wordsworth and Coleridge?"

VAN MORRISON

"Humility is not thinking less of ourself, it is thinking of yourself less."

C. S. LEWIS

"The foundation of most of the issues they have to deal with in daily life has their roots in their past."

BART HENDRIKS, SENSE OF WONDER, ENCOUNTERING VAN MORRISON

What is the importance of 1973-1974 in Van Morrison's career? What does this period demonstrate about his artistry and his life in the music business? Why was there, at times, a dark cloud over his career? Many biographers concentrated upon his drinking, think Clinton Heylin, his personal outbursts, the Troubles and his contradictions, think Johnny Rogan. There is some excellent analysis on Van's writing and the thought behind it, think Peter Mills, and those who attempt to explain his character, contractions and intellectual drive are prone to saying it can be done, think Eric Hage. But Hage said it best when he was asked to define Van. He replied: "I can't." The religious spiritual side of Van's life is not ignored, think Steve Turner, who has done a superb job discussing spiritual matters. John Collis, **Van Morrison: Inarticulate Speech Of The Heart**, was maligned by many fans but praised by reviewers. Collis presents the early years with Them and Bang Records skillfully, but his description of Van into the 1990s has more emphasis on the tirades than the music. Too much emphasis on personality not powerful songwriting doomed Collis' book. But it is a well written, nicely researched and interesting book.

There are also a number of under the radar books. Bart Hendriks **Sense of Wonder: Encountering Van Morrison**, published in 2020, is a unique work. Hendriks is a therapist living in Europe. He has a window into psychotherapy using the words and music of Van Morrison. Not only does this brilliant writer use Morrison's words, he had a real life encounter with the Belfast Cowboy. As Hendriks remarked it was Van's "messages, feelings, observations and experiences" that had a "healing effect." This book is unique. Read it and you will experience another type of Van Morrison experience.

Rock and roll writing is one of the culprits in misinterpreting Van's career. Unlike literary interpretation, analytical history and in depth biography, rock and roll is often written by those with an ax to grind. Those with too much interpretation, think the Shakespeare of Telegraph Avenue, Greil Marcus or Lester Bangs, as well as a knowledgeable fan who wrote the first biography, think Ritchie Yorke. They all do an excellent job detailing Morrison's life. This allowed me to synthesize and place him into perspective.

The problem is we learn too much about wives, girlfriends, money problems, drinking and boring subjects. These books are too critical while lacking background. There is too much material no one cares to digest. The media has a field day with information it fails to verify. When a rock album comes out it is a throwaway or a hit. At least that is what the reviewers conclude. Rock and roll is a throwaway society. That is until recently there has been little analysis of the literary side of rock music. That has changed since the 1980s. By 2014, when Van's first book of lyrics appeared, literary rock 'n' roll was in vogue.

Quality is seldom analyzed in rock and roll biographies To understand Morrison in the 1970s is a simple task. He was an Irishman living in America. When he moved to Marin County two key events defined his future creative life. The first was the It's Too Late To Stop Now tour and subsequent legendry double album. The second was a new muse. For Van to create he needed a muse. His wife, Janet Planet, was the original "Brown Eyed Girl." Then Carol Guida entered the picture. She began Van's muse until early 1977. By this time an absence from the limelight helped him re-define his career.

The best way to examine who Van Morrison is and why he is important is to analyze his lyrics and blend them with his environment. His life emerges. By combining journalism and history the biography can flush out his life. You need to examine both sides of his life to understand him. The enormous creativity, the brilliant in concert appearances and the day to day drive to maintain his career defines a legendary musician who has fought for his personal freedom while taking his art to millions.

VAN REINVENTING HIS ART: OCTOBER 1973 IN IRELAND

In 1973-1974 Van began reinventing his career and set out on restructuring his life. That process led him to Ireland. But not to Belfast. He avoided it due to the Troubles. When Van and Carol Guida landed in Dublin, in October 1973, his reinvention was in progress. His manager Stephen Pillster was there for a few days.

After Van rented a car he drove Carol to Cork, Cashel, Killarney and Arklow. They checked into hotels as Mr. and Mrs. Guida. It was idyllic. In Cork Van passed by the Cork Opera House, built in 1855, admiring its recent 1965 replacement after a fire destroyed it. Then it was on to Cashel where the Rock of Cashel, a medieval complex sits on a hilltop overlooking the town. With a fifteenth century castle and the Cashel Folk Village it was a relaxing spot. In Killarney, Van's Irish roots took on a special meaning. The nineteenth century buildings with St. Mary's Cathedral standing out impressed tourists. A stop in Arklow was the inspiration for more new songs and one in particular was a reflection of the new Van.

That song "Streets of Arklow," appearing on **Veedon Fleece**, captured the magic of the trip. Van wrote of being "filled with poetry." He used "love," as well as "grass" to reinforce the beauty of the Irish countryside. When Van wrote of "God's green land," he indicated where his writing heart resided. That was the precursor to **Veedon Fleece**. He stretched his lyrics into a new and more creative direction. The "sha la las" were a thing of the past as were reflection on "Wild Children."

The new writing direction continued after **Veedon Fleece**. It was apparent in **A Period of Transition**, his ninth studio album, contained remnants of the 1973 Ireland visit. He was taking the first steps in becoming the new Van Morrison.

When Van and Carol returned to Fairfax and finished the songs. The album took only four days to record. It was more complex than it appeared. The stage was set for what some critics called the "return to **Astral Weeks**." It wasn't.

VAN'S NEW THEMES BECAME CAREER BITCHES

What were Van's new themes? "Fair Play" summed up his mind set. When it appeared on **Veedon Fleece**, it was an elegy to the past.

On the October, trip to Dublin, Van and Carol Guida talked at length with journalist Donal Corvin. Amidst Corvin's heavy drinking and over the top behavior, he said "fair play to you." It was a means of welcoming the Belfast Cowboy back to Ireland. The phrase simmered in Van's psyche. When he stopped in Killarney with Guida, Van thought of poets Edgar Allan Poe and Oscar Wilde while name-checking Henry David Thoreau in the lyrics. Van described "Fair Play" as a return to a stream of consciousness writing.

Looking out on the shimmering, moon lit Killarney waters with a lithe, beautiful twenty year old vixen, Van was relaxed, writing productively and planning his future. Unwittingly, what became **Veedon Fleece** gestated in this brief trip. He looked to past experiences.

This led to pulling out an old tune, "Country Fair," and he reworked it. As Van recalled Ireland's beauty and Belfast's influence, he saw his future writing in the Emerald Island.

CAROL GUIDA AND THE OCTOBER 1973 IRISH TRIP: HER MEMORIES

Carol Guida: "We arrived at Sutton Place. It was a grand hotel. It was a former castle made into a hotel. You had to climb up these stairs to get into bed. Donal Corvin came to Sutton Place. I thought it was a joke when these Irish promoters, comb overs and pot belly's accosted Van with what they thought was hip language. They would say: 'Hey Van baby.' He had trouble not laughing in their faces. They were greasy and smarmy."

When they were dropped off at Sutton Place, twenty year old Guida was impressed. "It was a grand hotel." Then the couple went to Dublin. "He asked me to marry him," Guida continued. "He bought me a diamond ring in Dublin on Grafton Street." The engagement continued. The wedding didn't take place.

There were those waiting in the wings to get rid of Guida. "I have heard that Stephen Pillster said it was my idea to get married. That is bullshit." After two days at Sutton Place, Guida agreed to marry Van. She didn't. That is a story she is saving for her in-progress memoir.

VAN LOOKED BACK ON THE OCTOBER 1973 TRIP

Looking back in 1987 on the Ireland trip, Van observed: "You have to pretend that there is...something you are searching for...." In this convoluted utterance Van confessed the brilliance of his songwriting method. He continued: "You're searching but in fact you're just telling little stories."

When Clinton Heylin and Johnny Rogan completed their biographies, they depended heavily on Van's manager Stephen Pillster for the October 1973 trip. Big mistake! His interviews allegedly were unreliable. Carol Guida confronted him for his ill thought out comments. He went to Van and wanted her fired. Van was flummoxed. She wasn't an employee. She was his fiancée. Pillster worked for Van on and off until 1990 then he left. Pillster was a self-promoter. He allegedly had a penchant for grandiose overstatement. He gave numerous, in depth, interviews about the October, 1973 trip. He was there for only two days.

Pillster told Heylin: "Morrison has never taken pride in authorship; he thinks of himself more as a channel." This was typical Pillster. He took a grain of truth and blew it into the truth. While Van has remarked he channels, he has more often alluded to the hard work and the pride he takes in his writing.

If 1973-1974 is significant in Van's life it is because he perfected his autobiographical lyrics. Certain themes intensified. One song stands out in the new phalanx of Morrison tunes. Some say that song represents a combination of Irish themes and California influences molding Van's increasingly sophisticated songwriting. Whether "Linden Arden Stole The Highlights" fits that mold or not is insignificant. What is important is Linden Arden represents the hybrid mind that was Van Morrison. He was an Irishman. The end product was sheer songwriting brilliance with a mixture of the Golden State and Belfast. Always the outlier, Van wrote with the sophistication of a newly arrived poet. Those who interpreted his lyrics claimed he had the observation powers of a historian. He struck Irish gold in prose destined for the Songwriting Hall of Fame.

Love was a constant in the 1973-1974 writing years. "Comfort You" and "Come Here My Love" extolled his feelings for Carol

Guida. Perhaps the same conclusion could assumed about other songs on **Veedon Fleece**. Van has never explained.

Although Van rediscovered his Irish heritage, he continued to live in the San Francisco Bay Area. The intellectual ferment in Marin County intensified his self-education. He was on a reading and writing binge bringing the next fifty years into focus. Ironically, as Van looked back on his Irish education in a 1991 interview, he complained in school he didn't read Irish writers. "All we got was Shakespeare...." He recalled he had never heard of W. B. Yeats while in school. "I didn't know him. I never read him," Van continued. "I discovered all these connections later on..." That was the beauty of Marin County. It gave Van a roadmap to his fierce intellectual direction.

LANGUAGE AND THE CALEDONIA SOUL ORCHESTRA

Van's joy was employing language in his writing. He was a furtive poet. That poetry was written on the back of restaurant bills, bank deposit slips, hotel bills, royalty statements and any small piece of paper suitable for catching an image. Organization was in Van's head. He could produce songs quickly. He could write and file a tune away bringing the song back years later. Daoud Shaar remarked: "The vibe was the most important thing in the studio."

When he formed the Caledonia Soul Orchestral, Van put together a touring-recording band sympathetic and in tune with his every musical nuance. Perfection ensued. The It's Too Late To Stop Now tour and double album remains legendary.

Van was neither critical or praiseworthy over the years about his 1973-1974 successes. He wondered why people asked. He was after all just a blue collar guy working for a living. At least this was his line during interviews. The press pounced on Van's words with a ferocity. Van's close friends pointed out he began a trend of dismantling successful albums or not discussing them. He moved on continually to new, fertile interpretive grounds. Along the way some fans, some critics, and some industry insiders tried to figure it out. They couldn't. It was simply Van being Van. Ambivalence was something only those close to Van understood. He set the template in Marin County for the remainder of his career.

Phil Coulter saw Van's triumphs. His good friend put it into perspective. He recognized Van changed his musical course after praise ore acclaim. In a 1980 interview with former Manfred Mann vocalist, John Paul Jones, on BBC radio, the host praised the **It's Too Late To Stop Now** album. Van responded "You can hear it. I can't." Ray Ruff told me Warner Bros. believed Van didn't do enough to promote the live album. He wanted it to stand on its merits. It did!

By 1974 Van's performing makeover was complete. The days of turning his back on the audience, taking a quick smoke break during the show or leaving the stage in a huff ended. The consummate in concert Van was born. He was bred in Marin County. The San Francisco Bay Area was his training ground providing an assist with clubs, restaurants, bars, coffee shops, book stores and a fertile intellectual climate influencing his intellectual development. This was not possible in Belfast. Becoming Van Morrison was a product in Marin County.

Despite all this Irish themes dominated. That would continue. In the next book in the series, volume four, **Van Morrison: Made In Martin County, 1974-1979**. This book is one where **Veedon Fleece** takes center stage suggesting a great deal about Van's future. Marin County, Carol Guida, the San Francisco Bay Area clubs, the management of Bill Graham Presents and the renewed creativity of Van created his career.

BECOMING VAN MORRISON: WHAT DOES IT MEAN?

Defining the Belfast Cowboy's creativity is a complex puzzle. But one that can be unraveled. This brief time span, 1973-1974, began Van's emergence as a sophisticated and brilliant songwriter. Along the way he became a smooth in concert performer and a consummate businessman. Van's relationships and surroundings drove his creativity. Combine that with an unshakeable work ethic. Bam! You have "Becoming Van Morrison."

Bad behavior didn't derail Morrison's career. He explained his moments of rage. They were predictable. It was due to Van's single minded devotion to his craft. Over the years the press has been kinder to Morrison. For the last thirty years he has reciprocated with transparent interviews looking back on his career. For the first twenty-five years in the music business he was guarded with the press with a half dozen open ended interviews. Jonathan Cott, Cameron Crowe and his old Belfast drinking buddy cum journalist Donal Corvin were young personalities he opened up to in the 1970s. In later years in discussions with his wife Michelle Rocca, band member journalist Leo Green and premier Irish mainstream news reporter, Fintan O'Toole. Van was open, thoughtful and precise.

VAN'S MARIN COUNTY ROLE MODELS: WHAT HE LEARNED, WHAT HE DIDN'T LEARN

There were role models for Van's future. Some were positive. Some were negative. All of them were helpful to "Becoming Van Morrison." There were ten Marin County-San Francisco Bay Area influences shaping the Belfast Cowboy.

First, the musicians who arrived and departed were important to his developing talents as a producer. The primary influence upon Van in the studio in 1973-1974 came from virtually unknown session musicians. They included Jerome Rimson, Joe Macho, Mark Isham and John Tropea among others. These session men were primarily jazz or soul artists.

Second, Van was enamored with local sights. They included the simple and the mundane as well as the famous tourist attractions. The International House of Pancakes intrigued Morrison. One night he took Carol Guida to dinner in a Marin County IHOP. They ate pancakes. They drank coffee. Van smoked cigarettes. Then, as they prepared to leave, Van said he didn't have his wallet. They ran out laughing. "It was one of my favorite nights," Carol Guida said.

Third, Van learned to live with and understand the media. The Shakespeare of Telegraph Avenue, Greil Marcus, drove Van around the San Francisco Bay Area. He took the Belfast Cowboy over to jazz critic Phil Elwood's home where they listened to 78s in Elwood's Berkeley basement. The blues legends Elwood collected intrigued Van. He learned how this obsessive-compulsive music scholar and writer viewed his career. Along the way Van talked with and observed two music store owners who were inveterate collectors and skilled businessmen. John Goddard of Village Music in Mill Valley had a record store like no other. His massive inventory stretched over two stores with new, used and rare recordings. Blues, rhythm and blues, soul and rock 'n' roll had equal status. In Emeryville, next to the University of California, Berkeley campus, Downhome music was the brainchild of a small record label owner who specialized in the Oakland blues and every other rare, unknown or impossible to find record. If you wanted a Bob Geddins produced 45 you came to Downhome Music. The founder and owner Chris Strachwitz had the Arhoolie label to release unknown Delta blues artists. Van took note. He educated himself on the obscurities as well as the Junior Wells and Bobby Blue Bland records he favored.

WRITING THEMES AND THE COMING INELLECTUAL EXPLOSION: THE REMAINDER OF THE 1970s AND WHY 1973-1974 FORMED MORRISON'S CREATIVE GENIUS

Ball breaking creativity with a demeanor. That is how one of Van's musicians described him. "He is not able to see how others feel," Chris Michie continued. "That doesn't mean he is a bad person. He is simply about his career. That's it." I have heard this comment for the past fifty years I have researched Van Morrison. Since I picked up the first Them album, I have tried to figure out the man. I confess I failed. After four books, this is the fourth one and the fifth is written and will follow, I have learned to accept the contradictions and enjoy the genius. Van is unsentimental, strong, determined and predictable.

He has a one dimensional addiction to the blues. Soul and rhythm and blues feed his original songs. He introduced a new vocabulary to rock lyrics. Much like Jack Kerouac, he envisioned a different America. Coming from Belfast many people could accept his vision.

What is Van's magic? It is recalling the past. Whether he is skewering Bert Berns. Whether he is complaining about a record label. Whether he is claiming he is disrespected. Whether he is observing whatever happened to P. J. Proby. Whether he is complained about an ex-wife or girlfriend. We know these complaints make him Van Morrison. It is part of his creative genius.

INTO THE MYSTIC: HOW IT DEFINED VAN'S FUTURE

If there is a song defining the 1974 Van Morrison it is "Into The Mystic." Why? Because of the way the lyrics interpret Van and his harrowing march through the 1970s. It was fitting this song was on **Moondance**. That was the vinyl masterpiece launching the commercial and increasingly mystical Morrison. Poetic lyrics through a spiritualism prism. That is how to describe "Into The Mystic."

When this book ends with Van's appearance at the Montreux Jazz Festival, it was fitting the highpoint was his poignant re-creation of that song. The spiritual tone was an indication of his future. When Van looked back on writing the song, he remarked "Into The Misty." The songs lasting appeal came to the forefront in 2022 when it charted at number one on Ireland radio airplay.

LOOKING AT 1973-1974: CONCLUSIONS

Van looked for a long term career. How to do that? That was the question Van addressed from 1974 through 1979. After the commercial failure of **A Period of Transition**, Van wrote and recorded a hit album. The nineteen months from January 1973 through July 1974 was when Van crafted his career for the long term. Time was on Van's side. He had the money in the mid-1980s to daily address his creativity. By 1978 **Wavelength** demonstrated the finished product of "Becoming Van Morrison."

When **Wavelength** was released, it became Morrison's fastest selling album. He was back. No one addressed Marin County's influences.

BEING INTENSELY PRIVATE: VAN MORRISON SUFFERED FROM IT

If there is a constant in writing about Van Morrison it is his intensely private, thoughtful intellectual life. Van reads his press. He attempts to control it. Not a chance! This bothers him. Endless eruptions with the media are never forewarned. They continue to provide a window into his life. One the biographer mines.

Van was always ready to alter his writing, his musical direction and his image to suit his needs. He was never predictable. Van shrewdly crafted his image. His magnificent voice aged like a Stratovarius violin getting better every year.

Van's strength evolves around selecting and shaping musicians. Long before he was a best-selling artist Van hired Ronnie Montrose. Long after he left the Paul Butterfield Band, Mark Naftalin played piano in the studio and in concert with Morrison. Some of the musicians forming Huey Lewis and the News performed with Van when they were known as Sound Hole. Mark Isham before he became an under the radar movie soundtrack guru performed and recorded with Van. Ronnie Montrose played with Van before going on to a legendary solo career. It goes on and on those who worked with him. Van recognized talent. He brought many artists into the creative arena.

Privacy brought paranoia. Van worried about what people thought of him. He was angry at times with personal perceptions. Morrison's working class, blue collar background hovered around his psyche. He demanded privacy and respect. As he approached eighty, Van failed to understand fame's burden.

In 2021 when Van's album **Latest Record Project, Vol. 1** was released one was shocked, Jonathan Bernstein wrote Van's latest work was a "terrible study in casual grievance." What did he mean? He meant that Van's fame gave him the concert venue necessary to sell his anti-lockdown arguments. How did Van get there. It was through decades of reading and self-education.

THIS BOOK IS THE STORY OF 19 MONTHS: WHY?

This book is the story of roughly nineteen months of Van Morrison's life. It was the period of maturation he had sought out since the Monarch days. Morrison's musical gifts were undeniable. His personality was another factor. He won the war with the music industry. In process a negative image thrust forward like a runaway locomotive. He retained an air of mystery. That helped him survive. He planned. He schemed. He worked hard.

The story of the first transition to stardom that evolved in a long and varied road filled with obstacles. It is a tale of how he gained control of his intellectual property. It is not a linear story. There are twists and turns. The road was never smooth. As Joe Smith said of Van: "I have never seen anyone do more to derail their career." That said it all. Morrison was a survivor in a jungle that ate its young. That jungle was the record business.

What did Van achieve in this period? Fiscal stability! Career continuity! Personal freedom! That was enough to ensure his drive developing new musical themes. He. was on his way to a legendary career. "Becoming Van Morrison" was in the works.

There is one virtually forgotten or ignored aspect of Morrison's career. That is an examination of Van as a critic. In his songwriting themes, in his interviews, in his two books of songwriting lyrics, in his off handed remarks to friends, he is the essence of a critic. If an at times quietly ebullient observer of the world around him. Like Bob Dylan he can be opaque with the vision of a trickster but with the mind of a visionary in blue collar clothing. Happy surprises and exasperation are the rewards for Van's songwriting. In the 1980s his themes were more mature, increasingly spiritual and alternately simple and complex. These forces allow him to evolve into a finished writer. That finished product was the Van Morrison trademark "Made In Marin County," which I'll be covering in the next volume in this recurring multi-volume biographical tome. Stay tuned.

It takes time to find truth. That truth is an insight into one of the most talented, irascible and mysterious forces in the history of rock 'n' roll. This is a story about dedication to your craft. No one did it better than Van Morrison.

A NOTE TO THE READER

"Truth takes time."

HOWARD A. DEWITT

"Turn every page."

ROBERT CARO

"I have trespassed on Van Morrison's life."

HOWARD A. DEWITT IN CONVERSATION WITH PAT THOMAS

"To understand Van Morrison in 1973 into mid-1974 you need to listen to his YouTube interviews, newspaper-magazine interviews and read his lyrics. Van is his own biographer."

HOWARD A. DEWITT

"Van Morrison is an enigma. But when he sings, we forget that."

HOWARD A. DEWITT

I never recovered from my first Van Morrison live show. Authentic! Driven! Talented! Enigmatic! These were my thoughts.

Howard A. DeWitt

In 2008, Van Morrison announced he would recreate his seminal album **Astral Weeks** live. There were only two shows scheduled at the Hollywood Bowl November 7th and 8th. These two appearances would recreate his legendary album on the concert stage. The live **Astral Weeks** would appear in 2009. Unwittingly, this decision opened Van's eyes to the 1970s, not 1968 when the album was released. It was the success of the legendary It's Too Late To Stop Now tour and the release of the February 1974 double live album that persuaded Van to rehearse, perform and release a live **Astral Weeks**.

Van reflected on his time in Marin County when he made this decision. He has always looked back on his career to move forward. He loves to recreate, rewrite, reperform and redo his career. Van is in own biographer in lyrical form. This book employs Van's technique. While technically examining the period from January 1973 into mid-1974, the use of Van's words from that time to the present day were employed in this book. In other words, Morrison has mentioned Marin County, his 1970s dealings with Warner Bros. and the struggles solidifying his career. He invariably reflects on his time from 1974 through 1979 in Marin County. This is the first of two books on that small sliver of his career. Why so much material on a six year period? It was, as I have shown, the time frame when he was "Becoming Van Morrison."

This is the third volume in my six book examination of Van's life and career. The emphasis on life is the key. It is from his daily working habits that this book emerged. His environment, his reading, his thinking, his writing, his cup of tea and his tirades and complaints from the litany of his life. This is a maximalist biography reflecting every facet of his life. Those around him, the events influencing him and his reaction to his environment is what this book is about. The information in these pages proves conclusively that Van Morrison was finalized as a brilliant writer, a stupendous concert act and an intransigent businessman in the 1970s. How was this accomplished?

This book is based on hundreds of interviews with people at every level of Van's life. Some are close friends. Some are not close to Van. Some are family. Some talked in anonymity. Those who spoke on the record are cited by name. Those who insisted on anonymity were fact checked with others in order to make sure their sensitive experiences not just with Van, but in the industry, were vetted with interviews from people close to them. The confidential sources were not used if they had an axe to grind, a petty dispute or a hatred for Morrison. The primary sources were working musicians, close friends and those with whom Van did business.

One of the primary research aspects of this book comes from the hundreds of interviews, off-hand comments and observations about the music business from Van. Since music is first and foremost a business, I have spent a good portion of the book on Morrison's business genius. He can be criticized for not getting the best deals in redoing the rights to his albums. That is a minor complaint. His business model is one most music industry professionals should emulate.

The materials collected for this book represent more than fifty years of research. When using quotations which are attributed to an individual quotation marks are used. They are verbatim quotes. When I write about what Van thinks or how he reacts it is from a source I can't make public. Hence, no quotation marks. In every instance the story is told honestly, directly and with a fidelity to the facts.

When my three volume Van Morrison biography was conceived in 1984, after the publication of **Van Morrison: The Mystic's Music**, the intention was to finish about 2000. The first volume came out in 2005 and the second in 2022. This book and its companion covers the period 1973-1979 in almost 400,000 words. The reason is a simple one. This 1970s gave birth to the Van Morrison legend.

Why 400,000 words? I realized the story was more than just a Van Morrison biography. If was about the record business and the music industry. It was also about Van's obsessive-compulsive blue-collar work ethic and his penchant for overproduction. To craft a proper music biography is a difficult task. Why? There are no archives? The result is a dependence on the rock 'n' roll press, popular periodicals and books of high and dubious quality. To capture the personality and creative essence of Van Morrison is not an easy task. I feel privileged to tell this story. While it was a joy to write this material there were many sobering moments. The coronavirus pandemic slowed me down. It also provided a window into how middle aged Van Morrison dealt with the restrictions. The windows into his mind since an interview with Michelle Rocca in 1995 is a constant reminder of his creative genius.

The most important source in a biography examining, analyzing and dissecting an intellectual is through publications. In Van's case this would be songwriting. As I have demonstrated he laid his life bare in lyrical form. I have made extensive use of song lyrics. Once I embarked on this project, decades ago, I realized those who knew him were the best sources. I tracked down who I could and most were forthcoming. This presented a paradox. Invariably, these interviews described two Van's. The cooperative "good Van." He was followed by the often irrational off the wall "bad Van." I decided time, place and circumstances produced both Vans and I did my best to describe his roller coaster personality.

Given the limits of human longevity many of the people I have interviewed are no longer with us. When they talked of Van, I had three other sources to verify what I wrote. The tricky part was describing how Van saw his life. These descriptions came from drinking sessions, coffee klatches, chance remarks before or after concerts and the over three thousand pages of personal interviews. In other words there was plenty of research material to delve into Van's mind.

Memories must be treated with caution. When I use an oral interview, I do my best to juxtapose it with a print article. This is an attempt to keep tall tales out of the book. Van says his personal life is private. It is in his view. To understand the man his personal reactions, his continual view of being disrespected, his lack of compassion for some people and his getting even mentality tarnishes a portions of the story. What is doesn't tarnish is an incredible vocal gift matched with a production genius. The cycles in Van's life define his ability to turn out a product.

Van is a hypomanic. This is a person who has a liveliness, an interpersonal charm and a high degree of perception concerning people. A hypomanic finds vulnerable spots in people and exploits them. Many of Van's highly pleasurable points end up in painful consequences. Think Bert Berns. Think Blue Note Records. Intellectual energy defines Van. This is the reason for the mood swings. Van is both charismatic and puzzling. To write about him one must understand that trait.

In the end Van Morrison was an ambivalent and ambitious singer-songwriter. That trait is at times lost in the jungle of information defining his life. He was brighter. He was more intelligent. He was better at business. He was better read. He took songwriting risks. These multiple traits led to the Rock 'n' Roll Hall of Fame. The journey continues.

When the Shakespeare of Telegraph Avenue, Greil Marcus, wrote that Van Morrison had a work ethic where "the process is beyond words" he described the Belfast Cowboy's mystique.

There is more to this book than Van Morrison. The purpose of biography is as much to explore the environment, the family dynamics, the public side of a prolific musician and in the end find out what makes him tick. I never recovered from my first Van Morrison live show. Authentic! Driven! Talented! Enigmatic! These were my thoughts. Since that time in the 1960s I have maintain a fascinating with, interest in and sense of his life and professional career. Van is one of a kind. He beat the recording industry at its own game. That in itself is enough for a book. After reading this volume there is no need to tell you his genius. It is on every page of this book. I hope that I separated the mythology from the man. That was my intent.

The responsibility of telling this story is not one I took lightly. The friendship, partnership and open nature of those close to Van Morrison and the industry made this book a joy to write. The sources, named and unnamed, made this book possible. Van will dispute legitimate facts. He often attacks reporters. He is unhappy when someone writes how he operates, what he thinks and how he meticulously planned his career. This volume and the next one tell you how he "Became Van Morrison." Enjoy! I did!

Howard A. DeWitt

ACKNOWLEDGEMENTS

"I am the Doulas Southall Freeman of rock music."

VAN MORRISON

John Hicks
Larry Catlin Ron Vega
Zaire Brian Young Jesse Hector
Bill Graham B Lee Cooper
Jeff Hughson Jack Schroer
Phil Solomon John Lee Hooker Marc Bristol
Paul Vincent Tom Bradshaw Steve Rowland Ed Diaz
Haik Arakail Brian Epstein Delbert McClinton
John Goddard John L. Wasserman Jeanette Heinen
Mark Naftalin Scott Amonson
Dan Hicks
Lee Cotton Roger Armstrong Clive Epstein Marie Bainer
Tony Dey Opal Louis Nations Steve Turner
Miles French Jimmy Witherspoon Charles Brown David Leaf
Nick Clainos Solly Lipsitz Lowell Fulson
Hank Ballard
Ken Burke Terry Dolan Carol Guida
Sal Valentino Herb and Mike Schott Johnny Otis
Dan Bourgoise Harry Balk
Ronnie Montrose Art Siegel Chris Michie
Fred Worth Jimmy McCracklin Russ Dugoni
Duane DeWitt Simon Gee
Pat Thomas Michael Seltzer
Mervyn Solomon

I never intended to write six volumes on Van Morrison's life. My admiration for him knows no bounds. He is brilliant. He is charismatic. He is complex. He is a great guy. He is a world class asshole. He is a solid family man. He is loyal to friends. You can count on him. These were only some of the comments I have received since I started researching Van in 1972 and since that time, I have published four books on him. He is all of those things his friends suggested. For the biographer this is a challenge. How to put all of Van's character strengths and flaws, his moods, his peccadilloes and his career triumphs and challenges in a book on less than two years of his life is a formidable task. His talent has grown every year. Carol Guida, who lived with Van from September 1973 until February 1974 said it best when she went to the **Astral Weeks Live** shows in Los Angeles. "I couldn't believe it. Van had a better voice and a career charisma like no other." Guida's remark about the 2008 shows came in 2023 when she finished a marathon set of interviews with me. This comment was echoed by hundreds of people I interviewed. The wealth of material on Van makes it necessary to sift through an enormous amount of material. So mistakes in interpretation, spelling, environment and fact has occurred. Could I do the job. I asked myself this as I finished volumes 3 and 4 of my 6 volume work. I am the Doulas Southall Freeman of rock music. I have tried to let Van, his friends, his critics and the general public do the commentary. Did I do a good job? You decide.

I think I was up to it. I will let the reader decide. This book was a wonderful experience. I have relived a period in my life where I attended most of Van's shows in small clubs. I was ready to write a book. Now forty-nine years later after attending an Inn Of The Beginning show, this book is completed.

In 1983, after **Van Morrison: The Mystic's Music** came out, I began taking notes and making files for a three volume biography. That was more than forty years ago. I am, still taking notes. Then it was five and now it is six. I promise to hold to that formula. This is the first of two volumes on the period 1974-1979 and so far, this book covers only about nineteen months. But, in my opinion, these nineteen months formed Van's future artistic direction. The key point is Marin County took his Irish heritage and blended it with the hippie subculture undergoing cataclysmic changes in the U. S. in the 1970s with disco and punk making many of feel the world was coming to an end. Morrison's music convinced me there was still hope for rock 'n' roll music. The problem in writing about Van is his private nature. He doesn't understand that he is a public figure. He will sue at a drop of the hat. Fortunately, living forty miles from Van's Mill Valley residence I was a regular at his small and larger shows when he lived on the hill in Fairfax. The people listed in this section who helped me are a smattering of over 200 Vanatics, industry insiders and musicians who helped me with this book. I want to thank all of them. If your name is not here, please accept my apologies.

As I completed this volume in the hot days of summer in Scottsdale, Arizona, I received a book by Bart Hendriks. He is a therapist living in the Netherlands who met Van and was encouraged by the Belfast Cowboy to write a book using Van's lyrics. Hendriks' **Sense of Wonder: Encountering Van Morrison**, published in 2020, examines Morrison's lyrics with the mission of employing the complex wisdom in Van's words to understand life. As Hendriks states: "Lyrics and music do have a healing effect on clients and the therapist as well." Great writing. The lyrics and music also placate the biographer. The intriguing aspect of this book is Van encouraged, had a meal with and was in some ways a co-author to Hendriks' book. This is a complex, but simple, book. Does that sound like a contradiction? Yes! Is Van a contradiction? Yes! Hendriks' text recalls "the poet-musician can be inspired by the mundane in ways that most of us can't." After writing about Van for more than forty years, I knew this but I didn't know it. What became obvious to me after reading this book is that what I and others see as "mundane" provides writing inspiration for Morrison.

In writing about seven years of Van Morrison's life I had no intention of turning this work into two volumes. That happened! How? Why? The how was simple. Van spent seven years carefully crafting his career. It wasn't just the new found maturity in his songwriting. It was also the attention to detail whether on the concert stage or in the intricate business web he established to protect his intellectual property. Van's personal life was of little concern to me. That is unless it impacted his professional life. Then I dealt with it. Those I interviewed who told me long, salacious tales of his life were relegated to the dust bin.

The interviews for the two books making up the years 1973 through 1979 occurred over a long period of time. They began in the mid to late 1980s when I made the acquaintance of Chris Michie. He was related to a colleague at Ohlone College, and he spent many hours regaling me with Van Morrison stories. He loved playing with Van. He had only positive stories. Michie's main influence was to show me the tender, positive and friend based side of Van. It was Michie who introduced me to a coterie of Van acolytes who worked with him in the 1970s. Many requested anonymity. Some spoke for the record. Their impact? They convinced me the influence from Marin County was as important as Morrison's Irish roots. They believed there was a melting pot of influences leading to what Chris Michie said was "Van becoming the Belfast Cowboy we all know to the present day." The chapters in both books were often set up by chance comments from those interviewed. Many interviews were anonymous for a variety of reasons. No quotes or material was corroborating evidence. All quotes used were carefully vetted and used without reference to Van's personal life.

Each chapter has a bibliography suggesting the material for that particular part of the book. A note on sources is necessary to understand how and why my fourth book on Van Morrison took shape and came to fruition. Unlike the traditional history-political science books I write, the rock and roll books generally do not have archive material. What is archive material? It is a library collecting the papers of an individual or organization that are catalogued and available to researchers and scholars. To understand how this book was conceived it is important to examine the sources. After spending more than forty years collecting Van Morrison albums, publicity releases, magazine articles, books, memorabilia and interviews I have built up an archive. That said the archive needs an explanation.

For my 1983 book **Van Morrison: The Mystic's Music**, I depended upon Paul Vincent at KMEL-FM, Mark Naftalin of the Paul Butterfield Band now gone solo, Chris Michie, one of Van's guitarists, Art Siegel a fan and friend, Simon Gee, editor of the best Van fanzine, **Wavelength** and two Sacramento musicians Tony Dey and Ronnie Montrose for large segments of his book. Conversations with Steve Turner at a Beatlefest was significant in understanding Van's search for spiritual matters. Michael Seltzer shared his vast knowledge of Morrison's concerts, his bands and the atmosphere in and around the Morrison phenomenon. Seltzer is truly the Belfast Cowboy's number one fan, Sorry Roma Downey.

Sacramento's Jeff Hughson provided information on Morrison's 1970s Northern California concerts. In Sacramento former Beau Brummel vocalist, Sal Valentino, discussed Them and early Morrison solo efforts. Although he played with Van in the 1980s Chris Michie helped recall Van's tales of Marin County as did writer Marie Bainer. Long before I started writing about rock 'n' roll San Francisco Chronicle columnist John L. Wasserman encouraged me to do so. John Goddard of Village Music and musician-entrepreneur Mark Naftalin provided insight into Van's ability to handle the business end of the music business. He also became a life-long friend. The extraordinary prolific writer and musician Opal Louis Nations was a fountain of information. On Van's connection to the blues; Jimmy McCracklin, Johnny Otis, John Lee Hooker, Charles Brown, Jimmy Witherspoon, Lowell Fulson, Delbert McClinton and Hank Ballard offered their opinions. Tom Bradshaw at the Great American Music Hall and Nick Clainos with Bill Graham Presents were helpful describing the larger venues Morrison played.

In London Jesse Hector of the Hammersmith Gorillas and Roger Armstrong of Ace Records were helpful. Dave Williams shared his vast knowledge of the British blues scene. From his retirement Penthouse in Bournemouth Phil Solomon filled me in on the 1970s London rock scene. Mervyn Solomon in Belfast added to the story as did Solly Lipsitz.

The legendary London record producer, Steve Rowland, was important to all aspects of this book. He provided information on record labels, production methods and the inner workings of the industry. Steve also provided contacts in the recording industry, he helped me understand the rigors of touring and he always had a coffee ready for me when I dropped into his Palm Springs life. He went from a valued source to one of my closest friends.

In the San Francisco record collecting community and elsewhere the observations of Art Siegel, Ed Diaz, Ron Vega, Zaire, Russ Dugoni, Haik Arakail, Herb and Mike Schott, Larry Catlin, Dennis DeWitt, Duane DeWitt, Marc Bristol and Lee Cotton provided information on Morrison collectibles as well as his truncated life. Miles French provided a comment on Van's personality leading to conclusions on each chapter as to Van's personal interaction with people and how it impacted his career. In Paul McCartney's management two members of his business and public relations staff provided comparisons with how Paul dealt with the press and they compared this to Morrison's relationship with the media. Fred Worth provided trivia information and general consul on Van's life. The Paul McCartney people offered a reasoned account as why Van had problems with the press and Paul didn't. Earlier in my research Clive Epstein gave his view of Van from Liverpool and suggested why his brother, Brian, had success and was a real manager. Van, said Mr. Epstein, never had a real manager.

A number of people around the legendary, quirky Dan Hicks talked of how he viewed Van Morrison and a brief conversation with a number of Hick's former band mates helped with the influence of and material on Marin County. Hicks took me up to see Van's Fairfax home when the Belfast Cowboy was out of town. It may have been my strangest research experience.

Terry Dolan, a Marin County musician who almost became a star, led Terry and the Pirates amongst other bands. I talked with him half a dozen times at the Silver Peso Bar in Larkspur while completing the research for the Marin County material. He was always in awe of Van's talents and praiseworthy of his advice the few times he had talked with him.

During my early years following Van I met saxophonist Jack Schroer a number of times in San Francisco. He lived in the Marina with his stewardess girlfriend. He recalled me from the shows. We talked at length. I didn't have a formal interview but I talked with him about playing with Morrison. These conversations took place before Van's shows and at times I caught him walking in the Marina in San Francisco. His girlfriend was a flight attendant and they were dabbling in drugs. This led to an untimely end for Schroer at fifty one. He provided a few anecdotes about Van. He said how much he appreciated the solos and Van's recognition of him after the solos to the audience. He remarked Van was easy to work with and paid well. Schroer is one of the tragedies of the rock 'n' roll lifestyle. But his horn genius has left a brilliant legacy for his family.

The management of half a dozen acts who appeared with Van talked with me on the condition of anonymity. They had little to say that was negative and, in fact, were complimentary about Morrison. They feared his litigation and his demeanor.

A series of in-depth conversations with Professor B. Lee Cooper helped to formulate the approach to biography. Discussions with a wide variety of academics including Nathan Rubin helped the analysis in the music end. The business end of the industry was helped by previously for my Del Shannon book talking with Bug Music owner and Del Shannon manager Dan Bourgoise. The kid, Brian Young, was important to this book. Harry Balk came into the picture on the Del Shannon book and he became a friend.

My long-time collaborator Ken Burke and of course my editor, illustrator, book creator, idea person Scott Amonson have been babysitting me for decades. All I can say is thank you for your good writing, editing, research and friendship.

As I was finishing this book David Leaf provided contacts and information that was important to the final product. His brilliant work on Brian Wilson and his book **Only God Knows: The Story Of Brian Wilson, The Beach Boys Of The California Myth** (New York, 1978, revised edition 2020) is the most complete book on Wilson and the Beach Boys. Leaf is a brilliant writer and he has always been helpful on my projects.

John Hicks, the Sunday waffle chef at Scottsdale's AJ's, made it easy for me to work on the sabbath. Thank John for years of blueberry waffles. Also, thanks for coming up with the title of this book. We talked. He said: "It sounds like what you are writing is "Becoming

Van Morrison." I used the title. No royalty, John, but you have my thanks. The waffles you made allowed me to finish this book.

Jeanette Heinen was a good friend providing a window into Van's life as was former Monarch Roy Kane. The Dude, Ron Sexton offered his views of Morrison on the 1970s.

INDEX

B

C

D

E

F

H

K

L

M

N

Q

R

S

T

U

V

W

Y

Z

ABOUT THE AUTHOR

Howard A. Dewitt is Professor Emeritus of History at Ohlone College, Fremont, California. He received his B. A. from Western Washington State University, the M. A. from the University of Oregon and a PhD from the University of Arizona. He also studied at the University of Paris, Sorbonne and the City University in Rome. Professor DeWitt is the author of thirty-six books and has published over 200 articles and more than 200 reviews in a wide variety of popular and scholarly magazines. DeWitt's graduate degrees were with honors.

DeWitt has also been a member of a number of organizations to promote the study of history. The most prestigious is the Organization of American Historians where he was a reviewer for a decade. His membership in the Community College Association, while publishing in their journal, combined his scholarship with the pursuit of teaching rock 'n' roll in the classroom. He did this at Ohlone College for three plus decades.

For more forty-five years he taught full and part time at a number of U. S. colleges and is best known for teaching two college level courses in the History of Rock 'n' Roll music. He continued to teach the History of Rock and Roll music on the Internet until 2011. In a distinguished academic career, he has also taught at the University of California, Davis, the University of Arizona, Cochise College and Chabot College. In addition to these teaching assignments, Professor DeWitt was a regular speaker at the Popular Culture Association annual convention and at the National Social Science Association meetings. He has delivered a number of addresses to the Organization of American Historians, the Pacific Coast Branch of the OAH and the American Historical Association.

DeWitt is an award nominated writer. His 2017 book **Searching For Sugar Man II: Coming From Reality, Heroes and Villains** was a finalist for the best pop music book by the Association for Recorded Sound Collections. This was DeWitt's eleventh book on rock music.

The two Sixto Rodriguez books provided more than 1200 pages of material on how the music industry systematically ignored Rodriguez songwriting and performing talent while his records sold in the millions in South Africa. Steve Rowland, who produced the Sugar Man's second album provided e-mails from Malik Bendjelloul, the documentary director, providing an inside view of the music business.

He wrote the first book on Chuck Berry, which was published by Pierian Press under the title **Chuck Berry: Rock N Roll Music** in 1985. DeWitt's earlier brief biography, **Van Morrison: The Mystic's Music**, published in 1983, received universally excellent reviews. He is completing a six volume biography of Van Morrison. The first two are out with positive reviews and steady sales. On the English side of the music business DeWitt's, **The Beatles: Untold Tales**, originally published in 1985, was picked up by the Kendall Hunt Publishing Company in the 1990s and is used regularly in a wide variety of college courses on the history of rock music. Kendall Hunt also published **Stranger in Town: The Musical Life of Del Shannon** with co-author Dennis M. DeWitt in 2001. In 1993's **Paul McCartney: From Liverpool To Let It Be** concentrated on the Beatle years. He also co-authored **Jailhouse Rock: The Bootleg Records of Elvis Presley** with Lee Cotten in 1983. His two books on Sixto Rodriguez are benchmark studies of the record business and how it is difficult for obscure performers from collecting their royalties.

The Library of Congress commissioned Dr. DeWitt to write an essay included in the Library of Congress and the Smithsonian's 500 Best Rock 'N' Roll songs. The essay "Blueberry Hill-Fats Domino 1956" went viral in 2022. This essay on Fats Domino was commissioned after Professor DeWitt published a kindle on his career. This was one of over 100 articles he wrote for **Blue Suede News**.

DeWitt is working with Ken Burke on a study of Gary S. Paxton, Kim Fowley and how they had success despite the music industry, as well as a biography of Gene Vincent's last decade.

Professor DeWitt's many awards in the field of history include founding the Cochise County Historical Society and his scholarship has been recognized by a number of state and local government organizations. DeWitt's book, **Sun Elvis: Presley In The 1950s**, published by Popular Culture Ink, was a finalist for the Deems-ASCAP

Award for the best academic rock and roll book. His first book on Sixto Rodriguez was a finalist for a Michigan Notable Book Award.

In his research for any and all of his books, Professor DeWitt employs the Gay Talese method: interview everyone around and connected to the project! Turn every page in the Robert Caro fashion.

Professor DeWitt is a renaissance scholar who publishes in a wide variety of outlets that are both academic and popular. He is one of the few college professors who bridge the gap between scholarly and popular publications. His articles and reviews have appeared in **Blue Suede News**, **DISCoveries**, **Rock 'N' Blues News**, the **Journal of Popular Culture**, the **Journal of American History**, **California History**, the **Southern California Quarterly**, the **Pacific Historian**, **Amerasia**, the **Western Pennsylvania Historical Magazine**, the **Annals of Iowa**, the **Journal of the West**, **Arizona and the West**, the **North Beach Review**, **Ohio History**, the **Oregon Historical Quarterly**, the **Community College Social Science Quarterly**, **Montana: The Magazine of the West**, **Record Profile Magazine**, **Audio Trader**, the **Seattle Post-Intelligencer** and **Juke Box Digest**.

For forty plus years DeWitt has combined popular and academic writing. He has been nominated for numerous writing awards. His reviews are combined with articles to form a body of scholarship and popular writing that is frequently footnoted in major works. As a political scientist, Professor DeWitt authored three books that questioned American foreign policy and its direction. In the Philippines, DeWitt is recognized as one of the foremost biographers of their political leader Jose Rizal. His three books on Filipino farm workers remain the standard in the field.

During his high school and college years, DeWitt promoted dances in and around Seattle, Washington. Such groups as Little Bill and the Bluenotes, Ron Holden and the Playboys, the Frantics, the Wailers and George Palmerton and the Night People among others played at such Seattle venues as the Eagle's Auditorium and Dick Parker's Ballroom.

Howard and his wife Carolyn have two grown children. Darin is a Professor of Political Science at California State University, Long Beach and Melanie is a Special Education teacher with two children Natalia and Katarina. They both live in Los Angeles. Howard's wife of fifty plus years, Carolyn, is an educator, an artist and she continues to raise Howard. She is presently retired and vacationing around the world. The DeWitt's live in Scottsdale, Arizona. That is when they are not in Paris looking for art, books and music. Howard is working on a book on Portugal's secrets. That is a year or two away.

His book on the president **Obama's Detractor's: In The Right Wing Nut House** is a marvelous look at the radical right and the tragedy of Fox TV News, right wing book authors and political kooks like Laura Ingraham and Ann Coulter. His novels **Stone Murder** and **Salvador Dali Murder** feature a San Francisco P.I. Trevor Blake III and a gay mobster Don Gino Landry, and much of the story line will evolve around crimes that DeWitt witnessed while working four years and two days as an agent with the Bureau of Alcohol, Tobacco and Firearms. He was a street agent for the BATF and his tales of those years are in manuscript waiting for publication. He was also a key figure in the BATF Union.

Meeting Hitler: A Tragicomedy, published in 2016 was a best seller with excellent reviews. In 2017 **Sicily's Secrets: The Mafia, Pizza and Hating Rome** was a number one best seller for travel books on Amazon. DeWitt is working on a like-minded book on Portugal. In 2018 DeWitt's **Trump Against The World: A Foreign Policy Bully, Russian Collusion** was the first in-depth examination of his European foreign policy and how it impacted American domestic politics.

Any corrections or additions to this or the subsequent volumes that will follow this study can be sent to Horizon Books, P. O. Box 4342, Scottsdale, Arizona 85258. DeWitt can be reached via e-mail at Howard217@aol.com. For personal correspondence send your requests to 7525 E. Gainey Ranch Road, Unit 169, Scottsdale, Arizona 85258.

Made in the USA
Monee, IL
06 January 2024

51323618R00454